SAINT
VINCENT DE PAUL

CORRESPONDENCE

CONFERENCES, DOCUMENTS

CORRESPONDENCE

VOLUME VII **(December 1657 - June 1659)**

NEWLY TRANSLATED, EDITED, AND ANNOTATED

FROM THE 1922 EDITION

OF

PIERRE COSTE, C.M.

Edited by:

SR. MARIE POOLE, D.C., *Editor-in-Chief*
SR. JULIA DENTON, D.C.
SR. ELINOR HARTMAN, D.C.

Translated by:

SR. MARIE POOLE, D.C.
REV. FRANCIS GERMOVNIK, C.M. (Latin)

Annotated by:

REV. JOHN W. CARVEN, C.M.

NIHIL OBSTAT
Very Rev. Jerome R. Herff, C.M.
Censor Deputatus

IMPRIMATUR
Right Rev. Msgr. W. Francis Malooly
Vicar General, Archdiocese of Baltimore

July 29, 1997

To commemorate
the beatification of Frédéric Ozanam

This book is dedicated

to

Eugene B. Smith

Vice-President of the Society of St. Vincent de Paul
Council of the United States

and through him

to

the other committed men and women
of the extended Vincentian Family

who collaborate to accomplish the Mission of Christ
in the Church and the World today

Published in the United States by New City Press
202 Cardinal Rd., Hyde Park, NY 12538

Printed in the United States of America

Library of Congress Cataloging-in-Publication Data:

Vincent de Paul, Saint, 1581-1660.
Correspondence, conferences, documents.

Translation of: Correspondance, entretiens, documents.
Includes bibliographical references and index.
Contents: I. Correspondence. v. 1. 1607-1639. —
v. 7. December 1657-June 1659.
1. Vincent de Paul, Saint, 1581-1660—Correspondence.
2. Christian saints—France—Correspondence. I. Coste, Pierre, 1873-1935. II. Title.
BX4700.V6A4 1985 271'.77'024 [B] 83-63559
ISBN 0-911782-50-8 (v. 1)
ISBN 1-56548-102-X (v. 7)

TABLE OF CONTENTS

APPENDIX

INTRODUCTION

The correspondence of Saint Vincent de Paul contains a wealth of information about the man, the Saint, and his milieu. To facilitate the informed reading of this volume, the editors felt it would be useful to preface the work with some explanatory remarks regarding language, style, and placement. In this way, a fuller image of the multifaceted personality and influence of the Saint will emerge from these pages, giving the reader a broader understanding of his life and the world in which he lived and worked.

In placing new letters within the volume or changing the placement of letters we have relied on Coste's corrections given in volumes VIII and XIII, the listings found in the *Annales*,[1] the dates on recently discovered letters or, in the absence of a date, on internal evidence. To facilitate research in Coste's work, we have chosen to keep the letter numbers of the original volumes and to indicate material newly added or relocated within each volume by adding a, b, c, etc., to the number of the preceding item. We have also decided to adhere to the span of years assigned by Coste for each volume.

In some cases, the finding of an original has enabled us to join fragments formerly considered separate letters. Such combined letters have been assigned a single number followed by a letter to differentiate the whole from the segments as published in the

---

[1]*Annales de la Congregation de la Mission* (1937), pp. 234-237.

original Coste volume. Where variations of a single letter exist, only the most correct version has been included in the volume. Likewise, although Coste chose to publish letters originally written in Latin both in that language and in French, the present edition sometimes bears only the English translation of the original Latin.

Three different types of letters are presented in these volumes: letters *from* Saint Vincent, letters *to* Saint Vincent and, at times, mere summaries of letters where the existence of a letter is known but no text is available. The letters written by Saint Vincent appear in regular type, while those addressed to him are printed in italics. Smaller type has been used to differentiate the summaries.

As Coste states in his introduction, almost all the letters we now possess are either in Saint Vincent's handwriting or in that of one of his secretaries. The term *original autograph* found in the citation of a letter indicates that the manuscript was written entirely in the Saint's hand. If the citation uses the term *signed letter,* the manuscript was written by a secretary and signed by the Saint. For some letters only a facsimile, a handwritten copy, a photocopy, or a photograph is known. Such indications are given in the citation of the letters for which this information is available.

The citations usually state as well the actual location of the manuscript or copy used for the present edition. Great care has been taken to verify these locations where possible. Letters drawn from other publications and those belonging to special collections, private or museum, have not been checked due to the near impossibility of such a task. However, an attempt has been made to verify all letters belonging to private houses of the Daughters of Charity, the Priests of the Mission, other religious houses, churches, and various religious institutions. In checking these locations and in the search for unpublished letters, we have at times been fortunate enough to locate the originals of letters for which only copies were known formerly. In these instances as well no mention has been made of the correction—the citation simply states that the manuscript is an original.

We have updated as well the department names given in the footnotes. Several departments have had name changes since the time of Coste, while two others have been subdivided.[2]

Although the project has undergone many delays, each has contributed in some way to the overall quality of the work. The appearance, in 1983, of the revised edition of Saint Louise de Marillac's writings[3] has permitted us to check her letters to Saint Vincent and her spiritual writings for any corrections which may have come to light. We have also adjusted all the footnote references to the appropriate indication as given in the new edition.

In any work of translation the question of style invariably arises, so it was not strange that we should be faced with the problem. Should we smooth out clumsy or elliptical phrasing in the interest of producing a more "readable" translation or should we preserve the roughness and unpolished style of the original in order to reflect the flavor and spontaneous quality of Saint Vincent's expression, supplying explanations where needed to make the sense clear? As our response to this question, we have attempted to make our translation as "readable" as possible while adhering closely to the style of each correspondent. For that purpose we have made an effort to give as literal a meaning as we could to the expressions used, while still adapting them to modern terminology. We have tried to reproduce even the grammatical constructions used by each correspondent unless the true meaning of the sentence would suffer thereby. Very long sentences have been shortened and short phrases joined together to render thoughts more readily intelligible,

---

[2]*Department* is the term used to designate each of the principal divisions of French territory. It denotes a geographical area similar to that of the American *state*. In the names of several departments, the word *maritime*, indicating *near the sea*, has replaced the word *inférieure* of the same meaning: Charente-Maritime, Seine-Maritime, Alpes-Maritime. In 1964, the Department of Seine was subdivided into Hauts-de-Seine, Paris, Seine-Saint-Denis, and Val-de-Marne; Seine-et-Oise became Essonne, Val-d'Oise, and Yvelines.

[3][Sr. Elisabeth Charpy, D.C., ed.] *Sainte Louise de Marillac. Ecrits Spirituels* (Tours: Mame, 1983), trans. Sr. Louise Sullivan, D.C., *Spiritual Writings of Louise de Marillac, Correspondence and Thoughts* (New York: New City Press, 1991).

though still preserving the sense of the original. The vocabulary and expression have deliberately been kept simple. Saint Vincent's love for and practice of simplicity are no secret to anyone familiar with his life; therefore, it was judged fitting to follow his own simplicity in the choice of words and style unless he himself opted for more elegant forms.

To retain the French atmosphere of the work we have left certain terms and expressions in the original French. General terms of greeting such as *Monsieur, Madame, etc.*, have not been translated, nor have we attempted an English version for expressions such as *O mon Dieu!, O Jésus!* Land-holding titles which often form part of a proper name—*Comte, Duc, Marquis*—have also been left in French. Other titles have been translated by the closest English equivalent possible. Proper names are given in the original language unless there is a familiar English form. This holds true for both people and places. Therefore, *Sainte Jeanne-Françoise Frémiot de Chantal* has been rendered as *Saint Jane Frances* Frémiot de Chantal, whereas *Pierre Séguier* remains in French. For places, *Brittany* is used instead of *Bretagne,* while *Granada, Villeneuve,* and similar names remain in the original language. Proper foreign names within the text of the manuscripts have been left as written by the correspondents. However, the footnotes and index present the name in its original language form—*Alessandro* Bichi for *Alexandre* Bichi; *Patrick Walsh* for *Patrice Valois.*

An attempt has been made to standardize name variations appearing in the original manuscripts: *Gondi* is always used in this edition although the form *Gondy* is often seen in the manuscripts. We have, however, left the variations *Pollalion* and *Poulaillon.* Although the correct spelling is the former, Saint Vincent always wrote the latter.

We have also standardized the various forms of the phrase used by Saint Vincent after his signature: *unworthy priest of the Congregation of the Mission.* Throughout this edition the abbreviation *i.s.C.M. (indignus sacerdos Congregationis Missionis)* has been used.

The word *fille,* meaning girl, daughter, young woman, appears in many of the manuscripts. In the seventeenth century, this word also denoted a woman religious or nun. We have tried to adjust the meaning of *fille* to the context of the various letters and have sometimes rendered the word as *Sister* rather than *Daughter* when referring to a member of Saint Louise's nascent community.

Monetary terms—*livre, écu,* etc.—have not been translated for it would be difficult to assign them an equivalent value in modern currency. Several other words and phrases have likewise been left in French—*Parlement, Chambre des Comptes, collège*—since English has no corresponding institution. These terms have been explained in footnotes. For other words of foreign origin used in English and found in English dictionaries no explanation has been given, for example, *faubourg.*

Saint Vincent often makes use of scriptural references which, however, are not always direct quotes. Where he has done so, the translation has been adjusted to flow with the meaning of the sentence. The scriptural quotations given in the footnotes are usually taken from the *New American Bible,* unless a passage cannot be found in that edition or a more suitable rendering of the phrase is found elsewhere. In such instances, the *Douay-Rheims Bible* has been used. In the case of the psalms, both versions have been cited because of the variations.

Coste almost always refers to Vincent de Paul as Saint Vincent or the Saint. In the present edition we have added this title to the names of Louise de Marillac and any other individual who has been canonized since Coste's time.

Generally speaking, in the titles of the letters, Coste gave the location of the addressee only when he was sure of it and when the locality was outside the then city of Paris. We have continued this practice and have attempted to make it more consistent. We have also followed Coste's custom of placing within brackets dates that are uncertain or conjectural. Brackets have also been used to indicate words either missing from the manuscript or inserted by the editors.

The capitalization forms of the original manuscripts have been adjusted to American usage as has the punctuation. Number forms—words versus figures—follow common American practice as well.

In addition to our goal of producing a smooth English translation which is faithful insofar as possible to the meaning and style of the original French, we have also purposed to present a work which is interesting and informative with regard to Saint Vincent, his correspondents, and his times. Both the scholar who may wish to use this work as a research tool and the ordinary reader unfamiliar with the Vincentian Family and with the religio-political history of the period have been kept in mind. A great effort has been made to update, correct, and amplify Coste's footnote material. Irrelevant notes have been eliminated and new annotation added whenever this has been deemed necessary or helpful. In the case of new matter, no indication has been given to distinguish Coste's footnotes from the annotation added by our editor.

A biographical sketch of each personage has been supplied throughout the work the first time that he or she appears in a volume. To facilitate reference to this data and also to the explanations of terms and places given throughout the text an index has been added to each book. The index indicates the number of the letter to which the reader should refer for the information sought. A general index will also be provided as an appendix to the entire work.

All references in the indices and the footnotes have been given by citing the volume and the number of the item rather than the page. Since Coste's volume span and his numbering of items have been retained, this practice should facilitate research in both his edition and the present translation.

In order to enjoy these volumes more thoroughly, the reader would do well to keep in mind that, as now, so then, one correspondent did not spell out to the other details that were already known and understood by both. Reading these letters at a distance of some three hundred years will often arouse a curiosity which in many cases must remain unsatisfied. The allusions made will not always be clear, nor can they be. However, a familiarity beforehand with the life of Saint Vincent will greatly aid one's knowledge and understanding of the situations mentioned and the people involved. The three-volume definitive biography written by Coste[4] provides extensive information, but many shorter versions of the Saint's life can be found. Placed against such a background, these writings take on still more a life of their own and make the Saint vividly present once again. The twinkle in his eyes and the smile or tenderness in his voice seep through the words and we meet the delightful, charming man known to his contemporaries. The severe, ascetic Saint takes on a new personality and somehow becomes more human.

Let us not fail to seek the man beyond these words, the man of compassion, warmth, humor, savoir faire, authority, and, most of all, the mystic whose sanctity was carved amid the bustle and involvement of very human situations. He will give us hope that we, too, can find holiness in an ordinary, busy life. May this personal acquaintance with the real Vincent de Paul lead us to encounter the dynamic force behind his life, Jesus Christ, who, for him, was all things.

NOTE TO THE READER

The editors felt that it was not necessary to reproduce in each volume the lengthy "Introduction to the French Edition" and the entire "Introduction to the English Edition," which appear at the beginning of Volume I. They would like to remind the reader, however, that these introductions contain valuable information regarding the background and major sources of the letters and facilitate an informed reading of the correspondence.

---

[4]Pierre Coste, C.M., *The Life and Works of Saint Vincent de Paul,* trans. Joseph Leonard, C.M., 3 vols. (Westminster, Maryland: Newman Press, 1952; repr., New York: New City Press, 1987).

ACKNOWLEDGEMENTS

Special thanks should be given to Vincentian Fathers Thomas Davitt, Ignatius M. Melito, and John E. Rybolt for their dedication in reading the manuscript of this volume and of the preceding ones. Their expertise in history, theology, Sacred Scripture, and/or English, and their knowledge of Vincentian history and spirituality have allowed us to correct errors, clarify the text, and make stylistic changes which render it more readable. By the invaluable contribution each has made to this translation of Saint Vincent's correspondence, they have merited the gratitude, not only of the editorial staff, but of all who will be enriched by reflective reading of the Saint's own words.

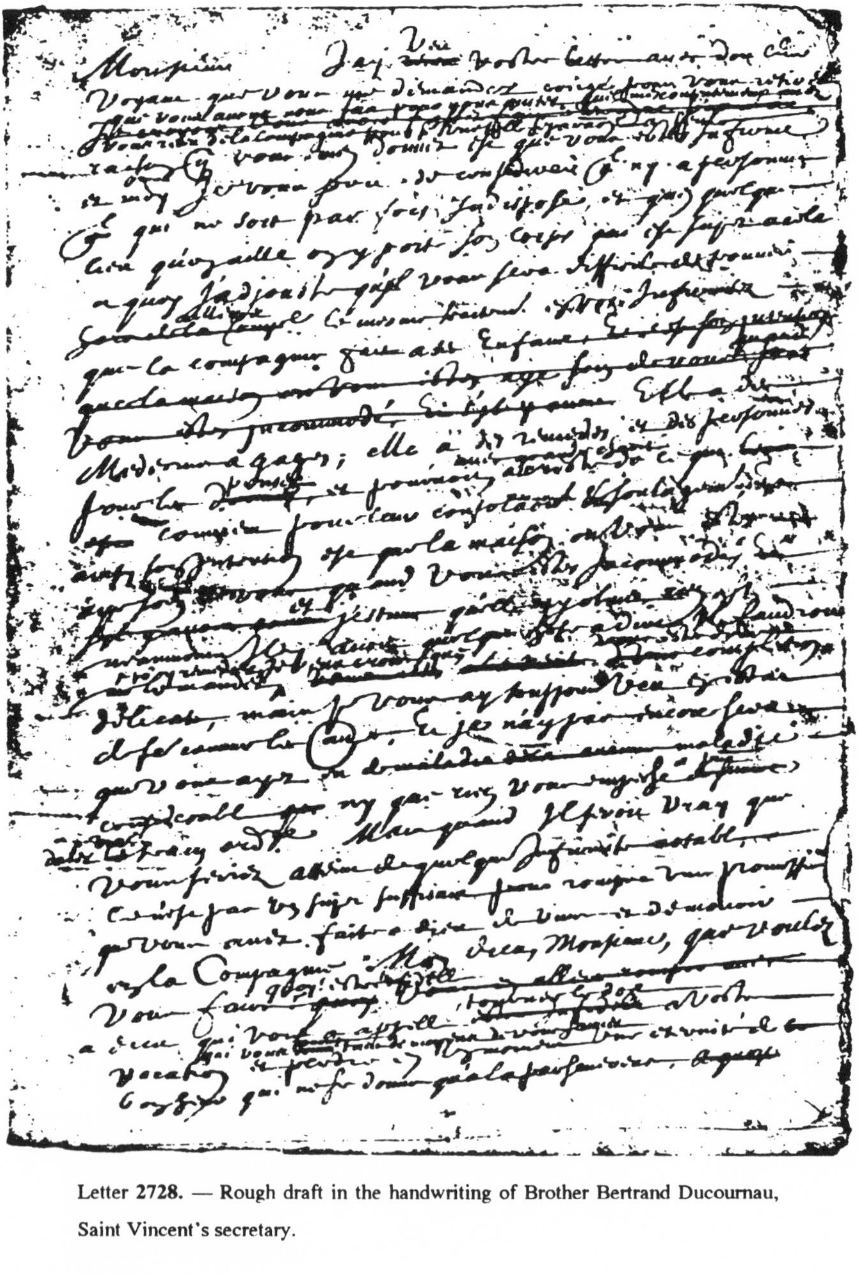

Letter 2728. — Rough draft in the handwriting of Brother Bertrand Ducournau, Saint Vincent's secretary.

a Mr. B[illegible] Vicaire pbre de la Compie au Mans 26 d'8bre 1698

A Vous permettez [illegible] sorti de la compagnie [illegible] par consequant vous accordez [illegible] vous demande [illegible] de la bonne [illegible] de N. S.

Monsieur Vre tres h[umbl]e

A. G.

Monsieur que vous aviez eu grand regret a vostre [illegible] Dieu aura fait [illegible] car elle est de la nature de [illegible] que [illegible] abandonnement [illegible] vous deviez grand [illegible] aussi [illegible] abandonnement [illegible] que vostre [illegible] volonte [illegible] gardez vous [illegible] de la sainte [illegible], faites quelque jour [illegible] connoistre la volonte de Dieu [illegible] d'accomplir vos voeux [illegible] vous estes obligé, aussi [illegible] je vous [illegible] la lettre [illegible]

Vous [illegible] congé de parol [illegible] A

[illegible] le premier voeu que vous fistes [illegible] de vostre [illegible] obligé de les garder tous [illegible] vous [illegible] de devoir [illegible] du Bref [illegible]

Vous [illegible]

SAINT VINCENT DE PAUL

CORRESPONDENCE

2475. - TO GEORGES DES JARDINS,[1] SUPERIOR, IN TOUL

Paris, December 1, 1657

Monsieur,

The grace of O[ur] L[ord] be with you forever!

I received your letter concerning the arrival of Brother Jean Proust.[2] It is clear to me that you are willing to do without him; besides, we need him here. For these reasons I ask you to send him back to us as soon as possible, unless you need him for something no one else can do; if so, you can keep him for another ten to fifteen days.

I praise God that you have gone back to giving missions. I ask His Divine Goodness to bless your work and fortify your health. I am, in His love, Monsieur, your most humble servant.

VINCENT DEPAUL,
i.s.C.M.[3]

At the bottom of the page: Monsieur des Jardins

Letter 2475. - Archives of the Mission, Turin, original signed letter.

[1]Georges des Jardins, born in Alençon (Orne) on January 6, 1625, was ordained a priest in September 1649, entered the Congregation of the Mission on August 15, 1651, and took his vows on August 17, 1653. Later, he was Superior in Toul (1655-57) and Narbonne (1659).

[2]Brother Jean Proust, born in Parthenay (Deux-Sèvres) on March 12, 1620, entered the Congregation of the Mission on June 25, 1645, and took his vows on October 28, 1647.

Saint Vincent refers to clerical students as "Brothers." The context usually determines whether the one referred to is a coadjutor Brother or a student destined for the priesthood.

[3]Saint Vincent subscribed the initials, *i.p.d.l.M.* (*indigne prêtre de la Mission*) [unworthy priest of the Mission], to his signature. It has been traditional in the Congregation of the Mission

2476. - TO PIERRE DAVEROULT,[1] IN SAINTES

Paris, December 2, 1657

Monsieur,

The grace of O[ur] L[ord] be with you forever!

I am replying to the letter you wrote me concerning the Mass stipends you want, saying that I will send them to you if we get any, but I must tell you also that it is rare that anyone comes to us to give us such alms. It is not that people do not request Masses of us—we are often overwhelmed with them, and right now we have about one thousand for the poor Genoa house, which owed them but could not take care of them because it lost six or seven priests—I mean, however, that we scarcely ever receive any money for them. So, Monsieur, I dare not give you any hope of a single one, although I will be happy to send them to you, if we do get any, so you can finish paying off the little debt that is worrying you.

I have nothing to say to you about the difficulty you are experiencing on the part of the persons with whom you are at present, except that we will remedy that as soon as possible, God willing. Meanwhile, I ask O[ur] L[ord] to give you a share of His humility and patience to overcome these difficulties. I am, in His love. . . .

I praise God that the seminary where you are working is doing better and better, and I ask His Divine Goodness to make it grow in numbers and in virtue. I think this will not depend on you, since you are contributing to it by your instructions and example.

---

to append to one's name the Latin of this phrase, *indignus sacerdos Congregationis Missionis* or the initials, *i.s.C.M.* The editors have adopted this traditional practice, substituting the initials of the Latin phrase for the French used by Saint Vincent.

Letter 2476. - Archives of the Mission, Turin, unsigned rough draft.

[1]Pierre Daveroult, born in Béthune (Pas-de-Calais) on January 20, 1614, was ordained a priest during Lent of 1638. He entered the Congregation of the Mission on April 13, 1653, and took his vows on January 13, 1656. Twice he embarked for Madagascar and twice returned to Paris without being able to set foot on the island.

2476a. - TO PIERRE CABEL,[1] SUPERIOR, IN SEDAN

Paris, December 2 [1657] [2]

I ask M. Cabel to go to see Messieurs des Maretz, the sons of the Duc de Richelieu's [3] Intendant,[4] who are in the army and are stationed at the Sedan citadel.[5] I ask him to offer them his services

---

Letter 2476a. - Archives of the Religieuses Hospitalières de Saint-Joseph, 251 Ouest, avenue des Pins, Montreal H2W IR6 (Canada), original autograph letter; photograph in the Archives of the Congregation of the Mission, 95 rue de Sèvres, Paris. The text was published in *Annales C. M.*, vol. 126 (1961), p. 222, and reprinted in *Mission et Charité*, 19-20, no. 95, pp. 119-120. This edition uses the latter text.

[1]Pierre Cabel, born in Chézery (Ain), was ordained a priest on March 13, 1642, and entered the Congregation of the Mission in Annecy in January 1643, at twenty-six years of age. He arrived in Paris on February 24, 1644, and was sent to Sedan, where he took his vows on August 9, 1645, and was Superior (1657-63). He was also Superior in Saint-Méen (1670-71), Visitor for the Province of Champagne, and a member of the General Assembly that elected René Alméras as Superior General. Cabel died at Saint-Lazare on September 26, 1688, leaving the reputation of an exemplary priest. His biography, written by one of his contemporaries, was published in vol. II of *Notices sur les prêtres, clercs et frères défunts de la Congrégation de la Mission* (10 vols. in two series, Paris: Dumoulin, 1881-1911), pp. 315-37.

[2]On the sheet containing the address, an old notation gives the year as 1657; there is no information to contradict the exactitude of this date.

[3]Armand-Jean du Plessis, Duc de Richelieu, was born on October 2, 1631. He succeeded his father, François de Vignerod, brother of the Duchesse d'Aiguillon, as General of the Galleys (1653-81). In virtue of that office the hospital for galley slaves came under his jurisdiction. He died on May 10, 1715.

[4]Jean Desmarets, Seigneur de Saint-Sorlin, member of the French Academy, and Intendant of the Duc de Richelieu, was born in Paris in 1595. He wrote some very successful tragedies and comedies before devoting himself mainly to works of piety, translations of the *Imitation of Christ* and the *Spiritual Combat, Avis du Saint-Esprit au Roi,* and some articles attacking the Jansenists, Simon Morin, Homer, Virgil, and the pagan authors. His principal work, *Les Délices de l'esprit,* a poetic apology of Christianity, was printed in 1658. He often consulted Saint Vincent and called him his "good spiritual Father"; Saint-Cyran was frequently the topic of their conversations. Despite the strong influence of the Saint, after his death Desmarets fell into strange ways, not only on the spiritual and religious level but also in the literature he wrote, leading people to think that he had more or less lost his mind. Desmarets died in Paris on October 28, 1676. No further information concerning his sons is available.

[5]The Missionaries had been working in Sedan since 1643; the previous year the principality of Sedan had been annexed to the kingdom of France from the Spanish dominions in the Low Countries (Spanish Netherlands). In 1644 the King, by his endowment of twenty-four thousand livres (cf. vol. XIII, no. 92), had tried to procure missions, if not to convert the Calvinists to the Catholic faith, at least to confirm the Catholics in their faith (cf. vol. II, no. 660, p. 435, n. 10, and no. 723, p. 524, n. 1). The Governor, Abraham de Fabert, and a reliable garrison were supposed to win hearts and minds to France, and thereby, according to prevalent thought, to Roman Catholicism. Saint Vincent is recommending that his Missionaries help the Catholics to

and those of the house and to ask either M. Michel[6] or M. Sevant[7] to converse with them in the spirit of piety and devotion and to encourage them to receive the Holy Sacraments once a month. I assure M. Cabel that he and either M. Michel or M. Sevant will console me more than I can say because they will give me the means of acknowledging in some way the infinite obligations we have toward the elder M. des Maretz.

VINCENT DEPAUL,
i.s.C.M.

Addressed: Monsieur Cabel, Superior of the Priests of the Mission, in Sedan

2477. - TO EDME MENESTRIER,[1] SUPERIOR, IN AGEN

Paris, December 5, 1657

Monsieur,

The grace of O[ur] [Lord] be with you forever!

Enclosed is a short note of reply for Father du Bourg.[2]

---

become better and, by the example of a truly Christian life, dispel the preconceived ideas of the Calvinists.

[6]Guillaume Michel, born in Esteville (Seine-Maritime), left his parish in Saint-Valery to enter the Congregation of the Mission on June 19, 1646, at thirty-nine years of age. He withdrew from the Congregation of his own accord before taking vows but later returned. In 1657 he was a member of the Sedan house and was in Fontainebleau in 1666.

[7]Jean Sevant, born in Vaucelles, a faubourg of Caen (Calvados), on April 14, 1617, entered the Congregation of the Mission on October 9, 1654, at the Paris seminary, took his vows on January 20, 1657, in the presence of M. Berthe, and died in Richelieu on November 5, 1665.

Letter 2477. - Archives of the Mission, Turin, original signed letter.

[1]Edme Menestrier, born in Rugney (Vosges), on June 18, 1618, entered the Congregation of the Mission on September 10, 1640, took his vows in October 1646, and was ordained a priest in 1648. He spent the rest of his Community life at the Agen Seminary, where he was Superior (1651-65, 1672-85) and Procurator (1665-72). Saint Vincent always called him by his first name only.

[2]Moïse du Bourg, S.J., was born in 1598 and died in Limoges on March 3, 1662. He was the author of the book entitled: *Le jansénisme foudroyé par le bulle du Pape Innocent X, et l'histoire*

Has the Bishop of Agen[3] written to his clergy on your behalf, as he led you to hope?

Please give me a little more time to think about the Brother cleric you are requesting of us, and let me know what you think about M. Admirault[4] because they would like to have him in Notre-Dame de Lorm for the seminary. Now, if he could be more suitable and effective there than with you, we would give you in his place M. Thieulin,[5] who is a good priest.

We have no news here. I am always, in the love of O[ur] L[ord], Monsieur, your most humble servant.

VINCENT DEPAUL,
i.s.C.M.

Addressed: Monsieur Edme

---

du jansénisme, contenant sa conception, sa naissance, son accroissement et son agonie (Bordeaux: I. Mongiron-Millanges, 1658). As stated in the preface, the idea of the author was that this book was to serve primarily "for zealous Catholic missionaries . . . , especially in rural areas, during their missions."

[3]Barthélemy d'Elbène, Bishop of Agen (1638-63).

[4]Claude Admirault, born in Chinon (Indre-et-Loire), entered the Congregation of the Mission on September 20, 1648, at sixteen years of age, took his vows in 1651, was ordained a priest in December 1656, and was placed at the Agen Seminary. He was Superior of the Montauban Seminary (1665-75, 1686-90), and the Agen Seminary (1690-94).

[5]René Thieulin, born in Argentan (Orne) on January 29, 1629, entered the Congregation of the Mission on January 18, 1653, was ordained a priest on December 25, 1654, and took his vows in January 1655. He was Superior at the Collège des Bons-Enfants (1674-76, 1685-89) and acting Assistant General (1677-79). At the General Assembly of 1679 he was named Assistant General, remaining in office until the generalate of Nicolas Pierron (1697). Thieulin died in Paris on November 7, 1706.

2478. - TO FIRMIN GET,[1] SUPERIOR, IN MARSEILLES

Paris, December 7, 1657

Monsieur,

The grace of O[ur] L[ord] be with you forever!

I received your two letters of November 20 and 26.[2] I praise God for M. Berthe's [3] arrival and the good results for which you are hoping from his visitation.

I have not yet been able to read the letters from Barbary you sent me because I received your packet just a few hours ago. I will try to answer them as soon as possible.

You were a little too hasty in drawing a bill of exchange on us for 500 livres,[4] after writing us that you were unable to find that

---

Letter 2478. - Archives of the Mission, Paris, copy made from the original in the Hains Family Collection, Marseilles.

[1]Firmin Get, born in Chépy (Somme) on January 19, 1621, entered the Congregation of the Mission on January 6, 1641, and took his vows in January 1643. In 1648 he was placed in Marseilles, where he was Superior (1654-62), except for a very short time spent in Montpellier (1659-60) to open a seminary, which lasted only a few months. Later he became Superior in Sedan (1663-66, 1673-81) and in Le Mans (1670-73), and Visitor of the Province of Poitou, an office he held until April 4, 1682.

[2]These letters are no longer extant. It is evident from innumerable references in the Saint's letters that a great many letters written to him are now missing. Except for what he himself might not have preserved, much of this loss can be attributed to the pillage of Saint-Lazare during the French Revolution.

[3]Thomas Berthe, born in Donchery (Ardennes), entered the Congregation of the Mission on December 26, 1640, at the age of eighteen, and took his vows on December 8, 1645. After ordination in 1646, he was assigned to Sedan. Convinced that he had been sent there as Superior, he felt humiliated to see less important work entrusted to him, and he returned to his family. A short time later he came to his senses, and Saint Vincent, who recognized his virtues and appreciated his talents, joyfully took him back. He subsequently served the Community as Superior in Picardy and Champagne and in other important positions: Superior at the Bons-Enfants Seminary (1649-50) and in Rome (1653-55), Secretary of the Congregation (1660), Assistant to the Superior General (1661-67), Superior in Lyons (1668-71), at Saint-Charles Seminary (1673-82, 1687-89), and Richelieu (1682-85). In October 1659 Saint Vincent decided that among his Missionaries none was more suitable to succeed him as head of the Congregation than René Alméras or Thomas Berthe. He proposed the two names in advance, in writing, to the General Assembly that was to choose his successor. (René Alméras was elected.) There were some clashes between Berthe and Edme Jolly, the third Superior General (1673-97), which clouded his last years. Berthe died in 1697. (Cf. *Notices*, vol. II, pp. 247-313.)

[4]Throughout this edition the various denominations of French money have been left in French, since no adequate, unchanging value in American dollars can be assigned. In the time

amount, and for having asked that Messieurs Simonnet [5] be given here the money we had that was to be forwarded to you, which is only around 330 livres. For, in line with that, we had already sent you a letter to get 160 livres from M. Napollon,[6] so now you will be getting 660 livres, which is twice the amount we owe you. God willing, we will still pay the 500 livres to preserve your credit, but remember to credit us with this additional amount.

I approve of the reasons you give me for sending M. Le Vacher of Tunis[7] the first money we will receive for Algiers, since it is only just that he be reimbursed for the sums he sent to Brother Barreau[8]

---

of Saint Vincent, one écu equaled three livres; one thousand livres could support two priests and a Brother for one year on the missions (cf. vol. V, no. 1972, p. 485).

[5]Bankers in Paris.

[6]Jean and Louis Napollon were bankers in Marseilles. As with the Simonnets in Paris, Saint Vincent often used their bank when transferring funds.

[7]Jean Le Vacher, born in Écouen (Val-d'Oise) on March 15, 1619, entered the Congregation of the Mission with his brother Philippe on October 5, 1643. He took his vows in 1646 and was ordained a priest in 1647. When Julien Guérin, a Missionary in Tunis, needed help, Saint Vincent decided to send him Jean Le Vacher. On August 23, 1647, as the Founder and his young disciple were leaving Saint-Lazare, they met Nicolò di Bagno, the Nuncio. "Excellency," said the Saint, "you are just in time to give your blessing to this good priest, who is leaving for the Tunis mission." "What! this child!" exclaimed the astonished Nuncio. "Excellency," replied the Saint, "he has the vocation for that."

Le Vacher arrived in Tunis on November 22, 1647. Guérin's death on May 13, 1648, followed two months later by that of the Consul, Martin de Lange, placed on Le Vacher the double burden of Consul and head of the Mission. In 1650 he added Vicar Apostolic to these titles. Since the Holy See would not allow priests to be in charge of the consulate, Saint Vincent sent a layman, Martin Husson, a parlementary lawyer, who arrived in Tunis in 1653 and left in April 1657, expelled by the Dey. For two years Jean Le Vacher acted as Consul. He returned to France in 1666, and was sent to Algiers in 1668 as Vicar-General of Carthage and Vicar Apostolic of Algiers and Tunis. His life in Algiers was that of an apostle, and his death that of a martyr. On July 16, 1683, Algiers was being bombarded by Duquesne. After the Turks had used every device to make Le Vacher apostatize, they finally tied him to the mouth of a cannon, which shot his body into the sea. (Cf. Raymond Gleizes, *Jean Le Vacher, vicaire apostolique et consul de France à Tunis et à Alger (1619-83)* [Paris: Gabalda, 1914].) Frequent mention of the Le Vacher brothers appears in the letters. In this volume, unless stated otherwise, Jean is usually associated with Tunis and Philippe is mentioned in conjunction with Algiers.

[8]Jean Barreau was born in Saint-Jean-en-Grève parish, Paris, on September 26, 1612. While still a young man, he left the position of parlementary lawyer to enter the Cistercian Order. He later asked Saint Vincent to receive him into his Community and began his novitiate on May 14, 1645. In 1646 Saint Vincent sent him, while still a seminarian, to Algiers as French Consul, in keeping with the wish of the Holy See not to have a priest in the office of Consul. There his

when he was in need. However, Brother Barreau should give us some assurance that he has received them. I will see if the letter says anything to me about this, and we will act in conformity with it.

God be praised for the payment that same Brother was about to receive of the 1600 piastres M. Gaspard Vancamberg [9] owed him! That amount, together with the 1000 écus his brother sent him and the 600 or so piastres M. Le Vacher of Tunis says he had him withdraw, should have helped to pay off his most pressing debts. With 9000 livres, he should have been able to fill quite a few holes.

I am, in O[ur] L[ord], Monsieur, your most humble servant.

VINCENT DEPAUL,
i.s.C.M.

2479. - TO CHARLES OZENNE,[1] SUPERIOR, IN WARSAW

Paris, December 7, 1657

Monsieur,

The grace of O[ur] [Lord] be with you forever!

I received your two letters of October 17 and 25, which gave me

---

dedication to the slaves was limitless. The goodness of his heart moved him more than once to commit himself for sums he did not possess or which did not belong to him; for this he was ill-treated by local authorities and reproved by Saint Vincent. When his companion, Jacques Lesage, became gravely ill, Barreau took his vows before him, although he had not yet been released from the simple vow of religion he had taken as a Cistercian. This dispensation was not requested until 1652. Finally, on November 1, 1661, he was able to take his vows validly in the Congregation of the Mission. He was in Paris at the time, summoned by René Alméras, second Superior General, and had only Minor Orders. He was ordained a priest in 1662 or 1663 and spent the remainder of his life at Saint-Lazare as Procurator. In 1672 he was associated with the Procurator General, Nicolas Talec. On May 24, 1675, during a serious illness, he made his will, to which he added a codicil on April 7, 1679. (Cf. Arch. Nat. M 213, no. 8.)

[9]A slave in Algiers from Antwerp.

Letter 2479. - Archives of the Mission, Krakow, original signed letter.

[1]Charles Ozenne, born in Nibas (Somme) on April 15, 1613, was ordained a priest in 1637 and entered the Congregation of the Mission on June 10, 1638. After his Internal Seminary

both joy and fear: joy, in seeing that you, M. Desdames,[2] and M. Duperroy[3] are now together in Warsaw—to their great pleasure and yours—for which I thank God; and fear because of what you say about the countryside being contaminated and the city being in some danger. May God be pleased to deliver it from this scourge and from any new troubles, since it has already been tried by them so many times! I have recommended to the members of our community that they entreat Him earnestly for this grace.

I am consoled that good M. Falibowski continues to show his kindness to you; if God blesses his efforts to see that you have a house in Krakow, we should hope that His Divine Goodness will provide the other things necessary for an establishment.

You say that the war has ruined three houses you had in Warsaw and five in your area. That is a heavy toll, but it was not just that you should be exempted from the public affliction. God, who has allowed this, will have the goodness to restore these losses in due

(novitiate), he was assigned to Troyes, where he took his vows on August 29, 1642, and became Superior in 1644. Saint Vincent recalled him in 1653 to direct the mission in Poland. "He is a zealous and detached man of God," he wrote to Nicolas Guillot, "with a talent for leadership and for winning hearts within the Company and outside of it." (Cf. vol. IV, no. 1624, p. 573.) Unfortunately, this excellent Missionary's career was brief: he died in Warsaw on August 14, 1658. (Cf. *Notices*, vol. III, pp. 148-54.)

[2]Guillaume Desdames, born in Rouen, entered the Congregation of the Mission on June 19, 1645, at twenty-three years of age, took his vows on March 10, 1648, and was ordained a priest on May 31, 1648. He was stationed in Toul shortly afterward, then sent to Poland where he arrived with Lambert aux Couteaux in November 1651. He worked there with praiseworthy dedication amid numerous difficulties, first as a simple confrere and, after the death of Charles Ozenne (August 14, 1658), as Superior of the Mission. René Alméras recalled him to France in 1669, but he returned to Poland a few years later and assumed the direction of the house in Chelmno. He returned to France for the General Assembly of 1685. Desdames ended his days as Superior of the foundation in Krakow, June 1, 1692. (Cf. *Notices*, vol. III, p. 166, and *Mémoires de la Congrégation de la Mission* [11 vols., Paris, 1863-99], vol. I, pp. 24-33.)

[3]Nicolas Duperroy, born in Maulévrier (Seine-Maritime) on January 16, 1625, entered the Congregation of the Mission on September 13, 1651, was ordained a priest on April 4, 1654, and took his vows on December 13, 1663. After the capture of Warsaw, he was brutally treated by the Swedes and left for dead, caught the plague twice, and for a long period of time suffered from a painful bone condition. René Alméras appointed him Superior in 1670. His house sent him as delegate to the General Assembly of 1673. Returning to Poland, he continued as Superior until 1674, after which there is no further trace of him.

time, if He so pleases. Oh! how kind is the Queen[4] who, seeing that your church had no vestments, has already given it some gifts! Our Lord, whom she honors everywhere, will not let this good work, nor any of the others she is constantly doing, go unrewarded.

We will do whatever Her Majesty commands us with regard to M. Turin, the father of Mademoiselle Cornuty. I am going to commission someone to go to find out the place and situation in which he is and to try to reassure him regarding his residence and his religion. I will let you know about this.

I feel deeply indebted to Mademoiselle de Villers[5] for the generous services that she in her charity renders you on occasion.

M. Sergent came here recently, but I was away, to my great regret, for I would have been consoled to see him and to hear some news in detail from him. He brought me some letters that were written a long time ago; nothing in them requires an answer.

We have no news here. We have more than forty seminarians,[6] most of whom are very promising. A few of the men have been sick but they are better now. We sent the confreres out to open two missions at the same time—not to mention a third, which is being given in Champagne.

I will send your packet on to Nibas.[7]

---

[4]Louise-Marie de Gonzague, Queen of Poland, was the daughter of the Duc de Nevers. Despite her attachment to the Jansenist party, this former Lady of Charity, wife of King Wladyslaw IV, then of his brother, Jan Casimir, held Saint Vincent in the highest esteem. She summoned to Poland the Priests of the Mission, the Daughters of Charity, and the Visitation nuns; gave them housing, took care that nothing was wanting to them, and never failed to protect them. She died in 1667.

[5]Lady-in-waiting for the Queen of Poland.

[6]In the Congregation of the Mission, those in the years of formation went through the Internal Seminary, which corresponded to the novitiate in Religious Orders. All new applicants were received there to be formed to the practice of the virtues of their state and to be trained for the lifestyle and duties of the Missionaries. Saint Vincent readmitted to the seminary Priests of the Congregation who felt the need to withdraw for a month or two from exterior occupations so as to recapture the first fervor of their vocation.

[7]Birthplace of M. Ozenne. It is situated in the Somme region.

I recommend myself to your prayers and to those of our dear confreres and our good Sisters, to whom I send greetings.

I am, in the love of O[ur] L[ord], Monsieur, your most humble servant.

VINCENT DEPAUL,
i.s.C.M.

If M. Falibowski makes any progress with what his incomparable charity may procure for you in Krakow, please let me know so we can get a few members of the Company ready. O Monsieur, how fervently I pray that God will sanctify more and more the soul of that good gentleman! [8]

Addressed: Monsieur Ozenne, Superior of the Priests of the Mission of Warsaw, in Warsaw

2480. - TO EDME JOLLY,[1] SUPERIOR, IN ROME

Paris, December 7, 1657

Monsieur,

The grace of O[ur] L[ord] be with you forever!

The regular mail from Lyons has arrived but not the mailbag from Rome, so I have not received any letters from you.

---

[8]The postscript is in the Saint's handwriting.

Letter 2480. - Archives of the Mission, Turin, original signed letter.

[1]Edme Jolly, born in Doué (Seine-et-Marne) on October 24, 1622, was acquainted in his youth with the Marquis de Fontenay-Mareuil, the French Ambassador in Rome, who took him to that city. He even entrusted Jolly with a delicate mission in the service of the King, which the young man handled most successfully. Before being admitted to Saint-Lazare on November 13, 1646, he had a post in the Apostolic Datary, an office of the Roman Curia in charge of examining the fitness of candidates for Papal benefices and of handling the claims of those with rights to pensions. After his seminary he returned to Rome, reviewed philosophy, theology, and

I am waiting for you to send me the letters of appointment for the Gignac benefice, for which you have registered the dates: one for M. Cuissot, as a graduate in Cahors,[2] and the other for M. Grimal.[3]

I have not yet received Cardinal Bagni's[4] reply regarding the clarification I requested concerning the priests H[is] E[minence] had instructed me to send to Ireland and Scotland. Perhaps the plans

---

Canon Law, and was ordained a priest on May 1, 1649. In May 1654 he became Director of the Saint-Lazare Seminary, and in 1655 he was appointed Superior of the house in Rome, from where Thomas Berthe had just been recalled by order of the King. Jolly rendered immense service to his Congregation because of the concessions he obtained from the Holy See. After the Saint's death he became Assistant to the Superior General and Assistant of the Motherhouse. The General Assembly of 1673 elected him successor to René Alméras as Superior General. His generalate was one of the most fruitful the Company has ever known. Jolly died in Paris on March 26, 1697. His biography, written by a contemporary, was published with some alterations in vol. III of *Notices*, pp. 387-512.

[2]The death of Élie Laisné de la Marguerie, archpriest of Gignac, left vacant this simple benefice of the diocese of Cahors. Gilbert Cuissot was named to succeed him. In his letter of November 9, 1657, to Edme Jolly, Saint Vincent requests that he obtain this provision from Rome for "Gilbert Cuissot, priest of the Autun diocese, designated a graduate of the said diocese of Cahors." (Cf. vol. VI, no. 2452.)

Cuissot, born in Moulins (Allier), on November 5, 1607, had been a priest for six years when he entered the Congregation of the Mission on May 14, 1637. After serving as Superior of the Luçon house, he was appointed to the same office in La Rose (1640-44), then at the Collège des Bons-Enfants (1644-46), where he took his vows on November 11, 1644. From there he went to the Le Mans Seminary (1646), then to Saint-Lazare (1646-47). He was Director of the Cahors Seminary (1647-62) and Superior of the Richelieu house (1662-66). He declared that, at the time of the election of Saint Vincent's successor, he was hesitant about voting for René Alméras, who was in poor health. The Saint, however, appeared to him and determined his choice. He also said that in 1662, while exorcising a possessed woman, he drew from the demon an acknowledgment of the Founder's holiness and the reward reserved by God for Missionaries faithful to their vocation. Cuissot died in 1684.

[3]François Grimal, born in Paris on March 6, 1605, began his Internal Seminary on June 6, 1640, and took his vows on October 9, 1646. He rendered outstanding service to his Congregation as Superior in Crécy (1645-46), Montmirail (1646-49, 1654-55), and Agen (1650-51); as Second Assistant to Saint Vincent (1652); and in more humble positions in Fontainebleau and elsewhere. The introduction of vows into the Company corresponded to his wishes, and he made every effort to have this measure accepted by those around him. He renewed his vows on October 3, 1665, in the presence of M. Portail.

[4]Nicolò di Bagno (Saint Vincent always refers to him as *Nicolas Bagni*), Archbishop of Athens, Nuncio in France from June 25, 1643 to 1657, was made a Cardinal with the titular church of Sant'Eusebio, and Bishop of Senigallia on April 9, 1657. He died in Rome on August 23, 1663, at the age of seventy-nine. Saint Vincent, with whom he had a close relationship, was very pleased with his benevolence.

have been changed. On this point, I will tell you that God has not granted me the same favor with the present N[uncio] [5] as I had with his predecessor, and I think he was a little annoyed that we were approached[6] about sending those priests. Still, I do not know this for certain, but you can use this information in whatever way you deem appropriate.

I am, in O[ur] L[ord], Monsieur, your most humble servant.

VINCENT DEPAUL,
i.s.C.M.

Addressed: Monsieur Jolly, Superior of the Priests of the Mission of Rome, in Rome

2481. - TO JEAN PARRE,[1] IN RETHEL[2]

Paris, December 8, 1657

Dear Brother,

The grace of O[ur] L[ord] be with you forever!

I have not had a letter from you since last week. This kept me from going to the meeting[3] yesterday, but no new orders for allocating funds were given there.

---

[5]Celio Piccolomini, a member of the ancient Sienese family that furnished many Bishops of Siena and Pienza and several Cardinals and Popes, as well as political and military leaders. Titular Bishop of Caesarea, and Nuncio in France (1656-63), he became a Cardinal in 1664 and was Archbishop of Siena from 1671 until his death in 1681.

[6]First redaction: "that he was not approached." The change is in the Saint's handwriting.

Letter 2481. - Archives of the Mission, Turin, original signed letter.

[1]Born in Châtillon-en-Dunois (Eure-et-Loir), Jean Parre entered the Congregation of the Mission on April 16, 1638, at twenty-seven years of age, took his vows in 1643, and died after 1660. He and Brother Mathieu Régnard were two of the most intelligent and active instruments that Divine Providence placed in Saint Vincent's hands. Brother Parre traveled all over Picardy and Champagne assessing and remedying needs. (Cf. *Notices,* vol. II, pp. 223-40.)

[2]Town in the Ardennes that had suffered greatly from the war, especially since 1651. Brother Jean Parre made several trips there to organize the distribution of the aid sent from Paris. He also started a Confraternity of Charity there.

[3]A meeting of the Ladies of Charity of the Hôtel-Dieu. Through Missionaries like Jean Parre, they were assisting provinces devastated by the Fronde and its aftermath.

I pray to O[ur] L[ord] that your health may always be good and your work pleasing to God. I am, in Him, dear Brother, your very devoted servant.

VINCENT DEPAUL,
i.s.C.M.

Addressed: Brother Jean Parre, of the Mission, in Rethel

2482. - TO A PRIEST OF THE MISSION

[November or December 1657] [1]

So you have not heard about the losses we have suffered! O Monsieur! how great they are, not only because of the number of

---

Letter 2482. - Abelly, *La vie du Vénérable Serviteur de Dieu Vincent de Paul* (3 vols., Paris: Florentin Lambert, 1664), bk. III, chap. XXI, p. 311.

Louis Abelly was born in Paris in 1604. From the earliest years of his priesthood he took part in Saint Vincent's apostolic labors. The Saint spoke so highly of him to François Fouquet, Bishop-elect of Bayonne, that the latter appointed him his Vicar-General. Abelly's stay in Bayonne was not long; he accepted a simple village parish near Paris, and shortly afterward (1644) was given charge of Saint-Josse parish in the capital, where he formed an ecclesiastical community. He later became Director of the Sisters of the Cross (1650), chaplain of the General Hospital (1657), and Bishop of Rodez (1664). In 1666 he resigned his diocese for reasons of health and retired to Saint-Lazare, where he spent the last twenty-five years of his life in recollection and study. We have about thirty of his books on devotion, history, and theology. Abelly is not merely the sponsor of *La vie du Vénérable Serviteur de Dieu Vincent de Paul,* as has been asserted, but is truly its author. His task was greatly facilitated by Brother Ducournau, one of the Saint's secretaries, who collected and classified the documents. Abelly made a donation to the Saint-Lazare house of some property in Pantin, which became the country house of the students. He died on October 4, 1691, and, according to his wish, was buried in the church of Saint-Lazare, under the Saints-Anges chapel. (Cf. Pierre Collet, *La vie de St Vincent de Paul* [2 vols., Nancy: A. Leseure, 1748], vol. I, pp. 5ff.)

[1]Saint Vincent wrote this letter after learning of the death of Dermot Duggan, i.e., after October 30, 1657, and very probably within two months after receiving this news.

Duggan (Saint Vincent spells his name *Duiguin*), born in Ireland in 1620, was already a priest when he entered the Congregation of the Mission on August 26, 1645. In November of the following year he was sent back to Ireland, returning to France in 1648. Two years later he left for Scotland, where he spent the rest of his life amid great dangers, animated with the zeal of an apostle and the courage of a martyr. He died on May 17, 1657 on the isle of Uist, where an ancient chapel still bears his name and recalls his memory. (Cf. *Notices,* vol. III, pp. 114-121.)

men—ten or eleven—whom God has taken from us, but also because of their high caliber, since all of them were priests and among the best workers in the Company! Moreover, all of them died in a very holy, extraordinary way, while serving their neighbor directly. They are Messieurs . . . ; six of them and one of the Brothers died of the pestilence in Genoa, while nursing the plague-stricken. The others gave their earthly lives to procure eternal life for the islanders of Madagascar and the Hebrides.[2] They are so many Missionaries we now have in heaven. There is no room to doubt this, since they all made the supreme sacrifice of their lives for charity, and there is no greater love than to give one's life for the neighbor, as Jesus Christ Himself said and practiced.[3] May God then be glorified, Monsieur, by the glory He has given our confreres, as we have good reason to believe, and may His good pleasure be always the peace and tranquility of our afflicted hearts!

I cannot tell you how grieved we were at receiving such sad news, all of which reached us almost simultaneously; it would be impossible for me to express it to you.[4] You can judge from the sorrow you yourself will experience on hearing it—you who love the Company so much—that we could not receive a greater blow without being completely crushed by it.

---

[2]Many confreres died in the spring-summer of 1657; among those in Genoa were Luca Arimondo, Étienne Blatiron, Domenico Boccone, Louis Duport, John McEnery, Antoine Tratebas, François Vincent, and Brother Giovanni Damiani. At the same time Saint Vincent heard of the deaths of the above, he was also receiving news of the death of Mathurin de Belleville, en route to Madagascar, and of Claude Dufour and Nicolas Prévost, shortly after their arrival there.

[3]Cf. Jn 15:13. (NAB)

[4]This is evident from the many letters in vol. VI in which these deaths are mentioned.

2483. - TO DOMINIQUE LHUILLIER,[1] IN CRÉCY

Paris, December 11, 1657

Monsieur,

The grace of O[ur] L[ord] be with you forever!

It is true that I have not written to you for a long time; please accept my apologies for this. Thank you for not failing to give me news of you, which always consoles me. I thank God for the good disposition He gives you and for Madame's [2] gifts for your chapel.

It is much to be desired that the lawsuit [3] be settled soon so that you will not remain alone and unable to give missions, for which God has brought us together. I am not putting any pressure on the Bishop of Meaux[4] to speed up his proceedings because he did what he had to do in that matter, and I am glad not to get involved in it so that the less we have to do with the outcome, the more we may see the Will of God in it. Meanwhile, it is only right for you to turn to us for small expenses. That is why I ask you to let me know when

---

Letter 2483. - Archives of the Mission, Turin, unsigned rough draft in the secretary's handwriting.

[1]Dominique Lhuillier, born in Barizey-au-Plain (Meurthe), entered the Congregation of the Mission as a priest in Paris on July 11, 1651, at the age of thirty-two. He took his vows there on May 5, 1659, in the presence of M. Alméras. Lhuillier was a Missionary in Crécy (1654-60) and in Toulon, where he died.

[2]Marie Séguier, widow of César de Coislin; she later married the Marquis de Laval-Boisdauphin.

[3]When the house was first established in Crécy (1641), Pierre Lorthon, the King's secretary, had promised the Congregation of the Mission a revenue of four thousand livres from five large farms he had obtained from the King and Queen. On further reflection, he preferred to give two thousand livres to the hospital in Crécy and to keep the balance for himself. This resulted in a lawsuit between Lorthon and the Bishop of Meaux, Dominique Séguier, which did not close until 1659 in favor of the Missionaries. Saint Vincent would have preferred to renounce everything rather than bring a benefactor to court. Deprived of the resources on which he was counting, he left only one priest and a Brother in Crécy. The priest said Mass daily in the chapel, heard confessions of those who came to him, and visited the sick of the parish who asked for him.

[4]Dominique Séguier (1595-1659), brother of the Chancellor, Pierre Séguier, was named Bishop of Auxerre in 1631 and transferred to Meaux in 1638. He resigned in 1659 and died in Paris the same year.

you need something; with God's help, we will provide it. The Montmirail house is not in a position to pay you. It will be a good idea for you to get what is owed you from elsewhere and use it for the little provisions you need the most.

So you have not heard about the losses we have suffered! O Monsieur! how great they are, not only because of the number of men—eleven of them—whom God has taken from us, but also because of their high caliber, since all but one, who was a coadjutor Brother, were priests and among the best workers in the Company! All of them died in a very holy, extraordinary way while serving their neighbor directly.

We had sent Messieurs Dufour,[5] Prévost,[6] and de Belleville[7] to Madagascar, but all three of them went to God, after giving proofs of their zeal and good conduct during the voyage and after their arrival at the site of their mission. They have left there only M. Bourdaise,[8] whom God is blessing in a marvelous way.

---

[5]Claude Dufour, born in Allanche (Cantal) in 1618, entered the Congregation of the Mission on May 4, 1644, shortly after his ordination to the priesthood. He was first sent to Montmirail (1644), then put in charge of the seminary in Saintes (1646-48). He was very virtuous but of a rigid and unobliging kind of virtue. In his eyes the life of a Missionary was too soft; he persuaded himself that the life of a Carthusian was more suited to his love for prayer and mortification. Saint Vincent was of an entirely different opinion, so Dufour, always docile, abandoned his plans. To free him from temptations of this kind, the Saint put him on the list of priests to be sent to Madagascar. While awaiting the day of departure, the Saint assigned him first to Sedan, then to Paris, entrusting him with the Internal Seminary there during the absence of M. Alméras, and finally to La Rose as Superior (1654-55). Sea voyages were long in those days; Dufour left Nantes in 1655 and arrived in Madagascar in August of the following year, but died on August 18, 1656, just a few days after his arrival. (Cf. *Notices,* vol. III, pp. 14-23.)

[6]Nicolas Prévost, born in La Roche-Guyon (Val-d'Oise), entered the Congregation of the Mission on October 20, 1646, at thirty-four years of age. He was sent to Madagascar in 1655 and died there in September 1656, leaving the reputation of being a very zealous and virtuous Missionary.

[7]Mathurin de Belleville, born in Brix (Manche), entered the Congregation of the Mission on May 1, 1654, at twenty-seven years of age. He contracted an illness as soon as the ship left the Saint-Martin roadstead, died on January 18, 1656, and was buried at sea off the coast of Sierra Leone (cf. *Notices,* vol. III, p. 160). On September 7, 1657, Saint Vincent gave a conference to the Congregation of the Mission on his virtues (cf. vol. XI, no. 173).

[8]Toussaint Bourdaise, born in Blois (Loir-et-Cher) in 1618, entered the Internal Seminary of the Congregation of the Mission in Paris on October 6, 1645, and took his vows there on October

In Genoa God has taken to Himself M. Blatiron the Superior[9] and Messieurs Duport,[10] Ennery,[11] François Vincent,[12] Tratebas,[13] and Boccone,[14] along with a coadjutor Brother.[15] Of these seven who died of the plague, only one did not risk his life and catch the

---

7, 1647. He was ordained a priest in 1651, even though his talent and knowledge had been questioned a number of times (cf. vol. XI, no. 177). In 1654 he was sent to Madagascar, where he died on June 25, 1657 (cf. *Notices*, vol. III, pp. 180-214).

[9]Étienne Blatiron was born in Saint-Julien-Chapteuil (Haute-Loire) on January 6, 1614. He entered the Congregation of the Mission on January 6, 1638, was ordained a priest in 1639, and was placed in Alet (1639-41), Saintes (1641), Richelieu, Rome (1644-45), and Genoa (1645-57). He distinguished himself particularly in the latter post where, as Superior of a new house, he had to organize everything. Saint Vincent considered him one of his most competent Missionaries and "a very great servant of God." (Cf. Abelly, *op. cit.*, bk. III, p. 70.) Blatiron died in Genoa on July 24, 1657, a victim of his dedication to the plague-stricken. His biography was published in vol. II of *Notices*, pp. 151-203. In the Lyons manuscript there is a report on his virtues addressed to Saint Vincent.

[10]Nicolas Duport, born in Soissons (Aisne) on March 22, 1619, was ordained a priest on June 15, 1647, entered the Congregation of the Mission on May 5, 1648, and took his vows on May 6, 1650. He was assigned to Genoa in 1652, where he died of the plague on July 14, 1657. (Cf. *Notices*, vol. III, pp. 82-87, for an account of several Missionaries who died of the plague in Genoa that year.) A brief summary of Duport's virtues is given in Ms. 774 of the municipal library of Lyons (fol. 232-33).

[11]John McEnery (Saint Vincent refers to him as *Jean Ennery*), born in December 1616 at Castle Mak Ennery, today Castletown (Ireland), entered the Congregation of the Mission on September 23, 1642, and took his vows on October 11, 1645. According to Saint Vincent, he was "a wise, pious, and exemplary man" (cf. Abelly, *op. cit.*, bk. III, p. 48). He taught theology at Saint-Lazare (1652), aided the unfortunate people of Champagne impoverished by the war (1653), and assisted his countrymen who had fled to Troyes (1654). His last assignment was Genoa, where he died of the plague in 1657.

[12]François Vincent, born in 1611 in Gandelu, Meaux diocese (Seine-et-Marne), entered the Congregation of the Mission on April 2, 1649, and died of the plague in Genoa on July 13, 1657.

[13]Antoine Tratebas, born in Allauch (Bouches-du-Rhône), near Marseilles, in October 1632, entered the Congregation of the Mission in Paris on October 7, 1651, took his vows on October 20, 1653, and died of the plague in Genoa in August 1657. His family gave hospitality to Antoine Portail and other Priests of the Mission in 1649 during the plague that was ravaging the city of Marseilles.

[14]Domenico Boccone was born in Tirane, Albenga diocese (Italy), on November 12, 1613, and entered the Congregation of the Mission in Genoa on November 9, 1655. He was ordained a priest on December 25, . . . and died of the plague in Genoa on August 3, 1657. According to *Notices*, vol. I, p. 485, Boccone (Bacone) was ordained a priest on Christmas 1657 and died on August 3, 1657. *Notices* then states, "Therefore, there is an error either in the date of his ordination or in that of his death." *Notices*, vol. V (Supplement), gives no information about his ordination.

[15]In his Index (vol. XIV) Coste states that this is Brother Jean (Giovanni) Damiani, but gives no biographical data; none can be found in *Notices*, vols. I or V (Supplement).

disease while nursing the plague-stricken, but he was just as ready and willing as the others to go to serve them, except that he was one of the first to die of it. Only three priests are left in that afflicted house, and one is still in the lazaretto, where he is nursing the sick. He himself was sick but is completely cured, thank God.

So we have ten persons who, according to Scripture, have saved their lives by losing them; [16] and the eleventh is M. Duiguin, who worked in the Hebrides with unusual and almost incredible success. He gave up his earthly life there to procure eternal life for those poor islanders, who all wept for him as for their own father. They are so many Missionaries we now have in heaven; there is no room to doubt this, since they all gave their lives for charity, and there is no greater love than to give one's life for the neighbor, as O[ur] L[ord] has said and practiced.[17] If, then, we have lost something on the one hand, we have gained something on the other because God has been pleased to glorify our confreres, as we have good reason to believe, and the ashes of these apostolic men will be the seed of a large number of good Missionaries. At least, these are the prayers I ask you to offer to God.

I cannot tell you how grieved we were at receiving such sad news, all of which reached us almost simultaneously; it would be impossible for me to express it to you. You can judge from the sorrow you yourself will experience on hearing it—you who love the Company so much—that we could not receive a greater blow without being completely crushed by it.

I am, in the love of Him who gives life and takes it away, Monsieur, your most humble servant.

---

[16]Cf. Mt 16:25. (NAB)
[17]Cf. Jn 15:13. (NAB)

2484. - TO JACQUES THOLARD,[1] IN BRUYÈRES [2]

Paris, December 12, 1657

Monsieur,

The grace of Our Lord be with you forever!

I have often told the Company, Monsieur, that no ill comes to it except through my fault. The difficulty being encountered in that mission makes this clear enough, and I ask your pardon for that, prostrate in spirit at your feet and those of the men who are with you.

It seems you are right, Monsieur, to wonder whether you should go on working or should leave what you have begun and return home, since you have no proper lodging, are obliged to stay at the inn, your congregation is very small—only about one hundred persons, most of whom are children—and, lastly, five or six hamlets are far away.

On the other hand, however, it seems that you should give yourself to Our Lord to persevere to the end of the mission because:

(1) you have been welcomed by the Pastors;

(2) the local lord has consented to it;

(3) no authorities are opposing you;

(4) those poor people—or many among them—are coming to the exercises, especially the young people, whom Our Lord was so glad to see at His sermons and who have such great need of them;

(5) perhaps Our Lord intends to save some good soul whose salvation is in jeopardy and is to die soon but, being damned for

---

Letter 2484. - Archives of the Mission, Turin, original autograph letter.

[1]Jacques Tholard was born in Auxerre (Yonne) on June 10, 1615, and entered the Congregation of the Mission on November 20, 1638. He was ordained a priest on December 17, 1639, and died after 1671. He manifested throughout his life, in Annecy (1640-46), Tréguier, where he was Superior (1648-53), Troyes (1658-60), Saint-Lazare, Fontainebleau, and elsewhere, the qualities of an excellent Missionary. During the generalate of René Alméras, he was Visitor of the Provinces of France and Lyons.

[2]Bruyères-le-Châtel, in the district of Corbeil (Essonne).

lack of assistance, will make you—and me along with you—responsible for its loss, if we do not do His Will in these circumstances;

(6) this is a test God wants to make of your patience in the midst of the difficulties you present to me. In addition, the evil spirit is using this situation to divert the good He sees you do. He is taking advantage of the feelings of your nature, which is mortified because you have not been welcomed as you usually are in other places, such as Conflans,[3] or because you are not lodged as elsewhere but rather at an inn.

All these reasons and several others, Monsieur, cause me to ask you to continue to the end the work you have begun, despite any reasons to the contrary, such as the refusal of the concierge to lodge you and your being housed at the inn. Remember that the Missionary of Missionaries did not have a stone on which to lay His head,[4] that He was sometimes refused entry to places where He was going to work, and that He and His Apostles were driven out of some provinces.[5] God has not yet found the Mission worthy of such treatment.

As for the remote hamlets, very few country parishes do not have some, and it happens at times that these are more zealous in participating in the exercises of the mission than the others. All you need in each hamlet is one or two persons whom Our Lord has touched, who will become the preachers to the rest of the people. In addition, if it should happen that attendance is poor there, recall that Our Lord preached to a very small number of persons—even to just one—and that perhaps Our Lord has permitted these causes of repugnance in order to preach to you yourself and to protect you from the empty satisfaction we imperceptibly seek in our work.

Now, this being the case, I entreat you in the name of Our Lord,

---

[3]Probably Conflans-Sainte-Honorine, in the district of Versailles (Yvelines).
[4]Cf. Mt 8:20. (NAB)
[5]Cf. Mt 8:34. (NAB)

Monsieur, to continue to work, even if there should be only a single soul who might need you. Do so in keeping with the mind of Our Lord that the good shepherd should leave his flock of ninety-nine sheep to go in search of the hundredth that is lost.[6] It rarely happens in these circumstances that a mission which starts out in this way does not succeed in the end, if the Missionaries practice the necessary virtues of patience, humility, prayer, and mortification. This, Monsieur, is what I hope you will do and that you will edify M. Caset[7] and M. de Fleury.[8] I am, in the love of Our Lord, your most humble servant.

VINCENT DEPAUL,
i.s.C.M.

If you need furnishings, you can rent them from the landlady of Châtres—the one across the street from the church. Do not expect any lodging from the priory. I venture to tell you that this wretch that I am has never given better missions than when he was lodged in inns.

---

[6]Cf. Lk 15:4. (NAB)

[7]Michel Caset, born in Vautortes (Mayenne), entered the Congregation of the Mission on October 31, 1649, at twenty-four years of age, took his vows in November 1651, and was ordained a priest in 1653. He was Superior in Toul (1659-60), then in Crécy (1662-70), after having spent some time in Fontainebleau. He later became a diocesan priest and died as Pastor of Crouy-sur-Ourcq (Seine-et-Marne).

[8]Antoine Fleury, born in Bully (Rhône) in September 1624, entered the Congregation of the Mission as a priest on August 28, 1657, and took his vows in Saintes on January 18, 1660, in the presence of M. Dehorgny.

2485. - TO PIERRE CABEL, IN SEDAN

Paris, December 12, 1657

Monsieur,

The grace of O[ur] L[ord] be with you forever!

I am replying to Mademoiselle de Santeuil that Mademoiselle Le Gras [1] cannot send a third Sister to Sedan because she has none left and that it is better for her to get a woman or girl from there to help the sick Sisters than to subject one from here to a difficult journey at great expense.

Father Annat [2] sent here two copies of a book he wrote,[3] one for

---

Letter 2485. - Archives of the Mission, Turin, original signed letter.

[1]Saint Louise de Marillac, Foundress, with Saint Vincent, of the Daughters of Charity, was born in Paris on August 12, 1591. Her father was Louis de Marillac, brother of the devout Michel de Marillac, Keeper of the Seals (1616-30), and half-brother of another Louis, Maréchal de France, renowned for his misfortunes and tragic death. Louise married Antoine Le Gras, secretary of Queen Marie de Médicis, on February 5, 1613, and they had one son, Michel. Antoine Le Gras died on December 21, 1625. The devout widow had implicit confidence in her spiritual director, Vincent de Paul, who employed her in his charitable works, eventually making her his collaborator in the creation and organization of the Confraternities of Charity. The life of Saint Louise, whom the Church beatified on May 9, 1920, was written by Gobillon (1676), the Comtesse de Richemont (1883), Comte de Lambel (n.d.), Monsignor Baunard (1898), and Emmanuel de Broglie (1911). Her letters and other writings were copied and published in part in the work entitled: *Louise de Marillac, veuve Le Gras. Sa vie, ses vertus, son esprit* (4 vols., Bruges, 1886). Saint Louise was canonized on March 11, 1934, and on February 10, 1960, was named the patroness of all who devote themselves to Christian social work. Therefore, in this English edition of the letters of Saint Vincent, "Saint" has been added to her name in titles of letters and in the footnotes. To the above bibliography should be added some of her more recent biographers: Alice, Lady Lovat, *Life of the Venerable Louise de Marillac (Mademoiselle Le Gras)* (New York: Longmans, Green & Co., 1917); Monsignor Jean Calvet, *Louise de Marillac, a Portrait*, translated by G. F. Pullen (1959); Joseph I. Dirvin, *Louise de Marillac* (1970); the compilation by Sister Anne Regnault, D.C., editor: *Louise de Marillac, ses écrits* (1961), of which the section containing the letters was translated by Sister Helen Marie Law, D.C.: *Letters of St. Louise de Marillac* (1972); and the revised edition of Sister Regnault's work entitled: *Sainte Louise de Marillac. Écrits spirituels* (Tours: Mame, 1983), ed. Sister Élisabeth Charpy, D.C., trans. by Sister Louise Sullivan, D.C., *Spiritual Writings* (Brooklyn: New City Press, 1991).

[2]François Annat, born in Estaing (Aveyron) on February 5, 1590, entered the Society of Jesus on February 16, 1607. For thirteen years he taught philosophy and theology in Toulouse and was Rector of the Collège de Montpellier and the Collège de Toulouse. He became Assistant to the Superior General, Provincial of France, and confessor of King Louis XIV (1654-61). To him we owe many works against Jansenism. Annat died in Paris on June 14, 1670.

[3]Annat wrote several books. In 1657 he published: *Défense de la vérité catholique touchant*

you and the other for the Pastor in Stenay. I had them forwarded to you on the coach that left here yesterday, I think. Please pick them up and have the one for the Pastor delivered to him.

I am, in Our Lord, Monsieur, your most humble servant.

VINCENT DEPAUL,
i.s.C.M.

Addressed: Monsieur Cabel, Priest of the Mission, in Sedan

2486. - TO JEAN MARTIN,[1] SUPERIOR, IN TURIN

Paris, December 14, 1657

Monsieur,

The grace of O[ur] L[ord] be with you forever!

I am replying to your latest letters. Your absence from Turin may deprive me of receiving any others for a while. Provided God keeps you in good health and blesses your missions, I will willingly accept this deprivation that is due to such a good reason. This letter, then, is simply to accompany the enclosures. There is one for M. Berthe, who is going to make the visitation of your house. I think I informed you of this so that you may welcome him and

---

les miracles contre les déguisemens et artifices de la réponse faite par MM. de Port-Royal à un escrit intitulé: "Observations nécessaires sur ce qu'on dit estre arrivé à Port-Royal au sujet de la Saincte-Espine," by the Sieur de Sainte-Foy, Doctor of Theology (Paris: F. Lambert, 1657); and *Rabat-joie des Jansénistes ou Observations nécessaires sur ce qu'on dit estre arrivé au Port-Royal au sujet de la Saincte-Espine.* In the same year, in collaboration with his confreres Fathers Jacques Nouet, De Lingendes, and Brisacier, he published *Réponses aux "Lettres provinciales" publiées par le secrétaire de Port-Royal contre les PP. de la Compagnie de Jésus sur le sujet de la morale desdits Pères* (Liège: J.M. Hovius, 1657).

Letter 2486. - Archives of the Mission, Turin, original signed letter.

[1]Jean Martin, born in Paris on May 10, 1620, entered the Congregation of the Mission on October 9, 1638. He was ordained in Rome on April 25, 1645, and that same year was sent to Genoa to found a new house. Saint Vincent probably had no Missionary more gifted in drawing crowds and converting souls. In 1654 Martin was recalled to France and placed in Sedan as

prepare your family [2] to profit by his visit. He has greatly edified and consoled all the houses through which he has passed. I think he has just left Marseilles to head for your house. I do not know if he will go to Annecy first or will save it for the return trip; I left all that up to him.

We have no news here except for the ordinands. Our men are out giving three missions simultaneously, and I am, in O[ur] L[ord], Monsieur, your most humble servant.

VINCENT DEPAUL,
i.s.C.M.

At the bottom of the page: Monsieur Martin

2487. - TO EDME JOLLY, SUPERIOR, IN ROME

Paris, December 14, 1657

Monsieur,

The grace of O[ur] L[ord] be with you forever!

I am writing to you to observe the custom,[1] and not to reply to

---

Superior and Pastor; then he was sent to Turin in 1655 for the new establishment founded by the Marchese di Pianezza, Prime Minister of State. There, as in Genoa and Sedan, the zealous Missionary knew how to soften the most hardened hearts. He was given the name "Apostle of Piedmont," and his fellow Missionaries were called "the holy Fathers." In 1665 René Alméras asked him to head the house in Rome. This was a painful sacrifice for Martin, but he resigned himself to it. Subsequently, he was named Superior in Genoa (1670), Turin (1674), Rome (1677), Perugia (1680), and again in Rome in 1681, where he died on February 17, 1694. His obituary, written by one of his contemporaries, is in the Archives of the Mission in Paris. It was published, with some corrections, in vol. I of *Notices*, pp. 269-372.

[2]Saint Vincent often uses the term *family* to designate the local community of confreres.

Letter 2487. - Archives of the Mission, Turin, original signed letter.

[1]It was Saint Vincent's desire to establish a regular pattern of communication between the confreres and Superiors. To one he wrote, "It will be a consolation for me to receive letters from you every month" (cf. Vol. IV, no. 1627, p. 578); Étienne Blatiron and Edme Jolly usually wrote to him every week (cf. Vol. VI, no. 2142, p. 99).

any of your letters, since I received none either this week or last. I am a little worried about this. Maybe the snow or floods have delayed the mail.

As for news, I can tell you that Messieurs Portail,[2] Alméras,[3]

[2]Antoine Portail, born in Beaucaire (Gard) on November 22, 1590, came to Paris to study at the Sorbonne. He met Saint Vincent there around 1612 and became devoted to him. From the time of his ordination (1622) to that of his death (1660), he was the Saint's auxiliary. Vincent employed him in the service of the galley slaves, received him as the first member of his new Congregation, initiated him into the ministry of the missions and the work of the ordinands, chose him as First Assistant in 1642, and entrusted to him the direction of the Daughters of Charity. In 1646 Portail left Paris to make visitations in the houses of the Congregation. He began in the west of France, then went south, crossed into Italy, and did not return to Saint-Lazare until September 1649. Except for a fairly long absence in 1655, he hardly ever left the Motherhouse again and died on February 14, 1660, after an illness of nine days. (Cf. *Notices,* vol. I, pp. 1-94.)

[3]René Alméras, nephew of Madame Goussault, was born in Paris on February 5, 1613, and was baptized the same day in Saint-Gervais Church. By coincidence Saint Louise was married in this church that very day. A Councillor in the Great Council at the age of twenty-four, Alméras left everything—family, position, and hopes—despite the opposition of his father (who was to follow him later) to enter the Congregation of the Mission, into which he was received on December 24, 1637. He was ordained a priest at Easter in 1639. Saint Vincent entrusted to him important positions, such as Assistant of the Motherhouse and Seminary Director. He appointed him to his council and often relied on his prudence to deal with lay persons in delicate matters; he also gave him charge of the retreatants. So much work ruined Alméras' health. The Holy Founder, convinced by personal experience that a change of air could improve one's health, sent him in 1646 to make the visitation of several houses in France and Italy. When he reached Rome, Alméras was notified that he had been appointed Superior of the house, where he remained until 1651. On his return to France he took over the direction of Saint-Charles Seminary. In 1654 he was involved in distributing relief to the poor of Picardy and Champagne. He made visitations of some houses of the Congregation and was again named Assistant of the Motherhouse, in which position he remained until the death of Saint Vincent. He was also Visitor of the Province of Poitou. Alméras was in Richelieu when the Saint, realizing that his own death was near, begged him to return to Paris immediately. Alméras was ill and was brought back on a stretcher but had the consolation of receiving a last blessing from the Saint. Appointed Vicar-General by Saint Vincent, then elected Superior General by the Assembly of 1661, he governed wisely the Congregation of the Mission and the Company of the Daughters of Charity until his death on September 2, 1672.

Brin,[4] and Perraud,[5] who have all been very ill, are convalescing right now, thank God. The rest of the community are well; they are now busy with the ordination retreat. The Bishop of Pamiers[6] is giving one of the talks, and it is being very well received; a young Doctor of the Sorbonne is giving the other. Our seminary is more crowded than ever; there are forty seminarians, most of whom are very promising. God is also blessing the one in Richelieu. M. De-

---

[4]Gerard Brin, born near Cashel (Ireland), entered the Congregation of the Mission on October 14, 1639, at the age of twenty-one. He took his vows on November 2, 1642, and was ordained a priest in 1644. Of all the Irishmen whom Saint Vincent received into his Congregation, Brin was perhaps the most accomplished. He was sent from Le Mans in 1646 to the mission in Ireland, which was financed by the Duchesse d'Aiguillon; there, with several other confreres and compatriots, he did boundless good (cf. Abelly, *op. cit.*, bk. II, chap. 1, pp. 154-55). Driven back to France by persecution, Brin went as a missionary to Saint Vincent's native region. Some time later he was named Superior in La Rose (1652-54), and subsequently held the same position in Troyes (1657-58), Meaux (1658-60), and Toul (1660-62). He returned to Ireland in 1662 or 1663, resuming his apostolic work with a zeal that age had not slackened. Neither illness, which brought him twice to the brink of the grave, nor a month in prison could stop this heroic Missionary. Brin died in Thurles (Ireland) sometime between October 9, 1683, the date of his will, and February 25, 1684, the date of its admission to probate.

[5]Hugues Perraud, born in Arguel (Doubs) on October 3, 1615, entered the Congregation of the Mission on January 5, 1640, took his vows on March 23, 1644, and was ordained a priest in 1646. He was placed in Saintes (1646) and Richelieu (1651) and died in Paris on December 26, 1659.

[6]François-Étienne de Caulet, born in Toulouse on May 19, 1610, was endowed in 1627 with Saint-Volusien Abbey in Foix. Attracted by the spirit of Jean-Jacques Olier, he accompanied him on his missions in Auvergne, in the Chartres diocese, and in other places in the kingdom. He supported him in his parish ministry and, together with him and du Ferrier, founded the Vaugirard Seminary. Saint Vincent, who knew the Abbot of Saint-Volusien, thought he would make a good Bishop. Thanks to him, de Caulet was consecrated Bishop of Pamiers on March 5, 1645. In 1638 he had testified against Saint-Cyran; as Bishop, he continued for a long time to combat Jansenism, forbade in his diocese the reading of books by adherents of the movement, and made every effort to bring back those who had strayed from the truth. However, his association with Nicolas Pavillon, Bishop of Alet, won him over to Jansenism. The Bishop of Pamiers died on August 7, 1680, without having made an act of submission to the Church. (Cf. Jérôme Besoigne, *Vies des quatres évesques engagés dans la cause de Port-Royal, d'Alet, d'Angers, de Beauvais et de Pamiers* [2 vols., Cologne: n. p., 1756]; Georges Doublet, *Un prélat janséniste, F. de Caulet, réformateur des châpitres de Foix et de Pamiers* [Paris: A. Picard et fils, 1895].) M. Gazier, an authority on Jansenism, had, among the rare manuscripts in his extensive library, one entitled: *Histoire abrégée de la vie de M. François de Caulet, évêque de Pamiers,* by Father Gabaret.

horgny [7] is still Superior at the Bons-Enfants,[8] where the seminary is filled with diocesan priests. They are short of rooms, not persons. Saint-Charles Seminary [9] is also doing well. Many of our priests are giving missions; they went out in three bands. God has been pleased to bless the visitations of M. Berthe, who is now in Savoy, I think. He will go no further in Italy than Turin this time because we need him here.

M. Le Vacher,[10] who came from Algiers, has not yet gone back there but will do so as soon as we have the money needed to release

---

[7]Jean Dehorgny, born in Estrées-Saint-Denis (Oise), entered the Congregation of the Mission in August 1627 and was ordained a priest on April 22, 1628. When Saint Vincent made the move to Saint-Lazare in 1632, Dehorgny took over the direction of the Collège des Bons-Enfants, which he retained until 1635, then took up again (1638-43, 1654-59). He was Assistant to the Superior General (1642-44, 1654-67); Superior of the house in Rome (1644-47, 1651-53); and Director of the Daughters of Charity (1660-67). In 1640, 1641, 1643, 1644, 1659, and 1660, he made the visitation of several houses of the Company, reestablishing good order wherever necessary. His sympathy for Jansenist ideas merited for us two beautiful letters from Saint Vincent, who had the joy of seeing him return to sounder beliefs. Dehorgny died on July 7, 1667. We still have twenty-three of his conferences to the Daughters of Charity and several letters.

[8]On March 1, 1624, Jean-François de Gondi, Archbishop of Paris, turned over to Saint Vincent the direction of the Collège des Bons-Enfants so that he might have a place to lodge priests wishing to join him in giving missions in the country. Situated near the Porte Saint-Victor, on the site of the building now standing on the corner of rue des Écoles and rue Cardinal-Lemoine, this collège, over three hundred years old, was one of the oldest of the University of Paris. It was not a teaching center, but simply a hostel in which students were provided with shelter and sleeping quarters.

[9]In 1645 Saint Vincent established, within the enclosure of Saint-Lazare, Saint-Charles Seminary (also known as the Petit Saint-Lazare) for youths completing their studies in the humanities; not all the students, however, aspired to Holy Orders. Before he died, Cardinal Richelieu endowed twelve students; others paid room and board.

[10]Philippe Le Vacher, born in Écouen (Val-d'Oise) on March 23, 1622, entered the Congregation of the Mission on October 5, 1643, and took his vows on August 5, 1646. He was part of the first group sent to Ireland in 1646. Recalled to France in 1649, he was sent to Marseilles, where he was ordained a priest on April 2, 1650, and sailed for Algiers as Vicar Apostolic and Vicar-General of Carthage. He returned to France in 1657 to collect alms for the slaves. His absence, which was supposed to last only a few months, was prolonged for two years. He set out again in September 1659, reached Barbary, and in 1661 accompanied Brother Jean Dubourdieu to Algiers, where the latter was destined to replace Jean Barreau, French Consul in that city. Le Vacher paid Barreau's debts, settled a number of business matters, and finally left Barbary in 1662, accompanied by seventy slaves whom he had ransomed. He was sent to Fontainebleau, where he led a most exemplary life until August 5, 1679, the day of his death. (Cf. *Notices*, vol. III, pp. 595-606.) In this volume, the Le Vacher brother mentioned in connection with Algiers is usually Philippe, unless stated otherwise.

the Consul.[11] His faculties have expired; I think the same is true for his brother in Tunis. Please have them renewed for both of them, Monsieur. I say nothing more to you about the permission for priests to take charge of the consulate because I know you have presented this request to the Sacred Congregation.

I hope to send you with this letter the report on Madagascar that we are getting copied. We thought a ship would be going there this fall, but its departure has been postponed until spring.

I cannot conclude without reminding you again about your packets that are late in coming; I have a special reason for wanting to receive them soon. I hope to get two or three of them the day after tomorrow.

I ask O[ur] L[ord] to sustain your health and to bless your leadership and your missions. I am, in His love, Monsieur, your most humble servant.

VINCENT DEPAUL,
i.s.C.M.

Addressed: Monsieur Jolly, Superior of the Priests of the Mission of Rome, in Rome

2488. - TO FIRMIN GET, SUPERIOR, IN MARSEILLES

Paris, December 14, 1657

Monsieur,

The grace of O[ur] L[ord] be with you forever!

I am writing to you to observe the custom, and not to reply to any of your letters because I have not yet received the ones from

---

[11]Jean Barreau.

Letter 2488. - Archives of the Mission, Paris, Sister Hains Collection, original signed letter.

the last regular mail. I am expecting it to bring me the results of the visitation M. Berthe made to your house and the news of his departure for Turin or Annecy.

Since writing the above, I received your letter of December 4. I praise God for all the things you tell me, which require no reply. I thank Him above all for the grace He grants you of abandoning yourself entirely to His guidance.

Since you have not drawn a bill of exchange on us, I will send you one by the next regular mail, God willing, for the 183 livres M. Huguier [1] advanced to the convicts.

You say that a boat has gone to Algiers and another to Tunis. You do not say whether you sent any money there. I have asked you, and I ask you once again, not to send any unless I tell you to do so, especially the one thousand écus of the Basques.

I am, in O[ur] L[ord], Monsieur, your most humble servant.

VINCENT DEPAUL

At the bottom of the first page: Monsieur Get

---

[1]Benjamin-Joseph Huguier, born in Sézanne (Marne) on March 10, 1613, was an attorney at the Châtelet of Paris before his admission into the Congregation of the Mission on September 15, 1647. He served in Tunis (1649-52), returning to France by way of Marseilles in May 1652, took his vows that same year, and was ordained a priest in February 1655. After ordination, he became chaplain of the galleys in Toulon; however, he felt drawn to Barbary, and on September 19, 1662, was sent to Algiers with the title of Vicar Apostolic. While nursing the plague-stricken there, he contracted the illness and died of it himself in April 1663. (Cf. *Mémoires C.M.*, vol. II, pp. 221-30.)

2489. - TO JACQUES RIVET,[1] IN GENOA

Paris, December 14, 1657

Dear Brother,

The grace of O[ur] L[ord] be with you forever!

The letter you wrote me on October . . . has revived my sorrow by the losses you have sustained and has consoled me by the good report you give me of our living and deceased confreres. God be praised, dear Brother, that some have given their lives for charity and the others have given their attention to the relief and consolation of the sick and the good order of the family. I know you have done your part in this, for which I thank His Divine Goodness, who has given you His own good heart for the service of the Company.

It is no surprise that it is moved by the death of good M. Blatiron, who loved you and was so dear to you. He is now in heaven with the others, in a position in which we have good reason to hope that he will be a great help to us before God. You see, dear Brother, how they persevered to the end in corresponding with God's plan in the place where His Providence had led them. Let us ask Him to grant us the same grace. We have prayed much to Him for your preservation, and we will still do so.

Continue always to be a consolation and relief to everyone, for the love of Our Lord; by this means you will make yourself very pleasing to Him. Your mother is still a Sister with the Daughters

---

Letter 2489. - Archives of the Mission, Turin, seventeenth-century copy.

[1]Jacques Rivet, coadjutor Brother, born in Houdan (Yvelines) on September 11, 1620, entered the Congregation of the Mission on December 16, 1641, and took his vows on April 22, 1646.

of Charity and is working with the elderly of the Nom-de-Jésus.[2] Both she and your brothers[3] are well.

As for me, I am always, in the love of Our Lord, dear Brother, your most affectionate servant.

VINCENT DEPAUL,
i.s.C.M.

---

[2]The Nom-de-Jésus [Name of Jesus] hospice. The foundation was made by an anonymous rich merchant of Paris, who one day brought 100,000 livres to Saint Vincent for a good work of the Saint's choice. After discussing his plan with the benefactor, the Saint decided to spend 11,000 livres for the purchase of the house called Nom-de-Jésus, which belonged to Saint-Lazare, and 20,000 livres for enlarging the living space, should it become too small. He also constituted an income of 60,000 livres, to which 20,000 were added from Saint-Lazare, which later retrieved them; he allocated 5400 livres for chapel furnishings, and 3600 livres for room and board for forty poor persons for a year. All this was on condition that the Superior General of the Priests of the Mission, together with the laymen from Paris whom he would employ, would have the spiritual and temporal direction of the hospital, and in this position would have the authority to receive and dismiss the poor. The contract was accepted on October 29, 1653, approved by the Vicars-General on March 15, 1654 (the Archbishop of Paris, Cardinal de Retz, was in exile in Rome), and ratified by the Parlement by letters patent in November. (Cf. Arch. Nat., M 53.) The work was already in operation in March 1653. Saint Vincent chose twenty male and twenty female artisans who, because of old age or infirmity, could no longer earn their living; to occupy their time, they were provided with looms and tools. Men and women were housed in separate wings; although they came together in the same chapel for Mass, they were not permitted to see or speak to one another. The Daughters of Charity served them; a Priest of the Mission, in conformity with the terms of the contract, acted as chaplain. Saint Vincent often used to come to visit and instruct them. (Cf. Abelly, *op. cit.*, bk. I, chap. XLV, pp. 211-13.) The Nom-de-Jésus later became the municipal health center (1802-16); its buildings were on the site now occupied by the offices of the Gare de l'Est.

[3]Fathers François and Louis Rivet.

François Rivet, born in Houdan (Yvelines) on July 28, 1628, entered the Congregation of the Mission on October 12, 1647, took his vows on November 6, 1650, and was ordained a priest on April 1, 1656.

Louis Rivet was born in Houdan (Yvelines) on February 19, 1618. He entered the Congregation of the Mission on June 13, 1640, took his vows on October 16, 1642, and was ordained a priest on September 19, 1643. In 1646 he was placed in Richelieu, then at the Saintes Seminary which he directed for several years (1648-50, 1656-62, 1665-73).

2490. - TO THE SUPERIOR OF THE SECOND MONASTERY OF THE VISITATION, IN PARIS

I ask the Reverend Mother Superior of Sainte-Marie in the faubourg to allow Mademoiselle de Lamoignon [1] to enter her monastery to see our dear Sister Marie-Élisabeth.[2]

2490a. - TO JEAN PARRE, IN RETHEL

Paris, December 15, 1657

Dear Brother,

The grace of Our Lord be with you forever!

At our meeting yesterday three hundred livres were allotted you for the needs of the Rethel area. Please get them and draw a bill of exchange for them on Mademoiselle Viole.[1] Your letter of December 6 gives me reason to praise God for the journey you made for

---

Letter 2490. - Reg. 1, fol. 66.

[1]Madeleine de Lamoignon was born in Paris on September 14, 1608, of Chrétien Lamoignon, a Presiding Judge of the Parlement of Paris, and of Marie des Landes, who initiated her from childhood in the traditions of the Confraternity of Charity. Mother and daughter were both very zealous in their dedication to the poor. They often went to visit them in their homes, dressed their wounds, cleaned their rooms, made their beds, and gave them clothing, linen, food, and money. She supported and took an active part in all the works the Saint founded. Saint Vincent used to say that she forged ahead so fast with her charitable works that nobody could keep up with her. Mademoiselle de Lamoignon died on April 14, 1687, at seventy-nine years of age; her life has been written by Father d'Orléans (*Vie de Mademoiselle de Lamoignon*, Bibl. Nat., Ms. fr. 23895) and by Mademoiselle Louise Masson (*Madeleine de Lamoignon* [Lyons, 1846]). Abbé Guy-Toussaint-Julien Carron gave her a place in *Vies des Dames françaises qui ont été les plus célèbres dans le XVII*e *siècle par leur piété et leur dévouement pour les pauvres* (2nd. ed., Louvain: Varlinthout et Vandenzande, 1826).

[2]Madeleine de Lamoignon's sister, who died in Paris on August 12, 1658.

Letter 2490a. - Congregation of the Mission, Florence (Italy), original signed letter; photocopy in the Archives of the Mission, Paris. The text was published in *Annales C. M.* (1947-48), p. 310, and reprinted in *Mission et Charité*, 19-20, no. 96, p. 121. This edition uses the latter text.

[1]Marguerite Deffita, widow of Jacques Viole, Counselor at the Châtelet in Paris. A very intelligent and active Lady of Charity greatly appreciated by Saint Vincent, she died in Paris in 1678.

the relief of the poor people and for the strength He gives you to continue your services for them. May His Divine Goodness be pleased to give you His blessings of body and mind.

I am, in His love, dear Brother, your most affectionate servant.

VINCENT DEPAUL,
i.s.C.M.

Addressed: Brother Jean Parre, of the Congregation of the Mission, in Rethel

2491. - TO FIRMIN GET, SUPERIOR, IN MARSEILLES

Paris, December 21, 1657

Monsieur,

The grace of O[ur] L[ord] be with you forever!

I have not yet received your letter from the last regular mail. While awaiting it, I will tell you that a bill of exchange on Messieurs Napollon for two hundred livres is enclosed to reimburse M. Huguier for the advances he made and will make for the poor convicts. I say "will make" because, since all of this sum is not due him, he will have a little left over for the basic items we will ask him to supply them.

Work continues here on the affairs of the Consul of Algiers.[1] The early stages gave us some hope of success, but we do not see much progress; this requires time and patience.

May God preserve and bless you! I am, in His love, Monsieur, your most humble servant.

VINCENT DEPAUL,
i.s.C.M.

Letter 2491. - Archives of the Mission, Paris, copy made from the original in the Hains Family Collection, Marseilles.

[1]Jean Barreau.

2492. - TO ANTOINE DURAND,[1] SUPERIOR, IN AGDE

Paris, December 21, 1657

Monsieur,

The grace of O[ur] L[ord] be with you forever!

I did not write to you last Friday so as to begin to put your advice into practice, namely, that we write to one another only every two weeks. On that day I received your letter of December 3. I praise God for the disposition He has given you to do willingly whatever is His good pleasure. This is an effect of the grace He has granted you and not of any virtue there might be in my words, for my sins make me unworthy that His Divine Goodness should bless what I say.

I approve of your admitting to your seminary classes the priests of the town who would like to attend them,[2] provided they have the right intention and the Vicar-General[3] has no reasons to the con-

---

Letter 2492. - Archives of the Mission, Turin, unsigned rough draft.

[1]Antoine Durand was a chosen soul. Born in Beaumont-sur-Oise (Val-d'Oise) in April 1629, he entered the Congregation of the Mission on September 15, 1647, took his vows in 1651, and was ordained a priest in September 1654, a few days after his arrival in Poland. He returned to France in 1655, was assigned to Agde, and became Superior there the following year. The Savoy Province sent him as its delegate to the General Assembly in 1661. In 1662 he was put in charge of the house and parish in Fontainebleau, a very important and delicate position because of the dealings the Pastor was obliged to have with the Court. In his interesting memoirs, published by Abbé Octave Estournet (*Journal de Antoine Durand, prêtre de la Mission, premier curé de Fontainebleau (1661-67)* [Fontainebleau: Libr. cathol., 1900]), he retraces the events in which he was involved during his stay in Fontainebleau. From there Durand went to Agde (1679-81), then to Dijon (1681-83), Sedan (1683-90), Saint-Cyr (1691-92), and the Arras Seminary (1692-95); in all these places he was Superior. Despite his age, he was given the duty of Secretary General, which he performed until 1707. For two years he was also Director of the Daughters of Charity. Besides his memoirs, he wrote three books, still in manuscript form: *Vie de la Soeur Julienne Loret, Fille de la Charité; Livre contenant les marques d'un homme juste* (Bibl. Maz., Ms. 1250); and *Réflexions sur les masques, le bal et les danses, avec quelques pratiques pour les trois jours qui précèdent le carême*, Ms. 1679. The exact date of his death is not known. His biography is in *Notices*, vol. II, pp. 389-424.

[2]In this place some words are scratched out: "It would be desirable for everyone to have the same love for learning."

[3]First redaction: "and M. Le Breton."

trary. As for me, I see none, but rather many that make me wish that they all had the same desire.

We are awaiting the contract you led us to expect regarding your foundation. We have no news except that there are about eighty ordinands, and the Bishop of Pamiers[4] is giving them the two talks, which are very well received.

I am, in O[ur] L[ord]. . . .

2493. - TO CHARLES OZENNE, SUPERIOR, IN WARSAW

Paris, December 21, 1657

Monsieur,

The grace of O[ur] L[ord] be with you forever!

I just received your two letters, dated November 3 and 8. It will be difficult for us to send back to you any of the priests who have come from Poland because they are needed in the houses where they now are. We have, however, thought about sending you five or six young men because, while they are completing their theological studies there, they will learn Polish and become acclimated to the country much more easily than if they were older. Please let me know how you feel about this. We will not fail to send you a priest and, at the same time, one or two coadjutor Brothers.

Meanwhile, we will ask God for the grace to correspond with His plans for the Company in that kingdom. We continue to ask Him to complete the work of restoring it to its pristine glory and, above all, to give it peace. I thank His Divine Goodness that there appears to be some likelihood of this. You consoled me greatly by that good news and the other news you gave me.

We have no news here.

---

[4]François-Étienne de Caulet.

Letter 2493. - Archives of the Mission, Krakow, original signed letter.

I embrace you tenderly. I am, in O[ur] L[ord], Monsieur, your most humble servant.

VINCENT DEPAUL,
i.s.C.M.

Addressed: Monsieur Ozenne

2494. - TO EDME JOLLY, SUPERIOR, IN ROME

Paris, December 21, 1657

Monsieur,

The grace of O[ur] L[ord] be with you forever!

I received no letters from you this week nor in the two weeks previous to it, except for an old one that I should have received five months ago because it is dated July 10. There are still one or two delayed since that time. This one was accompanied by the indulgence you obtained for a Pastor in the Aire diocese, for which I thank you.

Enclosed is the report from M. Bourdaise [1] that I failed to send you by the last regular mail. I do not know what God will do with our Madagascar mission. Someone told me that the Maréchal de la Meilleraye[2] asked the Capuchins for twelve of their priests, and they have promised to give them. There may be some truth in that because I had the honor of writing to inform him that we will have

---

Letter 2494. - Archives of the Mission, Turin, original signed letter.

[1]Probably Toussaint Bourdaise's letters of February 19, 1657 (cf. vol. VI, nos. 2215 and 2216).

[2]Charles de la Porte, Duc de la Meilleraye, born in 1602, owed his rapid advancement as much to the protection of Cardinal Richelieu as to his personal valor. He was appointed Grand Master of Artillery in 1634, Maréchal of France in 1637, Superintendent of Finance in 1648, and Duke and Peer in 1663. It was he who gave Saint Vincent the idea of sending Missionaries to Madagascar. He died in Paris on February 8, 1664.

two or three priests ready for the first ship to go out—which they say will be soon—and to entreat him to let us know the best time to have them go to Nantes, but he did not give me any answer. Then I wrote to a devout person who is close to him, and even had Abbé d'Annemont write to another man to find out his plans and what we should expect, but I still have learned nothing certain. Things will be as God so chooses.[3]

I just now received two of your letters, dated November 12 and 19. I will notify the Bishop of Le Puy[4] and the Provincial of the Mercedarians[5] of what you have written me concerning their affairs, and I will even send each of them an extract of it. The Provincial came while I was writing this, and I informed him of what concerns him.

I thank God for the good status of the Saint-Pourçain affair[6] and for the fact that the Cardinal Datary[7] has pronounced in favor of it. May God make us worthy by His grace of the benevolence with which H[is] E[minence] is pleased to honor us! We will gladly pay

---

[3]The arguments between the Duc de la Meilleraye and the Company of the Indies went back several years. This Company had received from the King the exclusive right to trade with Madagascar and the nearby islands, and this right was renewed in 1652 for a twenty-year period. But the disagreement among the members and a lack of funds paralyzed its operation. In November 1655 the Duke, on his own initiative, sent four ships to Madagascar. There was a lawsuit, soon followed by an agreement. Sébastien Cazet reconstituted the Society along other lines. (Cf. Bibl. Nat., Ms. fr. 10.209.) The rift seemed mended, but they did not reckon with the Duke's haughty character: he was confident of the backing of the Court, and the two Commandants he himself had established in Fort-Dauphin—MM. du Rivaux and Chamargou—were devoted to him. In November 1656 he ordered the *Saint-Jacques* to set sail without waiting for the Company's merchandise. From that day on the rift was complete. (Cf. Arthur Malotet, *Étienne de Flacourt ou les origines de la colonisation française à Madagascar (1648-61)* [Paris: Ernest Leroux, 1898], pp. 268ff.).

[4]Henri Cauchon de Maupas du Tour, a member of the Tuesday Conferences, Bishop of Le Puy (1641-61), and of Évreux from 1661 to August 12, 1680, the day of his death. He was a renowned orator and preached the funeral panegyrics for Saint Jane Frances de Chantal and Saint Vincent. He also wrote biographies of Saints Francis de Sales and Jane Frances, and was one of the two Bishops who approved Abelly's life of Saint Vincent.

[5]The Order of Mercy, whose members are commonly known as Mercedarians, was founded for the redemption of captives by Saint Peter Nolasco in the thirteenth century.

[6]Abbé Louis de Chandenier wanted Saint-Pourçain Priory united to Saint-Lazare.

[7]Giacomo Corradi, a very important member of the Roman Curia and one of the Pope's closest collaborators.

the thousand livres that this union is supposed to cost; it will be well for you to pay them without asking for a reduction, not only for the reason you mention but also to speed up the expedition of the Bull. Have no doubt that there will be difficulties in its execution, but Providence will remove them when God so pleases.

Since the Sacred Congregation of Propaganda Fide was unwilling to give its consent for our priests to be in charge of the consulates in Tunis and Algiers, we must acquiesce in its decision. I would really like to know if this lack of consent carries a prohibition or if, while refusing to allow it openly, it is at least disposed to tolerate it in the case of the Le Vachers, so that they can have a clear conscience about it. Otherwise, they may as well come home and abandon the slaves entirely, since it is impossible to help them, as has been done, without the backing of the consulates. Furthermore, suitable laymen cannot be found to carry out the office with the steadfastness and disinterestedness needed to sustain the work of God, after the harsh treatment the last ones have received there. Nevertheless, we will not resort to this total abandonment until the last possible moment; for it will be a great misfortune if this happens. So, please send us apostolic faculties for those two brothers.

I think your reply to Cardinal Ludovisio[8] concerning the Bishops' proposal is very good and judicious, and I do not think you could give one that is more in conformity with our Constitution. May God bless you!

You did the right thing if you went to hear Cardinal de Sainte-Croix,[9] since he wanted this so much and you need to take some fresh air in the country from time to time.

I approve of your receiving the young French gentleman who made his retreat at your house, and as many priests who come to

---

[8]Nicolò Albergati-Ludovisio, appointed Cardinal in 1645, was Grand Penitentiary (1649-87); he died in 1687.

[9]Marcello di Santacroce, born on June 7, 1619, was appointed Cardinal on February 9, 1652, at the urging of the King of Poland. He was made Bishop of Tivoli in October of that same year and died in Rome on December 19, 1674.

enter the Company, as long as they have their titles and the requisite qualities, and especially that they have the right intention.

Thank you for the letters of appointment for the Champvant priory that I received for M. Le Boysne.[10]

I have nothing to say about the reasons you gave Cardinal Bagni for not using your influence to gain entrance to the palace of Saint John Lateran, since it is a place that does not suit you. Still, if God in His Providence, through the Pope's order, were to lodge you there, I think some good could come of it, both because it would be a means of allowing the Company to be of service in the primatial see of the Church,[11] and also because it would be an opportunity to undertake the retreats for the ordinands. This would not prevent the Missionaries in time from having another more convenient house in the city.

I am not surprised at the difficulties you are encountering in the Sépulchre affair,[12] for it got off on the wrong foot. M. Le Vazeux [13] took it on without asking our advice and without taking the necessary precautions that had to be observed.

---

[10]Léonard Le Boysne, born in La Chapelle-Janson (Ille-et-Vilaine), was received at Saint-Lazare on May 6, 1638. Sent to Luçon, then to Richelieu, he went to Saint-Méen in September 1645 and died there on February 25, 1670. Monsieur Alméras, Superior General, praised him highly in his circular of March 13, 1670: "We have just lost a hidden treasure of grace and holiness. . . . He excelled in piety, meekness, mortification, regularity, obedience and good example, but especially in humility and charity. I consider myself fortunate to have made my seminary with him. . . . He was very virtuous and one of the most talented Missionaries in the Company." A biographical sketch of Le Boysne is given in the Lyons manuscript, pp. 234-37.

[11]First redaction: "of making the Company known." The correction is in the Saint's handwriting.

[12]An unsuccessful effort to unite the Saint-Sépulcre Priory to the Annecy Seminary. Saint Vincent abandoned these efforts.

[13]Achille Le Vazeux, born in Bonneval (Eure-et-Loir) on June 22, 1620, entered the Congregation of the Mission on August 24, 1639, took his vows on June 7, 1643, and was ordained a priest on April 3, 1649. Shortly after ordination he was sent to Rome, where he remained until 1653. He was Superior of the Annecy Seminary (1653-58), then was recalled to Paris and sent to the Collège des Bons-Enfants. He left there a few days before the Saint's death and returned to his family. To certain good qualities Le Vazeux added such noticeable failings (including doubts regarding the validity of the vows) that Saint Vincent regarded his withdrawal from the Congregation as a blessing from God. Hasty and obstinate in his decisions, he found it hard to take advice from Superiors and to submit his will to theirs. Saint Vincent had frequent occasion to reproach him.

Please seek counsel to find out if there is any danger in priests getting involved with dispensing remedies to the poor for certain diseases they have. I, for my part, see none, and I think that if others find none in it you will do well to allow M. d'Eu [14] to exercise his charity in such circumstances, provided these bodily remedies do not keep him from his spiritual duties and do not cost him too much trouble and expense.

I am, in O[ur] L[ord], Monsieur, your most humble servant.

VINCENT DEPAUL,
i.s.C.M.

Addressed: Monsieur Jolly

2495. - TO HIPPOLYTE FÉRET,[1] PASTOR OF SAINT-NICOLAS-DU-CHARDONNET

Saint-Lazare, December 22, 1657

After having an extract made of the letters from the Bishop of Boulogne[2] concerning the misfortunes of his diocese, I took it to

---

[14]Louis d'Eu, born on April 8, 1624, in Fresnay-sur-Sarthe (Sarthe), entered the Congregation of the Mission on May 20, 1651, left it, and reentered on March 6, 1655, taking his vows in Rome on March 7, 1657. After Saint Vincent's death, he again left the Congregation, for some important business, by order of the Archbishop of Paris, but returned as soon as he was able after the Archbishop died. The Bibliothèque Nationale has acquired one of his manuscript works, *L'homme accompli* (fr. 9625).

Letter 2495. - Archives of the Mission, Turin, original unsigned letter.

[1]Hippolyte Féret, born in Pontoise (Val-d'Oise), was a Doctor of Theology and later became Pastor of Saint-Nicolas-du-Chardonnet, Vicar-General of Alet, and then of Paris. Saint Vincent thought so highly of Féret that he proposed him as Coadjutor Bishop of Babylon.

[2]François Perrochel, a cousin of Jean-Jacques Olier, was born in Paris on October 18, 1602. Animated by the spirit of Saint Vincent, he was one of the devout, zealous priests who worked under the Saint's direction and gave missions in several places, especially in Auvergne, Joigny, and the faubourg Saint-Germain. He was a member of the Tuesday Conferences and was present at the meetings at which retreats for ordinands were organized. As Bishop-elect of Boulogne, he was invited to give conferences to the ordinands at the Bons-Enfants and was so successful that the Queen wanted to hear him. Moved by his words, she gave the Saint a generous donation

the meeting of the Ladies of Charity. They decided to donate three hundred livres to be used for clothing, and I was given the responsibility of notifying that good Bishop that, if he would take the trouble to get this amount from some merchant in his town and draw a bill of exchange on Mademoiselle Viole, it would be paid promptly. I most humbly ask the Pastor of Saint-Nicolas to inform him of this, since these alms are the result of his recommendation. There is no need to tell him that they are to clothe the most destitute of the poor; his paternal charity for them is too compassionate to use them for anything else.

The Ladies have not yet earmarked anything for the two religious houses because their funds are completely exhausted. We shall see whether a little relief can be sent to them in a while.

2496. - TO LOUIS DUPONT,[1] SUPERIOR, IN TRÉGUIER

Paris, December 26, 1657

Monsieur,

The grace of O[ur] L[ord] be with you forever!

I received your latest letter, but I could not read the date on it. There is reason to be consoled by the return of the person you mention. Since I was very surprised by his fall, I will also be

---

to help defray the retreat expenses. Perrochel was consecrated in the church of Saint-Lazare on June 11, 1645. His episcopate was one of the most fruitful and glorious known to the Boulogne diocese. In 1675, worn out by age and infirmity, and unable to govern his diocese properly, the Bishop resigned; he died on April 8, 1682. (Cf. Van Drival, *Histoire des évêques de Boulogne* [Boulogne-sur-Mer: Berger frères, 1852].)

Letter 2496. - Archives of the Mission, Turin, original signed letter. The rough draft is also in the Turin Archives.

[1]Louis Dupont, born in Nemours (Seine-et-Marne), entered the Congregation of the Mission on October 23, 1641, at twenty-two years of age, and took his vows in November 1644. He was Superior in Toul (1652-53), Tréguier (1654-61), Annecy (1662-63), and at Saint-Charles (1664-71).

overjoyed if he recognizes his faults. You must not, then, be too hard on him but welcome him and treat him cordially so as to give him the confidence to come to see you and consult you. Show him that you are happy to be of service to him, as if it were your idea, without telling him that I wrote to you about this—unless you think it is advisable. You can even advise him to come here to distance himself from the causes.[2]

I approved the settlement of accounts for the Canon Theologian,[3] but it is still with the notary. I will send it to you by the first regular mail or will put it in the Bishop's[4] hands to be forwarded to him, since it was given to him.

I greet your heart and your family tenderly and affectionately, asking O[ur] L[ord] to bless them so abundantly that the seminary will also share in the blessing, and all those priests in whom you are trying to instill and nurture the ecclesiastical spirit will ultimately be filled with it. I do not recommend them to you; you know that they are the treasure of the Church.

I am, in O[ur] L[ord], Monsieur, your most humble servant.

VINCENT DEPAUL,
i.s.C.M.

Addressed: Monsieur Dupont, Superior of the Priests of the Mission, in Tréguier

---

[2]First redaction: "to come here, and once he is here, we shall see."

[3]Maître Michel Thépault, sieur de Rumelin, Licentiate in Civil and Canon Law, Rector of Pleumeur-Bodou and of Plougasnou, then Canon of the Tréguier Cathedral, and Penitentiary of the diocese. Thépault was a great benefactor of the Missionaries and founded the Tréguier Seminary. He died on August 30, 1677. (Cf. Discourse of Canon Daniel in *Annales C. M.*, vol. LXIII [1908], pp. 191-201.)

[4]Balthazar Grangier de Liverdi.

2497. - TO PIERRE LAISNÉ,[1] IN SAINT-MÉEN

Paris, December 26, 1657

Monsieur,

The grace of O[ur] L[ord] be with you forever!

I received your letter, which consoled me more than I can tell you. Thank you for the advice you give me; I will make good use of it, God willing.

I am very concerned about M. Le Boysne's illness; I ask O[ur] L[ord] to preserve him for the Company and to restore him soon to perfect health, since he uses it so effectively. I am not recommending him to you, in the absence of M. Serre,[2] because I am well aware that your charity is careful to see that he lacks nothing that may help to console and cure him. I ask only that you continue to do so and to embrace him for me.

I praise God, Monsieur, that you have about twenty seminarians and are working to help them make progress. I cannot prevent myself from entreating you, in the name of O[ur] L[ord], who wants all of them to be good and perfect priests, to do your utmost to make them such, sparing neither prayers, reprimands, spiritual exercises, nor good example for this. [You] see, Monsieur, they are the treasure of the Church, which [God] has entrusted [to you], and the

---

Letter 2497. - Archives of the Mission, Turin, original signed letter.

[1]Pierre Laisné, born in Dreux (Eure-et-Loir) on November 9, 1623, entered the Congregation of the Mission on September 24, 1641, and took his vows on October 4, 1643. He received all the Sacred Orders in December 1648, with a dispensation *extra tempora*. In 1657 he was a member of the Saint-Méen house.

An *extra tempora* was an indult from the Holy See granting religious Institutes the privilege of having Sacred Orders conferred outside the times prescribed by church law.

[2]Louis Serre, born in Épinal (Vosges), was ordained a priest in September 1643. He entered the Congregation of the Mission on March 23, 1644, at the age of twenty-six, and took his vows in July 1646. His first assignment was Crécy, where he was Superior (1646-48). From there he was sent to Saint-Méen, where he spent nearly all his life as a Missionary, including his years as Superior (1655-65, 1671-75, and 1676-81).

field where you must k[now how to bring] [3] to fruition the graces He has given you. This is the prayer I make to God.

When M. Serre returns, tell him I received the book he sent me for M. Dolivet,[4] to whom I will have it forwarded. However, I am waiting for a favorable opportunity because postage is too expensive; it costs thirty-two sous from here to Rennes.

I send greetings to the dear Saint-Méen family. We have no news. I am, in O[ur] L[ord], Monsieur, your most humble servant.

VINCENT DEPAUL,
i.s.C.M.

Addressed: Monsieur Laisné, Priest of the Mission, in Saint-Méen

2498. - TO EDME JOLLY, SUPERIOR, IN ROME

Paris, December 28, 1657

Monsieur,

The grace of O[ur] L[ord] be with you forever!

Thank you for the privileged altar [1] for Saint-Sauveur of Melun and the faculties for those priests in the Hebrides, which I received with your letter of November 26. Since then, you have heard that God has been pleased to take M. Duiguin to Himself. I think I informed you of that.

---

[3]The original, damaged by mites, is missing a few words; these have been supplied here between brackets.

[4]Julien Dolivet, born in Cardroc (Ille-et-Vilaine), was ordained a priest on March 30, 1652, entered the Congregation of the Mission in Richelieu on January 2, 1653, and took his vows in Agde in March 1656 in the presence of M. Berthe. He was Superior in Sedan (1668-73) and in Narbonne (1673-82).

Letter 2498. - Archives of the Mission, Turin, original signed letter.

[1]An altar to which apostolic authority attaches the privilege whereby a plenary indulgence may be applied to the soul of a deceased person for whom Mass is celebrated on that altar.

So then, do not request an *extra tempora* for Brother Plunket,[2] since the reasons you give me are important enough to leave matters as they stand. He is in Tréguier right now; I think he must have received the subdiaconate at the last ordination there and will be able to receive the other Holy Orders between now and Easter. As for Brother Deslions [3] and the others from the same area, for whom I will ask you later to send us the *extra tempora* and who will not fulfill one of the requisite conditions for receiving them—either that of being subdeacons, nobles, professors in theology, or thirty years of age—please make an effort to get them, explaining the Company's need for priests. If that does not suffice, add to it *ob solatium parentum senio confectorum*[4] or any other reasons you deem proper, and do not worry about the cost.

We will pay your bill of exchange of 32 livres 15 sous for the money you gave Jean Félix[5] and will forward to his mother in Villenauxe[6] the letter he is writing to her.

I asked you to find out if our priests can in conscience take charge of the consulates in Tunis and Algiers, given the fact that the Sacred Congregation, which refuses to grant this permission, nevertheless does not forbid them to do so, although it knows that they are already carrying out the duties.

You were right to remark that, in Cardinal Bagni's proposal to you of an establishment in his diocese,[7] he did not let you know his

---

[2]Luke Plunket, born on October 18, 1630, in Girly, Meath diocese (Ireland), entered the Congregation of the Mission in Richelieu on September 24, 1653, and took his vows there in the presence of M. de Beaumont. In 1659 he was in Saint-Meen.

[3]Jacques Deslions, born in Arras (Artois), entered the Congregation of the Mission in Paris on December 28, 1654, at the age of twenty-three, and took his vows there in 1656 in the presence of M. Berthe. On December 28, 1657 (cf. vol. VII, no. 2498), Saint Vincent asked Edme Jolly to apply for a dispensation *extra tempora* for Deslions, and he was ordained in 1658.

[4]*For the consolation of his parents in their old age.*

[5]A servant in the Rome house.

[6]Today, Villenauxe-la-Grande, principal town in the canton of Aube, near Nogent-sur-Seine.

[7]Senigallia, to which he was appointed on April 9, 1657.

thinking regarding his foundation. He did me the honor of writing me a letter in which he offers to give a house for this purpose, but he says nothing about living expenses. Perhaps H[is] E[minence] assumes that the Rome house will support the Missionaries in his diocese or that we will find the means of funding them from here in the way that the Rome house itself is funded. But do not expect either one or the other. This is a long, drawn out affair, and it will be well for you to act accordingly, without, however, letting that good nobleman know that you have this plan.

As for what you tell me about several good proposals already made that have gone up in smoke, let me tell you, Monsieur, that the persons who made them may have had good intentions; however, no matter how holy new works may be, they amount to nothing if they do not have a promoter who follows them up. Since those in question did not, they have remained at a standstill. Thanks be to God, Monsieur, we have seen the affairs of which you were the prime mover succeed through the attention and good leadership you brought to them. We have, then, reason to believe that whatever was proposed would have had the same success if you had been the instigator of them—but there are some matters in which we must take only a passive role.

How do we know, Monsieur, whether God is not at work in the Saint John Lateran proposal? If you were to reside there, you would be citizens of Rome and in a position to render new services to God. Furthermore, that would not prevent you from having another house in the city for the summer. Since people are after you for that, you should not be too quick to reject the proposal but should listen to the overtures being made and seek counsel.

If you find any good priests there who are willing to work in the missions, and you have solid references for them, it will be well for you to accept them, without waiting for my reply. That is how the Company acted in the beginning, bringing in outside priests to work with it because it could not do everything. Furthermore, by this means those priests are formed in the service of souls.

I praise God that the Saint-Pourçain petition has been signed.[8] We will try to pay the bill of exchange you have to draw on us for it.

The books requested by Cardinal Brancaccio[9]—for which we received the note only twelve to fifteen days ago, although you addressed it to us more than five months ago—will cost seven or eight hundred livres, according to the estimate of M. Soly, the bookseller, whom we brought to this house expressly for the purpose of pricing them. This does not include the ones you request for Father Hilarion.[10] I do not know, Monsieur, if these are to be given as gifts to both of them, or whether they intend to pay for them. I will await your answer before doing anything about this.

Your most humble servant.

VINCENT DEPAUL,
i.s.C.M.

It was only ten or twelve days ago that I received your letter of July 6, mentioning the books for Cardinal Brancaccio and Father Hilarion.[11]

Addressed: Monsieur Jolly, Superior of the Priests of the Mission of Rome, in Rome

---

[8]The Bull uniting Saint-Pourçain Priory to the Congregation of the Mission bears the date of December 13.

[9]Francesco Maria Brancaccio, Bishop of Viterbo, Porto, and Capaccio, was created Cardinal in 1634, and died on January 9, 1675. He is also the author of a collection of Latin essays.

[10]Abbot Hilarion, born Bartolommeo Rancati in Milan on September 2, 1594, was the son of Baltasarre Rancati and Margherita di Bagno. He entered the Cistercians in Milan on March 10, 1608, and taught in Salamanca (1614-18), then in Milan. In May 1619 he was sent to the Convent of Santa Croce in Gerusalemme in Rome. Among the offices he held in the Curia was that of Consultor for Propaganda Fide, in which he provided many services for religious Orders and Founders. Saint Vincent considered him a friend and protector (cf. *Annales C. M.* (1951), p. 374).

[11]This sentence is in the Saint's handwriting.

2499. - TO FIRMIN GET, SUPERIOR, IN MARSEILLES

Paris, December 28, 1657

Monsieur,

The grace of O[ur] L[ord] be with you forever!

I received your two letters, dated December 11 and 18. I will gladly use my influence with the Duc de Richelieu for the choice of the new Administrators and will do whatever I can so that you will have the answer you desire as soon as possible.

We sent you a bill of exchange for two hundred livres for the money M. Huguier advanced to the convicts. I am sure you have received it by now.

You tell me that, if M. Le Vacher [1] hurries, he will still be able to get on the boat that is supposed to be going to Algiers. If it were question only of him, he would be ready to leave, but money is needed, and we do not have any. He is very worried about this, and so are we. We are doing our utmost to find some but are not making much progress. A collection is being taken up to supply for what we lack. All this requires patience.

M. Delaforcade[2] wrote to us by the last regular mail but made no mention of the chest you sent him; perhaps he had not yet received it.

M. Berthe has arrived in Turin; I received a letter from him.

I praise God for the opportunity He gave you to render service to Him with the ordinands and for the care you took to prepare them for the Orders they received. God grant that they have profited from your instructions and example and that this beginning will help them to continue to grow!

I am deeply indebted to the Bishop of Marseilles [3] for the

Letter 2499. - Archives of the Mission, Paris, original signed letter.

[1]Philippe Le Vacher.

[2]A merchant in Lyons.

[3]Étienne du Puget, Bishop of Marseilles (1644-68).

remembrance with which he honors me and for the favor he granted me through you. I thank him most humbly for this, and I ask you, Monsieur, to renew to him the offers of my obedience whenever you have the occasion to do so. Be assured of the affection of my poor heart and paltry prayers for you in particular, for Our Lord does not want me to be to no purpose, in His love, Monsieur, your most humble servant.

VINCENT DEPAUL,
i.s.C.M.

We received a gold louis for Marbais, known as La Source, a convict on the *Mazarine;* please ask M. Huguier to give it to him.

I will reply to M. de la Fosse,[4] whom I embrace tenderly for now because I am very busy.[5]

Addressed: Monsieur Get, Superior of the Priests of the Mission of Marseilles, in Marseilles

---

[4]Jacques de la Fosse, born in Paris on November 25, 1621, entered the Congregation of the Mission on October 8, 1640, took his vows on April 7, 1643, and was ordained a priest in September 1648. Immediately after his ordination, Saint Vincent entrusted to him the humanities at Saint-Charles Seminary. He "often reenacted there Christian tragedies," wrote Collet (*op. cit.*, vol. I, p. 326), "whose spirit and sublimity drew the applause of connoisseurs in Paris." In 1656 he went to Marseilles, where he served in turn as Missionary and seminary professor. Two years later he was sent to Troyes. He died in Sedan on April 30, 1674. De la Fosse was as generous as he was capricious, becoming easily enthused and just as easily discouraged. Several times he almost left the Company; only Saint Vincent's paternal encouragement kept him from doing so. His writings, all in Latin, made a name for him among the Latinists of the seventeenth century. Collet says he was "an orator, philosopher, and theologian all in one, and such a great poet that Santeuil considered him his rival and sometimes his master" (*ibid.*, vol. I, p. 277). Dom Calmet added: "In general, there is great passion and many noble, generous thoughts in de la Fosse's poetry, but his penchant for mythology, even in his sacred verses, sometimes renders them obscure because of his unusual expressions and frequent allusions to fable." (Cf. Augustin Calmet, *Bibliothèque lorraine* [Nancy: A. Leseure, 1751], p. 376.) His works are found in the Bibliothèque Nationale (Ms. L. 10.331, 11.365), in the Bibliothèque de l'Arsenal (Ms. 1137, 1138), and in the Bibliothèque Mazarine (Ms. 3910-19, 4312, imp. 10.877). See also [Édouard Rosset, C.M.] *Notices bibliographiques sur les écrivains de la Congrégation de la Mission* (Angoulême: J.-B. Baillarger, 1878).

[5]This sentence is in the Saint's handwriting.

2500. - TO GEORGES DES JARDINS, SUPERIOR, IN TOUL

Paris, December 29, 1657

Monsieur,

The grace of O[ur] L[ord] be with you forever!

Madame de Herse, the President's wife,[1] is very worried about the second bundle she sent you for the Carmelite nuns of Neufchâteau and about getting no reply from you to the letters she wrote you on this matter. Neither has she had any news from them to let her know whether they received this alms. She expressed to me her deep distress about this and has distressed me at the same time, since I see how she is suffering through our fault.

Please write to her as soon as possible, Monsieur, to assure her that you have received and delivered those clothes—if that is the case, which I do not doubt. Act very respectfully with her, and please apologize to her for having taken so long. I attribute this delay to the mission you gave, which prevented you from returning or from sending that bundle to those nuns. If that is true, tell her so; for, if she knows that you were absent for such a good reason, she will be satisfied, provided you did on your return what she asked you to do.

Be very careful, Monsieur, not to mention the transportation expenses for either the first or the second parcel; I promised her that you would pay them. Do not take anything from those poor

---

Letter 2500. - Archives of the Mission, Turin, original signed letter.

[1]Madame de Herse, née Charlotte de Ligny, was the daughter of Jean de Ligny, Seigneur de Ranticey, Master of Requests. She was also the widow of Michel Vialart, Seigneur de la Forest de Herse, Counselor to the King in his Parlement Court, President of Requests of the palace, then Ambassador to Switzerland, who died in Solothurn (Switzerland) on October 26, 1634. Madame de Herse was the mother of Félix Vialart, Bishop of Châlons, as well as a relative of Jean-Jacques Olier; Francis de Sales, a good friend of hers, was her son's godfather. A Lady of Charity, she was one of Saint Vincent's chief auxiliaries and a great benefactress of the poor of Paris, Picardy, and Champagne. Works for the ordinands and for abandoned children received her support, and she established the Daughters of Charity in Chars (Val-d'Oise). During the wars that ravaged the capital, the Queen Mother, Anne of Austria, entrusted to her and some other Ladies the distribution of her personal alms. Madame de Herse died in 1662.

Sisters either, even if they try to give you something; for if that Lady heard about it, she would be greatly disedified, knowing their poverty and our obligation to inconvenience ourselves for the relief of the poor. She is one of our Company's greatest benefactresses; for this reason, we must obey her and try to please her, but graciously. That is why, Monsieur, I ask you once again to write her a letter letting her know that you have this desire. Enclosed is one she has had written to you again and another for the coach mistress,[2] asking her to explain about the bundle, if she has not delivered it to you.

We have not finished with the business of the letters of union but are still working on it and are hoping to get them. Has God blessed your work in this latest mission? How are you? I ask His Divine Goodness to preserve and sanctify you, along with the little family, to whom I send greetings. I am, in the love of O[ur] L[ord], Monsieur, your most humble servant.

VINCENT DEPAUL,
i.s.C.M.

2501. - TO A PRIEST OF THE MISSION

Our Congregation does not allow those who have given themselves to God among us to go back home. This is because of our experience that a visit to relatives may lessen their first fervor and because Our Lord, who knew the harmful effects of too much contact with relatives on those who profess to follow Him, was unwilling to allow one of His disciples even to go to bury his father,[1] or another to return home to dispose of his property. After

---

[2]The woman in charge of the coach station.

Letter 2501. - Abelly, *op. cit.*, 2nd ed., bk. II, chap. XXIII, p. 250.
[1]Cf. Mt 8:21-22. (NAB)

examples such as these, you cannot fail to ask your family to excuse you for not going to see them, and I can give you no better piece of advice than what Our Lord Himself gave you, namely, to leave father, mother, brothers, sisters, and possessions, if you want to follow Him and be numbered among His disciples.[2]

If you are worried about a division in your family, try to remedy it by letter, asking some upright person there to mediate the reconciliation. If there is question of some temporal good which involves you, send your power of attorney to a relative or friend to do in your absence what you would do if you were there.

If you yourself were to handle the affairs of your relatives, there would be reason to fear that, instead of settling matters as you would wish, they might drag you into their disputes and embroil you in their affairs. This happens only too often to priests who try to interfere in them. If you say that it is only to have them profit spiritually by this, remember that frequent association with those who are close to you diminishes the spirit and often destroys it altogether. That is why a person is rarely a prophet in his own country.[3] Our Lord returned only once to His town of Nazareth after He had begun His preaching ministry, and that very time the inhabitants tried to hurl Him off a cliff.[4] Perhaps He allowed this to teach evangelical workers that by returning home they are in danger of falling from the high esteem to which their works have raised them and of plunging into some deadly abyss.

---

[2]Cf. Lk 14:26. (NAB)
[3]Cf. Mk 6:4. (NAB)
[4]Cf. Lk 4:28-30. (NAB)

2502. - TO FIRMIN GET, SUPERIOR, IN MARSEILLES

Paris, January 4, 1658

Monsieur,

I ask O[ur] L[ord] that this new year may bring you a thousand blessings to serve you as steps to attain a blessed eternity.

Enclosed is the Duc de Richelieu's letter with his choice of two new Administrators.

I have not yet received your letter from the last regular mail. In the meantime, please credit M. Huguier with twenty-one livres, which I ask him to give to Denis Dubois, a convict on the *Capitaine;* we have received them here from his father.

The elder M. Alméras [1] is seriously ill; everyone else in this house is in very good health.

Since writing the above, that good Brother has gone to God; he was around eighty-three years of age. We have reason to believe he is now in heaven, after the acts of virtue we saw him practice since he entered the Company, which edified the whole house. Nevertheless, since God's judgments are unknown to us,[2] I recom-

---

Letter 2502. - Archives of the Mission, Paris, original signed letter. The postscript is in the Saint's handwriting.

[1]René Alméras the elder was born in Paris on November 12, 1575. After the death of his first wife, Marguerite Fayet, he married Marie Leclerc, the future mother of his six children. He was Secretary to the King, became Treasurer of France in Paris on January 19, 1608, Secretary to Marie de Médicis, Comptroller (1622-56), Postmaster General (1629-32), and Secretary for the execution of the orders of Marie de Médicis, filling all these positions in a worthy manner. After he had given his son to the Congregation of the Mission, he himself entered it on March 2, 1657, at the age of eighty-one, and died at Saint-Lazare on January 4, 1658. (Cf. *Notices,* vol. II, pp. 453-61.)

[2]Cf. Rom 11:33. (NAB)

mend his soul—and mine as well—to your prayers. I am, in the love of O[ur] L[ord], Monsieur, your most humble servant.

VINCENT DEPAUL,
i.s.C.M.

Since writing the above letter, I received yours, which mentions only the effort to find some boats for Algiers.

We are working on taking up a collection for M. Le Vacher.[3] The end of that is still a long way off. We will lose no time in doing it.

I ask M. de la Fosse to excuse me for being unable to write to him this time; we are busy with the funeral of our dear Brother Alméras.

Addressed: Monsieur Get

2503. - TO EDME JOLLY, SUPERIOR, IN ROME

January 4, 1658

I am consoled that you have finally received the Rector of the Salviati College and the young postulant from Alençon for a trial period. So there you have the beginning of a seminary. May God be pleased to water these new plants and raise on this foundation the edifice of this good work so that gradually it will be able to supply a large number of good workers for the Church of God, especially for all of Italy! These are simply wishes, which I willingly submit to God's guidance.

---

[3]Philippe Le Vacher spent about two years in France (1657-59) collecting money for the Algiers mission.

Letter 2503. - Reg. 2, p. 238.

2504. - TO N.

January 9, 1658

The virtues I saw him [1] practice make me believe that he has gone to God, and I do not think that the saints can die with greater confidence and resignation.

2505. - TO FIRMIN GET, SUPERIOR, IN MARSEILLES

Paris, January 11, 1658

Monsieur,

The grace of O[ur] L[ord] be with you forever!

I told you in my last letter that the elder M. Alméras became ill on New Year's Day and died on the fourth and that the virtues he practiced in this house prepared him for a happy death after such a long life.

Since that time, God has chosen to call to Himself one of our good Brothers, named François Hémet,[1] who died the following day, the fifth of this month, at the age of forty-five or fifty. His death corresponded to his life, for he manifested in both that he was

---

Letter 2504. - Collet, *op. cit.*, vol. II, p. 29. According to Collet, these same words are in another letter, dated January 12, 1658, which we no longer have.

[1]René Alméras the elder.

Letter 2505. - Archives of the Mission, Paris, copy made from the original in the Hains Family Collection, Marseilles.

On October 28, 1989, Xavier Charmoy, an appraiser and seller of rare books and autographs, sold at public auction in Nîmes, France, thirty-four letters written by Saint Vincent: thirty-two to Firmin Get, one to Philippe Le Vacher (December 6, 1658), and one to Dominique Lhuillier (November 13, 1658). These were all part of what was called the Hains Family Collection. Two letters remained in France; the rest went to foreign buyers. The Archives of the Mission, Paris, has copies of all these letters.

[1]François Hémet, born in Campremy, in the Beauvais diocese (Oise), entered the Congregation of the Mission as a coadjutor Brother on January 27, 1650.

ready for anything and filled with such fine sentiments that none better can be expected from a devout man. The last two times I saw him I was permeated with the fragrance of the fullness of his faith, his confidence in God, and his resignation to God's good pleasure.

We received word that the chest M. Le Vacher [2] is expecting from you has left Lyons and that he may have it in two or three days.

I have not yet received any of your letters from this regular mail, so I have nothing more to say to you except to ask O[ur] L[ord] to draw His glory more and more from your leadership and your family.

One of your good brothers has come to Paris on business, and we are expecting him today to make a few days of retreat here in this house. I think Brother Get [3] prepared him for this.

I am, in the love of O[ur] L[ord], Monsieur, your most humble servant.

VINCENT DEPAUL,
i.s.C.M.

2506. - TO A PRIEST OF THE MISSION

[January 11, 1658] [1]

The Saint mentions a rumor concerning the Maréchal de la Meilleraye, whose displeasure he had incurred.[2] The Maréchal had asked the Capuchins for missionaries, and they had promised him twenty-four of them,

---

[2]Philippe Le Vacher.

[3]Firmin Get's brother, Nicolas, was born in Chépy (Somme) in May 1635, entered the Congregation of the Mission on October 5, 1655, and took his vows on October 6, 1657, in the presence of M. Berthe. He left for Poland in September 1660, before his ordination to the priesthood.

Letter 2506. - Collet, *op. cit.*, vol. II, p. 38.

[1]The date Collet seems to favor. Moreover, this letter seems to fit near no. 2509.

[2]See the Saint's letter to the Duc de la Meilleraye, no. 2509. More detailed information is given in no. 2494.

who were supposed to sail on the first ship going to Saint-Laurent Island. The Saint says that "if the Maréchal makes an arrangement with those good religious," he is ready to recall M. Bourdaise from Madagascar. "Our maxim," he states, "is always to give place to others, confident that they will do better than we."

2507. - TO JEAN MARTIN, SUPERIOR, IN TURIN

Paris, January 11, 1658

Monsieur,

I ask O[ur] L[ord] that this new year may be a happy one for you for eternity and be followed by many other similar ones that will lead you to God, our last end.

Good M. Alméras the elder has reached his at the end of the eighty-three years he lived on this earth. He became ill on New Year's Day, and on the fourth he went to God. We have reason to believe this, after the acts of virtue we saw him practice since his entrance into the Company, which edified the whole house and prepared him for a happy death after such a long life. Nevertheless, since God's judgments are unknown to us, it will be well for us to pray for his soul and for that of our good Brother François Hémet, who died the following day, the fifth of this month, at the age of forty-five or fifty. His death corresponded to his life, for he manifested in both that he was ready for anything and was filled with such fine sentiments that none better can be expected from a devout person. The last two times I saw him, I was permeated with the fragrance of the fullness of his faith, his confidence in God, and his resignation to His good pleasure.

I received two letters from you, dated December 10 and 29. I praise God that you were pleased with the visitation and are hoping

---

Letter 2507. - Archives of the Mission, Turin, original signed letter.

for good results from it, also for the fact that the last three priests we sent you are already in a position to help you with your missions. This is a great consolation to me. After the Bra mission, the Genoa house will need two of those priests; you know that we sent them to you with the intention that they go to help there, once they become a little accustomed to the climate of the country.

I have nothing to say to you about M. de Musy's [1] departure.

We will gladly keep on praying for your continued good health and the success of your work.

You must leave to God the time and manner of your foundation and, in the meantime, endure patiently the inconveniences of housing and other needs.

I have not been too well but am better now, thank God.

I am, in O[ur] L[ord], Monsieur, your most humble servant.

VINCENT DEPAUL,
i.s.C.M.

Addressed: Monsieur Martin, Superior of the Priests of the Mission of Turin, in Turin

2508. - TO EDME JOLLY, SUPERIOR, IN ROME

January 11, 1658

I am consoled to hear that a person who has made a vow to become a religious fulfills his promise by entering our Company, even though it is not a religious Order. Nevertheless, we will be careful not to accept such persons anymore, unless they are well-balanced and persevering.

---

[1]M. de Musy was a very gifted priest on whom Saint Vincent had placed great hopes. He was sent to Turin in 1656; there he allowed boredom to get the better of him and left the Company the following year. His name does not appear in the personnel catalogue.

Letter 2508. - Reg. 2, p. 18.

2509. - TO THE DUC DE LA MEILLERAYE

January 12, 1658

My Lord,

I had the honor of informing you in two letters that the former Company of the Indies had met once and was to meet a second time to settle the proposed union, thanks to Messieurs de Lamoignon and Cazet.[1] Now, My Lord, I will tell you that, because I had a fall and a head injury, I have not been able to continue my efforts, but M. de Lamoignon, who has taken responsibility for writing you what those gentlemen have decided, notified me this morning that he would do so today.

I received a letter from M. Couplier, who informs me that he has been negotiating with you, My Lord, about going to make a settlement on one of the Mascarene Islands,[2] and he wants me to send him a priest and a Brother to go there with his men. My reply to him is that I will gladly do so if you, My Lord, agree to our sending at the same time one or two other priests for Madagascar. The manner in which we were called there to work for the salvation of those poor people, which was not by our own choice but at the wish of His Holiness; the loss we have sustained there of six good priests, together with expenses amounting to eight thousand livres

---

Letter 2509. - Reg. 1, fol. 35.

[1]Both Guillaume de Lamoignon and Sébastien Cazet were members of the Company of the Indies. No further information is available on Cazet.

Lamoignon, Marquis de Bâville and Counselor in the Parlement of Paris, was a devout man of outstanding character. In 1644 he became Master of Requests and in 1658 Chief Judge of the Parlement of Paris. When announcing his appointment as Chief Judge, Louis XIV said of him: "Had I known a better man, a worthier subject, I would have chosen him." Lamoignon was a friend and patron of literary men, especially of Boileau, who addressed to him his sixth epistle and wrote the *Lutrin* at his request; he was also a close friend of Saint Vincent and gave hospitality to the Missionaries who fell ill while caring for the poor in Étampes. His mother and sister were very active in the Saint's works. Lamoignon died on December 10, 1677. (Cf. *Vie de M. le premier président de Lamoignon* [Paris, 1781].)

[2]Former name for the archipelago made up of Réunion (Ile de Bourbon) and Mauritius (Île de France). Today it also includes Rodrigues.

entailed in this mission; the assistance we have to give to the only surviving Missionary remaining there; the experience he has acquired of the country and language; and the blessing God has been pleased to give him have prompted me, My Lord, to ask whether it is your good pleasure that we continue this good work or, if not, that we recall M. Bourdaise, who is still there.

You did me the honor of writing me that our men have shown greater attachment to the former Company than to you. I entreat you, My Lord, to allow me to tell you that someone has done us a disservice with you. For my part, I have considered nothing but the service of God in this work, and I think they have also held this same view. Indeed, My Lord, all of us were consoled that God in His Providence looked to you to establish His empire in those countries, and we have asked God—and ask Him often—to bless you and this undertaking. If the reply that M. de Lamoignon is supposed to give you is not in conformity with your intention, it is to my great regret. I most humbly entreat you, My Lord, to believe that I have done my utmost in this and that only my sins may have made me unworthy of serving you effectively in this matter according to your desire.

If then, My Lord, it pleases you to do us the favor of allowing us to continue our modest services to God in Madagascar and to grant passage to the workers we have designated for that purpose, I most humbly entreat you, My Lord, to let me know as soon as possible so that we can have them leave quickly.

Meanwhile, My Lord, I am, in the love of Our Lord, your most humble and very obedient servant.

VINCENT DEPAUL,
i.s.C.M.

2510. - *JACQUES-BÉNIGNE BOSSUET*[1] *TO SAINT VINCENT*

Metz, January 12, 1658

Monsieur,

M. de Champin[2] *has informed me of your charity for this region, prompting you to send an important mission here; that you had proposed this to the Company;* [3] *and that you and all those priests had such a high*

Letter 2510. - *Les Grands Écrivains de la France, Bossuet, Correspondance,* C. Urbain and E. Lévesque, eds. (15 vols., Paris: Hachette, 1909-25), vol. I, p. 11, L. 6.

[1]Jacques-Bénigne Bossuet, Bishop, preacher, and author, was born in Dijon on September 27, 1627, into a family whose ancestors, both paternal and maternal, occupied judicial posts in France for over half a century. He pursued a classical education at the Collège de Navarre, where he came under the influence of Vincent de Paul, whose guidance prepared him for the priesthood, which he received on March 18, 1652. He was a Canon of the Cathedral Chapter of Metz and for seven years was engaged in preaching, discussions with the Protestants, and study of the Bible and the Fathers of the Church. In 1659 he went to Paris on Chapter business and was persuaded by Saint Vincent and the Queen Mother, Anne of Austria, to remain there as a preacher. In 1670 he was consecrated Bishop of Condom but had to resign later that year when he was named tutor and guardian of the Dauphin. He wrote a number of works for the latter, of which he considered the most important his "philosophy of history": *Discours sur l'histoire universelle.* After the Dauphin's marriage in 1681, Bossuet was named Bishop of Meaux but continued to have great influence at Court, especially on Louis XIV's religio-political policy with regard to the Protestants (revocation of the Edict of Nantes in 1685). It was he who inspired the promulgation of the Gallican Principles in 1682, which he also wrote at the behest of the Assembly of the Clergy of France. Bossuet was involved in the disputes both with the Jansenists and the Quietists of Fénelon. He died on April 12, 1704.

[2]Omer de Champin, Doctor of Theology, member of the Tuesday Conferences, was appointed Dean of Saint-Thomas du Louvre on November 4, 1666.

[3]The meetings known as the Tuesday Conferences began on June 13, 1633, as an outgrowth of the retreats for ordinands. They were to serve the clerical and spiritual development of priests selected for their proven holiness and learning. By the rules devised at the initial organizational meetings (cf. vol. XIII, no. 35), the members committed themselves to meet every Tuesday at Saint-Lazare or the Bons-Enfants "to honor the life of Christ the Eternal Priest"; to celebrate daily Mass and confess once a week to a regular confessor; to make a spiritual retreat annually; to spend some time each day in mental prayer and the Divine Office; to read the New Testament; to make an examination of conscience; to attend the funerals of members; and to offer three Masses for the souls of the deceased.

They met at three o'clock in the afternoon from All Saints' to Easter and at three-thirty from Easter to All Saints', beginning with the *Veni Creator,* followed by discussion on the topic proposed at the previous meeting. In his letters and conferences, Saint Vincent mentions some of these topics proper to priests, such as the Beatitudes, the sanctification of Lent, modesty, humility, the spirit of poverty in the use of ecclesiastical goods, and censures. Members also gave reports on the works undertaken: confession for the sick at the Hôtel-Dieu, exhortations for prisoners, missions, etc.

opinion of me as to believe I would willingly use my influence in favor of such a salutary work. When he informed me of this, I asked him to assure you that I would spare nothing on my part to cooperate in it in whatever way I might be judged capable.

Since the Bishop of Auguste[4] *and I had to make a short journey to Paris, I asked him also to find out the time of arrival of those priests so that we could plan accordingly. We both felt that we would be very guilty before God if we abandoned the harvest at the time His Sovereign Bounty was sending us such faithful, charitable workers. I do not understand, Monsieur, why I have not received a reply to that letter, but I am not sorry that this opportunity presents itself to renew my respects to you, assuring you above all else how well-disposed the Bishop of Auguste is to cooperate in this work.*

As for what regards me, Monsieur, I acknowledge that I am most incapable of rendering it the service I would like to give, but I hope from God in His goodness that the example of so many holy priests and the lessons I formerly learned in the Company will give me the strength to act together with such good workers, if I can do nothing on my own. I ask you the favor of assuring the Company of this, and I send it my wholehearted greetings in Our Lord, with a request that it give me a share in its prayers and Holy Sacrifices.

If you feel that something is necessary here to prepare the people, I will, by the grace of God, accept willingly and carry out faithfully the orders you give me.[5]

I am, Monsieur, your most humble and very obedient servant.

BOSSUET,
Priest, Grand-Archdeacon of Metz

The Superior of the Congregation of the Mission or his delegate directed the Conferences at Saint-Lazare, which were attended by more than 250 priests during Saint Vincent's lifetime. Of these priests, twenty-two became bishops. Similar conferences, modeled on those of Saint-Lazare, were organized in dioceses throughout France and Italy.

[4]Pierre Bédacier, a monk of Cluny, was Suffragan and Administrator of the Metz diocese from 1649 until his death on October 19, 1660. Auguste may refer to the second-century diocese of *Augusta Treverorum*, present day Trier.

[5]The mission of Metz was one of the most famous organized by Saint Vincent, both for the quality and number of the missionaries who participated in it and for its excellent results. Bossuet did the preparatory work; Louis de Chandenier (Abbé de Tournus) directed it, aided by such collaborators as Omer de Champin, Nicolas Gédoyn, Claude de Chandenier (Abbé de Moutiers-Saint-Jean) and some fifteen other outstanding priests. From March 6 to May 22 the inhabitants of that ancient town in Lorraine flocked around the pulpit to hear the preachers.

2511. - TO THE SISTER SERVANT, IN SAINT-FARGEAU [1]

[January 1658] [2]

The eagerness of that large number of young women who want to enter your Company is not a sure sign that God is calling them to it, especially if they have been motivated to do so by some human persuasion rather than by divine inspiration. Still, God's action may be present in this; that is why it will be well for you to encourage them in that good will, but it is not advisable to send all of them at the same time. Choose two or three of the best disposed and most suitable; Mademoiselle Le Gras will take them for a trial period, while you test the others. However, make them understand very clearly the following things:

(1) that your Company is not a religious Order, nor your house a hospital from which they must not budge, but rather a Society of Sisters who come and go constantly to various places and at definite times for the assistance of the sick poor, regardless of the weather;

(2) that, since the Daughters of Charity are servants of the poor, they too are poorly dressed and fed and may not change their white headdress or clothing;

(3) that they must have no other intention in coming to the Company than that of the service of God and the poor;

(4) that they must live in it in continual mortification of mind and body, with a firm will to observe all the Rules exactly, especially unquestioning obedience;

(5) that, even though they may go here and there in Paris, they

---

Letter 2511. - *Recueil des procès-verbaux des Conseils tenus par Saint Vincent de Paul et Mademoiselle Le Gras*, Ms, p. 307.

[1]Saint-Fargeau, a commune some thirty miles southwest of Joigny (Yonne). The Daughters of Charity went there in 1657, at the request of the Duchesse de Montpensier.

[2]Some of the recommendations given here are almost identical to those in a letter of January 1658 from Saint Louise to Brother Ducournau, for a reply to be given to the Sisters in Saint-Fargeau (cf. *Spiritual Writings*, L. 561, p. 583). It seems reasonable, therefore, to assign this date to Saint Vincent's letter.

are not permitted to go to visit their acquaintances without permission, nor allow any man to visit them in their houses;

(6) lastly, that they must have the wherewithal to pay for their journey and their first habit.[3]

In one of your letters you asked me if you might receive as a postulant in your house a woman of the upper class, while awaiting instructions to send her here. I am not in agreement with this, Sister, because experience has shown, with women who associate with Sisters working at a distance from the Paris house, that before receiving the habit and the instructions given them here, they usually do not succeed. The reason is that they are convinced that they will have to do only what they have seen practiced by those Sisters living at a distance. So, please do not take any of them into your house.

You make no mention of your work, except to say that you have many girls as pupils and two little girls as boarders. Please let me know if you have any patients in your hospital and, if so, how many; whether you take care of the sick poor in the town and its environs, and if there are many or few of them; your main occupations; and why you are requesting a third Sister.

It is to be feared that those little boarders may occupy too much of your time. You know that it is not customary in your Company to take them because it detracts from other more necessary work. In addition, you would have done well not to accept the care of those children without consulting us. If you say that Her Royal Highness[4] ordered you to take them in, perhaps it is because you did not explain to her that your Rule does not allow it; for had she known this, she would have given you time to write to Mademoiselle Le Gras and await her reply.

---

[3]This first part of the letter is almost identical to that of Saint Louise mentioned in note 2.

[4]Anne-Marie-Louise d'Orléans, Duchesse de Montpensier, was the daughter of Gaston d'Orléans, Louis XIII's brother. Born in Paris on May 29, 1627, she played an active part during the troubles of the Fronde. The Duchess wrote memoirs, composed two novels, and sketched portraits. She died in Paris on April 5, 1693.

In the period preceding the French Revolution, *Mademoiselle* was the stylized title given to

I ask you, Sister, not to undertake anything new on your own initiative but to do everything with consultation and the blessing of obedience. God will be honored by that, and your leadership will produce good, edifying results by this means.

2512. - TO SISTER NICOLE HARAN,[1] SISTER SERVANT, IN NANTES

Paris, January 16, 1658

Dear Sister,

The grace of O[ur] L[ord] be with you forever!

I received your letter of December 22. All I can do just now is to sympathize with you in your present dejected state and ask O[ur] L[ord], as I do, to inspire the Fathers to see that you get some relief. If they ask us for another Sister to increase your number, we will try to send one. If you have no one there to explain to them that there are too few of you to serve so many patients, we will soon send a Missionary to Nantes, God willing, to make them aware of your excessive workload and the danger of your being overwhelmed by it. Meanwhile, I ask God to be Himself your strength.

You are right in having no scruple about missing Mass to assist the poor, for God prefers mercy to sacrifice.[2] I ask only two things of God for you and your Sisters. The first is that He give you great

---

the eldest daughter of the King's younger brother. With the death of Louis XIII (1643), the Duchesse de Montpensier became known officially as *La Grande Mademoiselle*.

Letter 2512. - Archives of the Motherhouse of the Daughters of Charity, 140 rue du Bac, Paris, original signed letter.

[1]Nicole Haran, born in 1627, entered the Company of the Daughters of Charity on July 28, 1649. In October 1650 she was sent to Montmirail and in 1653 to Nantes, where she encountered many difficulties over the years. In May 1655 the Administrators of the hospital proposed her as Sister Servant; she was still in Nantes at the death of Saint Louise (1660). In 1673 she was named Superioress General for three years, after which she served the foundlings in the faubourg Saint-Antoine in Paris, where she died on June 5, 1679.

[2]Cf. Mt 12:7. (NAB)

concern for the salvation and relief of the sick; the second is that He grant you the grace to love and support one another. If you have these two things, you will practice the virtues O[ur] L[ord] has recommended to us the most, you will be a source of edification to everyone, and you will enjoy great peace.

People say that a ship is preparing to go to Madagascar. If so, we will be able to send a few priests there, who will visit you when they pass through.

Let me know if the clothes salvaged from last year's shipwreck are in good condition. I am not asking you to look after them because I know you will do your utmost to preserve them.

Mademoiselle Le Gras is very well, thank God, and your Company is doing better and better. May Our Lord be pleased to unite your hearts and bless your spiritual exercises! I recommend myself to the prayers of all in general and of each in particular, and I am, in the love of O[ur] L[ord], [Sister],[3] your most humble servant.

VINCENT DEPAUL,
i.s.C.M.

Addressed: Sister Nicole Haran, Daughter of Charity, Servant of the Sick Poor of the Nantes Hospital, in Nantes

2513. - TO CHARLES OZENNE, SUPERIOR, IN WARSAW

Paris, January 18, 1658

Monsieur,

The grace of O[ur] L[ord] be with you forever!

Since writing to you two weeks ago, I have not received any of your dear letters. I do not write to you weekly for fear that someone

---

[3]The original text has "Monsieur."

Letter 2513. - Archives of the Mission, Krakow, original signed letter.

say that this is too much. Since then, I have had a fall from my carriage and was injured slightly.[1] I am better now, thank God, but am still confined to my room. My indisposition is also the reason why I have asked M. Alméras to reply—for him and for me—to M. Duperroy,[2] who wrote to us; and I ask you, Monsieur, to embrace good M. Desdames for me.

Enclosed is a letter from M. Guillot,[3] who is writing to you; he is Superior in Montmirail.

I think I told you that God has taken to Himself good M. Alméras the elder, who died on the fourth of this month. The next day we lost one of our coadjutor Brothers, named François Hémet, who was about fifty years of age; in his younger days he was in the army in Poland. His death corresponded to the life he led in the Company, since in both he seemed ready for everything and filled with such fine sentiments that none better can be expected from a devout man. The last two times I visited him during his illness, I was permeated by the fragrance of the fullness of his faith, his confidence in God, and his resignation to God's good pleasure. I recommend his soul to your prayers.

A ship is being prepared to leave for Madagascar; God willing, we are going to send two or three Missionaries there. We have no

---

[1]This happened after a visit in the city. Saint Vincent was returning to Saint-Lazare in his little carriage, accompanied by one of his confreres; suddenly, the braces broke, the carriage turned over, and the Saint hit his head very hard on the pavement. A few days later his temperature rose, and he became so ill, stated Abelly (*op. cit.*, bk. I, chap. L, p. 246), that the Saint thought he was dying. Abelly mistakenly placed this accident at the end of 1658. Saint Vincent mentioned the episode for the first time on January 11 (cf. no. 2507).

[2]Cf. Appendix 1 in this volume.

[3]Nicolas Guillot, born in Auxerre (Yonne) on January 6, 1627, entered the Congregation of the Mission on June 12, 1648, took his vows on June 11, 1651, and was ordained a priest on December 24, 1651. While still a subdeacon, he was sent with the first group of Missionaries to Poland. There he devoted himself to the works of his vocation, but after the death of Lambert aux Couteaux he became discouraged and returned to France in May 1654. Saint Vincent gently reproved him for his fault, inspired him with regret, and persuaded him to go back in July. This was not for long, however: the misfortunes of Poland, which was invaded by the Swedes, obliged four of the seven Missionaries, including Guillot, to leave the country in November 1655. The Saint made him Superior of the Montmirail house, then in 1658 called him to Saint-Lazare to occupy the chair of philosophy. René Alméras later appointed him Superior in Amiens (1662-67); he filled the same duty in Le Mans (1667-70).

news in the Company. Everything is going well everywhere, thank God. We are working on filling the Genoa house again. We are greatly in need of men because we have requests for them from several places, even for new establishments. Pray that God will send good workers into His vineyard.[4] We continue to pray for you and your family, as well as for the King and Queen[5] and their States, that His Divine Goodness may be pleased to preserve Their Majesties and bless their plans.

I am, in the love of O[ur] L[ord], Monsieur, your most humble servant.

VINCENT DEPAUL,
i.s.C.M.

At the bottom of the first page: Monsieur Ozenne

2514. - TO FIRMIN GET, SUPERIOR, IN MARSEILLES

Paris, January 18, 1658

Monsieur,

The grace of O[ur] L[ord] be with you forever!

I received two letters from you, dated January 1 and 8. I thank

---

[4]Cf. Lk 10:2; Mt 9:37-38. (NAB)

[5]Jan Casimir and Louise-Marie de Gonzague.

Few Princes experienced as many vicissitudes of fortune as did Jan Casimir. Born in 1609, he went to France in his youth and was thrown into prison by Richelieu. He became a Jesuit, received the Cardinal's hat, and ascended the throne of Poland on the untimely death of his brother, Wladyslaw IV. Obtaining a dispensation from his vows, he married his brother's widow, Louise-Marie, and ruled Poland under the title of Jan Casimir V. His reign was unfortunate: Poland, attacked in turn by the Cossacks, Sweden, Brandenburg, Russia, and Transylvania, and torn asunder by internal dissensions, was forced to surrender a large part of its territory to its enemies. Jan Casimir lost his wife in 1667; he abdicated and withdrew to Flanders. From there he went to Saint-Germain-des-Prés Abbey and afterward to Saint-Martin Abbey in Nevers, dying in that city in 1672.

Letter 2514. - Niagara University Library, Niagara University, NY (USA). The original of this

God that the Bishop of Marseilles [1] has decided to establish his seminary [2] and to entrust it to the care of the Company. I hope this good work will be the source of many benefits and the blessing of his diocese. If he does me the honor of writing to me about it—as you say he intends to do—I will gladly congratulate him on the effort he is trying to make.

I sent you the Duc de Richelieu's reply on the appointment of the new Administrators. I do not know if he has commissioned someone by the same letter to receive in his name the accounts of the administration, for I had not had anyone mention this to him. I will do so if those gentlemen so desire, once they have been notified.

M. Le Vacher [3] is writing a letter to a Capuchin Father from Marseilles about a Turk[4] who is here and wants to convert. Please get his reply on that as soon as possible.

We have received six livres for Pierre Goubert, a convict on the galley *Reine*. Please have M. Huguier give them to him. At the first opportunity we will reimburse him for the money he advances.

Meanwhile, I am, in O[ur] L[ord], Monsieur, your most humble servant.

VINCENT DEPAUL,
i.s.C.M.

---

letter was part of the Hains Family Collection, Marseilles, which was sold at auction by Xavier Charmoy (cf. no. 2505). In 1996 Stephen C. Plumeri purchased it from Bernard Quaritch Ltd., a London antiquarian bookseller, and presented it to Niagara University.

[1]Étienne du Puget.

[2]Countless difficulties delayed the establishment of the diocesan seminary, which did not open until fifteen years later. In 1658 the Priests of the Mission were directing only a kind of collège (cf. no. 2582).

[3]Philippe Le Vacher.

[4]Saint Vincent used the term "Turks" both for the inhabitants of the Ottoman Empire and for the members of the Muslim religion. The context of the letter usually dictates to which group he is referring.

2515. - TO JACQUES THOLARD, IN MARCOUSSIS [1]

Paris, January 18, 1658

Monsieur,

The grace of O[ur] L[ord] be with you forever!

I am concerned about your telling me that you will have the children's communion next Sunday to close the mission, although only about 150 of the five or six hundred communicants have made their duty, and that I should send someone to give notice that there will be a mission in Montlhéry.[2] Now, I will tell you, Monsieur, that I think it advisable—unless you think better—to postpone leaving the place where you now are until those good people have benefited by the grace Our Lord is offering them through you. There is reason to hope they will do so if you will please give them time, especially if we send you workers, as we will do, God willing. We will send two priests from here, God willing, and will leave Montlhéry as it is, in the meantime. Our Lord saw the Gentiles perishing, and He wanted to help them; yet, he did not abandon the people of Israel, to whom He had been sent. Let us finish what we have begun, Monsieur, and Our Lord will help us.

It will be well for you to go to see those good Fathers, whom I admire and honor so much for their gratitude to their benefactor. It is one of the most touching and edifying acts of gratitude witnessed in the Church. I hope they will pray for you. Please assure them of

---

Letter 2515. - Archives of the Mission, Paris, photograph of original signed letter.

[1]The name of the recipient and his whereabouts were given by Pémartin (Jean-Baptiste Pémartin, *Lettres de Saint-Vincent de Paul* [4 vols., Paris: Pillet et Dumoulin, 1880], vol. IV, p. 12, L. 1590). He probably knew these details from the address, which was not photographed. Marcoussis is a locality of Essonne in the district of Rambouillet.

[2]District of Corbeil (Essonne).

my obedience. I am, in the love of Our Lord, your most humble servant.

VINCENT DEPAUL,
i.s.C.M.

I embrace tenderly M. d'Huitmille[3] and M. Hurpy.[4]

2516. - TO LOUIS RIVET, SUPERIOR, IN SAINTES

January 20,[1] 1658

From now on, Missionaries passing through your house will stay there only a day or two, unless they have instructions or a need to stay longer, and it will be a good idea for you after that to get them to agree to leave for the place where they are obliged to go.

Because the seminarian whose furnishings you are storing in your house had no other place to put them, you had to do him this charity, since you could do so conveniently.

If you had refused M. Rassary, who is ill, the charity he asked of you, I would be very annoyed because two things make him, above anyone else, worthy of our esteem: (1) his virtue is extraordinary (I know no one alive who is a finer man than he); and (2) we are indebted to him. In addition, I recommended him to you previously and, because you welcomed him when he was in good health, you would have acted badly if you did not do so now that

---

[3]Philippe Huitmille, born in Arras, entered the Congregation of the Mission as a priest on October 25, 1645, at the age of twenty-nine. He took his vows in Amiens on February 9, 1664, in the presence of M. Guillot.

[4]Pierre Hurpy was born in Beaussault (Seine-Maritime), entered the Congregation of the Mission on November 10, 1656, and took his vows on November 12, 1658, in the presence of M. Delespiney. He died in Saint-Méen in July 1679; *Notices*, vols. I and V (Supplement), lists him as Dehurpy.

Letter 2516. - Reg. 2, p. 112.

[1]Above the "20" someone else has written "10," probably because the number on the original is hard to decipher.

he is not well. I would like to think that you welcomed him respectfully and had him treated as best you could, disregarding the conclusions others may draw from this in favor of their staying in your house, since they do not have the reasons he has. I am well aware that you will be encumbered by him, but is it not right for us to inconvenience ourselves through charity and gratitude for a servant of God?

2517. - TO FIRMIN GET, SUPERIOR, IN MARSEILLES

Paris, Feast of the Conversion of Saint Paul,[1] 1658

Monsieur,

The grace of O[ur] L[ord] be with you forever!

While awaiting your letter, which I have not yet received from the last regular mail, I will tell you our little news items. Messieurs Portail, Alméras, Bécu,[2] Perraud, and Brin, who have been ill, are better, and so am I, thank God. I had to stay in my room for two weeks because of a fall I had. Most of our priests who are able to work are out giving missions, divided into three bands. We are going to send three or four of them and two Brothers to Madagascar. The Maréchal de la Meilleraye has informed me that his ship will leave on February 8 and is urging me to send them. I will tell

---

Letter 2517. - Archives of the Mission, Paris, copy made from the original in the Hains Family Collection, Marseilles. This is one of the letters sold at auction by Xavier Charmoy (cf. no. 2505).

[1]January 25.

[2]Jean Bécu, born in Braches (Somme) on April 24, 1592, and ordained a priest in September 1616, came to join the first companions of Saint Vincent in September 1626. Two of his brothers, Benoît and Hubert, followed him into the Congregation, the latter as a coadjutor Brother; two of his sisters, Marie and Madeleine, became Daughters of Charity. Bécu was Superior of the house in Toul (1642-46) and spent the rest of his life in Paris. He died on January 19, 1664, having been Vice-Visitor, then Visitor of the Province of France. (Cf. *Notices*, vol. I, pp. 125-33.)

you who they are, after they have left; meanwhile, I recommend their voyage to your prayers.

We are praying for your projected seminary, that the Bishop of Marseilles, whose idea it was, will make it a reality, and the Divine Goodness will bless its beginning and its development through the blessings of His Spirit and your leadership.

Our Algiers affairs are making very little progress. M. Le Vacher is so distressed and agitated about them that he is endangering his health. He comes and goes constantly; on my part, I am doing what I can to send him back as soon as possible with the satisfaction he desires. A collection will be taken up in the Paris parishes, but there are so many other ones for other needs that we cannot look forward to any great results from it. We shall see.

Meanwhile, I am, in O[ur] L[ord], Monsieur, your most humble servant.

VINCENT DEPAUL,
i.s.C.M.

2518. - TO JEAN MARTIN, SUPERIOR, IN TURIN

Paris, Feast of the Conversion of Saint Paul,[1] 1658

Monsieur,

The grace of O[ur] L[ord] be with you forever!

I am writing simply to give you our news and to ask you for yours. I replied to the last letters I received, and I thanked God, as I still do, for the good results of the visitation and your hope that they will last. I, too, hope for this from the goodness of God and your fine leadership.

I think you are now at grips with the enemy in Bra, where Providence has removed the obstacles that delayed the mission.

Letter 2518. - Archives of the Mission, Turin, original signed letter.
[1]January 25.

May God be pleased, Monsieur, to give you a double share of His Spirit to banish evil and establish good there! Extra grace is needed for extraordinary needs. As for the work, however, please do not take on too much but gauge it according to your strength and the way you still have to go. You now have a few men who can relieve you. True, all of them cannot stay with you because the Genoa house is badly in need of the two who are intended for there. I will let you know when you will have to send them there.

We are going to send three or four priests to Madagascar; a ship at Nantes is ready to sail. Once they have left, I will tell you who they are. I recommend their voyage to your prayers. Most of our men are out giving missions in three separate bands. We have no one sick, thank God, although we do have a few who are still weak and convalescent, such as Messieurs Portail, Alméras, Bécu, Perraud, and Admirault.[2] I myself was laid up—and still am—because of a fall from a carriage, but I am improving, by the mercy of God.

I am not sure if I have written to you this year.[3] I ask O[ur] L[ord] that it may be a happy one for you for eternity, followed by many others that may lead you to God, our last end.

Good M. Alméras the elder has reached his at the end of the eighty-three years he lived on earth. He became ill on New Year's Day and went to God on the fourth. We have reason to believe this because of the acts of virtue we saw him practice from the time he entered the Company, which edified the whole house and prepared him for a happy death after such a long life.

Nevertheless, since God's judgments are unknown to us, we will pray—as we ask you please to do—for his soul, as well as for that of Brother François Hémet, who died the following day, the fifth of this month, at about fifty years of age. His death corre-

---

[2]Charles Admirault, born in Chinon (Indre-et-Loire) on September 20, 1622, entered the Congregation of the Mission on December 1, 1640, took his vows on December 2, 1642, and was ordained a priest in December 1646. For several years he was assigned to the Bons-Enfants Seminary, where he died in August 1661, after a long illness. (Cf. *Notices*, vol. I, p. 462, which lists him as *Amiraut;* in vol. V (Supplement), p. 17, he is *Amirault.*)

[3]The Saint had written to him on January 11 (cf. no. 2507).

sponded to his life, for in both he seemed prepared for anything and filled with such fine sentiments that none better can be expected from a devout man. The last two times I saw him, I was permeated with the fragrance of the fullness of his faith, his confidence in God, and his resignation to His good pleasure, by which I am also, in His love, Monsieur, your most humble servant.

VINCENT DEPAUL,
i.s.C.M.

Addressed: Monsieur Martin, Superior of the Priests of the Mission of Turin, in Turin

2519. - TO DENIS LAUDIN,[1] SUPERIOR, IN LE MANS

January 26, 1658

I fully agree that you should comply with the decision of the senior Dean regarding your dispute with your boarders. So, you can give him your reasons, especially the following: since they enjoy all the revenues of the house free of charge—and have always enjoyed them since our priests have been there—and because our priests have had nothing left for their living expenses after the pensions, tithes, and other fees the house pays have been taken out, it seems only just that those gentlemen should now pay at least the full tax on the clergy, since they are bound to do so by the contract. Now, the proof that your family has subsisted only on the help

---

Letter 2519. - Reg. 2, p. 167.

[1]Denis Laudin was born in Provins (Seine-et-Marne) on January 15, 1622. He entered the Congregation of the Mission on April 21, 1647, took his vows in September 1649, and was ordained a priest on December 25, 1649. After ordination he asked and obtained permission to remake a little of his Internal Seminary. He was next sent to Montauban, then to Richelieu as Procurator (1651-57). He was Superior in Le Mans (1657-68), Troyes (1668-75), Angers (1675-79), and Fontainebleau (1679-90) and Visitor of the Province of Champagne (1682-86). In 1690 he was changed to Saint-Cyr, becoming Superior there the following year. Serious illness and poor eyesight prompted his return to Saint-Lazare, where he was given the direction of the coadjutor Brothers and where he died on April 12, 1693. (Cf. *Notices*, vol. II, pp. 365-88.)

given by Saint-Lazare is apparent in the fact that we have always paid four thousand livres a year for it. Whatever reasons you may have, however, tell the Dean that I told you to do whatever he orders, and I ask you to do so.

2520. - *PIERRE BÉDACIER TO SAINT VINCENT*

Metz, January 29, 1658

The lettre de cachet *from the Queen and the one you did me the honor of writing to me concerning the mission Her Majesty is sending to this town* [1] *were delivered to me on the same day; the first by M. Demonchy* [2] *and the other by M. Bossuet, Grand-Archdeacon of this church. I have nothing to say about either, except that I entreat you to assure Her Majesty that I will most willingly use any credibility and authority—spiritual as well as temporal—I may have in this town and diocese to support her holy, pious intentions. Assure her also that I will try to see that they will then succeed for the glory of God, the edification of our people, the salvation of souls, and the conversion of heretics and unbelievers, who are quite numerous here.*[3] *In addition, I will do my utmost to show my very special esteem for her piety.*

In truth, her effort to sustain the zeal I should have to put this diocese in order, through good and perfect discipline by means of this letter, makes me too greatly indebted to her not to show my gratitude for this to the extent she indicates that she desires. I would also be hypocritical in my ministry if I did not on this occasion show how important the work of God and the command of Her Majesty are to me. I will add to that the special appreciation I have for your guidance, which benefits the entire Church in these missions. Please rest assured, Monsieur, that I will spare nothing that may be desired of me to make them as successful as you can hope.

Letter 2520. - Urbain and Lévesque, *op. cit.*, vol. I, p. 421.

[1]Metz.

[2]Nicolas Demonchy, born in Eu (Seine-Maritime) on March 21, 1626, entered the Congregation of the Mission on August 19, 1646; and took his vows on March 6, 1649. He was ordained a priest on March 4, 1651, and was Superior in Toul (1653-55, 1657-58, 1669-74), Metz (1661-69), Tréguier (1680-84), and La Rose (1689-92).

[3]There were many Jewish people living in Metz. (Cf. Cahen, "Les Juifs de Metz," in *Mémoires de la Société d'archéologie lorraine* [3rd series, vol. III, Nancy, 1875].)

Only one obstacle hinders me, and I do not think I can overcome it unless you have the kindness to consider the simple solution to be applied to remove it. These priests say that, according to the method of your missions, when they are engaged in their functions all other sermons are suspended, except the ones they give at the appointed times, and that our regular Lenten preacher will be obliged therefore to stop and leave. I entreat you to give this some thought and to see the awkward position in which this might place us. The priest we have for next Lent is a very upright, capable Dominican and Doctor of the Sorbonne,[4] *who has already successfully and commendably preached the Advent sermons. I booked him for here in good faith, unaware of that method; I even asked him to refuse the invitation that had been offered him to preach in Angers. It would be an insult to cancel him at the beginning of Lent. If you agree, we could arrange matters by having him take the Mondays, Tuesdays, and Thursdays of the week; in that way, those priests could preach in the cathedral four mornings of the week and, in addition, would have the cathedral free for their exercises the rest of the time. I am really annoyed that we did not foresee this inconvenience but, since that is how things stand, they could very well preach in another church, which we will assign to them, and which is quite suitable for that.*

Beyond that, there is no other problem, except to provide what is necessary to receive and house the men you send us. They will be most welcome, coming in the name of the Lord and on behalf of Her Majesty. M. de la Contour[5] *has given us the King's lodgings in la Haute-Pierre,*[6] *where they will be very comfortably accommodated. As for food and furnishings, we will see to it that everything will be taken care of for them, and that an account of that will be given you as soon as possible.*

Meanwhile, please believe that I am only too happy to have this opportunity of assuring you of my continued service and obedience, since I am, Monsieur, your most humble and obedient servant.

BÉDACIER,
Bi[shop] of Auguste

---

[4]Father Antoine Guespier, of the Tours convent. He was a Master of Theology but not a Doctor of the Sorbonne.

[5]Françojs de Moussy, Sieur de la Contour, the King's lieutenant in Metz.

[6]The Kings of France stayed in this mansion whenever they came to Metz.

2521. - TO A SUPERIOR [1]

February 1658

What you informed me about M. . . and his answer to you have given me reason to tell you that several times I have noticed that you are not on friendly enough terms with members of the Company and, what is more, (please accept this piece of advice, Monsieur) you are the Superior in the Company the least united with the members of his family and others who visit you. I do not know if you have ever written me about anyone whomsoever, except in a disdainful way and with a negative judgment about many of the men. What pains me the most is that you do this even with persons in whom I have never seen anything but good, and who live—as others have always said—in an exemplary way in the Company and outside it.

In the name of God, Monsieur, give heed to what I am telling you; ask Our Lord for the grace of perfect charity and the spirit of humility that causes us to acknowledge that others are better than we and we are worse than demons. You can rest assured that you will then esteem and love others. If you fail in this, you will always be a trial to yourself and even more so to others, who will find this cross harsh and difficult to bear.

Letter 2521. - Reg. 2, p. 116.

[1]Most likely Achille Le Vazeux, Superior in Annecy.

2522. - TO GUILLAUME DELVILLE,[1] IN ARRAS

[February 1, 1658] [2]

You did the right thing, Monsieur, in preventing our Daughters of Charity from being made responsible for the sick soldiers placed in the Hôtel-Dieu in the town, given the fact that there are nuns there who are not only capable of this work but quite ready to undertake it. Furthermore, according to the opinion of Mademoiselle Le Gras and the custom of the Company, you must not allow those two Sisters to go to serve those patients in the Hôtel-Dieu under the direction of the nuns. Those same nuns must perform this service, since they were established there for that purpose; in addition, the Daughters of Charity are only for the neglected sick who have no one to help them, and it is for these latter that those two Sisters were sent to Arras.

2523. - TO FIRMIN GET, SUPERIOR, IN MARSEILLES

Paris, February 1, 1658

Monsieur,

The grace of O[ur] L[ord] be with you forever!

I received your letter of the fifteenth. I will gladly use my influence with the Duc de Richelieu, through the intermediary of

---

Letter 2522. - Archives of the Motherhouse of the Daughters of Charity, *Lettres choisies du Bienheureux Vincent de Paul,* Ms, letter 107.

[1]Guillaume Delville, born in Tilloy-lez-Bapaume, today Ligny-Tilloy (Pas-de-Calais), entered the Congregation of the Mission as a priest on January 19, 1641, at thirty-three years of age. He was Superior in Crécy (1644) and Montmirail (1644-46, 1650-51). He then retired to Arras, where, with Saint Vincent's permission, he continued his missionary work until his death in 1658.

[2]Date given by Pémartin (*op. cit.*, vol. IV, p. 18, L. 1597), who probably had at his disposal a source other than ours.

Letter 2523. - Archives of the Mission, Paris, copy made from the original in the Hains Family Collection, Marseilles. This is one of the letters sold at auction by Xavier Charmoy (cf. no. 2505).

M. Desmarets, to see if he will appoint M. Bausset the Provost,[1] or his nephew the Lieutenant Seneschal of Marseilles,[2] to receive in his name the statement of accounts of the administration of the Royal Hospital. I have not yet had the occasion to speak to him about this.

I continue to thank God for the holy dispositions He has given the Bishop of Marseilles,[3] and I pray that He will draw glory from the fulfillment of his plan.

I am notifying M. Jolly that the box he had entrusted to the young man who came from Rome has been mislaid, as you mention, and I am asking M. Durand to send you Brother Duchesne[4] without delay to help good Brother Louis [5] with the work of your house.

We are awaiting the opportunity to send you the Busées[6] you are requesting. If you find a more convenient way than sending them by the Lyons coach, please let me know.

I am, in O[ur] L[ord], Monsieur, your most humble servant.

VINCENT DEPAUL,
i.s.C.M.

---

[1]Pierre de Bausset.

[2]Antoine de Bausset.

[3]Concerning Bishop Étienne du Puget's proposal to entrust a seminary in Marseilles to the Congregation of the Mission.

[4]René Duchesne, born in Saint-Juire-Champgillon (Vendée) in August 1607, entered the Congregation of the Mission as a coadjutor Brother in Richelieu on February 16, 1654, and took his vows on November 1, 1658.

[5]Louis Sicquard, born in Nalliers (Vendée) on May 3, 1624, entered the Congregation of the Mission as a coadjutor Brother on October 18, 1645, and took his vows in November 1648.

[6]The work in question here is a highly esteemed book of meditations, first published in Mainz (1606) and then in Douay under the title *Enchiridion piarum meditationum in omnes dominicas, sanctorum festa, Christi passionem et caetera* . . . , Douai, G. Patté, 1624. It was translated into French by the Jesuits and in 1644 by Antoine Portail, who added several meditations. Its author, Jean Busée (Johannes Busaeus [De Buys]) was born in Nijmegen (Netherlands), on April 4, 1547. He entered the Society of Jesus in 1563, studied in Rome, and for twenty-two years taught theology in Mainz, where he died on May 30, 1611. Initially he produced polemic works against Protestantism but after 1595 turned to editing and writing ascetical works.

2524. - TO GUILLAUME DESDAMES, IN WARSAW

Paris, February 1, 1658

Monsieur,

May the grace of Our Lord continue to grow in you during this new year and for all eternity!

I cannot fail to send you my faithful wishes, even though I am deprived of your dear letters. For, since God has chosen to exercise His strength in and through you, keeping you steadfast in the midst of agitations and helping you to overcome so many difficulties that have tried your patience, such sentiments of esteem and tenderness for you and gratitude to God have remained in my soul that I can scarcely think of Him without thinking about you, nor think of you without offering you to Him. I often thank Him for the graces He has granted you and for the edification you have given to the entire Little Company, which considers you a model of constancy. I also ask His Divine Goodness to strengthen you more with His own strength so that, serving as a foundation for the Company in Poland, it will be firmly established there, like an immovable rock, for the service of this same Lord, whom you serve so faithfully and steadfastly.

Calm is not yet assured in Warsaw, nor have the Missionaries seen the end of their sufferings. We must hope that O[ur] L[ord] will continue to protect them and that, having founded and extended His Church through persecutions, He will likewise raise their little building up in the midst of storms. I ask Him above all

---

Letter 2524. - Archives of the Mission, Krakow, original signed letter.

to preserve you, Monsieur, and I recommend to you as strongly as possible to take care of your health.

I am, in His love, Monsieur, your most humble servant.

VINCENT DEPAUL,
i.s.C.M.

Addressed: Monsieur Desdames, Priest of the Mission, in Warsaw

2525. - TO CHARLES OZENNE, SUPERIOR, IN WARSAW

Paris, February 1, 1658

Monsieur,

The grace of O[ur] L[ord] be with you forever!

I received two letters from you, the last dated December 15. If M. Vszinski does us the honor of passing through here on his return from Naples, we will welcome him with open arms and will show him all the marks of service and gratitude proper to a person of his merit and the great charity he has for us. That means as far as we can.

God be praised, Monsieur, for rendering justice to the King with regard to the Transylvanian! [1] There is reason to hope that He will deal in the same way with the others who have served Him poorly. I pray that He will give success to his armies at the siege of Riga[2] and everywhere else, that He will preserve his royal person and that of the Queen and, in a word, will fulfill their just plans.

Letter 2525. - Archives of the Mission, Krakow, original signed letter. The postscript is in the Saint's handwriting.

[1]George II Rákóczi, Prince of Transylvania, had formed an alliance with Charles X Gustavus of Sweden against Poland. The retreat of the Swedes and a defeat suffered near the Vistula brought him to terms with King Jan Casimir who imposed his own conditions on him.

[2]Riga remained in the hands of the Swedes until 1710.

God willing, we will send you by the first favorable opportunity the report from Madagascar [3] and the copies of the Briefs you are requesting. If, however, you find an occasion for this before we do, remind me of it. We are going to send four priests and two Brothers to that island. Their belongings were packed yesterday, and they are preparing to leave in a few days. I recommend their voyage and their mission to your prayers.

M. Perraud has had a serious relapse. M. Bécu is in bed with gout. The rest of the men in this house are very well. We have two Brothers here—one a cleric and one a coadjutor Brother—with the same name as yours, who are closely related to you.[4] For this reason it is a joy for us to have them, and I hope that, through your fervent prayers, God will give them perseverance in His service and in their vocation.

Our men are out giving two or three missions simultaneously, and the Company everywhere is going along very well, thank God. I am, in Him, Monsieur, your most humble servant.

VINCENT DEPAUL,
i.s.C.M.

I just received a letter from you, dated December 22.[5]

Addressed: Monsieur Ozenne

---

[3]The long letter of Toussaint Bourdaise, dated February 19, 1657 (cf. vol. VI, nos. 2215 and 2216).

[4]Laurent Ozenne, born in Nibas (Somme) on December 6, 1637, entered the Congregation of the Mission at the Paris Seminary on September 26, 1656, and took his vows on December 3, 1658, in the presence of M. Delespiney.

Jacques Ozenne, born in Saint-Blimont, Amiens diocese (Somme), in 1635, entered the Congregation of the Mission as a coadjutor Brother at the Paris Seminary on January 20, 1658, and took his vows there on March 1, 1660, in the presence of M. Langlois.

[5]This letter is no longer extant.

2526. - *JACQUES-BÉNIGNE BOSSUET TO SAINT VINCENT*

Metz, February 1, 1658

I was deeply consoled that your priest who came here was M. Demonchy but am very sorry that his stay was so short. He may have told you, Monsieur, that the letters from the Queen were received with the respect due to Her Majesty and that the Bishop of Auguste [1] *and M. de la Contour did their duty on that occasion.*

I am giving an account to M. Demonchy of the state of affairs since his departure [2] *and am counting on him to transmit the information to you so as not to bother you with repetitions, but I feel obliged, Monsieur, to inform you of something that took place here a while ago and which will soon be reported to the Court.*

A Catholic servant woman, who died at the home of an important, well-off Huguenot merchant, had her conscience scandalously violated. From the very testimony of her master, it is obvious that she had been a Catholic all her life. It even seems certain that she had received Communion shortly before becoming ill. She never attended the sermons or took part in any service of the so-called reformed religion.[3]

Her master claims that she changed religions five days before her death. He says he summoned some ministers to receive her declaration but did not call either the Pastor, the magistrate, or any Catholic who could have been a witness to the fact. The day that poor young woman died, a Jesuit, who had been notified by one of the neighbors of the way the woman was being coerced, came to console her. They refused to allow him to enter the house, and it is certain that she was still alive. Some time later he returned with an order from the magistrate but found that she had died in the meantime.

All these facts have been verified and proven. There are even such strong indications that she asked for a priest, and the adversaries have given such contradictory replies on that point, that it can be considered a certainty.

I am not exaggerating, Monsieur, either the circumstances of this affair or its consequence; you yourself see it clearly enough, along with the

---

Letter 2526. - Urbain and Lévesque, eds., *op. cit.*, vol. I, no. 7, p. 14.

[1]Pierre Bédacier.

[2]This letter was published by Urbain and Levesque, vol. I, no. 8, p. 17.

[3]The Huguenot religion: the Reformed Church in France, a Protestant sect which espoused the spiritual and political tenets of John Calvin.

impudence of those who, having been granted by the King's favor freedom of conscience in his kingdom, deprive his subjects—their servants—of it in their household. That certainly cries out for vengeance; yet, the ministers and the consistory are supporting this encroachment of rights. M. de la Contour told me today that a representative of those men had the effrontery to tell him that this man had done nothing out of order. What is more, they added that they were going to register a complaint to the Court of the proceedings followed by the Lieutenant General.[4] All this, Monsieur, is doubtless intended to summon the case for review before the Council to remove it from the place where there is greater knowledge of the affair and to hush it up with the passage of time.

God will not allow their evil plan to succeed, and I ask you, Monsieur, to use all the means at your disposal in these circumstances to prevent this seditious delegation from being heard and to see that the matter remains in the ordinary course of justice. In that way those persons cannot avoid being punished for this outrage against the edicts and freedom of conscience. When the Queen was in this town, she manifested such devotion and zeal for religion that I am sure that, if she were made aware of this attempt, she would will only that justice be done regarding it.

Apart from that, Monsieur, since the King has allowed them to have two teachers for their children, on condition that these educators be Catholics, they are going to ask for wages for them. That is neither just nor plausible, but they want to make this poor town responsible for it. Since, however, they know that most likely their request will not be granted, I am very much mistaken if they are not planning to obtain permission that, should they be unwilling to pay them, they be allowed to choose their own teachers—consequently, those of their own religion. The Queen alone prevented their being given that permission here, and I am sure this is still her intention. I am not telling you now, Monsieur, what you have to do in this matter; it is enough for you to be aware of it. God will inspire you for the rest.

I anxiously await the excellent workers He is sending us through you, and I am, with profound respect, Monsieur, your most humble and very obedient servant.

BOSSUET,
unw[orthy] priest

---

[4]Philbert Estienne, Sieur d'Augny.

2527. - *SAINT LOUISE TO SAINT VINCENT*

February 2 [1658] [1]

Most Honored Father,

I most humbly entreat Your Charity to allow me to ask you for news of the true state of your health. For the love of God, do not be in a hurry to go out!

Sister Renée, one of the best young women to come from Angers, took her vows for the first time a year ago, with Your Charity's permission. Since she has been named for Sainte-Marie-du-Mont [2] *and may leave soon without knowing when, she asks to renew them tomorrow. She went to confession with this intention and spoke about it to her confessor—we do not know his name—and he advised her to go ahead. I most humbly entreat you, Most Honored Father, to let us know if you approve and to tell us how she should go about it, since she will not be able to be at Holy Mass when you celebrate it upstairs.*

All of us—even though I myself am most unworthy—beg Your Charity to offer us once again to Our Lord and to ask Him for the graces we need so as not to be unfaithful to Him any longer. Asking also for your holy blessing for this intention, Most Honored Father, I am your most obedient and very grateful daughter.

2528. - *SAINT LOUISE TO SAINT VINCENT*

February 4 [1658] [1]

Most Honored Father,

To spare Your Charity the trouble, I had asked Brother Ducournau[2] *to*

Letter 2527. - Archives of the Motherhouse of the Daughters of Charity, original autograph letter.

[1]Date added on the back of the original by Brother Ducournau.

[2]Locality in the district of Valognes (Manche). The Company had been established there since 1655. The two Sisters who were there on February 1, 1658, were sick.

Letter 2528. - Archives of the Motherhouse of the Daughters of Charity, original autograph letter.

[1]Date added on the back of the original by Brother Ducournau.

[2]Bertrand Ducournau, born in Arnou (Landes) in 1614, entered the Congregation of the

explain to you the interior dispositions of the good young woman who had been with the late Mademoiselle Noret. She has been very depressed since her parents made her leave Mademoiselle Noret's home a year ago. As a result, her poor spirit has a distaste for everything. She was deeply moved during her retreat, but her spirit was not strengthened in this matter. She would like to speak to her confessor at Saint-Eustache[3] *because she says he might make her better known to us. I also think, Most Honored Father, that it would be advisable for him to speak with you before allowing her to make any decision. If Your Charity agrees, we will ask him to take the trouble to come here. He will have more information to give you concerning this.*

Enclosed is the little booklet you requested. Permit me, Most Honored Father, to ask that the author remain anonymous—not that I fear it contains anything contrary to faith, but it might seem a slight weakness to have spent time on it and to appear to be carrying on this conversation with a woman.

Do me the charity of giving me your holy blessing, of offering to God the desire of our Sisters to go to Madagascar, and of doing me the honor of believing that I am always, Most Honored Father, your most obedient and very humble daughter and servant.

L. DE MARILLAC

Addressed: *Monsieur Vincent*

Mission as a coadjutor Brother on July 28, 1644, and took his vows on October 9, 1646. He had fine penmanship and common sense, and, from the various positions he had occupied in the world, including that of professional secretary, had learned to be shrewd, frank, and reliable in business affairs. Saint Vincent made him his secretary in 1645. By his devotion, tact, and love of work, this good Brother rendered inestimable services to Saint Vincent and his Congregation. It can be said that, through his preparation of materials and his personal notes, he contributed more than Abelly himself to the first biography of Saint Vincent. Brother Ducournau remained as secretary to the Superiors General René Alméras and Edme Jolly, and was Archivist of Saint-Lazare. He died in Paris on January 3, 1677. Brother Pierre Chollier, his assistant in the secretariat, wrote his biography, which is in *Notices*, vol. I, pp. 377ff.

[3]A parish in Paris.

2529. - *JEAN MARTIN TO SAINT VINCENT*

February 6, 1658

We have been working for a month in the locality of Bra, where God has been pleased to dispose the inhabitants to be reconciled with one another. They were first led to this by the distress Her Highness expressed at their disunion, and then by means of the mission, which has succeeded in disposing them entirely to do so. Both parties were together at our sermons and the exercises of the mission in the same church; in the beginning we felt this was very awkward and even dangerous. Before assembling them in the church, however, we persuaded both groups to lay down the weapons which, until that time, they had always carried everywhere.

Their close attention to the sermons and catechism classes, together with the sentiments God was pleased to give them, reunited them perfectly. The result was that they all embraced in the presence of the Most Blessed Sacrament, asking pardon of one another; even some of the prominent people did this publicly on occasion in the main square. Both parties were so satisfied by this that there is good reason to hope that the reconciliation will be steadfast and permanent.

All the people are deeply consoled to see those persons, who formerly sought each other in order to kill one another, now meeting, walking, and talking with one another as cordially as if they had never been at odds. Before this, all of them used to walk through the streets carrying weapons; now, by the grace of God, these have disappeared. Everyone is intent only on being truly reconciled with the Divine Majesty by means of a good confession.

When the Madame Royale heard this good news, she deigned to express to us in a letter how much it pleased her. The Marchese di Pianezza [1] *did*

Letter 2529. - Abelly, *op. cit.*, bk. II, chap. I, sect. VI, p. 86. This same letter is reproduced with some variations in the biographical sketch of Jean Martin (cf. *Notices*, vol. I, p. 290).

[1]Filippo Emmanuele Filiberto Giacinte di Simiane, Marchese di Pianezza, had distinguished himself by his bravery in the wars of Monferrato and Genoa, earning the title of Colonel-General of the Infantry. A clever diplomat, he attracted the attention of the Madame Royale, Christine of France, the Duchess-Regent, who made him Prime Minister. She had implicit trust in him, as did Charles Emmanuel II when he came of age. The sole aspiration of the Marchese, however, was to live in a religious house, far from the Court and its activities. After the death of Pope Alexander VII, who had persuaded him to defer the execution of his plan, the Prime Minister ceded all his possessions to his son, the Marchese di Livorno, and retired to San Pancrazio Monastery. Deeply grieved by this, Charles Emmanuel tried repeatedly to make him yield, but

likewise, saying that it gave him most extraordinary sentiments of consolation.

We are now busy hearing confessions, and there is such a crowd of penitents that, although we have asked all the priests and religious in the area to help us—and there is a large number of them—I do not know when we will be able to finish.

2530. - TO CHARLES OZENNE, SUPERIOR, IN WARSAW

Paris, February 8, 1658

Monsieur,

The grace of Our Lord be with you forever!

I just read your latest letter from Warsaw, showing me that you are in good health, by the grace of God, as are Messieurs Desdames and Duperroy. I thank God for this and ask Him to keep you well in the midst of those dangerous colds circulating throughout the kingdom. I ask Our Lord to protect from them also the King and Queen, whose presence you expect in Warsaw in two weeks. Since we are more obliged to do so than anyone else alive, we pray that He will bless their armies more and more and sanctify their sacred persons and, through them, their kingdom.

I am writing to you while recovering from a fall I took head first from a carriage; by the grace of God, I am improving, although I am still confined to my room because of the intense cold. I hope to go out as soon as we have a thaw.

We are working constantly on a collection being taken up to free

---

to no avail. He then suggested that the Marchese come to Turin and live in a religious house of his choice, leaving it only when called to Court to give his advice on some important affair. The Marchese accepted this proposal, choosing the house of the Priests of the Mission, which he himself had founded. He died there in July 1677, at sixty-nine years of age. Whenever Saint Vincent speaks to the men in Turin of their "founder," he is referring to the Marchese.

Letter 2530. - Archives of the Mission, Krakow, original autograph letter.

the Consul in Algiers [1] and to provide him with the means of paying off the sums of money the poor Christian slaves lent him to get him out of the clutches of the Pasha. The latter really mistreated him because of the bankruptcy declared in Algiers by a merchant from Marseilles,[2] involving a considerable sum of money.

Four of our priests, a Brother, and a black child from Madagascar who had a marvelous conversion[3] will be leaving to board ship at Port Louis[4] in three or four days to go to that island.

We are very worried about the news that reached us here yesterday from Rome. The plague has broken out again in Genoa and was carried back to the house by M. Judice[5] from the lazaretto, where he had been exposed to it while nursing the plague-stricken. He had caught the disease there but recovered from it.

I recommend to your prayers an unfortunate incident that occurred in Annecy between M. Le Vazeux, Superior of the Mission, and a lawyer from the town. Insults were exchanged in connection with a lawsuit that has been going on between them for four years now concerning the residence of the Mission, which we have lost. M. Le Vazeux is trying to recover the price paid on it from a property mortgaged as collateral, for which the lawyer is holding the mortgage.

For the past few years the Queen has spent some time in Metz, Lorraine. Noting the spiritual needs of that town, she did us the honor of ordering us to go to give the mission there; however, because we made the decision not to work in towns where there

---

[1]Jean Barreau.

[2]Rappiot.

[3]One of the young Malagasy boys whom M. de Flacourt had taken to France in 1655 and entrusted to Saint Vincent.

[4]Port of Morbihan, which lost its importance after the foundation of Lorient.

[5]Girolamo Giudice (Jérôme Lejuge), born in Diano, Albenga diocese (Italy), on September 30, 1611, was ordained a priest on December 22, 1635, entered the Congregation of the Mission on March 25, 1650, and took his vows on September 30, 1652. The terrible epidemic of 1657 that killed almost all the men in the Genoa house brought him to death's door (cf. *Notices*, vol. III, pp. 82-87). His self-sacrifice was admirable, but his character was difficult. He died on October 16, 1665.

is an archbishopric, bishopric, or presidial court[6] so as to reserve ourselves for the poor country people, we are sending there eighteen to twenty priests from our Tuesday Conferences, under the leadership of Abbé de Chandenier,[7] our benefactor.

We will await with great joy the good Officialis of Poznan. I am very much afraid that my stupidity and our boorishness may disedify him. O Monsieur, how happy we will be to see our benefactor! Please send me details of what he has done for us.

Our two bands of Missionaries are working successfully in the villages of this diocese. I think the same is also true everywhere, by the mercy of God.

I embrace Messieurs Desdames and Duperroy with all the affection of my heart. I renew also to good Mademoiselle de Villers the offers of my obedience, and I ask Our Lord to bless the poor but dear Sisters of Charity. I am, in the love of Our Lord, Monsieur, your most humble servant.

VINCENT DEPAUL,
i.s.C.M.

Addressed: Monsieur Ozenne, Superior of the Priests of the Mission of Warsaw, in Warsaw

---

[6]A royal court established in the sixteenth century to relieve the pressure of appeals to the Parlements. In certain cases it also served as a court of first instance.

[7]Louis de Rochechouart de Chandenier, Abbé de Tournus, was as remarkable for his virtue as for his noble birth. (Cf. Abelly, *op. cit.*, bk. I, chap. XLIX, p. 240.) One of the most assiduous members of the Tuesday Conferences, he took great pleasure in giving missions, especially to the poór. He declined several dioceses out of humility but accepted more modest but no less exacting functions, such as that of Visitor of the Carmelite nuns of France. To conform himself to the laws of the Church, he resigned all his benefices except Tournus. He died in Chambéry on May 6, 1660, after having been received on the previous evening into the Congregation of the Mission. Several conferences on his virtues were held at Saint-Lazare; the remarks made there are recorded in *Notices*, vol. II, pp. 511-39.

2531. - TO FIRMIN GET, SUPERIOR, IN MARSEILLES

Paris, February 8, 1658

Monsieur,

The grace of O[ur] L[ord] be with you forever!

I received your letters of January 22 and 29. We are not sending you any money to purchase the things our men in Tunis and Algiers are requesting of you because we are counting on sending you shortly their modest revenue from last year, namely, one thousand écus, from which you can take what they need for those items. Since M. Le Vacher [1] pledged himself to help Brother Barreau, it is only right that he be reimbursed. We are thinking of sending him that entire sum of three thousand livres (we shall see) or of splitting the fifteen hundred livres.

As for the rest of the Consul's affairs, we are working on them here without losing any time, and we hope that Providence will gradually provide for them, but this requires patient waiting.

We sent to Rouen the letter from Mariage, the slave in Tétouan.

I sent someone to ask M. Desmarets to use his influence with the Duc de Richelieu to appoint either M. Bausset the Provost [2] or the Lieutenant Seneschal of Marseilles [3] to receive the Administrators' statement of accounts in his name. He told me he would speak to him about it. So far, I have had no reply. There is reason to wonder if he is unwilling to give this responsibility to those gentlemen, since he does not know them, and whether he is more inclined to give it to the Marquis de Ternes, Lieutenant General of the galleys, rather than to anyone else, thinking he can safeguard his rights better in this way. That is what M. Desmarets told the

---

Letter 2531. - Archives of the Mission, Paris, copy made from the original in the Hains Family Collection, Marseilles. This is one of the letters sold at auction by Xavier Charmoy (cf. no. 2505).

[1] Jean Le Vacher.

[2] Pierre de Bausset, Provost of Marseilles.

[3] Antoine de Bausset, the nephew of Pierre de Bausset.

man I sent to him, who pointed out to him that the Baussets are among the leading citizens and most upright men in the town; that the officers of the galleys have always been opposed to the hospital; and that, if any of them became familiar with the administration, they would try, by getting one foot in the door this year, to get both feet in next year. In the end they would find a way either to get control of the King's alms or to destroy that good work. I will send someone to find out the Duke's decision.

I read the letter you wrote to M. Le Vacher.[4] I was very consoled to see the attention you are giving to the Rappiot affair to see if we can get any satisfaction from him for the harm he has done the Consul—I mean some sort of indemnification. I thank you for this and ask you to continue your efforts to have his possessions seized, in the event that you find any.

M. Le Vacher wants to go to see the Chevalier de Montolieu[5] to find out the truth from him about what you are telling him. He will write to you about this at another time.

I thank God for Chevalier Paul's[6] proposal of going to Algiers to obtain justice from the Turks. Please go to see him for me and congratulate him on this plan; tell him he is the only one who can do such deeds; that he has already done some very fine ones; that his courage, together with his fine leadership and good intentions, gives us reason to hope for the success of this undertaking; that I consider myself fortunate to bear his name and to have paid my respects to him in the past at the Cardinal's[7] residence; and that I renew to him the offers of my obedience.

---

[4]Philippe Le Vacher.

[5]Jean-Baptiste de Montolieu commanded five royal galleys in Marseilles. He happened to be in Paris just then, as was Philippe Le Vacher.

[6]Some historians, rightly or wrongly, claim that Chevalier Paul was the son of a laundress at the Château d'If (a national prison on an islet in the Mediterranean near Marseilles). He became a Knight of Malta, led his desert convoys like all the Knights of the Order, and then joined the French navy, where his bravery soon obtained for him the rank of Captain in 1640, Commodore on December 30, 1649, and Lieutenant General in 1654. He died around 1667.

[7]Jules Cardinal Mazarin (Giulio Mazarini) was born in Pescina in the Abruzzi (Italy) in 1602, studied in Spain as a youth, and served in the papal army and the papal diplomatic corps. He

I am, in the love of O[ur] L[ord], Monsieur, your most humble servant.

VINCENT DEPAUL,
i.s.C.M.

Let him know how the Consul in Algiers has been treated. You might also tell him that he will be avenging for France the insults those barbarians are committing against her and that he could not perform a work more pleasing to O[ur] L[ord] than this one.

2532. - TO EDME JOLLY, SUPERIOR, IN ROME

February 8, 1658

We have a distressing dispute going on in Annecy. I had asked M. Berthe not to leave there until it was settled one way or another, but he has come back because he found that there were too many obstacles to that. I do not know if you are familiar with the situation; it is advisable that you be so.

The Company had purchased a heavily-mortgaged house in that town, with the result that the creditors of the person who sold it took it from us in court, excepting our claim on his other property against the holders, among whom was a very skillful, influential lawyer from Annecy. M. [Le Vazeux]—who is hot-headed, as you know—was there, and he filed an onerous lawsuit against him

met Richelieu in 1630 and represented the Pope in negotiating the peace of Cherasco with France in 1631. Mazarin had hardly begun preparing for the priesthood—he received tonsure in 1632 but never became a priest—when he was assigned to other important diplomatic posts: Vice-Legate of Avignon (1634), then Nuncio in France (1635-36), in which positions he demonstrated the ability and flexibility of the most subtle statesman. He became a French citizen in 1639, and Richelieu obtained a Cardinal's hat for him in 1641. Before Richelieu's death (1642), he recommended Mazarin to Louis XIII. He became the principal minister of Queen Anne of Austria during the regency of Louis XIV (1643-61) and, until his own death in 1661, was the absolute master of France.

Letter 2532. - Reg. 2, p. 238.

before the Chambéry Senate. I think he even had him declared a perjurer or a forger and had him fined for some incident. The Bishop of Geneva,[1] who is a good friend of that man, took offense at this and, since he never could tolerate M. [Le Vazeux], he took a strong position against us in this affair, unwilling to see our side in anything that concerned us.

Now, when this man saw that he was being hard pressed by M. [Le Vazeux], who paid little attention to his threats, chicanery, or authority, he tried to come to an agreement with him, and a few mutual friends got involved. When they came together for that purpose, however, instead of minimizing the dispute, they made it worse by using reproaches and insults. The lawyer exasperated and offended M. [Le Vazeux], who lost his temper and called him a big fool. Thereupon the Officialis, on the urging of the Bishop, who had been informed of this, subpoenaed M. [Le Vazeux] personally. When the latter appeared before him for a hearing, he was told that he had to go to prison to be heard—which he refused to do.

When M. Berthe arrived, he went to the Bishop of Geneva, explained our concerns, and asked him to settle the affair; however, he found him totally against it and determined to treat M. [Le Vazeux] as badly as possible. This obliged M. Berthe to have notice served to the Officialis of the Brief of our exemption so that he would not disregard it, since he was on the point of decreeing a second personal subpoena against M. [Le Vazeux]. The Officialis did, in fact, desist and told the Bishop, who tried to oblige him to overrule it, that he could not and would not override this Brief, which exempted a Community from the jurisdiction of the Ordinary in matters of conduct.

---

[1]Charles-Auguste de Sales, born in Thoren (Haute-Savoie) on January 1, 1606, was the nephew of Saint Francis de Sales, Bishop of Geneva. Provost of the Saint-Pierre Chapter in Geneva, Vicar-General and Officialis for his uncle, he was elected Dean of the collegiate church of Notre-Dame in Annecy in 1635. In 1643 he was named Coadjutor to Dom Juste Guérin and was consecrated on May 14, 1645, with the Titular See of Hebron. On November 3, 1645, he succeeded Bishop Guérin in the Geneva diocese, which he governed until his death on February 8, 1660.

So what did that good Prelate do? He himself issued the second decree, showing thereby how warmly he embraced the cause of his old school friend. Thereupon M. [Le Vazeux] appealed it and went to Chambéry to consult the Presiding Judge of the *Chambre des Comptes,* who was Advocate General of the Senate and very experienced in these matters. The latter encouraged him to hold fast and to take his appeal to the Senate as dealing with an abuse committed by the Bishop of Geneva. He promised him a successful outcome and even offered to write against such proceedings for a minor insult.

Now, when a decision is appealed in that region, there is no obligation to say where the appeal is being made, and one has fifty days to raise it. If matters were to reach that point, I do not know whether it should be taken to the Holy See, which would uphold us in our privilege, or to Avignon, which is the metropolitan.[2]

Please seek advice on the matter, Monsieur. I am very worried that this affair may become public knowledge and people may see Priests of the Mission at grips with a Bishop. That is why we are sending M. Dehorgny to Annecy and why I am writing today to the Bishop of Geneva, and to our party as well—who is the cause of all this trouble—to try to sort things out in a friendly manner by the use of arbitrators or otherwise.

If, however, after we have done everything reasonable—and more—on our part to settle the dispute, they remain adamant in trying to get what they are after, namely, the ruin of our poor family in Annecy, I think we will be forced to have recourse to the ecclesiastical or secular court to protect ourselves from such damages, since fourteen or fifteen thousand livres in property are at stake, and it is a question of our exercising our privilege. Please send us the advice you will get there.

---

[2]In the organizational structure of the Church, a number of dioceses, known as suffragan Sees, are united to form an ecclesiastical province whose principal diocese is called a metropolitan See. It is governed by an Archbishop, and its judicial structure functions as a court of appeals for the suffragan dioceses of the ecclesiastical province.

2533. - TO A JUDGE IN CHAMBÉRY

[Around February 1658] [1]

I venture to write to Your Excellency to offer you the services of this poor Congregation of the Mission and my own in particular. I do so, My Lord, with all possible humility and affection. I most humbly entreat Your Excellency, My Lord, to accept them, along with my most humble thanks to Your Excellency for the protection you have been pleased to extend to the poor Priests of the Mission in Annecy in the encounters they have had there with a person with whom they have a lawsuit.

After keeping them in court for a long time, this person is now doing his best to have them banished from the area. If by some crime they have made themselves unworthy of serving God, to their own prejudice in the area, I most willingly consent to this; if not, I would like to hope that Your Excellency, My Lord, in your incomparable goodness, will continue to favor them with your protection. We will be forever grateful for this and will continue our poor prayers for the sanctification of Your Excellency's soul and the accomplishment of your holy plans. I am, in the love of O[ur] L[ord] . . . .

2534. - TO A JUDGE IN CHAMBÉRY

[Around February 1658] [1]

Your reputation for incomparable goodness, My Lord, gives me the confidence to write you this letter. Its purpose, My Lord, is to

---

Letter 2533. - Reg. 1, fol. 65v, copy made from the handwritten rough draft.

[1]In all probability, this letter is related to the dispute mentioned in no. 2532.

Letter 2534. - Reg. 1, fol. 66, copy made from the handwritten rough draft.

[1]As with the preceding letter, this letter most probably is related to the dispute mentioned in no. 2532.

offer you the services of the insignificant Company of the Mission and my own as well, and to entreat you, as I now do, to continue your protection of the poor Missionaries in Annecy regarding an accusation being made against them before you, My Lord, and the members of your Senate. If they are guilty of any crime that makes them unworthy of continuing the service they have tried to render to God for about twenty years in the area, I willingly consent to the abolition of that family; if not, I dare to hope that you, in your just goodness, My Lord, will not allow them to be oppressed.

That is the purpose of the humble request I have the confidence to make to you, My Lord. In addition to the merit you will have for it before God, we—and I in particular—will pray to His Divine Goodness for the sanctification of your dear person and for your leadership. I am, in the love of O[ur] L[ord] . . . .

2535. - TO LOUIS RIVET, SUPERIOR, IN SAINTES

February 10, 1658

If you cannot get those who owe you money to pay you in whole or in part, after waiting so long for them to do so, I see no reason why you cannot have them subpoenaed, given your present need, provided this be done discreetly. You must, nevertheless, be careful not to discredit the family through lawsuits or through a lack of charity.

Generally speaking, no money should be given to our men who come and go and pass through your house, unless they bring you an order to furnish them with some. Exception should be made, however, for those who, because of some unfortunate occurrence, might need something to get to the place where obedience is sending them; for example, if they have been robbed, or delayed by illness, or something else.

Letter 2535. - Reg. 2, p. 113.

2536. - *JACQUES-BÉNIGNE BOSSUET TO SAINT VINCENT*

Metz, February 10, 1658

I sent M. Demonchy in Toul the letter you sent me for him; he did not consider us worthy of having him stay here with us more than a day. I would have liked with all my heart to have been able to keep him, but his business did not allow that. We are trying, Monsieur, to prepare in the best way possible everything he deemed necessary. He wrote me that they thought it was advisable to have the Lenten preacher discontinue the sermons altogether. Since the Bishop of Auguste [1] *had the honor of writing you on that subject, he is waiting for your decision regarding the reasons he explained to you. After that, he will adapt the situation of the preacher to whatever you find most suitable for the work of the mission, which he is determined to favor above any other consideration. There will be no problem in that area, and he has asked me to assure you of this.*

In addition, I was very sorry to hear about your accident.[2] *I praise God with all my heart, Monsieur, that His Goodness has preserved you.*

I took the liberty of warning you about the insolent claims of our Huguenots, whose deputies have left for the Court. The two affairs about which I wrote you[3] *are of the utmost importance for religion. The Queen, who is so zealous for the service of God and so charitable to this town, will certainly be doing a good thing by putting a stop to the unjust proceedings of those gentlemen and by using in this the ardor and authority worthy of her that we have remarked here in similar circumstances.*

I rejoice, Monsieur, to see the season of Lent approach, in the hope that I will soon see the workers arrive whom God is sending us. I send greetings to them with all my heart in Our Lord, and most especially to Abbé de Chandenier.[4] *I pity them for having to make such a long journey in such bitterly cold weather, but their charity will overcome everything. So, in the name of God, let them come soon; the harvest is abundant, and the little difficulties that are arising will soon be smoothed out by their presence.*

I am, with all respect, etc.

Letter 2536. - Urbain and Lévesque, *op. cit.*, vol. I, no. 9, p. 21.

[1]Pierre Bédacier.

[2]The fall from the carriage, which Saint Vincent first mentioned in his letter of January 18 to Charles Ozenne (cf. no. 2513).

[3]In his letter of February 1 (cf. no. 2526).

[4]Louis de Chandenier, Abbé de Tournus.

2537. - TO FIRMIN GET, SUPERIOR, IN MARSEILLES

Paris, February 22, 1658

Monsieur,

The grace of O[ur] L[ord] be with you forever!

I received your letter of the fifth. Please let me know how long it has been since you gave any money to the chaplains of the galleys, how much you distributed to them at that time, and their number at present; then we will see what can be done to satisfy them. Their letter surprised us, but we cannot send you anything for them until we get your reply. Recently you told me that you were hoping to receive their stipends soon from the salt tax collector; let me know if you are still expecting this and for what years the stipends in question are due.

Enclosed is a letter the Duc de Richelieu is writing to M. Bausset the Provost, asking him to receive on his behalf the statement of accounts from the Administrators of the hospital.

I ask M. Huguier to give seven écus to the convict named Traverse, which we received here from his mother, and to give three livres to Antoine Auroy. Please credit his account for this as we will do for yours.

I wrote to M. Le Vacher in Tunis last week, and I am writing to him again today about some Knights of Malta who were made slaves.

Two days ago Messieurs Le Blanc,[1] Arnoul,[2] and de Fon-

Letter 2537. - The original signed letter belonged formerly to Captain Pérodon, Château de Saint-Germain-la-Poterie (Oise). Its present location is unknown.

[1]Charles Le Blanc, born in Roye (Somme) on July 15, 1625, entered the Congregation of the Mission on November 20, 1649, took his vows on November 21, 1653, and was ordained a priest the following month. In 1658 he set sail for Madagascar but had to return to Paris, after a violent storm snapped the masts and rudder and imperiled the lives of the passengers, forcing the ship to drop anchor at Lisbon. It is difficult to determine in some letters whether " M. Le Blanc" is this Frenchman (Charles) or one of the three Irish confreres named White.

[2]Marand-Ignace Arnoul, born in Cayeux-sur-Mer (Somme), entered the Congregation of the Mission on November 22, 1654, at twenty-six years of age, and took his vows on November 23, 1656, in the presence of M. Delespiney.

taines [3] left here for Nantes, intending to set sail for Madagascar with M. Daveroult, who left from Saintes, and young Brother Christophe,[4] who was in Le Mans. I recommend their voyage and their mission to your prayers. We are sending back with them the oldest of the young black natives we raised here. He is a fine young man and will be a brother and an interpreter—even a catechist—for the Missionaries.

Abbé de Chandenier, together with fifteen or sixteen good priests from our Tuesday Conferences, has gone to Metz to give the Lenten mission. The Queen requested it because of the great needs she noticed in that town last summer, when the Court was staying there. I also recommend this good work to your prayers because of its great importance.

Your most humble servant.

VINCENT DEPAUL,
i.s.C.M.

I have apologized to Her Majesty because our Company [cannot] [5] take on this mission, in keeping with our Rules, since the town of Metz has a bishopric and a Parlement.[6] I told her that we would have the priests of our Tuesday Conferences give it and that we have asked Abbé de Chandenier, one of its members, to take

---

[3]Pasquier de Fontaines, born in Bailleul-Sire-Berthoult (Pas-de-Calais) on September 9, 1630, entered the Congregation of the Mission on April 22, 1653, as a clerical student and took his vows on April 25, 1656, in the presence of M. Delespiney. He volunteered for Madagascar and was sent there twice, but both times conditions at sea prevented passage, and he had to return to France. Both vols. I and V (Supplement) of *Notices* refer to him as *Desfontaines*.

[4]Christophe Delaunay, born in Haute-Chapelle (Orne), entered the Congregation of the Mission as a coadjutor Brother on October 4, 1653, at nineteen years of age, and took his vows in Luçon on January 6, 1656. In vol. VI, no. 2171, we see with what courage and spirit of faith he acted when the ship that was to take him to Madagascar was wrecked. Saint Vincent spoke of him with deep admiration (cf. vol. XI, no. 160).

[5]Word left out of the original.

[6]*Parlement* refers to the French judicial system. At the time of Saint Vincent, France had eight Parlements, each with its own legal jurisdiction, chief of which was the Parlement of Paris. They registered or gave sanction to the King's edicts, ordinances, and declarations, and supervised their implementation.

charge of it. We have given him a coadjutor Brother to do the cooking. M. Demonchy, who is in Toul, will be with him awhile to get things started.

Next Wednesday or Thursday we will give four thousand livres to M. Simonnet to be forwarded to you. Three thousand livres are to be sent to M. Le Vacher in Tunis for his annual income and to pay back what you advanced him to lend to M. Barreau. The remaining thousand livres are for Algiers; keep them, do not use them for anything, and deliver them to the younger M. Le Vacher.[7]

Addressed: Monsieur Get

2538. - TO JEAN MARTIN, SUPERIOR, IN TURIN

Paris, February 22, 1658

Monsieur,

The grace of O[ur] L[ord] be with you forever!

I was worried about your dear self and your little family, when your letter of the sixth brought me news of you. That news greatly consoled me; I cannot thank God enough for giving you such good health and for the graces He is granting you and, through you, the people of Bra. I pray that He may be glorified by this and reunite perfectly those divided spirits.

The recent outbreak of illness in our Genoa house has had no bad effects, thank God, and the priest who had contracted it was out of danger on December 19, according to what M. Lejuge wrote me. Without that reassurance, I would have been upset for a long time by such an incident. That poor Genoa house is unable just now

---

[7]The postscript is in the Saint's handwriting.

Letter 2538. - Archives of the Mission, Turin, original signed letter. The postscript is in the Saint's handwriting.

to say all the Masses it is obliged to celebrate. We have ten thousand for which it is responsible, and M. Lejuge is asking if, while the two priests we sent you, named for Genoa, are in Turin, they can help them fulfill their obligations for those Masses. Please tell them that I ask them to do so and that I embrace them in spirit, together with the rest of your men, with all the extent of my affection. I am very consoled to hear that they are making progress in the language and are really devoted to this.

We received Brother Pronetti's [1] title, his baptismal certificate, and an attestation of his life and good conduct. It is to be desired that his letters of tonsure and Minor Orders be sent to him.

Messieurs Le Blanc, Arnoul, and de Fontaines left here two days ago for Nantes, with the intention of setting sail from there for Madagascar, together with M. Daveroult, who left from Saintes, and young Brother Christophe, who was in Le Mans. I recommend their voyage and their mission to your prayers. We are sending back with them the oldest of the young black men we have raised here. He is a fine boy and will be a brother, interpreter, and catechist for the Missionaries, God willing.

I was laid up but I am better, as are all our infirm men, thanks to O[ur] L[ord]. I am, in His love, Monsieur, your most humble servant.

VINCENT DEPAUL,
i.s.C.M.

I embrace you with all the tenderness of my heart and, prostrate in spirit at your feet and theirs, I send greetings to your family.

Addressed: Monsieur Martin, Superior of the Priests of the Mission of Turin, in Turin [2]

---

[1]A clerical student for whom there is no biographical information because he left the Company (cf. no. 2721).

[2]The secretary added to this: "Care of M. Delaforcade, merchant, rue Mercière, Lyons."

2539. - TO LOUIS RIVET, SUPERIOR, IN SAINTES

February 24, 1658

You must not worry about the complaints or suspicions of the relatives of that good priest who is a boarder at your house and whose furniture you have stored, since they are wrong about that. We must continue to do good, even though people of the world may criticize it. So then, despite these rumors, it will be well for you to keep that boarder in your house. Time will prove that you are interested only in his own progress and not in taking advantage of what he has.

2540. - TO MARTIN HUSSON [1]

March 1658

Monsieur,

The grace of O[ur] L[ord] be with you forever!

Enclosed is a letter from Tunis, which will inform you of the news from there. Your charity, which has extended even that far, causes you always to be concerned with the interests of that suffering Church and all that regards the service of God. The Consul in Algiers [2] has greater peace than he has had with the Turks

---

Letter 2539. - Reg. 2, p. 166.

Letter 2540. - Reg. 1, fol. 39v, copy made from the rough draft.

[1]Martin Husson, born in 1623, was a lawyer in the Paris Parlement and had been Intendant in the de Gondi household since 1650. Saint Vincent had great respect for him, as is evident from the Saint's letters, especially vol. IV, nos. 1614 and 1638. Husson accepted the offer the Saint made him of the position of French Consul in Tunis and took up residence there in July 1653. While in Tunis he was an invaluable help and a faithful friend to Jean Le Vacher. Ignominiously expelled by the Dey in April 1657, he returned to France and became Intendant for the Duchesse d'Aiguillon. When he died in December 1695, he left a reputation as a learned, pious, virtuous man and a celebrated author.

[2]Jean Barreau.

but is very worried about the money he owes. We are even more worried about finding some way to extricate him. M. Le Vacher, who came here for that purpose, has been working for seven or eight months with unparalleled enthusiasm but with very little success. Many people who are good to our Company have used their influence and have obtained permission to take up a general collection in the Paris parishes—but this is producing more talk than results. Still, there is reason to hope that the amount owed will be found by Easter and that this good priest will be able to return, pay the Consul's debts, and send him back to France. We are hard pressed, however, to find a suitable person to replace him and, even more, to find some way to stop those barbarians from infringing on the rights of the King's subjects and the Consuls. Several means of doing so have been proposed to M. de Brienne.[3] Please pray for success in this.

For our part, we pray often for you, since this is the only way we can show our gratitude for your goodness and patience toward us. I, in particular, scarcely ever think of you without sentiments of esteem and affection, causing me to hope for the grace of being able to serve you and of continuing to enjoy your precious friendship. May God be pleased to make us worthy of this and to fill your soul and your hidden life with His blessings!

I am, in His love. . . .

---

[3]Henri-Auguste de Loménie, Comte de Brienne et de Montbron, Seigneur de la Ville-aux-Clercs, and Secretary of State. He died on November 5, 1666, at the age of seventy-one.

Saint Vincent and the government had been wrestling with this problem as is evident from vol. VI, Appendix 1: Ordinance of Louis XIV concerning the rights of Martin Husson, French Consul in Tunis, July 14, 1656; and Appendix 4: Letter of Louis XIV to the Consuls of Marseilles, July 5, 1657.

2541. - TO CHARLES OZENNE, SUPERIOR, IN WARSAW

Paris, March 1, 1658

Monsieur,

The grace of O[ur] L[ord] be with you forever!

I received your letter of January 11. In keeping with your wishes, I have just written to M. Jolly in Rome about the new Nuncio. My own wishes will be fulfilled when I hear that the King and Queen are in Warsaw and that the Diet has had the results for which Their Majesties are hoping. I praise God for the good news you send me concerning their affairs. I pray and am having the Company pray that the Divine Goodness may be pleased to change things from good to better.

You tell me that the Bishop of Poznan [1] is getting a parish for you in his city, and M. Falibowski a house in Krakow, and that the latter wants to make a donation to you of some money that is due him. All that is worthy of our gratitude, even though those things are only in the planning stage. May God in His mercy make you worthy of the effects of their good will, for which, after God, we are indebted to the Queen's charity!

If the mail had not been delayed by a huge flood caused by the thaw, I think I would have received another letter from you today. It is so bad that in many of the streets of Paris we see more boats than carriages go by. Water from the river is coming right into our enclosure. This extraordinary overflow must have caught by surprise four of our priests who were on their way to Nantes. They sailed from there for Madagascar with Brother Christophe and a fine young black man from that island, whom we raised here in this house and are sending back to his own country to serve our Missionaries as brother, interpreter, and catechist for the instruc-

---

Letter 2541. - Archives of the Mission, Krakow, original signed letter.

[1]Albert Tholibowski, Bishop of Poznan (1654-63).

tion of his compatriots. Those priests are Messieurs Le Blanc, Daveroult, Arnoul, and de Fontaines. Two are from Artois and the other two from Picardy. I recommend their voyage and their mission to your prayers.

We are very worried about them and about fifteen or sixteen good priests from our Tuesday Conferences who have gone to Metz to give the mission there, under the direction of Abbé de Chandenier. They go by order of the Queen who, when the Court was in residence there last summer, noticed the great need of that town. I apologized to her for not sending priests from the Company because it is an episcopal town, in which we must not preach or hear confessions. This obliged us to have recourse to those priests to do this good work. Nevertheless, we gave them one priest and two Brothers to serve them.

Just when the city of Genoa seemed to be entirely cleansed of the plague, it attacked one of our priests. This put the rest of the family in danger and frightened the whole city. From what I have been told, however, God has chosen not to allow the disease to spread; the patient is cured, but they are all obliged to remain in quarantine. So much for our little news items.

I embrace with all the affection of my heart Messieurs Desdames and Duperroy. I wish them, and you as well, an abundance of heavenly blessings.

I am, in the love of O[ur] L[ord], Monsieur, your most humble servant.

VINCENT DEPAUL,
i.s.C.M.

Addressed: Monsieur Ozenne, Superior of the Priests of the Mission of Warsaw, in Warsaw

2542. - TO FIRMIN GET, SUPERIOR, IN MARSEILLES

Paris, March 1, 1658

Monsieur,

The grace of O[ur] L[ord] be with you forever!

Since M. Bausset the Provost has been delegated by the General of the Galleys [1] to receive the accounts of the Administrators of the hospital, I think you should also present to him the ones you have that list the disbursements for the c[haplains'] stipends. Show him as well the King's order and the receipts releasing you from responsibility for the money with which you supplied them and for what you paid for the building. I would be very glad to see a copy of that statement, with both the receipts and the expenditures. Please send it to me. I will see if it is advisable to have it received by the Duc de Richelieu. I do not think it is expedient right now.

I am not surprised that, after looking to the State for the alms of the hospital and the stipends of the c[haplains] for the years 1656-57, they have now deducted them, because wherever the King finds something to retrench, he does so; and I have always been afraid that that hospital would have great difficulty supporting itself, since its maintenance was founded on a stroke of the pen and without the backing of the General. I will see if the Duchess [2] can

---

Letter 2542. - Archives of the Mission, Paris, copy made from the original in the Hains Family Collection, Marseilles.

[1]Armand-Jean du Plessis, Duc de Richelieu, General of the Galleys of France.

[2]Marie de Vignerod de Pontcourlay, Duchesse d'Aiguillon, was born in 1604, in the Château de Glenay near Bressuire, of René de Vignerod and Françoise de Richelieu, eldest sister of the great Cardinal. She married the nephew of the Duc de Luynes, Antoine de Beauvoir de Grimoard de Roure, chevalier, Seigneur de Combalet, whom she had never seen and did not love. During the two years this union lasted, the couple lived together only six months. The Marquis de Combalet, kept away from home by the war, died at the siege of Montpellier on September 3, 1622. His wife, widowed at the age of eighteen, left the Court and entered the Carmelite convent in Paris. After a year of novitiate, she received the habit from the hands of Father de Bérulle and took her first vows. Richelieu, who loved her dearly, did his utmost to bring her back to the Court. At his request the Pope forbade her to remain in the cloister, Marie de Médicis chose her as lady of the bed chamber on January 1, 1625, and the King elevated her estate of Aiguillon to a duchy-peerage on January 1, 1638.

do anything to have reinstated the amounts that were deducted for those two years.

That is all I can reply to your letter of February 12. I have not yet received the one from February 19 because the mail has been delayed by a huge flood in this area, caused by the thaw. It is so bad that we see more boats than carriages going down the streets of Paris. People have never seen the water so high as it is now; all Paris is in dread of it, and it is doing great damage both indoors and outside. Someone just told us that last night it swept away four entire arches of the Pont Marie, together with the houses that were built on it.[3] It would have caused much greater damage were it not

The Cardinal gave her a small mansion on rue de Vaugirard, one of the dependencies of the Petit Luxembourg Palace, where he lived. The Duchess made noble use of her immense wealth and great influence. She frequented and protected men of letters and took charge of all works of charity. She established the Priests of the Mission in Notre-Dame de La Rose and in Marseilles, entrusting them in the last-named place with the direction of a hospital she had built for sick galley slaves. The Richelieu and Rome houses subsisted on her generosity. She had the consulates of Algiers and Tunis given to the Congregation of the Mission. She contributed to the foundation of the General Hospital and of the Society of the Foreign Missions, took under her protection the Daughters of the Cross and the Daughters of Providence, and was a great benefactress of Carmel. She was President of the Confraternity of Charity at Saint-Sulpice, and replaced Madame de Lamoignon as President of the Ladies of Charity of the Hôtel-Dieu. The Duchesse d'Aiguillon must be placed, along with Saint Louise de Marillac, Madame de Gondi, and Madame Goussault, in the first rank of Saint Vincent's collaborators. No one perhaps gave him more; few were as attached to him. She watched over his health with maternal solicitude; the carriage and horses the Saint used in his old age came from her stables. Saint Vincent's death grieved her deeply. She had a silver-gilt reliquary made in the shape of a heart, surmounted by a flame, to enclose his heart. The Duchess died on April 17, 1675, at the age of seventy-one and was buried in the Carmelite habit. Bishops Bresacier and Fléchier preached her funeral oration. (Cf. Comte de Bonneau-Avenant, *La duchesse d'Aiguillon* [2nd ed., Paris: Didier, 1882].) Le Long mentions in his *Bibliothèque historique de la France* (Fontette ed., 5 vols., Paris: Hérissant, 1768-78), vol. III, no. 30.854, a manuscript collection of her letters, which has since been lost. Any further mention in the text of "the Duchess" refers to her, unless a footnote indicates otherwise.

[3]A letter of Gui Patin, dated February 26, 1658, to his friend Spon in Lyons, gives some interesting details on this flood (cf. Armand Brette, ed., *La France au milieu du XVIIe siècle, 1648-61, d'après la correspondance de Gui Patin* [Paris, 1901], p. 240): "The floods have caused great damage here. The river is so swollen that everyone is afraid of drowning; it is as wide as ever but is flowing about twenty times more swiftly than it did in this same month of February in 1651. We see wood, straw, mattresses, and beds floating down the river, signs of the powerful destruction it has wrought wherever it has passed on its way to Paris. The little Bibara River of Bièvre, popularly called the Gentilly River or the Gobelins River, caused great damage in the faubourg Saint-Marceau, where it drowned many persons and washed houses away. The Grève

for a canal that runs above the arsenal, passes outside the faubourg Saint-Denis, and goes on to empty out at the end of its course. This canal has helped a great deal by diverting the waters from the city and weakening the force of the river.

I ask O[ur] L[ord] to have pity on His poor people. This extraordinary overflow must have caught our priests by surprise as they went on their way to Nantes, and also those priests who are going to give the mission in Metz. We are really worried about them.

I am, in O[ur] L[ord], Monsieur, your most humble servant.

VINCENT DEPAUL,
i.s.C.M.

2543. - TO JEAN MARTIN, SUPERIOR, IN TURIN

Paris, March 1, 1658

Monsieur,

The grace of O[ur] L[ord] be with you forever!

I answered your last letter this past week. This one is simply to accompany the enclosed letters that Brother Pronetti is sending you and to share our news with you. A huge flood, caused by the thaw, has hit this area. It is so bad that we see more boats than carriages going down many of the streets of Paris. People have never seen the water so high as it is now; all Paris is in dread of it; it has done great damage both indoors and outside. Someone just told us that last night it swept away four entire arches of the Pont Marie, along

---

is so flooded that it can be reached only by boat; all the surrounding streets are inundated." The Pont Marie, connecting the Île Saint-Louis with the Quai des Ormes, collapsed on March 1, with twenty-two houses on it. This catastrophe caused the death of fifty-seven persons.

Letter 2543. - Archives of the Mission, Turin, original signed letter.

with the houses that were built on it. It would have caused much greater damage were it not for a canal that runs above the arsenal, passes outside the faubourg Saint-Denis, and goes on to empty out at the end of its course. This canal has helped a great deal by deviating the waters from the city and weakening the force of the river. I ask O[ur] L[ord] to have pity on His poor people.

This tremendous overflow caught by surprise our priests who were on their way to Nantes to leave from there for Madagascar, as well as those priests who went to preach the mission in Metz. We are very worried about them.

May God bless you, Monsieur, and strengthen you for His glory and our consolation! I am, in His love, Monsieur, your most humble servant.

VINCENT DEPAUL,
i.s.C.M.

At the bottom of the first page: Monsieur Martin

2544. - *JACQUES-BÉNIGNE BOSSUET TO SAINT VINCENT*

Metz, March 2, 1658

My most humble thanks to you for your charity in informing the Queen of the affair about which I had the honor of writing you.[1] *From the letters Her Majesty has had written about it in this area, I see that your recommendation was most effective. I ask God to bless the holy intentions of this devout Princess, who is so zealous in furthering the interests of religion.*

Brother Mathieu,[2] *who arrived here almost miraculously in the midst*

Letter 2544. - Urbain and Lévesque, *op. cit.*, vol. I, no. 10, p. 24.

[1]In his letter of February 1 (cf. no. 2526).

[2]Mathieu Régnard was born in Brienne-le-Château, now Brienne-Napoléon (Aube) on July 26, 1592. He entered the Congregation of the Mission in October 1631, took his vows on October 28, 1644, and died on October 5, 1669. He was the principal distributor of Saint Vincent's alms in Lorraine and during the troubles of the Fronde. His daring, composure, and savoir-faire made him invaluable to the Saint. Régnard made fifty-three trips to Lorraine, carrying sums of money

of a flood that was engulfing us on all sides, will give you an account, Monsieur, of what we prepared for those priests. Things are almost ready for the opening; time will arrange everything, and everything that can be done to give satisfaction to those servants of Jesus Christ will certainly be done. I was afraid—and rightly so—that there would be many problems with the preacher,[3] *especially if the floods kept those priests from arriving here before the beginning of Lent. That good Father was so reluctant to relinquish his pulpit to someone else while waiting for them, or to give it up once he had started, that I was really quite worried about the scandal that might have arisen here if the Bishop of Auguste*[4] *had been obliged to use his authority, although he was prepared to do so. But God, who provides for everything, Monsieur, set us at rest on that point, by the order the syndic of this town received to tell the Bishop of Auguste and M. de la Contour that the Queen would be very pleased if the preacher were to leave his pulpit entirely and accept the one hundred écus Her Majesty had someone give him, in addition to the ordinary stipend, and be scheduled to preach next year. This settled everything peacefully, and I must admit that it has greatly relieved my mind. All there is to do now is to ask God to open a path in the middle of the waters soon for His servants, give success to their work, and make their words efficacious. In His charity I am, etc. . . .*

2545. - *SAINT LOUISE TO SAINT VINCENT*

March 2, 1658

Most Honored Father,

If the poor woman on whose behalf you were asked to write is in a fit

---

varying between twenty thousand and fifty thousand livres. Bands of thieves, who had been alerted to his passage and knew what he was carrying, watched him closely, but he always arrived safely at his destination with his treasure. His company was considered a safeguard: the Comtesse de Montgomery, reluctant to journey from Metz to Verdun, decided to do so only after having procured Brother Mathieu as a traveling companion. Queen Anne of Austria used to enjoy listening to him tell of his adventures. Régnard's biography is in *Notices*, vol. II, pp. 29-33.

[3]Father Antoine Guespier.

[4]Pierre Bédacier.

Letter 2545. - Archives of the Motherhouse of the Daughters of Charity, original autograph letter.

state to be a wet nurse, I can think of nothing better to keep her out of harm's way than to have her come to nurse the foundlings. Were it to be feared that she might try to go back, if she had been banished in punishment for her fault, this would be a means to keep her here. Provided she has enough milk, she could nurse for two or three years. Otherwise, Most Honored Father, I see nothing sure in that area to prevent her from falling into the same fault—or a more serious one—depending on the place where she is. If she has been banished, she could be secretly placed as a servant in a locality five or six leagues from here, especially if her sentence has not been widely publicized, lest shame drive her to sin again because her honor has been completely lost.

Perhaps I am saying too much about this; I most humbly ask your pardon for it, taking advantage also of this opportunity to ask for your holy blessing and the assistance of your prayers that I may obtain mercy. I fear that my past obstinacy, perhaps even that of the present or the future—miserable creature that I am—may be the cause of my being lost, like those poor people who have perished only bodily during these floods. To move Your Charity to do this, I beg you to believe that I am by the Will of God, Most Honored Father, your most humble daughter and very grateful servant.

L. DE MARILLAC

Addressed: *Monsieur Vincent*

2546. - TO FIRMIN GET, SUPERIOR, IN MARSEILLES

Paris, March 8, 1658

Monsieur,

The grace of O[ur] L[ord] be with you forever!

I received your letter of February 19. Enclosed is one for Brother Barreau. I am letting him know where we stand with his affairs.

Letter 2546. - Archives of the Mission, Paris, copy made from the original in the Hains Family Collection, Marseilles. This is one of the letters sold at auction by Xavier Charmoy (cf. no. 2505).

We are working at them constantly but are not making much progress. A collection is going to be taken up, which will produce more talk than results. We will not know until around Easter what it will yield. I praise God that you have a trustworthy person at the Bastion [1] to write to Algiers. We have not yet received the three thousand livres for Barbary from the coach-tax farmer, so I was unable to send you the bill of exchange for them; I hope to do so by the next regular mail.

M. Durand told me he was going to send you Brother Duchesne; I think he is with you now.

I praise God for the charity the city of Marseilles is showing to the poor in their present need and for the timely help you have procured for the convicts suffering from the cold weather and poverty. God will grant you the grace, Monsieur, of softening our hearts toward the wretched creatures and of realizing that in helping them we are doing an act of justice and not of mercy! They are our brothers, whom God commands us to help, but let us do so through Him and in the way He intends in today's Gospel.[2] Let us no longer

---

[1]To protect their coral fishing grounds, merchants from Marseilles established around 1650 a fort on the North African coast, near El Kalá. This fort, known as the Bastion of France, became an important commercial center and was sacked repeatedly by the Turks during the seventeenth century. In 1692 the Sultan Achmet recognized it officially as a French possession, along with the other African concessions, when the French promised an annual payment of seventeen thousand francs. Later, the demands of the Dey, who wanted an increase in this tax and who had insulted the French Consul in Algiers in 1827, were among the causes of the incursion of a French expeditionary force in 1830 to depose the Dey. The Bastion was abandoned in 1827; its ruins can be seen at Mers-el-Kerraz.

[2]Cf. Mt 25:43-48; 6:1-4 (NAB) for Friday after Ash Wednesday.

say: "I am the one who did this good work," for anything good must be done in the name of O[ur] L[ord] Jesus Christ, in whom I am, Monsieur, your most humble servant.

VINCENT DEPAUL,
i.s.C.M.

As I was signing this letter, I received yours of February 26. You did well to urge the Bishop of Marseilles [3] to do something about his seminary because I think he needs that.

2547. - TO N.

March 8, 1658

Vincent de Paul announces to his correspondent that Louis de Chandenier and his companions have arrived in Metz, where they are to give a mission.

---

[3]Étienne du Puget.

Letter 2547. - Collet, *op. cit.*, vol. II, p. 41.

2548. - *ALAIN DE SOLMINIHAC [1] TO SAINT VINCENT*

Puy-la-Roque,[2] March 8, 1658

Monsieur,

Thank you for the trouble you are taking for the Chancelade business. Please press for a decision on the Gignac affair and do not lose any time. Meanwhile, I am and remain, Monsieur. . . .

ALAIN,
Bi[shop] of Cahors

2549. - *A PRIEST OF THE MISSION TO SAINT VINCENT*

1658

Our mission in Vassy [1] received every possible blessing that could be expected. We were assisted by four Pastors and another good priest, who

---

Letter 2548. - Archives of the Diocese of Cahors, Alain de Solminihac Collection, file 22, no. 42, copy made from the original.

[1]Alain de Solminihac was born in the Château de Belet in Périgord on November 25, 1593. He was only twenty-two when one of his uncles resigned in his favor Chancelade Abbey (Dordogne), which depended on the Order of Canons Regular of Saint Augustine. He replaced the old buildings and had discipline restored. On January 21, 1630, Cardinal de la Rochefoucauld sent him full powers to make visitations of the houses belonging to the Canons of Saint Augustine in the dioceses of Périgueux, Limoges, Saintes, Angoulême, and Maillezais. Solminihac was sought after in many places to establish the reform. Appointed to the Cahors diocese on June 17, 1636, he devoted himself body and soul to the Church of which he was the shepherd. He procured for his people the benefit of missions, visited the parishes of his diocese regularly, created a seminary for the formation of his clergy, and entrusted its direction to the sons of Saint Vincent. By the time he died on December 21, 1659, the Cahors diocese was completely renewed. Since God had manifested his sanctity by several miracles, his cause was introduced in Rome at the request of the clergy of France. (Cf. Léonard Chastenet, *La vie de Mgr Alain de Solminihac* [new ed., Saint-Brieuc: Prud'homme, 1817]; Abel de Valon, *Histoire d'Alain de Solminihac, évêque de Cahors* [Cahors: Delsaud, 1900].) He was beatified by Pope John Paul II on October 4, 1981.

[2]Locality in the district of Montauban (Tarn-et-Garonne).

Letter 2549. - Abelly, *op. cit.*, bk. II, chap. I, sect. II, §7, p. 48.

[1]In Haute-Marne.

were all capable and virtuous. Two of them have so well adopted the method of the Company in their sermons that, although they were little inclined to speak in public, they now do so effectively, with as much ease as I know among persons of their profession.

The Catholics whom heresy had tainted and infected with many bad maxims have abandoned them, have been confirmed in good sentiments, and have adopted a lifestyle that is truly Christian. Not only the local inhabitants but also people from four or five leagues around have profited from this in a wonderful way. . . .

We are now busy with the Holmoru[2] *mission, where there is still more good to be hoped for, given the throngs of people and the zeal of the Pastors. Their zeal is so great that today twelve of them came expressly from three or four leagues away to be present for the exercises and to learn the method of instructing the people.*

2550. - ***JEAN MARTIN TO SAINT VINCENT***

March 9, 1658

We have now closed our mission in Bra, where God was pleased to shower abundant graces on those poor souls, who had been for so long in the deplorable state about which I informed you in my previous letters. We spent seven full weeks there, and the whole time, of which people usually spend a part in the frivolities of the carnival, was for the local inhabitants a time of penance and, as it were, a continuous feast of very great devotion. There were around nine or ten thousand general confessions, made with such fervor that many persons spent entire days and a good part of the night in church in order to be able to approach the confessional, despite the very bitter cold that lasted the duration. By this means God was pleased to fill hearts with such abundant peace and charity that the inhabitants are amazed to witness such perfect reconciliation that they never recall seeing such union and cordiality.

They themselves have informed the Madame Royale of this. Yesterday I went to give her an account of all that took place and my hope for total

---

[2]Today Heiltz-le-Maurupt (Marne).

Letter 2550. - Abelly, *op. cit.*, bk. II, chap. I, sect. VI, p. 87. The same extract of this letter, with some variations, is in the biographical sketch of Jean Martin (cf. *Notices*, vol. I, p. 292).

perseverance. She experienced such joy and consolation at this that her heart was deeply moved by it and tears came to her eyes. To put the finishing touch on this and wipe out entirely the memory of the past, she granted them pardon and complete amnesty from all the crimes and excesses committed in the course of their dissensions.

Since, however, one act of mercy and grace ordinarily draws down another from the goodness of God, the Divine Goodness was pleased to extend the same blessing He had bestowed on the locality of Bra to another place nearby, where for forty years discord and dissension worked such havoc among the inhabitants that the entire place was almost destroyed by it. A large number of persons had been killed on both sides, many houses had been torn down and demolished, and many of the inhabitants had to go elsewhere to live. Several times the Senate of Piedmont had intervened to bring about a reconciliation, but to no avail, and all the other means they tried to use for this end were futile.

Finally, after the mission in Bra, where some people from there had participated in the exercises, the local landowner, who is one of the leading citizens of Piedmont, and very virtuous and wise, thought it advisable to convoke all of them from both sides to see if there were some way of bringing about a reconciliation after the example of their neighbors. We gave a few sermons and the spiritual exercises of the mission there for only three or four days, and God was pleased to touch their hearts. The result was that, in the presence of the Blessed Sacrament and a great number of people from the environs, they embraced and pardoned one another, swearing on the Holy Gospels to observe perpetual peace. As a proof of this, they invited one another to share a meal, which they did with as much union and cordiality as if they were brothers. Her Highness has had the goodness to grant them the same pardon and amnesty as the people of Bra, so that they can return to live in their abandoned homes and farm their land.

2551. - TO LOUIS DUPONT, SUPERIOR, IN TRÉGUIER

March 13, 1658

We have not yet given anyone permission to send us the postu-

---

Letter 2551. - Reg. 2, p. 191.

lants they judge suitable for the Company, unless they propose them to us beforehand and have received our reply. I think you should not desire this permission for yourself because you would be disappointed to see us send back some whom we do not think have the requisite qualities. In addition, they themselves would have reason to complain about having made a useless journey. So, when someone presents himself, do not send him without testing him for a time, no matter how accomplished he may seem and how good his intention.

During this trial period you can send us the following information: his name, age, situation, level of studies, whether his parents are still alive and whether they are poor or well-off, if he has his title or the means of obtaining it, if he has practiced virtue in the past or has been depraved, his motives for leaving the world and for becoming a Missionary, if he is well-balanced, has no physical deformity and is in good health, can speak clearly, has good eyesight, and, in a word, is disposed to do and suffer everything, and to come and go everywhere for the service of God, as will be indicated to him by holy obedience. You must sound them out on everything and, before making any promises, forewarn them of the difficulties they might encounter in the seminary and afterward in the works and in our manner of life.

We will think about your suggestion of opening an Internal Seminary in Saint-Méen for the Breton postulants. You have given me pleasure.

2552. - TO FIRMIN GET, SUPERIOR, IN MARSEILLES

(Now 2796a.)

2553. - TO FIRMIN GET, SUPERIOR, IN MARSEILLES

Paris, March 15, 1658

Monsieur,

The grace of O[ur] L[ord] be with you forever!

I received your letters of February 26 and March 5. For the present, please postpone giving your statement of accounts to M. Bausset the Provost, which shows how you used the c[haplains'] stipends, until I send you word to do so. I want to get some advice to see if it is advisable for you to render this account because of the consequences it may entail for the future. In the event that it is advisable, I also want to find out whether they should not be rendered to the General [1] himself rather than to M. Bausset, especially since the latter has been commissioned to receive only the accounts of the Administrators and not yours, for which I asked you to send me the rough draft. Mention will have to be made that there were only very few or no resident chaplains on the galleys in the years for which you received the stipends, so the religious from the city used to go to say Holy Mass there on holy days; for this they received the bread it is customary to give daily to the chaplains on duty. Say also that, even at the time when the province was in a disturbed state, the galleys were used against the King's service—or at least they refused to carry out his orders. It was partly for these reasons that His Majesty designated the stipends for the construction of your house to lodge the chaplains while the galleys are in the port of Marseilles, and to form and train them like seminarians in the duties of their state, under the direction of the Royal Chaplain and in accord with the letters patent of the foundation.[2] If, however, these arguments are not in reality such as I put

---

Letter 2553. - Original signed letter, formerly the property of the Daughters of Charity, 22 rue Vincent-Leblanc, Marseilles; its present location is unknown.

[1]Armand-Jean du Plessis, Duc de Richelieu.

[2]Documents relative to this foundation are included in vol. XIII: no. 90—Foundation of the

them forward and have been led to understand, do not use them.

I am very annoyed at the reproaches you have received from the Consul in Algiers.[3] He is wrong to lose his temper with you as he is doing, since you wrote only what I asked you to write. True, that poor man is so upset by his bad business affairs that we have to excuse his complaints, but he is still at fault in the way he is proceeding, since he took on the commitments for which he is suffering—and we as well—because he failed to follow the orders given him in the beginning about not taking on a commitment for anyone under any pretext whatsoever. I have never recognized more clearly the harmful character of disobedience than I have in these circumstances which are implicating and obligating the Company far beyond what I can tell you.

And now, according to what you inform me, M. Le Vacher of Tunis has also been negligent in his duty since, despite our prohibition, he has taken on a commitment for eleven hundred piastres on behalf of Brother Barreau. This is ruining everything and is making two evils out of one because he is following the other in his swift plunge downward and is not extricating him from it. Without knowing whether we can pay back the money he is borrowing and replace the deposits that have been entrusted to him for the slaves, he is putting himself in danger of doing them an irreparable wrong, of ruining his own credit and reputation, and, in a word, of putting himself in a position of no longer being able to continue his work in that country, as Brother Barreau has done in Algiers. We must, of necessity, withdraw the latter because he is the cause of the Company's now being subject to great embarrassment.

That is what happens to persons in Community who act on their

---

Marseilles house by the Duchesse d'Aiguillon (July 25, 1643); no. 91—Appointment of the Superior General of the Mission as Chaplain General of the Galleys (January 16, 1644); no. 96—Rules for the Priests of the Mission in Marseilles entrusted with the galley slaves; and no. 102—Resolutions concerning the establishment in Marseilles (July 9, 1650).

[3]Jean Barreau.

own initiative. When they are truly obedient, God most certainly makes use of them to do His work; on the contrary, the devil avails himself of their disobedience to thwart God's plans and to sow disorder everywhere. If they had been steadfast in not overstepping our known intention, God would be on their side and would have delivered them from their present state of despondency—and us from the difficulties we are experiencing because of this.

I am writing again to M. Le Vacher, telling him not to let that Brother take him by surprise and not to pay anything for anyone whomsoever if he cannot do it from his own resources, without using that of others. Please tell him also that, if he draws any other bills of exchange on you, you will send them back without paying them. However, for the one you have already accepted for two hundred écus, I consent to your paying it from the one thousand écus I am sending you to be forwarded to him. You will find enclosed for this purpose a letter from Messieurs Simonnet on Messieurs Napollon, containing four thousand livres, payable to you within eight days on presentation. Please hold on to the one thousand livres until further orders, and take what you need from the other three thousand livres for the necessary items requested by those priests in Tunis and Algiers, which I asked you to send them.

We have a Brief to read certain forbidden books, but we cannot use it until we have shown it to the local Bishops; in addition, private individuals in the Company must still have the express permission of the Superior. I will have a verified copy sent to you another time.

We received thirty livres for Denis Dubois, a convict on the *Capitaine;* eight for Nicolas Moreau, who is on the *Richelieu,* and six for Marc Mansart on the *Capitaine.* I ask M. Huguier to deliver these small amounts to them, and I ask you to credit him for them.

You propose giving thirty or forty livres to each chaplain who is now on duty so as to put a stop to their complaints.[4] If you can

---

[4]The rest of this letter is in the Saint's handwriting.

satisfy them with ten écus, please do so, and have included on the receipts the fact that we are advancing them this amount, even though we have received nothing for this year or last—if that is true for last year. I assure you that we have not received a single sou of it here since the Mission has been in Marseilles. Please do this with your usual prudence. Get the money to be given to them; we will pay it off here. The thousand livres M. Napollon will give you—besides the three for Tunis—are to pay off the debts in Algiers; please do not mention this to anyone else—I mean, about paying them off in that same town.

I am, Monsieur, your most humble servant.

VINCENT DEPAUL,
i.s.C.M.

I ask you once again not to use those one thousand livres for Algiers under any pretext whatsoever.

At the bottom of the first page: Monsieur Get

2554. - TO CHARLES OZENNE, SUPERIOR, IN WARSAW

Paris, March 16, 1658

Monsieur,

The grace of O[ur] L[ord] be with you forever!

I received your very short letter of January 18, and I have nothing to reply to it. I thank God that there is serious talk of peace. May His Divine Goodness grant that it be made for the tranquility of Their Majesties and the entire kingdom! I thank His Divine Goodness also that the little family is now enjoying a little respite

Letter 2554. - Archives of the Mission, Krakow, original signed letter.

and good health. I hope that both will continue to increase for the service of O[ur] L[ord], to whom all of you are consecrated. I often give the Company the example of your abandonment to God, your patience in difficulties, and your steadfastness in the midst of the past disturbances. I speak also of those men who are with you, whom I embrace with all the tenderness of my heart. I never think of you or of them without a feeling of consolation that my soul experiences above every other consolation. So as not to make the packet too big, I am not writing to them individually, as I would like to do, because this makes things difficult.

Enclosed is a letter for M. Duperroy from his brother,[1] who says he would like to come back when his health has improved somewhat. One of these days I will write and tell him that he will be welcome.

We have no news here except that four of our priests and two Brothers have set sail for Madagascar. We have about seventy ordinands here in the house and two Doctors of the Sorbonne who are giving them the conferences. We also have three bands of Missionaries who have been working in the rural areas for three months for the salvation of the country people.

Oh! how I hope you will soon be in a position to be able to give a few missions!

I ask O[ur] L[ord] to animate all of you with His Spirit for the salvation of souls. I am, in His love, Monsieur, your most humble servant.

VINCENT DEPAUL,
i.s.C.M.

Addressed: Monsieur Ozenne, Superior of the Priests of the Mission, in Warsaw

---

[1]Victor Duperroy, born in Maulévrier (Seine-Maritime), entered the Congregation of the Mission as a priest in June or July 1656. Shortly after his admission he was sent to Montmirail because he was suffering from headaches. Allowing boredom to get the best of him, he came back to Paris only to return to his family.

2555. - TO LOUIS DE CHANDENIER

[Spring 1658] [1]

I spoke to M. de Saint-Jean[2] about engaging the preacher [3] for next year; he will take care of it.

Mademoiselle de Chandenier[4] is still anxious to have news of your health and that of M. de Saint-Jean; [5] the Sisters of Saint-Thomas[6] and the Visitation nuns are anxious to hear about that of M. de Blampignon. I am not writing to him this time because I am very busy. I send my most humble greetings to M. de Moutiers-Saint-Jean and him, with all possible humility and affection. I am not writing to anyone else either.

I almost forgot to tell Abbé de Blampignon that M. Moufle told Abbé de Saint-Espir that he is doing wonders with the vine he gave him to tend; he will find it well cultivated on his return, in full bloom, and perhaps with bunches of grapes. Tell him please not to say anything to him about it.

That, Monsieur, is all I can tell you for now, except that your

---

Letter 2555. - Autograph rough draft, formerly the property of the Daughters of Charity, Moissac. Its present location is unknown.

[1]The reference to Antoine Guespier in the first sentence and to the meeting outside Paris of the Chandenier brothers and Abbé de Blampignon, a member of the Tuesday Conferences, seems to indicate that this letter dates from the time of the famous mission given in Metz.

[2]Nicolas Saint-Jean, chaplain to the Queen Mother, Anne of Austria.

[3]Father Guespier.

[4]His unmarried sister, Marie de Chandenier, who died in Paris in 1701, at eighty-seven years of age. She left her estate to Guillaume de Lamoignon, Chief Justice of the Parlement.

[5]Claude-Charles de Rochechouart de Chandenier, Abbé de Moutiers-Saint-Jean. Like his brother Louis, he was remarkable for his virtue, especially his humility. After the death of his uncle, François Cardinal de la Rochefoucauld (1645), he and his brother went to live at Saint-Sulpice Seminary, which they left in 1653 to stay at Saint-Lazare. Claude-Charles died on May 17, 1710. François Watel, Superior General at the time, announced his death to his priests and recommended the deceased to their prayers. A long, beautiful epitaph placed on Claude de Chandenier's tomb is found in Collet, *La vie de St Vincent de Paul* (2 vols., Nancy: A. Leseure, 1748), vol. I, pp. 584-88.

[6]The Sisters of Saint Thomas Aquinas, or Dominican nuns, lived on rue Neuve-Saint-Augustin, Paris. M. de Blampignon was their director.

business manager has left for Burgundy, very eager to do everything as you would wish. I am, in the love of Our Lord, Monsieur, your most humble and very obedient servant.

VINCENT DEPAUL,
i.s.C.M.

2556. - TO CHARLES OZENNE, SUPERIOR, IN WARSAW

Paris, March 22, 1658

Monsieur,

The grace of O[ur] L[ord] be with you forever!

Just yesterday I received your letter of January 26. We will wait until you let us know when to send you our young men. I greatly fear that we cannot send you the two priests you request because of pressing needs elsewhere. We will still do all we can to send them and the two Brothers you would like to have; but it will not be soon, and do not expect M. de Brière [1] because he is needed at the Bons-Enfants.

I will discuss with Mademoiselle Le Gras what you tell me about her Daughters, and we will try also to remedy the inconveniences you fear in their regard.

The Queen of Sweden[2] is in Paris, but I do not know if the master and the servant you mention are here. I will find out so as to try to separate them, in case they are together. God grant that peace will be made so that the people can get back on their feet! We are still praying for the King, the Queen, and the kingdom.

Letter 2556. - Archives of the Mission, Krakow, original signed letter.

[1]Nicolas de La Brière, born in Saint-Deniscourt (Oise), entered the Congregation of the Mission on May 15, 1648, at twenty-two years of age, and was ordained a priest on May 22, 1655. He took his vows on August 15, 1650, and renewed them on January 25, 1656.

[2]Hedwig of Holstein-Gottorp.

You can well believe that we do not forget your dear person nor that of Messieurs Desdames and Duperroy. I embrace all of you together and each separately with all the tenderness of my heart. I praise God for the union and good health you are enjoying.

All our sick men here are also doing better. Our ordination [retreat] went very well, thank God, and His Divine Goodness is blessing the missions being given in this diocese and in others, particularly the one in Metz. I told you that the Queen sent about twenty priests there from our Tuesday Conferences, under the direction of Abbé de Chandenier. He and his brother, Abbé de Moutiers-Saint-Jean, have been living with us for the past few years. Both of them are great servants of God, to whom we are most especially indebted and who edify us in a wonderful way. Our four priests and two Brothers who left for Madagascar have been at sea since the fourteenth of this month. Pray for them and for all of us.

I am, in O[ur] L[ord], Monsieur, your most humble servant.

VINCENT DEPAUL,
i.s.C.M.

Addressed: Monsieur Ozenne, Superior of the Priests of the Mission of Warsaw, in Warsaw

2557. - TO MONSIEUR PINON

March 24, 1658

Monsieur,

The grace of O[ur] L[ord] be with you forever!

I received with respect the letter you did me the honor of writing me, and I read it with very tangible consolation, seeing your tender,

---

Letter 2557. - Reg. 1, fol. 31v.

devout sentiments for your son Brother Pinon,[1] which are all the more edifying as they are contrary to nature. I thank God, Monsieur, that you have consecrated this son of yours to Him with such enthusiasm that his life and death are indifferent to you, provided they are for the greater glory of the Creator. That is a sign that Divine Love reigns over paternal love in your heart, and there is reason to hope that God will bless the son through the father, as it has already pleased His Divine Goodness to preserve him despite the high mortality rate, not only in Genoa, but in the house where he was and where we lost six priests and a Brother. Indeed, Monsieur, in this great affliction of the plague, we have been consoled to know that this Brother has been preserved from it, for he is a fine young man who always does good, through the mercy of God, and gives us hope of being a good Missionary some day.

Speaking of that title, however, I must tell you, Monsieur, that we are not religious, although we make simple vows, and that the vow of poverty does not deprive those who have made it of the freedom to dispose of the assets of their property, nor the interest and revenue from it while they are alive. True, they may dispose of them only with the permission of their Superiors. I do not think, Monsieur, that you would want him to deprive himself of what the Providence of God has given him through you, in the uncertainty that he will persevere in the state he has embraced, because, since the Pope and the General can dispense us from our vows, it may happen that he will leave us, and if he no longer had anything, he might find himself out on the street.

I hope, however, that neither thing will happen and that you will do him the favor of forwarding his modest revenue here, since he will use it well, and you do not need it, thank God.

---

[1]Pierre Pinon, born in Tours on June 19, 1630, entered the Congregation of the Mission on August 30, 1655, and took his vows in Genoa on October 14, 1657, in the presence of M. Simon.

I ask O[ur] L[ord] to continue to bless you and your family, Monsieur, and to provide me with occasions to be of service to you. I am, in His love, Monsieur, your. . . .

VINCENT DEPAUL,
i.s.C.M.

2558. - *JEAN MARTIN, SUPERIOR IN TURIN, TO SAINT VINCENT*

March 26, 1658

A mission given in Cavallermaggiore,[1] a locality with five thousand communicants, was very successful.[2]

Although there are not as many serious disorders as in the other places where we gave our past missions, still, there are so many disputes and lawsuits that they do not leave us a moment's rest. Because God has given all those good inhabitants such confidence in us, they are entrusting to us all the concerns of the lawsuit and all their disputes, civil as well as criminal. By the grace of God, we hope to settle them during Lent.

2559. - *SAINT LOUISE TO SAINT VINCENT*

March 26 [1658] [1]

Most Honored Father,

Three months ago I was bled and still needed a second bleeding but had to defer it because the last time I was ill the doctors told me that, given my age, I should have it done only in case of great necessity. For this reason

---

Letter 2558. - Abelly, *op. cit.*, bk. II, chap. I, sect. VI, p. 88.

[1]A locality in Piedmont, Cuneo province (Italy).

[2]This sentence from Abelly is the introduction to the following paragraph, which he quoted from a letter written by Jean Martin.

Letter 2559. - Archives of the Motherhouse of the Daughters of Charity, original autograph letter.

[1]Year added on the back of the original by Brother Ducournau.

I have put it off but, knowing my condition, I think I should have it done. I will do so today if Your Charity will kindly let me know that I can go ahead without seeking another opinion. I am not ill, thank God, but simply have some discomfort in my chest and other indications of this need.

I have reason to fear that I am trying too hard to end my days too comfortably, being more sensitive than ever to pain. Nevertheless, Most Honored Father, I remain always your most humble daughter and very obedient servant.

L. DE MARILLAC

Addressed: *Monsieur Vincent*

2560. - *LOUIS SERRE, SUPERIOR IN SAINT-MÉEN, TO SAINT VINCENT*

[March or April 1658] [1]

Every day—workdays included—more than twelve hundred persons came to the catechism lessons; even the most influential people in the place[2] *did not fail to come to them or to the sermons. Several servants and maids left their masters and mistresses who were unwilling to give them the time to come; they preferred to lose their wages rather than lose such a beautiful opportunity to be instructed. Some mothers, after having done their duty during this mission, replaced their daughters at their work to give them the means of doing the same. Other servants and maids asked their masters and mistresses for permission to come to the instructions and to deduct from their wages the time they spent there, which kept them away from their work.*

Such a huge, unusual crowd of people came to receive the Holy Eucharist on Quinquagesima Sunday [3] *and the two days following that we had to continue distributing Communion until seven in the evening. Since the close of the mission, I have learned that not a single one of the large number of cabarets that were in that area is still open because they heard*

Letter 2560. - Abelly, *op. cit.*, bk. II, chap. I, sect. II, §6, p. 43.

[1]Abelly gives the year; the contents of the letter allow us to pinpoint the months.

[2]Mauron, in the district of Ploërmel (Morbihan).

[3]Sunday of the liturgical year immediately preceding Ash Wednesday.

us say in one of our sermons that it was very difficult for tavern keepers to be saved if they gave people drink to excess, as is customary in this area. What is more, in their dealings with one another, instead of spending money on drink—which is the custom in the area—they give it to the Confraternity of Charity we established there for the sick poor of the locality.

2561. - ***LOUIS DE CHANDENIER, ABBÉ DE TOURNUS, TO SAINT VINCENT***

[Metz, March, April, or May 1658] [1]

I thought you would not mind, Monsieur, if I shared with you a thought that came to me. It is that you might write a short note of congratulations to the Bishop of Auguste[2] *for the honor of his patronage, which has been very advantageous to us, and a similar note to M. Bossuet for helping us by his sermons and instructions, to which God is giving many blessings.*

2562. - TO FIRMIN GET, SUPERIOR, IN MARSEILLES

Paris, April 5, 1658

Monsieur,

The grace of O[ur] L[ord] be with you forever!

I received your letters of March 19 and 26. You did well to inform me of the rough treatment to which poor Brother Barreau has once again been subjected. You were right, however, in thinking that this would be painful to me, for I indeed find it almost impossible to express my sorrow to you. What increases it is that

---

Letter 2561. - Urbain and Lévesque, *op. cit.*, vol. I, p. 29, n. 5.

[1]The Mission in Metz was preached during these months.

[2]Pierre Bédacier.

Letter 2562. - Archives of the Mission, Paris, copy made from the original in the Hains Family Collection, Marseilles. This is one of the letters sold at auction by Xavier Charmoy (cf. no. 2505).

in all the avanias [1] committed against that poor man, I see something he did previously to give the Turks reason to do so. In this last instance, for example, if he did not answer completely for that Greek merchant residing in Marseilles, as the witnesses have attested, he may have told the Jews that he was an upright, solvent man and that there was nothing to lose with him. I conjecture this from what M. Le Vacher has told me about it, in which case he gave those creditors the possibility of attacking him because of the foul temper to which their debtor has reduced them.

I agree that he must be recalled, but I am not convinced of the reasons you write me for abandoning the work that has been started. I think that a Missionary is essential in that country, both to assist the slaves when they are sick and to strengthen them in the faith at all times. True, the slaves who are priests and religious can substitute, but they do not do so. They themselves are so unruly that a man with authority is needed to keep them in line. Furthermore, there is reason to wonder if the sacraments administered by many of them would be valid for the poor captives.

Now, if the salvation of a single soul is so important that we should risk our temporal lives to procure it, how could we abandon such a large number of them for fear of what it might cost? Even if no other good were to come out of these situations than to reveal to that wretched land the beauty of our holy religion by sending there men who cross the seas, who willingly leave their own country and comforts and subject themselves to a thousand outrages for the consolation of their afflicted brothers, I feel that the men and the money would be well spent. Nevertheless, we will give special attention to this because of what you write me about it, and we will settle the matter among ourselves.

Our difficulty right now is knowing how we will send safely—from here to Marseilles and later from Marseilles to Algiers—the money that is being collected, and, once it arrives there, how to safeguard it from the insatiable greed of the Turks and use it for

---

[1]Payment extorted by the Turks; an insult or affront.

the purpose for which it is intended. Several good souls here are working to find the way to do this and are reflecting on it before God. I ask you to do likewise.

We will try to pay the bill of exchange you will draw on us for the chaplains, but see if you can satisfy them with ten écus apiece.

I am consoled by the two hundred piastres you sent to Tunis and for the opportunity presenting itself to send the rest there.

I praise God for the missions you are giving on the galleys, and I ask O[ur] L[ord] to bless them.

Enclosed is a bill of exchange for one hundred livres, payable to you by M. Jean Abeille. Please send that sum to Nicolas Renouard in Algiers for his return to France. They say he is free and all he needs is money for the exit tax. In addition, we were told that, if one hundred livres is not enough, M. Abeille has been requested in the notification letter to give whatever more he needs. That young man is from Le Havre de Grâce.

Please let me know if you have been paid the rest of the money that a boat captain owed the slaves from Le Havre, for which you went to court in Marseilles and Aix. We are being asked to give an account of it. Please inform me of the state of this affair.

We received a letter and one écu for Martin de Lancre, a convict on the *Mercares,* now in Marseilles. Please give them to him.

God has been pleased to take from us good M. Senaux,[2] who was the soul of the Troyes house and one of the wisest, most patient, gentle, and zealous priests in the Company. He was always sickly and always seeking God. I recommend him to your prayers and to those of your little family.

---

[2]Nicolas Senaux, born in Auffay (Seine-Maritime) on May 9, 1619, entered the Congregation of the Mission on June 22, 1639, was ordained a priest on February 20, 1644, took his vows on March 23 of the same year, and died in Troyes on March 28, 1658. Saint Vincent praised his regularity, resignation, and spirit of indifference in a letter of April 12, 1658 (no. 2570), and in a conference on the following June 28 (cf. vol. XII, no. 184).

I am, in the love of O[ur] L[ord], Monsieur, your most humble servant.

VINCENT DEPAUL,
i.s.C.M.

2563. - *JEAN PARRE TO SAINT VINCENT*

Saint-Quentin, April 6, 1658

Most Honored Father,

Your blessing, please!

Here are those two good young women about whom I had the honor of writing you again. They come to cast themselves at your feet to receive your blessing and to be enrolled among the number of your children, as two victims who have consecrated themselves to His Divine Majesty to give Him glory in eternity. Because means must be found for reaching this goal, they are going there in the hope of receiving them from your goodness. They go with great confidence and sincerity, however, for I can assure you that this is a work of God and not of humans because everyone has tried to dissuade them from it. That is why I hope God will be glorified by these two virgins.

I ask Our Lord to be pleased to keep you in good health in His love and for His glory. I am forever, Monsieur, your most humble and very obedient servant.

JEAN PARRE,
Unworthy Brother of the Congregation of the Mission

Addressed: *Monsieur Vincent, Superior General of the Congregation of the Mission, at Saint-Lazare, Paris*

Letter 2563. - Archives of the Motherhouse of the Daughters of Charity, original autograph letter.

2564. - TO LOUIS DE CHANDENIER, IN METZ

Paris, April 6, 1658

Monsieur,

I am replying to your dear letter of March 30, and I begin by most humbly asking your pardon for still not being able to write to you by my own hand because of a slight ailment that prevents me from doing so.

I thank God, Monsieur, for the health He gives you and the blessings He continues to grant you and all those priests in general and in particular.[1] I am having everyone who takes an interest in your preservation and works pray for you, especially our own Community and the members of our assembly.[2] Last Tuesday I had some excerpts from your letters and those of M. de Blampignon read to them. Everyone was delighted to hear of the fine progress of the work and the holy results of your good direction, and they left there afire with joy and gratitude.

M. de Saint-Jean[3] was there and wanted to take the excerpts with him to study their main points so he could report to the Queen, which he did the following day. It was such a consolation to Her Majesty that her whole expression changed—so much so that he noticed it immediately. He was holding the excerpts in his hand and, when her Majesty asked him what that paper was, he replied that he had taken from it what he had just told her. "Give it to me," she said, "I want to see it; " and she kept it. She showed above all that she was very satisfied with the spiritual and corporal assistance you are giving the poor and said that if more money is needed she will donate it. I most humbly entreat you to let me know how much the expenses will be.

Letter 2564. - *Lettres et Conférences de S. Vincent de Paul,* supplément, p. 529, letter 3136.

[1]Members of the Tuesday Conferences who were preaching the mission in Metz.

[2]The priests of the Tuesday Conferences in Paris.

[3]The Queen's chaplain.

We have not yet been able to send the help you are expecting because we have been unable to find suitable priests. We have only three, and they will leave on Friday, God willing, arriving in Metz on Tuesday or Wednesday of Holy Week. If you need more of them, Monsieur, I think you should have no trouble finding some in that area, either seculars or religious priests such as the Jesuits. I really wish our house in Toul could give you someone, but I strongly fear that it is not in a position to do so.

The sermons of Abbé de Moutiers-Saint-Jean[4] are so effective that their influence is being felt even as far as here, where I often contemplate his gentle, pleasing manner of acting, and I think his great modesty induces me to become simple, country bumpkin that I am. I greet him with respect and tenderness, and I am, in the love of O[ur] L[ord], Monsieur, your. . . .

2565. - TO LOUIS RIVET, SUPERIOR, IN SAINTES

Paris, April 7 [1658] [1]

Monsieur,

The grace of O[ur] L[ord] be with you forever!

I received two letters from you and your power of attorney from Brother Robineau.[2]

---

[4]Claude de Chandenier.

Letter 2565. - Archives of the Mission, Paris, seventeenth-century copy.

[1]The announcement of the death of Nicolas Senaux confirms the date given in Register 2, p. 113. The copyist, whose text we have used for the remainder of the letter, erroneously wrote "1659."

[2]Louis Robineau, coadjutor Brother, born in Neuvy-en-Dunois (Eure-et-Loir), entered the Congregation of the Mission on November 8, 1642, at twenty-one years of age, and took his vows on November 1, 1650. He was Saint Vincent's secretary for thirteen years; the notes he wrote for the Saint's biographer are still in the Archives. (Cf. André Dodin, *Monsieur Vincent raconté par son secrétaire* [Paris: O.E.I.L., 1991].)

What has happened to the Benedictine nuns of Cognac [3] is a source of great affliction. May God have pity on them! All we can do is to ask this of Him, and that is what we will do. You did the right thing to excuse yourself from being one of the exorcists and will do even better to ask those who might try to involve you in that to dispense you from it. There are many good religious who could perform this function in a holy manner.

I praise God that you are so pleased with the priests who are with you. Please take good care of them, both in mind and body, giving them reason to praise God for having fallen into your hands.[4] Since M. Bréant [5] has stomach trouble and has too much to do when he is the only one in the house, it is to be desired that you relieve him of the chant and, therefore, not send Brother Fricourt[6] to work on the mission. Or, if there is a cantor in the town who can teach chant, you might get him to come to your house to teach it to your boarders in the absence of this Brother. This is what I ask you to do.

God has chosen to take good M. Senaux from us. He was the soul of the Troyes house and one of the wisest, most patient, gentle, and zealous priests in the Company. He was always sickly but always seeking God. I recommend him to your prayers. I am, in the love of O[ur] L[ord], Monsieur, your most humble servant.

VINCENT DEPAUL,
i.s.C.M.

---

[3]Text of Reg. 2: "You tell me that some of the Benedictine nuns in Cognac are possessed by the evil spirit."

[4]The copyist of Reg. 2 added at this point: "I hope they will always do well and that your good example will be a great help to them. Usually, subjects are what their Superiors are."

[5]Louis Bréant, born in Beu, near Houdan (Chartres diocese), entered the Congregation of the Mission on February 12, 1654, at twenty-five years of age, and took his vows on November 13, 1656, in the presence of M. Berthe. He is listed as a priest in *Notices*, vols. I and V (Supplement), with no ordination date given. He was Superior in Saintes (1662-64), Tréguier (1664-70), Saint-Brieuc (1670-80), and Saint-Méen (1681-89).

[6]Jean de Fricourt, born in Nibas (Somme) on March 7, 1635, entered the Congregation of the Mission on June 20, 1656, and took his vows in Saintes on October 20, 1658, in the presence of M. Louis Rivet. He was still there in September 1660. *Notices*, vols. I and V (Supplement), lists him as *Defricourt*.

2566. - TO CARDINAL BRANCACCIO

Paris, April 8, 1658

Monseigneur,

I feel extremely honored that Your Eminence was pleased to ask us to purchase and send you the enclosed books. It is the least service we can render you since, whatever we may do, we could never repay what we owe you for the benevolence and protection with which you honor us in all circumstances.

I would like, Monseigneur, to express to Your Eminence my sentiments of gratitude for this, along with those of our Little Company. In token of this I most humbly entreat you to accept the little present I offer you of a four-part breviary printed at the Louvre,[1] which is quite highly regarded because it is clear and very correct. It is also, in a sense, rare because it is out of print. It is a trifle, Monseigneur, to be offered to a person in such a prominent position, but I thought that Your Eminence would consider not so much the gift in itself but the very great affection with which it is presented to you by the person who is, Monseigneur, your. . . .

2567. - TO FRANÇOIS DUPUICH,[1] SUPERIOR, IN TROYES

April 10, 1658

You can be sure that our sorrow at the departure of good

Letter 2566. - Reg. 1, fol. 52, copy made from the unsigned rough draft.

[1]*Breviarium Romanum*, 1647, 4 vols. with engraved illustrations. (Cf. Auguste Bernard, *Histoire de l'Imprimerie Royale du Louvre* [Paris, 1867, p. 127].)

Letter 2567. - The first part of this letter is taken from the Lyons manuscript, which gives neither the date nor the name of the recipient; the second part is from Reg. 2, p. 137. The contents show clearly that the fragment taken from the Lyons manuscript is part of a letter addressed to François Dupuich around April 10, 1658, which is the known date for the second part. It is quite probable that both parts belong to the same letter.

[1]François Dupuich was born in Arras on July 3, 1616. After his ordination to the priesthood

M. Senaux for the other life is equal to our loss, which is very great—greater than we could express. We had a treasure whom we did not know sufficiently well; he was a man filled with God and was the soul of your house. My sins make us unworthy of having him with us any longer. He is in heaven now, as we have reason to hope, while we are still groveling on earth; he is in the port, and we are still storm-tossed; he is in safety, and we are still in jeopardy; he is enjoying the fruits of virtue, of which he left us the example, but if we imitate him in practicing it, we will follow him in receiving the reward.

We have prayed for his soul and, to preserve the pious custom, I will write everywhere for others to do likewise. I am giving him to all our houses as a mirror of wisdom, patience, gentleness, and zeal, hoping that, through the help of this good servant of God and his prayers, His Divine Goodness will give them a stronger inclination to practice these virtues. Your leadership has always been good, but now it also seems to me to be very pleasant and kind in the way you have helped that dear departed man during his illness and in the way you share in our affliction. I thank you warmly for this.

You present your reasons for being relieved of your office of Superior; however, far from making us look for someone else, they only strengthen our determination to give you this duty entirely. The sight of your faults and inability should serve to make you humble yourself, as you are doing, and not to discourage you from what Our Lord wants to be done. He has enough virtue and competence for both of you. Let Him be the guide, and you can be sure that, if you remain in the humble sentiments in which you now

---

in September 1640, he entered the Congregation of the Mission in Paris on April 19, 1641, and took his vows in Troyes in November 1643, in the presence of M. Dehorgny. He was Superior in several houses: Troyes, Marseilles, Warsaw, Metz, Saint-Charles, and twice in Richelieu. In 1679 he was sent to Poland on a very delicate mission, of which he acquitted himself with competence and success. Dupuich had the title of Visitor in both Champagne and Poland; on January 2, 1683, he was asked to substitute for Thomas Berthe as Assistant General when the latter was detained outside Paris. Dupuich was still alive in 1697.

are, and have special trust in Him, His guidance will sanctify yours. This is what I hope from His goodness and from the holy use you make of His grace. In this hope I am sending you the letter of appointment as Superior of the family. Have it read to the confreres so that from now on they will consider you in Our Lord and Our Lord in you, as I pray will be the case.

2568. - TO DENIS LAUDIN, SUPERIOR, IN LE MANS

April 10, 1658

If your brother . . . ,[1] who is asking to be received as a Benedictine, is determined to leave us for them, it will be difficult to restrain him. Nevertheless, you can advise him to make a retreat before carrying out his plan and point out to him that he is well aware of what he is leaving but does not know what he is taking on. Tell him also that the pretext prompting him to make this change is, in fact, a pretext that is prompting him and not a reason, for if he had confidence in God and a true desire to belong to Him, he would not fear dismissal; furthermore, if he wants to be perfect, what virtues will he practice in religious life that he does not have the opportunity to practice in the Company?

I approve of your admitting M . . . to vows. I think that, if the only impediment you see is his difficulty in rising in the morning, that should not exclude him from performing a good action like the former, by which he will make a sacrifice to God of all the others in his life and all that he is. On the contrary, there is reason to hope that by this means God will grant him the grace of offering Him in a special way the first action of the day by rising the moment the bell calls him.

Letter 2568. - Reg. 2, p. 168.

[1]Gabriel Laudin, born in Provins (Seine-et-Marne), entered the Congregation of the Mission on May 10, 1654, at the age of twenty-five, and took his vows on May 14, 1656. He was Superior in Amiens (1667-70) and was Procurator General (1677-79).

2569. - TO A PRIEST OF THE MISSION

April 11, 1658

We have just lost M. Senaux, a treasure whom we did not know sufficiently well, a man filled with the Spirit of God, a mirror of patience, wisdom, gentleness, and zeal. I have good reason to fear, Monsieur, that my sins are indeed the cause of this loss. May God, by His grace, grant me mercy! I pray for this with all my heart, and I ask you to help me to do so.

2570. - TO JEAN MARTIN, SUPERIOR, IN TURIN

Paris, April 12, 1658

Monsieur,

The grace of O[ur] L[ord] be with you forever!

I was so busy when the last regular mails were going that I could not write to you; yet, I wanted very much to do so to express to you the joy I received from your letter of March 9,[1] which contains great reasons for consolation. God alone can make known to you my consolation at the happy results of your missions, as He is also the only one who could have brought them about. I thank His Infinite Goodness, Monsieur, for the spiritual and temporal mercies those people have received through you, and for the divine clemency and that of their Prince, by which they are now at peace and determined to live better in order to stay that way. May the Holy Spirit, who has reunited them, be pleased to perfect their union and to perpetuate in them all the fruits of your labor, worthy of eternal gratitude!

Letter 2569. - Collet, *op. cit.*, vol. II, p. 197.

Letter 2570. - Archives of the Mission, Turin, original signed letter.

[1]Cf. no. 2550.

O Monsieur, what great reason you have to humble yourself before God to refer the glory to Him for this, and even before others, who may applaud you for it! What can you do without the grace of God? Or rather, what could this grace not do, if you did not put obstacles in its way? How many faults have you not committed amid the little good that was done? And how many are you not capable of committing, if God were to abandon you to the inclinations of corrupt nature? These are the sentiments you should have—even though they are not my own—for I esteem you highly and have great hope that the good use you make of God's blessings will always draw down fresh ones on you.

I must confess that, after the honor God receives from your work—which should be our only aspiration—what gives me the most joy is the great satisfaction the Marchese[2] is receiving from it, for it is only just that he should begin to experience, even in this world, the blessed effects of his charity, which keeps on increasing in our regard. May God make us worthy of the attention he pays to our needs and for the residence he is procuring for you!

God has chosen to take from us good M. Senaux, who was the soul of the Troyes house and one of the wisest, most patient, gentle, and zealous priests in the Company. He was always sickly but always seeking God. I recommend him to your prayers and to those of your little family, whom I embrace cordially. I am, in O[ur] L[ord], Monsieur, your most humble servant.

VINCENT DEPAUL,
i.s.C.M.

Addressed: Monsieur Martin, Superior of the Priests of the Mission of Turin, in Turin [3]

---

[2]Marchese di Pianezza.

[3]The secretary added to this: "Care of M. Delaforcade, merchant, rue Mercière, Lyons."

2571. - TO FIRMIN GET, SUPERIOR, IN MARSEILLES

Paris, April 12, 1658

Monsieur,

The grace of O[ur] L[ord] be with you forever!

We have paid on receipt of the bill of exchange the 165 livres you drew on us, although it was payable only two weeks at sight. We will try also to pay the 235 livres you still have to draw to make up the 400 you have to distribute to the chaplains.

I examined the statement of account of receipts and expenditures that you sent me. You make no mention in it either of the money I think we sent from here to help pay for the site and construction of your house or of the sum we sent to mollify the chaplains. All you tell me is that, if I want further clarification on this account, you will give it to me. This is what I am asking you to do.

I thought you no longer had sore eyes. From what I can gather, however, you are still suffering from them. I am very worried about this, and I ask you to do what you can to be healed.

Madame de Romilly [1] gave us 100 livres to be given to her son, a Knight of Malta and a slave in Tunis,[2] for his little necessities. Please forward them to M. Le Vacher,[3] along with the enclosed letter, and take it from the 1000 livres you have for Algiers.

I am writing to tell M. Get to send you 1000 livres, besides the 3000, to pay your debts, so that you will have no balance. Please give 100 livres of that directly to the Chevalier de Romilly, without

---

Letter 2571. - Archives of the Mission, Paris, copy made from the original in the Hains Family Collection, Marseilles. This is one of the letters sold at auction by Xavier Charmoy (cf. no. 2505).

[1]Louise Goulas, wife of Pierre Sublet, Seigneur de Romilly. She was a Lady of Charity very devoted to the work of the foundlings.

[2]Michel Sublet, Chevalier de Romilly.

[3]Jean Le Vacher.

letting anyone know it. I recommend to you especially the Chevalier de Tonnerre.[4]

By mistake, I added the preceding paragraph in my own hand, thinking I was writing to M. Le Vacher. Please send him the 900 livres you have left from the 1000 livres we were thinking of keeping for Algiers, which I had asked you not to use. This is in addition to the 3000 livres you already have instructions to send to M. Le Vacher in Tunis. With these 3900 livres, he will have enough for his release and living expenses.

Enclosed is a letter the Duchesse d'Aiguillon is writing to a Carmelite nun about the proposal made by Commander Paul. She wants her to use her influence with her brother, who is—I think—the First Consul in Marseilles,[5] so that the Commander will do what he has proposed. Let me know if you have mentioned this to him and if it seems likely to happen.

I am, in the love of O[ur] L[ord], Monsieur, your most humble servant.

VINCENT DEPAUL,
i.s.C.M.

2572. - TO JEAN-JACQUES PLANCHAMP,[1] IN TURIN

Paris, April 19, 1658

Monsieur,

The grace of O[ur] L[ord] be with you forever!

---

[4]Louis de Clermont, who was also a slave in Tunis. Coste originally had *Fournier* here but corrected it (vol. XIII, p. 850) to read *Tonnerre*.

[5]Antoine de Bausset.

Letter 2572. - Original signed letter, formerly the property of Comte Allard du Chollet, 114 *bis* Boulevard Malesherbes, Paris; its present location is unknown.

[1]Jean-Jacques Planchamp, born in Mionnay (Ain) on December 8, 1627, was ordained a priest in 1651. He entered the Congregation of the Mission on April 29, 1655, and took his vows in Turin on May 12, 1657, in the presence of M. Martin. Planchamp left the Company in 1659.

I received your letter with joy and gratitude. I thank God for your good dispositions, and I thank you for the items of information you give me. They are so many marks of the esteem and affection you have for M. Martin and of your zeal for his preservation and his method of leadership. I have always regarded you as a good servant of God, but now that you have written me so well, I consider you a man of common sense and sound management. I ask Our Lord, Monsieur, to continue to grant you His graces and to increase them so that you may go on growing from strength to strength.

I will write to M. Martin, as I have already done several times, asking him to moderate his work and that of the family, and I ask God, Monsieur, to strengthen you personally to bear yours.

I do not have time to write you as long a letter as I would really like to do, so I could converse with you awhile; the offices of this holy day [2] prevent me from doing so and oblige me to close with this sentiment: Happy are those who consume their lives for the service of O[ur] L[ord], as He Himself consumed His for the salvation of mankind. Nevertheless, I ask you to take care of your health and to ask Him to give me the patience to make good use of the sufferings of our state, for it lays us open to suffer a great deal, both from within and from without, after the example of our Master, who was betrayed, denied, and abandoned by His disciples[3] and mistreated by those whose conversion and salvation He was procuring.

I am, in His love, Monsieur,

VINCENT DEPAUL,
i.s.C.M.

Addressed: Monsieur Planchamp, Priest of the Mission, in Turin

---

[2]Good Friday.
[3]Cf. Mk 14:30-31. (NAB)

2573. - TO JEAN MARTIN, SUPERIOR, IN TURIN

Paris, April 19, 1658

Monsieur,

The grace of O[ur] L[ord] be with you forever!

Never has a letter from you consoled me more than the one you wrote on March 26! [1] I read it last evening at the very time I had just been told that someone in this city had received news that you were seriously ill on mission, and added a few other things. Your letter, however, assured me of the contrary, thank God. May His Holy Name be ever glorified for it!

The strong impression this bad rumor made on my soul left me with a renewed fear that you may give way beneath the weight of your missions. You are taking on too many and ones that are too heavy, given the small number of workers you have. The latter are neither formed for nor accustomed to such strenuous work, they lose their breath in the middle of the race, along with the courage to continue, and you end up by ruining your health. I am well aware that it is difficult for you to restrain yourself when you see such an abundant harvest, but there may also be some excess in the way you go about it.

The Marchese, whose zeal you are trying to satisfy, knows full well that a person cannot work constantly, as you are doing, and go very far; so, the fear that the labor may overwhelm you, and the work will still remain to be done, will undoubtedly cause him to agree to your going at it more calmly, conserving your strength and your men, and taking some rest. In the name of God, Monsieur, do so, go easy, and be attentive to the needs of those whom God has entrusted to your guidance. That is the reason for this letter, since I have nothing to reply to what you write me, except that we have

---

Letter 2573. - Archives of the Mission, Turin, original signed letter.

[1] Cf. no. 2558.

no news of M. Richard[2] and that I will write to Metz to get some.

We are very well here, thank God. Our men, separated into three bands, have been out giving missions for five or six months. Right now we have eighty ordinands here in this house. Pray for our needs as we are doing for your preservation and for God's continued grace for you, your family, and your work.

I am, in the love of O[ur] L[ord], Monsieur, your most humble servant.

VINCENT DEPAUL,
i.s.C.M.

Addressed: Monsieur Martin, Superior of the Priests of the Mission, in Turin

2574. - TO FIRMIN GET, SUPERIOR, IN MARSEILLES

Paris, April 19, 1658

Monsieur,

The grace of O[ur] L[ord] be with you forever!

I received your letter of the ninth. I praise God for the journey you made to Toulon and for its success. I asked you to send M. Le Vacher,[1] in addition to the 3000 livres already sent, the 1000 livres remaining from the 4000 livres of the last bill of exchange, namely, 900 livres for him and 100 livres for the Chevalier de Romilly. We

---

[2]François Richard, born in Metz on February 3, 1622, entered the Congregation of the Mission on September 24, 1641, took his vows in 1643, and was ordained a priest in Rome on March 31, 1646 (cf. *Notices,* vol. I, p. 464).

Letter 2574. - Archives of the Mission, Paris, copy made from the original in the Hains Family Collection, Marseilles. This is one of the letters sold at auction by Xavier Charmoy (cf. no. 2505).

[1]Jean Le Vacher.

will try to pay the remaining 181 still to be drawn on us of the 352 livres you paid the chaplains, in addition to what was received here and paid out there for the convicts. We will be thinking about you shortly regarding the help you are requesting.

We received 30 livres for Renaud Le Page; [2] I am writing to tell M. Huguier to give them to him.

I am, in the love of O[ur] L[ord], Monsieur, your most humble servant.

VINCENT DEPAUL,
i.s.C.M.

2575. - TO FIRMIN GET, SUPERIOR, IN MARSEILLES

Paris, April 26, 1658

Monsieur,

The grace of O[ur] L[ord] be with you forever!

I praise God that you have found someone who offers to give you in Marseilles the money we have here for Algiers, at no cost for the exchange. When we have collected it all, it may amount to fifteen or twenty thousand livres. You can begin to draw it on us; it is better to do so at different times rather than by one bill of exchange. If, however, you do not get the sums by giving your bills of exchange, as is to be desired, be very sure to get them at least as soon as you hear that we have delivered them here; otherwise, we will have recourse to Messieurs Simonnet. Since they are trustworthy persons, they will forward the money to us safely, with some small profit for themselves.

You inform me that you have dismissed the Saint-Victor novices. Now, given the reasons you say you had for acting in such a

---

[2]A galley slave in Toulon.

Letter 2575. - British Museum, *Foreign Private Letters*, Egerton 27, fol. 164, original signed letter. The postscript is in the Saint's handwriting.

way, I think you did the right thing,[1] but it would have been even better if you had proposed this plan to me before putting it into effect. I take that back—I think you did write to me about it.[2]

We will try to pay your bill of exchange for 400 livres, which, together with the one you have already drawn for 165 livres, amounts to 565 livres, to reimburse you for the 355 livres you paid out to the ch[aplains], and the 210 livres given, or to be given, to the poor captives. I will have our little account checked against our reports to see if they correspond. Meanwhile, see what else has to be added to them: first, four écus for Pierre Le Gros, called Lapointe, which we have received here and are to be sent to Toulon for him; and second, 7 livres 5 sous for M. Esbran, a priest-prisoner on the *Bailliebault.* I am writing to tell M. Huguier to give both of them those amounts.

I am, in the love of O[ur] L[ord], Monsieur, your most humble servant.

VINCENT DEPAUL,
i.s.C.M.

M. de la Fosse writes me that, since he is now out of work and feels that the climate does not suit him, he would like to be changed from there. I am asking him to go to Troyes, where the climate is considered one of the best in the kingdom. Please give him, Monsieur, what he will need for his journey. When he gets to

---

[1]We know these reasons from an old notebook from the Marseilles house, preserved today in the Arch. Nat., S 6707: "Since most of these young men had no other vocation to the religious life than the will of their parents, who wanted to relieve their households of them and provide for them from the revenues of a religious Order as from a benefice, these young men, having no idea what it meant to be monks, followed their own feelings and inclinations and were dissolute rogues, seeking only to gratify their senses. As a consequence, since they showed no improvement nor hope of reform after a year's tryout, the Prior [of the Saint-Victor Monastery] and their parents had to be asked to withdraw them from our house. This they did, although regretfully and after having implored the Superiór of that house to bear with them for a few more years." Once the Saint-Victor novices left, there were no longer any other students in the Marseilles house.

[2]This sentence is in the Saint's handwriting.

Lyons, he can take the river or the public carrier to go to Chalon-sur-Saône and from there to Dijon, where he can take the coach to Troyes. If it is necessary to send a priest to replace him, we will do so.

I embrace M. Parisy [3] with all the tenderness of my heart.

It is not advisable to divulge the sum that will be received.

Addressed: Monsieur Get

2576. - TO PIERRE CABEL, SUPERIOR, IN SEDAN

May 1, 1658

It is the maxim and custom of the Company that Superiors of houses not allow individuals to go on pilgrimages, travel, or absent themselves except for the exercise of their ministries, without consulting the General.

M . . . is an upright man, inclined to virtue, who was esteemed and highly respected in the world. If he is restless now that he is among us; if he is concerned about his little temporal goods and the affection of his relatives; if, in a word, he distresses those who are with him; bear with him. If he did not have these faults, he would have others; and if you had nothing to put up with either from him or from others, your charity would not have much practice nor would your leadership resemble closely enough that of Our Lord. He willed to have uncouth disciples, subject to various failings, so that He might have the opportunity to practice humility and patience toward them. He did so to show us by His example how those in authority should act.[1] Please pattern yourself, Mon-

---

[3]Antoine Parisy, born in Mesnil-Réaume (Seine-Maritime) on December 7, 1632, entered the Congregation of the Mission on November 18, 1651, took his vows in 1653, and was ordained a priest in 1657. In 1659 he was sent from Marseilles to Montpellier, returning to Marseilles in 1660. He was Superior there (1672-75), then in Metz (1676-85) and Saint-Méen (1689-1701).

Letter 2576. - Reg. 2, p. 124.

[1]Cf. Mk 10:42-44. (NAB)

sieur, on this holy model, who will teach you these two things together: forbearance with your Brothers and the way to help them rid themselves of their imperfections. You must not tolerate the evil but try to remedy it in a gentle way. For the rest, I sympathize with you in your present difficulties, and I ask Our Lord to strengthen you with His Spirit.

2577. - TO JEAN MARTIN, SUPERIOR, IN TURIN

Paris, May 3, 1658

Monsieur,

The grace of O[ur] L[ord] be with you forever!

I think I have written you twice since I last received any of your dear letters, expressing to you some of my consolations and my gratitude for the special graces God is granting you and, through you, the people you serve. I cannot sufficiently thank His Holy Name for this nor ask Him often enough to strengthen you and continue to bless you abundantly.

This letter has two purposes. The first is to tell you that I received a letter from your brother asking to be received into our Company. I am writing to tell M. Jolly to assure him of that, if you are in agreement and let him know,[1] and for him to send him to Genoa to begin his seminary there. I did not want to see any reasons against this in a person who is so close and so dear to you. However, since I desire in it only what you judge to be most advisable for his welfare and your consolation, I ask you to let M. Jolly know your own sentiments so that he may take them into account as if they were mine. I hope that the blessings you enjoy will extend to your

---

Letter 2577. - Archives of the Mission, Turin, original signed letter.

[1]These last words, from "if you are in agreement," are in the Saint's handwriting.

only brother, if God is calling him to the same state to which He has called you. All that remains now is to discern his vocation well.

My second reason for writing is to ask you to send to Genoa as soon as possible Messieurs Stelle[2] and Beaure.[3] M. Jolly has to go there around June 15 to make the visitation, along with a priest he is supposed to take there from Rome. M. Cruoly,[4] whom we will send from here as Superior, is also going there with a few young people to learn the language. Now, your two priests have to be there at the same time, so please have them leave Turin as soon as possible.

We have no news here; everything is going along as usual.

I send greetings to your little family, and I am, for you and for it, in the love of O[ur] L[ord], Monsieur, your most humble servant.

VINCENT DEPAUL,
i.s.C.M.

Addressed: Monsieur Martin, Superior of the Priests of the Mission of Turin, in Turin

---

[2]Gaspard Stelle, born in the Sisteron diocese (Alpes-de-Haute-Provence) on April 5, 1624, entered the Congregation of the Mission as a priest on January 16, 1657, and took his vows in Genoa on January 7, 1659, in the presence of M. Simon. Both vol. I and vol. V (Supplement) of *Notices*, list him as *Estelle*.

[3]Jacques Beaure, born in Saint-Léonard-de-Noblat (Haute-Vienne) on March 22, 1627, entered the Congregation of the Mission for the second time on September 2, 1656.

[4]Donat Crowley (Saint Vincent spells his name *Cruoly*), born in Cork (Ireland) on July 24, 1623, entered the Congregation of the Mission on May 9, 1643, took his vows in November 1645, and was ordained a priest in 1650. He was among the group of Missionaries sent to Picardy in 1651 for the relief of the people reduced to destitution by the war. Later, he was named Director of Students and theology professor at Saint-Lazare (1653-54) and was sent after that to Le Mans as Superior. In 1657 he returned to Saint-Lazare to teach moral theology. Crowley also became Superior in Richelieu (1660-61), at Saint-Charles (1662-64), Montauban (1664-65), Agen (1665-66), and Saint-Brieuc (1667-70). Sent to Le Mans in 1676, he was Superior there (1687-90), after which there is no trace of him.

2578. - TO FIRMIN GET, SUPERIOR, IN MARSEILLES

Paris, May 3, 1658

Monsieur,

The grace of O[ur] L[ord] be with you forever!

I simply want to thank you for the clarification you gave me regarding the sums of money you have received and used for the chaplains and for your house. I only glanced at it but will study it more closely when I have time.

Thank you also for having sent to Tunis the last thousand livres I asked you to send.

Please hold on to the four hundred livres M. Perriquet [1] sent you for Algiers, until a way is found to send the rest there.

It would have been a good idea for you to have seen M. Paul, as I had asked you to do—even though it was most unlikely that he would follow through on his proposal—for at least you would have been able to find out in greater detail how he felt about such a venture and to learn something from it that could be helpful to us in the event that someone else may do it. For, if it is feasible, the Duchesse d'Aiguillon has her mind set on having it done by M. de Beaufort [2] who, so I hear, is to be in command of the navy. However, all you have to do is mention it.

I am writing to ask M. Huguier to give eight livres to a convict named Alexis Leyo on the galley *Reine;* please credit him for them.

Letter 2578. - Archives of the Mission, Paris, copy made from the original in the Hains Family Collection, Marseilles. This is one of the letters sold at auction by Xavier Charmoy (cf. no. 2505).

[1]Vicar-General of Bayonne.

[2]François de Vendôme, Duc de Beaufort, was born in Paris in 1616 to César, Duc de Vendôme, the illegitimate son of King Henry IV and Gabrielle d'Estrées. In his youth he distinguished himself in the war against the Spaniards and became a great favorite of Anne of Austria, the French Queen. His intrigues earned him four years in prison at the Château of Vincennes. He had barely been set free when he joined the Frondeurs and became a popular idol. De Beaufort fought the Algerians at sea in 1665 and died in 1669 at the siege of Candia (Heraklion), a seaport of Crete.

I ask O[ur] L[ord] to accomplish in you and through you His most holy Will, in which and by which I am, Monsieur, your most humble servant.

VINCENT DEPAUL,
i.s.C.M.

2579. - TO CHARLES OZENNE, SUPERIOR, IN WARSAW

Paris, May 3, 1658

Monsieur,

The grace of O[ur] L[ord] be with you forever!

I am replying to your dear letter of March 27 almost as soon as I have received it. While the King prepares to fight his enemies, all we can do is lift our hands to heaven that he may overcome them by the virtue and strength of the God of armies. We ask Him also to grant that the peace now being negotiated will be made, and that ultimately, in one way or another, His Divine Goodness will restore things to their pristine state. These are the graces we ask most often and most earnestly of Him and will continue to ask of Him until the end, along with the preservation and sanctification of Their Majesties.

I thank God, Monsieur, for your good health and that of Messieurs Desdames and Duperroy.[1] I embrace all of you together and each one in particular with all the tenderness of my heart and with a deep sentiment of gratitude to the Goodness of God for the union existing among you and the perfect trust all of you have in His protection. I am indeed sure that it is very special for you and that, after so many disturbances and dangers and so much patience,

---

Letter 2579. - Archives of the Mission, Krakow, original signed letter.

[1]Nicolas Duperroy.

O[ur] L[ord] will place you in a stable, acceptable situation, suitable for carrying out His plans for you.

I would like to think that you have now made the Krakow journey and expressed to M. Falibowski there our profound gratitude for his benefits to you, and that he has signed over to you the deed of the purchase he made. If God blesses the action you plan to take to get the Bishop's [2] permission for your house and the King's privilege, we will send you a few of our young men to be placed in that city, where they can learn the language and customs of the country and be trained in our works, but we have to wait until matters are a little clearer.

Not finding Mademoiselle Cornuty's father at the château de Bicêtre, I learned that he was sick and has been taken to the Hôtel-Dieu. I will send someone to find out how he is and will recommend him to our Daughters of Charity.

I send greetings to the Daughters in Warsaw. There is no news in their Little Company—nor in ours either. Everything is going very well, thank God, in whom I am, Monsieur, your most humble servant.

VINCENT DEPAUL,
i.s.C.M.

Addressed: Monsieur Ozenne, Superior of the Priests of the Mission of Warsaw, in Warsaw

---

[2] Andrzej Trzebicki.

2580. - *SAINT LOUISE TO SAINT VINCENT*

[May 1658] [1]

I was unaware, my very dear and Most Honored Father, that you were ill. For the love of God, take care of yourself!

What I am anxious to know from Your Charity is whether we should have the young Sister assigned to Cahors [2] *accompany Sister Anne*[3] *on the journey she will be making with the Duchesse de Ventadour.*[4] *We are sure*

Letter 2580. - Archives of the Motherhouse of the Daughters of Charity, original autograph letter.

[1]Date added on the back of the original by Brother Ducournau.

[2]It was Sister Avoie Vigneron who accompanied Sister Anne Hardemont to the hospital of Ussel; perhaps she is the one Saint Louise had in mind here.

Avoie Vigneron entered the Daughters of Charity around 1646-47. She was in Paris in August 1655 and was sent to Ussel in May 1658. There she encountered many difficulties; she made her sufferings known to Saint Louise (cf. vol. VII, no. 2767) and to Saint Vincent (cf. vol. VIII, no. 3241). In 1672 she was Sister Servant in Corbeil. Her two sisters, Geneviève and Marie, were also Daughters of Charity.

[3]Anne Hardemont. There was question of sending her to the hospital in Ussel, which the Duchesse de Ventadour wanted to entrust to the Daughters of Charity.

We get to know Sister Anne Hardemont from the many letters she preserved. In 1640 she was missioned to Saint-Paul parish; in 1647 she was chosen to establish the mission in Montreuil-sur-Mer, and in 1650 the one in Hennebont (Morbihan). In 1651 she was stationed in Nantes, and the following year in Châlons-sur-Marne. Because of illness she returned to Nantes, where she remained until 1653, at which time she went to Sainte-Menehould, then to Sedan in 1654, and La Roche-Guyon in 1655. She was present in Paris on August 8, 1655, and signed the Act of Establishment of the Company of the Daughters of Charity (cf. vol. XIII, no. 150). In 1656 she was at the Petites-Maisons in Paris and in Ussel in 1658. Because of her leadership ability, she was named Sister Servant in all these places, despite what Saint Vincent wrote to Saint Louise (cf. no. 1405) that she was "somewhat to be feared"; this was undoubtedly the cause of her many changes. (Cf. vol. IV, no. 1342, and *Spiritual Writings*, L. 110, pp. 120-21.)

[4]The Duchesse de Ventadour, née Marie de la Guiche de Saint-Gérand. On February 8, 1645, she married Charles de Levis, Duc de Ventadour, widower of Suzanne de Thémines de Montluc, who had bequeathed forty thousand livres to Saint Vincent for the foundation of a mission in Cauna (Landes). After her husband died (May 19, 1649), she sought consolation in works of charity, becoming one of Saint Louise's principal auxiliaries and best friends. On the eve of Saint Louise's death, the Duchess came to be with her, caring for her with all the devotedness of a Daughter of Charity. She spent part of the night with her and, after a short rest, stayed by her bedside until the end, holding the blessed candle herself. (Cf. Abbé Nicolas Gobillon, *La vie de Mademoiselle Le Gras, fondatrice et première supérieure de la Compagnie des Filles de la Charité* [Paris: A. Pralard, 1676], pp. 178, 181.) In 1683 the Duchess was elected President of the Ladies of Charity. She died at the age of seventy-eight at her château, Sainte-Marie-du-Mont (Normandy), during the night of July 22-23, 1701. Thanks to her generosity, this locality had an establishment of Daughters of Charity as early as 1655.

of this Sister's stability in the service of God. She is exact in observing the Rules; she also knows how to write, which is essential so we can be accurately informed of what goes on. The Lady would like our Sisters to be ready to leave on May 8.

I think we should ask Mademoiselle de Lamoignon to make up her mind once and for all about what will be done with Mademoiselle de Chisé. If she wants us to keep her, and she is healthy, should we grant her request? If she is sick, and remedies have to be provided for her, would four hundred livres be enough to request, without including clothing?

One of our new Sisters, who has been doing very well for more than two months, has asked to be clothed in the habit of the Daughters of Charity. If you agree to grant her request, I hope she will be capable of replacing Monsieur Ablet's sister, who left yesterday after having spoken to Monsieur Portail.

I will tell the good Brother [5] the rest, if Your Charity will kindly send him here.

2581. - TO BENJAMIN HUGUIER, IN MARSEILLES [1]

May 5, 1658

I asked you to stay in Marseilles, especially since you wrote me that you were happy to remain there and because I think God will be glorified by the service you are rendering to souls there. You mentioned something in your last letter that confirms me in that sentiment, when you said you wanted to spend the rest of your days usefully. I am very consoled by that, for this desire will cause you to use for that good purpose whatever state in which you find

---

[5]Bertrand Ducournau.

Letter 2581. - Reg. 2, p. 116.

[1]The letter is addressed to "A priest of the Company who seemed anxious to direct the others." This priest is undoubtedly Benjamin Huguier because the contents do not apply to Firmin Get, the Superior; or to Jacques de la Fosse, who had just been assigned to Troyes; or Antoine Parisy, the only other priest living with them in Marseilles. Apparently the Saint was trying to distract him from his temptation by sending him on a voyage to Algiers.

yourself and the opportunities God will give you to do some good.

In keeping with that, Monsieur, I do not want to take literally something else you mentioned later, when you said that, unless you have some occupation to divert you, you will only get depressed. The way you have lived for the past twelve years or more that [you] have been in the Company convinces me enough that you want no other satisfaction than what is to be found in doing the Will of God. This satisfaction is entirely spiritual and far removed from imitating worldly people, who seek to satisfy themselves in pleasures of the senses, for that would be unworthy of a priest and a Missionary.

I would not dare to think that you are saying you would like to be a Superior. Alas! that is no way to be happy; those who have the duty groan under its weight because they do not feel strong enough to bear it and think they are incapable of guiding others. Otherwise, if someone were to presume the contrary, he would make his subjects groan because he would lack humility and the other graces necessary to be a consolation and good example to them.

You know, Monsieur, that God's gifts vary and He distributes them as He sees fit: one man is learned but is not suited to governing others; another is on the road to sanctity but is not apt for leadership. So, it is up to His Divine Providence to call us to the works for which He has given us some talent, and it is not our place to aspire to them. Our Lord, who had destined the Apostles to be the heads of all the Churches in the world, tells them that it is He who has chosen them.[2] Another time, seeing the rivalry among them for primacy, He gave them this beautiful precept: that the one who would wish to be first should be the servant of the others [3] to teach us that of ourselves we should tend only to submission. This is also what He taught us by His own example, since He came to serve, taking the form of a servant.

Now, the wretched man who goes against this rule and wants to

---

[2]Cf. Jn 15:16. (NAB)
[3]Cf. Mt 20:26-28. (NAB)

raise himself above others renounces the maxims of the Son of God; he takes another course and yields to pride, which is a source of disorders. If he attains that to which he aspires—if, unfortunately, he is made Superior through his own ambition—he does only harm and, being responsible for the souls under his care, is guilty of all the failings that arise because of his bad conduct. This causes even the best Superiors to tremble and makes them ask constantly to be relieved of the care of others. There are several such men in the Company. They are also the ones God blesses because this fear humbles them and makes them more conscientious in their duty. Our experience of these truths puts us very much on our guard against giving the principal responsibility for any office whatsoever to a person who has shown an inclination to having it.

Perhaps what I am saying to you is out of place since, in my opinion, these are not the kinds of duties you are requesting; if, however, you want only lesser ones, I think you have no shortage of these in Marseilles. There is plenty to be done within and outside the house for the salvation of the neighbor and, if you love to obey, you will find peace of mind in that, and the sanctification of your soul as well. So, Monsieur, please limit your desires and aspirations to that for now. I have a special tenderness for your heart, causing me to offer it frequently to Our Lord.

2582. - TO FIRMIN GET, SUPERIOR, IN MARSEILLES

Paris, May 10, 1658

Monsieur,

The grace of O[ur] L[ord] be with you forever!

Letter 2582. - Archives of the Mission, Paris, copy made from the original in the Hains Family Collection, Marseilles. This is one of the letters sold at auction by Xavier Charmoy (cf. no. 2505).

Nine or ten months ago you received 3150 livres for the ransom of three Basque slaves detained in Algiers. One of them, named Martisans de Celhay, was taken to the Levant and is in danger of not returning. For that reason his father sent word here to M. de Lafargue, who forwarded that sum to you, that he wants his son's share—which is 945 livres—to be given for safekeeping to M. Roman [1] in Marseilles, while awaiting some news of that poor slave. In line with that, Monsieur, I ask you to give the 945 livres to M. Roman and get a receipt from him for them.

It will be well for you to hold firm about no longer taking responsibility for the Saint-Victor novices, regardless of any pretense they may assume and no matter how insistent their Superiors and relatives may be with you. For, since God did not give you the grace on the first attempt to correct them—although you did everything on your part that could be done—I see no cause to hope you would succeed on a second try. What removes any hope of this for me is that we have no calling to work in collèges, except in the way you know, which is for secular priests; consequently, in no way do I feel that you should receive these monks.

If you have kept a copy of the short compilation of the acts of virtue you remarked in the late M. Coqueret,[2] please send it to me; but if you have not kept a summary of it in writing, do not bother to do a new one because I will have someone look for the one you sent me at the time.

I ask O[ur] L[ord] to shower on your soul and your family the

---

[1]A merchant.

[2]The "short compilation" Saint Vincent mentions here was published in L.D.C. Gueriteau, *Opuscules Biographiques. Vie de Jean Coqueret, Vie du Docteur André Duval, Vie de Robert Gueriteau*, ed. J. Depoin (Pontoise: Société historique du Vexin, 1901), pp. 12-21.

Jean Coqueret, Doctor of the Collège de Navarre, was head of the Collège des Grassins and Superior of the Discalced Carmelites of France. He was a friend of Saint Francis de Sales, André Duval, and of Saint Vincent with whom he had given a mission in Villepreux in 1618. Born in Pontoise (Val-d'Oise) in 1592, he died in Marseilles on October 7, 1655. Saint Vincent consulted him before introducing vows into the Company and invited him to the conferences on Jansenism given at Saint-Lazare.

graces of His Spirit. I am, in the love of O[ur] L[ord], Monsieur, your most humble servant.

VINCENT DEPAUL,
i.s.C.M.

2583. - TO EDME JOLLY, SUPERIOR, IN ROME

May 10, 1658

Since the Procurator General of Saint-Maur opposed the execution of our Bulls for Saint-Méen, it has not yet been done.[1] I have always feared this setback but am, nevertheless, resigned to whatever God will be pleased to ordain. I think this opposition is groundless because those good reformed monks have no right to enter any house of Saint Benedict if they have not been called there, in accord with the Bull of their establishment. No matter if they say that, since they are the children of that saint, they can reclaim his property when someone wants to alienate it from his Order, for all church property belongs to the Church; and if Saint Benedict were still alive—he who was a child of the Church—he would not deny this truth. In addition, he would declare that the property of his

---

Letter 2583. - Reg. 2, p. 240.

[1]In 1645 the Bishop of Saint-Malo gave the Priests of the Mission permanent direction of the seminary he had just established in Saint-Méen Abbey, near Boursel (Côtes-du-Nord). He guaranteed them a tenth of the yearly annuity of five hundred livres and added to the establishment the revenue of the abbey, on condition—among other things—that there be five Missionaries: three for the seminary and two for the missions; that for two or three years they would teach gratis twelve young seminarians; and that they would give a pension to the monks of the abbey until the last one died (cf. vol. III, no. 829, n. 11). The Benedictines of Saint-Maur had looked askance on the transformation of Saint-Méen Abbey into a seminary and instituted legal proceedings that became heated and protracted (cf. vol. III, no. 832, n. 8).

Saint Vincent is referring here to the latest stumbling block. The reason alleged was that in his petition Edme Jolly had "not mentioned the monastic offices." He was obliged to appear before the Cardinal Datary with the Procurator General of Saint-Maur, where arguments were heard on both sides. The report was read to the Pope, who, on April 3, despite the opposition, ordered the Bulls to be sent. The text is published in *Acta apostolica in gratiam Congregationis Missionis* (Paris: Georges Chamerot, 1876), pp. 18-23, Arch. Nat. S 6711, and in vol. XIII, no. 117. This letter informs us that fresh difficulties had arisen.

Order was given to it by the Church because of the help the latter received from him at the time, through the seminaries of priests he opened to fill benefices in a worthy manner.

Now, they no longer do this, and since the Church has ordered Bishops to open seminaries, and Kings to unite benefices and other revenues to them, is it not just for the same Church to use a modest part of that property, by authority of the Prince and the Prelate and with the consent of the legitimate owners, to make up for what the Benedictines did in the past but no longer do now? We will be waiting patiently for the outcome of this affair.

2584. - TO THE MEMBERS OF THE CONGREGATION OF THE MISSION

[May 1658]

Vincent Depaul, Superior General of the Congregation of the Mission, to our dear brothers in Jesus Christ,[1] the priests, seminarians, and lay coadjutors of the same Congregation, greetings in Our Lord.[2]

Here at last, my very dear brothers, are the Common Rules or Constitutions of our Congregation, which you have so ardently desired and so long awaited.[3] True, almost thirty-three years have

---

Letter 2584. - Archives of the Mission, Paris, *Regulae seu Constitutiones communes Congregationis Missionis* (Paris, 1658), original in Latin. This letter forms the preface of the document. Coste printed both the Latin text and a French translation; Saint Vincent used the latter for the French edition of the Rules prepared that year for the coadjutor Brothers. The editors have translated the French text here, noting any significant differences from the Latin.

[1]The Latin has: "in Christ."

[2]Latin text: "in the Lord."

[3]The little book of *Common Rules* that Saint Vincent presented to his Missionaries in 1658 was a second edition. The first, completed in 1655, contained so many printing errors that he ordered it to be destroyed (cf. vol. V, no. 1851). He went over the text with Antoine Portail and sought the advice of theologians and renowned canonists, many of whom were in prominent positions in Rome itself (cf. vol. V, no. 2053; vol. VI, nos. 2289, 2299, 2315, 2365, 2402, and 2446). Finally, on May 17, 1658, after giving one of his most beautiful conferences (cf. vol.

elapsed since our Congregation was instituted, without our having given them to you in printed form; but we acted this way both to imitate Our Savior Jesus Christ,[4] who began by doing rather than by teaching, and to avoid several inconveniences that might have arisen[5] from a too hasty publication of the same Rules or Constitutions, whose use and practice might later have seemed perhaps either too difficult or less suitable. Now, our delay and line of action in this have safeguarded us, by the grace of God, from all these inconveniences[6] and have even brought it about that the Congregation gradually and gently practiced them before they were published. And, in fact, you will note nothing in them that you have not already practiced for a long time, even to our very deep consolation and the mutual edification of all of you.

So then, my very dear brothers, receive them with the same affection with which we give them to you. Consider them, not as a product of the human spirit, but rather as something inspired by God,[7] from whom proceeds all good and without whom we are incapable of thinking anything good of ourselves as coming from ourselves. For what will you find in these Rules that does not serve to inspire and spur you on to avoid vices, to acquire virtues, and to practice the evangelical maxims?

That is the reason why we have done our utmost to try to derive all of them from the Spirit of Jesus Christ and to draw them from the actions of His life,[8] as may easily be seen. We felt that persons

---

XII, no. 180), he had the joy of distributing personally to his Missionaries the first copies. The corrections to the 1655 edition, approved by the Archbishop of Paris, were of minor importance. Saint Vincent was able to write to Cardinal de Retz on July 15, 1659: "We did not alter the essentials of the Rules nor anything of consequence" (cf. vol. VIII, no. 2907). The 1655 version has survived in manuscript form in what is known as the CODEX SARZANA, preserved in the Archives of the Congregation of the Mission, Curia Generalitia, Rome, and published in *Vincentiana* (4-5), 1991, pp. 303-406.

[4]Latin text: "Christ our Savior."

[5]Latin text: "that doubtless might have arisen."

[6]Latin text: "dangers."

[7]Latin text: "emanating from the Divine Spirit."

[8]Latin text: "from the Spirit of Jesus Christ and the actions of His life."

called to continue the mission of the same Savior [9] (which consists chiefly in evangelizing the poor) must share His sentiments and maxims,[10] be filled with His same Spirit, and walk in His footsteps.

That is why, my very dear brothers, we ask and entreat you by the very heart of this same Savior Jesus Christ to do your utmost to observe these Rules exactly,[11] holding for certain that if you keep them they will keep you and will lead you assuredly to the long-desired goal, that is, to heavenly bliss. Amen.

2585. - TO N.

May 13, 1658

Saint Vincent sings the praises of Nicolas Senaux.

2586. - *EMERAND BAJOUE [1] TO SAINT VINCENT*

Fontaine,[2] 1658

God, who blessed the previous missions, seems to be increasing His graces in this one, for the illicit unions that had endured for twenty-five years have been dissolved; all lawsuits have been terminated; and a very large number of persons from this area and from the environs, who made

---

[9]Latin text: "of Christ Himself."

[10]Latin text: "must share the sentiments and maxims of the same Christ."

[11]Latin text: "As well as this, Brothers, we therefore ask and entreat you in the Lord Jesus to do your utmost to observe these same Rules exactly."

Letter 2585. - Collet, *op. cit.*, vol. II, p. 197.

Letter 2586. - Abelly, *op. cit.*, bk. II, chap. I, sect. II, §5, p. 40.

[1]Emerand Bajoue, born in Céaux (Vienne), entered the Congregation of the Mission as a priest on December 1, 1640, at thirty-one years of age, and took his vows on April 24, 1657, in the presence of Antoine Portail. He was Superior in La Rose (1649-52) and Notre-Dame de Lorm (1652-54). Bajoue died on February 28, 1671.

[2]A small commune in the canton of Ay (Marne).

ill use of the sacraments for twenty, thirty, and even thirty-five years, have acknowledged and detested their crimes. The inhabitants of this locality are calling and assembling their relatives from the most far-flung places to come and share the fruits of the mission, and the nobles are coming from seven, ten, and fourteen leagues away from around Rethel.

2587. - TO EDMUND BARRY,[1] SUPERIOR, IN NOTRE-DAME DE LORM

Paris, May 15, 1658

Monsieur,

The grace of O[ur] L[ord] be with you forever!

I received your letter of April 20. In the name of O[ur] L[ord], please excuse us for not having yet sent the help you await and for not even being able to send you any for some time. Our priests were scarcely back from their missions when we were obliged to send them out on others, some in the Troyes diocese, others in the Châlons diocese, and the men who have been in the Reims diocese for six or seven months are continuing. There is no way they will be back before the month of July, and we cannot send you anyone until they return.

The inhabitants of Brial and Falguières are right to complain that they do not see you until it is time to collect the revenue. If you have not already done so, please take the opportunity to speak to

---

Letter 2587. - The original signed letter was made available to Coste by Abbé Colombel, Pastor of Saint-Jean-Baptiste-de-Grenelle parish in the Paris diocese. Its present location is unknown.

[1]Edmund Barry, born in the Cloyne diocese (Ireland) on June 24, 1613, was ordained a priest in Cahors in 1639 and admitted into the Congregation of the Mission on July 21, 1641. He took his vows at Saint-Lazare a few days before his departure for Ireland in 1646, returning to France in 1652, after Limerick had been captured by Cromwell's army. He was then placed in Richelieu (1652-53) and Montauban (1653-80). While in Montauban, he directed the seminary and was Superior there (1657-64, 1675-80). Barry was also a Doctor of Theology and was still alive on May 31, 1680, as two legal documents show. He died later that year.

the Bishop of Montauban [2] about releasing the Company from this responsibility in one way or another.

I praise God that your seminary is growing and the Bishop has decided to transfer it to Montauban. May God, in His infinite goodness, bless this plan and the work this worthy Prelate is doing for the conversion of heretics!

We have no news here.

I send greetings to your little family, and I am, in O[ur] L[ord], Monsieur, your most humble servant.

VINCENT DEPAUL,
i.s.C.M.

At the bottom of the first page: Monsieur Barry

2588. - TO FIRMIN GET, SUPERIOR, IN MARSEILLES

Paris, May 17, 1658

Monsieur,

The grace of O[ur] L[ord] be with you forever!

I received your letter of May 7. God willing, we will pay your bills of exchange for up to 25,000 livres, if you find as much

---

[2]Pierre de Bertier, Doctor of the Sorbonne, former Canon and Archdeacon of Toulouse, Coadjutor of Bishop Anne de Murviel and then his successor (1652). In 1636 he was consecrated Bishop *in partibus* of Utica. He had to tolerate a great deal from the elderly Bishop of Montauban and several times was on the point of resigning. Some time before the Prelate's death, he wrote to Mazarin: "His health is so good and his humor so bad that I cannot hope for his succession nor even his favor. Therefore, Excellency, not only am I unemployed in my ministry and deprived of sufficient revenues for my position, I am, in addition, constantly persecuted and believed guilty for no reason." (Cf. Arch. Nat., KK 1217, p. 207.) De Bertier was Bishop of Montauban until 1674.

Letter 2588. - Archives of the Mission, Paris, copy made from the original in the Hains Family Collection, Marseilles. This is one of the letters sold at auction by Xavier Charmoy (cf. no. 2505).

without having to pay for the exchange and have received the last ones before giving your bills.

I sent the Duchesse d'Aiguillon the letter from the Administrators and will have delivered to the Duc de Richelieu the one they are writing to him. He is in the country and will spend the whole summer there. I will take the honor of writing to him at the same time about the case of the ship from Algiers, which is being heard before him and for which the Turks are trying to put the blame on the Consul. My age and infirmities prevent me from taking action in person, as I would really like to do, in this affair and that of the hospital. May God Himself be pleased to put His own good hand to it!

I am, on the one hand, quite worried about M. Parisy's illness, and I pray that O[ur] L[ord] will see fit to restore him to health. On the other hand, however, I am very consoled to see that M. de la Fosse has made up his mind not to depart until the former has recovered, so as not to leave you on your own, unable to do everything. I embrace both of them with all the extent of the tenderness of my heart, and you along with them. I am, in the love of O[ur] L[ord], Monsieur, your most humble servant.

VINCENT DEPAUL,
i.s.C.M.

Please let me know if you are taking action against Rappiot and are doing something to have the ship with those adventurers returned in order to free M. Barreau.

Enclosed is a passport for a Jewish merchant from Tunis, which M. Le Vacher urged us to obtain. Now, for that Jewish man to be able to use it, you would have to get the approval of the Admiral of France attached to it and have it registered in the Admiralty of Marseilles. However, since it is only for one year, I do not know if it is worth the trouble and expense involved. We had requested it for twenty years, but they were willing to grant it for only one. Since

M. de Vendôme [1] is in Paris, we are keeping the passport here to try to get the approval attached.

2589. - *EMERAND BAJOUE TO SAINT VINCENT*

Ay,[1] 1658

Upon our arrival here, some of the leading citizens tried to close the gates on us, having prepared the people poorly for what we were going to do. However, after we had practiced patience for a few days, God, who had sent us to this place by order of our Superiors, so changed hearts that no mission ever began so well. They were very exact in their confessions, showing all the signs of true contrition; they are now making restitution; they go down on their knees to ask pardon of one another; they pray morning and evening and show that they are determined to turn their lives around and to lead truly Christian ones; and they cannot get their fill of the Word of God. The minister who was staying here has left town, and the small number of heretics in this place—poor, very ignorant vine-dressers—never miss any of our sermons.

2590. - *JACQUES-BÉNIGNE BOSSUET TO SAINT VINCENT*

Metz, May 23, 1658

I cannot let these dear Missionaries depart without expressing to you

---

[1]César de Bourbon, Duc de Vendôme, the illegitimate son of Henry IV and Gabrielle d'Estrées, was born at the Château de Coucy. He married Françoise de Lorraine, daughter of the Duc de Mercoeur, and died in Paris on October 22, 1665. The Duke was involved in the troubles during the regency of Louis XIII, fought against Richelieu's political policies, and under him was jailed and exiled. He accepted the politics of Mazarin, who appointed him Minister of Navigation in 1650 and lavished many favors on him. His eldest son married Laura Mancini, the Cardinal's niece.

Letter 2589. - Abelly, *op. cit.*, bk. II, chap. I, sect. II, §5, p. 40.

[1]Principal town of a canton in Marne.

Letter 2590. - Bossuet, *op. cit.*, vol. I, letter 11, p. 26.

the universal regret and marvelous edification they are leaving behind. It is such, Monsieur, that you have every reason in the world to rejoice in Our Lord about it. I would pour out my heart with joy on that point, were it not that the effects go beyond all my words. Nothing better organized, more apostolic, or more exemplary has ever been seen than this mission.

What could I not tell you about each man, especially the leader [1] *and the others who preached the Gospel to us in such a holy, Christian way, if I did not think that you have been informed about them from elsewhere through more important testimonies and through your knowledge of them, added to the fact that I am not sure how much their modesty might suffer from the praises? They have stolen all hearts here, and now they return to you, tired and worn out in body, but rich in spirit from the spoils they have snatched from hell and from the fruits of penance God has produced through their ministry.*

So, Monsieur, welcome them with blessings and thanksgiving, and please be so kind as to thank them together with me for the honor they were willing to do me of sharing their company and part of their work with me.[2] *I thank you yourself as well and entreat you to pray that, having once been united with such holy priests, I may remain so eternally by truly taking on their spirit and profiting by their good example.*

By means of them God has been pleased to establish here a company closely modeled on yours,[3] *since God in His goodness allowed the Rules for it to be found among the papers of that excellent servant of God, M. Blampignon. It is looking forward to the honor of having you as Superior, since we have been led to hope for the favor of being associated with that of Saint-Lazare and that you and those priests will approve this. I have been given the responsibility of asking this of you, Monsieur, and I do so with all my heart. May God in His mercy give all of us perseverance in the things that have been so well established through the charity of those priests! I ask you to kindly give me a share in your Sacrifices and to believe that I am, etc.*

---

[1]Louis de Chandenier, Abbé de Tournus.

[2]Bossuet had participated actively in the mission; he preached at the church of the citadel and taught catechism there twice a week; he also preached some sermons at the Cathedral.

[3]The Tuesday Conferences.

2591. - TO ANTOINE DURAND, SUPERIOR, IN AGDE

[Around May 1658] [1]

Prayer is a great book for a preacher: from it you will draw the divine truths of the Eternal Word, who is their source, and you in turn will pour them forth on the people. It is to be hoped that all Missionaries may have a great love for this virtue, for without its help they will do little or nothing useful, but with its help it is certain that they will touch hearts. I ask God to give us the spirit of prayer.

Do not be surprised nor frightened if you have a bad year—or several. God has riches in abundance; until now, you have lacked nothing; why are you fearful for the future? Does He not take care to feed the birds, who neither sow nor reap? How much more will He have the goodness to provide for His servants! [2] You would like to see all your provisions before you to be sure of having everything you want—I mean, according to nature because I think that, according to the spirit, you are glad to have an opportunity to entrust yourself to God alone and, like a truly poor man, to depend on the generosity of such a rich man. May God have mercy on the poor people, who are greatly to be pitied in this time of want because they do not know how to make use of it, nor do they seek first the kingdom of God and His justice to make themselves worthy of having the essential things in life given to them besides! [3]

You ask me how you should act toward the friars.[4] You should try to be of service to them and show them, if need be, that you have this attitude. Go to see them sometimes, never take sides against them, do not get involved in their affairs except to defend

---

Letter 2591. - Reg. 2, p. 140. Despite some differences of expression, it would appear that the passage from the letter given by Abelly (cf. *op. cit.*, bk. III, chap. XIII, sect. 1, p. 214) is an excerpt from this one.

[1] A detail—the illness of Julien Dolivet—allows us to give an approximate date to this letter; no. 2605, of June 14, 1658, informs us that he is well on the way to recovery.

[2] Cf. Lk 12:24. (NAB)

[3] Cf. Mt 6:33. (NAB)

[4] There was a convent of Franciscan Friars in Agde.

them in charity, speak well of them, say nothing in the pulpit or in private conversations to offend them, even though they may not treat you in kind. That is what I would like all of us to do because they are religious, living in a state of perfection, so we should honor and serve them.

Your last letter grieved me deeply by informing me of the serious illness of good M. Dolivet, making me fearful that God might take him from the Company because of my sins. If we should suffer this loss, we will really have to conform ourselves to the good pleasure of God and kiss His hand that strikes us; but, if His Divine Goodness is pleased to preserve him for us, we will also bless Him eternally for it, and I will experience one of the greatest joys I can receive. Thank you, Monsieur, for doing everything possible for this. You can well imagine how heartily we join our prayers to your care, that God may be pleased to restore him to health because of the good use he has made of it and can still make of it for the honor and service of Our Lord and the edification of souls. If he is still alive, Monsieur, please embrace him for me and express to him my present sorrow and the consolation I await of his precious recovery. We recommended him this morning to the prayers of the community and will continue to do so until you have assured us of his convalescence.

2592. - TO GUILLAUME DESDAMES, IN WARSAW

Paris, May 24, 1658

Monsieur,

The grace of O[ur] L[ord] be with you forever!

Although your letter of March 17 is dated a long time ago, and

---

Letter 2592. - Archives of the Mission, Krakow, original signed letter.

I am very busy today, I still cannot prevent myself from telling you that I received it, that it is very precious to me, and that it is a great joy for me to have learned from you of the good health and union of the family. I thank God, Monsieur, that things are as you tell me. I thank Him particularly for the strength of mind He gives you amid the great disturbances in the kingdom, which have not yet been able to shake your courage. I am so filled with consolation at this that I have to pour it forth often into the hearts of the Company by edifying them with the abandonment and trust you exhibit with regard to the good pleasure of God. Having tried you until now by many losses and sufferings, He has disposed you to accept fresh ones with the same patience and resignation. I think that everyone is moved by your example and is determined to suffer for God and serve Him with the same constancy with which you have served Him for so long.

M. Ozenne informed me that he was going to Krakow with M. Duperroy. That makes me anxious about you, knowing that in their absence you will have the whole burden of the parish and business affairs. God grant that the new troubles with which you have been threatened may not add new crosses to your work! We constantly ask His Divine Goodness to give peace to the entire kingdom or to bless the King's armies and the plans of the Queen.

Please take the best possible care of your health, Monsieur, and give me news of you frequently, especially until the return of M. Ozenne, who perhaps may not be able to send me any during his journey to Krakow.

We have no news here worth writing you, busy as I am right now. The Company is very well everywhere, thank God. I am, in Him, Monsieur, your most humble servant.

VINCENT DEPAUL,
i.s.C.M.

Addressed: Monsieur Desdames, Priest of the Mission, in Warsaw

2593. - TO FIRMIN GET, SUPERIOR, IN MARSEILLES

Paris, May 24, 1658

Monsieur,

The grace of O[ur] L[ord] be with you forever!

I received your letter of May 14. We will have a meeting here in this house the day after tomorrow, God willing, to see what we have to do about the Algiers business. Two very intelligent, experienced men with sound judgment will be there, so we will see if the boat being prepared in Marseilles to go to Algiers can be useful for carrying out what will be decided. Meanwhile, I am waiting to hear if you have seen Chevalier Paul, what he told you, and what we can expect from him for the projected undertaking. We have letters from the King and the Cardinal [1] for this purpose but, before sending them there, I would be consoled to know his plans.

I felt sure you would have trouble finding such large sums there as the ones we have to pay; we will see M. Simonnet.

I have nothing to say about the resignation of the Bishop of Marseilles, except that I ask O[ur] L[ord] not to allow the diocese to suffer any loss in this change.[2]

We received fifty-six livres for Denis Dubois, a convict on the *Capitaine*. I am writing to tell M. Huguier to give them to him, and I ask you to credit him for them, as we will do for you.

I am so busy that I can add nothing else just now, except that God has chosen to take to Himself M. Delville, a priest of our Company, who died in Arras. I am told that his zeal consumed him

---

Letter 2593. - Archives of the Mission, Paris, copy made from the original in the Hains Family Collection, Marseilles. This is one of the letters sold at auction by Xavier Charmoy (cf. no. 2505).

[1]Cardinal Mazarin.

[2]Étienne du Puget was Bishop of Marseilles until his death on January 11, 1668.

there through his excessive work. I recommend his soul to your prayers, and the preservation of your health to your own care.[3]

I am, in His love, Monsieur, your most humble servant.

VINCENT DEPAUL,
i.s.C.M.

2594. - TO CHARLES OZENNE, SUPERIOR, IN WARSAW

Paris, May 24, 1658

Monsieur,

The grace of O[ur] L[ord] be with you forever!

I received two letters from you, one undated and the other from April 21. You did well to separate Sister Françoise [1] from the other Sisters, and you will also do well to try other remedies if that one does not suffice to restore her peace of mind and to reunite them. The one you suggest, namely, to send another Sister, can be done in a while but is difficult just now when the situation is unclear.

I admire the benefits M. Falibowski bestows on you and his efforts to establish the Company in Krakow. I thank God a thousand

---

[3]In a note preserved in the Archives of the Mission, Sister Radegonde Lenfantin claimed that Guillaume Delville had left the Congregation before his death (1658). This was not the case; proofs of his continued membership are seen in this letter and the following one and in the conference Saint Vincent held on May 24 at Saint-Lazare concerning his virtues.

We have knowledge of this conference only from its inclusion on one of the two lists in the Archives of the Mission of conferences given at Saint-Lazare: one, compiled by René Alméras, the Assistant Superior of the house, covers 1656-60; the second, written by Jean Gicquel, the Sub-assistant Superior, includes the last ten years of Saint Vincent's life. (Cf. vol. XII, Appendix 2.)

Letter 2594. - Archives of the Mission, Krakow, original signed letter.

[1]Françoise Douelle was the youngest of the three Sisters sent to Poland in September 1652 (the others were Marguerite Moreau, the Sister Servant, and Madeleine Drugeon). After overcoming some difficulties, she adapted herself so well that she became known by her Polish name *Duelska* (cf. *La Compagnie des Filles de la Charité aux Origines. Documents (1617-60)*, ed. by Sister Élisabeth Charpy [Tours: Mame, 1989], Doc. 556, no. 1).

times for the blessing He gives to his efforts, and I ask His Divine Goodness to carry this plan to completion, if it is for His glory. We will prepare a few young priests to send you, when you let me know the proper time and see that it will be safe for them to travel and stay there, as a result of either a peace accord or the success of the King's army. We will continue to pray for both and for the preservation of Their Majesties. Thank you for the news you give me about this.

M. Buffier delivered your letters to me. I am taking the honor of replying to the ones from Madame de Villers and Mademoiselle Cornuty, whose father died recently.

I am very busy today so I have to cut this letter short.

God has chosen to take to Himself M. Delville, a priest of the Company, who was working in and around Arras. It is felt that his zeal hastened his death. I recommend his soul to your prayers.

I am always, in the love of O[ur] L[ord], Monsieur, your most humble servant.

VINCENT DEPAUL,
i.s.C.M.

Addressed: Monsieur Ozenne, Superior of the Priests of the Mission of Warsaw, in Warsaw

2595. - TO PIERRE DE BEAUMONT,[1] SUPERIOR, IN RICHELIEU

May 26, 1658

I laud your prudence regarding the person who could not decide

Letter 2595. - Archives of the Brothers of St. John of God, St-Barthélemy (France), original signed letter. The postscript is in the Saint's handwriting. This letter is also found in Reg. 2, p. 187, and p. 52, but the latter is less complete and has many variations.

[1]Pierre de Beaumont, born in Puiseaux (Loiret) on February 24, 1617, entered the Congregation of the Mission on February 23, 1641, took his vows on October 4, 1643, and was ordained

to come to Paris and who refused to go to Le Mans.[2] You are afraid he may leave the Company if we pressure him to change his place of residence. You say he is a capable, good worker [with a talent for all our functions. My reply to that, Monsieur, is that I would really like to keep him],[3] but also, Monsieur, it certainly is not advisable to leave him in Richelieu because he so desires, in the proximate occasion of offending God, of being the cause of others offending Him, and in danger of giving scandal. It is better for a man to go than for us to keep him in this perilous situation, for we must run to remedy those things as to a fire.

The Company loses nothing but rather gains by losing a person who is dissolute and unwilling to leave. Furthermore, I see no better means to save that person than to be firm with him, since the latitude that has been given him is not making him any better. If disobedience reigns among us who have promised to imitate Our Lord in His virtues and works, what can be expected from that except results that are adverse and harmful to the Church?

If, however, he promises you not to enter any house in the town again, Monsieur, I consent to your keeping him in your house; otherwise, please give him my letter, in which I have asked him to come here when he has rested for two weeks after his return from the mission. If he comes, he will be welcome; if not, *in nomine Domini,* we will have reason to be grieved by his leaving, on the one hand, and to be consoled, on the other, for having done all we could within reason to maintain him in the place and state to which God has called him.

I ask you not to waste time at the house where the Sisters are staying; that is an alms you give to the poor they are nursing. Please

---

a priest in March 1644. He was imprisoned as a result of the lawsuit over the establishment of the Saint-Méen house. De Beaumont became Director of the Internal Seminary in Richelieu, and was twice Superior of that house (1656-60, 1661-62).

[2]In his note Coste conjectures that this may be François-Ignace Liébe; however, the biographical sketch in vol. IV, no. 1613, n. 2, states that Liébe had left the Company in 1657.

[3]The words in brackets were taken from p. 52 of the register. On page 187, the copyist was content with writing "capable, etc."

tell them not to worry about this but to do their little duty well. Encourage them to mutual support and union and the practice of virtue; help them to bear with their little sufferings and treat them a little more gently so that they will have all the confidence in you they should have.

2596. - *A PRIEST OF THE MISSION TO SAINT VINCENT*

Ludes,[1] 1658

Everything is proceeding as you desire; that says it all. One result we have had is that the finishing touches were put on the church building—which would never have been done without the mission. Cabarets are forbidden, as are night meetings. There is no more cursing, and the Most Holy Name of God is used only with the greatest respect. People go into homes and kneel down to ask pardon of those they have offended.

2597. - TO FIRMIN GET, SUPERIOR, IN MARSEILLES

Paris, May 31, 1658

Monsieur,

The grace of O[ur] L[ord] be with you forever!

I thank God that M. de la Fosse has left and that you are completely freed of the Saint-Victor novices.

I showed M. de Verthamon [1] and M. de Lamoignon, two of the most intelligent men in Paris, what you informed me about the Algiers business in your letter of May 21. They think that, whether

---

Letter 2596. - Abelly, *op. cit.*, bk. II, chap. I, sect. II, §5, p. 39.

[1]A locality in the district of Reims (Marne).

Letter 2597. - Archives of the Mission, Paris, photograph of the original signed letter.

[1]François Verthamon, Master of Requests.

or not Chevalier Paul goes to Algiers, it will be a good idea to send a man there to handle the arrangements for the Consul[2] and his return and to make sure that the money is used only to pay off his creditors and not those of M. Rappiot or anyone else.

I also feel that M. Huguier and Brother Duchesne are the most suitable persons we could choose for this purpose. I am well aware that they do not possess all the necessary qualities, but where will we find someone who does? They can set sail from Leghorn, make the crossing, then stay in Algiers, as if they were going there to ransom some slaves. Under this pretext—which, however, will be the truth, since they will be bringing some money we will give them to ransom three or four of them—they can handle the rest discreetly, or at least get an inkling of what can be hoped for and give us the information we will need. We will agree among ourselves here how to do all that; I will be able to write you more and speak about it another time, as also about remitting the money. Meanwhile, I am waiting to hear what Chevalier Paul will have to say to you. People here think that he, and no other, will be the one who will command the navy.

Thank you for having paid M. Roman the 945 livres earmarked for the ransom of Martisans de Celhay. I told the person here who is representing those Basque slaves that, if he wants you to give the rest of the 3150 livres to the same merchant, I will ask you to do so. He has not yet made a decision on this.

We received 25 livres here for a convict in Toulon named Traverse, and 36 livres for André Le Sueur. I ask M. Huguier to give them to them.

The Lord has been pleased to see to it that our Rules are finally ready to be given to the Company. We have added nothing new in them that has not already been practiced by it. We have had them printed, and I have distributed them here. We will send you a few

---

[2]Jean Barreau.

copies at the first opportunity, and I will tell you at that time why this has taken us so long.

Meanwhile, I am, in O[ur] L[ord], your most humble servant.

VINCENT DEPAUL,
i.s.C.M.

2598. - TO CHARLES OZENNE, SUPERIOR, IN WARSAW

Paris, June 2, 1658

Monsieur,

The grace of O[ur] L[ord] be with you forever!

Since M. Buffier is returning to Poland, I have asked him to be responsible for a little packet I am sending you. It contains an authentic copy of Our Holy Father's Brief on the confirmation of our vows,[1] six copies of another Brief for the indulgence granted in favor of our missions, four copies of our printed Rules, with an accompanying memo, and a report from Madagascar.

When you distribute our Rules to the priests who are with you, you should recommend that they take good care of them and not let them go astray, since they are not something that should fall into the hands of persons outside the Company. I am writing to tell all the Superiors to write down the names of those to whom they distribute them and to send the list to Saint-Lazare so that Missionaries who come here from other houses may not ask for another copy, and we will know what members of the Company have had them. If after receiving one, someone should lose it and ask for another, his Superior should tell him he will write to us to get another and to see if it is advisable to give other copies to all those who lose them.

Letter 2598. - Archives of the Mission, Krakow, original signed letter.

[1]The Brief *Ex commissa nobis* of September 22, 1655 (cf. vol. XIII, no. 113).

I am also sending back to you a letter Mademoiselle Cornuty had sent me for her father, who has died, so that you might return it to her.

I am, in O[ur] L[ord], Monsieur, your most humble servant.

VINCENT DEPAUL,
i.s.C.M.

Addressed: Monsieur Ozenne, Superior of the Priests of the Mission, in Warsaw

2599. - TO LOUIS RIVET, SUPERIOR, IN SAINTES

June 3, 1658

Monsieur,

The grace of O[ur] L[ord] be with you forever!

It will be well for you to keep an eye on M. Fleury to see that he does not work too hard at prayer or study because, being choleric by nature, he might easily give himself headaches. Recommend to him that he go at it gently and not strain himself. Encourage him in his difficulties, which everyone has in one form or another—at least those who are trying to serve and follow Jesus Christ. That is the narrow, rough path that leads to life.[1] We must not let difficulties prevent us from taking it. It is wise to be on the watch that no one who should be edifying him does the contrary, for the biggest thing that discourages newcomers who desire to work at virtue is to see that the oldest members do not give them sufficient example in this.

Letter 2599. - Avignon manuscript.

[1]Cf. Lk 13:24. (NAB)

I will have our printed Rules sent to you by the first public carrier so that everyone may be inspired to observe them; all of us will be sanctified in this, especially since they contain what Our Lord did and what He wants us to do.

2600. - TO JACQUES CHIROYE,[1] SUPERIOR, IN LUÇON

June 5, 1658

I received the foundation contract from M. Pignay,[2] for whom I have great respect because he is so good to us, and I have a similar gratitude for his benefits, which continue to increase. I cannot express to you my sentiments concerning this nor the ardent desire God gives me to please and obey this servant of His, who gives your little family the means of rendering some small service to the poor. I ask Our Lord to be Himself his thanks and reward for it.

You tell me that he gave you twenty-five *boisselées* [3] of tax-free land, which he acquired for eleven hundred livres; that you received eighteen hundred livres from him in silver; that you are to receive another thirteen hundred livres, which he gave you to be collected from his debtors; and that with these two sums you want to buy more land. I do not know what revenue can be drawn from these funds, but I see clearly that it will hardly take less than fifty écus income to pay the expenses of the foundation. Still, for the

---

Letter 2600. - Reg. 2, p. 118.

[1]Jacques Chiroye was born in Auppegard (Seine-Maritime) on March 14, 1614, and entered the Congregation of the Mission on June 25, 1638. He served as Superior in Luçon (1640-50, 1654-60, 1662-66) and Crécy (1660-62). He did not take his vows until March 9, 1660. Chiroye died on May 3, 1680.

[2]Nicolas Pignay, priest of the Rouen diocese and Doctor of the Sorbonne. In his will, dated August 10, 1671 (Arch. Nat., M 213, n. 8), he is mentioned as "Headmaster of the Collège de Justice . . . living at the Bons-Enfants."

[3]The amount of land required by a bushel *(boisselée)* of seed.

consolation of that good Doctor, I would have approved the contract, but without the right to dividends you accepted for these goods, acquired and given for your personal use during your lifetime, to become effective upon his death. That is something I cannot approve.

If he reserved the revenue for himself, fine; he should have done so; if not, I would still be ready to give our consent to this because it seems just to me. But as for you, Monsieur, who have given yourself to Our Lord to follow Him in His poverty and to serve Him in our Company, according to the vows you have taken in it, far from having any reason to use this money, you have several for not possessing anything of your own. If this were some property given you by a natural right of succession, you could in that case reserve to yourself the disposition of it, in accord with our Rule. You should, however, make it a matter of conscience to accept any other by way of a donation or for your private use and to give such an example to the Company because both you and I would cause an irreparable breach in it were this foundation made in the way you stipulated.

You will tell me, perhaps, that this condition regarding you is only in case of need; but what need will you have, Monsieur (you who want to live an apostolic life and are assured of always being supported from the common funds), of also having that for your personal use? Please do not even think of doing so, and I ask you not to settle any matter of importance again without having sought and received our advice on it beforehand, for I have remarked that you inform me of things only after they have been done. I am writing to tell M. Pignay my objection, and I am holding the contract until he lets me know if he wants me to return it to him.

2601. - TO A BISHOP

I ask God, Excellency, to form those two Missionaries according to His own heart and according to yours. I would like to be able to send you some others, but we have too few workers and a great number of works. Would to God, Excellency, that I might be part of this so as to spend my whole life, under obedience to you, working among your poor people. His Divine Goodness knows that I desire nothing more than that. Wherever I am, however, you will always have in me a servant as eager to obey you as any other you may have in this world.

2602. - TO FIRMIN GET, SUPERIOR, IN MARSEILLES

Paris, June 7, 1658

Monsieur,

The grace of O[ur] L[ord] be with you forever!

I was very consoled by your letter informing me of your Toulon journey and your negotiations with Commander Paul. I do not think you could have acted more discreetly or successfully than you did. I thank God, Monsieur, for the favor He allowed you to find in the heart of that valiant man and for his intention to go to Barbary to do the things you tell me. I pondered whether I should have taken the honor of writing to thank him for this, but I felt unworthy of finding words corresponding to the honor of his affection and the greatness of his courage. I plan simply to celebrate Holy Mass in

---

Letter 2601. - Abelly, *op. cit.*, second edition, second part, p. 77.

Letter 2602. - Archives of the Mission, Paris, copy made from the original in the Hains Family Collection, Marseilles. This is one of the letters sold at auction by Xavier Charmoy (cf. no. 2505). Henri Simard (*Saint Vincent de Paul et ses oeuvres à Marseille* [Lyons: E. Vitte, 1894], p. 151), who owned the letter after M. Hains, states that it is in the Saint's handwriting.

thanksgiving to God for the proofs he has given you of both of these, asking His Divine Goodness to preserve him for the welfare of the State and to bless his armies more and more.

I am waiting for you to let me know the decision those gentlemen in Marseilles have taken in response to the remonstrance you were supposed to make to them in his name. To my way of thinking, if they refuse to provide maintenance for the army for two months, I do not think it should be expected from the King because of the major siege by land and sea of the town of Dunkirk [1] and of another important place he is going to attack at the same time, so I am told. He is devoting not only his effort and presence to this, but I think he is putting all he can afford financially into it as well. Therefore, any proposal that might be made to him just now of funneling part of it into another project on which he does not really have his heart set would not be well received.

This being the case, Monsieur, I think that, while awaiting whatever God will be pleased to ordain regarding this projected undertaking, we should send someone to Algiers to negotiate with the Pasha and the Customs House about the Consul's [2] release, Rappiot's debts, and the ship for which they are trying to hold him responsible. That person must also try to make him acknowledge his just debts and actual creditors so that the money will not be misspent.

We discussed here whether to send M. Huguier, Brother

---

[1]One outgrowth of the Thirty Years' War (1618-48) was the ongoing friction between France and Spain, which continued to abet the French Frondeurs, notably Condé. England allied itself with France to break the Spanish hold on the Low Countries (Belgium and the Netherlands). The French-English allies, led by Maréchal Turenne, defeated the Spanish army of Don John of Austria and Condé at the battle of the Dunes (June 14, 1658); subsequently, the besieged city of Dunkirk, the last Spanish outpost in the Low Countries, surrendered (June 25). Among the agreements of the Treaty of the Pyrenees, signed November 7, 1659, England acquired Dunkirk, which in 1662 she sold to France; France reembraced Condé and reinstated him as a Maréchal of France; and Louis XIV became engaged to Maria Teresa, eldest daughter of Philip IV, King of Spain.

[2]Jean Barreau.

Duchesne, or a Brother we have here who is very intelligent and courageous.[3] We certainly think Brother Duchesne would do a good job of it, but we are afraid they would pay no attention to him and treat him contemptuously because he was once a slave there. As for the Brother from this house, he does not know the language, which is a great hindrance. So, that has brought us back to M. Huguier, who does not have these shortcomings but rather several good qualities to help make him more successful than the others in this negotiation. Still, M. Le Vacher[4] told us that, because he is a priest, the Turks might commit some avania against him. I find that hard to believe, however, because he will declare to them first of all who he is and what he is going to do—which is to ransom a few slaves, since we will, in fact, give him some money to do so. Therefore, I am proposing this journey to him in the letter I am writing him today to find out how he feels about it.

M. Le Vacher will leave for Marseilles in ten to twelve days, God willing, since it is inadvisable for people to see him around Paris once the collections have been made. He has worked very hard at them.

We sent thirty thousand livres to Messieurs Simonnet; I am awaiting their bill of exchange so that they may be obtained from M. Napollon in Marseilles. We have arranged for payment to be

---

[3]Probably Brother Jean-Armand Dubourdieu. According to the author of his biography (cf. *Notices*, vol. IV, p. 22), Saint Vincent intended to offer Dubourdieu the consulate of Algiers in 1658.

Jean-Armand Dubourdieu, born in Garos (Pyrénées-Atlantiques), entered the Congregation of the Mission in La Rose on November 8, 1644, at eighteen years of age, and took his vows on December 13, 1647. In 1658 Saint Vincent chose him for the position of Consul in Algiers, but circumstances delayed his departure until 1661. He set sail with Brother Louis Sicquard, who had been given him as chancellor, and Philippe Le Vacher, who was going to settle the affairs of Jean Barreau. The new Consul carried out his office with intelligent zeal. His correspondence testifies to his concern for the interests of religion and of France and how touched he was by the sad plight of the slaves, whose well-being was the object of his constant care. He returned to France in 1673 and died at Saint-Lazare on April 15, 1677. Edme Jolly announced his death and eulogized him in a circular letter to all the houses of the Company. Brother Dubourdieu's biography is published in vol. IV of *Notices*, pp. 21-24.

[4]Philippe Le Vacher.

made to you in French currency. In the event that you are unable to come to an agreement over the price of piastres, and so that they will be able to find other money, the bill will be payable only two weeks after sight. Enclosed is your own bill, which I am sending you.

I am worried about the place where you will keep this money; I am afraid it will not be safe in your house, since you live outside the city. The thought occurred to me that it might be well for you to have the Carmelite nuns keep it for you. There would be nothing to fear if you took your strongbox with the double lock there—I think you have one. Still, if you think the money is safe in your own house and in this strongbox, use your usual prudence about it. Ask M. Napollon not to mention that you have it, for fear lest news of it may reach Algiers.

I do not think you should accept just now the offer someone made you to deliver three hundred piastres to Algiers if you give them to him in Marseilles. Do not send the Consul anything else, unless the entire amount is sent to him and we know how he uses the money.

We received two écus here for two convicts: one for Nicolas Bonner and the other for Antoine Auroy. I ask M. Huguier to give them to them, for I think they are both in Toulon.

I am, in O[ur] L[ord], Monsieur, your most humble servant.

VINCENT DEPAUL,
i.s.C.M.

M. de Brienne told M. de Lamoignon—who reported it to me—that he placed in the secret orders he is sending to Commander Paul the order to go to Algiers. Enclosed is a letter the King is writing to him and another from the Cardinal.[5] Please take them or have them delivered by M. Huguier. The first way seems better to me, unless you think otherwise. Use your usual prudence in this.

---

[5]Jules Cardinal Mazarin.

2603. - TO PIERRE DE BEAUMONT, SUPERIOR, IN RICHELIEU

June 9, 1658

We should manifest deep gratitude to that good Canon from Poitiers who is offering to allow the Company to be established in his parish of Saint-Étienne.[1] I, for my part, am deeply grateful for his kindness in this and for the honor he does us. Please thank him on my behalf and on your own and tell him that one of our maxims is never to establish ourselves in a place unless we have been called there by those in whom that authority resides. Tell him also that we do not accept parishes in episcopal towns because it is not permissible for us to preach and hear confessions in them. This will not prevent us from being as indebted to that good Canon for his good will in our regard as if this were put into effect.

2604. - *SAINT LOUISE TO SAINT VINCENT*

This holy feast of Pentecost [June 9, 1658] [1]

Most Honored Father,

I remind Your Charity kindly to recall that the election of officers takes place during Pentecost week. I ask if it could be today,[2] *for fear lest you cannot come another day.*

The Act of Establishment states that the Superioress shall be elected every three years; until now, however, she seems to be in office for life. I

Letter 2603. - Reg. 2, p. 55.

[1]Saint-Étienne-la-Cigogne, a small commune of Deux-Sèvres.

Letter 2604. - Archives of the Motherhouse of the Daughters of Charity, original autograph letter.

[1]Date written on the back of the original by Brother Ducournau.

[2]Three officers were chosen on that day: Mathurine Guérin, Françoise-Paule Noret, and Jeanne Gressier.

Mathurine Guérin was born in Montcontour (Brittany), on April 16, 1631. Despite the opposition of her parents, she entered the Company of the Daughters of Charity on September 12, 1648. After her formation period, she was sent to Saint-Jean-de-Grèves parish and then to Liancourt. Recalled to the Motherhouse in 1652, she became Seminary Directress and Saint

think it would be most fitting, if Your Charity judged it appropriate, to begin to make this an elective office, provided this presents no danger because of the weakness and ambitions to which persons of lowly condition are inclined.

The Rule makes no provision for the continuation of the three officers; nevertheless, Most Honored Father, I think this would be essential because nearly three to four months go by before they assume their responsibilities. If Your Charity thinks this is a good idea, you could begin it this year, since it is impossible to find other Sisters because of the need to provide such a large number elsewhere.

May Our Lord in His goodness continue to realize His plans for the Company under your holy guidance for many years to come. May He also grant me the grace to be all my life, Most Honored Father, your most obedient daughter and very grateful servant.

L. DE MARILLAC

Addressed: *Monsieur Vincent*

Louise's secretary. In 1655 she was made Treasurer but was sent to the hospital in La Fère (Aisne) in 1659. Saint Vincent recalled her in May 1660 for the Belle-Isle Hospital. She served a first six-year term as Superioress General in 1667 and again (1676-82, 1685-91, 1694-97) and died at the Motherhouse on October 18, 1704. A long sketch of her life and virtues is written in *Circulaires des supérieurs généraux et des soeurs supérieures aux Filles de la Charité et Remarques ou Notices sur les Soeurs défuntes de la Communauté* (Paris: Adrien Le Clère, 1845), pp. 556-68.

Françoise-Paule Noret, born in Liancourt, entered the Daughters of Charity at the end of 1640 or the beginning of 1641. She spent the greater part of her life at the Motherhouse. In 1645 she went to Saint-Denis; during July-August 1646 she accompanied Saint Louise on her trip to Nantes. She signed the Act of Establishment of the Company of the Daughters of Charity on August 8, 1655. She was named Assistant of the Company in 1658.

Jeanne Gressier, born in Senlis (Oise), entered the Company of the Daughters of Charity around 1654. Although very young, she was named Procuratrix in 1655 and remained at the Motherhouse. She assisted Saint Louise on her deathbed (March 15, 1660) and wrote the details of her last moments. It was she to whom Saint Vincent confided the governance of the Company, while awaiting the naming of a new Superioress General in August 1660.

2605. - TO FIRMIN GET, SUPERIOR, IN MARSEILLES

Paris, June 14, 1658

Monsieur,

The grace of O[ur] L[ord] be with you forever!

M. Dolivet has been very ill in Agde. He would like to spend a month in the air of Marseilles to help him recuperate. Please welcome him and send him back when he recovers.

Like you, I think nothing is to be hoped for from the city of Marseilles in the matter of the Algiers project. We must await from Providence alone whatever God will be pleased to ordain in that regard. Please let me know exactly when M. Roman's boat will be leaving and whether another one is being made ready. I hope to tell you as soon as possible whom we have chosen to go to negotiate the Consul's [1] release. Perhaps we will fall back on M. Huguier. It would be a shame to lose the opportunity provided by M. Roman, upright man that he is. Because of that, I would like to entrust to him the money you still have for the ransom of two Basques, but the man who represents them here told us not to do so without his permission, for which we are waiting. The man we send to Algiers could bring the money with him and deliver it to the slaves themselves.

M. Delaforcade has two hundred livres to be paid in Tunis and added to the amount sent previously to Dominique de Lajus. I am telling him to take from it what we owe him for postage on the letters, and the one hundred livres he gave M. Le Vazeux in Annecy for us. I am also informing him that, when you receive the balance, you will send that sum of two hundred livres to M. Le Vacher in

---

Letter 2605. - Archives of the Mission, Paris, copy made from the original in the Hains Family Collection, Marseilles. This is one of the letters sold at auction by Xavier Charmoy (cf. no. 2505).

[1]Jean Barreau.

Tunis, which I ask you to do. We will reimburse you whatever you advance, or you can draw it on us.

What that Chevalier told you about the return of the two or three renegades from Algiers is unlikely. I approve your discretion in not lodging him in your house. I am, in O[ur] L[ord], Monsieur, your most humble servant.

VINCENT DEPAUL,
i.s.C.M.

I am sending you the second bill of exchange for thirty thousand livres, which we have paid M. Simonnet here to have it accepted, in the event that the first one, which I sent you last week, may not have been given to you. See about withdrawing payment of this bill in piastres or in another currency more advantageous to you and with less loss.

2606. - *SAINT LOUISE TO SAINT VINCENT*

Monday [June 1658] [1]

Most Honored Father,

The uncertainty as to whether the Queen will ask that Sister Marthe[2] *leave La Fère troubles me greatly, since I am not sure that Sister Manceau*[3] *can be the Sister Servant, although she has been in the Company for a*

Letter 2606. - Archives of the Motherhouse of the Daughters of Charity, original autograph letter.

[1]Date added on the back of the original by Brother Ducournau.

[2]Marie-Marthe Trumeau had been sent to Angers in March 1640; she returned to Paris in June 1647 after becoming dangerously ill in Angers. In 1648 she served the poor in Saint-Paul parish. In 1653 she was named Sister Servant in Nantes, where she remained for two years (cf. no. 1672). She was sent to La Fère on July 31, 1656, and from there to the establishment in Cahors in September 1658.

[3]Françoise Manceau, a native of Laumesfeld (Moselle), entered the Company of the Daughters of Charity around 1643 and was in Chars in 1650. In June 1658 she was sent to Calais, where she died in September, a victim of her devotion.

good fifteen years. This leads me to suggest, Most Honored Father, that we send a Sister to La Fère. If this can be done, the coach could pick up our Sister when it passes that way, or we could tell her to go wait for it in some nearby town. In this way, there would be five Sisters there. We have Sister Clémence[4] here; either she or that Sister from Lorraine who offered to return for Metz would be quite suitable as Sister Servant.

If the news I just heard is true, I wonder if it should prevent their journey. I await your permission to go to see you and to send to the parishes for the Sisters I proposed to you. I am, with all my heart, Most Honored Father, your most humble daughter and very grateful servant.

L. DE MARILLAC

Addressed: *Monsieur Vincent*

2607. - TO LOUIS DUPONT, SUPERIOR, IN TRÉGUIER

June 19, 1658

In the same letter in which you ask if you should accept two benefices being offered to you in your native place, you give us fresh indications of your attachment to the Company, saying that you plan to have it enjoy the fruits of those benefices some day. I thank you for this, especially since your intention is that God may be honored and the people assisted more by it. These are the results of your zeal, and they will not go unrewarded.

However, I must tell you in reply, Monsieur, that we should desire no other good for the Company nor any other works but those God is pleased to give it on His own initiative without us—I mean without our having sought after or procured them. If the local

[4]Clémence Ferré, a native of Champignière, near Nancy (Meurthe-et-Moselle), went to Angers in January 1640 and remained there until April 1644. She was then sent to Liancourt, and in 1657 to Chars.

Letter 2607. - Reg. 2, p. 192.

Bishop, in whom resides the authority to call us, had made this proposal, God's Will would then be clear enough for us. As for you, Monsieur, I think that, because you have given yourself to His Divine Goodness in the way you have done, you may neither receive nor retain benefices, especially those that have the responsibility for souls attached to them. You have taken Our Lord for your benefice and have renounced the goods of this earth to follow Him as a poor man and to serve Him in an apostolic life. Is that not a motive for great consolation to you who, having lacked none of the necessities of life until now nor any opportunity to use your own life in a holy manner, should hope that you will not lack them in the future either?

If you say you would not want to be a burden to the Company, you will not be; for the infirm are no burden to it, thank God. On the contrary, it is, in a certain sense, a blessing to have some. And if you were to convince yourself that your health would improve in your native place and you would have greater means to procure God's glory there than elsewhere, that would be a ruse of the evil spirit who, by showing you a seeming, uncertain good, would try to make you leave an actual, real one. By distancing you from the Spirit of Our Lord, he would try to make you enter once again, if possible, into the spirit of the world. I ask God, Monsieur, to preserve us from this misfortune and to strengthen us in our original dispositions to sacrifice ourselves in the state to which He has called us and in the practice of the humility, patience, and charity of Jesus Christ.

2608. - TO FIRMIN GET, SUPERIOR, IN MARSEILLES

Paris, June 21, 1658

Monsieur,

The grace of O[ur] L[ord] be with you forever!

I would have been very distressed about your latest ailment had I heard of its onset before hearing of its abatement, but God be praised that, in informing me of the former, you assure me that a bloodletting has halted its progress! Please take care of the little health you have.

You gave me very great pleasure by welcoming M. Pastour into your house. He is a good servant of God, who is very kind to the Company. I ask you not only to allow him to stay in your house as long as he wishes to remain there, but also to take good care of him and render him all the services and marks of affection and gratitude we owe him. We should do so, not only for his personal merit but also in consideration of the Bishop of Saint-Flour,[1] to whom he belongs.

We persist in our decision to send someone to Algiers before sending any money there and before M. Le Vacher returns there. We also maintain our choice of M. Huguier for that purpose. I would like him to be ready to go there on M. Roman's boat. I proposed that journey to him two weeks ago to see how he felt about it. I hope to receive his reply this week and to send him next Friday the order to leave, along with instructions about what he will have to do.

I hope M. Le Vacher will leave here for Marseilles in ten to twelve days at the latest. We still have some money to give you to be added to the thirty thousand livres for which I sent you the first

---

Letter 2608. - Archives of the Mission, Paris, copy made from the original in the Hains Family Collection, Marseilles. This is one of the letters sold at auction by Xavier Charmoy (cf. no. 2505).

[1]Jacques de Montrouge, Bishop of Saint-Flour (1647-61).

and second bills of exchange by the last two regular mails. Let me know if the bill was accepted and if you expect a good rate of payment for it. Above all, please act in such a way that the silence of O[ur] L[ord] is honored with regard to those sums of money—I mean by Messieurs Napollon and all those who will know about it—for fear lest news of it reach Algiers. For, besides the fact that the slaves might expect these funds for their ransom and then complain about the way they are used, Rappiot's creditors might take measures to pounce on them when they arrive.

Enclosed are four bills of exchange from M. Simonnet on M. Napollon; please get them accepted and withdraw the payment for them. They are to be used for the ransom of certain slaves whom I cannot name just now because M. Le Vacher, who has the names, has gone to the country for some fresh air. I do have one, however, for whom someone is writing to you. He is Jacques Varlet, whose brother, a Barnabite friar, sends him 1200 livres; the letter is dated June 4. The second, dated April 10, is for 500 livres; the third, dated May 11, is for 350 livres; and the fourth, dated the fourteenth of this month, is for 250 livres. The second and third are a little old because M. Le Vacher kept them by mistake. We went to ask M. Simonnet to renew them, but he replied that there was no need to do so and said he would write to Messieurs Napollon telling them to raise no objection about paying them. So much for the 2300 livres from the bills of exchange, of which 750 are for the slaves from Le Havre, whose names I will give you in a week.

Speaking of Le Havre, the Duchesse d'Aiguillon has gone there and informs me that other small sums will be sent to us for certain men whose relatives are sending them to them. At the same time, she mentions the balance which the boat captain still owes the slaves from Le Havre; she seems to want to use these funds to contribute to the ransom of some of them. Please let me know the amount of this balance, if you have received it; or—if you hope to receive it soon—why it has not been done, and what expenses and loss there will be, etc. You clarified these matters for me a while ago; but, besides the fact that I do not remember enough to give an account of them to the Lady, there may have been some changes since then.

You tell me that M. Roman is the one who is chartering the boat being prepared for Algiers. I do not really understand what you mean and am not sure if he is the one who fits it out and sends it or if he himself is going there. Since he is such an upright man that you think we can entrust him with the money for the slaves—either to ransom them personally or give it to the slaves so they can help themselves to do so—I agree to your making him responsible for it, provided he brings you back a receipt for each slave, registered in the Chancellery, or returns the money to you. That presupposes that his boat sails before M. Huguier leaves; but, if M. Huguier is going at the same time, it will be better to give him personally this commission. If you have not already done so, please remember to send there the 300 livres I gave you in April 1657 for Laurent Cramoisant from Le Havre and 316 livres a month later—that is, 16 livres for Cramoisant and 300 livres for Gilles Marguerin, alias Beaupré, from the same place, plus 100 livres for Nicolas Renouard, who is also from Le Havre, which you received last April. In addition, please send the 180 livres I sent you last August to Roch-Sébastien Hardy from Nancy, who is a slave in Algiers. I do not remember if you forwarded to Félix Begat from Nogent-sur-Seine, who is in Tunis, the 50 livres we received here for him. I think you did, but his sister has not been assured of it by him.

When I tell you to send the slaves their money through M. Roman, I do not mean the 2205 livres you have for the ransom of Joannès de Hirigoyen and Adamé de Lissardy from Saint-Jean-de-Luz because M. de Lafargue, who gave us that money, told us not to give it to M. Roman unless he tells us specifically to do so; but you can give it to M. Huguier. I ask you also, Monsieur, to send 506 livres, by one or the other, to two Basque brothers, Jean and Bernard de la Roquette, who are slaves in Algiers, and give instructions that, if this amount is sufficient to ransom only one of them, it should be the elder, if possible. Take this sum of 506 livres from the large sum you have.

It is inadvisable to send any money for all that to Brother Barreau because, when I went over the list of his debts that he sent me, I noted that he had spent for his own use the money he had received for the slaves—and even what I sent him to ransom one who was in the greatest danger of apostatizing. He might still use the money you would send him again. You can write to tell him you are not sending it to him for fear lest, if it were addressed to him, Rappiot's creditors might seize it, thinking that it was his [Rappiot's].

Thank you for having written to Agde that you would welcome M. Dolivet in your house to convalesce there. I hope God will give the Company that spirit of charity that makes all our houses one single house and that all the members will have one and the same will in God, in whom I am, Monsieur, your most humble servant.

VINCENT DEPAUL,
i.s.C.M.

M. de la Fosse has arrived in Troyes.

2609. - TO ANTOINE DURAND, SUPERIOR, IN AGDE

[June 21, 1658] [1]

You will be hard hit for having sent your confreres out to give missions, as I asked you to do. I clearly foresaw this, and I sympathize with you, but you know we have to quicken our pace and redouble our ordinary exercises on certain occasions when the service of God requires it, and then God does not fail to redouble

---

Letter 2609. - Reg. 2, p. 142.

[1]The next-to-last sentence in this letter indicates that it was written on the same day as the preceding one.

our courage and strength as well. That, Monsieur, is what I hope He will do in your regard.

I continue to thank God that M. Dolivet is recovering and for the foresight of M. Get, the Superior in Marseilles, in offering you his house so you could send him there for a while to recover the rest of the strength he lost during his serious illness. I was so consoled to see M. Get's charity in this that I have expressed my gratitude for it in the letter I am writing him. Oh! how I hope that God will give this spirit to the Company so that all its houses will be one single house and all the members will have but one heart and one soul! [2]

2610. - TO SISTER MARGUERITE CHÉTIF,[1] SISTER SERVANT, IN ARRAS

Paris, June 22, 1658

Dear Sister,

The grace of O[ur] L[ord] be with you forever!

I received the letter of annuity you sent me, compiled by the Bridgettines. Thank you for this and for the watch you obtained.

---

[2]Cf. Acts 4:32. (NAB)

Letter 2610. - Archives of the Motherhouse of the Daughters of Charity, original signed letter.

[1]Marguerite Chétif, born in Paris, was baptized at Saint-Sulpice on September 8, 1621, and entered the company of the Daughters of Charity on May 1, 1649. She was first sent to Chars and in May 1651 went to Serqueux. Chosen for the mission in Poland, the war between that country and Sweden prevented her departure. She took perpetual vows in Paris on April 4, 1655. When the Company was officially erected on August 8, 1655, she signed the Act of Establishment. In 1656 she went to Arras as Sister Servant and was there when Saint Louise died. Saint Vincent appointed Sister Marguerite Superioress General (1660-67); in 1667 she became Seminary Directress, and in 1670 Sister Servant in Angers. In 1674 she was named Treasurer General under Sister Nicole Haran; upon completion of her term of office (1677), she went as Sister Servant to the Nom-de-Jésus [Name of Jesus] hospice. She died at the Motherhouse on January 9, 1694. Two conferences given after her death are preserved in *Circulaires des supérieurs généraux et des soeurs supérieures*, pp. 470-78.

Please send it to us with some trustworthy person who will be coming here. I think you can entrust it to that good priest who wants to enter our Company, if by chance he is leaving soon to come here.

I have not seen Madame Fouquet [2] for a long time because she has gone to the country.

I do not have enough influence to get that poor mentally ill man, about whom you wrote to me, into the Petites-Maisons.[3] There is never an opening because the places are reserved long before they are vacant. Please tell his children that I am very sorry I cannot procure this consolation for them and that they should be careful not to send him.

How are you, Sister, and how is Sister Radegonde? [4] I ask O[ur] L[ord] to bless and unite you more and more.

---

[2]Marie de Maupeou, wife of François Fouquet, Vicomte de Vaux, Master of Requests, and then Councillor of State. Among her eight children were Nicolas, the celebrated Superintendent of Finance; François, Bishop of Narbonne; Louis, Bishop of Agde; and several daughters who entered the Visitation Order, one of whom, Marie-Thérèse, became Superior of the Visitation in Toulouse. Marie de Maupeou was a woman of exceptional piety and immense charity, of whom Saint Vincent said that "if through some mischance the Gospels were lost, their spirit and maxims would be found in the conduct and sentiments of Madame Fouquet." "She makes devotion so attractive," he added, "that she encourages everyone to be devout." (Cf. *Année sainte des religieuses de la Visitation Sainte-Marie* [12 vols., Annecy: Ch. Burdet, 1867-71], vol. I, p. 627.) When she heard that her son, Nicolas, had fallen into disgrace, she exclaimed: "I thank You, O my God. I asked You for the salvation of my son, and this is the way to obtain it." She died in 1681, at the age of ninety-one, mourned by everyone, but especially by the poor, who called her their mother. In the catalogue of the Ladies of Charity, she is listed under the title of Madame Fouquet, the President's wife.

[3]This hospice, composed of cottages for the patients, housed nearly four hundred elderly and infirm persons of both sexes, afflicted with skin disorders, dementia, or social diseases. It was located near the intersection of rue de Sèvres and Boulevard Raspail, mainly on the site of Boucicaut Square, next to the present-day Bon Marché department store. Saint Vincent himself had preached a mission there before the establishment of the Congregation of the Mission (cf. Abelly, *op. cit.*, bk. II, chap. I, sect. II, p. 20). He later sent members of the Tuesday Conferences there, where they did considerable good (*ibid.*, bk. II, chap. III, sect. III, p. 257).

[4]Radegonde Lenfantin was sent to Arras on August 30, 1656. Born around 1637, she entered the Company of the Daughters of Charity in 1653. In September 1660, after the departure of Sister Marguerite Chétif, who had been named Superioress General, she went through a period of discouragement and left Arras. She returned, however, and would die as a Daughter of Charity (cf. Coste, vol. VIII, no. 3288, n. 1). In 1705 and 1713, she testified at the beatification process of Saint Vincent (cf. *Documents D.C.*, Doc. 663, n. 2).

Mademoiselle Le Gras was not feeling well, but she is better now, thank God.

The Queen sent for six of your Sisters to nurse the sick and wounded of the army who are being brought to a hospital in Calais.[5] Only four could be sent[6] because another four have to be sent to Metz for the establishment there.

I recommend myself to your prayers, and I am, in the love of O[ur] L[ord], Sister, your most affectionate servant.

VINCENT DEPAUL,
i.s.C.M.

Addressed: Sister Marguerite Chétif, Daughter of Charity, Servant of the Sick Poor, in Arras

---

[5]The hospitals in Calais were filled to overflowing with soldiers who were wounded at the battle of the Dunes or were victims of a serious epidemic.

[6]Françoise Manceau, Marguerite Ménage, Marie Poulet, and Claude Muset. The disease they were coming to combat struck all four, and the first two died of it. The Queen had a memorial erected to the two victims.

Marguerite Ménage entered the Daughters of Charity at the end of 1650. Three of her sisters, Françoise, Madeleine, and Catherine, were also members of the Company.

Marie Poulet entered the Daughters of Charity around 1649. She went to Châlons-sur-Marne in October 1653, returning to Paris the following year. In 1657 she was in Chars and was chosen in June 1658 to nurse the wounded soldiers in Calais.

Claude Muset, born in 1637, entered the Daughters of Charity late in 1655 and was chosen in 1658 for the mission in Calais. On August 3 she wrote a beautiful letter to Saint Louise, telling her of the deaths of Sisters Françoise Manceau and Marguerite Ménage, her own illness, and that of Sister Marie Poulet (cf. *Documents D.C.*, Doc. 723, pp. 828-29). In 1705 and 1713, she testified at the process of canonization for Saint Vincent.

2611. - TO MADEMOISELLE CHAMPAGNE [1]

June 25, 1658

Mademoiselle,

The grace of O[ur] L[ord] be with you forever!

Thank you for the confidence with which you have honored me. I received your letter with a desire to be of service to you, and I read it with joy, seeing the sentiments of your heart.

(1) I am not surprised at the distaste you feel for the exercises of religious life; on the contrary, I would have been surprised if you had none. Sooner or later God tests by similar trials the souls He calls to His service, and it is better for you to have experienced them from the beginning of your vocation than in the course of it or at the end because you will learn early to know and humble yourself, to be mistrustful of self, and to rely on God—in a word, to lay a foundation of patience, strength, and mortification, which are virtues you will need to practice throughout your life.

(2) I am sure you would be satisfied to remain free as you are, but this satisfaction would be natural and would not last. We cannot serve two masters,[2] and if you want to enjoy the freedom of the children of God,[3] you must follow J[esus] C[hrist] on the narrow path of subjection that leads to salvation.[4] For, regardless of how disposed you may be to do good by walking on the broad way of your own freedom, you might fall by the wayside. That is where those usually fall who are attached to God only by silk threads, so great is the inconstancy of human nature.

(3) Mademoiselle, please reflect a little on the Son of God, who came into the world not only to save us by His death but to submit

---

Letter 2611. - Reg. 1, fol. 55.

[1]Niece of Mademoiselle du Fresne and a novice in Notre-Dame-de-Sézanne Abbey.

[2]Cf. Mt 6:24. (NAB)

[3]Cf. Rom 8:13. (NAB)

[4]Cf. Lk 13:24. (NAB)

to all His Father willed [5] and to draw us to Him by the example of His life. He was still in His mother's womb when He was obliged to obey the Emperor's edict. He was born outside of His own native place in a harsh season and in dire poverty. Shortly after that, we see Herod persecuting Him, causing Him to flee and to suffer in exile His own hardships and, out of compassion, those of the Blessed Virgin and Saint Joseph, who had to endure much because of Him. When He returned to Nazareth and grew up, He was subject to His parents and the rules of a hidden life. He did so to serve as a model to religious souls who, having embraced a similar life, must submit to their Superiors and the observances of their state.

Doubtless, He had you in mind at that time, in His eternal plan to save you by the life of complete withdrawal you have begun. Now, if you, in your turn, look to this Divine Savior, Mademoiselle, you will see how He suffers constantly, how He prays, how He works, and how He obeys. "If you live according to the flesh," says Saint Paul, "you will die"; [6] and to live according to the Spirit that gives life we must live as O[ur] L[ord] lived: renounce ourselves, do the will of others rather than our own, make good use of contradictions, and believe that sufferings are better for us than gratification. "Was it not fitting that the Christ should suffer these things? " said He to the disciples, who were speaking of His Passion.[7] This is to make us realize that, as He entered into His glory only by afflictions, we must not expect to attain it without suffering.

(4) People suffer in different ways. The Apostles and the first Christians suffered the persecutions of tyrants and all sorts of trials, and it is said that all those who wish to follow J[esus] C[hrist] will undergo temptation.[8] If you reflect on your past life, you will see

[5] Cf. Jn 6:38. (NAB)
[6] Cf. Rom 8:13. (NAB)
[7] Cf. Lk 24:26. (NAB)
[8] Cf. Mt 16:24. (NAB)

that you have not been exempt from this; in whatever state you are—even were you married, and well married—you will find crosses and bitterness. There are few persons in the world who do not complain of their situation, even though it seems pleasant. The best one is certainly the one that makes us more like O[ur] L[ord] tempted, praying, acting, and suffering. That is the path by which He leads souls He wants to raise to higher perfection.

(5) Do not, then, become discouraged, Mademoiselle, if you have no taste for the practice of virtue: virtue is virtue only in so far as we make the effort to practice it. "Man's life is but a warfare," says Job.[9] We must, then, struggle so as not to be overcome. Since the devil is a roaring lion, always prowling around seeking to devour us,[10] he will not fail to attack you and your good resolution to belong entirely to God. He wants to discourage and dishearten you in this endeavor, if possible, foreseeing that he will be disconcerted if you persevere.

It is to your advantage, then, to resist him strongly by prayer and by fidelity to Community practices, doing so above all with a completely filial and admirable confidence in God. His grace will never fail you; on the contrary, it will abound in your soul in proportion to the adversities you encounter and your determination to overcome them with His same grace. God never allows us to be tempted beyond our strength.[11]

(6) For all these reasons, Mademoiselle, I think it will be well for you to brace yourself against difficulties. The more you give to O[ur] L[ord], the greater blessings you will receive. His yoke is easy to those who welcome it willingly, and your burden will be light [12] if you compare it with that of J[esus] C[hrist], who suffered so much for you, or if you consider the consolation and reward He

---

[9]Cf. Jb 7:1. (DR-B)
[10]Cf. 1 Pt 5:8. (NAB)
[11]Cf. 1 Cor 10:13. (NAB)
[12]Cf. Mt 11:30. NAB

promises to those who serve Him constantly, with no regret, in the place and in the manner he wills, as I hope you will do.

These then are my humble thoughts, Mademoiselle, which I submit to your better ones. I would be wary of sharing them with you if you had not desired this and if I did not see at the end of your letter that you are seeking to know God's Will in order to carry it out. I pray that He will grant you this grace.

I am, in His love, Mademoiselle. . . .

2612. - TO DENIS LAUDIN, SUPERIOR, IN LE MANS

[Saint-Denis] June 26, 1658

[Monsieur,]

The grace of O[ur] L[ord] be with you forever!

. . . and I am at Saint-Denis and, [conse]quently, not in a position to [write] to you [at] length. I thank God for having given you sufficient strength and help to open the mission in Pressigny [1] and to bring it to a successful close. May His Divine Goodness be pleased to preserve the good results of it!

Send us M. Gorlidot along with M. Rivet,[2] since he needs remedies and rest for his recovery. We will try to have him take them in order to preserve him for the Company, particularly for your house.

Since you have M. Grainville with you, it will be well for you to treat him graciously; he is a good gentleman, whose son[3] is in the Internal Seminary in Richelieu, and he deserves that you look

---

Letter 2612. - Archives of the Mission, Paris, original signed letter. The upper left-hand corner is missing.

[1]Probably one of the two localities in Indre-et-Loire that bear this name.

[2]François Gorlidot and François Rivet.

Gorlidot, born in Charly (Aisne) on January 10, 1623, entered the Congregation of the Mission on March 3, 1647, took his vows on September 30, 1649, and was ordained a priest in 1650.

[3]Eustache-Michel de Grainville, born in the Paris diocese on May 18, 1633, entered the Congregation of the Mission in Richelieu on November 10, 1657, and took his vows in the

after him, treating him as one of the family, for as long as his business affairs keep him in Le Mans.

You must obey the Bishop[4] and be of service to him during his visitations, since this is his wish. If you are in a situation to do so, it will be well for you to go with him.

As for the priest who [indicated to you] a desire to enter the [Company], we [will have him begin] retreat at the time he told you, and he [will talk things over with] us; then [we] will see.

I will give you an answer some [other time] about opening letters [that] come from Saint-Lazare. We have no news here just now.

I am, in the love of O[ur] L[ord], Monsieur, your most humble servant.

VINCENT DEPAUL,
i.s.C.M.

At the bottom of the first page: Monsieur Laudin

2613. - TO FRANÇOIS CAULET, BISHOP OF PAMIERS

June 26, 1658

Excellency,

I took the honor of writing you within the past few days and to forward to you a letter from Rome. Enclosed is another I received since then.

---

presence of M. de Beaumont on December 11, 1659.

[4]Philibert de Beaumanoir de Lavardin. Although Saint Vincent did not recommend him for the episcopacy, he took up residence in Le Mans even before receiving his Bulls. He was not a model Bishop; in fact, after his death, a rumor spread that, on his own admission, he never had the intention of ordaining anyone. Several persons believed this and had themselves reordained. The rumor, however, was false. (Cf. Collet, *op. cit.*, vol. I, p. 473.)

Letter 2613. - Reg. 1, fol. 18v.

My most humble thanks, Excellency, for the marks of kindness you have shown to our poor Cahors house. M. Cuissot wrote me about them with a deep sense of gratitude, and I will add this obligation to all the others we have toward you.

The Bishop of Sarlat [1] is very worried about his affair. He is anxiously and patiently waiting to hear what you and the Bishop of Cahors [2] have decided.

The other day your sister [3] sent someone to ask me for a time when she could talk to me. I excused myself because of my ailment, which was keeping me in my room at the time and which I had since you left. Now that I am better, by the grace of God, I will take the honor of going to see her at her home.

I ask the Divine Goodness, Excellency, to keep you always in good health and that your works may abound in blessings. Prostrate in spirit at your feet, I ask for your blessing, since I am, in the love of O[ur] L[ord], Excellency, your most humble servant and very obedient servant.

VINCENT DEPAUL,
i.s.C.M.

---

[1]Nicolas Sevin.

[2]Alain de Solminihac.

[3]Catherine Caulet, Baronne de Mirepoix. As will be seen in no. 2802, she asked to be admitted to the Ladies of Charity of the Hôtel-Dieu in March 1659. Perhaps she is seeking Saint Vincent's advice about that here.

2614. - TO FIRMIN GET, SUPERIOR, IN MARSEILLES

Paris, June 28, 1658

Monsieur,

The grace of O[ur] L[ord] be with you forever!

God be praised that the bill of exchange for thirty thousand livres has been accepted and at the good rate of exchange for which you are hoping! I have no doubt of your discretion in being very sure of the persons to whom you will consign it; the large amount of money and its destination demand that you be very careful to do so. You will have to do it again for some other money we will be sending you shortly.

M. Le Vacher will be leaving in a few days and will remain in Marseilles until M. Huguier sends word from Algiers that it is safe for him to go there with those sums of money. M. Huguier writes me that he is ready to make that journey, and I ask him to do so at the first opportunity, leaving Toulon as soon as you send him someone to do what he has been doing. I have not yet been able to make the report I promised him; I will get to work on it one of these mornings. Meanwhile, if there were a boat preparing to leave, as you told me, it would be a good idea for you to summon him to Marseilles and to send M. Parisy to replace him. You can manage without the latter because you have M. Dolivet with you, who is supposed to be spending some time there, and M. Le Vacher, who is making haste to leave. In addition, we will send you someone from here, if need be.

I am glad you did not go to Toulon to take the letters to Commander Paul but sent M. Parisy instead, since you were not well. Do nothing to aggravate the inflammation in your eyes but

---

Letter 2614. - Archives of the Mission, Paris, copy made from the original in the Hains Family Collection, Marseilles. This is one of the letters sold at auction by Xavier Charmoy (cf. no. 2505).

make good use of all the appropriate remedies to clear it up and to avoid a recurrence.

If M. Dolivet is with you, I embrace him very warmly in spirit. I am writing him a note in reply to the letter he wrote me, but I am sending it to Agde because I am not sure that he has left there.

In the last regular mail I sent you four bills of exchange: the first for 1200 livres to ransom Jacques Varles; the second for 250 livres for Guillaume Legrand from Le Havre; the third for 500 livres to be used by M. Le Vacher when he is in Algiers, in line with the special instructions he received from the Pastor in Le Havre; and the fourth for 350 livres for Jacques Jobe—or Jove—from Honfleur.

Because M. Le Vacher knows all these slaves, and people have gone to him to have these sums of money delivered, it will be a good idea for you to keep them until he gets to Marseilles and not send them to Algiers with M. Roman or M. Huguier ahead of time, as I had asked you to do. Perhaps he will arrive before they leave, and you will then be able to discuss when and how to send these sums, along with the others you have and the ones you will soon be receiving for other slaves, whose names you already have and will have.

I am writing to ask M. Huguier to give André de Brie six livres, which we received here; he is a convict on the galley *Reine*.

I am, in the love of O[ur] L[ord], Monsieur, your most humble servant.

VINCENT DEPAUL,
i.s.C.M.

I will send the reports for M. Huguier by the first mail.

2615. - TO JEAN D'ARANTHON D'ALEX [1]

[1658] [2]

Monsieur,

The grace of O[ur] L[ord] be with you forever!

I received your letter with all due respect for the grace God has given you. It has always seemed very great to me and has given me sentiments of special veneration for you that will last me a lifetime. I have thought of this many times since I have had the honor of knowing you. I thank you most humbly, Monsieur, for the honor you did me of writing to me in such a gracious, cordial style and about so worthy a subject as that of the Prior of La Pérouse.[3]

I was very consoled to see him and to offer him my services because you recommended him to me and because of his personal merit. I did not have the pleasure of speaking very long with him because I had to leave in a hurry on some important business, but he led me to hope for the favor of seeing him here again soon. In that case, I will offer him once again our modest services and

---

Letter 2615. - Innocent Le Masson, *La vie de messire Jean d'Aranthon d'Alex* (2nd ed., Clermont-Ferrand: Tribaud-Landriot, 1834), p. 46.

[1]Saint Vincent's relationship with Jean d'Aranthon d'Alex dated back to the time when the latter was studying in Paris. One day, after the Saint had heard him speak at a priests' meeting, he introduced himself to d'Aranthon and asked him to come to Saint-Lazare from time to time, which he did. Shortly after ordination to the priesthood on December 17, 1644, he was appointed Canon of Geneva and Pastor in Ceury. The services he rendered the diocese and the Court of Savoy, his great learning, and his indefatigable zeal in combating heresy made him a likely candidate to succeed Charles-Auguste de Sales, who died on February 8, 1660. Some time before, Saint Vincent had foretold that he would be appointed to this position and had recently repeated his prediction to the Prelate's nephew, the Prior of La Perouse. Jean d'Aranthon enjoyed one of the longest and more fruitful episcopates ever known to the Geneva diocese. He died on July 4, 1695, at seventy-six years of age. The Priests of the Mission, directors of the Annecy seminary—who had nothing but praise for his benevolence—inherited his library, his chapel in the country, a precious chalice, and all of his paintings.

[2]The information about d'Aranthon's nephew coming to study in Paris enables us to assign this date for the letter.

[3]The Prior of La Pérouse came to Paris in 1658 to prepare for the priesthood under the direction of the Priests of Saint-Sulpice. He later became a Doctor of the Sorbonne and Dean of the Sainte-Chapelle in Chambéry.

whatever we have, as I have already done with regard to our house and the Collège des Bons-Enfants. It would be a blessing for us if he agreed to take a room there.

I will welcome in the same way, Monsieur, the opportunities God will give me to obey you. I am obligated to do so by your precious remembrance of me, who am so unworthy of this, and by the special esteem God has given me for you who, by your fine leadership, have merited the latest dignities and holy duties you have at the Court of Savoy.

I ask the Divine Goodness to preserve you, Monsieur, for a long time for His glory, to fulfill your desires, and to make you realize how much I am, in His love, Monsieur, your most humble servant.

VINCENT DEPAUL,
i.s.C.M.

2616. - TO JEAN MARTIN, SUPERIOR, IN TURIN

Paris, July 5, 1658

Monsieur,

The grace of O[ur] L[ord] be with you forever!

It has been a long time since I wrote to you and even longer since I received any letters from you. I do not know to what I can attribute this except to your absence from Turin and your heavy duties in the rural areas. Still, I find it hard to convince myself that you could not find an hour to let me know the state of your health and the outcome of your work since Lent. You can well imagine how worried I am. Please be more exact, Monsieur, in giving me news of you.

In my last letter I asked you to send Messieurs Stelle and Beaure to Genoa.[1] I thought you had done so, but M. Lejuge writes me that

---

Letter 2616. - Archives of the Mission, Turin, original signed letter.

[1]Cf. no. 2577.

they are still in Turin. Please have them leave as soon as possible, Monsieur, and keep M. Laurence[2] with you. Having spent two years in the seminary, he is ready to take vows. If he is disposed to do so, please allow him to take them.

Please let me know if you paid M. Delaforcade any postage for the letters since you have been in Piedmont, for it is only just that he be reimbursed for what he advanced.

Our news is that, by the grace of God, all of us are now in very good health, after most of us had been bothered by a cold that was going around. We have two or three bands of Missionaries out at work; and, from what I hear from the other houses, all is going very well with them, thank God.

The boat that sailed for Madagascar last March, with four of our priests [3] on it, was caught in such a terrible storm the day after its departure and the entire week that followed that they were on the point of being submerged during that time. The masts and the rudder were smashed, and those poor people were at the mercy of wind and waves. Finally, however, God brought them ashore at Lisbon, Portugal; and once the boat was repaired, they put out to sea again. Very soon after that, they were attacked by a Spanish man-of-war, which captured them and took them to Spain. We are waiting for God to be pleased to bring them back here. This is a strong motive for adoring the guidance of Providence and submitting to it our poor way of thinking.

I am, in His love, Monsieur, your most humble servant.

VINCENT DEPAUL,
i.s.C.M.

Addressed: Monsieur Martin, Superior of the Mission, in Turin

---

[2]Yves Laurence, born in La Roche-Derrien (Côtes-du-Nord) on March 1, 1632, entered the Congregation of the Mission as a deacon on June 28, 1656, and took his vows in Turin on July 25, 1658, in the presence of M. Martin. He was Superior in Marseilles (1686-92) and Vicar Apostolic for the Regencies of Algiers and Tunis (1693-1705). Laurence died in Algiers on March 11, 1705. (Cf. *Notices*, vol. IV, pp. 39-46.)

[3]Fathers Pasquier de Fontaines, Marand-Ignace Arnoul, Charles Le Blanc, and Pierre Daveroult. Brother Christophe Delaunay was also with them.

2617. - TO FIRMIN GET, SUPERIOR, IN MARSEILLES

Paris, July 5, 1658

Monsieur,

The grace of O[ur] L[ord] be with you forever!

I received your letter of June 25 and was overjoyed to hear of your second journey to Toulon and to learn that Commander Paul is so well disposed toward the Algiers project. I am distressed, however, to see no way of our being able to supply him with what he requests nor what you suggest. I told you clearly that we would give him twenty thousand livres from the money you have, but that is understood to mean after he has ransomed the slaves, extricated Brother Barreau, and installed another Consul; for, if he cannot do that by armed means, the money must be used to obtain those results by the ordinary channels, which is to secure that Brother's release and return to the poor Christians what they gave him so they can use it for their ransom. I am waiting to hear what he has to say to you about this proposal, which is being made on condition of a successful outcome and with no money being given in advance.

The question you ask me about whether it is advisable for M. Huguier to go to Algiers, seeing that the Consul has obtained a release from Rappiot's debts, makes me wonder about the need for this voyage now. I will reflect on this between now and the first regular mail and will tell you the decision at that time.

It is true that we owe M. Delaforcade almost three hundred livres, as he made clear to us in his accounts. He will receive in payment the two hundred livres you will send to Tunis for Dominique de Lajus, and we will pay them here on your bill of exchange.

Letter 2617. - Archives of the Mission, Paris, copy made from the original in the Hains Family Collection, Marseilles. This is one of the letters sold at auction by Xavier Charmoy (cf. no. 2505).

I wrote you a letter two or three days ago, which I entrusted to M. de Lafargue. He gave you the money for the Basque slaves, asking you to give M. Roman the remaining 2205 livres you have, allocated for the ransom of Joannès de Hirigoyen and Adamé de Lissardy from Saint-Jean-de-Luz. I ask you once again to do so and to have M. Roman write the receipt for them on the back of my last letter.

The boat that sailed for Madagascar last March with our four priests on it was caught in such a terrible storm the day after its departure and the entire week that followed that they were on the point of perishing the whole time. The masts and the rudder were smashed, and those poor people were at the mercy of wind and waves, but God brought them to the shores of Portugal; and once their boat was repaired in Lisbon they put out to sea again. Soon after that they were attacked by a Spanish man-of-war, which captured them and took them to Spain. We are now waiting for God to be pleased to bring them back here. This is a good motive to adore the guidance of Providence and to submit our poor way of thinking to it.

I am, in His love, Monsieur, your most humble servant.

VINCENT DEPAUL,
i.s.C.M.

2618. - *JEAN MARTIN TO SAINT VINCENT*

July 6, 1658

We are leaving Fossano, a small, thickly-settled town, where we gave the mission. God was pleased to bestow on it great blessings in proportion to its great needs. The crowd was so large that, although the church was quite spacious, there was not enough room for the people who came to

---

Letter 2618. - Abelly, *op. cit.*, bk. II, chap. I, sect. VI, p. 89.

take advantage of the sermons and the other activities of the mission. Not only the laity came but the clergy and religious also participated.

Besides the bad secret and public practices that were abolished, the enmities that were done away with, and the other usual good results of a mission, some good works were established there for the future:

(1) the public evening prayers we had begun are being continued in the church of the Oratorian Fathers of Saint Philip Neri, and many people attend every evening;

(2) to maintain the people in their present sentiments of piety, the Canons have decided to have a general Communion every three months in their church;

(3) these Canons and all the clergy are resolved to continue the weekly spiritual conferences we gave them during the mission. This can be very effective, please God, in reestablishing and preserving a true ecclesiastical spirit among themselves. Several of those priests, who are intelligent, virtuous persons, seem to be strongly attracted to it.

In a word, this place now seems completely renewed in a truly Christian life. May God in His goodness keep the people in this good state by continuing and increasing His graces to them!

2619. - TO LOUIS RIVET, SUPERIOR, IN SAINTES

July 7, 1658

You did well to represent to the Bishop of Saintes [1] your reasons for being dispensed from the service of nuns. There are so many other priests in the town, and the Bishop has so many other means of meeting the needs of the nuns of Notre-Dame,[2] that I cannot imagine that he would want to make your family, which has always been at the service of the diocese, responsible for this, especially if you represent to him humbly and sincerely that we have a Rule

---

Letter 2619. - Reg. 2, p. 78.

[1]Louis de Bassompierre, Bishop of Saintes (1649-70).

[2]These nuns had just come to Saintes, where they undertook the education of young women and girls of the nobility and upper middle class.

of not being involved in any way with nuns, and that our experience has even been that the men who devote their time to them can scarcely work at anything else.

It was for this reason that, foreseeing from the very beginning the things that might divert the Company from its functions, we felt it necessary to be wary of any kind of communication with such women, and we have been very exact about this. It is true that, in my particular case, I have done the contrary, since I have the care of the Sisters of Sainte-Marie; [3] but it must be known that I had it before the Mission existed because it was imposed upon me by the blessed Bishop of Geneva,[4] or rather, by the Providence of God, to punish me; for, it is a cross—the heaviest one I have—that I am obliged to carry, after having tried several times to be freed of it.[5] So I hope that, when your good Bishop has been informed of our custom, our reasons for refraining from the service of nuns, and the inconveniences to be feared from the contrary, he will not oblige you to work with them. This is what I ask of O[ur] L[ord].[6]

---

[3]The Visitation nuns.

[4]Saint Francis de Sales was born in Thorens, near Annecy, on August 21, 1567, and died in Lyons on December 28, 1622. Saint Vincent was honored with his friendship. "Many times I have had the honor of enjoying the close friendship of Francis de Sales," he said at the beatification process of his illustrious friend on April 17, 1628. He always spoke of the Bishop of Geneva with great admiration, considering him worthy of the honors reserved to the saints. According to Coqueret, a Doctor of the Sorbonne, Saint Francis de Sales, on his part, used to say that "he did not know a more worthy or more saintly priest than M. Vincent." (Postulatory letter from the Bishop of Tulle, March 21, 1706.) When it came to appointing a Superior for the Visitation convent in Paris, he chose Vincent de Paul.

[5]For some eighteen months, beginning in October 1646, Saint Vincent did not fulfill the functions of Director of the Visitation nuns. Jean-François-Paul de Gondi, Cardinal de Retz, at the insistence of Marguerite de Gondi, Marquise de Maignelay, obliged him to resume them. Whenever Saint Vincent counseled members of his Community against assuming the direction of nuns, he referred to the Rules of the Congregation of the Mission and the obligation forced on him by Cardinal de Retz.

[6]Collet (*op. cit.*, vol. II, p. 39) mentions two letters, one dated July 6, the other July 7, in which Saint Vincent spoke of the adventures of the Missionaries who had embarked for Madagascar. One of these is probably this letter to Louis Rivet, of which we only have a fragment.

2620. - TO PIERRE CABEL, SUPERIOR, IN SEDAN

Paris, July 10 [1658] [1]

Monsieur,

The grace of O[ur] L[ord] be with you forever!

We have accepted your bill of exchange and will try to pay it.

You must know clearly the reasons supporting your rights with regard to the new tithes and the roofing for the choir, for which you say you are going to be at odds with the inhabitants. You have to be able to give the Governor [2] full information on this so he can give you his opinion on it.

I praise God that your little family is going along as usual. If the person who is the exception in it is trying the patience of the others, he is still useful, since he gives you the means of practicing humility, forbearance, gentleness, and charity toward him, as well as providing an opportunity to make progress in these virtues. If, however, his behavior were to become scandalous, a remedy would have to be applied.

The ship that left for Madagascar last March, with our four priests aboard, was caught in such an extraordinary storm the day of its departure and the entire week that followed that everyone on it was on the point of being engulfed by the water—I do not mean fully alive because they were all half-dead. The masts and the rudder were smashed, and those poor people were at the mercy of wind and waves. In the end, however, God brought them ashore at Lisbon, Portugal; and once their ship was repaired, they put out to sea again. Soon after that, they were attacked by a Spanish ship,

---

Letter 2620. - Archives of the Mission, Paris, original signed letter. The postscript is in the Saint's handwriting.

[1]A very old note written on the back of the original mistakenly dates the letter *1657*. The details of the departure for Madagascar—the same as in no. 1617—leave no doubt about the year.

[2]Abraham de Fabert.

which captured them and took them to Spain. We are now waiting for God to be pleased to bring them back here. This is a good motive for adoring the guidance of Providence and of subjecting our poor way of thinking to it.

I am, in the love of O[ur] L[ord], Monsieur, your most humble servant.

VINCENT DEPAUL,
i.s.C.M.

Consult a good lawyer; then tell the Governor what he thinks and submit yourself to his will. He is a just man and will not order you to do anything unreasonable.

At the bottom of the first page: Monsieur Cabel

2621. - TO MONSIEUR MOISET, IN LA FÈRE

July 10, 1658

I thank God, Monsieur, for the sacrifice you wish to make to Him of yourself, and I thank you most humbly for choosing our Company in which to consume yourself in the service of His Majesty. It would be an honor and a consolation for us to see you practice your piety and patience in it, but I must tell you, Monsieur, that one of our maxims is to accept only young people to work in it. Since you are beyond the age of being able to devote yourself to the work we assign them, we have reason to believe that God is not calling you to it.

True, in the past we did receive two upper-class persons who were quite elderly, but that is because one [1] was the brother-in-law

---

Letter 2621. - Reg. 2, p. 43.

[1]Charles d'Angennes, Seigneur de Fargis, was a member of a family distinguished in military and diplomatic circles. By his marriage to Madeleine de Silly, Madame de Gondi's sister, he

of our founder, and the other [2] bestowed important benefits on us before and after being among us. We were then obligated in their regard to make an exception to the general rule. Furthermore, they were not married, as you are, Monsieur, and you have your wife with you; consequently, you have a two-fold impediment. If you say that she will go to live with the Daughters of Charity, this cannot be expected of them, as it could not be expected of us because we have never received anyone in either Community except persons who are free and in a position to do what the others do in them. I entreat you most humbly to hold us excused.

I ask Our Lord to make known to you the place and manner in which He wants you to serve Him to assure your salvation. Have no fear that He will not take care of you and what concerns you if you truly seek His glory—which I am convinced you do. Put your trust in His great goodness and offer yourself frequently to Him that He may accomplish His good pleasure in and through you. If some other opportunity presents itself in which I may be in a position to be of service to you, I will do so with the same affection with which I am. . . .

---

became Comte de la Rochepot; he was also Ambassador in Spain (1620-26). The Queen Mother, dissatisfied with the politics and influence of Richelieu, wanted to oust the powerful minister. Madame de Fargis, her lady-in-waiting, who belonged to the opposition, was involved in the intrigues. In 1631 she was condemned to death but fled abroad, dying in Louvain in 1639. Her husband was imprisoned in the Bastille for the same reason on February 14, 1633. On June 2, 1640, his twenty-seven-year-old son was killed in the siege of Arras. For many years, his daughter, Henriette, was Abbess at Port-Royal, where she died on June 3, 1691. On December 21, 1647, M. de Fargis entered the Congregation of the Mission. His conduct in the seminary was so exemplary that Saint Vincent stated that "he never saw him commit a single venial sin." He died on December 20, 1648. (Cf. *Notices*, vol. I, pp. 425-30.)

[2]René Alméras the elder.

2622. - TO MONSIEUR DUTOUR, VICAR-GENERAL OF SOISSONS

Paris, July 10, 1658

Monsieur,

The grace of O[ur] L[ord] be with you forever!

I received, with the respect God has given me for you, the letter you did me the honor of writing me. In reply to what you proposed to me, Monsieur, it is not up to a poor priest like me to become involved in something God has placed over my head. I will tell you nevertheless that the ordinance drawn up at the synod is in conformity with the decree of the Congregation of Rites and that the Bishop may dispense from it for a just reason.

My most humble thanks for thinking of us for Orbais Abbey.[1] We are greatly indebted to you for desiring such a benefit for us, even though it is beyond our hopes. The union of abbeys is very difficult in France; for the ten years I worked with ecclesiastical affairs I saw only one that was granted. It is no less so for the union of conventual revenues. The late Bishop of Saint-Malo[2] had united the one in his Saint-Méen Abbey to his seminary and had established the Company there, but we have had a great deal to suffer from the monks, until now that our Holy Father the Pope has been pleased to confirm this union.[3]

You do me the honor of telling me that the inhabitants of Montmirail are complaining, but I do not know the reason why they are complaining. If it is about the hospital, that is groundless; first of all, because it belongs to the local lord and not to them. He is the one who founded it and gave its direction to the Priests of the

---

Letter 2622. - Reg. 1, fol. 44v.

[1]Orbais-l'Abbaye (Marne) was thus named because of a Benedictine abbey situated there.

[2]Achille de Harlay de Sancy, born in Paris in 1581, entered the Oratory in 1620 and in 1631 was named Bishop of Saint-Malo, where he died on September 20, 1646.

[3]Cf. vol. XIII, no. 117, Bull by which Saint-Méen Abbey is united to the seminary established in that place.

Mission—I went two years from the time Father de Gondi[4] first mentioned it to me before I was willing to accept it—in the second place, because it is run better than it was when the nuns or the district tax collector were in charge. We placed two Daughters of Charity there and things are now going very well. If it is the leper hospital, that is another story; we will discuss that the first time I have the honor of seeing you.

Teaching the youth of Condé[5] is not our line of work, and neither is it our place to seek out any establishment. The ones we have came to us without asking, thank God; furthermore, of all people alive, I am perhaps the one most unworthy of obtaining some favor from the Princesse de Carignan.[6]

As for Madame de Bécherelle's foundation,[7] it is true that we were not paid for it, Monsieur, but that is not why the mission has not been given in Beuvardes for a long time. It is, rather, because the late Bishop of Soissons[8] gave us a hard time with it, and since his death I have not thought about it. Besides, our little house in Fontaine-Essart, to which we transferred that foundation, suffered so many losses that it could only support one or two priests, and they also contracted debts that we had to pay.

I hope that one of the first missions we give, Monsieur, will be that one, God willing. Do us the favor of always reminding us of

---

[4]Philippe-Emmanuel de Gondi entered the Oratorian Fathers after becoming a widower (June 23, 1625) and spent the rest of his life in the practice of Christian and religious virtues. He died in Joigny on June 29, 1662. The Congregation of the Mission, the Oratory, and Carmel honor him as one of their greatest benefactors.

[5]There were several places with this name in the Soissons diocese.

[6]Daughter of Charles de Bourbon, Comte de Soissons. In 1624 she had married Thomas-François, Prince de Carignan, who became Grand Master of France. In an earlier letter (cf. vol. VI, no. 2237, dated March 31, 1657) Saint Vincent claimed that she would never forgive him for refusing her entrance to the Visitation monastery to visit one of the nuns.

[7]Madame de la Bécherelle had funded a mission for Beuvardes on July 3, 1643; it was supposed to be given every five years (cf. vol. II, no. 733, n. 8).

[8]Simon Le Gras, born in Paris in 1598, was appointed Bishop of Soissons in 1623 and died at the Château de Sept-Mons, near Soissons, in 1656.

our duty and of praying that God will do us that of carrying it out for His glory and the service of souls.

I am, in His love, with all the affection of mine, Monsieur, your. . . .

2623. - TO FIRMIN GET, SUPERIOR, IN MARSEILLES

Paris, July 12, 1658

Monsieur,

The grace of O[ur] L[ord] be with you forever!

I received your letter of July 2. I noticed a difference between the last letter you sent me from Brother Barreau and the previous one. One speaks with uncertainty about his being released from Rappiot's debts and from others for which they could make him responsible; the other assures me that he has in his possession the authorization from the Pasha, which is to be confirmed by the customs office.

Because of this conflicting information I am suspending my judgment until M. Huguier has witnessed that release and declared that it is in the proper form. So, we think M. Huguier should make this journey, in line with the report I sent him and which he will share with you. I ask you, Monsieur, to send M. Parisy to replace him there until he gets back from Algiers so he can leave on the first boat.

M. Le Vacher is making his retreat so he can leave here in eight to ten days at the latest. He will stay with you while M. Huguier is traveling; please give the latter the 3300 livres I am sending you by a bill of exchange from Messieurs Simonnet on Messieurs

---

Letter 2623. - Property of the Congregation of the Mission, Beirut (Lebanon), original signed letter. The postscript is in the Saint's handwriting.

Napollon. You can see from my report where the money is to go, namely, 3000 livres for the ransom of three French priests or religious who are slaves, or of three other men who are in the greatest danger of apostatizing, and 300 livres for M. Huguier's expenses.

Thank you for the explanation you gave me about the business of the slaves from Le Havre and for following through on it with the captain. If you cannot be paid from the expenses and the unexpended balance, you must leave that to Providence and use the 270 livres you have to help ransom some of those slaves.

We have received 150 livres here for one of them named Louis Lefebvre. At the first opportunity, we will send them to you along with some other money, I hope. Meanwhile, if you have occasion to forward those 50 piastres to Lefebvre, please take them from the money you have and do not let the boat leave without them because the Duchesse d'Aiguillon, who is in Le Havre, has urged us to hurry.

Please tell Brother Louis [1] that M. Berthe has gone to give a mission and will be able to answer his letter when he gets back. In the meantime, I ask him to make to God the sacrifice of his desire to read the New Testament in French, so he will be in conformity with our Brothers here, who do not read it—except perhaps Brother Alexandre[2] and a few of the older ones.

---

[1]Louis Sicquard.

[2]Alexandre Véronne, coadjutor Brother, born in Avignon on May 15, 1610, entered the Congregation of the Mission on July 22, 1630. He was infirmarian at Saint-Lazare and was so dedicated and capable that he won the esteem of all, especially Saint Vincent. His death on November 18, 1686, was announced to the whole Company in a circular from Edme Jolly, Superior General (1673-97). Brother Chollier wrote his life, which was published in *Miroir du frère coadjuteur de la Congrégation de la Mission* (Paris, 1875), pp. 145ff. This work also served as the basis for his biography in *Notices*, vol. III, pp. 528-48.

I embrace good M. Dolivet; please take good care of him. Enclosed is a letter written to him from his native place.

Your most humble servant.

VINCENT DEPAUL,
i.s.C.M.

Please share this letter with M. Huguier.

The money we have sent and will send you from now on is to remain in your hands to be sent or retained in the time and manner I will write you, for the specific purpose I will tell you, and not otherwise.

Addressed: Monsieur Get

2624. - TO EDME JOLLY, SUPERIOR, IN ROME

July 12, 1658

I attach no importance to those projected establishments that are made, not by persons having the authority to do so, but by those who have only desires and are unwilling to meet the expense for them. You do well to make it clear to them that it is not enough for the Missionaries to be housed; they must also have the wherewithal to work, since it is neither permissible nor suitable for them to beg. We lack neither work nor foundations, thank God, but we do lack men; for few can be found who have—or are willing to acquire—the apostolic spirit we should have.

Letter 2624. - Reg. 2, p. 240.

2625. - TO PIERRE DE BEAUMONT, SUPERIOR, IN RICHELIEU [1]

Paris, July 14, 1658

Monsieur,

The grace of O[ur] L[ord] be with you forever!

It does not suffice for the Sisters of Charity in your town to think that the two postulants are suitable for their Company, unless you yourself share their opinion. So, if you think they have the strength for this state of life, that it is the desire to serve God and the poor that prompts them to embrace it and not the thought of being more comfortable than they now are, and, in a word, if you see that they intend to persevere, as far as that can morally be foreseen; in that case you can send them, although they may have no money, even to return home—because, God willing, they will not have to do so—or for their clothing, since what they will be wearing will do.

We do not look too closely at those things when the subjects are good; on the contrary, we would have them come from a great distance at considerable expense if we could be assured of this, since the people need those young women so much and they are being requested from all sides. Four Bishops and several towns have asked us for some but could not have them. Still, Monsieur, let me tell you that, if their parents are so poor that they need their presence and service to survive, it is better for them to assist them until they die or can manage without them.

Letter 2625. - *Recueil des procès-verbaux des conseils tenus par Saint Vincent,* p. 306.

[1]No. 115 of the collection of selected letters preserved at the Motherhouse of the Daughters of Charity gives us the name of the recipient and the date of this letter. This manuscript adds to the text a fragment from no. 2595.

2626. - TO DENIS LAUDIN, SUPERIOR, IN LE MANS

July 17, 1658

I fear that the liberty being taken by the Brother cleric about whom you write me and the Company's tolerance in his regard may give others cause to behave as he is doing. Be that as it may, his unruliness can produce only bad results. That is why I ask you to see that he is kept in line and to give him a penance at Chapter so he will mend his ways. You could, for example, deprive him of wine at meals or give him some other punishment of the senses. If that does not work, and you have a room where you could lock him in—as we have in this house—it will be a good idea to use it; for there has to be a good reason to dispense him from his vows, and there is none. His faults are only flightiness and the ardor of youth that we should curb and not tolerate and, still less, encourage, as would happen if we let him continue.

Once you have tried to remedy this by gentleness, forbearance, and long-suffering, it is time to apply to his misconduct both oil and wine together. Perhaps when he sees that pressure is being put on him, he will break with us completely. In that case I will be very sorry, on the one hand, because of the good he could do in the Company and the danger he will be in if he leaves contrary to his vow; on the other, however, it will be a relief for it to be rid of such an incorrigible person.

Since the two Brothers who have been with you for the past eighteen months do not wish to be Brothers, it is unwise for them to remain with you as servants, so please send them away. If the third one wants to stay even if you do not admit his father, well and good. You must not, however, saddle yourself with an elderly man because of the consequences. There are many men in the Company with poor relatives, and they might demand the same thing; if we

---

Letter 2626. - Reg. 2, p. 118.

had to be subjected to that, it would be too great a burden. Tell that good lad that it is enough that his father has another son a priest to help him. If you see that he is determined to leave in order to assist him, let him go, and get some servants in the place of those three Brothers; or we will send you some other Brothers.

2627. - TO FIRMIN GET, SUPERIOR, IN MARSEILLES

Paris, July 19, 1658

Monsieur,

The grace of O[ur] L[ord] be with you forever!

Thank God you are still trying to convince the city of Marseilles to contribute to Chevalier Paul's undertaking and to encourage the other maritime towns in the kingdom to do likewise. We have to await the decision and results of this from God. If you offer the Chevalier the sum of money I mentioned to you, do not tell him you have it, or where it comes from, or—still less—promise it to him, except on condition that he will ransom not just a few slaves but all the French ones in Algiers and will receive nothing until that is done.

I had already raised here to some intelligent persons, who highly approve this undertaking, the objection that was raised to you there, namely, that the Grand Lord [1] might be angry about this and have all the French merchants in the Levant arrested. They replied, however, that we should not fear this nor that the Grand Lord will disapprove of the King's seeking justice for the insults he has received from the town of Algiers and for the harassments his

---

Letter 2627. - Archives of the Mission, Paris, copy made from the original in the Hains Family Collection, Marseilles. This is one of the letters sold at auction by Xavier Charmoy (cf. no. 2505).

[1]Sultan Mehemet IV.

subjects are receiving there. He will not do so once he hears how the city mistreated His Majesty's Consul [2] and the continual unjust seizures it makes on the French. He has already sent a dispatch to M. de la Haye, Ambassador in Constantinople,[3] telling him to register his complaints with the Grand Lord and the Porte.

You tell me that M. Monstier is willing to grant you passage through his land to bring water from the city aqueducts to both your garden and his, provided you alone pay the expenses of this conduit, which could amount to three hundred écus. You say that your friends advise you to do so because it is advantageous for your house. My reply, Monsieur, is that I agree with them and consent to your using the money for that purpose, if you can borrow that amount; but do not expect it from us because we are too short of cash to provide you with it and put ourselves further in debt.

Let me go back to affairs in Algiers. Even if it were true that the Consul had a declaration from the Pasha and the customs office stating that he was no longer being held responsible for others' debts for which he has no written obligation, M. Huguier must still be sent there, as I told you. We are not sending him simply to negotiate this settlement but to see with his own eyes and put his finger on the affairs of the Consul and the true state of his commitments; for, whatever he may write us about them and whatever people may tell me about them here, I have reason to doubt and mistrust the proceedings of both. I am even obliged by the rules of good government to be apprised of everything by a Visitor in order to judge whether or not so many avanias and expenses could have been avoided, and whether the Brother behaved in such a way that he alone went too far and the other could not restrain him. It is hard to believe that, if both of them had been unwilling to make a show of things, the priest would not have tried to control the other one

---

[2]Jean Barreau.

[3]M. de la Haye-Vantelay.

and to urge him to be faithful in not giving or promising what he did not have.

Be that as it may, we have to find out if similar inconveniences can be avoided in the future, whether we leave those persons there or send others. That is why a third person has to go there before M. Le Vacher[4] returns. I hope he will be able to leave Tuesday by the Lyons coach to go to Marseilles. You can put him in M. Parisy's place when you send the latter to replace M. Huguier in Toulon. Please have him [M. Huguier] leave on the first boat that sails for Algiers, where he will be able to see things differently from the way we see them—or at least assure us that they are such as we are being led to understand. He can observe what orders have to be established there for the future and explain to us exactly what has to be done to remedy the past. He will be able to prepare the Consul to return—in the event that he is changed—and give us information in more ways than one that will enable us to know whether God wants to make further use of the Company there.

I sent you a bill of exchange for 3300 livres to be obtained from Messieurs Napollon and given to M. Huguier when he leaves. If by chance you have not received the first one, the second is enclosed. Enclosed also are two bills of exchange drawn by M. Simonnet on Messieurs Napollon. One is for 350 livres, payable eight days after sight to M. Le Vacher, or on his order, which he has given you on the back of the bill. This sum is to be used by him to ransom Jean Senson, alias Bruslotte, from Le Havre, who is a slave in Algiers. He asks you not to send it until he is with you. The other bill of exchange is for 420 livres. Please send them as soon as possible to Roch-Sébastien Hardy from Nancy, who is also a slave in Algiers, together with the 180 livres you received for the same

---

[4]Philippe Le Vacher.

slave last August. I ask you to have these bills of exchange accepted, Monsieur, and to withdraw the payment.

I am, in O[ur] L[ord], Monsieur, your most humble servant.

VINCENT DEPAUL,
i.s.C.M.

2628. - TO EDME JOLLY, SUPERIOR, IN ROME

July 19, 1658

There is reason to praise God that the Pope was willing to be informed about our Institute and the good results of our works by a holy Cardinal who has full knowledge of them. He gave an account of them to His Holiness with such simplicity, clarity, exactness, sound judgment, and kindness toward our Company that Our Holy Father has finally given instructions to the Congregation of Apostolic Visitation to set in motion the means of having us exercise our functions in Rome as we do in Genoa and elsewhere. What consoles me more, however, is that we had nothing to do with all that; it was done by the guidance of God alone, and the less we are involved in it, the better the Will of God will be made known to us. The favorable testimony Cardinal Durazzo [1] gave of us should certainly prompt us to become such as he describes us and to do all the good he attributes to us. Please help us to ask this grace of God.

Letter 2628. - Reg. 2, p. 241.

[1]Stefano Durazzo, Legate in Ferraro, then in Bologna, was created a Cardinal in 1633 and was Archbishop of Genoa (1635-64). He died in Rome on July 22, 1667. Cardinal Durazzo was always most gracious and very devoted to Saint Vincent and his priests.

2629. - TO JEAN MARTIN, SUPERIOR, IN TURIN

Paris, July 19, 1658

Monsieur,

The grace of O[ur] L[ord] be with you forever!

Your dear letter of July 6 [1] has removed our anxiety and filled us with joy. I thank God both for having brought you back to Turin in good health after so much work and for the good results of your big mission, which was greatly blessed by God, from what I can see.

I will have a copy made of the regulations for our Tuesday Conferences and will have it sent to you.

Since the town of Fossano made you the same proposals as Savigliano,[2] and under the same conditions, I think you must have also given it the same reply expressing to it, first of all, profound gratitude for the favor being offered you and, second, our disappointment at not being able to give it the satisfaction it desires because we are forbidden to preach and hear confessions in the towns in which we are established.

You were right to wonder if your brother would be steadfast in his desire to enter our Company, for M. Jolly informs me that he has not seen him for three weeks—which gives us reason to think he has changed his mind. Nevertheless, I am telling him to welcome him if he presents himself for that purpose.

If you have not sent Messieurs Stelle and Beaure to Genoa, please keep the latter and send M. de Martinis [3] with M. Stelle.

Letter 2629. - Archives of the Mission, Turin, original signed letter.

[1]Cf. no. 2618. Only a few of the letters that Saint Vincent received during this period are still extant.

[2]A town in Piedmont.

[3]Girolamo di Martinis (Jérôme de Martinis), born in Fontana Buona, Genoa diocese, on May 15, 1627, entered the Congregation of the Mission in Rome on August 6, 1650, and was ordained a priest in September 1651. He took his vows in October 1652 and renewed them on October 22, 1655. He was Superior in Naples (1673-76).

What you tell me about M. Beaure will oblige us to recall him here, and at that time we will send you another priest in his place. We have not yet sent off M. Cruoly and the others named for Italy; I have been told that it will be time enough if they reach there by September.

I can imagine that, instead of encouraging your men to make an attempt to preach, the grace God has given you for preaching discourages them because they are afraid that there is too great a distance between their conventional style and your too lofty one. I hope, however, that you will help them to determine to do so and to present their topics simply, in the manner with which Our Lord and the Apostles formerly instructed the people and inculcated in them the love of virtue and the hatred of vice.

I praise God for the incomparable acts of kindness of the Marchese, your founder, and for the new house he has procured for you. If it is not large enough, remember that good establishments are not made all at once but gradually. Perhaps God is reserving something better than that for you; you must await His time. Meanwhile, serve Him faithfully in small things so that He will set you over important ones.[4] If you give the missions in the Spirit of O[ur] L[ord], perhaps He will see that you get a seminary and the ordinands.

I highly approve of your sending to Genoa for their seminary the postulants who want to enter the Company and whom you judge suitable, healthy, and having the right intention. Since Brother Pronetti has not finished his, he will not take Holy Orders beforehand.

---

[4]Cf. Mt 25:21. (NAB)

I am, in the love of O[ur] L[ord], Monsieur, your most humble servant.

VINCENT DEPAUL,
i.s.C.M.

Addressed: Monsieur Martin, Superior of the Priests of the Mission of Turin, in Turin

2630. - TO FIRMIN GET, SUPERIOR, IN MARSEILLES

Paris, July 26, 1658

Monsieur,

The grace of O[ur] L[ord] be with you forever!

I am sending you a bill of exchange for twelve hundred livres, drawn by M. Jamen on Messieurs Giraudon and Rimbaud, merchants in Marseilles. This money is for Amable Coquery, a slave in Tunis; it was given me by the Superior of the Oratorian Fathers of Dijon, who sent me the letter the slave wrote him, which I am also sending on to you. Please forward it, along with the money, to M. Le Vacher [1] to help him to know better the person he is supposed to ransom.

M. Le Vacher [2] left for Marseilles Tuesday, traveling there by coach and by water to await M. Huguier's return from Algiers. I ask you to send the latter there on the first available boat, for the reasons I wrote you. I ask you also to change nothing in the

---

Letter 2630. - Archives of the Mission, Paris, copy made from the original in the Hains Family Collection, Marseilles. This is one of the letters sold at auction by Xavier Charmoy (cf. no. 2505).

[1] Jean Le Vacher.

[2] Philippe Le Vacher.

instructions I have given or will give from now on, without first having written me and received my reply, regardless of any proposal M. Le Vacher may make to you about them.

We still have some hope that M. Paul will take on the much-desired project. I think you replied to his secretary as you should have done. If the approval of the Duc de Vendôme is needed, the King's order will have to be deferred.

At the first opportunity, we will send you the two hundred livres we owe M. Delaforcade, which you sent Dominique de Lajus for him, and will add to that another two or three hundred livres to help with your living expenses.

If you gave M. de la Fosse fifty écus for his journey, I do not think there was any reason to get another three pistoles from M. Delaforcade. We have to reimburse him for them; for M. Dupuich, the Superior of the Troyes house is asking me to do so.

I praise God that you are no longer responsible for the three thousand or so livres you had on deposit for three Basque slaves and that you obtained the receipt for them from M. Roman.

On the nineteenth of this month M. Billain[3] went to God. He was a priest of the Company who was in charge of the Troyes Seminary and taught there with exceptional assiduousness and zeal. His soul had a sovereign influence over his body, which it mortified in all its senses in order to subject it to the service of His Divine Majesty. His dedication to that Majesty was such that, if a person could have too much, his would have been excessive. He had a special gift for speaking about God and holy matters, and he expressed his thoughts so clearly that no one could hear him without being moved. Since men of this caliber are rare, we lost a

---

[3]This is obviously a misprint and should read *Villain.* François Villain was born in Paris on April 10, 1605, and possibly baptized on the same day (cf. *Notices*, vols. I and V [Supplement]). He entered the Congregation of the Mission on December 24, 1649, three months after ordination, and took his vows on August 11, 1653. Villain died at the Troyes Seminary on July 19, 1658. (Cf. *Notices*, vol. III, p. 165.)

great deal when we lost him. He was our benefactor, and for that reason we have a double obligation to pray for him. Please have your family offer at least the customary prayers due him.

I had led M. Huguier to hope for a passport from the King, but I have been told that objections would be raised to one being given us because His Majesty has not yet registered his displeasure with the city of Algiers for mistreating the Consul. It seems, furthermore, that this passport would be of no use to him, since the Turks would not honor it. It will suffice for him to get one from the City Magistrates of Marseilles, stating that he is going to Algiers to ransom some slaves—so that no one will think he is going there for some other purpose.

I am, in O[ur] L[ord], Monsieur, your most humble servant.

VINCENT DEPAUL,
i.s.C.M.

2631. - TO JEAN MARTIN, SUPERIOR, IN TURIN

Paris, July 26, 1658

Monsieur,

The grace of O[ur] L[ord] be with you forever!

Even though the letter I wrote you last week may serve as a reply to the one dated July 12, which I have received from you since then, I still thought I should let you know that I received yours. I also want to ask you once again to send Messieurs Stelle and de Martinis to Genoa, if you have not already sent M. Beaure there with M. Stelle, in accord with the first order.

I consent to your sending to the Genoa Seminary those persons whom you will find truly suitable for the Company, after testing

---

Letter 2631. - Archives of the Mission, Turin, original signed letter. The postscript is in the Saint's handwriting.

their desire and their vocation for a certain time. To judge from appearances, Brother Pronetti, whom we have here, will not last long.

Enclosed at last is a dimissorial letter [1] for Brother Demortier.[2] If you need priests, just write to M. Jolly to send you an *extra tempora* to make a good priest [3] of this good Brother soon.

Since progress on your establishment is slow, you must be patient. In this world, things that of their nature must last longer are the ones that take the longest to develop. If your family is very faithful to God, His rules, and His works, nothing will be wanting to it, God willing.

I will take the honor of writing to the Marchese di Pianezza at another time to thank him for all the care he deigns to take of his Missionaries and for the affection he certainly shows you.

On the nineteenth of this month M. Villain went to God; he was a priest of the Company, who was in charge of the Troyes Seminary and taught there with exceptional assiduousness and zeal. His soul had a sovereign influence over his body, which it mortified in all its senses to subject it to the service of God. He had so much dedication to it that, if one could have too much, his would have been excessive. He had a special gift for speaking about God and holy matters, and he expressed his thoughts so clearly that no one could listen to him without being moved. Since such men of great prayer and action are rare, we have lost a great deal in losing him. He was our benefactor, and for that reason we have a double obligation to pray for him. Please have your family pay him the

---

[1]Statement giving a subject permission to be ordained by a Bishop other than his own Ordinary. Exempt religious cannot be ordained by any Bishop without dimissorial letters from their own Major Superior.

[2]Raymond Demortier, born in Marquay (Dordogne) on November 15, 1634, entered the Congregation of the Mission on March 18, 1655, and took his vows on May 20, 1657, in the presence of M. Bertier. He was one of the witnesses at the process of inquiry with regard to the virtues of Saint Vincent.

[3]The words "good priest" are in the Saint's handwriting.

customary respects due him. I embrace it, and you in particular, with all the tenderness of my heart, and I am, in the love of O[ur] L[ord], Monsieur, your most humble servant.

VINCENT DEPAUL,
i.s.C.M.

If both Messieurs Stelle and Beaure have not left, please send them as soon as you have received this letter.

Addressed: Monsieur Martin, Superior of the Priests of the Mission, in Turin

2632. - TO LOUIS RIVET, SUPERIOR, IN SAINTES

July 28, 1658

It is true, Monsieur, that it is not advisable to speak about our vows to persons outside the Company. If it is necessary to let them know that we are bound to practice the virtues we have vowed, we can do so in terms of the virtues and not that of the vows because people of the world may take them as vows of religion—although they are simple and can be dispensed—and may take us for religious, which we are not.

Letter 2632. - Reg. 2, p. 21.

2633. - TO FIRMIN GET, SUPERIOR, IN MARSEILLES

Paris, August 2, 1658

Monsieur,

The grace of O[ur] L[ord] be with you forever!

You did well to send M. Parisy to Toulon; he will get some experience and, when M. Huguier is in Marseilles, he can submit his difficulties to him, if he has any.

I am not of the opinion that M. Huguier should go to Leghorn to look for an opportunity to get into Algiers, but rather that he—and we along with him—should wait in Marseilles, and wait patiently if it is long in coming. Apparently, there is no urgency regarding the Consul,[1] who seems to be at peace.

And what is to be done regarding the slaves? You cannot send them their money if no boat is leaving from your port, but you can have it forwarded to them by the first one that goes—I mean the money you have received or may receive for specific slaves whose names you have—but I am afraid that, if you make M. Huguier responsible for it, he will be considered a ransomer there, and that may be prejudicial to him. If the captain of the boat could be relied on to hand over the money to the slaves or to use it for their ransom, it would be better to give it to him, with the instructions and list for its use, while still making M. Huguier responsible for seeing that it is done. Do whatever God inspires you to do.

I will write to Le Havre to find out if the one hundred livres you received for Nicolas Renouard the father, who has returned to his own country, will be given to the son, who is still a slave; it seems that this is what the relatives want. I will be glad to know if the bill of exchange for 3300 livres has been paid punctually. I fully

---

Letter 2633. - Archives of the Mission, Paris, copy made from the original in the Hains Family Collection, Marseilles. This is one of the letters sold at auction by Xavier Charmoy (cf. no. 2505).

[1]Jean Barreau.

approve of your having had seized from M. Fabre[2] the 1800 livres he owes the Jews, as insurance for the 950 piastres paid by the Consul in Algiers because of the avania they committed against him. To prove that they are the ones, Brother Barreau will have to send you a well-authenticated attestation and the other documents that can serve to have his reimbursement awarded him in Marseilles for that amount, which you will decide.

We will pray most willingly that God will restore calm amid the troubles that have arisen there. I would have been very pleased to know the cause of them and how many men were killed.[3]

We received eight livres for a convict in Toulon named Alexis Deleau, who is on the *Reine;* please have someone give them to him.

I am, in O[ur] L[ord], Monsieur, your most humble servant.

VINCENT DEPAUL,
i.s.C.M.

2634. - TO EDME JOLLY, SUPERIOR, IN ROME

Paris, August 2, 1658

Monsieur,

The grace of O[ur] L[ord] be with you forever!

---

[2]This Marseilles merchant absconded from Algiers and returned to France to avoid paying a debt of twelve thousand écus, which resulted in another jail term for the Consul.

[3]The people of Marseilles had been against their Consuls from the time when the King reserved to himself the right to choose these public servants. They revolted on July 13, 1658, after hearing that one of them had stated that he was accountable for his actions only to the King and the Governor of the province and would assert his authority by force, if need be. Fifteen persons died that day, and many were wounded. On July 19, a riot broke out again, more violent than ever, leaving in its wake a greater number of victims. (Cf. Augustin Fabre, *Histoire de Marseille* [Marseille: M. Olive, 1829], pp. 269ff.)

Letter 2634. - Archives of the Mission, Turin, original signed letter.

I did not get any letters from you this time. They say that the mail from Italy was intercepted by the Spanish and taken to Milan. I fear that your packet may be lost. I think it contained the Bulls for Bussière.[1] If we hear any other news about it, I will let you know.

M. Le Blanc [2] is here with us; he left Messieurs de Fontaines and Arnoul sick in the hospital of Santiago[3] in Galicia, but they are beginning to recover. M. Daveroult has stayed in Portugal, and Brother Christophe in Saintes, where he fell ill. That is how God has been pleased to disperse our Madagascar Missionaries.

I ask you once again to see about the dispensation for M. Geoffroy,[4] a priest in our seminary.

Your most humble servant.

VINCENT DEPAUL,
i.s.C.M.

There is reason to fear some troublesome consequence if we spell out in detail the value of the Saint-Lazare property in the way the Bull for the union with Saint-Pourçain[5] seems to be dictating. We make a distinction between two kinds of goods: the first, those belonging to the Saint-Lazare Priory, and the second, from the foundations made since our establishment at Saint-Lazare. These foundations state that they are given to the Mission of Saint-Lazare. If we declare everything, the total is very high because of gifts granted to the house in the city of Paris[6] and from the *aides*,[7] of

---

[1]In 1656 Claude de Blampignon had resigned Bussière-Badil Priory in favor of Gilbert Cuissot, who resigned it in his turn in favor of Denis Laudin. The Bulls substituting Laudin for Cuissot, for which Saint Vincent was waiting, were signed in Rome on June 4, 1658. (Cf. Arch. Nat., S 6703.)

[2]Charles Le Blanc.

[3]Santiago de Compostela in Spain.

[4]Yves Geoffroy, born in Quimper-Corentin (Finistère) in July 1624, was admitted to Saint-Lazare as a priest on August 1, 1657.

[5]The Bull of Union of Saint-Pourçain Priory to Saint-Lazare.

[6]The Collège des Bons-Enfants. Saint-Lazare was outside the city of Paris.

[7]Indirect taxes on consumer goods such as meat, fish, wood, and especially wine.

which a stroke of the pen can deprive us, and which happens only too often. If we declare only that of the Saint-Lazare Priory, we fear that the union will be null and void. Here are the terms of the Bull: *Quique dudum inter alia voluimus et ordinavimus quod petentes beneficia ecclesiastica aliis uniri tenerentur exprimere verum annuum valorem secundum communem aestimationem, etiam beneficii cui aliud unire petetur, alioquin unio non valeret.*[8] Please seek some advice, Monsieur, and let me know as soon as possible if it suffices for us to show the revenue of the priory alone; please consider the meaning of the word "benefices."

I ask you not to work on that yourself but to get someone else to do it, and for you to go off to Frascati or Tivoli to take a very good rest until after the rains.[9]

At the bottom of the first page: Monsieur Jolly

2635. - TO LOUIS RIVET, SUPERIOR, IN SAINTES

August 4, 1658

Please indicate to me the particular cases of usury for which you desire a solution. I will give a reply for each one. In the meantime, follow the maxims of the Sorbonne, never speaking disparagingly of those who have contrary opinions. In this way, you will honor and cherish them as our Fathers. Do not tell anyone what I am writing to you, unless you do so confidentially to our confreres, and never to others.

---

[8]*Some time ago we had already decided and ordained, among other things, that those who ask that ecclesiastical benefices be united to other benefices must declare their true annual income according to common estimation, as well as the income from the benefice to which they ask that another benefice be united; otherwise the union would be invalid.*

[9]The entire postscript is in Saint Vincent's handwriting.

Letter 2635. - Reg. 2, p. 114.

2636. - TO DENIS LAUDIN, SUPERIOR, IN LE MANS

August 7, 1658

I am consoled to hear that you intend to put up a little longer with the Brother I had advised you to dismiss rather than to retain him as a servant. Bear with him, then, Monsieur, but see that he keeps the Rules as much as possible, according to the Spirit of Our Lord, which is both gentle and firm at the same time. If a man cannot be won over by gentleness and patience, it will be difficult to do so otherwise; but neither is it advisable to let him do and say whatever he pleases, which is not proper to his situation.

Brother . . . has a brother who is studying in Le Mans and is thinking about entering the Company. You know that; please inform me of his age, studies, intellectual abilities, health—in a word, anything that can give us sufficient knowledge to judge whether we should admit him now or put him off to a later time, and whether to have him come here or send him to Richelieu.

I am afraid he may be attracted by regard for his brother or curiosity to see Paris—or both of these together—rather than by the desire to renounce the world entirely. Will you please let me know your opinion on this?

2637. - TO JEAN MARTIN, SUPERIOR, IN TURIN

Paris, August 9, 1658

Monsieur,

The grace of O[ur] L[ord] be with you forever!

I received your letter of July 20, which consoled me by inform-

---

Letter 2636. - Reg. 2, p. 169.

Letter 2637. - Archives of the Mission, Turin, original signed letter.

ing me of your dear news and the departure of the three priests you sent to Genoa. But what you tell me about M. B[eaure] filled me with a sadness more intense than anything I have heard in a long time. It is absolutely imperative to remove him from where he is. All that is needed to ruin the reputation of the Company and hinder the good results it can produce there is a Missionary who takes the liberty he does. Please try, Monsieur, to send M. Martinis to Genoa so you can recall the other man. M. Berthe is supposed to go there soon and will stop and see you in Turin on his way.

What increases my anxiety is the failure you have noticed in Brother Dum . . . in such a risky matter. Please let me know the specific things he has done that have given you reason to inform me of it. In the meantime, do your utmost by corrections, penances, kind and gentle admonitions, and other ways with which God will inspire you, and above all by keeping an eye on him, to see that he corrects those faults and breaks off completely, now and for always, useless conversations with persons of the other sex. Otherwise, he should not be allowed to take Holy Orders.

I praise God for the total offering M. Laurence has made to Him, for his progress in the language, and for the satisfaction you hope to receive from him.

M. Delaforcade has been paid his postage for the letters. Until now we have given him almost sixty francs for you; but, for the future, it is to be desired that you take care of paying him either every six months or annually, according to what he wishes. He keeps an exact account of the money. Poor Saint-Lazare is too overburdened to be able to help other houses with that, when they can do so themselves.

We have no news.

I am, in the love of O[ur] L[ord], Monsieur, your most humble servant.

VINCENT DEPAUL,
i.s.C.M.

I am not sure that M. Berthe will be stopping in Turin. Do not send M. Martinis to Genoa until I tell you. I want him to be there at the same time as the Visitor, and not sooner. Meanwhile, prepare him to go, without mentioning the reason. If he were unable to go, I would ask you for M. Mugnier [1] or someone else. We will send in his place M. Chardon,[2] who is a good priest from Savoy. I am taking the honor of writing a word of thanks to your founder, as you wish—I have not yet written but will do so as soon as possible.

At the bottom of the first page: Monsieur Martin

2638. - TO THE MARCHESE DI PIANEZZA

August 9, 1658

My Lord,

I can no longer refrain from intruding on you; your continued benefits demand that I write you this little note of thanks. From what I hear, My Lord, your charity is unparalleled, and I do not know how to thank you for the favors you shower upon your poor Missionaries. I pray that the ones O[ur] L[ord] bestows on you may increase infinitely and serve as an eternal thanks to you for all the services you render and have others render Him, especially those poor priests. You have once again housed them, you maintain them with your resources, you tolerate their shortcomings, and you protect them as your own children.

---

[1]Jean-Jacques Mugnier, born in Esvière, Geneva diocese, on November 30, 1608, was ordained a priest on December 18, 1632, entered the Congregation of the Mission on December 15, 1642, and took his vows on March 16, 1645. He was Superior of Agde (1654-56).

[2]Philbert Chardon, born in Annecy in November 1629, entered the Congregation of the Mission on October 3, 1647, took his vows in October 1649, and was ordained a priest during Lent of 1654. That same year he left the Company but was readmitted in Rome; from there he was sent to Genoa (cf. no. 1771).

Letter 2638. - Reg. 1, fol. 36.

Mon Dieu! My Lord, how indebted we are to you! My realization of this makes me hope that the Divine Majesty will either destroy us or make us worthy of honoring Him according to your holy intentions. Since His intention is that we obey you perfectly, I assure you, My Lord, that I, personally, will strive to do so all my life, and I venture to promise that all of us will do the same, such as we are. We will pray especially for the preservation of your dear self and that God may be pleased to sanctify your beautiful soul more and more and to bless your illustrious family.

I entreat you most humbly, My Lord, to accept these tender affections of my heart, which is filled with respect and reverence for yours.

I am, in the love of O[ur] L[ord], My Lord, your. . . .

VINCENT DEPAUL,
i.s.C.M.

2639. - TO FIRMIN GET, SUPERIOR, IN MARSEILLES

Paris, August 9, 1658

Monsieur,

The grace of O[ur] L[ord] be with you forever!

I am very concerned about M. Le Vacher in Tunis because I have received no news of him since he has been ill. Let me know if you have heard anything. As for his brother, I think he is now with you in Marseilles.

Letter 2639. - Archives of the Mission, Paris, copy made from the original in the Hains Family Collection, Marseilles. This is one of the letters sold at auction by Xavier Charmoy (cf. no. 2505).

We have not yet sent you the balance of the money for the poor slaves. This is due to the bankruptcies that have occurred—causing us to fear the worst—and the disturbances that have arisen in the city of Marseilles, which have made us decide to wait awhile. I hope we will send you some money for your living expenses next week without fail, but we cannot give you any for your water conduit.

Since the Duchesse d'Aiguillon is not here, I could not discuss with her the sale of the Tunis consulate so I am unable to settle that for you until she returns from Le Havre. Still, let me tell you in advance that, if it is sold, it is to be feared that the Consul may be unwilling to have a priest with him and may find a way to get rid of him so as to have greater freedom to do what he wants. If we lease it out, the tax farmer may instigate some avanias against that priest or have him expelled to safeguard the cost of the lease. In which case, the poor slaves could no longer be assisted. Now, the deprivation of that benefit would be disastrous for them.

If Messieurs Le Vacher and Huguier are with you, I embrace them most cordially.

I am really distressed by the blockade of Marseilles, and I ask O[ur] L[ord] not to allow this incipient disturbance to go any further, for it can have only disastrous results.

I am writing to M. Huguier in Toulon and, if he is not there, to M. Parisy, to give Vincent Traverse five sous a day for three months, beginning September 1. We received seven écus from his mother for that purpose, and the money M. Huguier received should last until the end of this month. Please send us the account of what you have given him for the poor convicts so I can reimburse you for it.

I am, in O[ur] L[ord], Monsieur, your most humble servant.

VINCENT DEPAUL,
i.s.C.M.

2640. - TO EDME JOLLY, SUPERIOR, IN ROME

August 9, 1658

I praise God, Monsieur, for the decree given by the Congregation of Apostolic Visitation, stating that we will be provided with a house in Rome. This is the result of your efforts, and we owe this favor—as well as many others we have received—to your good leadership. If the opportunity to put this decree into effect does not present itself now, it will do so some day. We must await it patiently and expect it from God rather than from men.

2641. - TO SISTER ANNE HARDEMONT, SISTER SERVANT, IN USSEL

Paris, August 10, 1658

Dear Sister,

The grace of O[ur] L[ord] be with you forever!

I have had several letters from you and a great deal of sorrow because of what you are suffering. Yes, I pity you, when I see your poor heart groaning, oppressed by that terrible aversion you are experiencing there. May God in His merciful gentleness lessen your suffering and make you see that you are happier than you think! Yes, Sister, our happiness lies in the Cross, and Our Lord willed to enter His glory only through the difficult things He endured. He is leading you along the path of the saints; please do not be surprised at this, but be patient, allow Him to act, and tell Him that you want His Will and not yours to be done. I am well aware that you observe this practice and offer yourself to Him to do and to suffer whatever He pleases, but you must continue to do

---

Letter 2640. - Reg. 2, p. 241.

Letter 2641. - Archives of the Mission, Paris, original signed letter.

so with confidence and not allow yourself to be overwhelmed by discouragement. If you are steadfast in remaining in the place where you now are and to rise above yourself in the service of the poor, you will deserve that His Divine Goodness will change your sorrow into joy and your aversion into pleasure—which is what I hope He will do. You will also edify your Sister and encourage her in the practice of virtue.

You thought that Mademoiselle Le Gras sent you to that area to get rid of you. *O Dieu!* Sister, how far from the truth that statement is! For I know that she appreciates and loves you and has tried to do what is good for you by sending you with a very devout Lady for the service of O[ur] L[ord] and the relief of His poor members. You must indeed thank God for the choice Providence has made in selecting you to go to Ussel; [1] for, if you had been here, you would have been sent to Calais, where the Queen ordered us to send four Sisters to nurse the wounded soldiers. All of them became ill, and two of them died there.[2] I do not know if the others will recover, which has obliged us to send another four, who left here with great determination, despite the danger. When Sister Henriette,[3] the oldest member of the Company, heard about the illness and death

---

[1]At the request of the Duchesse de Ventadour, Saint Louise had sent Sisters Anne Hardemont and Avoie Vigneron to Ussel in May 1658 for the purpose of founding a hospital. They were overwhelmed by the difficulties of starting a work and allowed themselves to yield to discouragement.

[2]Cf. no. 2610, n. 6.

[3]Henriette Gesseaume, a highly intelligent, resourceful, but very independent Daughter of Charity. She was one of the first members of the Company, which she entered in 1634 at the age of twenty-six. Her early years in Community were spent in and around Paris: Saint-Germain-en-Laye (1638), Fontenay-aux-Roses (1643), and Saint-Germain parish (1644). A skilled pharmacist, she was of great assistance at the Nantes Hospital (1646-55). Assigned once again to Paris, she served the poor in Saint-Séverin parish. As mentioned here, she left to nurse the wounded soldiers in Calais. Upon her return, she served the galley slaves. Two of her nieces, Françoise Gesseaume and Perrette Chefdeville, also became Daughters of Charity. Her brother Claude and a nephew, Nicolas Chefdeville, were coadjutor Brothers in the Congregation of the Mission.

Of those being sent to Calais, Saint Vincent mentions only Sister Henriette here and in his conference of August 4, 1658 (cf. vol. X, no. 100). We know from Saint Louise's *Spiritual Writings* (L. 595, p. 615) and from *Documents* (Doc. 725, p. 831) that Sister Marie Cuny, a Sister Françoise, and a Sister Jeanne accompanied Sister Henriette. In a letter of September 10

of her Sisters, she was inspired by God to risk her life for the neighbor by asking to take their place—an act of love of God that is most pleasing to His Majesty.

Blessed are those souls who have died in the practice of charity, whose name they bear! And you, Sister, who also bear it, are likewise fortunate to be in a place and in a situation where you can give your care, your work, and even your life for charity, so as to win the same crown—and perhaps an even greater one. So, I ask you, Sister, to make up your mind to remain at peace where you are, not allowing yourself to think about returning here or being sent to Cahors. The first suggestion is not advisable and the other is not timely. I ask O[ur] L[ord] once again to strengthen and bless you.

I am, in His love, Sister, your most affectionate brother and servant.

VINCENT DEPAUL,
i.s.C.M.

Addressed: Sister Anne Hardemont, Daughter of Charity, Servant of the Sick Poor, in Ussel

---

(cf. *Documents* Doc. 729, p. 837), Sister Henriette wrote that Sister Marie was ill. She was brought back to Paris on a stretcher at the end of the month; Sister Françoise accompanied her. Sister Élisabeth Charpy, D.C., editor of *Écrits spirituels* (cf. *Spiritual Writings,* L. 590, p. 608), tells us that Sisters Marie Poulet, Claude Muset, Henriette Gesseaume, and a Sister Françoise returned to Paris at the end of October.

2642. - TO FIRMIN GET, SUPERIOR, IN MARSEILLES

Paris, August 16, 1658

Monsieur,

The grace of O[ur] L[ord] be with you forever!

In your letter of the sixth you tell me you are sending back the bill of exchange for twelve hundred livres drawn by M. Jamen on Messieurs Giraudon and Rimbaud because they refused to accept it; however, I did not find it in your packet. No doubt you left it on your desk; I am very sorry about that because the delay may be prejudicial to the person to whom we have to give it to obtain the money for M. Jamen's reimbursement. You also say that, since the bill of exchange was protested, he can be obliged to make restitution. You do not say, however, if you are the one who had it protested, as should have been done, or whether you are assuming that the protest will be made here to M. Jamen. I would like to think that, when you noticed that you left the bill of exchange out of the last packet I received from you, you put it in the one I hope to receive next week. Therefore, I am not asking you to have it protested there, if it has not already been done, nor to send it to me in haste because you know that is necessary.

I just sent four hundred livres to M. Simonnet so you can obtain them in Marseilles for what you need, until I can send you something else by some members of our Company whom we have to send to Italy shortly.

We no longer dare to entrust large sums of money to the merchants because of the inconveniences that have arisen recently.

I do not think M. Huguier should go to Algiers either by way of the Bastion [1] or by way of Leghorn but rather that he should wait

---

Letter 2642. - Archives of the Mission, Paris, copy made from the original in the Hains Family Collection, Marseilles. This is one of the letters sold at auction by Xavier Charmoy (cf. no. 2505).

[1]The Bastion of France.

in Marseilles for the first boat leaving for Algiers. M. Le Vacher of Tunis has informed me that, in his opinion, no one should go until the King has registered his displeasure—not even M. Le Vacher his brother [2] nor M. Huguier. However, I do not think there will be any problem for the latter, since he is going there to ransom three slaves. Please let me know your opinion on this.

I praise God for the settlement between Marseilles and the Governor.[3]

We received ten livres ten sous for Renaud Le Page, three livres for Jacques Mauge, and thirty sous for a priest named M. Esbran; all three are convicts. I ask M. Parisy to give each one his share, and I ask you to credit him for it.

Send us M. Huguier's account of what he advanced to the convicts by our order since the last account we paid; I will forward to you what we have for that.

Madame de Romilly just sent us fifty livres for her son, a slave in Tunis. Please send them to M. Le Vacher to be given to him. We will credit you for this. Enclosed is a packet from that good lady.

We have just been told that Messieurs Giraudon and Rimbaud will give you the twelve hundred livres allocated for the ransom of Amable Coquery, a slave in Tunis—not by virtue of M. Jamen's bill of exchange, which they refused, but on another order to be sent to them today. When you receive this letter, I ask you to find out if they will accept delivering that amount to you.

I am, in O[ur] L[ord], Monsieur, your most humble servant.

VINCENT DEPAUL,
i.s.C.M.

---

[2]Philippe Le Vacher, who was still in Europe.

[3]Following the troubles of July 13 and 19, the Duc de Mercoeur, Governor of Provence, agreed to negotiate with the rebels. The agreement was based on the following conditions: a full and complete amnesty to be granted to the rebels; a promise to withdraw the royal troops and send the ships away, provided that the Consuls and the Assessor be reinstated in their positions and the citizens lay down their arms (Fabre, *op. cit.*, pp. 279ff.).

2643. - TO JACQUES PESNELLE,[1] SUPERIOR, IN GENOA

August 23, 1658

You do very well to be attentive to the physical health and intellectual abilities of the postulants so as not to burden yourself, if possible, with any who are unlikely to succeed. It suffices, however, for them to have good health, intelligence, and the right intention, although they may have no extraordinary gifts or even no talent for preaching. We have so many other things to do that no one who wants to work with us remains idle, thank God. On the contrary, the simple, most ordinary workers are, as a rule, the ones best suited for us and most useful for the poor people. God knows how to raise up children of Abraham from stones; [2] and Our Lord chose rough persons for His disciples and made apostolic men of them. Without any formal learning, lofty minds, or commanding presence, they still served as instruments of their Divine Master to convert everyone. Provided Missionaries are truly humble, very obedient, mortified, zealous, and filled with confidence in God, His Divine Goodness will use them effectively everywhere and will supply for other qualities they might lack.

Letter 2643. - Reg. 2, p. 40.

[1]Jacques Pesnelle, born in Rouen (Seine-Maritime) on June 5, 1624, entered the Congregation of the Mission on September 4, 1646, was ordained a priest in Rome on November 30, 1648, and took his vows there. He was Superior in Genoa (1657-66, 1674-77), and Turin (1667-72, 1677-83). A very gifted man, highly esteemed by Saint Vincent, Pesnelle died in 1683.

[2]Cf. Lk 3:8. (NAB)

2644. - TO EDME JOLLY, SUPERIOR, IN ROME

Paris, August 23, 1658

Monsieur,

The grace of O[ur] L[ord] be with you forever!

I received your letter of July 22. We sent M. Gicquel [1] to Clermont for the fulmination of the Bull for Saint-Pourçain[2] and are going to send to Dol[3] the Bulls and reports concerning Saint-Méen. We obtained the new written consent of the Abbot—but not without difficulty. We are now going to set to work in good earnest on these two important affairs.

We made no mention to the Officialis of Paris of the Saint Lazare affair because I think he is only the vicegerent, and also because he is very wary of getting involved in the official proclamation of the Bull, or of saying what he will or might do, before he has the documents in his hands. If he becomes too difficult, we will have recourse to higher authority, who will give us letters to have the Bulls registered in the Parlement, where we have nothing to fear.

I had made up my mind yesterday to write to you today in my

Letter 2644. - Archives of the Mission, Paris, original signed letter.

[1]Jean Gicquel, born in Miniac (Ille-et-Vilaine) on December 24, 1617, was ordained a priest during Lent of 1642, entered the Congregation of the Mission on August 5, 1647, and took his vows on May 6, 1651. He was Superior of the Le Mans Seminary (1651-54) and at Saint-Lazare (1655-60) (cf. vol. V, nos. 1908 and 1912; vol. VI, no. 2157), and was Director of the Company of the Daughters of Charity (1668-72). Gicquel wrote an interesting diary of Saint Vincent's final days (cf. vol. XIII, no. 57), which is preserved in the Archives of the Mission, Paris. He died in 1672.

[2]As noted earlier (cf. no. 2494, n. 4), Abbé Louis de Chandenier had offered Saint-Pourçain Priory to Saint-Lazare. The Bishop of Clermont-Ferrand, Louis d'Estaing, demanded that as the price of his approval Saint Vincent engage the Congregation of the Mission to preach a "continual and perpetual mission" in his diocese; Saint Vincent proposed that a mission be given every five years at Saint-Pourçain. Jean Gicquel was sent to Clermont to make the official proclamation (fulmination) of the Papal decree of union. As will be seen in this volume, Saint Vincent feared that the formalities of this were not fulfilled. Finally, on March 2, 1660, the Officialis of Clermont proclaimed publicly the Bull of Union, and on March 6 Gicquel took possession of the priory in the name of the Congregation of the Mission (cf. vol. VIII, no. 2934).

[3]A locality near Saint-Malo (Ille-et-Vilaine). A problem similar to that of Saint-Pourçain existed with regard to Saint-Méen (cf. no. 2583).

own hand the notes on the regular meetings held in Paris for various good works and the good the members are doing. I do not know if I will have the time; if not, I will make time between this letter and the next regular mail. So much for my reply to your dear letter.

Enclosed is a memorandum signed by M. Portail. Please send us the books and replies he is requesting.

I am, in the love of O[ur] L[ord], Monsieur, your most humble servant.

VINCENT DEPAUL,
i.s.C.M.

Addressed: Monsieur Jolly

2645. - TO FIRMIN GET, SUPERIOR, IN MARSEILLES

Paris, August 23, 1658

Monsieur,

The grace of O[ur] L[ord] be with you forever!

I received M. Jamen's bill of exchange, together with the act of protest made to Messieurs Giraudon and Rimbaud, who refused it.

I also think that M. Huguier should leave on the first boat sailing to Algiers, and not to the Bastion. What has made me a little hesitant about that is the letter from M. Le Vacher in Tunis urging us not to send his brother or anyone else to Algiers until the King first registers his displeasure to the Turks over what has taken place. He is right in saying that with regard to M. Le Vacher [1] and anyone else we might send there to replace him or the Consul. I think,

---

Letter 2645. - Archives of the Mission, Paris, copy made from the original in the Hains Family Collection. This is one of the letters sold at auction by Xavier Charmoy (cf. no. 2505).

[1]Philippe Le Vacher.

however, that, if he knew that M. Huguier was going there only to ransom three slaves and, incidentally, to get the lay of the land, with no intention of staying, he would have felt the same as we do. Therefore, please do not allow M. Huguier to lose the first opportunity. I have no other reply to your letter of August 13.

We just received two écus, one for Martin de Lancre on the galley *Mercoeur* and the other for Jean Meglat on the galley *Manse*. Please give—or have someone give—them this little aid. Enclosed is a letter for the former, and I am sending another to M. Parisy for the latter.

I am, in O[ur] L[ord], Monsieur, your most humble servant.

VINCENT DEPAUL,
i.s.C.M.

2646. - TO SISTER AVOIE VIGNERON, IN USSEL

Paris, August 24, 1658

Dear Sister,

The grace of O[ur] L[ord] be with you forever!

I have written two letters to good Sister Anne;[1] I wanted to write to you as well at the time but was unable to do so because I was so busy. Now I am replying to your letters, including the one you wrote to M. Portail.

You say that God is testing you to try your patience. That is a good thing, Sister, for it is a sign that His Divine Goodness wants you to make progress in that virtue so that, through its practice, all the trials and tribulations of this world will turn to your honor and benefit.

Letter 2646. - Archives of the Motherhouse of the Daughters of Charity, original signed letter.

[1]Anne Hardemont. One of these is no. 2641 (August 10); the other is not extant.

It is a general rule that only through sufferings do we attain heaven; yet, not all those who suffer will be saved, but only those who suffer willingly for love of Jesus Christ, who first suffered for us. When you consider this, you should rejoice instead of becoming discouraged; and instead of becoming depressed, trust in God, who will never allow you to be tempted beyond your strength.[2] You add that you have already shed many tears, prayed, and made novenas. All that is good. "Blessed are those who weep," [3] said Our Lord, and "those who ask will receive," [4] but He did not say that we would be answered as soon as we have prayed; this is so that we will not stop praying.

That is why, Sister, you should not have said what you allowed to slip out: that the more you pray, the less you obtain; for that shows that you are not really resigned to God's Will and do not trust enough in His promises. Often, by refusing what we ask, He grants us a greater grace than by giving it to us, and we should realize that, since He knows what is good for us better than we do, what He sends us is best, even if it is disagreeable to nature and contrary to our wishes.

Mon Dieu! Sister, how I pity you in your trials and how I sympathize with poor Sister Anne, weighed down by her repugnances! *Mais quoi!* this is a trial God is permitting to test you, as you say, so welcome it as a favor from His paternal hand and try to make good use of it. Help your Sister to carry her cross, since yours is not as heavy as hers; remind her that she is a Daughter of Charity and must be crucified with Our Lord, submitting to His good pleasure so as not to be totally unworthy of such a worthy Father. Alas! if she does not surmount these petty repugnances of spirit, how could she put up with greater afflictions? I am afraid we may be too sensitive to little difficulties and not sufficiently

---

[2]Cf. 1 Cor 10:13. (NAB)
[3]Cf. Mt 5:5. (NAB)
[4]Cf. Lk 11:10. (NAB)

determined to overcome the ones to be encountered in the service of God and the poor. We would like to find consolations in it and for everything to go our way; we are unwilling to serve God when it costs us something, but we want to receive, even in this world, peace of mind as a reward for bodily labor. That, however, is not how you will make yourself pleasing to God, Sister, but by suffering patiently interior as well as exterior trials.

You are wrong to blame Mademoiselle[5] for these troubles or to be determined not to write to her any more because you are not happy with her letters. Nor should you attribute to others, as you do, the choice made of you by Divine Providence, who alone has called both of you to the place where you now are. You will acknowledge this when you obey your Superiors for the love of God, and you will consider Him alone in the orders you receive.

I have replied to Sister Anne regarding her desire to go to Cahors. If this desire came from God, as you think, she would not be upset by it, as she is, and would leave that to the persons who are guiding her. If she strives to do God's Will in Ussel, there is reason to hope that she will also do it elsewhere. Lastly, if she does not, in fact, feel at peace there, and a house is opened in Cahors or Montpellier, we could send her to one or the other, but those matters are not yet settled, and she must be patient in the place where she now is, since this is God's Will.

Neither she nor you should worry so much whether the hospital is well established, or well constituted, or sufficiently funded. Serve the poor to the best of your ability and entrust the rest to the goodness of God. All His works have their beginnings and development, and if the Duchess[6] is unable just now to put everything in the state that is to be desired, it can be done with time. As for you, do whatever God asks of you and remain at peace; above all, love and support one another in Our Lord.

---

[5]Saint Louise.

[6]The Duchesse de Ventadour.

I send my most affectionate greetings to you, and I ask God to give you His holy strength and many blessings. Mademoiselle is very well. Four of your Sisters [7] are going off to open a house in Metz.

I am, in O[ur] L[ord], Sister, your brother and servant.

VINCENT DEPAUL,
i.s.C.M.

At the bottom of the first page: Sister Avoie Vigneron

2647. - TO MARAND-IGNACE ARNOUL AND PASQUIER DE FONTAINES [1]

August 25, 1658

God alone can make you realize how worried we are about you—more worried than I can tell you because, since M. Le Blanc[2] arrived here a month ago and Brother Christophe arrived in Saintes, I know neither the place nor the state in which you are. They told us you remained in Compostela because you were sick but out of danger. I am taking a chance on sending this letter, addressing it to the Bishop of Ferns [3] in San Sebastian, to ask you, if you pass through there, to console us as soon as possible with a letter from you, while we await your much-desired presence here. And so that you will not lack money for clothing and the journey, I am asking the Bishop of Ferns to lend you enough to get you to Bayonne, and

---

[7]Françoise Manceau, Marguerite Ménage, Marie Poulet, and Claude Muset.

Letter 2647. - Reg. 2, p. 121.

[1]Captured on the high seas by the Spanish during their voyage to Madagascar, they were taken to Santiago de Compostela.

[2]Charles Le Blanc.

[3]Nicholas French, Bishop of Ferns (Ireland), who was exiled in Spain at the time; he died in Louvain on August 23, 1678.

the Bishop of Bayonne[4] to see that you get four hundred livres, if you need that much. I also wrote to M. Fonteneil,[5] the Archdeacon and Vicar-General of Bordeaux, to advance you whatever you will need. Even the coach master has orders to give you a place in the carriage and have your expenses defrayed as far as Paris, if need be.

Above all, Messieurs, please get a good rest and recuperate after the many hardships you have endured, and spare nothing for this. Then take your time getting back here. I cannot tell you how happy I will be to see and embrace you once again.

2648. - TO LOUIS RIVET, SUPERIOR, IN SAINTES

August 25, 1658

Please see that Brother Christophe gets some new clothes. *Mon Dieu!* Monsieur, what have you done since he arrived! You saw his need; you knew he was our Brother and that you would give us pleasure; yet, you left him in his rags!

---

[4]Jean Dolce, Bishop of Bayonne (1643-81).

[5]Jean de Fonteneil, born in Bordeaux around 1605, was a friend and admirer of Saint Vincent. His outstanding qualities earned him the highest positions in the diocese. He was appointed Canon of Saint-Seurin in July 1623, special archiepiscopal Vicar-General on November 1, 1639, Vicar in perpetuity of the parish church of Sainte-Colombe, then of Saint-Siméon in Bordeaux, Grand Archdeacon, Chancellor of the University of Bordeaux in 1650, and Vicar-General of the diocese on September 10, 1655. Like his friend Saint Vincent, he was convinced of the great good that could result from seminaries, missions, retreats, and weekly meetings of priests to discuss questions of theology, discipline, or piety. For this purpose, he founded the Congregation of the Missionaries of the Clergy, who directed the seminary for ordinands in Bordeaux and the seminaries in Aire and Sarlat. They were given the chapels of Notre-Dame-de-Montuzet and the parishes of Saint-Louis-du-Marais and Saint-Simon-Cardonnat (Gironde). This Congregation was short-lived, surviving its founder by only three years. He died in Bordeaux on March 2, 1679. In 1682 the *Prêtres du Clergé* (the title under which they were then known) transferred their works to the Priests of the Mission of Saint-Lazare. (Cf. Louis Bertrand, *Histoire des Séminaires de Bordeaux et de Bazas* [3 vols., Bordeaux: Féret, 1894], vol. I, pp. 207ff.)

Letter 2648. - Reg. 2, p. 114.

Furthermore, you let go—or rather, you sent away—those two young black men who stopped at your house, without welcoming them or having them take a rest, except for one night, after all the fatigue and hardships they endured. We have had no news of them since, and I am very much afraid that Louis,[1] who is a very fine lad, is offended at having found so little consolation and help in one of our houses. Here in this house he was treated like one of our Brothers, and he worked like one of them, too. I fear that, having been rebuffed in that way, he has made up his mind to leave us. It is to be wished, Monsieur, that you might have a little more charity for members of the Company passing through—or those who have some connection with the Company—when they are as destitute as those men.

2649. - TO JACQUES PESNELLE, SUPERIOR, IN GENOA

August 30, 1658

I am sure that holy humility is inspiring you with the sentiments you express to me concerning your office of Superior. Since, however, God is the one who governs all things in His adorable wisdom, we have to believe that He is also guiding the Company in general and each house in particular and that they will be very well guided if we, on our part, are faithful to the practice of the maxims of the Gospel and the observances of our Institute. Doubtless, this was your disposition when you resolved to maintain in the family union and exactness, the two principal ends of good government.

You even ask me for the means of doing so, but it would take me too long to write them to you. Just let me tell you that, to preserve peace and charity among your men, you must accustom

---

[1]Louis Voureq.

Letter 2649. - Reg. 2, p. 208.

them to ask pardon of one another on their knees whenever they happen to say or do anything that might affect this charity ever so little. One day the Superior of some nuns told me that there was great union in her community. I asked her to what she attributed the cause of this. She replied that, after God, it was to the Sisters' practice of asking pardon of one another for any harsh or disrespectful words. I have noted that this remedy is, indeed, very useful among us, for I have tried to introduce the custom and to practice it myself, whenever I fall into these failings. You will see, Monsieur, that if you put this practice into use, it will be like a precious balm in your house that will soften sharp tongues and resentment of hearts.

By being exact to the Rules and practices, in addition to the good means you are planning to use, which is to give the example yourself, you will find it very helpful not to tolerate their transgression in others without calling it to their attention, even giving them some penances at times for this, especially the backsliders.

You are acting according to the Spirit and Will of God in expressing deep gratitude to the Cardinal [1] for his incomparable benefits and in renewing often to him our most humble thanks. Do not fear being excessive in his regard, although his humility may find it difficult to endure, since his paternal goodness to us seems unbounded.

While awaiting the Visitor, you must not leave things just as they are, as you say you want to do, but you should try, rather, to set crooked things straight, put a stop to bad ones—if there are any—and make the good ones better. Perhaps you are referring to the conduct of the person who has a tendency to be independent.[2] In that case, since you have trouble managing him, you will do well to bear with him until the Visitor has spoken to him.

---

[1]Stefano Cardinal Durazzo.

[2]Probably Girolamo Giudice (Jérôme Lejuge).

I ask Our Lord, Monsieur, to help you to profit by the reasons for self-contempt you recognize in yourself, as well as by the praiseworthy actions you see in others. I ask Him also to enlighten you in doubts, encourage you in difficulties, and animate you with His Spirit of strength, graciousness, and forbearance.

2650. - TO EDME JOLLY, SUPERIOR, IN ROME

Paris, August 30, 1658

Monsieur,

The grace of O[ur] L[ord] be with you forever!

You tell me of the progress being made there to get a house for you and to engage you in the service of the clergy. We must thank God for this and pray that He will make use of us and of this plan according to His good pleasure. If His Divine Goodness chooses to see that it goes into effect, I will attribute it, after God, to your good leadership, as I already do for the good dispositions of the Pope and the Prelates. May Our Lord be pleased, Monsieur, to be ever more glorified in and through you, to enlighten you in your doubts, and to strengthen you in your heavy labors!

We will soon be thinking about sending you some help for the conferences of the ordination retreats, if God allows them to take place in Rome as in Paris. I will say nothing to you just now regarding the other business about which you write me, except for what concerns Saint-Lazare. I ask you as earnestly as I can to get the Bulls for it, regardless of the cost, and in the best possible form. I see clearly that one day this house will need all official documents to maintain its possession. A religious of Sainte-Geneviève told a member of the Company who is related to him that their Congregation plans to investigate ours about this and is waiting only for

---

Letter 2650. - Archives of the Mission, Paris, original signed letter.

my death in order to begin. They hope they will have a better chance then than they do now, while I am in a position to assert our rights. They must be basing theirs on some grounds—true or false—that we do not see. That is why we have to provide ourselves soon with whatever can serve for our defense. I hope we will have the Prelate's consent, if necessary, and that of the three religious who are still alive.[1]

I am, in the love of O[ur] L[ord], Monsieur, your most humble servant.

VINCENT DEPAUL,
i.s.C.M.

Addressed: Monsieur Jolly, Superior of the Priests of the Mission, in Rome

2651. - TO FIRMIN GET, SUPERIOR, IN MARSEILLES

Paris, August 30, 1658

Monsieur,

The grace of O[ur] L[ord] be with you forever!

The Duchesse d'Aiguillon, to whom I previously made the suggestion about turning the Tunis consulate over to one of the persons who asked for it, does not agree to this. Since these are persons who have a vested interest in this, she fears that, to rid himself of the Priest of the Mission and to have more elbow room,

---

[1]The Bulls Saint Vincent desired were received the following October, but he was clearly very concerned about this question.

Letter 2651. - Archives of the Mission, Paris, copy made from the original in the Hains Family Collection, Marseilles. This is one of the letters sold at auction by Xavier Charmoy (cf. no. 2505).

such a Consul might instigate some avanias against him. I will discuss it with her again to see if she has changed her mind.

In the present state of affairs, it is not at all advisable for M. Le Vacher to go to Algiers nor for any money to be sent there. I am writing the reasons for this to Brother Barreau so that he will please be patient, and I will tell you, Monsieur, that we have to wait and see if Chevalier Paul will pride himself on making an effort, or if the charity of Jesus Christ will urge him to go to set the slaves free. For, if he undertakes this and succeeds, things will change; if not, we will see what M. Huguier will do. In both cases, we will take other measures that are surer than the ones we can take right now.

I have nothing to say about the journey you are going to make to Toulon.

When I have received the accounts of the hospital that have been settled, I will show them to the Duchesse d'Aiguillon to let her see at the same time that the hospital can no longer survive.

I am, in the love of O[ur] L[ord], Monsieur, your most humble servant.

VINCENT DEPAUL,
i.s.C.M.

2652. - TO CHARLES OZENNE, SUPERIOR, IN WARSAW

Paris, August 30, 1658

Monsieur,

The grace of O[ur] L[ord] be with you forever!

Nothing has been lost: I received four of your letters at the same time; they were dated June 23, July 7 and 21, and August 4.[1] If I

Letter 2652. - Archives of the Mission, Krakow, original signed letter.

[1]None of these is extant.

suffered from their delay, I have been well paid for my trouble, for I received a double and triple consolation from them. God be praised for your safe return from Krakow and the good dispositions there for your establishment!

The Bishop has done only what he had to do in taking the time to be informed about the obligations of Saint-Roch Church. If the proposal meets with success, we will have to thank God for it; if not, we must adore His guidance, which perhaps has something better in store for you. Above all, Monsieur, do not commit yourself in any place where there will not be enough to live on. You do not tell me if Saint-Roch has any income, separate from that of the hospital, of which you write me that the town magistrates want to reserve the administration to themselves. You are acting wisely in this by resolving to follow the Queen's advice; for, since I perceive these things only from a distance, I can give you no other opinion on it.

I approve of your having refused the parish you were offered, since it was of so little advantage to you. As for the house M. Falibowski bought, it is up to you to judge whether it is suitable for you and if it is worth the burdens he wants to impose on you. Do nothing in that regard—nor, moreover, in anything else of importance—without discussing it with Messieurs Desdames and Duperroy and with the advice of your friends, especially M. Fleury.[2]

God be praised that M. Falibowski has given you the garden without any obligation, and may He in His infinite goodness be pleased to reward him eternally for it!

Since a priest will most likely have to be sent you soon from

---

[2]François de Fleury, chaplain to the Queen of Poland. Born in the Langres diocese (Haute-Marne), he secured for himself a canonry in the Verdun diocese. He approved the book *De la fréquente communion* and was presented by the Jansenists to Queen Louise-Marie de Gonzague on her departure for Poland to act as her chaplain. His relationship with Saint Vincent and the Missionaries sent to that country was always excellent—even cordial—as is evident from the letters of the Saint, who esteemed him highly. De Fleury died in France early in November 1658. Part of his correspondence with Mother Marie-Angélique Arnauld is extant.

here, we will wait until then to send you the Brother you request because there is no possibility of sending him alone to you.

I am really worried about the trouble you are having with your legs. *Mon Dieu!* what can that be? Whatever it is, I know from experience that cauterization will do you good, along with frequent purges and some bloodlettings. Even if you are purged every month, it would not be too much. Please take care of your health.

M. Jolly is still in Rome, and I must confess that his presence is so necessary and useful to us that we cannot bring ourselves to remove him from there.

We have no news here. We are very worried about Messieurs Arnoul and de Fontaines; they stayed behind in Galicia because they were ill, and we have heard nothing from them. Pray for them and for us, as we do almost constantly for you and our dear confreres, whom I embrace tenderly. We do the same for Their Majesties and their armies so that the Divine Goodness may be pleased to bless them.

I am, in His love, Monsieur, your most humble servant.

VINCENT DEPAUL,
i.s.C.M.

Addressed: Monsieur Ozenne, Superior of the Priests of the Mission of Poland, in Warsaw

2653. - TO THE COMMUNITY OF SAINT-LAZARE

[September 1658] [1]

Whatever God does, He does for the best; therefore, we must

Letter 2653. - Abelly, *op. cit.*, bk. III, chap. III, p. 14.

[1]The information on the loss of Orsigny allows us to assign this date. Saint Vincent accepted this farm in the commune of Saclay (Essonne) from Jacques Norais, notary and Secretary of the King, by a contract dated December 22, 1644. According to the Saint (cf. vol. IV, no. 1467),

hope that this loss [2] will be to our advantage, since it comes from God. All things work together for the good of the just; [3] and we have the assurance that when adversities are received from the hand of God, they are converted into joy and blessings. So then, Fathers and Brothers, please thank God for the outcome of this affair, the deprivation of this property, and the disposition with which He has prepared us to accept this loss for love of Him. It is great, but His adorable wisdom will certainly know how to make it turn to our advantage by ways unknown to us now, but which you will see some day.[4] Yes, you will see it, and I hope that the proper way in which you have all conducted yourselves in this unexpected event will serve as a basis for the grace God will grant you in the future of making perfect use of all the trials He will be pleased to send you.

---

the farms that supplied Saint-Lazare provided less than one-sixth of the needs of the Motherhouse.

[2]The loss of the Orsigny farm, as is clear from no. 2752, which Abelly noted after this letter and which he gives as pertaining to the same business. Saint Vincent was absent from Saint-Lazare when he heard this painful news from Brother Louis Robineau, his second secretary, on September 3. He had just dined and was on his way to church. "God be praised!" he exclaimed several times, and he remained kneeling before the Blessed Sacrament for a longer time than usual. The Saint lost his lawsuit by three or four votes because, among the twenty or twenty-one judges who were to vote on this affair, several could not forgive him his opposition to Jansenism (cf. Robineau manuscript, p. 97, and published in Dodin, *op. cit.*, p. 89).

[3]Cf. Rom 8:28. (NAB)

[4]Saint Vincent was not mistaken: shortly after this, a Counselor of the Grand'Chambre left him an estate that was worth as much as the Orsigny farm (cf. no. 2752).

2654. - TO MONSIEUR DESBORDES[1]

[September 5, 1658]

Monsieur,

Good friends share the good things and bad things that happen to them and, since you are one of the best friends we have in this world, I cannot refrain from letting you know of the loss we have suffered in the affair of which you are aware.[2] I do so, not as if it were an evil that has befallen us, but as a grace that God has granted us, and so that you may join us in thanking Him for it.

I call a grace of God the trials He sends us, especially those that are well received. Now, since God in His infinite goodness prepared us for this deprivation before it was ordained, He has also led us to acquiesce in this misfortune with total resignation and, I venture to say, with as much joy as if it had been favorable to us. To one not as versed in heavenly matters as you, Monsieur, and who might not realize that conformity to the good pleasure of God in adversities is a greater benefit than any temporal advantage, this might seem paradoxical. I most humbly entreat you to accept my pouring into your heart in this way the sentiments of my own heart.

2655. - TO EDME JOLLY, SUPERIOR, IN ROME

September 6, 1658

God be praised that the latest proposals for a residence and for

---

Letter 2654. - Abelly, *op. cit.*, bk. III, chap. XI, p. 176. The date and recipient of this letter are known from Collet, *op. cit.*, vol. II, p. 56.

[1]Vicomte de Soudé and Auditor of Accounts. He had been executor of the will of Commander de Sillery and Administrator of the Quinze-Vingts Hospital.

[2]This refers to the loss of the lawsuit concerning the Orsigny farm.

Letter 2655. - Reg. 2, p. 241.

the ordinations seem to be reaching the desired point! Our senior members who saw the Saint-Nicolas house say that it is situated in a very advantageous location, but I have to tell you two or three things on this subject.

The first is that perhaps it will be better to leave the parish as it is rather than separate the house from it. True, we have objected to taking responsibility for parishes, especially in episcopal towns and in places where there is a Parlement or Presidial Court, but experience has taught us that wherever there is a seminary, it is good for us to have a parish to train the seminarians, who learn parish functions better by practice than by theory. We have the example of this in Saint-Nicolas-du-Chardonnet, where all the priests who leave there are ready to serve in a parish because they have had practice in that one. For lack of similar experience, those at the Bons-Enfants Seminary are not so ready, although we have tried to train them for this.

That has made me think, Monsieur, that you will do well to represent what I am telling you to Father Spada [1] and the other good Prelates involved in the spiritual advancement of the clergy—not to ask them for a parish, but so that they may see whether it is advisable for His Holiness to designate one for that purpose, in the event that he plans to open a seminary in Rome and to ask us to run it. The Will of God will be made known to us by the decision that will be given on this by His Holiness, and you will know by this means that you will be doing nothing contrary to our intention in accepting a parish for such a reason. We must, however, neither seek nor desire one otherwise.

The second thing is that, assuming you are lodged at Saint-Nicolas or elsewhere, we are not in a position to pay anything, or to compensate the suppressed monks, or to satisfy any other interested parties.

---

[1]Commander of the Spirito Santo Hospital in Rome; he was the brother of Cardinal Bernadino Spada.

The third thing concerns expenses for the ordinands; for, even though we provide room and board for them gratis in Paris, we cannot do so in Rome, since we have only what is needed for the living expenses of the family. You will do well to represent early on our powerlessness in this matter and in everything else and to offer the solution, practiced in several dioceses in France, of obliging each ordinand to pay his own retreat expenses, if the Pope is unwilling to pay for all of them himself. Likewise, each seminarian who enters the seminary should pay his own room and board, everything according to the rate that will be fixed.

2656. - TO FIRMIN GET, SUPERIOR, IN MARSEILLES

Paris, September 6, 1658

Monsieur,

The grace of O[ur] L[ord] be with you forever!

I received your letter of August 24. Since you hope to obtain some money in Marseilles, please get 3795 livres 10 sous, which we will pay here on your bill of exchange to whomever you indicate, but get the money before giving the bill of exchange, if possible. It is to be distributed to seven or eight slaves, in accord with the memo I am sending you. In addition, please get 129 livres 2 sous for the money you advanced to the poor convicts up until August 19, in accord with the account you sent me for them, which we will also pay, God willing.

I am very pleased with the charity you are showing to Martin, who accompanied M. Le Vacher,[1] by keeping him in your house in an effort to get him well again.

Letter 2656. - Archives of the Mission, Paris, copy made from the original in the Hains Family Collection, Marseilles. This is one of the letters sold at auction by Xavier Charmoy (cf. no. 2505).

[1]Philippe Le Vacher.

I saw M. Pastour's letter. If you reply to him, thank him for his advice and tell him we are sending another Superior to Annecy,[2] who will leave next week, God willing. I am, in Him, Monsieur, your most humble servant.

VINCENT DEPAUL,
i.s.C.M.

Along with your letter, I received all the others enclosed in the packet; we will deliver the ones that are not for us.

2657. - TO JEAN MARTIN, SUPERIOR, IN TURIN

Paris, September 6, 1658

Monsieur,

The grace of O[ur] L[ord] be with you forever!

I failed to write you in the last two regular mails because I had too many other letters to do. I am writing one to Brother Demortier—not to tell him when he will take Holy Orders but so he will continue to be disposed to do so. Meanwhile, please let me know if you think he is sufficiently prepared, if he is inclined to virtue, and if he gives you promise of becoming a good Priest of the Mission.

---

[2]Mark Cogley (Saint Vincent spells his name *Marc Coglée*), who went there to replace Achille Le Vazeux. Born in Carrick-on-Suir, Lismore diocese (Ireland), on April 25, 1614, Cogley was ordained a priest on May 30, 1643, and entered the Congregation of the Mission the following July 24. In a period of stress and discouragement, he had the good fortune to meet Gerard Brin, a fellow countryman, who induced him to remain in the Congregation. After giving him time to make up his mind definitely by spending some time in the novitiate, Saint Vincent sent him to Sedan (1646), where he took his vows on December 13, 1649; the following year he was named Pastor of the parish and Superior of the house. Replaced in 1654 by Jean Martin, he resumed these same functions in 1655 and kept them for another year. For a few months in 1659 he was Superior of the Annecy Seminary; from there he returned to Saint-Lazare.

Letter 2657. - Archives of the Mission, Turin, original signed letter.

In your last letters of August 3 and 10, you ask us for a copy of the book containing sermons and catechetical instructions. We cannot send them to you because someone has taken that book. We are well aware who did it, but I do not know if it has been returned to us. Even if we did get it back, it is not an easy matter to have it copied, nor is it really necessary to send it so far off for one or two persons who might use it or not. As for the Rules, we will send them to you with the first Missionaries who leave here for Italy—which will be soon, God willing. And if we get our book of sermons back, we will send them to you.[1]

If you have the instructions for the establishment of the Charity, you will see at the end what is done during the visitation. We have not drawn up any special notes for that; we will do so, God willing.[2]

It is difficult for a new house like yours to be able to take on so many different works all at once. It can do so with time, but you must await that time patiently. Meanwhile, try to be faithful in doing small things so that God may be pleased to set you over big ones, according to His word.[3]

I send greetings to your dear little family with all the tenderness of my heart. I had intended recently to take the honor of writing to the Marchese, your founder, to renew to him the gratitude of my poor heart and the offers of my humble and perpetual obedience, but I have not yet been able to carry out this duty. When you have the opportunity, I hope you will make up for my shortcoming. I ask Our Lord to be the Spirit of your spirit and the strength of your arm in order to destroy ignorance and sin, two monsters in God's Church.

If you are urged to give a mission in Saluzzo,[4] do not object to doing so, even though it is an episcopal town, since in Piedmont those towns are small and numerous, and although there are many

---

[1]This sentence is in the Saint's handwriting.

[2]The clause "we will do so, God willing" is in the Saint's handwriting.

[3]Cf. Mt 25:21. (NAB)

[4]Town in the province of Cuneo, in Piedmont.

priests in them, the needs are still great. Nevertheless, Monsieur, always remember to prefer the poor country folk, as far as you can.

I am, in O[ur] L[ord], Monsieur, your most humble servant.

VINCENT DEPAUL,
i.s.C.M.

Addressed: Monsieur Martin

2658. - *SAINT LOUISE TO SAINT VINCENT*

[September 1658] [1]

I must seek Your Charity's consolation, Most Honored Father, for the loss of our poor Sister Jeanne-Baptiste.[2] *That was my fault because I did not have the courage to speak to her frankly about the bad behavior that went on at the Nom-de-Jésus, from which she suffered intensely because of her timidity. She left at seven o'clock in the morning, and I did not know it until four in the afternoon.*

What are we to do, Most Honored Father? I feel very sorry for her because I think she was innocent of those latest suspicions. Shall I send someone to look for her at the Magdalens' house, where she has a sister, or at the home of some of her relatives whom we know? Shall I send to the Nom-de-Jésus for the woman who always accompanied her when she went out so that, without telling her she has left us, I can find out how she behaved when she was out? Shall we see if we can get further information from the Sisters at the Nom-de-Jésus to try to learn what has become of her?

Letter 2658. - Archives of the Motherhouse of the Daughters of Charity, original autograph letter.

[1]Date added on the back of the original by Brother Ducournau.

[2]Jeanne-Baptiste the younger entered the Company of the Daughters of Charity at the end of 1648. Her first mission was apparently the Saint-Jean-de-Grèves parish (cf. vol. IV, nos. 1369-70), after which she was sent to Montmirail in October 1650. She signed the Act of Establishment of the Daughters of Charity on August 8, 1655 (cf. vol. XIII, no. 150). In 1658 she went to the hospice of the Nom-de-Jésus, from which she abruptly left the Company, as this letter indicates.

Oh, how this incident makes me see the need for the Daughters of Charity to be subject to those who act as their Superiors! For some time now, she has shown herself much more independent in her manner. I think that it was a groundless fear, rather than anything reasonable, that put her in her present state.

I am sure Your Charity will pray for her and will pardon the faults I have committed in this matter. Nevertheless, I ask you to remind me of these faults and others to help me to overcome them. I entreat you most humbly to do so for the love of God, in whom I am, Most Honored Father, your most humble daughter and very obedient servant.

L. DE MARILLAC

Addressed: *Monsieur Vincent*

2659. - TO FIRMIN GET, SUPERIOR, IN MARSEILLES

Paris, September 13, 1658

Monsieur,

The grace of O[ur] L[ord] be with you forever!

I am glad that boats are being prepared for Algiers. Once again I ask M. Huguier to go there, and I ask you to give him the 3300 livres and whatever instructions you deem appropriate.

I think the occasion you indicate to us for getting money to you is very good. Since you are sure about M. Rambert, we will send M. Colbert the balance of what we have for Algiers, and I will send you his bill of exchange, if it is thought advisable after the imprisonment of the Ambassador to Constantinople [1] and the bad treat-

---

Letter 2659. - Archives of the Mission, Paris, copy made from the original in the Hains Family Collection, Marseilles. This is one of the letters sold at auction by Xavier Charmoy (cf. no. 2505).

[1]The imprisonment of M. de la Haye-Vantelay, French Ambassador to Constantinople, was caused by a coded letter addressed to him by Grémonville, an Admiral in the service of the Venetians, that fell into the hands of the Turks. When the Ambassador and his son refused to reveal the contents of the letter, the Grand Vizier treated both of them roughly, then had them thrown into prison.

ment the Turks are giving the Consuls in Alexandria,[2] Aleppo, and Tripoli.[3] There is a Bishop here from Mount Lebanon for this reason. We have to call a meeting of capable persons to discuss it.

We received one écu for Nicolas Bonner, a convict in Toulon. I ask M. Parisy to give it to him and to give three livres to Antoine Auroy and twenty livres to Toussaint Le Cercieux, a convict on either the galley *Ternes* or the *Richelieu.* The money was received here from M. Haistrau, a merchant from Montfort,[4] in Anjou.

Your most humble servant.

VINCENT DEPAUL,
i.s.C.M.

2660. - TO GUILLAUME DESDAMES, IN WARSAW

Paris, September 13, 1658

Monsieur,

The grace of O[ur] L[ord] be with you forever!

Blessed be the Father of this same Lord J[esus] C[hrist] for the trial He has sent us in taking from us His servant M. Ozenne! [1] You can imagine how great is our sorrow, and I am judging by my own, which is very deep, that yours is no less so. Since, however, it is God who has done this, it is up to us to make good use of this visitation by conforming ourselves to His holy Will. That dear

---

[2]Christophe de Bermond, Consul in Alexandria.

[3]Tripoli and Aleppo shared the same Consul, François Picquet. In 1675 the administration of the diocese of Babylon was confided to him; he later succeeded to the See of Baghdad (cf. vol. VIII, no. 3020).

[4]Small locality in the district of Saumur.

Letter 2660. - Archives of the Mission, Krakow, original signed letter. The postscript is in the Saint's handwriting.

[1]He had died in Warsaw on August 14.

deceased man is very fortunate to have been freed of this mortal body, which subjects us to so many miseries, and to be now in the house of His Lord, as we have reason to believe. And perhaps we are not so much to be pitied at having lost him as we think, since he can be of more help to us where he is than if he were still where he used to be.

I am sure there will be difficulties with the establishment in Krakow, but, if it is God's good pleasure that it be made, Providence will find the means of removing the obstacles; if, on the contrary, the obstacles prevail, that will be a sign that Providence wants to postpone this project, seeing that you could not do all that would be required. Indeed, Monsieur, what would you do if you had to be in two places, with only two priests? For even if we sent you a few—which would be difficult for us just now—they would not be in a position to work for a long time because they would not know the language. The result is that, when I think of means to furnish good Missionaries for Poland, this one always comes to mind: to bring together about twelve good young men from there—if they could be found—and give them a sound preparation in a seminary, where they can be formed in virtue and ecclesiastical functions. Please think about this and discuss it with M. Fleury.

We will not be sending any other Superior or Rector [2] but you. Please do both duties yourself, Monsieur. I thank God for the way He has guided you. I hope He will bless your leadership and sanctify your soul more and more, as I ask Him to do with all my heart. I make the same prayer for M. Duperroy, whom I consider an object of the infinite goodness of God, who has tried him to the highest degree so that He might have reason to bless him to the highest degree as well. I embrace him, and you along with him,

[2]Director of the Daughters of Charity in Poland.

with all the tenderness of my heart. Prostrate in spirit at your feet, I am your most humble servant.

VINCENT DEPAUL,
i.s.C.M.

I am sending you a document of presentation concerning you to be given to the Bishop of Poznan[3] for the parish. Because I am not sure if M. Ozenne was provided with Holy Cross parish, I am sending you two different presentations: one, since the parish has become vacant through the death of the Pastor, who resigned it to the Company *per modum unionis,*[4] and the other, since it is vacant through the death of the late M. Ozenne. You can use whichever one is appropriate.[5] Get M. de Fleury's advice and please follow it in that and in everything else.

It is impossible for me to write to Madame de Villers in this mail; they are taking the pen from my hand to send me off to the meeting of the Ladies of Charity; I will write to her in the next mail.

At the bottom of the first page: Monsieur Desdames

2660a. - TO ALBERT THOLIBOWSKI, BISHOP OF POZNAN[1]

To the Most Illustrious and Reverend Lord Albert Tholibowski, Bishop of Poznan, or any other person having authority in what is

---

[3]Albert Tholibowski, appointed Bishop of Poznan in 1654. He remained in office in this diocese until the day of his death, July 22, 1663.

[4]*By means of union.*

[5]Both these documents form part of the archival material of Krakow.

Letter 2660a. - Archives of the Mission, Krakow, original signed letter, written in Latin. The text was published in *Annales C. M.* (1940), p. 73. Although Coste referred to the letter, he forgot to include it in vol. VII; the present editors have inserted it in its correct chronological place.

[1]The two versions of this letter were included with no. 2660, which was sent to Guillaume Desdames.

written below, Vincent de Paul, Superior General of the Congregation of the Mission.

At the present time, the parish church bearing the title of Holy Cross, in a suburb of the city of Warsaw in the Poznan diocese, is vacant upon the voluntary resignation of the Very Reverend Jan Scaillicz, its last and immediate possessor.[2] According to our right and in conformity with the union granted us by the Most Illustrious Local Ordinary, we present to this parish church, vacant in the way mentioned above, Reverend Guillaume Desdames, priest of our Congregation, whose life, morals, and knowledge are well known to us. We request exclusively for him and with him that Your Most Illustrious and Reverend Excellency deign to install him, and no one else, in the said parish church and entrust to him in a special way the care and administration of the spiritual affairs of this parish church.

In witness of which, we have issued the present letter in the usual authentic form.

Given in Paris at Saint-Lazare on the thirteenth day of September in the year of Our Lord sixteen hundred fifty-eight.

VINCENT DEPAUL,
Unworthy Superior General
of the Congregation of the Mission

By order of the aforesaid Lord, my Superior General.

Thomas Berthe

September 13, 1658

---

[2]For reasons indicated in the preceding letter, Saint Vincent sent Desdames a copy of this presentation, identical except for the phrase *upon the voluntary resignation . . . possessor,* which he replaced with *through the death of the late Charles Ozenne, during his lifetime.*

2661. - TO BALTHAZAR GRANGIER DE LIVERDI, BISHOP OF TRÉGUIER

September 17, 1658

Excellency,

The reason I recalled Brother Plunket and sent him to Saint-Méen is that M. Dupont had informed me that he was teaching the classes Brother Plunket used to teach. He said that the latter was no longer doing so because the seminarians did not understand him clearly, since he does not speak French well. When I heard this from the man himself, I felt, Excellency, that it was not just for you to be burdened with him in your seminary and that you needed no one else to teach, since M. Dupont was taking the class. If you absolutely need someone else, I will try to send him, if you do me the honor of believing that I will never give you any reasonable cause for dissatisfaction and that, if there is any indication of the contrary in some of my actions, I hope you will suspend your judgment until you have heard my side, Excellency. I would prefer to die or to recall the poor Priests of the Mission rather than to fail in my duty toward you and for them and me to be a source of pain and displeasure to you.

We had the honor of having here in this house Abbé de Liverdi, your nephew, who made his retreat with us in a manner that edified us greatly. I hope, Excellency, that some day he will make a good Prelate of God's Church. That is what I ask of God. I am, in His love and in that of His Holy Mother, Excellency, your. . . .

Letter 2661. - Reg. 1, fol. 69v, copy made from the original in the Saint's handwriting.

2662. - *SAINT LOUISE TO SAINT VINCENT*

September 19, [1658] [1]

Most Honored Father,

I did not know that my son had spoken to you about Champlan,[2] *but his brother-in-law told me he would talk to you about it. He indicated that it was a rather important family matter caused by a minor breach in the friendship between my daughter-in-law and her de la Prontière and Lestang cousins. It would be distressing if this were to continue. Please God, I will explain the reason to you.*

A Sister came from Saint-Roch to tell me she could not adjust to our Sister or to the parish and did not want to return there. There is much fault to be found in her. I sent her back and promised to speak to Your Charity about the matter. I think, however, that you would have to know the whole situation in order to make a decision on it.

For persons our age, Most Honored Father, I think the best time for bloodletting is during the full moon; for purgatives, the waning moon is best, for fear lest evacuation be too violent.

This morning I forgot to get instructions from Your Charity concerning the retreat for that good nun whom the chaplain[3] *in Chantilly mentioned to you. He is here today about the matter. The poor woman seems to be in a sad state, but perhaps her soul needs assistance. Can she speak to one of your priests, or shall our Sisters and I do what we can to help her?*

Would Your Charity please let me know if I may take this short trip, if I am able? And, in keeping with my needs, kindly grant me the powerful assistance of your holy advice and prayers to raise me from my misery and rid me of my illusions, if I am in that state. Continue to honor me by

---

Letter 2662. - Archives of the Motherhouse of the Daughters of Charity, original autograph letter.

[1]Because of the reference in both letters to Saint-Roch parish in Paris and to the Sisters there, this letter must be placed near no. 2667, whose date is certain.

[2]Small locality in the canton of Longjumeau (Essonne). The parents of Gabrielle Le Clerc, Saint Louise's daughter-in-law, lived there.

[3]M. Delahodde.

believing that I am, by the Will of Our Lord, Most Honored Father, your most humble and very grateful servant.

LOUISE DE MARILLAC

Addressed: *Monsieur Vincent*

2663. - TO SAINT LOUISE

[September 19 or 20, 1658]

If Mademoiselle Le Gras can find a carriage, we will give her the coachman and horses. I think she will do well to make this little journey to unite the hearts of the family more closely.[1]

Business will prevent me from seeing her today. I ask her to inform me briefly of the problem with the Sisters at Saint-Roch,[2] along with the other matters I should know.

I pray that God will keep her well on her journey and bring her back in perfect health; I ask Him also to give her His Spirit to unite hearts.

Addressed: Mademoiselle Le Gras

Letter 2663. - Archives of the Motherhouse of the Daughters of Charity, original autograph letter. Saint Vincent wrote his response to the previous letter at the bottom of that letter.

[1]There was some friction between Gabrielle Le Clerc and her cousins (cf. no. 2662).

[2]The Sisters working in the parish often experienced difficulties.

2664. - TO FIRMIN GET, SUPERIOR, IN MARSEILLES

Paris, September 20, 1658

Monsieur,

The grace of O[ur] L[ord] be with you forever!

My reason for asking you last week to keep M. Huguier in Marseilles until further orders is that the Ambassador of France in Constantinople and his son, who was sent there to replace his father, were imprisoned there. We gather from this that, since those persons were treated in that way, there would be no guarantee either for M. Huguier or M. Le Vacher in Algiers, but a clear danger that they would be mistreated there. At the least, it would be imprudent on our part to put them at risk there before we have seen the consequences of this mistreatment of the Ambassadors, which redounds on the King, and the decision His Majesty will take on it.

So, since some enlightened persons have advised us that this delay would be very timely, I hope you will find it appropriate; that M. Huguier will postpone his journey and will, nevertheless, be ready to leave whenever it is deemed advisable; and that M. Le Vacher will be patient in his desire to relieve his suffering brothers. I am sure this is hard for him, but I must follow the opinion of several persons rather than his alone and believe that, in the present circumstances, this will help the Consul and the slaves, instead of exposing them to the risk of losing their money to the attacks of the Turks. These latter would most likely seize it if we were rash enough to send it there. They have reason to think that they can do anything they want to the French, seeing the great encroachment of the Grand Lord.

I am not replying to your letter from the last regular mail because I have not yet received it.

Letter 2664. - Archives of the Mission, Paris, copy made from the original in the Hains Family Collection, Marseilles. This is one of the letters sold at auction by Xavier Charmoy (cf. no. 2505).

We received six livres for Marc Mansart, a convict on the *Capitaine;* I am writing to ask M. Parisy to give them to him and to give one pistole to Antoine Marbais.

Here is some news that will sadden you: God has chosen to take to Himself M. Ozenne, Superior of our poor family in Poland. A raging fever carried him off from earth to heaven on the eve of the Assumption, the fifth day of his illness. He was fortified by all the sacraments and as well prepared to leave this world to be united to his Sovereign Lord as anyone could wish. He had also prepared himself for it from the time of his entrance into the Company, in which he always shunned evil and did good most ardently and effectively. He was very sincere, gentle, and exemplary. God is now his reward for this. He is deeply regretted by all who knew him, and we have lost a great deal in him—if we can call loss what God gains. May His Will be done always in us and in all that concerns us! Please pray, and have others pray for this dear departed man, since the Church orders prayers for the just as for sinners like myself.

God has consoled us, on the other hand, by the arrival of Messieurs de Fontaines and Arnoul, who were sick and had remained in Spain. We were very worried about them because we had no news of them. Please thank God for having brought them back to us in good health, although M. de Fontaines has been in bed for two days with double-tertian fever.

I just received your letter of the tenth. I am very anxious about your eye trouble; since your health is more precious to us than anything else, I think you should have a change of air, and I ask you to take it. It would be desirable that this be at our nearest house, which is Agde; but, since the town is by the sea, like Marseilles, and the air is even worse there, you will do well to go to Annecy or Notre-Dame de Lorm in the Montauban diocese, where the air is good, the countryside is beautiful, and the Garonne, a lovely river, flows through it.

I ask M. Le Vacher to fill in for you in your absence; please give him any information you think advisable and familiarize him with the running of the house. Please put in the strongbox with the double lock the 3300 livres you were supposed to give M. Huguier; he will have one key to it and M. Le Vacher the other. Please let us know the place you choose for your rest. You will be useful and welcome in both.

I am, in O[ur] L[ord], Monsieur, your most humble servant.

VINCENT DEPAUL,
i.s.C.M.

2665. - TO JEAN MARTIN, SUPERIOR, IN TURIN

Paris, September 20, 1658

Monsieur,

The grace of O[ur] L[ord] be with you forever!

God has chosen to take to Himself M. Ozenne, Superior of our poor family in Poland. A raging fever carried him off from earth to heaven on the eve of the Assumption, the fifth day of his illness. He was fortified by all the sacraments and as well prepared to leave this world to be united to his Sovereign Happiness as anyone could wish. He had also prepared himself for it from the time of his entrance into the Company, in which he always shunned evil and did good most ardently and effectively. He was very sincere, gentle, and exemplary. God is now His reward for this. We have lost a great deal in him—if we can call loss what God gains. May His Will be done! Please pray and have others pray for this dear departed man, as is customary in the Church, which prays for the just as well as for sinners.

God has consoled us, on the other hand, by the arrival of Messieurs de Fontaines and Arnoul, who were sick and had remained in Spain, where they had been taken by a man-of-war which

---

Letter 2665. - Archives of the Mission, Turin, original signed letter.

captured them at sea; they were on their way to Madagascar with M. Le Blanc. For a long time we were very worried about them because they had not sent us any news. Finally, however, they brought us the news themselves by returning in good health. It is true that M. de Fontaines became sick again two days ago.

I received your letter of August 23 and have nothing to reply to it. Enclosed is a letter for M. Cauly informing him of the departure of his brother; after spending a while in the Bons-Enfants Seminary, he has returned to Savoy to serve in his parish there. He would do good there if his health were as sound as his intentions.

I send greetings to the little family, and I am, in the love of O[ur] L[ord], Monsieur, your most humble servant.

VINCENT DEPAUL,
i.s.C.M.

Addressed: Monsieur Martin

2666. - TO EDME JOLLY, SUPERIOR, IN ROME

Paris, September 20, 1658

Monsieur,

The grace of O[ur] L[ord] be with you forever!

I received your letter of August 20. Thank you for all you have done to expedite the Bulls for Saint-Lazare. In so doing, you make us more indebted to you than I can tell you, and I am most grateful. We will await patiently the reply of the Cardinal Datary,[1] the dispensation for M. Geoffroy, and the one for that good nobleman and lady near Montmirail. Thank you also for your efforts in these matters, especially for M. Geoffroy's dispensation.

Letter 2666. - Archives of the Mission, Paris, original signed letter.

[1]Giacomo Corradi.

God be praised, Monsieur, for what you wrote me about the devotedness that good priest from Piedmont has shown to the Company in his will! Tell him of our deep gratitude for it. God be praised again for having restored him to health! We will ask Him to continue to grant it to him for many long years to come.

May God in His infinite goodness bless the beginning and growth of the seminary that is going to open at the College of Propaganda Fide. May He also give to the proposal discussed in the Congregation of the Apostolic Visitation the outcome that will be pleasing to Him! Meanwhile, we will remain as resigned as possible to His good pleasure, regardless of how things turn out.

Please send us a letter of provision for the parish of Chavagnac,[2] in the Sarlat diocese, made vacant by the death of the last titular or by M. Gilbert Cuissot's resignation given to the Bishop[3]—who has not made an appointment to this benefice in the past six months—or for some other reason that it is vacant. Have it drawn up on behalf of M . . . , a priest of the . . . diocese.

Here is some news that will sadden you. God has chosen to take to Himself M. Ozenne, Superior of our poor family in Poland. A raging fever carried him off from earth to heaven on the eve of the Assumption, the fifth day of his illness. He was fortified by all the sacraments and as well prepared to leave this world to be united to his Sovereign Lord as anyone could wish. He had been just as prepared for it from the time of his entrance into the Company, in which he always shunned evil and did good with great ardor and good results. He was very sincere, gentle, and exemplary. God is now His reward for this. He is deeply regretted by all who knew him, and we have lost a great deal in him—if we can call loss what God gains. May His Will be done and accomplished in us and in all that concerns us! Please pray and have others pray for this dear

---

[2]Small locality near Sarlat (Dordogne).

[3]Nicolas Sevin.

departed man, since the Church orders us to pray for the just as well as for sinners like me.

God has consoled us, on the other hand, by the arrival of Messieurs de Fontaines and Arnoul, who were sick and had remained in Spain. We were very worried about them because we had no news of them. Please thank God for bringing them back to us in good health, although M. de Fontaines is in bed now with double-tertian fever.

I am, in O[ur] L[ord], Monsieur, your most humble servant.

VINCENT DEPAUL,
i.s.C.M.

Addressed: Monsieur Jolly

2667. - *SAINT LOUISE TO SAINT VINCENT*

[September 1658] [1]

Most Honored Father, I informed Your Charity that you should know about the behavior of the Sister who is unwilling to be supervised at Saint-Roch or to be with someone who is strict. She has gone back, so that can await my return, if I can go.

I am a little fearful that Madame de Marillac and her entire family [2] *will be offended if I am so near them and do not pay them a visit—as they were in previous years when I refused them. If Your Charity has no objection to this, I ask to stay two days and to return the horses on Sunday morning, provided I feel strong enough.*

The other thing I had to tell you, Most Honored Father, concerns the

---

Letter 2667. - Archives of the Motherhouse of the Daughters of Charity, original autograph letter.

[1]Date added on the back of the original by Brother Ducournau.

[2]Jeanne Potier, Madame de Marillac, and her husband, Michel de Marillac, a Counselor in the Parlement. They resided at the family estate in Ollainville, some eight miles south of Champlan (Essonne). Michel de Marillac was the Lord of Ollainville.

disagreement between the people I am supposed to visit there and how I can be of service to them in the future by giving them advice. This is not urgent but Ollainville is.

Would Your Charity please give me a reply on this? I await it with entire submission, as God has always granted me the grace to do, since I am your poor daughter and most humble servant.

L. DE M.

I have just been assured of a carriage for tomorrow morning, with the help of your horses and the coachman Your Charity is willing to lend us.

Addressed: *Monsieur Vincent*

2668. - TO JEAN DOLCE, BISHOP OF BAYONNE

Paris, September 22, 1658

Excellency,

It is only just that, after having been granted the favor I requested of you, I should thank you most humbly for it, as I now do, Excellency, with all the tenderness of my heart. I am referring to the two poor Missionaries who were in Spain [1] and who, on your orders received all possible assistance and offers in Bayonne, extending far beyond their needs and their hopes. I will be deeply grateful for this all my life and will have a very ardent desire to manifest it by my obedience.

I entreat you most humbly, Excellency, to rest assured that I will always welcome your orders with all the respect and submission due you on the part of the lowliest priest from your diocese.

Letter 2668. - Archives of the Mission, Paris, original signed letter.

[1]Pasquier de Fontaines and Marand-Ignace Arnoul.

Consequently, I am more than anyone, in the love of O[ur] L[ord], Excellency, your most humble and very obedient servant.

VINCENT DEPAUL,
i.s.C.M.

At the bottom of the page: The Bishop of Bayonne

2669. - TO FIRMIN GET, SUPERIOR, IN MARSEILLES

Paris, September 27, 1658.

Monsieur,

The grace of O[ur] L[ord] be with you forever!

I have not sent M. Colbert the three thousand or so livres we have for certain slaves whose names you have because I did not know if you would draw them on us, as I wrote you to do. Since, however, you are referring us to him, I am going to send someone to find out if he is willing to accept this sum, and I will inform M. Lambert to deliver the money to you. It will be difficult to be able to do this today; God willing, we will do so next week.

If the Consuls send for you to find out what you think about Rappiot, you will do well not to demand his expulsion but simply to give the pros and cons without coming to any conclusion, leaving to their discretion to ordain whatever they judge advisable concerning him. You can, nevertheless, suggest the seizure of his belongings that were taken by the coast guard, to be applied to M. Barreau's reimbursement, in the event that Rappiot should win his case against M. de Montolieu.

Letter 2669. - Archives of the Mission, Paris, copy made from the original in the Hains Family Collection, Marseilles. This is one of the letters sold at auction by Xavier Charmoy (cf. no. 2505).

Last week the Duchesse d'Aiguillon took care to inform the Superintendent [1] that the Royal Hospital is no longer able to admit sick convicts unless it is paid from the King's alms. If the Lady is at the meeting today, I will find out what she has done. As for the Duc de Richelieu, he has gone to take the waters in Bourbon, and I am keeping the letter from M. Bausset the Provost until he gets back.

We have received four écus for Charles Ballagny, a convict in Toulon. Please have them given to him; I am notifying M. Parisy of this.

I see from your letter in this regular mail that your handwriting is very good and, consequently, that your eyes must be better. That is why I ask you, Monsieur, in the name of O[ur] L[ord], to stay in Marseilles a little while longer—at least until the Algiers business is settled or until M. Berthe arrives. He is leaving today for Marseilles and then for Italy with nine or ten other Missionaries. However, if the ailment is still giving you trouble, go to one of the houses I mentioned, namely, Notre-Dame de Lorm and Annecy—or, if you think the Paris air is better for you, then come here; it will be a great consolation for me to see you.

M. Berthe is bringing you the printed Rules and the Busées you requested earlier.[2]

I embrace Messieurs Le Vacher and Huguier with all the tenderness of my heart. I have no time to write to them.

---

[1]Nicolas Fouquet, born in Paris on January 27, 1615, became Attorney General of the Parlement of Paris in 1650 and Superintendent of Finances in 1653. Accused of embezzlement and arrested in Nantes on September 5, 1663, he was judged, condemned to life imprisonment, and incarcerated in the Château de Pignerol where he died in March 1680. He became reconciled with God in his last years and even composed some books of devotion. (Cf. Jules Lair, *Nicolas Fouquet, procureur général, surintendant des finances, ministre d'État de Louis XIV* [2 vols., Paris: Plon et Nourrit, 1890].)

[2]Cf. no. 2523, n. 6.

Please discuss with M. Le Vacher whether it is advisable to show Martin Jolly [3] the letter from his uncle.

I am, in O[ur] L[ord], Monsieur, your most humble servant.

VINCENT DEPAUL,
i.s.C.M.

2670. - TO JEAN MARTIN, SUPERIOR, IN TURIN

Paris, September 27, 1658

Monsieur,

The grace of O[ur] L[ord] be with you forever!

God be praised that you are finally lodged in more spacious quarters and in better air! However, it is still a rented house. Is there no further talk of the Sant'Antonio affair? [1]

You should not be surprised, Monsieur, at the malaise you detect in the little family; the same thing happens everywhere for the same reasons for which God allowed repugnance and changes among Our Lord's companions, namely, to try those who endure them and to humble Superiors. The remedy for that is patience, forbearance, and prayer that God will restore the men to their original serenity and the openness of heart they should have. You can also help in this by being the first to show them expressions of esteem, affection, and cordiality.

What happens to an individual person happens also to a community; that is, it becomes downhearted, unfeeling, and turned in on itself. When you see others in this state, it seems you become

---

[3]A slave in Tunis.

Letter 2670. - Archives of the Mission, Paris, original signed letter.

[1]Proceedings were under way to unite the Sant'Antonio Abbey in Piedmont to the Congregation of the Mission, which had a seminary there.

just like them, and so boredom, then discouragement, take hold of you. Instead of giving in to this, however, as long as it lasts you must, first of all, strive to honor the acts of patience and resignation practiced by Our Lord in similar circumstances, especially when several of His disciples, disheartened by His holy leadership and admirable teaching, left Him. "Do you also want to leave me?" [2] He said to His Apostles. It will be well to find out from someone the cause of the trouble and try to remedy it.[3] Second, you should redouble your trust in Our Lord, making Him and regarding Him as the Superior of your house. Ask Him constantly to be pleased to guide it according to His ways, considering yourself only a poor instrument which, if it were not in the hand of such an excellent Craftsman, would spoil everything.

Lastly, Monsieur, M. Berthe, who is leaving for Italy with a number of others, will go to see you on his way back from Genoa, God willing. Talk everything over with him heart to heart. I hope that by all these means you will find peace and joy for you yourself, as well as for your men, and progress in virtue for all in general and each one in particular. Remember, however, that patience is as necessary to bear with ourselves as charity is to bear with the neighbor. May God be pleased to give us both!

I am, in His love, Monsieur, your most humble servant.

VINCENT DEPAUL,
i.s.C.M.

M. Berthe is bringing you the printed Rules of the Company to be distributed to each confrere. Perhaps he will leave them with M. Delaforcade when he passes through Lyons to be forwarded to you, for he is going straight to Marseilles.

Addressed: Monsieur Martin

---

[2]Cf. Jn 6:68. (NAB)

[3]This sentence is in the Saint's handwriting.

2671. - TO EDME JOLLY, SUPERIOR, IN ROME

September 27, 1658

I really think there is nothing to be hoped for from the Toledo proposal [1] before peace is concluded between the two crowns. In my opinion, that is also what M. du Loeus [2] is trying to get across to you by his vague, general answers, without actually saying so. Since, by the grace of God, we want only what He wills, we will await with great patience the time His Providence has ordained for the fulfillment of His plans. I say the same regarding a residence for your family since apparently the one you looked at will not be given to you because of the difficulties involved, and it may take a long time to find another that suits you or does not also have its inconveniences. God grant that we may receive whatever happens with one and the same heart! I mean accepting the good and the bad indifferently. He will doubtless do so if we reduce our own desires and ways of action to nothing in His presence, allowing ourselves to be governed by His wisdom in the belief that whatever happens is best for us, even though it may be contrary to our feelings. If God chastises those whom He loves, we ought to believe that He is favoring us when things do not go well for us.

I am delighted that you are speeding up the expedition of the Bulls for Saint-Lazare. That is the seal which should strengthen this community and even the whole Company, which, after God, has its center and foundation in this place. You see from over there the importance of the service you render in giving it the means of defending itself against the attacks with which it is being threat-

---

Letter 2671. - Reg. 2, p. 247.

[1]This was a proposal to establish the Congregation of the Mission in that city. Since France and Spain did not sign a peace treaty until 1659 (Treaty of the Pyrenees), it appears that Saint Vincent was showing some hesitancy about embarking on that project during the unsettled times before the peace.

[2]The Latinized version of the name of James Dowley (Duley), future Bishop of Limerick.

ened; for, as I told you, there is a scheme afoot to get us removed from here, if possible. We must fear everything after a lawsuit we have just lost, contrary to all divine and human appearances, involving the Orsigny farm, which we have also lost. But God be praised! He has given us the grace to receive this blow as coming from His paternal hand, which deprives us in a small way of temporal goods to increase in us trust in His goodness and patience in adversity, so necessary for Christians and Missionaries.

2672. - TO A SUPERIOR

September 28, 1658

The next time you have the ordinands at your house, please do not leave them as you did this last time, going to the country to check out a place to give a mission. That is taking on too many things at once, and apparently it was useless for you to go since you are being asked for on all sides. Could you not have made your choice of a parish without having seen it beforehand?

I am surprised, Monsieur, that you are still urging me to send you your books, since I wrote you several times that it is contrary to the practice of the Company for anyone to have his own books, and still more to take a large number of them from house to house. I even told you that I am obliged to see to it that this Rule is observed. That was sufficient to make you consider God's Will and abide by it in that matter, without making further requests that I exempt you from it.

What is more annoying, however, is that your letters are always filled with bitterness and complaints, either about things that concern you or against others who do not please you. Not content to write to me, you also tell your troubles to a third and fourth party,

---

Letter 2672. - Reg. 2, p. 120.

as you did about those books, expressing your resentment to the men who are with you and writing to Messieurs . . . about it, thus making public your discontent, as do sensitive persons who cannot bear a slight mortification. I hope you will not do that again.

I am worried about the illness of Brother . . . , and I ask Our Lord to restore him to health. If I thought this good Brother would get better in Paris rather than in the place where he now is, I would be happy for him to come here, but usually a change of place does little to improve one's eyesight and rebuild lost strength. In addition, when townspeople are ill, I do not see them leaving their homes and going to some far-off place to try to get better; everyone puts up with his illness at home and uses the remedies at hand. Now, since this Brother has worked in your house for ten to twelve years, is it not right for it to bear with and care for him now that he is sick, without trying to unload him on to another that already has too many invalids? Please keep him, Monsieur, and take care of him.

2673. - TO DENIS LAUDIN, SUPERIOR, IN LE MANS

September 28, 1658

The Brother cleric's resistance to humbling himself for his fault gives us reason to hope for nothing from him, regardless of any pretense he makes. His spirit is such that, apart from some extraordinary grace or great fidelity on his part in responding to ordinary graces, he is in grave danger—I do not mean of leaving the Company, for he has already left or is close to it, but of being lost in the world, God forbid! I have no further advice to give you with regard to him, except to please remain firm so as to curb his unruly practices and little fits of temper and make him docile to obedience

---

Letter 2673. - Reg. 2, p. 169.

and to the Rule. If he leaves on that account, it will be without cause; but, if he changes and remains, we will see what we can do with him.

Since your council feels that M . . . , a former confrere from your house, has no right to ask for your late Pastor's residence, tell him, among the other reasons you will give him to prevent him from doing so, that women should not be living among priests, nor should Missionaries allow them in their enclosure.

2674. - TO DENIS LAUDIN, SUPERIOR, IN LE MANS

Paris, October 2, 1658

Monsieur,

I am writing you from the city, where I now am and it is very late, simply to ask you to send us a power of attorney as Prior of Bussière-Badil, with the name of the proxy left blank. By it you will give him authority to rent out the property of the priory for the price and years he will deem advisable, to receive its revenues and arrears, to exact payment, to go to law, to effect compromises, to give receipts, to substitute one or several proxies, both in court and for using the present power of attorney, and in general to do and carry on negotiations for the spiritual and temporal affairs of the said priory—just as you would do if you were present, etc. The notaries know the formalities of such documents. It is advisable for you to go and have this done in some place where you are not known.

Letter 2674. - Archives of the Mission, Paris, original signed letter. The postscript is in the Saint's handwriting.

While awaiting it, I am, in the love of O[ur] L[ord], Monsieur, your most humble servant.

VINCENT DEPAUL,
i.s.C.M.

The power of attorney must have the most extensive authority that can be given, and it should be sent here as soon as possible.

At the bottom of the first page: Monsieur Laudin

2675. - TO PIERRE CABEL, SUPERIOR, IN SEDAN

Paris, October 2, 1658

Monsieur,

The grace of O[ur] L[ord] be with you forever!

I had our printed Rules sent to you by the last coach that left for Sedan; they are in a small, linen-covered packet addressed to you. Please have someone pick it up. There are seven copies in Latin and three in French.[1] You will find in it a short circular letter containing instructions on this subject, signed by M. Alméras. I think there is also a Brief of an indulgence for those persons, both members and non-members, who make a retreat in the Company.

I praise God for having blessed your retreats and restored the sick to health. I am well aware that these retreats made for eight consecutive days inconvenience the service of the parish, but you must do the best you can, as has been done in the past; for, to make a retreat in two sessions, or for five days each twice a year, would be to do something that is not done in any place I know—not only

---

Letter 2675. - Archives of the Mission, Paris, original signed letter.

[1]The latter were for the coadjutor Brothers in the house.

in the Company, but in other Communities, with the exception of novices and seminarians. Please do not make any innovations in this matter.

M. Maillard[2] is writing to you about the donation made by young Jeanne Payon.

We here will try to pay your bill of exchange for this quarter.

M. Coglée[3] did not take any books with him, and I do not understand what books you are talking about when you say you have not found any of the ones Superiors should have, for there are none that are intended particularly for them. If you are talking about a register where we write down how we have solved the problems proposed to us, M. Coglée did not do that, and he says that the only sermon outlines he made were for his own use and not for the use of anyone else.

God has chosen to take to Himself M. Ozenne, Superior of our poor family in Poland. A raging fever carried him off from earth to heaven on the eve of the Assumption, the fifth day of his illness, fortified by all the sacraments and very well prepared for death. In fact, he had prepared himself his whole life long for this passage by avoiding evil and doing good, which he did most zealously and with good results. He was very sincere, gentle, and exemplary, and God is now his reward. He is sadly missed, and we have lost a great deal in losing him, if we can call a loss what God gains. May His Will be done always in us and in all that concerns us! Please pray and have others pray for this dear deceased man because the Church prays for the just as well as for sinners.

---

[2]Antoine Maillard, born in Veney (Meurthe), entered the Congregation of the Mission on May 21, 1644, at twenty-six years of age. He took his vows in 1646 and renewed them on January 25, 1656. Maillard was Procurator of Saint-Lazare for a long time and Procurator General (1679-86).

[3]Mark Cogley, predecessor of Pierre Cabel in the Sedan parish.

I am, in the love of O[ur] L[ord], Monsieur, your most humble servant.

VINCENT DEPAUL,
i.s.C.M.

Addressed: Monsieur Cabel

2676. - TO MADEMOISELLE DE LAMOIGNON

[October 1658] [1]

Vincent de Paul congratulates Mademoiselle de Lamoignon for the honor conferred on her brother Guillaume, who has just been named Presiding Judge by the King.

2677. - *SAINT LOUISE TO SAINT VINCENT*

[October 3, 1658] [1]

Most Honored Father,

Sister Françoise Fanchon[2] *consulted Monsieur Portail today concern-*

Letter 2676. - Collet, *op. cit.*, vol. II, p. 57, *note.*

[1]Since Guillaume de Lamoignon was appointed Presiding Judge on October 2, 1658, "October 1658" has been assigned as the date for this note.

Letter 2677. - Archives of the Motherhouse of the Daughters of Charity, original autograph letter.

[1]Brother Ducournau added "October 1658" on the back of the original. The contents allow us to pinpoint the day of the month because of the reference to the feast of Saint Francis of Assisi (October 4).

[2]Françoise Fanchon, born in Conche-les-Pots (Picardy), on June 25, 1625, entered the Company of the Daughters of Charity on August 9, 1644. She remained at the Motherhouse, where she worked in turn as gardener and cook, taking her vows for the first time in 1649. Françoise did not know how to write and made a simple cross on the Act of Establishment of the Company in 1655. She later became Sister Servant in Saint-Médard parish. She died

ing her desire to make the annual renewal of her vows tomorrow, the feast of Saint Francis, and he had no objections. If you approve of this, she entreats Your Charity to offer her to God, in the way she should make it, and I, still full of my miseries, ask for your holy blessing and prayers.

I am somewhat distressed at having been so long deprived of speaking with you. God wills it, since He permits it to be so.

Madame de Marillac the Carmelite [3] *would really like me to visit her to give her news of Ollainville, and her daughter told me she would be returning there Saturday. If Your Charity allows me to go, I will take advantage of her carriage tomorrow so as not to displease the mother.*

I am worried because I have had no news of our Sisters in Calais or Metz since their departure, although I have written to them. Permit me to ask you for some, and allow me to believe that I truly continue to be, Most Honored Father, your very lowly and most unworthy daughter and servant.

LOUISE DE MARILLAC

Addressed: *Monsieur Vincent*

2677a. - TO LOUISE-MARIE DE GONZAGUE, QUEEN OF POLAND

Paris, October 4, 1658

Madame,

I venture to thank Y[our] M[ajesty] for the favor she did me in

---

unexpectedly on May 12, 1689. Her companions stated that her charity and compassion extended to everyone.

[3]Marie de Creil, the daughter-in-law of Michel de Marillac, Saint Louise's uncle and Keeper of the Seals, entered Carmel in 1622, after the death of her husband, René de Marillac. There she was reunited with three of her daughters.

Letter 2677a. - Cathedral of Lucca (Italy), original autograph letter; Archives of the Mission, Paris, copy.

writing to me about the death of the late M. Ozenne.[1] I ask Our Lord to be Himself Your Majesty's thanks and reward.

I have done what Y[our] M[ajesty] did me the honor of ordering me to do regarding M. Desdames and have sent him the letters for the office of Superior and a presentation of himself to the Bishop of Poznan for Holy Cross parish.

The good people of this city admire Y[our] M[ajesty's] ways of acting and offer frequent prayers here that God may be pleased to bless the sacred persons of the King and Y[our] M[ajesty] and your kingdom as well. I personally am praying that God will make these Missionaries worthy of the incomparable acts of kindness Y[our] M[ajesty] does for them.[2]

I am the most humble and very obedient servant of Y[our] M[ajesty].

VINCENT DEPAUL,
i.s.C.M.

2678. - TO JEAN MONVOISIN,[1] IN MONTMIRAIL

Paris, October 8, 1658

Monsieur,

The grace of O[ur] L[ord] be with you forever!

I do not have time to write to you at length; I am simply writing

---

[1]He had died on August 14, 1658.

[2]Some words that follow have been crossed out and made illegible; the word "Mission," which apparently was not deleted, is also here, but it makes no sense in isolation. Saint Vincent must have forgotten to delete it along with the others.

Letter 2678. - Archives of the Mission, Paris, original signed letter.

[1]Jean Monvoisin, born in Arras on October 16, 1616, was ordained a priest in December 1640 and entered the Congregation of the Mission in Paris on July 13, 1641.

to tell you that I fully approve of your giving the Beuvardes[2] mission with those priests who are with you, and I embrace both them and you with all the tenderness of my heart. I ask O[ur] L[ord] to accept this service you will render to souls and to bless your work.

I have not yet given sufficient thought to your last letter to give you an answer just now concerning that good lady who is offering her property in return for a lifetime annuity. I would be glad to know what she gets from it in ordinary years, after all the expenses are paid.

I am, in the love of O[ur] L[ord], Monsieur, your most humble servant.

VINCENT DEPAUL,
i.s.C.M.

Before going to Beuvardes, you and M. Cornuel[3] will please go to see the Bishop of Soissons.[4] Discuss with him or with M. Dutour, his Vicar-General, whether there is any way of finding a good priest to say daily Mass in Beuvardes and to run a school there, and of getting the lord, who has to pay him in accord with the foundation, to accept this. Once the mission has been given, try also to get him to pay the revenue and arrears he owes you.

Addressed: Monsieur Monvoisin, Priest of the Mission of Fontaine-Essart, in Montmirail

---

[2]A village in Aisne.

[3]Guillaume Cornuel, born in Bar-sur-Aube (Aube), entered the Congregation of the Mission on November 29, 1644, at twenty-three years of age. He took his vows in 1646, was ordained a priest in December of that same year, and died in the Troyes diocese in 1666. Cornuel was Superior in Montmirail (1649-50 and 1658-59), at the Collège des Bons-Enfants (1652-54), and Troyes (1665-66). Pierre de Vienne, Seigneur de Torvilliers, his first cousin, mourned his death with several lyric poems in Latin, published in Troyes, to which Jacques de la Fosse, C.M., made a suitable response with several odes. (Cf. Abbé Jean-Baptiste-Joseph Boulliot, *Biographie ardennaise* [2 vols., Paris: n. p., 1830], vol. I, p. 420; Bibl. Maz., Ms. 3912.)

[4]Charles de Bourbon.

2679. - TO FIRMIN GET, SUPERIOR, IN MARSEILLES

Paris, October 11, 1658

Monsieur,

The grace of O[ur] L[ord] be with you forever!

I received your letter of the first of the month and am greatly consoled to hear that your sore eye is getting better. I thank God for this and for your attachment to the Will of God alone, causing you to have a holy indifference toward all things, instead of being attached to places and employments. That is the means to remain always at peace and to be blessed everywhere. May God be pleased to confirm us, as we are, in this blessed state!

I am, then, very glad that you are staying in Marseilles, since your health allows you to do so. I ask you to take care of it, and I ask Our Lord to work with you for the reestablishment of the conference [1] and the growth in virtue of those priests in the town who are to participate in it.

I am consoled to hear you talk of [giving] a mission soon. The change. . . .

The Duchesse d'Aiguillon is doing what she can to continue to have the salaries for the hospital paid; as for me, I can do nothing further. The first time I have the honor of seeing her, I will find out if she has made any progress.

I am sending M. Rambert's letter back to you, since it is inadvisable to present it to M. Colbert after his refusal to accept our money and the reason he gave us for it, as I told you. My opinion is that we should give the money to M. Simonnet, and we will do so this week. I think there is nothing to fear.

Letter 2679. - Archives of the Mission, Paris, copy made from the original in the Hains Family Collection, Marseilles.

[1]An assembly of priests modeled after the Tuesday Conferences of Paris.

I am, in the love of O[ur] L[ord], Monsieur, your most humble servant.

VINCENT DEPAUL,
i.s.C.M.

2680. - TO JEAN BARREAU, CONSUL, IN ALGIERS

Paris, October 11, 1658

Dear Brother,

The grace of O[ur] L[ord] be with you forever!

I am answering your dear letter of September 3, as I have already done for your previous ones to me. I forwarded to your brother all the letters you addressed to me and sent him your power of attorney, assuming that he will still be answerable to you for your property, which you have put completely at his disposal.

I really wish that the slaves could be paid and that M. Le Vacher[1] were with you, but several things oblige us to keep him and his money in Marseilles a while longer. First of all, there is the danger that Rappiot's creditors may seize some of the money and, consequently, instead of those poor people being relieved, they may be reduced to never getting any help because we were in too much of a hurry. You yourself acknowledge this danger in your last letter and would like the Tunis route to be used in order to avoid it. All things considered, however, there is danger on all sides.

Second, M. Le Vacher of Tunis writes us that it is not at all advisable to send anyone either to Algiers or to Tunis. He says, on the contrary, that those who are there should be withdrawn, if possible, until the King has registered a complaint against the Turks about what has happened and made some arrangement for the future; otherwise they will continue their attacks.

Letter 2680. - Archives of the Mission, Paris, original signed letter.

[1]Philippe Le Vacher.

In the third place, what has further obliged us to resolve to wait awhile is the G[rand] L[ord]'s imprisonment of the Ambassador of France and his son, M. de la Haye, who replaced his father in the office. That is an extraordinary act of violence, giving us reason to fear everything, or at least not to risk anything new until we see the outcome of this affair, which the King has good reason to resent.[2]

That is why, dear Brother, I ask you, in the name of O[ur] L[ord], to be patient. Our Lord is not permitting all these things without some reason; it is unknown to us just now, but we will see it some day. Delay has not spoiled anything up until now, and I hope it will spoil nothing in the future. As long as Our Lord grants you the grace to abandon yourself to His guidance, rest assured that you will be well with it. I ask His Divine Goodness to continue to protect you and to fill you with confidence in His strength and in His love for you, which is greater than you can imagine.

We have no news here. Our confreres are now making their retreat, after which they will go to render some small service to God, some in one place, some in another. Ten or twelve of them left a short while ago for Italy. From all sides we are being asked for men. The harvest is great; ask God to send good workers into His vineyard.[3]

God has been pleased to take one of our best ones from us—I do not know if I already told you this. I mean good M. Ozenne, Superior of our poor family in Poland; he died on the eve of the Assumption. This is a great loss for us, if we can call a loss what God gains. He always avoided evil and did good most zealously and with good results. I recommend his soul to your prayers, since the Church wants us to pray for the just as well as for sinners.

---

[2]This international brouhaha was detailed in no. 2659, n. 1.
[3]Cf. Mt 9:37-38. (NAB)

I am, in the love of O[ur] L[ord], dear Brother, your most humble servant.

VINCENT DEPAUL,
i.s.C.M.

Addressed: Monsieur Barreau, Consul in Algiers

2681. - TO JACQUES PESNELLE, SUPERIOR, IN GENOA

Paris, October 15, 1658

Monsieur,

The grace of O[ur] L[ord] be with you forever!

I received simultaneously your letters of October 1 and 9. I can only thank God for all the graces He has granted you. You should humble yourself greatly at the sight of what His Divine Goodness does in and through you and for the obstacles you perhaps put in the way of the working of His grace, which would produce even greater good works otherwise. Be very careful not to attribute any of these to yourself, Monsieur; you would be committing larceny and insulting God, who alone is the author of every good thing. Always tend toward lowliness, the love of your own abjection, and the desire for contempt and shame—contrary to our natural inclination, which makes us strive to be noticed and to achieve success. This is the best means to honor God, to truly edify and guide the family in a holy way, and, in a word, to draw down the special blessings of heaven on all your works. I ask His Divine Goodness to draw His glory from your retreats and ours. He will surely do so, if they incline us more and more to zeal and humility.

Letter 2681. - Archives of the Mission, Paris, seventeenth-century copy.

No matter what the doctor tells you about the nature of Brother Emmanuel's [1] illness, beware of it. His fainting spells give reason to fear he has epilepsy or at least a tendency to it and, regardless of what remedy is applied, it is difficult to remove the cause of it, even though you may be promised that it will be cured. Even the slightest suspicion of such an [illness] is sufficient to have a man dismissed from a Community. One of the nuns in the Sainte-Marie Monastery, for which I am responsible, has an acute form of this disease. Since she was disturbing the entire family, she was separated from it and put in a place apart. It so happened that, when the nun who had been appointed to look after her and help her saw her foaming at the mouth and thrashing about, she was so deeply affected that she herself is now having similar fits. You know that a man is irregular[2] because of this. If, then, the Church rejects him, how much more should a Company where brothers live together!

Our maxim is not to receive anyone into our houses to live there and do as he pleases. The late M. de Fargis, a distinguished lord of this kingdom who had been Ambassador in Spain and was the brother-in-law of our founder,[3] wanted to retire here in this house. I told him we no longer received anyone here except to make a retreat or to become a member of the Company. When he saw that he could not live here on his own with servants, he decided to take the habit of the Company and to adapt himself to the community. He lived in it for a year in this way, to our great consolation and his, and we never remarked any fault in him.[4]

---

[1]This is the only reference in Coste's fourteen volumes to Brother Emmanuel. No further information can be gleaned from *Notices*.

[2]In this context an irregularity is a perpetual impediment established by ecclesiastical law forbidding primarily the reception of Orders and secondarily the exercise of Orders already received. Brother Emmanuel would be irregular by defect, since epilepsy was classified at one time as an irregularity, although there were good theologians who thought otherwise.

[3]Philippe-Emmanuel de Gondi.

[4]Collet (*op. cit.*, vol. II, p. 28) quotes this sentence, which he says is an excerpt from a letter of October 25, 1658, but he gave the wrong date; it should be October 15.

Some time after that, M. d'Alméras, Master of Accounts, requested the same thing of us, and we gave him the same reply. He, too, then made the same decision, adopting the same habit and the same way of life, although he was eighty-two years old. We were greatly edified by him, and he died a saint. So, Monsieur, those gentlemen participate in the repetitions of prayer, conferences, chapters, and other exercises, as far as their age and health permit, and we avoid the inconveniences that would arise if they were separated from us. I tell you this in reference to M. Spinola and his wishes, so you can explain to him gently whatever you can and what solution he can adopt. The respect we owe his name—and even more his person, since he is as you tell me—will cause us to do whatever he may desire for his service and consolation.

M. Berthe has arrived in Marseilles and is only awaiting the opportunity to go to Genoa.

We have forwarded the letter you sent me from the religious.

If those Piedmontese gentlemen who are supposed to enter your Internal Seminary were willing to be satisfied with the order observed by others, that would remedy several inconveniences that might arise from singularity.

You tell me that M. Simon[5] is adding something to the author he is explaining. We do not readily allow that here, and I think it would be better if he were satisfied with a simple explanation.

I am, in O[ur] L[ord], your most humble servant.

VINCENT DEPAUL,
i.s.C.M.

---

[5]René Simon, born in Laval (Mayenne) on September 21, 1630, entered the Congregation of the Mission on August 5, 1650. He was a professor at Saint-Charles Seminary, then a Missionary in Poland, where he was ordained a priest in 1654. He returned to France the next year, took his vows on January 25, 1656, and was sent to Genoa. Simon became Superior of the Annecy Seminary in 1663 and of the Turin house (1665-67). He was named Secretary General in 1668 and, after participating in the General Assembly of that year, was appointed Superior in Rome and Visitor of the Province of Italy. In 1677 he was recalled to France; the following year he was made Superior of the Cahors house, where he died in 1682 or shortly thereafter. Simon was very useful to the Congregation, especially because of the favors he obtained for it from the Holy See. His biography is published in *Notices,* vol. II, pp. 447-51.

2682. - TO JACQUES DE LA FOSSE, IN TROYES

Paris, October 16, 1658

Monsieur,

The grace of O[ur] L[ord] be with you forever!

It is true that your question surprised me at first glance, as you yourself thought it might. Actually, Monsieur, how could it not surprise me, when I see that you now have doubts about your vocation, after having been in the Company for eighteen or twenty years, reflected on it in your entrance retreat, spent two years in the seminary, and vowed to God to remain in it, as you did several years ago? For, even though you have not renewed them since the Brief, those original vows remain promises to God, which one is obliged in conscience to keep.

After working so hard and successfully in various duties in the Company, after all that, I repeat, you write to ask me if you are called! Should I not be surprised at this question? I am replying to you, nevertheless, since you wish it, and I am telling you, Monsieur, that, after all that, God is asking you to persevere to the end. Any thoughts that may come to you contrary to this are temptations from the evil spirit, who is envious of the happiness you have to serve God.

"But I feel some repugnance to this; the vows and practices as well as the spirit of the Mission do not suit my temperament, although I appreciate them." And where, Monsieur, will you not have any repugnance? Is not every state in life beset by difficulties? And where do you see persons satisfied with their state in every detail? Take my word for it, Monsieur, that, besides the dangers to salvation to be encountered in the world, you will find many a cross and annoyance. And even if you should leave to enter another Community, do not think, Monsieur, that it will not have its

---

Letter 2682. - Archives of the Mission, Paris, rough draft and seventeenth-century copy. Both letters agree.

troubles as well, or that you will not have to practice obedience, or that it will not have its own practices, just as we have ours, and perhaps they might not suit your temperament either. When we are considering another state of life, we picture what is pleasing in it; but once we are in it, we experience what is annoying and contrary to nature. So remain at peace, Monsieur, and continue your journey to heaven on the same ship on which God has placed you. This is what I hope from His goodness and your desire to do His Will.[1]

I am, in His love, Monsieur, your most humble servant.

VINCENT DEPAUL,
i.s.C.M.

2683. - TO JACQUES THOLARD, IN TROYES

Paris, October 16, 1658

Monsieur,

The grace of O[ur] L[ord] be with you forever!

Your dear letter of the fourth of this month consoled me as much as or more than any I have received from you since you have been in the Company. This is because of the great openness of heart apparent in it and the graces and consolations I see you have recently received from Our Lord. I thank Him for this with all my heart.

What reply can I give to what you ask me, Monsieur, except what God Himself inspires you to do, what persons of learning and

---

[1]First redaction: "on the same ship on which God has placed you. Not that, if you decide to renew your vows, you will not be doing even better. Even if you do not, you will still be a member of the body of the Company, and I hope you will work in it to sanctify yourself and many others. I ask Our Lord to grant you this grace, and I am . . . ."

Letter 2683. - Archives of the Mission, Paris, original signed letter.

virtue have advised you to do, and what your own conscience dictates? Yes, Monsieur, have courage! If you give yourself entirely to God, He will also give Himself to you and will shower upon you His graces and choicest blessings. Do effectively what you could and—I will even say—what you should in a certain sense have been doing for a long time now. Do what so many other senior and new members have done, Monsieur, and believe that you will be consoled by it. If you have remained twenty years in the Company, you will remain in it another twenty or thirty more, since things will not be any more difficult in the future than they have been in the past. By binding yourself entirely to God like the others, besides the fact that you will edify them, Our Lord will bind Himself to you more closely than ever and will be your strength in weakness, your joy in sorrow, and your steadfastness in times of indecision.

(1) As for the doubts you say you have, these are only temptations of the enemy of your welfare and of the glory of Jesus Christ; for, with regard to the vow of working your whole life long for the salvation of the poor country folk, that means only in accord with the rules of obedience. So, if the Superior does not send you, you are not obliged to go. How many persons are there who cannot do that work and are still true Missionaries? House procurators, teachers—the Superior General himself—cannot go to do it very often; are they less members of the Company and are they not living their vows? You have been giving missions for twenty years; will you not be doing so for another twenty? And if God has helped you during that time when you still had not given yourself totally to Him, will He not help you in the future when you will be entirely His? But, taking this to the extreme, if the Superior judges that the danger is too clear, could he not dispense you from going?

(2) As for what you say about the vows—that sins against them will be greater—this is true, but does it prevent all religious, and even all the seculars who take all sorts of vows, from making promises to God? And just as the same God, who finds in these promises such pleasing testimonies of the love we bear Him, gives

His help in carrying them out, He will not refuse you His help in carrying out yours; furthermore, He will give you a share in many other favors. But, Monsieur, you fear God too much to fail in this in such an important matter.

(3) As for assisting your poor relatives, it is the intention of the Company that the income from property be used especially for that purpose, and that is how we have always acted.[1] Have you ever seen anyone from whom the revenue from the title[2] has been demanded? And I guarantee you, Monsieur, that this will not be done to you either by me or by any Superior who comes after me. For your assurance, keep this letter, which can be a proof in future that I promised you this, and no one will be able to oblige you to do anything to the contrary.

Courage then, Monsieur, give glory to God, give this good example to the Company, which will see that you, one of the senior members, are not lagging behind, and give yourself and your own conscience this consolation, which will doubtless be very great—greater than all worldly joys and satisfactions. I ask Our Lord to strengthen your spirit for this good resolution and to fill you with His grace. I am, in His love, Monsieur, your most humble servant.

VINCENT DEPAUL,
i.s.C.M.

Addressed: Monsieur Tholard, Priest of the Mission, in Troyes

---

[1]The last phrase is in the Saint's handwriting. The secretary had written "and I give you full permission for this now."

[2]To be admitted to Holy Orders a person must have a source of support, a title, such as incardination into a diocese, with an income from a benefice, or, as in this case, the guarantee of support which comes with membership in the Congregation of the Mission, under the title of *common table*. As indicated here, Saint Vincent would extend that support to a confrere's needy relatives.

2684. - TO JEAN MARTIN, SUPERIOR, IN TURIN

Paris, October 18, 1658

Monsieur,

The grace of O[ur] L[ord] be with you forever!

The last letter I wrote you is almost an answer to the one I received from you since then. You inform me that three or four of your men were sick and had not yet fully recovered. God grant that they have done so now and that M. Berthe will find all of you in good health and closely united!

I am sure you have made every gesture of kindness toward those whose hearts are set against you, so that when you open your fraternal, charitable embrace to them, they will have for you the respect and confidence due you. Do not be surprised at their coldness; all Superiors often endure something similar, especially those who are firm regarding the Rule and in waging war against the flesh. For all that, they keep going, and in the end God allows their patience and exactness to cause them to be honored and respected by everyone. If anything else has to be taken care of, the visitation will set everything right. Please be courageous, Monsieur, and put your trust in God. Desire that He alone be honored, and always take as your portion and that of the Company humility and love of abasement and contempt.

M. Berthe is now in Marseilles, with nine or ten others, whom he is taking to Italy. I sent you our printed Rules with him, and I think he will have left the packet with M. Delaforcade in Lyons to be forwarded to you.

I think what you tell me about the Brother who is studying is very important. I have a mind to write to him in my own hand one of these days. No matter how he may accept admonitions, continue to reprove him as long as he continues to stray from the path of

---

Letter 2684. - Archives of the Mission, Turin, original signed letter.

perfection. Sooner or later he can only profit from them because you will proceed in this matter according to your usual prudence and charity.

You did well to make your excuses to those Visitation nuns who asked you to be their regular confessor. If even the Marchese should pressure you on this point, you would have to explain to him that it is completely contrary to our Institute and customs and ask him to dispense you from it.

I forwarded the letter you sent me.

If someone gives you money to be forwarded here to Madame Bachelet, who lives with Madame de Lamare, on rue Saint-Jacques in this city, please send it to me. A young man who left there, led her to hope that he would send her something by you.

I am, in the love of O[ur] L[ord], Monsieur, your most humble servant.

VINCENT DEPAUL,
i.s.C.M.

Addressed: Monsieur Martin, Superior of the Priests of the Mission, in Turin

2685. - TO LOUIS D'ESTAING, BISHOP OF CLERMONT

Paris, October 18, 1658

Excellency,

The favor Your Lordship has done us in making the official proclamation of Our Holy Father's Bull regarding Saint-Pourçain is so great, and the mark of benevolence with which you honor us

---

Letter 2685. - Unsigned rough draft. This document was made known to Coste by M. La Caille, residing at the time at 50 Boulevard Malesherbes, Paris.

by deigning to want to have us give the mission in your diocese and to teach theology there is so outstanding, that I have no words to express our gratitude and to thank you for it. That is why I ask Our Lord to be Your Lordship's thanks and reward; I do so now, Excellency, and the Company will continue to do so always.

Abbé de Chandenier's [1] intention in resigning Saint-Pourçain in our favor—which was confirmed by His Holiness—was to unite this benefice to the Saint-Lazare house to provide it with the means of meeting the heavy expenses it incurs for the ordination retreats held for all the priests in the kingdom. These number from eighty to one hundred at each ordination retreat, which is given five times a year. The ordinands are fed gratis for eleven days, as is done for other retreatants, which usually number from eight to ten priests and as many laymen. They come from all over and succeed one another, so there are always twenty persons here from outside making their retreat, which they also do free of charge.

Accordingly, Excellency, Your Lordship sees that the revenue of Saint-Pourçain is insufficient for Abbé de Chandenier's plan and for the maintenance of a continual, permanent mission in your diocese, as you, Excellency, do me the honor of writing me that Your Lordship desires. Our plan, Excellency, is to go to Saint-Pourçain to give the mission every five years and to invite to it the villages dependent on it, beginning as soon as possible, with Your Lordship's permission.[2]

I am deeply distressed, Excellency, that Your Lordship has not received the satisfaction you had expected from M. Chomel and that I am of no use to you in that respect. He did not do me the honor of asking my opinion; he simply sent me word of his regret at not being able to accept the honor that you, Excellency, offered him.

---

[1]Louis de Chandenier.

[2]The Saint then added these words which, after reflection, he crossed out: "And when we are there, we shall see if we can leave two or three priests to go to preach the mission wherever Your Excellency sends them, helped by the reduction on the tithes with which the Priory has been burdened recently, beyond what it can bear, if you agree, Excellency."

Abbé Gedoyn[3] is a very virtuous priest. The Prince de Conti[4] says that, when he was a student, he was the first to speak to him about devotion and was, even then, already very virtuous. He preaches well and effectively; he is gentle but nonetheless firm. He is the son of the Head Commissioner of the Treasury, who died a few years ago, with the result that the latter has the use of his property, which he spends for good, holy works.

I have not yet made him the proposal [of] the honor you, Excellency, are doing him. I will do so in three or four days, when he is to be at the priests' meeting held here every Tuesday, of which he is the prefect. Please take my word that I will do all I can to be of service to you in this and in everything else. I will take the honor of then letting you know his decision, which I hope will be in line with your will, Excellency. Mine will be entirely so all my life; therefore, I renew to Your Lordship the offers of my perpetual obedience and am. . . .

---

[3]Nicolas Gedoyn, Abbé de Saint-Mesmin, became chaplain of the Duc d'Orléans and Superior of the Ursulines of Saint-Cloud. The missions he gave in Paris and in the provinces were very effective. Toward the end of his life he retired to the General Hospital of Paris, where he died on June 10, 1692, at sixty-four years of age.

[4]Armand de Bourbon, Prince de Conti, brother of the Grand Condé, was born in Paris on October 11, 1629, and became the head of the Conti house, a cadet branch of the house of Bourbon-Condé. His father, who had earmarked him for the ecclesiastical state, had conferred on him a large number of abbeys, including Saint-Denis, Cluny, Lérins, and Molesme, but the military attracted him more than the Church. His passion for the Duchesse de Longueville drew him into the intrigues of the Fronde. After having him locked up in the prison of Vincennes, Cardinal Mazarin gave him his niece, Anna Martinozzi, in marriage. The Prince became Governor of Guyenne (1654), General of the armies in Catalonia, where he captured several cities. He was also Grand Master of the King's house and Governor of Languedoc (1660). Before his death on February 21, 1666, his virtuous wife was able to bring him back to God and even to instill great piety in him. Two hours of his day were devoted to prayer. A friend of Saint Vincent, he offered his services to him more than once and was present at his funeral rites.

2686. - TO FIRMIN GET, SUPERIOR, IN MARSEILLES

Paris, October 18, 1658

Monsieur,

The grace of O[ur] L[ord] be with you forever!

I thank God once again that your sore eye is healing and is growing stronger and stronger.

I would like to think that M. Berthe and his group are now with you. They arrived safely in Lyons on the eighteenth of this month.[1] I praise God that they will find two good opportunities to get into Italy. M. Berthe informs me that not all of them will be going there because he plans to leave M. Brisjonc[2] in Marseilles to work a while longer in France before sending him to Italy. That is why I now ask you to send him to Agde, where M. Durand tells me they are badly in need of a priest for the chant. I am notifying M. Berthe of this same thing, in the event that he is still with you when this letter arrives. If, by chance, he has left, please send my letter for him to Genoa because it mentions a few other matters.

You will do very well, Monsieur, to send a priest to Toulon for a few days. . . .

The bankruptcies occurring in Paris a while ago—even recently—prevented us from giving the slaves' money to M. Simonnet, as I had planned to do. I have, nonetheless, been assured that they are being maintained, but I thought it well for us to wait until next week to be more certain of this. I hope, then, to send you a bill

---

Letter 2686. - Archives of the Mission, Paris, copy made from the original in the Hains Family Collection, Marseilles.

[1]The copy has the Arabic number *18*, but the date of the letter indicates that this had to be a misreading. Coste's corrections suggest either *8* or *10*.

[2]François Brisjonc, born in Tréfumel (Côtes-du-Nord) on April 13, . . . entered the Congregation of the Mission on August 7, 1654, in Richelieu, where he had been ordained on June 7, 1653. He took his vows there in the presence of M. Thieulin. Brisjonc left the Company of his own free will in 1659 but was readmitted on May 17, 1664.

of exchange for it in a week. Besides, we felt this delay was necessary to give to the nephew of Provost Bausset [3] the money he will need, in line with what you and he requested, namely, only five hundred livres, if he is paid by a bill of exchange for a similar sum which his uncle has sent for him, or one thousand livres, in the event that he is not paid by the above-mentioned bill. I have instructed M. Maillard to give him one of these sums he will request of him when he comes and to get a receipt from him to be sent to you. Meanwhile, I am, in the love of O[ur] L[ord], Monsieur, your most humble servant.

VINCENT DEPAUL,
i.s.C.M.

I almost forgot to tell you that we will send you something for the sums you have to advance and for your living expenses.

2687. - TO FIRMIN GET, SUPERIOR, IN MARSEILLES

Paris, October 18, 1658

I ask M. Get, Superior of the Mission in Marseilles, to use his influence with the Admiralty of Marseilles [1] on behalf of M. Jacques Gaultier, a merchant in that same city, for what he will ask of him and generally for whatever he desires. I ask this on the recommendation made to me of him by one of my friends. Please

---

[3]Pierre de Bausset, Provost of Marseilles. His nephew, Antoine de Bausset, was assistant Seneschal of Marseilles.

Letter 2687. - Archives of the Mission, Paris, copy made from the original in the Hains Family Collection, Marseilles. This is one of the letters sold at auction by Xavier Charmoy (cf. no. 2505).

[1]Antoine de Valbelle, Seigneur de Montfuron.

take the trouble also to write to M. Le Vacher of Tunis, requesting him to do what he can for M. de Beaulieu, a merchant residing in Tunis.

I am, meanwhile, in the love of O[ur] L[ord], your most humble servant.

VINCENT DEPAUL,
i.s.C.M.

2688. - TO EDME JOLLY, SUPERIOR, IN ROME

Paris, October 18, 1658

Monsieur,

The grace of O[ur] L[ord] be with you forever!

We received the Bulls for Saint-Lazare [1] and your advice for the official proclamation. I thank you most humbly for them and for the copy of the erection of the Congregation of Sainte-Geneviève. I thank God, Monsieur, for the grace He gives you of being attentive to business affairs, down to the least details, with the result that you have given us reason to say that nothing is lacking in what you do. I ask O[ur] L[ord] to preserve you for the Company, and I also ask you, Monsieur, to do whatever you can for it. You have saved us a great deal of money in this affair, given what has been asked of us on other occasions. We will pay your bill of exchange for 770 livres, God willing.

I will send the Abbot of Chancelade[2] a copy of the erection of Sainte-Geneviève.

Letter 2688. - Archives of the Mission, Paris, original signed letter.

[1]Concerning the union of the Priory of Saint-Pourçain to Saint-Lazare.

[2]Jean Garat, a monk of Chancelade and Vicar-General of the Bishop of Cahors. The monks of Sainte-Geneviève continued to put pressure on the Court of Rome to obtain the union to their Order of all the houses dependent on Chancelade Abbey.

I was greatly consoled by the note you sent me about the works of your house during the past year. God be praised, Monsieur, for the little services it renders Him through your fine guidance. May He grant all of you the grace of growing in humility, zeal, and good works for the salvation of souls!

I am really distressed about the illness of M. François.[3] I ask O[ur] L[ord] to cure him of it and to make him strong. I recommend myself to his prayers, to yours, and to those of the entire little family. I ask it to pray often and earnestly that God will be pleased to send good workers to His Church and to perfect those it has already—I mean the entire ecclesiastic and religious state. Through them may all nations know and serve Jesus Christ, and may all the souls He has redeemed avail themselves of the fruits of His Passion and the examples of His holy life in order to be able to glorify God with Him forever and ever. Amen.

I am, in His love, Monsieur, your most humble servant.

VINCENT DEPAUL,
i.s.C.M.

The Bishop of Le Puy[4] is writing to you. Please help him discreetly so that those who oppose him will know nothing about it.

I fear that the official proclamation of the Bull for Saint-Pourçain may not be as it should. The Bull is addressed to the Officialis[5] of Clermont. Since the office of Officialis is vacant, the

---

[3]Pierre François, born in Les Riceys (Aube) on November 11, 1627, entered the Congregation of the Mission on October 20, 1654, and took his vows in Rome on November 26, 1656, in the presence of M. Jolly. The Lyons manuscript gives a summary of the conference on his virtues, held in Rome after his death.

[4]Henri de Maupas du Tour. He was under a cloud in Rome because of his biography of Francis de Sales.

[5]The Officialis, or judicial vicar, is appointed by the Bishop and is given the ordinary power to judge, which is distinct from that of the Vicar-General. The Officialis constitutes one tribunal with the Bishop, but he cannot judge cases which the Bishop reserves to himself (cf. *Code of Canon Law,* Latin-English edition [Ann Arbor, Michigan: Braun-Brumfield, 1983], Canon 1420, p. 511). The duties of Officialis at the time of Saint Vincent did not differ markedly from what the present Code stipulates.

Bishop,[6] in his capacity of Ordinary, deputed by His Holiness because of the death of the Officialis, did it without summoning the Canons of Tournus or the religious, and without making enquiries about the property of Saint-Lazare and Saint-Pourçain. Please give me some advice on that.[7]

I ask you to do what the enclosed note says. M. Bardin, whom it mentions, is the one who had the official announcement proclaimed the way it is, and who said that it was valid.

Addressed: Monsieur Jolly

2689. - TO LOUIS DE CHANDENIER [1]

Paris, October 19, 1658

Monsieur,

Your brother the Abbé[2] is in good health. He was forced to give up his philosophy studies because, as soon as he exerts himself, he gets a headache. We have had two or three recreations together since you left, and they were spent very agreeably. For the rest of the time, we have a few of our men go and converse with him.

I thought I should tell you, Monsieur, that it is strongly rumored here that the King is leaving for Lyons on Thursday.[3] I do not think,

---

[6]Louis d'Estaing (1651-64).

[7]These first two paragraphs of the postscript are in the Saint's handwriting.

Letter 2689. - Archives of the Mission, Paris, original rough draft.

[1]Brother Ducournau wrote the name of the recipient on the back of the original.

[2]Claude de Chandenier.

[3]The twenty-year-old King, Louis XIV, accompanied by the Queen Mother, Anne of Austria, and Cardinal Mazarin, arrived in Lyons on November 24. There he had planned to meet members of the royal family of Savoy, who were supposed to introduce him to Marguerite de Savoie, his first cousin. There was some discussion of arranging a marriage between the two.

however, that this is really certain because yesterday someone told me that they were still waiting for a letter on the mail coach, which was supposed to settle the matter. See if it would be wise for you, Monsieur, to be in Tournus when the Court comes through.

The Bishop-elect of Chalon[4] paid me the honor yesterday of coming to see me. He wanted to tell me that his treasurer informed him that he spoke to the Dean of Tournus about the affair with which you are familiar and that he admitted the thing[5] to him with some slight modification.

M. Gicquel is back from Clermont. He brought us the official proclamation of the Bull of union,[6] which was proclaimed by the Bishop himself because he has not yet appointed an Officialis. I am not sure he had the right to do that, since the Bull was addressed to the Officialis, and I am worried because he did not observe any of the formalities.

May God be pleased to keep you in good health! I am, in His love, Monsieur, your most humble and very obedient servant.

VINCENT DEPAUL,
i.s.C.M.

2690. - TO NICOLAS DEMONCHY, IN TOUL

Paris, October 19, 1658

Monsieur,

The grace of O[ur] L[ord] be with you forever!

I am not answering your letters because we need you here.

---

[4]Jean de Maupeou.

[5]First redaction: "the truth."

[6]The Bull of union of the Priory of Saint-Pourçain to the Congregation of the Mission.

Letter 2690. - Archives of the Mission, Paris, original signed letter.

Please come and leave M. Caset in charge of the family in the interim, telling him what you know about the state of affairs. If Abbé de Chandenier [1] is returning to Paris, I hope he will be good enough to give you a place in his carriage. I will be consoled to see you again, since I am, in the love of O[ur] L[ord], Monsieur, your most humble servant.

VINCENT DEPAUL,
i.s.C.M.

At the bottom of the page: Monsieur Demonchy

2691. - TO LOUIS RIVET, SUPERIOR, IN SAINTES

Paris, October 20, 1658

Monsieur,

The grace of O[ur] L[ord] be with you forever!

I have nothing special to reply to your letter of October 2. It will be well for you to be on the alert that M. Fleury[1] does not strain himself too much at prayer or in his studies because, since he is choleric, that could easily excite him. Recommend that he apply himself gently and without strain, and encourage him in his difficulties. Everyone has them in one way or another—at least all those who want to follow Jesus Christ. That is the narrow, rough path that leads to life,[2] and difficulties must not prevent us from taking it. You should be careful above all to see that those who are supposed to be edifying him do not do the contrary, for what

---

[1]Louis de Chandenier.

Letter 2691. - Archives of the Mission, Paris, seventeenth-century copy.

[1]Antoine Fleury.

[2]Cf. Lk 13:24. (NAB)

especially puts off newcomers who want to work at acquiring virtue is to see that the older members do not give them sufficient example in this.

I will have our printed Rules sent to you by the first mail coach so that each man may be inspired to observe them. By so doing, we will find our entire sanctification, especially since they contain what O[ur] L[ord] did and what He wants us to do.

If Brother Christophe[3] has not left for Richelieu, keep him with you and tell him I would like him to spend the winter with you because you need a Brother for the missions. We have sent another Brother to Richelieu, with instructions for M. de Beaumont to send Christophe to Le Mans, if he arrives at his house, in line with our original orders.

I hope that the principal result of our retreats is that we tend to the practice of acts of humility because if O[ur] L[ord] is pleased to give us the virtue that produces them, He will also produce in us works that are pleasing to God and useful to His Church.

I am, in His love, Monsieur, your most humble servant.

VINCENT DEPAUL,
i.s.C.M.

Please forward the enclosed letter, which comes from Barbary.

2692. - TO PIERRE DE BEAUMONT, SUPERIOR, IN RICHELIEU

Paris, October 20, 1658

Monsieur,

The grace of O[ur] L[ord] be with you forever!

As you requested, I am sending you the copy of one of the

---

[3]Christophe Delaunay.

Letter 2692. - Archives of the Mission, Paris, original signed letter.

instructions of the Vicars-General of Paris for the missions in this diocese, drawn up like the ones of the late Archbishop of Paris.[1]

If M. Liébe[2] comes to your house to say Holy Mass, he should be made welcome and given vestments and whatever he needs. Ask him also, however, always to come to you alone and never to speak to any of the others and to excuse you for not inviting him to a meal because you are afraid that, if others in the house see him, they might be tempted to do what he has done. Moreover, I cannot believe that he would be so indiscreet—not to say ashamed—as to return to Richelieu, at least in order to stay there. I have a good mind to write to him, and I intend to do so. That is all that remains for me to reply to your last letter.

I am, in the love of O[ur] L[ord], Monsieur, your most humble servant.

VINCENT DEPAUL,
i.s.C.M.

After signing this letter, I was brought one from you.

At the bottom of the first page: Monsieur de Beaumont

---

[1]Jean-François de Gondi (1622-54).

[2]François-Ignace Liébe, born in Arras (Artois) on April 26, 1623, entered the Congregation of the Mission on May 12, 1641, took his vows in Richelieu on April 7, 1644, and was ordained a priest in June 1647. He was Superior at the Collège des Bons-Enfants (1650-51) and Notre-Dame de Lorm (1654-56). He was then placed in Richelieu; from there he left the Company in 1657.

2693. - TO FIRMIN GET, SUPERIOR, IN MARSEILLES

Paris, October 25, 1658

Monsieur,

The grace of O[ur] L[ord] be with you forever!

I am very sorry that the galley from Genoa had already left by the time M. Berthe and his companions arrived. We must wait patiently for another opportunity.

Money from collections must not be touched. If you have nothing else for the clothing, linen, and other things Brother Barreau is requesting, get some there—if you can find any—and we will repay it here, or you will do it there, from the first payment we receive from the coach-tax farmer.

I ask M. Le Vacher [1] to excuse me for not answering his last letter. It is night time and I am in the city, in no position to write to him. Besides, there is nothing urgent in his letter.

I send greetings to the whole family and am, in O[ur] L[ord], Monsieur, your most humble servant.

VINCENT DEPAUL,
i.s.C.M.

Letter 2693. - Archives of the Mission, Paris, copy made from the original in the Hains Family Collection, Marseilles. This is one of the letters sold at auction by Xavier Charmoy (cf. no. 2505).

[1]Philippe Le Vacher.

2694. - TO EDME JOLLY, SUPERIOR, IN ROME

Paris, October 25, 1658

Monsieur,

The grace of O[ur] L[ord] be with you forever!

With your letter of September 24, I received the memorandum you sent me countering the claims of the Fathers of Sainte-Geneviève.[1] You are one of the men in this world who most honors the Providence of God by preparing remedies against ills that are foreseen. I thank you most humbly for this, and I ask Our Lord to continue and increase His enlightenment to you so you can diffuse it throughout the Company.

I admit that it would be well to have the consent of Cardinal de Retz[2] for the official proclamation, but the difficulty of obtaining it in his present situation[3] prevents us from requesting it, especially since we have been assured here that it is not necessary:

Letter 2694. - Archives of the Mission, Paris, original signed letter.

[1]On Saint-Lazare Priory.

[2]Jean-François-Paul de Gondi was the son of Philippe-Emmanuel de Gondi, General of the Galleys, and Françoise-Marguerite de Silly. On June 13, 1643, he was named Coadjutor to his uncle, Jean-François de Gondi, Archbishop of Paris, and was consecrated on January 31, 1644. Although he played an active role in the Fronde, the Queen—no doubt to win him over—obtained the Cardinal's hat for him on February 19, 1652; he was known subsequently as Cardinal de Retz. Discontented with his influence and plots, Mazarin had him imprisoned at Vincennes. Becoming Archbishop upon the death of his uncle (1654), and consequently more dangerous to the Prime Minister, Retz was transferred to the Château de Nantes, from which he escaped to Spain and then to Italy. In Rome the Priests of the Mission gave him hospitality, on the orders of Pope Innocent X. Because of this, Mazarin very nearly let all the force of his anger fall upon Saint Vincent and his Congregation. After the accession of Pope Alexander VII (1655), who was less benevolent to him than his predecessor, Cardinal de Retz left Rome on a long journey to Franche-Comté, Germany, Belgium, and Holland. He returned to France in 1662, after Mazarin had died, renounced the archbishopric of Paris, and received in exchange Saint-Denis Abbey. Age and trials had made him wiser; during the last four years of his life, some persons even considered him pious. In this peaceful, studious, simple-mannered man, concerned with paying off his numerous creditors, no one would have recognized the ambitious, flighty, and restless Prelate who had stirred up Paris and made the powerful Mazarin tremble. Cardinal de Retz died on August 24, 1679.

[3]He was still hiding from the agents of Mazarin. Only after the latter's death (1661) did Cardinal de Retz return to France.

(1) Because the late Archbishop of Paris, his predecessor, resigned for himself and for his successors any rights they might have over this house by uniting it to the Company as a result of our agreement with the former religious. He subsequently confirmed the latter, after the opposition of Saint-Victor, because, although the decree of the Parlement maintained us in possession, it ordained, nevertheless, that we should apply to the King once again, through the Archbishop of Paris, for his authorization for the said union, which was done. That gave rise to a second decree, which ordained the registration of the letters patent for the execution of the said union.

(2) Because the Holy See granted its Bulls of confirmation while the Archbishop of Paris was still alive, as is set forth in those you have sent us; for, even though they may not have been officially proclaimed until after his death, they still have the same force as if they had been done so during his lifetime because the official announcement will be made now by the Officialis of Cardinal de Retz, who, in a certain sense, represents him. His decision, therefore, will serve as a consent for him, who made him his Officialis.

I delivered Cardinal Sachetti's[4] letter to Madame de Chastelain.

You could do no better than to dissuade M. du Loeus[5] from writing to tell the Cardinal of Toledo's[6] chaplain to go to Rome to enter our Company, since we must not accept anyone until we have seen and examined him and found signs of a true vocation, which that man perhaps does not have. In which case, his journey might have been detrimental both to him and to his intended plan. We will see what you have decided together as most suitable for him.

I will write to Saint-Flour the remark made by M. du Loeus concerning the article of the *Credo* you mentioned to me.

---

[4]Giulio Sachetti was born in Florence, became Nuncio to Spain, and in 1626 was created Cardinal; he died in Rome on June 28, 1663.

[5]James Dowley (Duley), future Bishop of Limerick.

[6]Balthazar Moscoso y Sandoval, Cardinal of Toledo (1646-65).

Like you, I am amazed at the admirable acts of kindness the Cardinal of Genoa[7] is doing for the Company. When I think of this, I do not know what to say or do except to hide in the abyss of my nothingness and poverty and to hope that the Company will humble itself profoundly at the sight of the great honor His Eminence does it.

I am consoled that the objection we raised about buying the Mattei house is in line with the sentiment of that holy Prelate, who does not approve of this purchase. So, we must let matters stand unless, by some turn of events, God disposes otherwise. We will be very wrong if we do not appreciate in this the happiness we have of being like Our Lord, when He said that He had nowhere to lay His head.[8] It is no small humiliation to be poorly lodged and in someone else's house in a large town that thinks highly only of well established Communities. Still, we should love to be unknown and ignored as long as God chooses to keep us in that state. If we have this love of our own abjection, perhaps God will make use of it to provide us with better lodgings. Oh! if God were pleased to lay this groundwork in us, we would have good reason to hope that our house would then be a house of peace and blessings.

You heard that M. Duiguin died two years ago[9] in the Hebrides. Since then, M. Le Blanc[10] has remained in the mountains, where I

[7]Stefano Durazzo.

[8]Cf. Mt 8:20. (NAB)

[9]The Saint says "two years ago," but Dermot Duggan [Duiguin] did not die until May 17, 1657.

[10]Francis White (Saint Vincent refers to him as *François Le Blanc*), born in Limerick (Ireland) in 1620, entered the Congregation of the Mission on October 14, 1645, took his vows on October 15, 1647, and was ordained a priest in 1651. He first went to Genoa, but his stay there was very short. Sent to Scotland, he evangelized the Highlands with unflagging zeal. The exercise of his ministry there was forbidden; he was accused of saying Mass and in 1655 was imprisoned for five or six months in Aberdeen. On his release, he was warned that he would most certainly be hanged if he did not stop ignoring the laws. He left the district but continued his apostolate. Except for two sojourns in France (1658-62, 1665-68), White continued to work in Scotland until his death on February 7, 1679. He left the reputation of being a saint and an apostle. His portrait was long preserved and venerated in what was known as the "Father White Room" in Invergarry Castle. He is praised in several official reports addressed to Propaganda Fide. (Cf. "*Hibernia Vincentiana*, or the Relations of St. Vincent de Paul with Ireland," Irish Ecclesiastical

am told he is in straitened circumstances. We are on the point of recalling him. I do not think Cardinal Charles Barbarin's[11] chaplain is referring to them, when he says that there are some Irishmen in Scotland who do not have faculties from the Congregation of Propaganda Fide, since we obtained them for those two Missionaries at the time they were sent. Perhaps, however, other priests, who do not have them, have gone there. Two who recently arrived from there are supposed to be coming to dinner here tomorrow. They worked for a while in that country; I will find out from them by what authority they did so.

If a synopsis of the minutes of the canonization of Blessed Thomas of Villanova is printed, I would be glad if you sent us a copy, so we may place ourselves under the protection of this saint.[12]

I am really distressed and quite worried about the illness of M. François. May God be pleased to cure him of it! I do not recommend him to you, knowing that your charity spares nothing for his health. I ask only that he, on his part, do all in his power to get better—not so much for himself as for the salvation of souls, who are in such great need of assistance.

We find a difficulty in the dimissorial letter you sent us for Brother Pierre Butler,[13] a cleric from the Cashel diocese, in Ireland because: (1) it does not state that he is a member of the Company;

Record, 4th series, 14 [October 1903], pp. 289-316, published in French in *Notices*, vol. III, pp. 172-78, as "Les relations de Saint Vincent de Paul avec l'Irlande," and reprinted in *Annales C. M.* (1907), vol. 72, pp. 354-62.)

[11]Carlo Barberini was the grandnephew of Pope Urban VIII (Matteo Barberini). Born on June 1, 1630, he was created a Cardinal on June 23, 1653, and died on October 11, 1704.

[12]Saint Thomas of Villanova was an Augustinian writer, educator, and Archbishop of Valencia (Spain) [1545-55]. Canonized on November 1, 1658, his feast day is September 22.

[13]Peter Butler (in *Notices*, vol. I, p. 482, and vol. V [Supplement], p. 102, he is listed as *Pierre Buthleer*), born in Drom, Cashel diocese (Ireland), in April 1632, entered the Congregation of the Mission in Richelieu on August 22, 1654, and took his vows in the same house on August 15, 1656. This same letter and others speak of Saint Vincent's persistent attempts in 1658-59 to obtain dimissorial letters for his ordination. The title for ordination in the Congregation of the Mission and the authority of the Superior General were at variance with the attempts of Propaganda Fide to have all Irish clerical students ordained on the continent take an oath to return as missionaries to Ireland.

(2) the dimissorial states that he will have to make a promise—to be inserted in the Acts of the Chancellor or Secretary of the diocese in which he will receive Orders—to go to Ireland as soon as possible after having completed his studies; (3) this will be to exercise there his functions as a Missionary, under the direction of the Sacred Congregation of Propaganda Fide, to which he will send annually a written report of what he is doing. There seems to be a disadvantage in this last condition above all, seeing that this would be passing from obedience to his own Superior to that of the Congregation of Propaganda Fide. Could it not be obtained at least without this last stipulation?

I am, in the love of O[ur] L[ord], Monsieur, your most humble servant.

VINCENT DEPAUL,
i.s.C.M.

At the bottom of the first page: Monsieur Jolly

2695. - TO DENIS LAUDIN, SUPERIOR, IN LE MANS

Paris, October 26, 1658

Monsieur,

The grace of O[ur] L[ord] be with you forever!

A young man, the brother of our Brother Hennebert,[1] left here today to go to study at your house. Please welcome him and look after him.

Letter 2695. - Archives of the Mission, Paris, original signed letter.

[1]François Hennebert, born in Hesdin (Pas-de-Calais) on November 18, 1634, entered the Congregation of the Mission in Paris on January 25, 1656, and took his vows on February 27, 1658, in the presence of M. Delespiney. Although he is listed as a priest in *Notices,* no ordination date is given.

It has been a good month since I had our Rules sent to you by the mail coach, and our Brother forgot to notify you of it by letter. If you have not already received them, you can send someone to pick them up.

I have received several letters from you, to which I am unable to reply in detail. I simply thank God that Brother Carpentier[2] is now so well disposed. It is not advisable for him to go to Richelieu. Test his resolution yourself and put him to work.

I am writing to M. Bienvenu[3] in conformity with his needs. Look over the letter; it is open.

I have just received a packet from you, which I cannot open now. It is too late to reply to it.

We will make an effort to send you one or two priests, but I strongly doubt that we can do so. We will send you back Brother Christophe.[4] I informed him in Luçon that he was to go to Richelieu, and I told M. de Beaumont to send him to you.

If the subdeacon about whom M. Herbron[5] wrote to me wants to come to make a retreat the better to make up his mind, he will be welcome. He will see us and we will see him.

I am, in the love of O[ur] L[ord], Monsieur, your most humble servant.

VINCENT DEPAUL,
i.s.C.M.

At the bottom of the first page: Monsieur Laudin

---

[2]Augustin Carpentier, born in Bapaume (Pas-de-Calais) on October 18, 1637, entered the Congregation of the Mission in Paris on October 19, 1655, to study for the priesthood and took his vows on October 23, 1657, in the presence of M. Delespiney. He, too, is listed as a priest in *Notices*, but no ordination date is given.

[3]Étienne Bienvenu, born in Mehun-sur-Vèvre (Cher) on March 29, 1630, entered the Congregation of the Mission in Paris on November 19, 1650, and took his vows on November 23, 1652.

[4]Christophe Delaunay.

[5]François Herbron, born in Alençon (Orne) in November 1617, was ordained a priest on September 22, 1646, entered the Congregation of the Mission on August 20, 1653, and took his vows on January 6, 1656. When the ship on which he was to sail for Madagascar sank, he was reassigned to Le Mans.

2696. - TO ÉTIENNE BIENVENU, IN LE MANS

Paris, October 26, 1658

Monsieur,

I am really taken aback by your letter because, coming from a person whom I cherish, it sets forth a proposal very far removed from the esteem I have for you and for the treatment you have received from the Company. What reason has the latter given you to withdraw from it? Has it not supported you, provided for you, and raised you as a mother does her own child? And does not God, to whom you have given yourself, deserve that you serve Him now as well as before? You will tell me that you intend to serve Him everywhere. However, to anticipate such a reply, I will tell you, Monsieur, that it is quite clear that you are seeking something other than God when you request a dispensation from your vows, and it is the evil spirit which is suggesting that to you to turn you aside from the good you have begun to do.

Are you not aware, Monsieur, that promises made to God cannot be broken by men? If yours were null, there would have to be other reasons for nullity than the ones you give me. You make no mention to me of the first vows you took at the end of your seminary, and yet you are obliged to keep them just as well as if you had not renewed them. You mention only the final vows that you took in consequence of the Brief of His Holiness. You say you had no intention of taking them. If that is the case, you have committed a mortal sin, so do not fail to be committed to keep the promise you made because the external act is binding on the internal. A priest would not be dispensed from the Holy Orders he received if he were to say that he had no intention of taking them, nor would a marriage be declared null if the husband or the wife

---

Letter 2696. - Archives of the Mission, Paris, unsigned rough draft in the secretary's handwriting.

were to say that they consented only with their lips and not with their heart, because hidden things are judged by those that are apparent.

You say furthermore that two things made you take vows. The first is the determination of your father, who wants you to remain in the Mission; the second is your fear that the Company would dismiss you if you did not do as the others did, and you would not know where to go or have any means of subsistence. Do you not see that these are human considerations that oblige you to do penance, and not reasonable motives for dispensing you from your promises? If your rationale were admissible, a person could, with impunity, utter blasphemies, commit sacrileges, abuse holy things, and deceive people with false words and fine pretexts.

Take my word for it, Monsieur, do not listen to nature; for it will furnish you with ample motives to do as you please and put you on the path to perdition. Think, however, about death, which is near—perhaps even nearer than you imagine—and about the terrible judgment of God, when your words and actions will be weighed on the scales of the sanctuary. If you are burdened by those vows, it is because you do not submit your will to the yoke of Jesus Christ. You would like to enjoy the conveniences of our common life and to spurn the trials and tribulations to be encountered in it. That cannot be: every walk of life has its joys and sorrows; we have to drink both of them. Heaven suffers violence,[1] and we must renounce ourselves to follow Our Lord. I ask you to work at that and to give yourself anew to God as you should to observe the Rules and practices of the Community. In this way you will be content, give good example, and experience how good and glorious it is to serve Our Lord God, who is our Master.

I am, in His love. . . .

At the bottom of the first page: Monsieur Bienvenu

---

[1]Cf. Mt 11:12. (NAB)

2697. - TO JEAN MONVOISIN, IN MONTMIRAIL

Paris, October 26, 1658

Monsieur,

The grace of O[ur] L[ord] be with you forever!

I am sending you the dispensation I received from Rome for that good gentleman and his wife, who were Huguenots and converted to our holy religion. Since they were related, they needed this marriage dispensation to assure their salvation. God grant that their good lives will correspond to their desire to be saved!

I cannot reply this time to your last letter, nor to the one Mademoiselle Serisé wrote me. I will do so some other day, when I have finished my retreat, which I began yesterday.

I am, in O[ur] L[ord], Monsieur, your most humble servant.

VINCENT DEPAUL,
i.s.C.M.

M. Dupuich told me that you are giving the mission in Beuvardes and that you volunteered to help him with the one in Vendeuvre;[1] I am greatly consoled by this. Please give this assistance to the Troyes house. Meanwhile, Messieurs Cornuel and Brière could help the Prior of Montmirail[2] and preach in his church, if he so wishes and their health permits. I embrace them cordially.

At the bottom of the first page: Monsieur Monvoisin

Letter 2697. - Archives of the Mission, Paris, original signed letter.

[1]Vendeuvre-sur-Barse, in the district of Bar-sur-Aube (Aube).

[2]Philippe Coquebert.

2698. - TO CANON PIERRE DULYS [1]

[Between October 1657 and July 1659] [2]

I thank you once again, Monsieur, with all possible humility and gratitude, for your goodness to us and your patience in putting up with our slowness and helplessness. The difficulty that has kept us undecided still persists, since we do not have any men suitable for the proposed project. Still, Monsieur, we do have one who could hear the confessions of the Germans, and we are being led to hope for another to preach to them in their own language—German or the Lorraine dialect. He will not be a member of our Congregation but will help us out for a time. We will, then, gladly accept the favor you offer us of wishing to install us in your Priory to render our services to God in that place, under the protection of the glorious Mother of His Son Our Lord, according to the Bishop's good pleasure and with your paternal assistance.

We will undertake this establishment, then, with a priest from outside the Company, if God is pleased that this be done, especially

---

Letter 2698. - Reg. 2, p. 61.

[1]Canon of Saint-Dié (Vosges) and Director of the Shrine of the Trois-Épis. He was a very zealous priest, but of a "restless, agitated, interfering, and inconstant" disposition (cf. J. Beuchot, *Notre-Dame des Trois-Épis dans la Haute Alsace* [Rixheim: A. Sutter, 1891], p. 48). The Shrine of the Trois-Épis in Ammerschwihr, near Colmar, which is said to date from the fifteenth century, owes its name to a lovely legend: a consecrated host, thrown away by an unworthy profaner, fell on three ears of wheat growing from the same stem; some bees gathered there immediately and built an elegant wax monstrance around it. After the destruction of the chapel by the Swedes in 1636, pilgrims no longer went there. Canon Dulys reestablished the shrine, which he entrusted in 1652 to the Canons Regular of Saint Peter Fourier. He dismissed them in 1655 and replaced them with the monks of the Benedictine Abbey of Pairis, who by 1657 no longer satisfied him. That was when he turned to Saint Vincent. The suggestions of the latter did not satisfy the Canon, and on July 31, 1659, he began negotiations with the Canons Regular of Saint Anthony of Egypt (Antonines). That very day two Antonines of Isenheim came to be installed in the Priory.

[2]This letter certainly postdates the one to Georges des Jardins (no. 2406 of October 6, 1657), in which Saint Vincent alludes to the work of the Shrine of the Trois-Épis and the dearth of German-speaking confreres. In vol. VIII, no. 2894, to M. Favier, dated July 5, 1659, the Saint remarks that Canon Dulys has begun to look elsewhere. This allows us to conjecture that the present letter was written some months before July 31, 1659, when the Antonines assumed the duty of confessors at the shrine.

since our own Congregation of the Mission began in this way. Two of us priests had joined together, and we paid a third to go with us to work for the salvation of the poor country folk, and another man to look after the house. Since God was pleased to give that His blessing, we hope He will do the same in Alsace, if He calls us there.

In order to know this, Monsieur, we need to find out when and how you and the Bishop of Basel[3] want this foundation to be made, the conditions you and he want to set down for us, whether you agree to commend your Priory to us first to be united to our Congregation and whether the said Bishop will effect the union. We must also know its revenue, responsibilities, and your own reservations.

It is to be desired, Monsieur, that you will be good enough to inform us fully of your intentions before going any further so that you, on your part, may be sure of what we can or cannot do, since it is a question of a foundation in perpetuity. That is the way we are accustomed to act everywhere. Since God has been pleased to inspire you with this good work and to cause you to cast your eyes on us, His Divine Goodness wills also that we proceed in it simply and openheartedly. That is why, Monsieur, I take the liberty of asking you for these clarifications, so as to try to correspond to God's plan and to give you, as to our father and founder, all possible satisfaction, in the event that we agree on everything.

---

[3]Johann Conrad Roggenbach.

2699. - TO GILBERT CUISSOT, SUPERIOR, IN CAHORS

Paris, October 30, 1658

Monsieur,

The grace of O[ur] L[ord] be with you forever!

We had given up any hope of settling the Gignac affair because of the great authority of your opposing party and the rapporteur he had engaged, who is entirely on his side. Then, however, God raised up a very devout soul, who explained to M. de la Marguerie the harm he was doing to the diocesan clergy of Cahors by trying to deprive it of a benefice intended for its spiritual growth. That person succeeded in persuading him to release it to the seminary and to leave it to you to enjoy it in peace, on condition of paying a pension of fifteen hundred livres to M. Le Camus, who will resign his right to you.

I must confess that this arrangement seems not only advantageous to you but even miraculous in the present circumstances, when we were thinking that the affair was a lost cause, after having so often experienced the great influence of that man. For the past six months he kept the affair from coming to trial because we had a good rapporteur, and he had another to his liking appointed for it, despite the powerful recommendation of Madame Fouquet, who was asking for one less suspect to us. So, we must thank God for the means He is offering us to preserve the said benefice and half the profits of the years that have passed, since it has been agreed that they will be shared in this way.

Nothing, however, has yet been done. Nevertheless, send us a blank power of attorney[1] authorizing your proxy to negotiate the title and right of possession of the said archpriestly benefice with

---

Letter 2699. - Archives of the Mission, Paris, original signed letter.

[1]First redaction: "Nothing, however, can be done unless you send us your power of attorney." The Saint corrected this with his own hand.

M. Le Camus—and everyone else who may have or claim to have an interest in it—with whatever clauses and conditions he will deem appropriate. I ask you, then, Monsieur, to send it to me as soon as possible. I hope that the Bishop of Cahors will then accept it, and I fear that delaying may cause us to lose the opportunity; for, since the arrangement has not been settled but simply outlined, M. de la Marguerie may change his mind. Have many prayers offered for the outcome of this affair.

We will have the Daughters of Charity leave in five days; their places have been reserved on the coach.[2]

I received your letter of October 14 and a document that mentions Saint-Barthélemy, which I have not yet been able to study. I found nothing in your packet, however, regarding what the Pastor of Caussade[3] said concerning your seminary, about which you wish to justify yourself.

I am, in O[ur] L[ord], Monsieur, your most humble servant.

VINCENT DEPAUL,
i.s.C.M.

Addressed: Monsieur Cuissot

2700. - TO DENIS LAUDIN, SUPERIOR, IN LE MANS

Paris, October 30, 1658

Monsieur,

The grace of O[ur] L[ord] be with you forever!

I approve the exchange of the land you have near Alençon for

---

[2]The last two sentences, from "Have many prayers offered," are in the Saint's handwriting.
[3]Principal town of a canton in Tarn-et-Garonne.

Letter 2700. - Archives of the Mission, Paris, original signed letter. The postscript is in the Saint's handwriting.

other land that is more useful to you, provided you do nothing without getting some sound advice, especially from M. Duval.[1]

You will see in our Rules that individual members of the Company are not permitted to give or change anything without the Superior's permission, so you will do well to prevent the contrary.

We are going to have a seal made for this house, different from that of the Superior General, to distinguish which letters do not come from him, so that the local Superiors may open the latter before giving them to those under their guidance.

If the gentleman you have disposed to make a retreat with us, in order to discern the inspiration he has had to leave the world, perseveres in wanting to be a Missionary, and if it is your opinion that we should accept him, we will gladly send him to the Genoa Seminary.[2]

You did well to tell the good man who wants to give himself to your house and bring his property there that, in order to remain in our Company, the members must be uniform in their clothing and spiritual exercises and be ready to submit to everything. You should not have added, however, that special attention is paid to those who have given property, because we treat them no differently from the others—take, for example, M. Alméras, Brother Mathieu,[3] etc. They brought what they had but have not enjoyed any privileges or special treatment on that account. Neither is it advisable to have any of this among persons in Community, where each one considers that he has given enough by giving himself unreservedly.

Your advice to him to refrain from discussing this with us until he has spent two years in the Company is not the best because, if he does not give his property to your house before entering it, he cannot do so once he has been received, except by selling it and

---

[1]Noël Duval, whom the Superior in Le Mans often consulted on legal matters.

[2]The secretary had then written, "provided he assume the expenses for it." The Saint erased these words or had them erased.

[3]Mathieu Régnard.

giving you the price, without its being apparent, because the moment a man enters a Community, he loses the freedom of donating his real estate to the same Community. Furthermore, this may give his relatives grounds for saying he was led astray and forced into it, which does not happen when the donation is made beforehand.

Since we find it difficult to send you a priest in place of M. Gorlidot, it will be well for you to get a few good, well-chosen priests from outside the Company, well suited to help you with your missions this year. I ask God to bless them and to sanctify you and your leadership more and more.

I am, in O[ur] L[ord], Monsieur, your most humble servant.

VINCENT DEPAUL,
i.s.C.M.

We will try to send you by the end of the year, God willing, the priest you are requesting.

At the bottom of the first page: Monsieur Laudin

2701. - TO FATHER SYLVESTRE, CAPUCHIN

Paris, October 31, 1658

Reverend Father,

The grace of O[ur] L[ord] be with you forever!

Thank you once again for the honor you did me in sharing your memorandum with me. I have heard it read, and I find it very well written, tactful, and moving. I also think it is animated with the

---

Letter 2701. - Archives of the Mission, Paris, original signed letter in the secretary's handwriting.

Spirit of God and quite suitable for conveying sentiments of distress and compassion. I experienced them myself, and I hope it will produce even more effective ones in others who can be of service more effectively than I for the purpose Your Reverence has written it.

Now, because you order me to tell you my thoughts, I will mention two things, Reverend Father, in my usual simple way, and I do so only out of obedience to you. The first is that it is preferable that this document be shorter so that those in authority might read it more readily. Because they are so taken up with business affairs, they balk at reports that take too much of their time. I am well aware, Reverend Father, that it is difficult to express so many things in few words and that it is necessary to make the evil known in order to remedy it, but that is what came to my mind. Your Reverence apparently had the same thought, since this narrative is very concise; and you would doubtless have shortened it even more if you could have done so without weakening the force of what you had to say.

The second point regards the content. Your Reverence sets forth the need of all the Christians in various kingdoms and the whole of Greece, oppressed by the Pashas of the cities. What can be done to help them when they are so numerous? Huge sums of money would be required—which are not available. Even if they were, it would only be throwing a few drops of oil on the fire of persecution; for, since those tyrants are insatiable, the more they are given, the more they demand. The result is that, if those poor people pay up one year, they are treated more harshly the next, especially since the Turks think they have money, and they believe they are making a sacrifice to God in persecuting them.

Your Reverence says that you are not asking for help for all the Christian nations you mention but only for twelve thousand écus to purchase the administration of Mount Lebanon to remove a tyrant who abuses it; it can then be given to a prominent man of the area who will protect the Christians in that locality, as Your Reverence recently suggested. In that case, there would be reason to fear[1] that the new Governor might not be supported for long, either because he might not be to the liking of the Turks or because the Grand Vizier is changed frequently, causing instability in the offices and duties he assigns. What so often happens is that what one does, his successor abolishes. For these reasons, considerable expense would be incurred with few good results.

I would not venture to express my sentiments in this way, Reverend Father, if Your Reverence had not manifested his confidence in me by wanting me to do so. I do so to submit them entirely to yours and not to excuse myself from furthering your plans, for I hope God will grant me the grace of contributing some little drachma to the treasury of your charitable proposal for your consolation,[2] the salvation of our brothers, and the glory of our Master.

I am, in Him, Monsieur, your most humble and very obedient servant.

VINCENT DEPAUL,
i.s.C.M.

2702. - TO JACQUES PESNELLE, SUPERIOR, IN GENOA

November 1, 1658

I ask the Saint of Saints, on their feast day, which we celebrate today, to include you among them. By His mercy, you are following in their footsteps. Continue to raise yourself from earth to heaven by works and practices that lead to God and are most suited to draw others to Him, as are the Rules and functions of the Company. It is through them that Our Lord and Master calls all Missionaries to

---

[1]First redaction: "there is reason to fear." The correction is in the Saint's handwriting.

[2]First redaction: "for I am determined, with the help of God's grace, to contribute whatever I can to this for your consolation."

Letter 2702. - Reg. 2, p. 217.

follow Him, and through them the people whose salvation is entrusted to their care. May He in His goodness be pleased to animate you with His Spirit and with the virtues that accompany it!

2703. - TO EDME JOLLY, SUPERIOR, IN ROME

Paris, November 1, 1658

Monsieur,

The grace of O[ur] L[ord] be with you forever!

I sent the excerpt from your letter of October 1, which mentions the incestuous uncle and niece, to the Assistant of their parish, who had given me the report on them, so he may see if the money and attestations being requested can be obtained.

I will be consoled to see a copy of the letter M. du Loeus was supposed to write to Spain for the project you discussed together.

Since Father Virgilio Spada sees no likelihood of our getting a house in Rome unless we buy one, and since we are in no position to do so, we must leave things as they are and believe that this is what God wants for us. Can we be any better off or more pleasing to Him, Monsieur, than by remaining in the state He asks of us, provided we indeed remain in it willingly, out of submission to His guidance, acknowledging that we are unworthy of a more advantageous post, and even that the one we have surpasses our merit and is more suited to God's plan for us? If it is our calling to go out, then we should have no lasting dwelling place nor a home of our own if we want to follow O[ur] L[ord], who had none.[1] If we do not love humiliation when God gives us the opportunity to

---

Letter 2703. - Archives of the Mission, Paris, original signed letter.

[1]Cf. Mt 8:20. (NAB)

practice it, how will we seek it out if we are placed in some respectable position? Let us remain lowly, Monsieur, and be glad to be poor because, when the world sees us debased in this way, it will despise us. Then we will begin to be true disciples of O[ur] L[ord]. "How blessed are the poor in spirit," says today's Gospel, "because the kingdom of God is theirs."[2] That, then, is where they will be lodged. Is that not a beautiful lodging for us? Grant us, O my God, the grace to prefer the means that lead us there to all the pretentiousness and comforts of earth! Let us allow Him to act, Monsieur, and have no doubt that all will go well for all your works and for you yourselves.

At the time the Provincial of the Mercedarians requested us to recommend his affair to you, I think I told you he had given us twenty écus, which we still have, to cover the cost of the document he was soliciting. So, Monsieur, you can pay the person there who forwarded it. Even though his letters and packets sent and received have used up a good part of it, we will still pay the bill of exchange you draw on us for that purpose, since you told me that it amounts to only forty-five livres.

God be blessed and forever glorified for the favor He has granted the Company to find in the heart of the Cardinal Datary,[3] and may He be pleased to grant us that of deserving its continuation! We will doubtless encounter greater obstacles in the unions of Coudres[4] and Bussière[5] than in the ones that have already been effected. We will have great difficulty in obtaining the consent of Commander de Souvré[6] and the religious of his abbey, on which

---

[2]Cf. Mt 5:3. (NAB)

[3]Giacomo Corradi.

[4]The main obstacle to the union of the Coudres Priory stemmed from the opposition of the religious of Bourgueil.

[5]Bussière-Badil, another priory in the process of being united to the Congregation of the Mission.

[6]Jacques de Souvré, who had been received into the Order of Saint-Jean de Jérusalem at the age of five, was appointed Grand Prior of France in 1667. He died on May 22, 1670, in his seventieth year of age.

the Coudres Priory depends. Before we make any commitment to this, I would be glad to know: (1) if there is reason to hope to obtain the union from Rome with the consent of the titular alone, which we can have whenever we like; (2) if there is a set time within which one is obliged to have the Bulls proclaimed officially, and what is that time; (3) in the event that there is no time limit, if the benefice will be assured for us or for the titular up to four or five years from now, in case we cannot obtain the consent of the other interested parties any sooner. I say this because I think the Oratorian Fathers went beyond that interval from the time they obtained the Bulls of union for Notre-Dame-des-Vertus[7] until the religious consented to it. Lastly, I would like to know if those Bulls would be useless to us if we did not have the Bulls proclaimed officially within the given time, with the result that, by getting the necessary consent subsequently for the union, new Bulls would have to be obtained and additional expense incurred. If that were the case, then it would be better to wait rather than to risk these inconveniences.

Please get information about all that and send me the reply in writing. Let me know also the possible cost for the Bulls of union for that priory, which is not a conventual priory and can be held by a person with simple tonsure; also, for the Bulls for the Bussière union, which is conventual and under the King's nomination. There is no likelihood of getting the King's consent for this one; do not even give it a thought.[8]

Please let me know also of what diocese in Ireland M. du Loeus[9] is said to become Bishop because, if it were Cashel, he could give the dimissorial letter for Brother Butler, about whom I wrote to you in my last letter. I am also adding to the questions I asked you on this subject:

(1) In giving a dimissorial *sub titulo missionis in Hibernia,* does

---

[7]In Aubervilliers.

[8]The last sentence of this paragraph is in the Saint's handwriting.

[9]James Dowley (Duley), future Bishop of Limerick (Ireland).

the Sacred Congregation of Propaganda Fide mean that a man must go there as soon as he becomes a priest? [10]

(2) Is its intention that he remain in Ireland his whole life, or just for a few years, and for how many years, with the result that afterward we will be free of this obligation?

(3) Is it for the man to go there for any period of disaster whatsoever—such as the present one—when there is great danger? If that were the case, or if it were for an entire lifetime, Brother Butler does not want a title under that condition, and the Company would also find this a great drawback, having maintained and educated him for eight to ten years now.

With all this in mind, Monsieur, I am not sure if you should go to the trouble of getting another dimissorial letter for him from the Sacred Congregation unless, to fulfill the obligation it imposes on him, it agrees to leave it up to his Superiors to send him to his own country or elsewhere, when and where they judge it advisable. It would be very troublesome if the Company were unable to prepare for all sorts of places the Irishmen it receives and educates at great expense, when they have no title, except on condition of going to their own country and depending solely on the Sacred Congregation. In which case, it would be wrong for us to receive any of them; and yet, God is pleased to do good through them wherever we send them. If there were reason to hope for as much in Ireland, we would gladly send them there; but right now there is little success to be had and many dangers to be undergone there. What does it matter where God is served, provided He is served, that it be done on behalf of souls for whom Jesus Christ has died, and that it be done

[10] Saint Vincent had added in his own handwriting: "and remain there permanently." He scratched out these words after noticing that what followed was a repetition of this.

through ways most advantageous for them, such as are the functions of the Company!

I am, in the love of O[ur] L[ord], Monsieur, your most humble servant.

VINCENT DEPAUL,
i.s.C.M.

On October 16 Brothers Le Gouz [11] and Le Mercier,[12] accompanied by a coadjutor Brother named Dufestel,[13] left Marseilles for Rome on a ship from Leghorn. I hope that, if they are not with you now, they will soon be there.

At the bottom of the first page: Monsieur Jolly

2704. - TO PHILIP DALTON, IN TROYES [1]

Paris, November 2, 1658

Monsieur,

The grace of O[ur] L[ord] be with you forever!

After receiving your letter, I had planned to reply to you as soon as possible but was unable to do so. I cannot express my joy at the

---

[11]This is probably Jacques Legouz (Legouts in *Notices,* vol. I and vol. V [Supplement]). Born in Dollon (Sarthe) on April 6, 1633, he entered the Congregation of the Mission on September 2, 1654, and took his vows on September 17, 1656, in the presence of M. Berthe. His brother René had entered the Congregation of the Mission just one month before this letter was written.

[12]This name does not appear in the personnel catalogue of the Mission.

[13]Claude Dufestel, born in Moyenville (Somme) in June 1637, entered the Congregation of the Mission in Paris as a coadjutor Brother on September 4, 1657, and took his vows in Rome on September 8, 1659, in the presence of M. Jolly.

Letter 2704. - Archives of the Mission, Paris, signed rough draft.

[1]Philip Dalton, born in Cooleeney, Cashel diocese (Ireland), entered the Congregation of the Mission in Paris on May 16, 1656, and took his vows in Troyes on November 11, 1658, in the presence of M. Dupuich.

inclination God is giving you to make the unreserved gift of yourself to Him in the Company, with indifference to whatever country in the world, and with total submission to holy obedience and the Will of God, which will be indicated to you by your Superiors. That is how truly apostolic souls speak and act. Entirely consecrated to God, they desire that His Son Our Lord be known and served likewise by all the nations on earth, for whom He Himself came into the world; like Him, they wish also to work and die for them.

That is how far the zeal of Missionaries should extend; for, even though they cannot go everywhere, nor do the good they desire, they still do well to desire this and to offer themselves to God to serve Him as instruments for the conversion of souls in the times, places, and manner He pleases. Perhaps He will be satisfied with their good will; perhaps also, if this will is strong and well regulated, He will use them, poor workers though they be, to accomplish great things. I see nothing that makes them more like Him than this, nor more worthy of His blessings.

So then, Monsieur, go ahead! Take your vows whenever you like, in the presence of M. Dupuich. I ask O[ur] L[ord] to be pleased to accept them and to give Himself more closely to you at the same time you will be giving yourself more completely to Him.

I really would like to procure some help for those valiant people of your country who are living in poverty and suffering in Troyes, but I do not know to whom I can turn.[2] The Ladies of Charity of

[2]In *Relations*, the first account for 1654 states: "When five regiments of Irish Catholics were defeated in the war of Bordeaux, the remnant of three hundred persons, including women, children, the elderly, and the crippled, sought refuge in the town of Troyes as in an asylum. . . . A good Irish priest has been sent there. Paris and Troyes have joined forces for this holy task. . . . The naked have been clothed; young women and widows have been placed in Saint-Nicolas Hospice, where they will be taught spinning and sewing; little orphans are being cared for; all receive instruction and are confirmed in the Catholic faith for which they had left their native land." (Cf. also, the second account of 1654 and that of 1655.)

The Ladies of Charity came up with the idea of using publicity to come to the aid of the provinces devastated by war. With the most interesting and touching passages from the letters of charitable persons working with the poor in those regions, they compiled accounts, which

Paris, who helped them in the past, are sending almost nothing more to the border areas or elsewhere because they cannot find any more money, so I dare not suggest any new acts of charity to them, knowing that it would be useless.

We did what you wanted with regard to that good priest who came from Ireland, whom you recommend to us.

I recommend myself to your prayers and am, in O[ur] L[ord]. . . .

V. D.

2705. - TO EDME MENESTRIER, SUPERIOR, IN AGEN

Paris, November 3, 1658

Monsieur,

The grace of O[ur] L[ord] be with you forever!

In reply to your letter of October 11, I ask O[ur] L[ord] that the waters you have taken may be beneficial to you both for your bodily health and the consolation of your soul, which suffers from not being able to act in conformity with the extent of its devotion.

---

were printed and distributed throughout Paris and the large towns. This publication lasted from September 1650 to December 1655. The Bibliothèque Nationale (R 8370) possesses a collection, 130 pages long, entitled: *Recueil des relations contenant ce qui s'est fait pour l'assistance des pauvres, entre autres ceux de Paris et des environs, et des provinces de Picardie et de Champagne, pendant les années 1650, 1651, 1652, 1653, et 1654* (Paris: Charles Savreux, 1655). These reports were used extensively by Abbé Maynard in *Saint Vincent de Paul, sa vie, son temps, ses oeuvres, son influence,* vol. IV, pp. 164ff., and by Alphonse Feillet, who published the text in 1856 in *Revue de Paris,* and used it in *La misère au temps de la Fronde et Saint Vincent de Paul* (Paris: Perrin, 1862). Feillet's work is extensively documented and highly recommended as a source of information on the pitiful state of France during the wars of the Fronde and the charitable activities of the Saint during this period.

Letter 2705. - Archives of the Mission, Paris, original signed letter. The postscript is in the Saint's handwriting.

I sent the Duchesse d'Aiguillon for the second time M. Grimaud's change of office and spoke to her myself about it a few days ago. She told me she will have her lawyer look at it and will send his reply to M. Grimaud. Perhaps she has already written about it to her collector there.

It is not through humility that I am excusing myself from seeing the Bishop of Agen [1] about your house but to observe the proper protocol, which requires the Superior of each house to inform the Bishop of the diocese to which it belongs, of any temporal needs it has, when it is up to him to remedy them. He should not shift this responsibility to the General, who has other things to do and who should not get involved in the details of such matters.

A place has been reserved for the long-awaited Brother cleric in the Bordeaux coach that will leave here Tuesday. We are sending with him for Cahors two Daughters of Charity, who will pass through Agen. I will write to you by them. Meanwhile, I am, in the love of O[ur] L[ord], Monsieur, your most humble servant.

VINCENT DEPAUL,
i.s.C.M.

It will be a good idea to have the Daughters of Charity stay with some devout woman or in some other respectable house, and to provide them with hired horses and a man to take them to Cahors, where the Bishop has requested them.

Addressed: Monsieur Edme, Superior of the Priests of the Mission at the Agen Seminary, in Agen

---

[1]Barthélemy d'Elbène.

2706. - *EDME JOLLY, SUPERIOR IN ROME, TO SAINT VINCENT*

[Rome, November 5, 1658] [1]

Of the three Brothers M. Berthe sent here on your orders, Monsieur, and who arrived the same day I wrote, as I informed you in my last letter, one,[2] *who has not yet completed the two years of his seminary, is very upset because he did not find a theology course here, as he expected, since he said that you, Monsieur, had promised him he would be studying it. I did what I could to explain that we would help him as best we could with his studies and to encourage him to be truly indifferent in all things, as is required for a Missionary. However, it is pitiful to see the enormity of his temptation, making him incapable of any human or divine reasoning, even though he shows himself steadfast in his vocation otherwise. He thinks he is totally detached from all worldly things, saying that he has become indifferent to everything, but not to this point of studies, since he was promised the contrary.*

I think you had me propose, among other things, something similar to this to the seminarians during a retreat, Monsieur, namely, to see that they were well grounded in indifference with regard to studies. I realize now that this is more necessary than I considered it then, for this poor Brother is lost in this temptation; and if he does not banish it from his mind—or rather if Our Lord does not take it from him—it is an open door to a thousand worries and can render him unsuitable for the service of his vocation. He told me he wanted to ask you and to have someone ask that he be sent to Genoa so he can study there, in accord with his ardent desire. I told him he could write to you, but I advised him not to have someone else make the request to you, nor even to ask it himself, because he would not be happy about having yielded to the temptation. I said that it was much better to adapt ourselves to God's plan for us than to do our own will, contrary to His good pleasure.

Lastly, I urged him to be very patient, since it is unlikely that so strong a temptation and such great restlessness will last long in a person who wants to belong entirely to God. Unfortunately, however, we cannot make

---

Letter 2706. - Archives of the Mission, Paris, *Life of Edme Jolly*, Ms, p. 142 (cf.*Notices*, vol. III, pp. 387-512; this letter is on pp. 462-63).

[1]In no. 2741 to Edme Jolly, dated December 6, 1654, Saint Vincent mentions a letter from this date.

[2]Le Mercier. (Cf. no. 2703, n. 12.)

him understand that this is an inordinate attachment. Our Lord will do so through your prayers, Monsieur, if He so chooses.

He is now on retreat, together with the two men who came with him. After the retreat we will see if the course he will be taking, and the help someone in the house will give him, will calm him down a little. He keeps referring to the promise he says was made to him of having him study with some other students under the direction of a teacher.

2707. - TO EDME MENESTRIER, SUPERIOR, IN AGEN

Paris, November 6, 1658

Monsieur,

The grace of O[ur] L[ord] be with you forever!

Here at last is Brother Didolet,[1] whom we are taking from our seminary to be given to you. You have lost nothing by waiting for him; for, even though he is very young, he is nevertheless intelligent and wise and is even sufficiently capable of teaching the subject you requested. He is a lad who shows good promise and is worthy of your attention. I recommend him to you with all my heart.

We are sending with him two Daughters of Charity for the Bishop of Cahors because of the convenience of the Bordeaux coach and the river, which they can take there as far as Agen. Once they arrive, please put them up with some good widow or in a house with which you are familiar; then have them taken to Cahors on

---

Letter 2707. - Archives of the Mission, Paris, original signed letter.

[1]Christophe Didolet, born in Aiguebelle (Savoy) on February 3, 1639, entered the Congregation of the Mission at the Paris Seminary on July 27, 1657, and took his vows on December 27, 1661, in the presence of M. Berthe.

some hired horses either by one of our Brothers or by some other trustworthy person.

I am, in the love of O[ur] L[ord], Monsieur, your most humble servant.

VINCENT DEPAUL,
i.s.C.M.

Addressed: Monsieur Edme, Superior of the Priests of the Mission at the Agen Seminary, in Agen

2708. - TO GERARD BRIN, SUPERIOR, IN MEAUX [1]

Paris, November 6, 1658

Monsieur,

The grace of O[ur] L[ord] be with you forever!

I received your letters of October 31. I can only respect whatever the Bishops ordain for the welfare of their seminary, and I have nothing to say about the care of the temporal affairs of which they have made you responsible,[2] except that we cannot send you anyone to help or train you in them. I imagine that you explained to them that you have little aptitude for business matters; so, if they have put you in charge of them despite this avowal, you should remain at peace and hope you will not spoil anything, especially if you take the Vicar-General's [3] advice in important matters.

Letter 2708. - Archives of the Mission, Paris, unsigned rough draft.

[1]The Priests of the Mission had just been given the direction of the Meaux Seminary, which they left three years later. (Cf. Abbé O. Estournet, *L'hôpital Jean Rose et le grand séminaire de Meaux* [Lagny: Colin, 1905].)

[2]The Superior of the seminary was also Principal of the collège and Administrator of the hospital.

[3]Antoine Caignet, Doctor of Theology, later Canon, Chancellor, Theologian, and Vicar-General of Meaux. He was a renowned preacher and the author of two works: *L'Année Pastorale* (7 vols., Paris: Jean de la Caille, 1659) and *Le Dominical des Pasteurs ou le Triple emploi des curés* (Paris, 1675, 2nd ed.). Caignet died in 1669.

If, as you hope, the state of the seminary may change in two months, do not make the changes you are suggesting so soon. In line with that, please be satisfied with Brother Pierron[4] and leave Brother Claude[5] in Crécy.

I ask Our Lord to be your guide and your strength. I am, in his love, Monsieur, your most humble servant.

At the bottom of the page: Monsieur Brin

2709. - TO JEAN DE FONTENEIL, IN BORDEAUX

Paris, November 6, 1658

Monsieur,

The grace of O[ur] L[ord] be with you forever!

I renew to you the offers of my obedience with all possible humility and affection. I entreat you to accept them, Monsieur, along with the most humble recommendation I make to you of two Sisters of Charity, Servants of the Sick Poor, whom we are sending to the Bishop of Cahors by way of Bordeaux and Agen because of the opportunity to travel by coach and the river. They will venture to turn to you, Monsieur, as I now do, to entreat you most humbly

---

[4]Nicolas Pierron, born in Monceaux-lès-Provins (Seine-et-Marne) on May 9, 1635, entered the Congregation of the Mission on May 14, 1657. He did not remain long in Meaux because on May 15, 1659, the day of his vows, he was at Saint-Lazare, where he was a professor after his ordination. He directed successively the establishments of Saint-Flour (1673-79), the Bons-Enfants (1679-81), Châlons-sur-Marne (1681-84), Bayeux (1684-86), Tours (1686-94), and Chartres (1694-97). On April 21, 1692, he became Visitor of Poitou, and on August 1, 1697, Visitor of France. The General Assembly of 1697 elected him Superior General of the Congregation of the Mission to succeed Edme Jolly. During his generalate he made every effort to maintain strong discipline in the Company and to fortify it against Jansenism. In 1703 he suffered a paralyzing stroke and died on August 17, 1703, twenty days after handing in his resignation as Superior General. (Cf. *Notices,* vol. IV, pp. 11-15.)

[5]Claude Gesseaume, coadjutor Brother, born in Villers-sous-Saint-Leu (Oise) in 1615, entered Saint-Lazare on December 6, 1643.

Letter 2709. - Archives of the Mission, Paris, original signed letter.

to find an occasion for them to travel by boat to Agen (it is said that one they call the mail boat leaves regularly twice a week) and to add to this favor that of recommending them to the most respectable persons who will be leaving with them.

I am ashamed to bother you with these things, but I am obliged to do so because you are the only person I know in your town, Monsieur.

I am, in the love of O[ur] L[ord], Monsieur, your most humble and very obedient servant.

VINCENT DEPAUL,
i.s.C.M.

If by some chance these good Sisters should need money, I entreat you to give them some to complete their journey. I will reimburse you through the coachmaster, as soon as you let me know about it.[1] We are sending with them one of our seminarians who will be remaining at the Agen Seminary.

Addressed: Monsieur Fonteneil, Archdeacon and Vicar-General of Bordeaux, in Bordeaux

2710. - TO ANTOINE FLEURY, IN SAINTES

Paris, November 6, 1658

Monsieur,

The grace of Our Lord be with you forever!

I am worried because I have had no letters from you since you

---

[1]This sentence is in the Saint's handwriting.

Letter 2710. - Archives of the Mission, Paris, unsigned rough draft in the secretary's handwriting.

have been in Saintes. I am sending you mine to find out the state of your health, how the missions are succeeding there, whether the people are profiting by your spiritual exercises, and if they are assiduous in coming to your instructions. I want to hope so from the goodness of God and your fine manner of giving them.

On the other hand, however, since that is an area influenced by heretics and where heresy established its reign in the past, I fear that some bad impressions of this, given by fathers to their children and by the children to their children, may remain among the poor Catholics. You must be patient and hope that the light of faith will gradually disperse all those shadows, and Jesus Christ will be the Master over the faith and morals of those poor people, whom the evil spirit has always tried to corrupt. You must also hope, Monsieur, that His great mercy will make use of you for that purpose; for, in the ordinary course of events, God tries to save men through men, and Our Lord became man Himself to save all of them.[1]

Oh! what a happiness for you to work at doing what He did! He came to bring the good news to the poor,[2] and that is your lot and your occupation, too. If our perfection lies in charity, as is certain, there is none greater than to give oneself to save souls and to sacrifice oneself for them as Jesus Christ did. This is what you are called to do, Monsieur, and you are ready to respond to it, thank God. It was for this purpose that you entered the Company, which is totally dedicated to the imitation of Our Lord, and this is the resolution you would again take if you had not already taken it. Oh! what an example you are to so many, many priests who are like workers sent into the Lord's vineyard, but who do not do His works! [3] Blessed be God, Monsieur, for the grace He has granted you in choosing you from among thousands to help destroy the ignorance and sin that are devastating the Church! And blessed

---

[1]Cf. Lk 19:10; 1 Tm 1:15. (NAB)
[2]Cf. Lk 4:18. (NAB)
[3]Cf. Mt 9:37-8. (NAB)

forever be His Holy Name for the grace He grants you to succeed so well in this holy work, as M. Rivet [4] has informed me! I cannot thank Our Lord sufficiently or ask Him often enough to continue to bless you and your works, although I do so very often.

I am sure, Monsieur, that the devil, foreseeing the victories you will gain over him, is making efforts to draw you away from it. He will show you even greater good to be done, but there is none so do not listen to him. No, make him utterly confused by devoting yourself to the opportunities God is now giving you to advance His glory against the schemes of this enemy, who will try to make you set it aside for deceitful, remote, and uncertain purposes.

On the other hand, the world may present its pleasures and vanities to you—but too late, since you wish to be crucified with J[esus] C[hrist] [5] and to find your delight and honors in Him alone.

Your relatives also may try to undermine your determination, but you know what O[ur] L[ord] said: "Whoever loves father or mother more than me is not worthy of me," [6] and "Anyone who leaves brothers, sisters, home, etc. because of me will have a hundred times as many and will inherit eternal life." [7] Blessed are your relatives, Monsieur, for giving the Divine Master such a servant as you, who can procure for them more benefits and consolations by serving Him in the vocation in which you now are than in some other state they might wish for you, since you will draw down upon them and yourself the blessings of heaven and earth.

You might have yet another temptation: the boredom of seeing yourself doing the same thing over and over, or discouragement at seeing only little or no success in them. But the remedy for the first is to think that only perseverance wins the crown and that all is lost

---

[4]Louis Rivet.
[5]Cf. 1 Cor 2:2. (NAB)
[6]Cf. Mt 10:37. (NAB)
[7]Cf. Mt 19:29. (NAB)

without it. For the second, it is to be convinced that God asks of you only that you cast your nets into the sea, and not that you catch the fish, because it is up to Him to make them go into the nets.[8] Have no doubt that He will do so if, having fished all night long despite the difficulties of the undertaking and the hardness of people's hearts—almost all asleep to the things of God—you wait patiently for day to come, for the Sun of Justice to awaken them, and for His light to illuminate and warm them.[9] To this work and patience, you must join humility, prayer, and good example; then you will see the glory of the Savior, and you will see in these words of advice, Monsieur, the sincere affection of your most humble servant.

2711. - TO MICHEL CASET, IN TOUL

Paris, November 6, 1658

Monsieur,

The grace of O[ur] L[ord] be with you forever!

I thank God for the good results of the mission in Charmes; [1] I ask Him to grant the people the grace of availing themselves of it for eternity and to grant you that of procuring similar ones all your life, in keeping with your great ardor, which is a gift of God. Use it well; for, provided your zeal is accompanied by indifference with regard to duties and by submission with regard to obedience, God will bless its effects.

I praise God also, Monsieur, for your repugnance for positions of authority; I am sure it stems from a sentiment of humility rather

---

[8]Cf. Lk 5:4-6. (NAB)
[9]Cf. Mal 4:2. (NAB)

Letter 2711. - Archives of the Mission, Paris, unsigned rough draft in the secretary's handwriting. He states on the back that the letter was never sent.

[1]Charmes-la-Côte, near Toul.

than a desire to avoid the care of business affairs or the trouble of serving your confreres. When I asked you to replace M. Demonchy, it was not my intention to make you Superior but only to be the representative of the one who is to be named for the office, while awaiting his arrival.[2] I am well aware that you have other good qualities for being a success in it, if only you had the necessary leadership experience. This does not prevent you from going to give missions—no more than the Superiors of other houses are prevented, most of whom are the first at this work.

So, once M. Demonchy is here, we will send you someone to give you the means of devoting yourself totally to the instruction and salvation of the poor people. Meanwhile, I ask Our Lord to accept the services you are rendering Him and the little family, to whom I send greetings. I am, in the love of this same Lord, Monsieur, your most humble servant.

At the bottom of the first page: Monsieur Caset

2712. - TO EDME JOLLY, SUPERIOR, IN ROME

Paris, November 8, 1658

Monsieur,

The grace of O[ur] L[ord] be with you forever!

I received your letter of October 8. You are right in saying that our religious [1] will find that our Bull[2] makes their pensions secure. It has been drawn up very well both for them and for us. We are

---

[2]The Saint's choice was Caset himself.

Letter 2712. - Archives of the Mission, Paris, original signed letter.

[1]The religious of the old Saint-Lazare.

[2]The Bull of union of Saint-Lazare Priory to the Congregation of the Mission.

going to work on the official announcement without losing any more time, God willing.

People say here that the one [the official proclamation of the Bull] for Saint-Pourçain, pronounced by the Bishop, is invalid. I shall await your reply to my request asking you to get information about that, before we go to any trouble about it.

I am very much obliged to the Assessor of the Holy Office for the honor of his remembrance and for the kindness he shows me. This is a grace I cherish highly, because of the esteem and reverence God has given me for his worthy person. Whenever the opportunity presents itself, please assure him of my deep gratitude for his charity and my perpetual obedience in whatever he chooses to command me.

I notified the Assistant at Saint-Jean-en-Grève[3] of what you inform me regarding the dispensation for those unfortunate incestuous persons. He thinks we should go through the Datary and for this purpose is trying to obtain the attestation of their poverty[4] and the letter that must accompany it. He hopes to send them to you by the first regular mail. As for the eight pistoles needed for this, get them there; he will reimburse them here at the rate of exchange.

I would like to hope that God in His goodness has put all of you more closely in touch with His Spirit during your retreats so that you will be able to convey His gifts to the souls that Providence will send you at your house and during your missions. In addition, so that His infinite mercy may not stop there, it is to be hoped that by it each one will become more humble and zealous.

If it is God's good pleasure that the seed Cardinal Brancaccio[5] has sown in the hearts of those good priests in Naples, for the union he proposed to them, grow and bear fruit, *in nomine Domini;* that affair will then have to be studied more closely. However, neither

---

[3]In the absence of the Pastor, who had been relegated to Compiègne by Mazarin's order.
[4]This attestation was necessary to avoid the customary fees.
[5]Francesco Maria Brancaccio, Bishop of Viterbo (1638-70).

now nor at any time should we make any overtures for that purpose, either by word or act. We belong to God; let us allow Him to act. As for them, they are in good hands, since they are in the hands of such a devout, wise Cardinal.

You did well to welcome into your house the priest who is going to work in the seminary of the Congregation of Prop[aganda] Fide. I would have been glad to know where he comes from and, if he is French, from what Province.

I began some time ago to write a report on the Paris meetings, but it is still incomplete, and I had already forgotten about it. God willing, I will finish it in my first free moments.

Please use your influence to obtain the indulgence requested by M. Simon, whose letter I sent you. If you get it, remind me that it is for a Pastor near Notre-Dame de la Rose, so I can have it sent to M. Chrétien,[6] the Superior at that chapel.[7]

Enclosed is the attestation of poverty of those poor unfortunate persons from Saint-Jean parish here in the city. I will send you by the next mail the other document that is needed.

I just received some letters from Messieurs Desdames and Perroy[8] in Warsaw. O Monsieur, what men God has given the Company in them!

We have reason to fear that Brother Barreau has been extremely maltreated because of a horrible outrage committed by a French merchant, named Picquet, from Marseilles. The latter took with him, from Algiers to Leghorn, four Turkish bailiffs and sixty Arabs. He then torched the Bastion of France, since it was fifty leagues from Algiers and a safe place for trading in Barbary, and because those bailiffs had gone to ask him for tribute money and

---

[6]Jean Chrétien, born in Oncourt (Vosges), on August 6, 1606 was ordained a priest on April 5, 1631, and entered the Congregation of the Mission on November 26, 1640. He was Superior in Marseilles (1645-53), sub-Assistant at the Motherhouse (1654), and Superior in La Rose (1655-62). On November 26, 1667, he was a member of the house in Troyes.

[7]The rest of the letter is in the Saint's handwriting.

[8]This is obviously Nicolas Duperroy.

he had no means of paying it. We do not know how the Christians in Algiers, especially the Consul, were treated.[9] I recommend this affair to your prayers.

Your most humble servant.

VINCENT DEPAUL,
i.s.C.M.

Addressed: Monsieur Jolly

2713. - TO JACQUES PESNELLE, SUPERIOR, IN GENOA

Paris, November 8, 1658

Monsieur,

The grace of O[ur] L[ord] be with you forever!

I received your letter of October 5. I thank God for having blessed your retreats. They are never made fruitlessly by souls who seek God and want to renounce themselves. I ask O[ur] L[ord] to unite you to Himself so that you may be more strengthened to go forth to win the souls that belong to Him and which the prince of this world has turned away from His obedience and love. This is a struggle in which there is more to be lost than gained by soldiers who lack zeal and humility. On the contrary, those who are armed with these virtues and with confidence in their Divine Captain will return laden with the spoils of the enemy.

I praise God that your brother has arrived at your house and for

---

[9]Having been informed that the Governor of Algiers had planned on sending a force of one thousand men to force him to pay his annual contributions, under threat of imprisonment if he refused, Thomas Picquet, Governor of the Bastion of France, armed the coral fishermen and set sail for Leghorn with all his possessions, including sixty Arabs and four Turkish officials. His conduct caused a riot among the population of Algiers, who maltreated the French residents. Their merchandise was seized as indemnity and the Consul thrown into prison.

Letter 2713. - Archives of the Mission, Paris, seventeenth- or eighteenth-century copy.

the mutual consolation of your meeting. I also thank O[ur] L[ord] that he acknowledges that your father's last will and testament cannot be executed in what concerns you so he has made up his mind to give you satisfaction. Is it not better that it should come to you peacefully in this way than if you had used harsh measures to pursue it? Our good God always sees to our business when we see to His. It is true, Monsieur, that the last time your brother came by here, I did not speak to him of your interest, through sheer forgetfulness; but I did so at other times when I had the honor of seeing him and would have also brought it up again when he was leaving for Italy, if it had not slipped my mind. My thought is that you should be steadfast in coming to an agreement on dividing the inheritance so you can use the interest and even the capital, as you will one day deem it more advisable, even though you may lead them to hope that you will never take it out of the family. Meanwhile, they should send you part of the income for the three years they have been enjoying the whole of it.

I think M. Berthe is now with you and has brought you some help. May God in His mercy sanctify his visitation and your work! I am, in His love, Monsieur, your most humble servant.

VINCENT DEPAUL,
i.s.C.M.

2714. - TO SISTER MARGUERITE CHÉTIF, SISTER SERVANT, IN ARRAS

Paris, November 9, 1658

Dear Sister,

The grace of O[ur] L[ord] be with you forever!

I have received two or three letters from you. You or Mademoi-

---

Letter 2714. - Archives of the Motherhouse of the Daughters of Charity, original signed letter.

selle Deslions can still hold on to the letter about the annuity of the Bridgettines, while waiting until we see if the heirs of the deceased will claim any of it.

Whenever he wishes, M. Caron can send us the young man who is so eager to enter our Company, provided he brings with him his patrimonial title and dimissorial letter for receiving Holy Orders. He should also bring one hundred livres or so for his first habit. In which case, we will accept him, first, for an eight-day retreat to study his vocation, and then to admit him to the seminary, which lasts two years, to ground him in virtue before he pursues his studies—provided he perseveres.

M. Rose [1] has arrived in good health; he brought us the watch, for which I thank you.

We received the letter and the money for Brother Roquet; [2] thank you for that, too.

I really wish that good man Dupuich[3] could get the fifty livres I have to send him. I will send them, God willing, to Madame Tintillier by the first regular mail. I cannot do so today because I received your last letter too late.

I thank Mademoiselle Deslions most humbly for her efforts to get Brother Cuveron's[4] title, and I ask her to continue until they

---

[1]Nicolas Roze, born in Transloy (Pas-de-Calais) in 1616, entered the Congregation of the Mission as a priest on December 7, 1641. He was Superior in Troyes (1653-57).

[2]Charles Roquet (Taquet), cleric of the Mission, was born in Arras on September 12, 1639, entered the Congregation of the Mission on January 5, 1657, and took his vows on January 17, 1659, in the presence of M. Delespiney. *Notices*, vol. I (p. 487) and vol. V (Supplement), p. 586, lists him as *Taquet*; the date of entry into the Congregation of the Mission (January 6, 1657) seems to confirm the latter spelling, since in a letter of January 6, 1657, to Guillaume Delville in Arras (cf. vol. VI, no. 2187), Saint Vincent speaks of three postulants from Arras, two of whom Coste mentions in a footnote: Charles Taquet and Maximilien-François Cuveron, to whom reference is made later in this letter. *Taquet* has been used in the index in this volume and in volume XIV.

[3]This man was not a confrere; he appears to have been a layman, about whom there is no information. This is the only time he is mentioned in the extant letters of Saint Vincent.

[4]Maximilien-François Cuveron was born in Arras (Pas-de-Calais) on January 6, 1634, entered the Congregation of the Mission in Paris on December 1, 1656, and took his vows there on December 3, 1658, in the presence of M. Delespiney. He spent some years at Fontainebleau before going to Madagascar in 1666, where he died a few months later.

send it to us. He is a young man of the right age and shows great promise.

Mademoiselle Le Gras is very well, thank God. Two of your Sisters, Sister Adrienne and Sister Louise,[5] have gone to Cahors, that is, to a place more than one hundred fifty leagues away.

I send greetings to Sister Radegonde,[6] and I am, in O[ur] L[ord], Sister, your most affectionate servant.

VINCENT DEPAUL,
i.s.C.M.

Addressed: Sister Marguerite Chétif, Daughter of Charity, Servant of the Sick Poor, in Arras

2715. - TO PIERRE CABEL, SUPERIOR, IN SEDAN

Paris, November 9, 1658

Monsieur,

The grace of O[ur] L[ord] be with you forever!

It has been a long time since I wrote to you. I made my retreat, I was not well, and I had several business affairs to take care of; all that has delayed my reply to your letters.

I am sending you, open, a letter for M. Daisne.[1] Once you have read it, seal it and give it to him whenever you think it advisable. We are working on sending you a priest in his place and will have him leave as soon as we can, but I am not exactly sure of the day

---

[5]Adrienne Plouvier and Louise Boucher.

[6]Radegonde Lenfantin.

Letter 2715. - Archives of the Mission, Paris, original signed letter.

[1]Chrétien Daisne, born in Sedan, entered the Congregation of the Mission on September 21, 1644, at twenty years of age, took his vows in 1646, and was ordained a priest in March 1651.

or the week because that depends on some business he is taking care of, which cannot last long.

As for M. Sevant, my advice is that you should continue to bear with him until the upcoming visitation. M. Berthe is making one in Genoa right now, and from there he will return by way of Turin, Annecy, and Troyes; then he will go to Sedan, where I hope you will have him with you in two or three months.

If, during the very cold weather, you want to wear hats instead of caps in the house and fur-lined slippers, that is a convenience contrary neither to good order nor propriety, so you may do so. Wearing muffs or gloves in town, however, is not done by any of our houses, so it would not be proper to introduce that custom, especially since, if the men became accustomed to wearing gloves during winter, they might not easily give them up in the spring—or maybe not even in the summer—because people wear them in all kinds of weather.

The Sisters should not be dispensed from making their retreat in that place so as to have an excuse to come to Paris for it, because only the Paris Sisters and those who are very close by come to make it with Mademoiselle Le Gras. Those like the ones in Sedan, who are far away, make theirs in the places where they are living, particularly if there are priests of the Company to conduct their spiritual exercises.

You will do well not to distribute our Common Rules while M. Daisne is wavering in his vocation. Please wait until he has left, unless he makes a strong resolution to remain and to renounce benefices. In a short time we will be able to send the Rules for Superiors.

If the nephew of the late M. Prévost [2] satisfies you as a house servant, admit him among the Brothers; I will be consoled by this because of his late uncle, of whom we have a very good recollection.

---

[2]It is not known whether Nicolas Prévost's nephew ever entered the Congregation of the Mission.

Brother Pintart [3] is beginning to do well since recovering from an illness he had. He asks you for his copies of paintings, and his Superior thinks they should be sent to him. Please do so.

If M. Daisne leaves, let him take the clothes he wears when he goes into town, and no others, and get him to agree amicably not to come to your house any longer for conversations because there are disadvantages in doing otherwise. That is why we have little or no communication with men who have left us.

Enclosed is a letter from M. Berthe for his brother.

I ask Sister Christine[4] to postpone her journey until the spring because the weather is already bad for traveling.

Our lawyer has the reports you sent.

It is not customary to insert in the Rules of a Company the Bulls authorizing them. Ours does not allow us to absolve persons from heresy. An express permission is required for your house. I will have it sent from Rome, God willing.

Your Ladies of Charity should not refuse to help new converts if they are poor and sick; for, the supplies you have are to be used for those who are well only if they have an extraordinary need.

It is absolutely essential to change the Ladies in office; but, because of the difficulty you foresee in this, I think you should wait until the visitation to do so. At that time the Visitor can prepare the people with you to accept a new election and help them to realize its importance.

Ring the bell for the general examination of conscience only at quarter past eight, and change nothing without necessity in the

---

[3]Guillaume Pintart, born in Vandy (Ardennes) on May 5, 1627, entered the Congregation of the Mission on August 4, 1649, and took his vows in Sedan on September 9, 1654. He was in Le Mans when Saint Vincent wrote this letter. *Notices*, vol. I and vol. V (Supplement), spells his name *Pintard*.

[4]Sister Jeanne-Christine Prévost had served the poor in Liancourt (1648), Fontainebleau (1651), and in Saint-Gervais parish in Paris. According to Saint Louise, she won the approval of the people everywhere she went. She was elected Assistant of the Company in 1660, but withdrawing her from Sedan was so difficult that Superiors were constrained to leave her there.

daily schedule or in the practices of the Company, for the men who go out from here would be very surprised to find them different elsewhere.

In your role as Superior and Pastor, you may continue to give certificates until the visitation.

I think I have replied to all the main points in your letters received until now. Enclosed are some letters from M. Coglée, the Superior in Annecy. He left an old breviary here to be sent to you; the priest who is going to help you will bring it.

I am, in the love of O[ur] L[ord], Monsieur, your most humble servant.

VINCENT DEPAUL,
i.s.C.M.

Addressed: Monsieur Cabel

2716. - TO CHRÉTIEN DAISNE, IN SEDAN

Paris, November 9, 1658

Monsieur,

The grace of O[ur] L[ord] be with you forever!

You have asked my permission to leave the Company to help your father, who is in need, and to accept a benefice being offered to you. Yes, Monsieur, I willingly consent to this, for your past behavior made it sufficiently clear that you were heading in that direction. I cannot, however, consent to your seeking a lapsed benefice for a parish while you are still with us, as the Pastor himself has told me you are trying to do. It is unheard of that a

---

Letter 2716. - Archives of the Mission, Paris, unsigned draft in the secretary's handwriting. This is the draft of the letter mentioned in no. 2715.

Missionary has ever taken a lapsed benefice from anyone. That is why I ask you, Monsieur, either to renounce this ambition or leave.

I ask O[ur] L[ord] to grant you the grace of living as a good priest in whatever state you are. I am, in His love. . . .

2717. - TO DOMINIQUE LHUILLIER, IN CRÉCY

Paris, November 13, 1658

Monsieur,

The grace of O[ur] L[ord] be with you forever!

Since the Coadjutor of Meaux [1] wants to know what arrears M. de Lorthon[2] owes your house, I ask you to make from your book an itemized account of the sums it has received from him, indicating the day, month, and year. Please send it to M. Brin and say nothing about it to anyone.

I praise God for the patience He is giving you in your present situation, which is very painful. It is, however, the right one for honoring the hidden life of Our Lord and for preparing you for His public functions, whenever He chooses to engage you in them. You will perform them all the more successfully the more closely you are united to Him now through the practice of prayer and the other virtues proper to persons who are alone.

Please take care of your health. We have no news here, except that we have a few sick men, including good Brother Soudin,[3] who

---

Letter 2717. - Archives of the Motherhouse of the Daughters of Charity, original signed letter. This is one of the letters sold at auction by Xavier Charmoy (cf. no. 2505). The postscript is in the Saint's handwriting.

[1]Dominique de Ligny.

[2]Pierre de Lorthon, the King's secretary. He was the founder of the Missionaries' house in Crécy.

[3]Claude Soudin, born in Crécy-la-Chapelle (Seine-et-Marne) on May 29, 1627, entered the Congregation of the Mission in Paris as a coadjutor Brother on October 2, 1657, and took his vows on December 4, 1659, in the presence of M. Langlois.

asks for your prayers. For three months now he has had an ulcer on his chest, which has grown larger. He is in a lot of pain but is patient and resigned. We are doing what we can to cure him, and there is hope that time and remedies will accomplish this.

I send greetings to Brother Claude,[4] and I embrace you in spirit with all the tenderness of my heart. I am, in the love of O[ur] L[ord], Monsieur, your most humble servant.

VINCENT DEPAUL,
i.s.C.M.

What we are requesting, Monsieur, is a list of what M. Lorthon owes, either for the alms or for the upkeep of the house. Send one copy to me and another to M. Brin.

2718. - TO DENIS LAUDIN, SUPERIOR, IN LE MANS

Paris, November 13, 1658

Monsieur,

The grace of O[ur] L[ord] be with you forever!

I received three letters from you, the last one dated the sixth of this month. You did well not to go out to give missions but to stay at home in the present circumstances. I am writing to encourage M. Molony [1] in his office of Procurator. I am sending you my letter open; please seal it before giving it to him, and try to help him to overcome his repugnance and to do his work.

I wrote to you and to M. Bienvenu at the same time, on October

---

[4]Claude Gesseaume.

Letter 2718. - Archives of the Mission, Paris, original signed letter.

[1]Thady Molony (Thaddée Molony) was born in Limerick (Ireland) in July 1623. He entered the Congregation of the Mission on September 4, 1643, was ordained a priest in Rome on March 6, 1650, and took his vows on November 14, 1655. He was in Le Mans in 1658-59.

26,[2] but you make no mention of those letters, although you were always talking to me about his opposition. If, after what I have written to him, he persists in being remiss, let him know that he either has to live like the others according to his vows and our Rules or provide for himself; for he cannot remain in the Company without living in dependence on it and loving it. Be sure, however, that he knows this is not a voluntary departure but one that is being imposed.

We will think about having Brother Descroizilles [3] pursue his studies, when he himself is not thinking about them so much—as he has been doing—that he is not indifferent to them. Let him leave the care of this to us and comply with our decision in everything. The immoderate attachment he has had for studies will oblige us to break his own will, as long as he continues to hold to it in this matter.

I instructed M. Alméras to choose a Brother for you in line with what you want in one and to send him to you as soon as possible. Brother Christophe[4] could then come here—even sooner, if you can manage without him. Give him whatever he needs for his journey.

If, after his retreat, the young gentleman who was thinking about the Company perseveres in wanting to enter, I will send you a letter for the Superior in Genoa, asking him to accept him there.

I do not think you should accept as a Brother that man who is offering us his property on the terms he proposed to you, even though he is no longer proposing them.

O Monsieur! most willingly do I consent to the arrangement with the Administrators, and it would be a great consolation to me

---

[2]Cf. nos. 2695 and 2696.

[3]Jean Descroizilles, a seminarian at this time, was born in Ault (Somme) on January 25, 1631, entered the Congregation of the Mission in Paris on August 10, 1654, and took his vows there on August 11, 1656, in the presence of M. Delespiney. In 1659 dimissorial letters were requested in preparation for his ordination (cf. vol. VIII, no. 3048).

[4]Christophe Delaunay.

to conclude everything by this means. It is not, however, advisable to seek them out, but let M. de la Bataillère[5] know that we want nothing better than to settle things this way and to live on peaceful terms with them.

I thank God for the opportunity Monsieur and Madame de Liancourt are giving you to show our obedience to them. I would be greatly consoled if other greater occasions of serving them were to arise.

May God bless the labors of your workers! We will try to send you one or two to increase their number.

Enclosed is a letter for Brother Guillaume.[6] I have written to Sedan asking them to send him his copies of paintings.

I am, in the love of O[ur] L[ord], Monsieur, your most humble servant.

VINCENT DEPAUL,
i.s.C.M.

At the bottom of the first page: Monsieur Laudin

2719. - TO EDMUND BARRY, SUPERIOR, IN NOTRE-DAME-DE-LORM

Paris, November 13, 1658

Monsieur,

The grace of O[ur] L[ord] be with you forever!

The last letter I received from you is dated October 13. I have not written to you for a long time. I praise God for the consolation

[5]Administrator of the Le Mans Hospital.
[6]Guillaume Pintart.

Letter 2719. - Archives of the Mission, Paris, original signed letter. The postscript is in the Saint's handwriting.

M. Cuissot brought you by his visitation and by our Rules.[1] I am sure your little family will make good use of them to become more closely united to God and among themselves.

I am greatly consoled that the seminary is growing. It would be a good idea if it were transferred to Montauban. *Mon Dieu,* Monsieur! Is there no way of doing this and for us to be released from the parishes? I am writing to ask M. Cuissot to go to see the Bishop of Montauban[2] to find out his final decision, since it is not expedient for us to have things remain any longer as they are. Depending on the answer, we will consider the help you are requesting. Meanwhile, please encourage Messieurs Lucas [3] and Treffort.[4] I am thinking about them, and God will doubtless be pleased with their patience and their work. I embrace them along with you and the rest of the little family, with all the tenderness of my heart.

We have no news here. Things are going along as usual. Several of our priests are out giving missions, in particular, M. Bajoue,[5] for whom I will have a power of attorney prepared on his return to authorize you to sell his annuity and collect its arrears because the transfer he already made is insufficient.

I am, in the love of O[ur] L[ord], Monsieur, your most humble servant.

VINCENT DEPAUL,
i.s.C.M.

It is inadvisable for me to write to the Bishop and for me to be

---

[1]The Common Rules, copies of which were distributed by Gilbert Cuissot during the visitation.

[2]Pierre de Bertier.

[3]Jacques Lucas, born in La Pernelle (Manche) on April 10, 1611, was ordained a priest in 1635 and entered the Congregation of the Mission on March 10, 1638. He was Superior in Luçon (1650-56) and La Rose (1662-68).

[4]Simon Treffort, born in Villiers-Herbisse (Aube) on October 2, 1611, entered the Congregation of the Mission on October 5, 1642, and took his vows on October 7, 1645. He was Superior in La Rose (1668-77) and died in Cahors on July 16, 1682. In a letter written a few days after his death, Edme Jolly, Superior General, highly praised his virtues.

[5]Emerand Bajoue, title holder for the benefices of Notre-Dame-de-Lorm and Saint-Aignan.

the one to urge the union. M. Dehorgny and the other titulars are finding it very difficult to bear the title of Pastor for so long and are pleading to be relieved of it.

See if you can find out what he will oblige us to do by the act of union. You can tell him that, if he wishes, we will make the [same] commitment the Bishop of Cahors[6] or the Bishop of Saintes[7] had us make. I am sending you a copy of it.

At the bottom of the first page: Monsieur Barry

2720. - TO JACQUES PESNELLE, SUPERIOR, IN GENOA

Paris, November 15, 1658

Monsieur,

The grace of O[ur] L[ord] be with you forever!

M. Turmeau [1] was very wrong not to send my letters on to you, in so far as it is his fault that you are not receiving them. I think that, since you have had charge of the family, I have written you by every regular mail but one. He is a man I do not know; he was suggested to us by the late M. Blatiron, to whom some other Genoese merchants who corresponded with him suggested him. So, you can get them to write to ask him to be more careful about our letters, or else find some other person.

May God bless the retreat exercises of the seminarians from the Cardinal's [2] seminary and grant them the grace of making good use

---

[6]Alain de Solminihac.
[7]Louis de Bassompierre.

Letter 2720. - Archives of the Mission, Paris, original signed letter.
[1]A merchant in Lyons.
[2]Stefano Durazzo.

of the help and advice you have given them! May He also bless your work on the missions! Is there no other priest from outside the Company who could go to help you?

On All Saints' Day M. Berthe left Marseilles with his little band to go to Genoa, but bad weather forced them to take shelter four leagues from there. I will be worried about them until I am sure they are with you.

I willingly give my consent for M. Stelle to take vows. It is easy for me to believe the good things you tell me about him and to have high hopes for him; I have always felt he would make a good Missionary.

You were right to assure the Cardinal that we would welcome his nephew [3] at Saint-Lazare, in view of the honor he has of being related to His Eminence, of being one of the leading Senators of the Republic, of his title of Resident in France, of the privilege he granted you, and of the endless obligations we have toward His Eminence, giving him sovereign authority over us and all that we have. We find it extremely difficult, however, to do what you have promised. First, because of a rule we have here in this house not to receive any layman[4] from outside the Company except to make a retreat. For that reason we made our excuses to an English Prince who was married to a relative of Cardinal de Retz, our Founder and Prelate, and I have never been willing to allow any French noblemen to erect a building here, as they wanted to do, because each wanted to have a room reserved there for himself in which to retire. It would take me too long to tell you the reasons for this rule; you can imagine some of them.

Secondly, because we have only two rooms that might be suitable for the Resident, one of which is occupied by the Abbés de Chandenier, and the other has been promised to the Bishop of

---

[3]The Marchese Durazzo, recently appointed chargé d'affaires of the Republic of Genoa at the court of the King of France.

[4]Word added by the Saint.

Sarlat,[5] who resigned his bishopric to become Coadjutor of Cahors and wants to live here until the door is open for him to go to work there. Now, we cannot put him out without offending him and, in his sacred person, all the Prelates of the kingdom, who would resent such an insult. In addition, we have a house in Cahors, where he is Coadjutor, and that house is responsible for the seminary, which is one of the fullest and best regulated in the kingdom. As for the Abbés, we cannot send them away either. They are the nephews of the late Cardinal de la Rochefoucauld[6] and are important benefactors, having given us two benefices worth four thousand livres each.[7] If we had shown such ingratitude toward them, heaven and earth would take up arms against us.

That is why, Monsieur, it is advisable for you to make known to His Eminence as soon as possible our good will and powerlessness; do so gently and tactfully so that this change in your word does not take him by surprise. If the Resident had only one servant, and a small room with a fireplace would suffice for him, we would be delighted by the honor of his presence and the opportunity we would have to show the Cardinal, in the person of his nephew, the respect and obedience we owe him. In a word, Monsieur, tell His Eminence that he is above any Rule and that we will do, now and always, whatever he may command us.

You may accept into your seminary the young man you mention as having a good spirit and who wants to enter the Company but

---

[5]Nicolas Sevin.

[6]François de la Rochefoucauld, born in Paris on December 8, 1558, became Bishop of Clermont on October 6, 1585, Cardinal in 1607, Bishop of Senlis in 1611, and Commendatory Abbot of Sainte-Geneviève in Paris in 1613. He resigned as Bishop in 1622 to dedicate himself to the reform of the abbeys dependent on the Benedictines, Augustinians, and Cistercians. With the support of men such as Saint Vincent, Father Grégoire Tarrisse, and Father Charles Faure, he restored order and discipline. Saint Vincent assisted him at his death on February 14, 1645. He was buried at Sainte-Geneviève, but his heart was given to the Jesuits. (Cf. M.M. La Morinière, *Les vertus du vrai prélat représentées en la vie de l'Eminentissime cardinal de La Rochefoucault* [Paris: Cramoisy, 1646]; Lallemand et Chatonnet, *La vie du Révérend Père Charles Faure, abbé de Sainte-Geneviève de Paris* [Paris: J. Anisson, 1698].)

[7]The benefices of Saint-Pourçain and Saint-Martin de Coudres.

cannot obtain a title. If he works hard at acquiring virtue and shows signs of persevering, we can get one for him after his vows. You suggest using the chapel of the late M. de Monchia[8] for that purpose. Before settling that, however, I would like to know what it is worth and who has its title now. If it could bring in the pension needed for that young man to enter Holy Orders, we could have it created. That seems more suitable than to have him made titular of the benefice because, if he were provided with it, he might leave and keep it.

I told you that it is better to dismiss the young Brother cured of epilepsy than to keep him, since he might have similar attacks again, which would have very bad effects on the Company. Discuss this with M. Berthe, to whom I send greetings and embrace, if he is still with you, as I have no time to write to him.

I am, in the love of O[ur] L[ord], Monsieur, your most humble servant.

VINCENT DEPAUL,
i.s.C.M.

At the bottom of the first page: Monsieur Pesnelle

2721. - TO JEAN MARTIN, SUPERIOR, IN TURIN

Paris, November 15, 1658

Monsieur,

The grace of O[ur] L[ord] be with you forever!

Since last writing to you I have received two of your letters. The

---

[8]Cristoforo di Monchia, a Genoese priest of noble lineage, had contributed to the foundation of the house in Genoa from his personal fortune and continued to assist it with gifts. (Cf. Abelly, *op. cit.*, bk. I, chap. XLVI, p. 223.)

Letter 2721. - Archives of the Mission, Turin, original signed letter.

retreat I made, some minor illnesses, and my usual press of business have prevented me from writing to you.

You tell me you have made your retreat, renewed your offering of yourself, and decided on a place for a mission. All that consoled me greatly as a disposition for doing much good, and it will be all the greater the more faithful you are to your resolutions and to the Rules. I ask O[ur] L[ord] to grant all of you the grace to do so. Today in the refectory the reading told us that virtues on which we meditate but do not practice are more harmful than profitable to us.

Another thing that consoles me is that you make no mention of the slight coldness you noticed with some of the men; this is a sign that the members are now closely united to their head and among themselves. It is a result of the retreat and your gentle, wise leadership, by which you must have won their hearts.

I am most grateful for the way your Founder and the Marquis de Saint-Thomas [1] were pleased to recommend the Sant'Antonio affair to the Ambassador who went to Rome.[2] Now we must await the outcome patiently and hope that, if it is not as we wish, it will nevertheless be according to God's Will, which is all that we should be seeking, [and in which we desire] [3] to see you firmly and solidly established. This is something Providence must do with time, and often our cares and hopes are of little use in such plans. Just look at our poor family in Rome that still has no house, even though it has been there fifteen to twenty years.

If the court of Savoy comes to Lyons, I will take the honor of writing to the Marchese di Pianezza, as soon as I hear it, to offer him all that depends on us and to renew our obedience to him.

I am really worried about Brother Demortier's long illness. How is he now and how is the rest of the family? I hope M. Berthe will

---

[1]Councillor and first Secretary of State for Savoy.

[2]Jeure-Millet, assistant tutor of Monsieur, Philippe d'Orléans, the younger brother of Louis XIV.

[3]One or two words at the top of the page are illegible here due to the ravages of time.

soon send me news of them. He should be in Genoa right now, if nothing has happened to him; and from there he is supposed to return by way of Turin.

Brother Pronetti has left the Company because, first of all, he seemed unwilling to want to put on its spirit, although he is a God-fearing young man with common sense, who has studied well enough. The most obvious reason, however, is that the doctor and the surgeon advised him to leave because he had an inflamed nerve arising from an impurity in the blood. This had gone to the lower part of his body, making him sick, and he had a hard time kneeling. The result was that he was often in the infirmary. He left satisfied with us, as he said. We did indeed treat him with greater support and affection than we would have done if he were from this country or had not been sent to us by you.

I am, in the love of O[ur] L[ord], Monsieur, your most humble servant.

VINCENT DEPAUL,
i.s.C.M.

Addressed: Monsieur Martin, Superior of the Mission of Turin, in Turin

2722. - TO JEAN PARRE, IN RETHEL

Paris, November 16, 1658

Dear Brother,

The grace of O[ur] L[ord] be with you forever!

Since we were out of the habit of writing to you every week, doing so last Saturday slipped our mind. Furthermore, I had nothing

---

Letter 2722. - Archives of the Mission, Paris, original signed letter.

in particular to tell you; also, Mademoiselle Viole wrote you a letter, which she addressed to M. de Séraucourt to be delivered to you. In it she instructed you to get some money—I do not know how much. I was not in a position to go to the meeting so she sent word to me yesterday that they would try to send you some vestments. I sent your letters to the meeting, but no decision was made, except that they would see at the first opportunity if they could get a small fund together to buy some wheat. The samples were viewed only by candlelight because it was night time, so they postponed discussion until next week. So much for that.

I thank God, dear Brother, that you arrived safely at the place where His service awaited you. If you give only very little to the poor out of helplessness, you give a great deal to God out of love, since you offer Him your own comfort, your heavy labors, and your life. Not only that, but you would like all people to make Him a sacrifice of their goods and their persons so that all the poor on earth may be assisted and all souls saved by Jesus Christ, who shed His Precious Blood for them. What more can you do, dear Brother? Is not that enough to console and humble you at the same time before God, who has granted you the grace of animating you with His charity, which consists in willing what His Son, our Divine Master, has willed, and in doing what He has done? You will tell me that you will it and do it only imperfectly. All right! Go on thinking this, and try to unite yourself more and more in action and intention with this same Lord, in whom I am, dear Brother, your most affectionate brother and servant.

VINCENT DEPAUL,
i.s.C.M.

Addressed: Brother Jean Parre, of the Congregation of the Mission, in Rethel

2723. - *SAINT LOUISE TO SAINT VINCENT*

Saturday [November 16, 1658] [1]

Most Honored Father, I think Your Charity really should speak to Sister Étiennette,[2] *who is supposed to go to Angers, to explain to her the dispositions she should have for the duty she will have there. She should make herself readily available to the Sisters wishing to speak with her; maintain confidentiality regarding all that is told her; divert as much as possible any tendency of mind or body that leads only to self-satisfaction; see to it that the Rules are faithfully observed, without detriment to the service of the poor; have a cheerful demeanor; respect the Administrators, and everything else, which you know better than I, who am incapable of doing anything worthwhile.*

We hope, with your approval, Most Honored Father, to have our Sisters[3] *leave Monday. If Your Charity could give us the conference continuing the explanation of the Rule, it would also benefit three or four Sisters who are returning to the country on the same day.*

I entreat Our Lord to give you the strength for this, and I ask you, for His holy love, for a small share in your holy prayers. I am, Most Honored Father, your very poor and unworthy daughter and servant.

L. DE M.

Addressed: *Monsieur Vincent*

Letter 2723. - Archives of the Motherhouse of the Daughters of Charity, original autograph letter.

[1]Brother Ducournau added "November 1658" on the back. Saint Vincent's reply (cf. no. 2724) leads us to suppose that the requested conference was given the next day, which was November 17 (cf. vol. X, no. 105: "On Rising, Prayer, Examen, and Other Exercises").

[2]Étiennette Dupuis was one of the elders in the Company of the Daughters of Charity. In 1658 she was sent as Sister Servant to Angers where she remained one year. She then went to Richelieu. In 1665 she returned to the Motherhouse and was at Maisons as Sister Servant in 1677.

[3]Étiennette Dupuis, Marie Bertrand, and Catherine.

2724. - TO SAINT LOUISE

[November 16, 1658] [1]

I have just sent Mademoiselle Le Gras a letter from the Vicar-General of Beauvais.[2]

I have been thinking that I could give the conference here in this house tomorrow, God willing, if it is likely that all the Sisters could fit in our parlor. Please let me know what you think.

Madame de Mirepoix [3] will come to Mademoiselle Le Gras' house this evening.

Tomorrow, God willing, I will speak to our dear Sister Étiennette.

2725. - TO FRANÇOIS-IGNACE LIÈBE

Paris, November 17, 1658

Monsieur,

The grace of O[ur] L[ord] be with you forever!

Since you left Richelieu, I have received three letters from you, which have two objectives: first, that I should dispense you from the vows you recently took in the Company, according to the Brief of His Holiness, or consent to your going to our house in Luçon, where you hope to work on the missions. Now, I will tell you,

---

Letter 2724. - Archives of the Motherhouse of the Daughters of Charity, original autograph letter.

[1]This is Saint Vincent's response to no. 2723.

[2]Claude Tristan, Seigneur de Maisoncelles, Canon, Grand Archdeacon, and Vicar-General of Beauvais for forty years. His refusal to sign the formulary against Jansenism brought upon him in 1666 exclusion from choir and the loss of the income from his prebend. He died on June 29, 1692.

[3]Catherine Caulet, Baronne de Mirepoix, was going to make a retreat at Saint Louise's house.

Letter 2725. - Archives of the Mission, Paris, seventeenth-century copy made from the original in the Saint's handwriting.

Monsieur, that you know as well as I that no one can dispense a person from vows without good reason, and you have had no good reason to leave the Company, since you tell me you have not been treated badly by it in any way. In keeping with that, Monsieur, you see clearly that I cannot dispense you from those promises you made to God.

As for your second request, you do not explain clearly enough whether you intend to return to the Company by going to the Luçon house and working at our functions there or simply as a person outside the Company. If it is in the second way, do not even think about it. And if it is in the first way, you must explain further and manifest deep regret for leaving and a great desire to return, accompanied by humility and appropriate prayers for that purpose. Then we will ask God to inspire us with what we will have to do, as well as where and how it will be advisable to effect this reentry into the Company.

This is something that well deserves your reflection. We must have a very high regard for the promises we make to God and, even more, for carrying them out. What is at stake is your salvation, which should be very dear to you and make you think before God and in conscience about what you have to do in these circumstances.

I felt obliged to point all this out to you, Monsieur, since you have given yourself to God in the Company whose care He has entrusted to me and, consequently, along with it, the care of the souls of those who have entered it. Moreover, I am, in the love of O[ur] L[ord], Monsieur, your most humble servant.

V. D.

2726. - TO ANTOINE GUESPIER,[1] IN TOURS

Paris, November 20, 1658

Reverend Father,

The grace of O[ur] L[ord] be with you forever!

It is true that I had the honor of receiving several letters from you which I have not answered. I ask your pardon for this. I was waiting to find out from Abbé de Chandenier,[2] who had gone to Metz, the state of the matter about which you wrote me.[3] However, instead of returning to Paris, he has gone farther away. This obliges me to tell Your Reverence without further delay what I know about it, namely, that we never had any intention of paying you twice for the same thing. I have always thought it was reasonable that, since you were good enough to give the pulpit over to the Missionaries, they should give you the same remuneration you would have had if you had actually preached. That is what they did with the money from the Queen. On what Your Reverence told me when you honored me with a visit—that they had not reckoned your account correctly—I had six pistoles from our own money given you, with which you were satisfied.

I recall nevertheless, Reverend Father, that you had claimed at the time that you should be given also the money the diocesan tax officer usually gives to Lenten preachers. Even though I told you that it was not at our disposal, Your Reverence still wanted me to take the honor of telling the Bishop of Auguste[4] that, although the

---

Letter 2726. - Archives of the Mission, Paris, unsigned rough draft in the secretary's handwriting.

[1]Dominican preacher; Master of Theology.

[2]Louis de Chandenier.

[3]In Lent of that year, there was a scheduling difficulty in Metz: a conflict between the Lenten sermons to be preached by Father Guespier and the missions to be preached at the same time in Metz by a team led by Abbé de Chandenier (cf. no. 2520).

[4]Pierre Bédacier, Titular Bishop of Auguste, Suffragan of the Bishop of Metz, and Administrator of the diocese.

Missionaries had given you one hundred écus, you were still hoping to get a similar amount from the tax officer. Then, if the Bishop judged it suitable to give you this double remuneration, he would know that, as far as I was concerned, I did not want to stand in the way of this. So, I gave you a letter stating these things in substance.

Now Your Reverence writes me, giving another side to this business. This, however, is what happened. I was in no way involved in it, having acted on our part according to the intention of the Queen, which was to give you thirty pistoles for not preaching, in place of a similar amount that the tax officer would have given you if you had preached. You received twenty-four in Metz from Abbé de Chandenier and six in Paris from the procurator of Saint-Lazare. I would not have been upset if you had also received what the tax officer had, but, as I told Your Reverence, that did not depend on me. In addition, I have just learned that this money, by order of Her Majesty and on the advice of the Suffragan Bishop, was used for the needs of the Confraternity of Charity in Metz, founded for the relief of the sick poor. I, however, was no way involved in the way the money was used.

I am really sorry, Reverend Father, that you did not obtain what you desired, either with regard to that money or with regard to a pulpit in Paris. If I had been able, I would gladly have been of service to you in this matter and will be so on every other occasion, whenever you are pleased to honor me with your orders. I assure you that I am, with all my heart, in that of O[ur] L[ord], Reverend Father, your most humble and very obedient servant.

2727. - TO SISTER BARBE ANGIBOUST,[1] IN CHÂTEAUDUN

November 21, 1658

Dear Sister,

I most humbly ask your pardon for not answering the letters you have written me since your arrival in Châteaudun.[2] The pressure of business has prevented me from doing so, but from now on I will be more exact, God willing, and you will continue to write to me as usual.

Monsieur . . . did me the honor of telling me about the reception given you, the confidence shown you in both town and country, and the blessing God has bestowed on your work. I was greatly consoled by this and thank God for it, asking Him to continue to grant you these same blessings. He will doubtless do so if you continue to serve Him with the zeal, charity, and humility with which you have done so until now and which I hope you will do, with the grace of O[ur] L[ord], in whom I am. . . .

Letter 2727. - Chambre des Députés, Paris, Ms, p. 138.

[1]Barbe Angiboust, who holds an important place in the first twenty-five years of the history of the Daughters of Charity, entered the Company on July 1, 1634, at the age of twenty-nine, and was admitted to vows on March 25, 1642. She was put in charge of the foundations of Saint-Germain-en-Laye (1638), Richelieu (1638), Saint-Denis (1645), Fontainebleau (1646), Brienne (1652), Bernay (1655), and Châteaudun (1657) where she died on December 27, 1658. In 1641 she was responsible for the Sisters serving the galley slaves. The conference on her virtues, held in the Motherhouse on April 27, 1659, is very edifying (cf. vol. X, no. 109).

[2]Saint Vincent forgot about his letter to her of August 20, 1657 (cf. vol. VI, no. 2343), shortly after her arrival in Châteaudun. Coste surmised that the copyist might have made a mistake in transcribing the date and that this letter could have been written on November 21, 1657. Perhaps he is correct, in view of what the Saint says here about Sister Barbe's reception by the townspeople and the letter written to Saint Vincent on October 25, 1657, by the Administrators of the hospital. Nevertheless, since the date on this letter does not seem to be uncertain, the editors have left it where Coste originally placed it.

2728. - TO ÉTIENNE BIENVENU, IN LE MANS

[November or December 1658] [1]

Monsieur,

I read your letter with sorrow, seeing that you are asking my permission to withdraw. What have we done to cause you to leave us? What displeasure have you received from the Company to cause such a separation? The only reason you give me is that you are not well. I ask you to reflect that there is no one who is not sometimes sick and that, wherever we go, we bring our bodies, subject to illness, with us.

To this I will add that it will be difficult for you to find elsewhere the same treatment in your ailments as the Company gives its children. It has salaried doctors, remedies, and persons to apply them, and provides with great charity whatever else is needed for their consolation and relief. So, its intention is that the house where you are should take care of you when you are ill—and I think it has spared nothing to do so. Nevertheless, if there were anything to complain about, you should have let me know so I could remedy it. I would like to believe that you have a delicate constitution, but I have always seen you able to do what the others do, and I have not yet been aware that you have had any serious illness nor that anything prevents you at present from doing as you usually do.

Even, however, if it should be true that you might have some serious illness, that is not sufficient reason to break a promise you made to God to live and die in the Company. *Mon Dieu,* Monsieur, what are you trying to do? What! To be unfaithful to God, who has

---

Letter 2728. - Archives of the Mission, Paris, unsigned rough draft in the secretary's handwriting.

[1]Coste originally notes that this letter must assuredly be placed between November 1658 and October 1659 and that, to all indications, it was sent shortly after the letter of October 26 (no. 2696). His subsequent corrections pinpoint the date to November 21, 1658. The secretary wrote the two rough drafts one after the other.

called you, to turn your back on your vocation, which provides you with so many means to save yourself, and to lose in one instant an eternity of happiness, which is granted only to perseverance! O Monsieur! what deep regret you would have at the time of your death if you had committed such a fault! For, it is of the nature of those that are irreparable, since, by abandoning the state in which God has placed you, you would be in great danger of His abandoning you to the one your own will would have caused you to embrace. Beware of following it. Make a few days of retreat to consider the importance of doing God's Will and of living the vows you have taken and renewed. You are bound to do so, as I explained to you in the letter I wrote you in October telling you that I cannot and will not, in word or in writing, allow you to leave the Company nor, consequently, grant you the rest of what you request because I am, in the right way, in the love of O[ur] L[ord], Monsieur, your most humble servant.

2729. - TO JACQUES PESNELLE, SUPERIOR, IN GENOA

Paris, November 22, 1658

Monsieur,

The grace of O[ur] L[ord] be with you forever!

I received two letters from you, dated October 29 and November 4. I am anxious for you to assure me of the arrival of M. Berthe and the others. By now, they must be in Genoa ten or twelve days. I am afraid you were in too much of a hurry to go off to give the mission; in that case, however, the Visitor will await your return or go to see you wherever you are.

Letter 2729. - Archives of the Mission, Paris, original signed letter.

I am consoled that M. Bruno [1] has come to your rescue. This gives you the opportunity to get to know him well so you can judge whether it will be advisable to grant him the consolation he is seeking, which is to be readmitted to the Company. He is very devout, but sickly and very melancholic.

I replied to you long ago about how to receive the blessing of the Pastors. I think it would be well for you to continue to do what the late M. Blatiron did rather than introduce a new way because that change could provoke criticism.

If the Cardinal [2] approves of giving the chapel of the late M. de Monchia[3] to the young postulant who has no title, after his two years of seminary, so he can receive Holy Orders, I approve it also, despite what I said to you about it in my last letter.

Most willingly will we pray for that good Senator, that God may make known to him His good pleasure during the retreat he intends to make. May He also grant him the grace of being truly detached from all perishable things, in whatever state he may be, and give him a great desire to be united to His Sovereign Good.

I will tell you two things about the uneasiness and melancholy you say you experience when things do not go well: (1) that it is not men who make things go well, but God, who sometimes allows them to go differently than the way we would like so as to make us realize that we can do nothing about them, or to try our patience; and (2) that you trust your own guidance too much when you think that, because you love good order, it is up to you to see that it is observed.

The result is that, not being able to succeed in all that, you become excessively sad, whereas if you were truly convinced that you are capable only of spoiling everything, you would be sur-

---

[1]Giovanni Antonio Bruno, born in Aprico, near Albenga (Liguria), on August 26, 1630, entered the Congregation of the Mission as a priest in Genoa on January 29, 1656, and took his vows on April 28, 1659, in the presence of M. Pesnelle.

[2]Stefano Durazzo.

[3]Cristoforo di Monchia.

prised that things do not go even much worse and would remain at peace in every outcome and event that seem unpleasant or unfavorable to you, since God ordains them thus.

I ask you, Monsieur, to consider all things in the order of His Providence and, by doing humbly and carefully whatever depends on you to see that everything goes well, to be submissive in all else to the good pleasure of God, in whom I am, Monsieur, your most humble servant.

VINCENT DEPAUL,
i.s.C.M.

Addressed: Monsieur Pesnelle

2730. - TO EDME JOLLY, SUPERIOR, IN ROME

Paris, November 22, 1658

Monsieur,

The grace of O[ur] L[ord] be with you forever!

I received your letter of October 22, which requires no reply. I thank God for the services you are rendering to Christianity in the person of the students of Propaganda Fide. You are instilling in them the spirit of prayer and the love of the Christian virtues so that they will go to different parts of the world to produce the fruits of these virtues by exercising priestly functions there. May God be pleased to animate them with His Spirit and to send good workers into His Church, which has such great need of them! [1]

I am consoled about the man who has gone to Moldavia, which

Letter 2730. - Archives of the Mission, Paris, original signed letter. The postscript is in the Saint's handwriting.

[1]Cf. Mt 9:37-38. (NAB)

you say is almost entirely Catholic and yet has only three or four priests. I have recommended to our community that they pray for this poor country and for that good priest who is going to its assistance. Oh! how willingly would I go as well, if I were of an age and state to do so!

I am also consoled to hear that you still have a good number of retreatants. You must be careful lest some, under the pretext of a retreat, come just for the free meals. There are persons who are only too glad to spend a quiet week or so at no cost to themselves.

I will be pleased to see the letter M. du Loeus [2] has written to Spain.

It is a very great novelty for a Turk to be admitted to the ecclesiastical state and even more to be accepted into a Community. Still, there may be some exception to the general rule that excludes such sorts of persons from our holy ministries, and the one who is asking you to enter our Company to become a priest may have such good dispositions that it would be well to accept him. It is up to you, Monsieur, to examine thoroughly the depths of his soul, his motivation, the firmness and quality of his mind, and, based on that, to admit him or to thank him. He must, however, be in possession of a title before being received, if you should reach that point.

I am, in the love of O[ur] L[ord], Monsieur, your most humble servant.

VINCENT DEPAUL

Please have the enclosed delivered to Cardinal Sachetti.

Addressed: Monsieur Jolly

---

[2] James Dowley (Duley), future Bishop of Limerick (Ireland).

2731. - TO FIRMIN GET, SUPERIOR, IN MARSEILLES

Paris, November 22, 1658

Monsieur,

The grace of O[ur] L[ord] be with you forever!

I would like to think that you have now received the help we sent you and, consequently, have the means of paying your debts and of giving the mission in Sisteron.[1]

I think I sent you word that there is now some hope of maintaining the hospital. A number of influential persons are working on it. I just sent your letter to the Duchesse d'Aiguillon so she could see how urgent the matter is and renew her entreaties to maintain this work—the work of her own hands—which is now in a desperate plight. I begged her once again to have letters written to the Court for the freedom of the Turks[2] in Tunis. She has already given a report of this to Madame de Vendôme[3] to get her to speak or write about it to the Admiral, who had already left—or was on the point of leaving—to go see the King. We must patiently await the reply.

I am sure you are doing your best to show the lawyer—who, as creditor of M. Despennes, is giving you trouble—that the price of your acquittance was used to pay the first creditors who held mortgages. I am very apprehensive about lawsuits and lawyers. God grant that M. Despennes did not catch you off guard by concealing the fact that this man's debt is the oldest one!

We received two gold écus, worth eleven livres eight sous, for a convict named Nicolas Chocart on the galley *Princesse,* and six livres for Charles Ballagny, a convict on the *Princesse de Morgue.*

Letter 2731. - Archives of the Mission, Paris, copy made from the original in the Hains Family Collection, Marseilles.

[1]Principal town of Alpes-de-Haute-Provence.

[2]The captives.

[3]Françoise de Lorraine, Duchesse de Vendôme, wife of César de Bourbon, Duc de Vendôme, Director of Shipping and Commerce. Their eldest son married Laura Mancini, the niece of Cardinal Mazarin.

I am writing to tell M. Huguier in Toulon, or his representative, to give each of them his due and the letter I am sending. If by chance none of your men is still there, please give instructions to have this done.

You do not tell me whether M. Brisjonc has gone to Agde or is still with you.

I had the two gold écus for Nicolas Chocart put into the packet we are sending to Toulon. They are the ones we received for him. I am doing so because they are a little light and we would lose something if we kept them here. So, do not put them on our account.

Your most humble servant.

VINCENT DEPAUL,
i.s.C.M.

2732. - TO PIERRE CABEL, SUPERIOR, IN SEDAN

Paris, November 23, 1658

Monsieur,

The grace of O[ur] L[ord] be with you forever!

God be eternally praised and glorified for having preserved our dear Brother Sirven! [1] I will have others thank Him for His infinite goodness and, in my own name will ask Him to be pleased to restore him to perfect health.

We received Brother Pintart's copies of paintings and have sent them to him.

Letter 2732. - Archives of the Mission, Paris, original signed letter.

[1]Pierre Sirven, coadjutor Brother, born in Verdun-sur-Garonne (Tarn-et-Garonne), entered the Congregation of the Mission on March 12, 1640, took his vows on January 1, 1643, and died on July 12, 1660, in Sedan. His outstanding qualities had earned the confidence of the Bishop of Montauban, and he was highly esteemed by Saint Vincent, who considered him "the living Rule of the Company; a wise, intelligent man, benevolent towards everyone."

I will reply to you at another time regarding the objection being raised at going to M. Lucas.[2]

I do not disapprove of your having M. Warin[3] preach in your church and letting him come to your house sometimes, since he makes good use of this and left the Company a long time ago. I cannot consent, however, to your going to supper at the new churchwarden's house the day he is elected. Let those who are accustomed to go there think whatever they like, and rest assured that those inside and outside your house will be more edified if you excuse yourself from eating in town than if you had done the contrary.

I persist in telling you what I told M. Daisne,[4] that whatever reason or pretext he may have for wanting to take a lapsed benefice,[5] I cannot tolerate that in a Missionary. In addition, if he wishes to remain in the Company, he must make up his mind as soon as possible to renounce the one he has taken. That is the reply I can make to his last letter. If he decides to leave your house rather than give up his parish, I consent to your giving him what you can for his bed and small furnishings.[6]

---

[2]In his first footnote for this letter, Coste identified this man as Antoine Lucas. This cannot be correct since Antoine Lucas had died in November 1656 (cf. *Notices,* vol. I, pp. 136-45, and vol. V [Supplement], p. 396). Luca Arimondo, whom Saint Vincent always called *M. Lucas,* had also died in 1656. It is, therefore, uncertain to whom he is actually referring.

[3]Simon Warin (Varin), born in Bazeilles (Ardennes), entered the Congregation of the Mission on October 6, 1645, at seventeen years of age, and took his vows on October 7, 1647. *Notices,* vol. I, p. 470, and vol. V (Supplement) p. 610, lists him as Simon Varin.

[4]Cf. no. 2716.

[5]This refers to the right of a Superior to confer a "devolved" (lapsed) benefice when a subordinate or customary collator has neglected to confer it within the approved time limit or had conferred it on an unfit person.

[6]The secretary had added: "so that he will not go away in need;" these words were subsequently crossed out.

I sent your packet to M. Coglée, and I ask O[ur] L[ord] to sanctify your dear soul more and more for the sanctification of many others.

I am, in His love, Monsieur, your most humble servant.

VINCENT DEPAUL,
i.s.C.M.

At the bottom of the first page: Monsieur Cabel

2733. - TO JEAN PARRE, IN REIMS

Paris, November 23, 1658

Dear Brother,

The grace of O[ur] L[ord] be with you forever!

I sent your letter to yesterday's meeting,[1] since I was unable to go myself. Nothing was decided there, except that you should take thirty écus to be used for the most urgent needs of Champagne or Picardy—either for clothing, grain, or food. Nothing more could be done this time, and no mention was made of the fabrics of which you sent me the samples. The funds are lacking.

As for me, I will never lack affection for you, God willing, since

---

Letter 2733. - Archives of the Mission, Paris, original signed letter.

[1]Of the Ladies of Charity. Parre was one of their agents in distributing aid to the devastated areas.

His Divine Goodness has filled me with it. I am, in His love, dear Brother, your most affectionate brother and servant.

VINCENT DEPAUL,
i.s.C.M.

Draw a bill of exchange on Mademoiselle Viole for those thirty écus.

At the bottom of the page: Bro[ther] Jean Parre

2734. - TO SISTER ANNE HARDEMONT, SISTER SERVANT, IN USSEL

Paris, November 24 [1658] [1]

Dear Sister,

The grace of O[ur] L[ord] be with you forever!

I have good reason to thank God for the graces He has granted you and, through you, has granted the poor; for, from what I can see, the Duchess,[2] who has perceived the excellent manner in which you have acted, is very pleased with it, and I am sure that God in His goodness is also pleased.

You have had a hard time getting used to the region, but you will also have great merit before God for having overcome your repugnance and for having done His Will rather than your own. Continue this, Sister, and you will see the glory of God, you will possess your soul in patience,[3] and if you once possess it well, Our Lord will be its Master, since you belong to Him by His mercy and

Letter 2734. - Archives of the Motherhouse of the Daughters of Charity, original signed letter.

[1]The year the Sisters arrived in Ussel. The postscript shows that the letter could not have been written as late as November 24, 1659.

[2]The Duchesse de Ventadour.

[3]Cf. Lk 21:19. (NAB)

you want to be His in time and in eternity. O Sister, how consoled you will be at the hour of death for having consumed your life for the same reason for which Jesus Christ gave His—for charity, for God, for the poor! If you only knew your good fortune, Sister, you would truly be overjoyed; for, in doing what you do, you are fulfilling the law and the prophets, commanding us to love God with all our heart and our neighbor as ourselves.[4] And what greater act of love can one make than to give oneself, wholly and entirely, in one's state of life and in one's duty, for the salvation and relief of the afflicted! Our entire perfection consists in this. It remains for you only to join zeal to action and to conform yourself to God's good pleasure, doing and bearing with all things for the same intentions Our Lord had and for which He suffered similar things. I pray that He will grant all of us this grace.

Please take care of your health, Sister, and send news of yourselves frequently to Mademoiselle Le Gras. Truly, she esteems and cherishes you tenderly. Take my word for it, honor her as your mother, and pray to Our Lord for me. I am, in His love, Sister, your most affectionate brother and servant.

VINCENT DEPAUL,
i.s.C.M.

This is the third letter I have written you since you have been in Ussel, not to mention one I also wrote to Sister Avoie. Enclosed is a second one for her.

Addressed: Sister Anne Hardemont, Daughter of Charity, in Ussel

---

[4]Cf. Mt 22:40. (NAB)

2735. - TO JEAN D'ARANTHON D'ALEX

Monsieur,

I received the letter you did me the honor of writing, with the respect I owe you and with a sentiment of special gratitude for the kind remembrance and benevolence with which you honor us. I thank you most humbly for this, Monsieur, and I ask Our Lord to make us worthy of them.

We will do whatever you command us to be of service to Monsieur . . .[1] and will give him one thousand livres in three installments at the time you indicate to me. God grant, Monsieur, that the opportunity might present itself to obey you in something of greater importance! His Divine Goodness knows how gladly I would do so.

From what I hear from all the men there, the blessings God is giving you and your leadership fill me with admiration, and I am deeply consoled whenever I think of it. My hope is that Our Lord will not stop at that but will lead you, for the benefit of His Church, to other states more in conformity with your condition and worthy of the special graces He has given you. I pray for this with all my heart, and with this desire I renew to you, Monsieur, the offers of my perpetual obedience. I am, with all possible humility and affection, in the love of Our Lord, Monsieur, your. . . .

VINCENT DEPAUL,
i.s.C.M.

Letter 2735. - Dom Le Masson, *op. cit.*, vol. I, p. 54.

[1]The name is missing in the text. It could well be Jean d'Aranthon's nephew, the Prior of La Pérouse (cf. no. 2615, n. 3), who was making his seminary at Saint-Sulpice.

2736. - TO LOUIS DUPONT, SUPERIOR, IN TREGUIER

Paris, November 27, 1658

Monsieur,

The grace of O[ur] L[ord] be with you forever!

I received your letter of the ninth of this month, which tries to point out to us your need for help. I have given much thought to that before it and since. The problem is to send you a priest who will be suitable for you. We are working on a choice, and I hope to have the man leave very soon.

I am returning to you the letter from the Bishop [1] that you request of me. From what I can see, the zeal of that good Prelate for the welfare and sanctification of his diocese, especially of his clergy, continues to grow; consequently, your work and your harvest are increasing. May God be praised for this, and may He will to strengthen and bless you more and more!

We have admitted to the seminary the priest you sent us.[2] Everything here is going along as usual.

I am, in O[ur] L[ord], Monsieur, your most humble servant.

VINCENT DEPAUL,
i.s.C.M.

Our dear Brother Plunket left his dimissorial letter at your house. Please send it to him or, if it has gone astray, find out from the Bishop—who already saw the dimissorial when he conferred the subdiaconate on him—if he will consent to confer the other Sacred Orders on him.

At the bottom of the first page: Monsieur Dupont

Letter 2736. - Archives of the Mission, Paris, original signed letter.

[1]Balthazar Grangier de Liverdi.

[2]Gilles Lemerer, born in the Tréguier diocese on September 22, 1633, entered the Congregation of the Mission on October 23, 1658, and took his vows in Agde on November 14, 1660, in the presence of M. Durand.

2737. - TO EDME JOLLY, SUPERIOR, IN ROME

Paris, November 29, 1658

Monsieur,

[The grace of Our Lord be with you forever!]

You inform me in your letter of October 29 that no further thought should be given to the establishment in Lombardy. We must praise God for everything and remain at peace. His Providence alone must settle these kinds of affairs, and we should neither desire nor seek any of them on our own or through others. In addition, the custom of the Company has always been to wait and not to run ahead of the higher order.

I say this, since we are on the subject of establishments, in reply to what you tell me about the one in Toledo, where I see no call for us. True, M. du Loeus did approach us previously on behalf of the Cardinal Archbishop,[1] who has the authority to call us there on the part of God; but he has not, in fact, called us, and we should make no further move to have him do so, except to tell M. du Loeus that we are prepared to respond to God's call, in the event that it does come.

That was my sole intention in asking you to mention it to him. If the Cardinal were to order us to send him some priests, and were it merely a question of travel expenses to put this into effect, we would gladly pay them—and something over and above that; but I would not want to go so far as to make the offer beforehand. Please tell M. du Loeus our maxim and leave matters at that. [We will try to pay your bill of exchange, which has not yet been presented to us.]

Letter 2737. - Bibl. de l'Institut Catholique, Paris, original signed letter; the last six lines are in the Saint's handwriting. Coste had first used a text published by Pémartin, *op. cit.*, vol. IV, L. 1761, p. 234, from a copy made available by M. Charavay. Later he was able to check the original and noted additions to be made, which the editors have added here in brackets. Part of the letter is reproduced in Reg. 2, p. 243.

[1]**Balthazar Moscoso y Sandoval (1646-65).**

I thank God that you have already assigned your men for the missions, and for the way you did it. All that seems good to me. We will ask God to bless them and their work. [I praise God also for the arrival of our dear Brothers Le Mercier, Le Gouz, and Dufestel.]

You say you have received the booklets of our Rules but not the circular letter telling what is to be observed in distributing them. That letter is from M. Alméras and not from me; in case you have not received it, I am sending it to you now.

Please have the interpretation[2] of our vow[3] sent as soon as possible, Monsieur, if there is any way to do so. We know not the day nor the hour when God will dispose of this miserable sinner. I will be consoled to see this matter settled before I die, if it is feasible and in order.

Your most humble servant.

VINCENT DEPAUL,
i.s.C.M.

Addressed: Monsieur Jolly

2738. - TO JEAN PARRE, IN REIMS

Paris, November 30, 1658

Dear Brother,

The grace of O[ur] L[ord] be with you forever!

I have nothing to tell you because the Ladies [1] have not allocated

---

[2]The original has "authorization."

[3]The Papal Brief *Alias nos,* on the vow of poverty taken in the Congregation of the Mission, was issued by Pope Alexander VII on August 12, 1659 (cf. vol. XIII, no. 120).

Letter 2738. - Archives of the Mission, Paris, original signed letter.

[1]The Ladies of Charity.

anything. I did, however, send them your letter yesterday because I could not be at their meeting, but I have had no reply to it. We are very well, and I ask God to keep you in good health and to give you an increase of His grace in order to be able to continue your services to Him. With this hope, I am, in His love, dear Brother, your most affectionate brother and servant.

VINCENT DEPAUL,
i.s.C.M.

I heard that good Brother de Hauteville[2] is sick in Reims. *Mon Dieu,* how this worries me! Please go to see him, offer him your service and everything he will need, and see that nothing is spared to have him well nursed and cared for. Assure him of our prayers and embrace him for me. Send me some news of him.

Addressed: Brother Jean Parre, of the Congregation of the Mission, at the home of Monsieur Séraucourt, Lieutenant for Criminal Affairs, in Reims

2739. - TO PHILIPPE LE VACHER, IN MARSEILLES

Paris, December 6, 1658

Monsieur,

The grace of O[ur] L[ord] be with you forever!

I have received no letters from Marseilles since last writing to

---

[2]There is some confusion regarding this person. Coste identifies him here as "François de Hauteville, a student in the Congregation of the Mission." *Notices,* vol. V (Supplement), states that he was Superior in Montmirail in 1660. The personnel catalogue lists the Superior in Montmirail in 1660 as François *Doriault,* who was received in Paris in 1655 and took his vows there on July 10, 1657. There is also a possibility that this is a François *Donault,* C.M., who was born in Hauteville in 1600.

Letter 2739. - Archives of the Mission, Paris, copy made from the original in the Hains Family Collection. This is one of the letters sold at auction by Xavier Charmoy (cf. no. 2505).

you. I am still going to send this one to you, in the absence of M. Get,[1] to ask you to send us some news of Algiers and Tunis, if you have any. I am more worried about them every day [2] and, while we await the remedy for the present state of affairs, I ask Our Lord to grant us the grace of considering those matters as they are in God and not as they appear apart from Him; otherwise we might deceive ourselves and act other than He wishes.

When M. Get returns, please tell him that the Attorney General[3] has had the Duchesse d'Aiguillon informed that the hospital for the convicts will not be abandoned; he will put the alms for her foundation on the account of the state so that it will be paid in the future. He will even have something given for the past and will do all this soon. His mother has taken the responsibility of reminding him of this, as he himself desired.

I am writing to tell M. Parisy to give four écus, which we have received here, to M. de Vassi, a convict on the *Bailliebault,* and thirty sous to Nicolas Bonner. I ask M. Get to keep count of all that for him, as we will do for him.

God bless you and keep you in perfect health, Monsieur! I am, in His love, your most humble servant.

VINCENT DEPAUL,
i.s.C.M.

---

[1]He was away giving a mission at the time.

[2]The Saint feared the consequences of the Picquet affair, the fire at the Bastion of France, and the flight of the Governor, Thomas Picquet.

[3]Nicolas Fouquet.

2740. - TO LOUIS DE CHANDENIER, IN TOURNUS [1]

Paris, December 6, 1658

Monsieur,

Thank you most humbly for the letter of November 23 with which you have honored me and for the good news it contains. I ask your pardon, Monsieur, for the liberty I take of replying to you by a hand other than my own.

I thank God, Monsieur, for having brought you safely and at such an opportune time to Tournus, for the satisfaction you have given everyone there by your fine leadership, and for that which you gave the Queen by your account of the things you did in Metz.[2] I ask His Divine Goodness, who gives life and movement to all your actions, to animate them more and more with His Spirit.

Your brother the Abbé[3] is very well, thank God, except that he is suffering a little from your absence. I am greatly in arrears with him for not giving him all I owe him.

Mademoiselle de Chandenier[4] was not feeling very well, but she is better now; she always shows great interest and affection for her relatives, especially you, Monsieur, who hold the first place in her heart. Right now, she is very much taken up with the interests of the Chief Justice,[5] who delighted everyone with a speech he made Monday at the Parlement. I learned this from several persons who heard him, especially M. de Moutiers-Saint-Jean. This great magistrate does everything so graciously and judiciously that he daily gives new reasons to hope that God will be glorified by his fine

---

Letter 2740. - The original signed letter was formerly the property of the Daughters of Charity, 20 rue du Cloître-Saint-Étienne, Troyes. Its present location is unknown. The postscript is in the Saint's handwriting.

[1]Today, principal town of a canton in Saône-et-Loire.

[2]During the mission given in the spring.

[3]Claude de Chandenier, Abbé de Moutiers-Saint-Jean.

[4]Marie de Chandenier, his sister.

[5]Guillaume de Lamoignon.

leadership, and the people will be more than satisfied. I tell you this, Monsieur, knowing that you love him for his virtue.

The condition of my legs, which is getting worse, is the reason why I am no longer allowed to go to the meeting,[6] now that it is being held at the Bons-Enfants. The five conferences since All Saints' Day were on the first five beatitudes, and they are supposed to continue with the other three, following the usual method; namely, the first point, the meaning of the beatitude and its acts; second, the motives for acquiring it; and third, the means.

Speaking of means, every day I ask God for those of being able to acknowledge in some way our infinite obligations toward you. I ask for myself the grace of bearing more effectively than I do the title He has given me and which you tolerate in me, in His love, Monsieur—that of your most humble and very obedient servant.

VINCENT DEPAUL,
i.s.C.M.

The Bishop-elect of Chalon[7] is making his retreat here the better to discover God's Will regarding his calling; he is counting on your help with these leadership responsibilities, and I am asking God to grant you the grace of corresponding with His eternal plan for you.

Addressed: Abbé de Chandenier, in Tournus

---

[6]Of the Tuesday Conferences.

[7]Jean de Maupeou.

2741. - TO EDME JOLLY, SUPERIOR, IN ROME

Paris, December 6, 1658

Monsieur,

The grace of O[ur] L[ord] be with you forever!

I received your letter of November 5 too late to reply to it in detail. When we receive the description of the house of Messieurs Mattei, for which you lead me to hope, we will take our final decision regarding the purchase and will weigh the reasons you give me. Meanwhile, let us try to be ever more firmly grounded in the confidence that, no matter what our situation, provided it is God who has placed us in it, we will be well off, even though it may seem to us that we would be better otherwise. If we had to make a choice, in order not to be mistaken we should always take the one that is more closely related to the state of O[ur] L[ord] on earth, where He had no house at all.[1]

I agree with you that no further action should be taken regarding Saint-Sépulchre in Annecy, and please see that none is taken, no matter how M. Le Vazeux may insist on it. Please tell this to the banker's correspondent, whom he has put in charge of this business.

When we sent Brother Le Mercier to Italy, it was for Genoa and not for Rome because of the theology classes given there, and we wanted him to study there; but M. Berthe has had some reason since then to act differently. Please send him to study in Genoa, according to the original plan, and I will have someone from Genoa sent to you in his place.

I will have M. Doublard's[2] letter forwarded, and if money is brought to us for him, I will let you know when we have received it so you or he can draw it on us.

Letter 2741. - Archives of the Mission, Paris, original signed letter.

[1]Cf. Lk 9:58. (NAB)

[2]M. de la Bouverie-Doublard, a priest in Angers.

Enclosed is a letter from the Abbot of Chancelade,[3] who wanted me to recommend his affair to you again.[4] I do so now, even though I know you do not need to have it recommended to you.

I told you my opinion regarding the proposal from Spain; that was in my last letter.[5]

In all that I have just said, I think I have covered all the points of your letter.

I am, in O[ur] L[ord], Monsieur, your most humble servant.

VINCENT DEPAUL,
i.s.C.M.

If you send us the reply to the letter I am enclosing for some doctor or surgeon, please remind me to send it to Brother Jean Parre, who is still helping the people of the poor border areas of Champagne and Picardy.

Addressed: Monsieur Jolly

2742. - *SAINT LOUISE TO SAINT VINCENT*

Sunday [December 8, 1658] [1]

Most Honored Father,

I have not dared to express to Your Charity, in the name of the entire

---

[3]Father Jean Garat.

[4]The monks of Sainte-Geneviève were continuing their efforts in Rome to have united to their Order the houses that were dependent on Chancelade Abbey.

[5]The Bishop of Toledo, Balthazar Moscoso y Sandoval, had proposed that the Congregation of the Mission establish a house there. Saint Vincent gave his opinion on this to Edme Jolly in no. 2737.

Letter 2742. - Archives of the Motherhouse of the Daughters of Charity, original autograph letter.

[1]Brother Ducournau has indicated the month and the year on the back of the original. The contents show that Saint Louise was writing on the eve of a feast of the Blessed Virgin. This can only be December 8, eve of the Immaculate Conception; because it fell that year on a Sunday in Advent, the feast was transferred to Monday, December 9.

Company of our Sisters, how very happy we would consider ourselves if you were to place us under the protection of the Holy Virgin at the holy altar tomorrow. Nor have I dared to entreat Your Charity to obtain for us the grace of being forever able to acknowledge her as our only Mother, since, until now, her Son has never allowed anyone to attribute this title to her in a public act. I ask you for this authorization, for the love of God, and also the favor of doing for us what we should and will do, if Your Charity approves of this and instructs us how to do it.

On this feast two years ago, our little Sister Barbe [2] *took her final vows, after having made them for five consecutive years. She entreats Your Charity, Most Honored Father, to offer her renewal to God.*

Another Sister has asked Monsieur Portail for permission to make them for the first time. However, I do not know her well enough to be able to assure you that the good Father has granted her request. Her name is Jacquette.

Allow me to entreat you most humbly to offer to God the renewal made by all the other Sisters, even if they did not take their vows on this feast. I beg you also to pardon me for all the faults I have the audacity to commit against the respect I owe you and to do me the honor of believing that I am, Most Honored Father, your most humble and very obedient daughter and servant.

L. DE M.

Addressed: *Monsieur Vincent*

[2]Barbe Bailly, born near Vitry-le-François (Marne) on June 1, 1628, and baptized the same day, entered the Company of the Daughters of Charity on October 8, 1645, and took her vows on December 8, 1648. Her first mission was with the foundlings, whom she helped install in Bicêtre in July 1647. During the Fronde, the constant presence of soldiers there and the difficulty in finding food caused great concern, but Sister Barbe handled these problems with great wisdom and devotion. In 1649 she went to the Motherhouse, where she worked as infirmarian and as secretary to Saint Louise. After the Saint's death, Sister Barbe was sent to Poland (September 1660). Illness necessitated her return to Paris in 1668. She served the Company as Treasurer General (1671-74) and first Superior at the Invalides, where she helped design the infirmary wing. In 1685 she was sent to Alençon, where she reorganized the hospital. She died there on August 21, 1699.

2743. - TO DENIS LAUDIN, SUPERIOR, IN LE MANS

Paris, December 11, 1658

Monsieur,

The grace of O[ur] L[ord] be with you forever!

As you informed me previously, M. Molony has written us that he is very upset about his duty, to the point where he says that, if he is not relieved of the care of temporal affairs, he will go off to become a Carthusian, where he already has a place reserved. Therefore, Monsieur, I ask you to send him to help your workers who are out giving a mission. Do not put him in charge but let M. Cornaire [1] direct it. Just because he has been Assistant in the house, it does not follow that he has to be in charge elsewhere. If he refuses to go, you must not go either; you cannot leave the care of the family and business matters, where new problems arise daily requiring your presence. You can write to those priests, telling them to moderate their work, not take on more than they can handle, and that you cannot send them anyone just now. We, on our part, will try to send you someone as soon as possible.

Your most humble servant.

VINCENT DEPAUL,
i.s.C.M.

It is important that you say nothing to M. Molony of what I have written you about him.

Letter 2743. - Archives of the Mission, Paris, original signed letter. Pope Leo XIII had given the letter to the Archpriest of Bruges; it subsequently became the property of the Conference of Saint Vincent de Paul in that city before being returned to Paris. The postscript is in the Saint's handwriting.

[1]Guillaume Cornaire, born in the Besançon diocese on June 4, 1614, was ordained a priest during Lent of 1639. He entered the Congregation of the Mission on December 2, 1647, and took his vows in Le Mans on November 23, 1653, where he provided for the spiritual needs of the sick in the hospital. He died there, perhaps in 1660. Brother Chollier wrote his obituary, but it is no longer extant.

We must wait and see what will happen regarding the affair of the main hospital before asking M. de la Bataillère to make some arrangement with the Administrators.

At the bottom of the first page: Monsieur Laudin

2744. - TO PHILIPPE LE VACHER, IN MARSEILLES

Paris, December 13, 1658

Monsieur,

The grace of O[ur] L[ord] be with you forever!

I received your letters of November 26 and the third of this month. I am glad that Messieurs Napollon have given you payment for M. Simonnet's bill of exchange and that you sent Bernusset [1] the sum that was for him. I have had your letters sent to Mesdemoiselles de Chandenier and de Lamoignon, and we will keep the one for the Abbé[2] here until his return from Burgundy; he is there now but will be back soon.

I received M. Beaure's letter. Let him know that I am consoled that he arrived safely in Marseilles, where I embrace him in spirit. I cannot reply to him today because I have many other letters to write; I will do so as soon as possible, God willing. I ask M. . . .[3]

We are trying to retrieve the alms for the hospital [4] and have some hope of success, as I informed you. Madame Fouquet has taken responsibility for getting that business settled.

I heard that M. Brisjonc has arrived in Agde.

Letter 2744. - Archives of the Mission, Paris, copy made from the original in the Hains Family Collection, Marseilles.

[1]Vital Bernusset, a slave in Nauplia, a citadel in southern Greece, in the Peloponnesus, near the head of the Gulf of Argolis.

[2]Louis de Chandenier.

[3]The bottom of the original has been cut off in this place.

[4]The hospital for convicts in Marseilles.

You make no mention to me of Algiers or Tunis; is nothing being said about them in Marseilles? O my God, protect our poor confreres! Please send me news of them, Monsieur, if you have any. I recommend them often to the Company as one of its greatest needs—the one that worries me the most.

Everything is going along as usual here. Please pray for our ordinands and for me, who am, in O[ur] L[ord], Monsieur, your most humble servant.

VINCENT DEPAUL,
i.s.C.M.

Enclosed is a memo for a slave in Algiers, in case you have occasion to write to our dear Brother Barreau.

2745. - TO EDME JOLLY, SUPERIOR, IN ROME

Paris, December 13, 1658

Monsieur,

The grace of O[ur] L[ord] be with you forever!

I am replying to your letter of November 12. I await by the next regular mail the reply for the Bishop of Le Puy [1] for which you lead me to hope and the opinion of the Prelate you are supposed to consult regarding the official proclamation of the Bull for Saint-Méen. Meanwhile, I thank you for the information you give me on this matter, which we will utilize, and we will soon begin to work on the verification in the Parlement for that and the other matters.

I already asked you not to make any move for the union of Saint-Sépulchre; for, besides the fact that the Annecy house has no

---

Letter 2745. - Archives of the Mission, Paris, original signed letter.

[1]Henri de Maupas du Tour.

money to pay for the Bulls, the official announcement would encounter insurmountable difficulties, since the religious and the Bishop of Geneva[2] are against it. I say the Bishop of Geneva because the priests in that poor house are unanimous in saying there is no assurance of it in the arrangement that has been made but that, instead of inhibiting a lawsuit, it will be the source of several, which are inevitable, and the cause of its losing about twelve thousand livres. That is why Messieurs Coglée, Charles, and Deheaume[3] insist strongly on not ratifying the transaction, without which it can have no effect. They say that, even should they lose that lawsuit, they will gain much more than if the transaction were carried out, and they will have nothing more to fear.

I told them to explain these things to the Bishop and ask that he himself be the judge of them so that, if he is unwilling to do so, he will not disapprove of their having a definite decision issued. I do not know what he will do, but I foresee clearly that he will not be favorable to us, either in this matter or with regard to the above-mentioned union. That is why I think it will be well for you to do nothing further regarding it.

I received Cardinal Brancaccio's letter and great consolation at seeing that Brother Le Mercier's temptation has abated. I am not retracting my request that you send him to Genoa, but if he has not left, I ask you to delay his departure until the men in Genoa have informed you whether they will be able to send you someone to replace him.

---

[2]Charles-Auguste de Sales.

[3]Mark Cogley [Marc Coglée] was the Superior in Annecy.

François Charles, born in Plessala (Côtes-du-Nord) on December 10, 1611, entered the Congregation of the Mission on March 12, 1640, and was ordained a priest during Lent of 1641. He died on January 26, 1673, after serving at Saint-Lazare as director of retreatants and of the coadjutor Brothers. Edme Jolly, Superior General, greatly praised his virtue in the circular letter addressed to the whole Company to announce his death.

Pierre Deheaume, born in Sedan (Ardennes) on August 20, 1630, entered the Congregation of the Mission on October 8, 1646, took his vows in 1651, and was stationed in Turin and Annecy (1656). He was Superior in Marseilles (1662-65) and Toul (1667-69).

I am waiting for the plan of the house of Messieurs Mattei, with the conditions of the sale for the price and the guarantee. Then we will make a decision. Meanwhile, my own is to be, all my life, as I am now and will be far beyond it, in the love of O[ur] L[ord], Monsieur, your most humble servant.

VINCENT DEPAUL,
i.s.C.M.

Addressed: Monsieur Jolly, Superior of the Priests of the Mission, in Rome

2746. - TO JACQUES PESNELLE, SUPERIOR, IN GENOA

Paris, December 13, 1658

Monsieur,

The grace of O[ur] L[ord] be with you forever!

I just received your letter of November 23. I thank God for the sentiments He gives you regarding the virtue of humility; they must be very pleasing to O[ur] L[ord] since they are the fruits of His Precious Blood. Please ask Him for the spirit of penance for me that I may lament my wretched past life, and I will ask Him to continue and increase those sentiments He is giving you.

Since God has inspired you to suggest to the Cardinal [1] that he establish a conference for the priests in his city, go ahead. It will be a good idea, however, not to pressure him about this; for, if it were established, it would require a member of the Company having the grace, ability, and seriousness you have, who would always have to be in the house to preside over those meetings. That might be awkward if it prevented you from going to give missions;

Letter 2746. - Archives of the Mission, Paris, seventeenth- or eighteenth-century copy.

[1]Stefano Durazzo.

and if you did go, which of your men would be capable of taking the place of leader with those priests? And if you were always there, what would become of your missions? If His Eminence talks to you about a plan to begin them, you can tell him, if you like, that you will write to me about it to get my advice.

I ask O[ur] L[ord], Monsieur, to grant your little family the grace to profit from the visitation and to put its recommendations into practice. I am writing to M. Berthe in Genoa and in Turin at the same time. This is in case he is no longer with you. If he is, give him the enclosed; if he has left, you can open it and do what I am asking him to do.

I am, in O[ur] L[ord], Monsieur, your most humble servant.

VINCENT DEPAUL,
i.s.C.M.

2747. - TO JEAN MARTIN, SUPERIOR, IN TURIN

Paris, December 13, 1658

Monsieur,

The grace of O[ur] L[ord] be with you forever!

Since M. Berthe already arrived in Genoa some time ago, he will be arriving without delay in Turin, which is why I am sending you this letter for him. I received one from you written at the time you were leaving to give a mission. I think you will return from it soon enough for the visitation, and I hope God has blessed the one and will bless the other.

We have the ordinands here in the house, and the whole family is well.

Letter 2747. - Archives of the Mission, Turin, original signed letter.

That is all the news we have. I await yours and am, meanwhile, in the love of O[ur] L[ord], Monsieur, your most humble servant.

VINCENT DEPAUL,
i.s.C.M.

Addressed: Monsieur Martin

2748. - TO GUILLAUME DESDAMES, SUPERIOR, IN WARSAW

Paris, December 13, 1658

Monsieur,

The grace of O[ur] L[ord] be with you forever!

I received two or three letters from you, the last one dated November 7. I cannot tell you how grieved I am by the loss of M. Fleury,[1] both for the sake of the Queen, who doubtless was deeply affected by it, and for the sake of the Company, which has lost a good protector and benefactor. As for him, I consider him fortunate to be out of the miseries of this world, after the good life he led in it. We are praying and having prayers offered for him and will continue, God willing, to pay him these last respects in gratitude for the great kindness O[ur] L[ord] gave him for us and for the great good he did and procured for you.

In addition to the young men I told you we are sending you, you feel it is necessary for us to send at least one older man with them, capable of guiding them and of doing all our works. That is what we are going to do, but, after all, this is not the right season: the weather is too severe for such a long journey; we will wait until it is milder. Meanwhile, the situation there may become clearer,

---

Letter 2748. - Archives of the Mission, Krakow, original signed letter.

[1]François de Fleury, chaplain of the Queen of Poland, had died in France at the beginning of November.

which is much to be desired before undertaking anything. I am greatly consoled by the good dispositions God is giving people in that regard. We will continue to pray for peace in the kingdom and the preservation of Their Majesties.

The gain you say you should have in return from your land by spending a thousand écus on it is too great not to use that amount for this purpose. You estimate that it will bring you fifteen hundred livres income in addition to what you are now getting from it. I agree, then, if God gives you peace, to your borrowing that money and trying to save two-thirds of this revenue so you can pay it back gradually.

I ask O[ur] L[ord] to fill you with His grace in your direction of the Daughters of Charity, who are giving you so much trouble by their little dissension. Please do not send Sister Françoise[2] back, as you are planning to do. You will avoid the rumors that a return might cause, the dangers of the journey, the trouble of sending someone else there and, in short, many difficulties. Do as I asked you to do: separate them; put Sister Françoise to work in some hospital or at something else that obviates frequent communication with Sister Madeleine.[3]

I am really distressed by what you tell me about the death of two servants of the Sisters of Sainte-Marie,[4] for I fear the latter might catch the disease, God forbid! We are praying for them. Please assure them of this and of my humble service. I will send their letter to Lyons today. Thank God that their confessor is better and that God is keeping you, Monsieur, and M. Duperroy[5] in good health. I ask O[ur] L[ord] to see that it remains strong.

---

[2]Françoise Douelle.

[3]Madeleine Drugeon, daughter of a rich Parisian merchant, entered the Company of the Daughters of Charity in 1647. She arrived in Poland on September 7, 1652, and died there in February 1671.

[4]The Visitation nuns.

[5]Nicolas Duperroy.

Everything here is going along as usual, and I am, more than ever—if this were possible—in the love of O[ur] L[ord], Monsieur, your most humble servant.

VINCENT DEPAUL,
i.s.C.M.

Addressed: Monsieur Desdames, Superior of the Priests of the Mission, in Warsaw

2749. - TO MONSIEUR DE GAUMONT, ON THE ÎLE NOTRE-DAME

Saint-Lazare, December 15, 1658

Monsieur,

One of our Brothers had the honor yesterday of entreating you most humbly on our part to do us the kindness of coming here today to give us your advice on a matter of some importance to us. He told me that you can only come late in the day because some arbitrations will keep you busy almost the entire day. For this reason, Monsieur, I entreat you most humbly to postpone this honor for us to another day in the week that is more convenient for you because we are having some other persons come who are informed on the matter. Please do me the favor, Monsieur, of letting me know if you can do us that of coming here, and what day and hour you prefer. If I did not have a slight ailment preventing me from going out, I would have the honor of going to your office, Monsieur, to get your advice.

I ask Our Lord to preserve you for all the good you do for people and to make me worthy of serving you according to my obligation

---

Letter 2749. - Municipal Library of Orléans, original signed letter.

and the desire He gives me to do so. I am, in His love, Monsieur, your most humble and very obedient servant.

VINCENT DEPAUL,
i.s.C.M.

Addressed: Monsieur de Gaumont, Parlementary Lawyer, on the Île Notre-Dame

2749a. - TO MOTHER MARIE-AGNÈS LE ROY,[1] SUPERIOR OF THE VISITATION NUNS

Saint-Lazare, December 18, 1658

Dear Mother,

The grace of Our Lord be with you forever!

M. Bucher[2] came here yesterday morning. He spoke to me in the same terms in which he spoke to you, saying that he is willing to give you only fifteen thousand livres and wants a prompt decision; otherwise he is determined to withdraw his daughter. I

Letter 2749a. - Archives of the Visitation Monastery of Mons (Belgium), original signed letter. The text was published in *Annales C. M.* (1929), pp. 726-28, and reprinted in *Mission et Charité*, 19-20, no. 97, pp. 122-23. This edition uses the latter text.

[1]Superior of the Second Visitation Monastery of Paris (faubourg Saint-Jacques). Born in Mons (Belgium) in 1603, she was, through her mother, the niece of Philippe de Cospéan, Bishop of Lisieux. In 1624 she entered the First Monastery, which she left at the request of the Marquise de Dampierre to join the group of Sisters who were sent to the Monastery in the faubourg Saint-Jacques at the time of its foundation. She became Directress there and then Assistant. Three times the votes of the Sisters entrusted to her the office of Superior (June 11, 1634-May 24, 1640; May 27, 1646-May 13, 1652; and June 6, 1658 to 1664). She went to inaugurate the Amiens and Mons Monasteries, remaining at the latter for three months; she also founded that of Angers and the Third Monastery in Paris, and played a prominent role in the establishment of the Warsaw Monastery. Mother Le Roy died on May 18, 1669. (Cf. *Année sainte des religieuses de la Visitation Sainte-Marie* [12 vols., Annecy: Ch. Burdet, 1867-71], vol. V, p. 547.)

[2]The father of a young woman who had expressed the desire to enter the Visitation Monastery in the faubourg Saint-Jacques.

must admit that I was as surprised at this as you were, although I was a little suspicious beforehand of what he might do.

Consequently, dear Mother, I do not see how anything else can be expected of him, nor that he is disposed to a postponement. That is why it will be a good idea for you to seek the advice of your councillors[3] to find out what you have to do, and give him a definite answer, as he asks. I will say nothing to you regarding the amount you should request because I have never been willing to get involved in the dowry of Sisters. As for the person, however, I cannot conceal from you the fact that the father's frame of mind causes me to fear that of the daughter; so, be careful of that.[4]

I ask Our Lord to help you to know and follow His Will. Please let me know the decision you take so that, when M. Bucher comes to see me again, as he told me he wanted to do, I can act in line with it.

As for the Demoiselles de Bouillon,[5] I think it will be well for you to excuse yourself from receiving them. I am well aware that they are very fine young women and that it would be very advantageous to them to spend some time in your house to become better. I am also considering the circumstance you point out to me—that this retreat would safeguard them from the close contact and plans of their aunt, the wife of the Maréchal de Turenne,[6] who belongs to the so-called reformed religion.[7] But, since they want to come for only three months and are reserving to themselves the freedom of going out whenever they please, I think it will be less of an inconvenience just to thank them than to receive them for such a

---

[3]First redaction: "of your community." The correction is in the Saint's handwriting.

[4]After writing this last sentence, Saint Vincent crossed it out; it has been inserted here, nevertheless, since it reflects the thinking of the Saint.

[5]The daughters of Frédéric-Maurice de la Tour d'Auvergne, Duc de Bouillon: Louise, Émilie-Léonor, and, perhaps, Hippolyte.

[6]Charlotte de Caumont, wife of Henri de la Tour d'Auvergne (1611-75), Vicomte de Turenne, Maréchal de France. She died in 1666.

[7]This term was often used at the time to designate Protestantism. Bossuet eventually converted the Maréchal to Catholicism.

short period and under that condition of being able to come and go.

That, then, is my opinion. I am, in the love of O[ur] L[ord], dear Mother, your most humble servant.

VINCENT DEPAUL,
i.s.C.M.

Please do not mention my name when you reply to those young ladies.

I almost forgot to tell you that M. Bucher also told me that, even though he promised his daughter only fifteen thousand livres, he intends, however, not to stop at that; but he does not want to make any commitment. He has a house worth twenty thousand écus, and he told me he wanted to save half of it. Yesterday he told me that he also has a son, twenty-one years of age, who is in Lyons. The young man wants to enter the Oratorian Fathers and, this being the case, he could give his children an equal share of his property.

I am not sure if you should put any faith in the above.

He told me, furthermore, that, if his son does enter, his wife is determined to come to your house. Together with your councillors, weigh all that before God, dear Mother.[8]

Addressed: Superior of the Visitation Monastery, in the faubourg Saint-Jacques

2750. - TO EDME JOLLY, SUPERIOR, IN ROME

Paris, December 20, 1658

We would almost prefer not to have any Irish priests than to have them without being able to use them as we wish. Now,

---

[8]This paragraph is in the Saint's handwriting.

Letter 2750. - Reg. 2, p. 243.

obliging them to go and work in their own country is to deprive us of making their assignments; for, even though the Sacred Congregation may not send them, later on this is a source of temptation for them to get themselves sent or a pretext for becoming independent of the Company, after it has formed them well. That is why I ask you, Monsieur, to make an effort to obtain another dimissorial letter for Brother [Butler] [1] without the obligation of the mission to Ireland, or at least with the clause that he cannot go there unless he is sent by us.

2751. - TO JEAN PARRE, IN LAON

Paris, December 21, 1658

Dear Brother,

The grace of O[ur] L[ord] be with you forever!

I had your letter delivered to Mademoiselle Viole, and the one you wrote me was read at the meeting.[1] One of the Ladies there said she would send you by coach or by the Laon messenger three bolts of fabric to clothe the poor people of the villages of Picardy and Champagne. They also earmarked one hundred livres for you, which you will draw on Mademoiselle Viole and use for the most urgent needs. That is all for this time.

You may go to Saint-Quentin[2] whenever you think it advisable. May God be pleased to deliver you from the soldiers and preserve you in good health and in His grace!

---

[1]Peter Butler.

Letter 2751. - Archives of the Mission, Paris, original signed letter.

[1]A meeting of the Ladies of Charity of the Hôtel-Dieu, of which Mlle Viole was the treasurer.

[2]A town in Aisne.

I am, in His love, dear Brother, your most affectionate brother and servant.

VINCENT DEPAUL,
i.s.C.M.

Addressed: Brother Jean Parre, of the Mission, at the home of the Cantor, in Laon

2752. - TO MONSIEUR DESBORDES, COUNSELOR IN THE PARLEMENT

Saint-Lazare, December 21, 1658

Monsieur,

We sent M. Cousturier [1] our documents against M. Norais.[2] He tells me he has examined them closely and thinks we will have solid grounds for filing an appeal in the civil courts. He wants to plead our case himself and is looking forward to winning it.[3] He even goes further, Monsieur, and says that, if we lose, he will compensate us for the loss.

Our senior members, however, cannot bring themselves to take this legal action because:

(1) The lawyers we consulted before the decision that deprived us of Orsigny always assured us—as does M. Cousturier—that our

---

Letter 2752. - Archives of the Mission, Paris, signed rough draft.

[1]A lawyer at the Parlement.

[2]The son of Élisabeth and Jacques Norais, the King's secretary. They had given the Orsigny farm to Saint Vincent and the Congregation of the Mission; their son was now contesting this bequest.

[3]This was followed by: "and although he is fond of money, he will not accept any for this affair," which was crossed out.

right was infallible, especially M. Deffita[4] and M. Lhoste,[5] who examined it thoroughly.[6] The former did so because he was supposed to plead our case if we could not reach a settlement on it, and the latter because he had worked on our documents. Both of them told us we had nothing to fear; yet, the court dispossessed us of that farm, as if we had stolen it. So true is it that opinions vary, and too much store must never be put in the judgment of men.

(2) We were not judged according to the law nor according to custom but on a maxim of the Parlement, which deprives the Church of whatever property it can and prevents it from accepting family property. That is why, when it saw the large pension we were giving the late Monsieur and Mademoiselle Norais, it paid too much attention to a calumny of our opponent, who convinced them [7] that we were trying shrewdly to ensnare others with this bait. That is what caused us to lose our case, as several of the judges admitted. Now, since we would have to deal with the same judges in the civil court, they will judge us also by the same maxim.

(3) We would cause great scandal if, after such a solemn verdict, we were to go to law to have it overturned. We would be criticized with being too attached to possessions—which is the reproach being leveled against priests—and, by making a public spectacle of ourselves in the law courts, we would do harm to other Communities and cause our friends to be scandalized in our regard.

(4) Since the Marsollier brothers, heirs of the late Mademoiselle Norais, sold to M. Norais, our opponent, any right they might have to the farm, one of their cousins is trying to have that right restored and has begun proceedings for this. He is a man recently appointed

---

[4]A lawyer in the Paris Parlement.

[5]Jean-Marie Lhoste was administrator of a number of hospitals in Paris.

[6]Saint Vincent had also consulted Messrs. Ozannet, de Gaumont, Martinet, Pucelle, Billian, and Mussot, lawyers to the Parlement, who had given him the same opinion. M. de Saveuses, its court reporter, had no doubts about the justice of the cause. (Cf. Manuscript of Brother Louis Robineau, pp. 96-97, published in Dodin, *op. cit.*, p. 89.)

[7]First redaction: "who slipped into the lawsuit."

Counselor in the Parlement of Rouen and is very skilled at lawsuits, so we would have two strong adversaries[8] to combat.

(5) We have reason to hope, Monsieur, that, if we seek the kingdom of God, as the Gospel says,[9] we will lack nothing and, if the world takes something from us on the one hand, God will give us something on the other. We have even experienced this since the Grand'Chambre deprived us of that land, for God permitted that, when a Counselor of that same court died, he left us almost as much as that property is worth.

(6) Lastly, Monsieur, to speak plainly, I have a very hard time—as you can imagine—going against the counsel of O[ur] L[ord], who does not wish those who have promised to follow Him to go to law.[10] And if we have already done so, it is because I could not, in conscience, abandon a property so lawfully acquired—a Community property of which I was administrator—without doing my utmost to preserve it. However, now that God has relieved me of this obligation by a sovereign decree that makes all my efforts useless, I think we should leave things as they are, Monsieur, especially since, if we fail a second time, it would be a mark of disgrace on us, which might be harmful to the service and edification we owe the people.

I most humbly entreat you, Monsieur, you whose spirit is filled with Christian maxims, to ponder all these reasons and be pleased to write me your opinion on them. This will be one more obligation we will add to the many others we have toward you.

I am, meanwhile, in the love of O[ur] L[ord], Monsieur, your most humble and very obedient servant.

Since one of our practices during missions is to settle differences, it is to be feared that, if the Company were to persist obstinately in a new dispute by this request to the civil court of law,

---

[8]First redaction: "enemies."
[9]Cf. Mt 6:33. (NAB)
[10]Cf. Lk 12:58. (NAB)

which is the refuge of those persons who love lawsuits the most, God might deprive us of the grace of working at reconciliations.

2753. - TO A PRIEST OF THE MISSION OF SAINTES [1]

Paris, December 22, 1658

Monsieur,

The grace of O[ur] L[ord] be with you forever!

I learned of M. Rivet's illness from two of your letters. This caused me great sorrow, but it would have been even greater had you not assured me at the same time that the doctor said he was out of danger. I thank God for this, and I thank you also, Monsieur, for the great care you take of him. I do not ask you to continue because I know that the same charity that made you begin will make you use every possible remedy for his relief. All I ask is that you spare nothing for this and do not allow him to return to work until he is completely cured. So then, please tell him that I ask him to moderate his zeal inside and outside the house so he will not overdo it and injure his health. We will ask God to keep him well.

I thank His Divine Goodness also for having preserved Brother Marin[2] and for the good health of mind and body He gives you. You find fault with your own proficiency, thinking that you are incompetent; but God has enough for both you and Him. Have no doubt, Monsieur, that if you have good will—as you do by His

---

Letter 2753. - Archives of the Mission, Paris, original signed letter.

[1]In an earlier letter to Louis Rivet, Superior in Saintes (no. 2565), Saint Vincent refers to Louis Bréant as a member of that house. It is probable that this letter was addressed to him since it also mentions Antoine Fleury, another member of the house.

[2]Martin Baucher, born in Epône, in the Chartres diocese, entered the Congregation of the Mission as a coadjutor Brother in January 1653 and took his vows in Saintes on January 13, 1656, in the presence of M. Berthe. Coste refers to him as *Marin* Baucher, but in the catalogue of Coadjutor Brothers (1627-1786) he is listed as *Martin*.

grace—He will give you what you need to serve effectively the ecclesiastical state to which He has given you. Trust in His goodness.

Please tell M. Fleury that I was very consoled by his letter and that I thank O[ur] L[ord] for the good dispositions He gives him.

For lack of time, I am writing to you alone. I am having more trouble than usual with my leg, which prevents me from going downstairs and obliges me to remain seated at all times.

The rest of this family is very well, and I am, in the love of O[ur] L[ord], Monsieur, your most humble servant.

VINCENT DEPAUL,
i.s.C.M.

2754. - *SAINT LOUISE TO SAINT VINCENT*

December 22 [1658] [1]

Most Honored Father,

Fearing that the frost may return, I am taking the liberty of telling you that I think the pain in your leg will subside when you have been purged. Let me tell you about a method I was taught, which produces no upset. Take some senna, the weight of an écu, infused for about an hour in a pint of ordinary bouillon, the first from the pot, drawn when it is at a full boil. Drink it at the beginning of the meal, or eat some soup after taking this small dose, good and hot, by itself.

Repeated for two or three days, this will have the same effect as a strong purgative but will not leave you feeling washed out. If you find it does you some good, continuing it once or twice a week will bring some relief to those poor legs of yours. I almost forgot to mention that this does not interfere with taking bouillon in the morning or having dinner at the first table.

Letter 2754. - Archives of the Motherhouse of the Daughters of Charity, original autograph letter.

[1]Year added on the back of the original by Brother Ducournau.

I think it was Monsieur de Lorme or some other skilled doctor who taught me this secret, which he has been using for more than thirty years. We would be very happy to prepare it for you to try out and even happier to continue to do so if God blesses its use. I think that experience has shown that trying it can do no harm.

Forgive me, as Your Charity has done so many other [times], for taking this liberty. Believe me, Most Honored Father, to be your most humble daughter and very obedient servant.

L. DE MARILLAC

Addressed: *Monsieur Vincent*

2755. - TO SAINT LOUISE

[Between 1645 and 1660] [1]

I thank Mademoiselle Le Gras most humbly for the many and varied acts of charity she does for me, and I ask Our Lord to be her reward.

I have taken the two remedies she sent me. The one I took before dinner worked on me four times with each dose. Since it is taken with the meal, however, I think it was the consistency of what we ate—except for the last two times, when it produced just a small amount of some sort of liquid.

Her charity will judge from that what she thinks advisable for me to take tomorrow, and at what time. I will do so, God willing.

I was feverish last night and this morning. I have just taken the tea.

Letter 2755. - Archives of the Motherhouse of the Daughters of Charity, original autograph letter.

[1]There is no internal evidence by which to date this letter correctly. Marie de la Guiche de Saint-Gérand became the Duchesse de Ventadour by her marriage to Charles de Lévis, Duc de Ventadour, on February 8, 1645; Saint Louise died on March 15, 1660. From a letter of Saint Louise to the Daughters of Charity in Ussel (cf. *Spiritual Writings*, L. 598, p. 617), dated October 26, 1658, we know that the Duchesse de Ventadour had just come to Paris from her ancestral lands in Corrèze.

I am more annoyed with myself than I have been in a long time because I was unable to give Madame de Ventadour the satisfaction she was seeking from us. We are compelled to act that way; all our Bulls oblige us to do so, and we would be offending God by doing what they forbid us to do. God forgive me if I have done so for her at some other time!

I ask Our Lord to sanctify her dear self and to bless her retreat.[2] I entreat her to offer, at the birth of Our Lord, the pain I have caused her. I renew to her the offers of my perpetual obedience; she is my only Lady, since Divine Providence has made me her subject by my birth[3] and even more so by my affection.

Addressed: Mademoiselle Le Gras

2756. - TO LOUIS DUPONT, SUPERIOR, IN TRÉGUIER

Paris, Christmas Day, 1658

Monsieur,

The grace of O[ur] L[ord] be with you forever!

I was deeply grieved to hear of the Bishop of Tréguier's [1] illness, and I shall be extremely anxious about him until you send me word that he is better. I have prayed and have had others pray for this, and we will continue to ask God for his preservation and complete recovery. Please send me news of him as soon as possible.

---

[2]The Duchesse de Ventadour was making her retreat at the home of Mademoiselle Le Gras.

[3]This part of the sentence would be sufficient to allay any doubt concerning Saint Vincent's place of birth, were it necessary. The Barony of Pouy, the village where the Saint was born, became the property of the Ducs de Ventadour through the marriage of Charles de Lévis to his first wife, Catherine-Suzanne de Lauzières, the daughter of Suzanne de Monluc and Antoine, Marquis de Thémines.

Letter 2756. - Archives of the Mission, Paris, original signed letter.

[1]Balthazar Grangier de Liverdi.

It is true that we have been a little tardy in sending you the priest you need, but this delay was against my will, for I really hoped to send you some relief and to give the Bishop this satisfaction. The various occupations that turned up unexpectedly for us, and the men we have had to send here and there—I mean the places for which we were strictly obliged, especially in Italy, where M. Berthe took eight or nine of them—have prevented us from meeting every need. Now that the ordination is over, we are going to prepare someone for you who will leave soon after these feast days.

I hope you will lose nothing for having waited so long. May God be pleased to strengthen you in the meantime! I am deeply consoled that He has blessed your leadership and the retreat exercises of those priests in the seminary, along with your own.

I am not sure if I asked you to send Brother Plunket's dimissorial letter to him in Saint-Méen and, in the event that it may be lost, to find out if the Bishop will agree to conferring on him the remaining Orders, since the former has already seen the dimissorial. If I had forgotten this, I ask you by the present letter to take care of it.

I am, in O[ur] L[ord], Monsieur, your most humble servant.

VINCENT DEPAUL,
i.s.C.M.

Addressed: Monsieur Dupont, Superior of the Priests of the Mission, in Tréguier

2757. - TO EDMUND BARRY, SUPERIOR OF THE PRIESTS OF THE MISSION, IN LORM

Paris, Christmas Day, 1658

Monsieur,

The grace of O[ur] L[ord] be with you forever!

Your letter of December 7 was a great consolation to me; it was even greater when I saw the various results of your fine leadership, which seems to me very wise and well received. I thank God who is using you for the various good works He accomplishes both inside and outside your house. I ask His Divine Goodness to continue and to increase in you the courage to bear the responsibility His Providence has laid on you.

I praise God for the arrangement that was supposed to be made with the priests of Castelferrus, and I pray that a settlement may result from it.[1]

I was informed that the Bishop of Montauban[2] would like to have some assurance about the two thousand livres that were previously offered to help with setting up the seminary in Montauban. On this I will tell you, Monsieur, that the person who mentioned doing this act of charity is still disposed to donate this sum but first wants to see the seminary transferred and the conditions settled. Make use of this information with your usual prudence. It is to be desired that the Bishop establish you in his town as soon as possible or that he confirm you in Lorm.

M. Bajoue is still out giving a mission; when he returns, I will see that he is given the power of attorney authorizing you to receive the capital and arrears of his income.

I tell you once again, Monsieur, that I cannot think of you

Letter 2757. - Archives of the Mission, Paris, original signed letter.

[1]There was some rivalry between the Priests of the Mission, who were the Directors of the shrine of Lorm, in the commune of Castelferrus, and the lord and the clergy of the locality.

[2]Pierre de Bertier.

without a deep sentiment of joy and tenderness, especially with regard to the good state of your family in general and of the present disposition of M. Lucas[3] in particular, which consoles and edifies the others. I am sure you have contributed to this happy change in him, even though you attribute it to his retreat.

It is true that this practice of the retreat, which God has given to the Company, is one of the most effective remedies we have for picking ourselves up again and moving forward, and I hear from elsewhere, especially from La Rose, that many other members of the Company have profited more from it this year than in others. I hope that, if we are faithful to God, His blessings will be multiplied for everyone in general and each one in particular.

Continue, Monsieur, to govern wisely, gently, and humbly, and you will see the glory of God. I am, in Him, Monsieur, your most humble servant.

VINCENT DEPAUL,
i.s.C.M.

Addressed: Monsieur Barry, Superior of the Priests of the Mission, in Lorm

2758. - TO EDME MENESTRIER, SUPERIOR, IN AGEN

Paris, Christmas Day, 1658

Monsieur,

The grace of O[ur] L[ord] be with you forever!

I have not written to you for a long time nor have I received any letters from you. I heard that the Daughters of Charity arrived in

---

[3]Jacques Lucas.

Letter 2758. - Archives of the Mission, Paris, original signed letter.

Cahors but have heard nothing so far about Brother Didolet's arrival in Agen, even though theirs gives me reason to believe he has arrived. How are you, Monsieur, and how is your little family?

You informed me that you see almost no women or nuns. That is a good thing. The more we avoid associating with them the better it will be for us.

You do well to consult M. Le Cat for your business affairs, provided it does not inconvenience him; and, if this is not satisfactory, write from time to time to the Bishop about them.

I do not disapprove of your giving part of what is due you to get the other part; that is the right way to do things today.

I ask Our Lord to be your spirit and your guide. I am, in His love, Monsieur, your most humble servant.

VINCENT DEPAUL,
i.s.C.M.

At the bottom of the first page: Monsieur Edme

2759. - *SAINT LOUISE TO SAINT VINCENT*

[December 1658] [1]

I most humbly ask your pardon, Most Honored Father; our remedy was ready at ten o'clock, and I completely forgot about it at ten-thirty. I consoled myself by the fact that, if Your Charity forgives me, we will start again tomorrow. If the preceding remedies helped you by drawing off the heavy fluids, then, if you think it advisable, the dose could be increased and taken tomorrow morning to finish drawing off the fluids. Use for this either twenty-four grains of cornachin powder or the weight of two écus

---

Letter 2759. - Archives of the Motherhouse of the Daughters of Charity, original autograph letter.

[1]Date added on the back of the original by Brother Ducournau. The table of contents has December 25 [1658]; *Spiritual Writings,* (cf. L. 604, pp. 623-24) has December 25, 1658.

of senna, a few crystals, and some rhubarb in an infusion of our good peach blossom syrup. I think this would do you good, Most Honored Father, and would help us have the honor once again of seeing you soon.

I hope that you in your goodness will give me a reply about this and will also help me so that my indifference to my interior state and everything pertaining to the service of God and my salvation will not lead to my condemnation. I flatter myself in the erroneous belief that God is willing to put up with everything from me—even my careless life—in what concerns my personal conduct. This leads me to fear, Most Honored Father, that I am, in name only, your most humble daughter and very obedient servant.

L. DE MARILLAC

Addressed: *Monsieur Vincent*

2760. - TO EDME JOLLY, SUPERIOR, IN ROME

Paris, December 27, 1658

Monsieur,

The grace of O[ur] L[ord] be with you forever!

I just received your letter of November 26 and the one from M. du Loeus, together with the copy of what he wrote to the Cardinal-Archbishop of Toledo.[1] I think it leaves nothing to be desired but rather that the contents and style of his letter show great wisdom and discretion. God be praised, Monsieur, for the benevolence with which this good Doctor honors us and for the evidence he gives us of it on this occasion! I will take the honor of writing to thank him as soon as possible, if I cannot do so today, as I fear. Meanwhile, you can thank him a thousand times on our part for all his acts of kindness and assure him of our entire gratitude.

Letter 2760. - Archives of the Mission, Paris, original signed letter.

[1]Balthazar Moscoso y Sandoval (1646-65).

What you tell me about Brother Le Mercier makes me feel very sorry for him. He is a young man who is basically a good soul, the son of a father who was a very fine man with keen intelligence, which the son does not lack. When he was here, however, I noticed that he was becoming attached from time to time first to some little thing,[2] then to another, but this had no bad results, thank God. He is a very good soul.[3] Be that as it may, he now has become extraordinarily obstinate about studying, to the point of wanting to interrupt and leave everything if his request is not granted.

What shall we do about that? As for me, I find it very difficult. I thought he would be satisfied with studying moral and scholastic theology, which is why I asked you to send him to Genoa. Since then, however, he has thought of nothing but wanting to study philosophy again. That is what troubles me because it is not being taught in Genoa this year, and the class here has already begun. Given these difficulties, I think that, if you have not already sent him to Genoa, it will be well to keep him in Rome until next year, when we will have him go to Genoa or bring him here to begin philosophy at the same time as the others. Meanwhile, he can be useful to you, even if he did nothing else than follow the seminary exercises with the new seminarian you have received, who might be bored at being alone.

If he is unwilling to wait, there is nothing we can do. It would be wrong for us to give in to his obsession, which has all the signs of a diabolical temptation, and I am amazed that he does not see this himself. Desires that come from God are gentle and leave the soul at peace; whereas inspirations of the evil spirit are, on the contrary, harsh and troubling to the person who has them. Now, since his determination to study is turbulent and accompanied by the anxious fear of a refusal, he can conclude that this unsettled state can come only from the devil, who is the author of disorder.

---

[2]First redaction: "to one thing." The correction is in the Saint's handwriting.

[3]This sentence is in the Saint's handwriting.

Furthermore, if he wants to be a Missionary, he must consider himself a member of the Company and, as such, allow himself to be guided. It is up to the Company to assign individual members either to studying or to the works, at the time and in the manner it deems appropriate; otherwise, if each man were at liberty to choose whatever he likes, it would no longer be a body composed of parts which constitute that beautiful harmony of well-regulated Communities, but rather a division of persons following their own inclinations. It is better to remain in the world to do that than to introduce, by this liberty, worldly maxims into a Company that has withdrawn from it and in which subordination is established.

So, that cleric's lack of submission can only come from the spirit of hell, which is a rebellious spirit and which, seeing him on the right path to render service to God and His Church, is doing its utmost to withdraw him from it. O my God, do not allow it to triumph over that poor Brother!

If he is still with you, Monsieur, please point out to him the wiles of the enemy and the malignity of his temptation so that, by allowing himself to be guided by the Spirit and example of O[ur] L[ord], he may fulfill God's plans for him. I ask this of His Divine Goodness.

I fully approve of your way of acting with regard to the new work God is offering you.[4] I also approve of the fact that, while assuring the Secretary of the Congregation of Propaganda Fide[5] of your entire, perfect attachment to following the orders and intentions of the Pope, with regard to the place and manner of serving these priests, you nevertheless pointed out to him the things to be done in order to direct and instruct them more effectively. After that, you must remain at peace and believe that, no matter how the affair turns out, the work will go well and God will bless those you assign to it. I have written to tell M. Berthe to go to Rome for that

---

[4]Probably the ordination retreats.

[5]Marius Alberici.

purpose. Meanwhile, the choice of M. d'Eu and Brother Le Gouz seems very good to me.

If God is not pleased to see that the proposal about the seminary is accepted, *in nomine Domini,* that is a sign that Our Lord has not willed it. If His Holiness absolutely wants it, we must obey; and if such is the case, write to M. Berthe about it in Turin, where I am writing to him, even though he is leaving for Rome, unless you send him word to the contrary.[6]

Your most humble servant.

VINCENT DEPAUL,
i.s.C.M.

Addressed: Monsieur Jolly, Superior of the Priests of the Mission of Rome, in Rome

2761. - TO SAINT LOUISE

[December 1658] [1]

I am better, thanks to the remedies of Mademoiselle Le Gras. I thank her most humbly for them. The only problem is that the tea acts as a stimulant on me and prevents me from sleeping.

I am very sorry about the state she[2] is in, which is such, they write, that it seems inadvisable to send a Sister there, nor even a priest (that is how I would act if there were question of a priest from here), because either Our Lord has taken her to Himself or, if she

---

[6]This paragraph is in the Saint's handwriting.

Letter 2761. - Archives of the Motherhouse of the Daughters of Charity, original autograph letter.

[1]Reference to the failing health of Sister Barbe Angiboust prompts us to assign this date to this letter.

[2]Barbe Angiboust, Sister Servant in Châteaudun.

is still alive, she will probably get better. It will be well to write tomorrow morning, by the Châteaudun coach, to ask the Sister who is with her[3] for news about her. Then we will see what it will be well to do. Meanwhile, let us honor the Blessed Virgin's acquiescence in God's good pleasure regarding the death of her Son.[4]

2762. - TO FIRMIN GET, SUPERIOR, IN MARSEILLES

Paris, December 27, 1658

Monsieur,

The grace of O[ur] L[ord] be with you forever!

May God be glorified for the results of your mission and for your safe return! If the troubles persist, it will be well for you not to go far away.

I am glad that the Turks from Tunis are in your hospital, awaiting the order and opportunity to be sent back. This will then give you the means of writing to our dear confreres in Barbary and perhaps to give them some help. See if that can be done safely. I think you are right in saying that sending things by the Spanish Mercedarian Fathers is very uncertain.

In my last letter to M. Le Vacher,[1] I included a note from

---

[3]Anne Bocheron, who entered the Company of the Daughters of Charity in 1654. She is mentioned in a letter of Saint Louise in 1657 as being in Châteaudun (cf. *Spiritual Writings*, L. 544, p. 568). Perhaps she was one of the Sisters from there who were in Paris in November 1659 and gave testimony to the virtues of Sister Barbe during a conference of Saint Vincent (cf. vol. X, no. 114).

[4]Barbe died on December 27, 1658. "Those who had seen her during her illness," relates Saint Louise (cf. *Spiritual Writings*, L. 634, p. 654), "confessed that they could not believe they were looking at the same person after her death; and the people, who came for two days in such numbers that the doors had to be closed, declared that she was so beautiful that she must have been wearing make-up."

Letter 2762. - Archives of the Mission, Paris, copy made from the original in the Hains Family Collection. This is one of the letters sold at auction by Xavier Charmoy (cf. no. 2505).

[1]Philippe Le Vacher.

Madame Fouquet stating that the Administrators of the hospital for the captives may take two thousand livres to continue assistance to the patients, and they should draw a bill of exchange on M. Bruand[2] who is with the Attorney General. I will send the letter from the Administrators to the Duc de Richelieu for the new election.

We do not yet have the results of the consultation from the Sorbonne on the case you sent us. I will have someone request them at the first opportunity.

I have nothing to tell M. Le Vacher, except that I received his letter.

I am glad M. Huguier has returned to Toulon and M. Parisy to Marseilles.

I am writing to you in haste because I received your packet just at the time my letters had to be sent to the post.

I am, in O[ur] L[ord], Monsieur, your most humble servant.

VINCENT DEPAUL,
i.s.C.M.

2763. - TO JACQUES PESNELLE, SUPERIOR, IN GENOA

Paris, December 27, 1658

Monsieur,

The grace of O[ur] L[ord] be with you forever!

I just received your letter of December 9; it was written from Ceranesi, where I ask O[ur] L[ord] to bless your work, and through it, the poor people. Since your acknowledgment of the need for the Divine Assistance is a motive for humbling yourself, it will also

---

[2]Clerk for Nicolas Fouquet, the Attorney General.

Letter 2763. - Archives of the Mission, Paris, original signed letter.

serve as a request to obtain from God the grace you need, especially if you accompany it with great confidence in His goodness.

It is the custom here that all official documents drawn up on behalf of the Community be done in the name of the Superior and not of the procurator. In line with that, any documents you sign before a notary must be signed by you—and not by your procurator—or by the entire assembled family for contracts involving important affairs concerning the Community; but, for receipts and farm leases, the S[uperior] is the one who does it.[1]

We should want all our disputes to terminate by mutual agreement rather than by lawsuits. That is why I am glad you are signing a compromise with the relative of the late M. de Monchia to settle by arbitration the inheritance question, especially since this is the opinion of the Cardinal.[2]

I want to believe that M. Berthe is now in Turin or is on the verge of leaving for there. He will find a letter there in which I have asked him to go to Rome. I have sent you a similar one in which you will see the reason for this order.

I am hurrying because it is night. I am, in the love of O[ur] L[ord], Monsieur, your most humble servant.

VINCENT DEPAUL,
i.s.C.M.

Addressed: Monsieur Pesnelle, Superior of the Priests of the Mission of Genoa, in Genoa

---

[1]The words from "for contracts involving important affairs" are in the Saint's handwriting.
[2]Stefano Durazzo.

2764. - TO DENIS LAUDIN, SUPERIOR, IN LE MANS

Paris, December 28, 1658

Monsieur,

The grace of O[ur] L[ord] be with you forever!

I received your letters of the eighth and the eleventh of this month. When you wrote the last one, I think you had already received mine, in which I asked you to send M. Molony to give a mission.[1] However, you make no mention of receiving it and have not told me since then whether M. Molony went to give the mission. It is true that you said something about it to Brother Robineau. Please acknowledge my letters so I will not be anxious about them.

If M. Molony seems different to you when he gets back—more content, submissive, and regular—please let me know, as well as whatever satisfaction he will have given his confreres; then we will see. But if, on the contrary, you find him as ill disposed as he was before, I think you will do well to speak to him about the valise he sent away; but do so respectfully and gently. Say to him, for example, "Monsieur, do you mind if I say something to you?" and tell him what you know about that business. Then ask him to tell you what was in it and where the books and other things he put in it came from. This is to see what he will reply and, in a word, to persuade him graciously to give everything back.

We will try to send you some help as soon as we can.

I consent to your having someone demolish the shed that is falling down, provided that has no serious consequences and you are being advised to do so.

We will see the young gentleman who wants to go to Genoa.

Letter 2764. - Archives of the Mission, Paris, original signed letter.

[1]Cf. no. 2743.

May God grant us the grace to finish this year well and to begin and continue the next one in a holy way.

I am, in His love, Monsieur, your most humble servant.

VINCENT DEPAUL,
i.s.C.M.

My advice is that, no matter what state M. Molony is in when he returns from the mission, it will be a good idea for you to speak to him in the way I told you.

At the bottom of the first page: Monsieur Laudin

2765. - TO PIERRE CABEL, SUPERIOR, IN SEDAN

Paris, December 28, 1658

Monsieur,

The grace of O[ur] L[ord] be with you forever!

The distribution being made of some pamphlets dealing with the opinions of the day [1] and my knowledge that some of them have been brought into one of our houses oblige me to warn you that, if any are brought to your house, neither you nor any other of your men should allow them in because reading these articles serves little purpose. They may even be very harmful, especially to persons in the Community who may discuss them with others and say what they think about them. Since everyone has his own interpretation, differences of opinion arise, leading to disputes and divisions.

Letter 2765. - Archives of the Mission, Paris, copy of the period.

[1]The rest of the letter shows that the propositions of the Jansenists, already condemned by Rome, were not involved here; it was a question of liberal opinions.

We must know and be firmly grounded in matters of faith but should leave those scholarly questions alone. O[ur] L[ord] did not want the Apostles to argue with the Scribes and Pharisees because of the leaven of their teachings,[2] which might have given them the wrong impression; and Saint Peter forbids the first Christians to argue over the Scriptures because, as he said, there are obscure, difficult things in them,[3] even in the Epistles of Saint Paul.

This being the case, we have much greater reason to avoid discussing those useless matters. By the grace of God, we do not talk about them here in this house because we have a thousand fine topics of conversation that are more edifying and more appropriate. We must, however, respect the diverse inspirations of those who stir up those questions, but we should not declare ourselves on one side or the other. Everyone has his reasons, and God allows them to have differing ones, as He did with Saints Peter and Paul,[4] Saints Paul and Barnabas,[5] and also among the angels,[6] when He revealed certain things to some differently than He did to others. That is why, Monsieur, I ask you once again not to allow any of those leaflets into your house, or any of those propositions to be put forward that can serve only to sow discord among the confreres and disedify persons outside the Company. The latter would criticize our curiosity and prattling if they saw us reading and discussing those scurrilous writings and novelties—and even more so if they saw us taking sides.

I told you already[7] that, if M. Daisne takes possession of his lapsed benefice, he is detaching himself at the same time from the Company because we cannot tolerate among us anyone who aspires to benefices—and even less those who want to gain posses-

---

[2]Cf. Lk 12:1. (NAB)
[3]Cf. 2 Pt 3:15-16. (NAB)
[4]Cf. Gal 2:11-14. (NAB)
[5]Cf. Acts 15:36-40. (NAB)
[6]Cf. Rv 12:17. (NAB)
[7]Cf. no. 2732.

sion of them in that way, which is odious. So, Monsieur, ask him to leave, and give him something rather than permit him to eat and sleep in your house, after that action, which is bound to put him in conflict with his competitor and would do the same in your family, if he were one of its members. We will send you another priest in his place as soon as possible.

We have not been able to get the results of the consultation concerning your tithes, although we have given three écus for it. I will send someone after it again.

There is no way of putting at the Incurables[8] the converted woman of whom you wrote me because all the places in that hospital are taken, and a large number of patients are waiting for the first vacancy.

There would be no major inconvenience if the administrators of your church were to assemble in your rectory only on Sundays and holydays, when the students are away. Nevertheless, because of the conclusion they might draw from this that they could meet there any time, it will be a good idea for you to dissuade them from doing so altogether, as tactfully as you can.

It is the distinctive duty of priests to procure mercy and to be merciful to criminals, so you must not always refuse to help those who seek your intervention, especially when there is more misfortune than malice in their crime. There is a letter in Saint Augustine on this topic (I forget which one it is), which points out that to free sinners and prisoners by way of intervention and leniency is not promoting or condoning vice; it also points out that it is part of the propriety and charity of priests to plead for them. Therefore, you may do so whenever you see that the case merits it, and you can prepare the minds of the judges by telling them that it is not your intention to defend crime but rather to practice mercy, by seeking it for the guilty and demanding it for the innocent, according to the obligation of your state.

---

[8]The Hospital for Incurables in Paris, known today as Laënnec Hospital.

It is the function of the Visitor to restore the practice of interior communications. We will soon send you one, God willing. You can tell him that your family has grown lax in this practice, so he can find a remedy for this.

Do not refrain from visiting the school just because the teacher does not like this or you fear that the students may think less of him. The Superiors of the Jesuits disregard these reasons because they have stronger ones for keeping abreast of what is going on in the classes.

As I was finishing this letter, I opened yours of December 23. We will try to pay your bill of exchange.

I am sending your packet to Annecy and will have prayers offered for the restoration of your health and that of those priests you mention who are ill.

You tell me that you gave M. Daisne a testimonial of his morals and ability so he can get his certification in Reims for the lapsed benefice in question. In so doing, you were too hasty; you should have written to me about it beforehand. And that gives me reason to ask you to do nothing from now on, in extraordinary matters that arise, without getting my opinion on them, especially when they are of some importance, as that one is. It has far greater consequences than I can tell you; for, if the Company has been publicly criticized in some dioceses for having had some persons who have taken parishes from the Prelates—to the extent of its being reproached during missions for going there only to be on the lookout to skim off all the good benefices—what will they not say if they see that there are others who not only take the parishes the Bishops give them but, in addition, take lapsed benefices with the authorization of their Superiors? I must admit that this distresses me greatly.

When I say you should give something to M. Daisne, I mean only once.

2766. - *SAINT LOUISE TO SAINT VINCENT*

Most Honored Father,

I praise God with all my heart that Your Charity foresees the expression of our needs, and I thank you most humbly for this. My heart is so reassured by it that, without it, I would find it very difficult to endure such a long deprivation. Reflect a little, Most Honored Father, on what means I might take so as not to go astray or be lost, living as I am without making known to you my state and without any advice or communication.

Permit me to ask if your leg is any better and if we can hope that it will soon be cured.

The last hours of the year are upon us. I throw myself at your feet to entreat Your Charity to obtain mercy for me, since I await only the one when God will call me to render an account to Him. It is for that moment alone that I implore Your Charity because my constant infidelities and lack of mortification cause me to offend Our Lord so often.

I think something still remains to be done for the spiritual strengthening of the Company. If Your Charity would allow me to send you a report on this, I would do so even if I should have to blush for shame because of it.

All our Sisters anxiously await the honor of seeing you. Offer us to God in the way He wishes, and do me the honor of believing, Most Honored Father, that I am your most humble and very obedient daughter and servant.

LOUISE DE MARILLAC

My ailment prevented me from finishing this letter yesterday, and I am beginning the year with great weakness and suffering of mind and body. I ask the blessing of Your Charity for this and for all my needs, as well as for the entire Company.

I had asked Monsieur Portail to ask Your Charity, for the love of God, to have a High Mass celebrated in your church for our deceased Sister Barbe,[1] since she was one of the oldest members of the Company and was very faithful to her vocation. All our Sisters would be assembled for it; I think it would be a great consolation for them and an encouragement to do good.

Letter 2766. - Archives of the Motherhouse of the Daughters of Charity, original autograph letter.

[1]Barbe Angiboust, who had died on December 27, 1658, in Châteaudun.

Enclosed are our holy pictures and maxims for the year. I am sending them to Your Charity so that, if you agree, we can distribute them as usual on your behalf, after you have blessed them to obtain for us the grace of using them well.

First day of the year 1659

Addressed: *Monsieur Vincent*

2767. - TO SISTER AVOIE VIGNERON, IN USSEL

January 4, 1659

Dear Sister,

The grace of Our Lord be with you forever!

My letter to Sister Anne [1] will serve as a reply to the one you wrote to Mademoiselle.[2] You go a little too far in the things you tell us, and you have sometimes failed in the respect you owe to Mademoiselle. I am well aware that your heart is not lacking in the latter, but you spoke too freely in justifying yourself for some slight reproach she made to you.

Mon Dieu! Sister, if you have no reverence and submission for your Superior, for whom will you have them? She is not complaining about this, but I have to tell you about it so that you will act with her as with your good mother, who esteems and cherishes you. Write to her when you have occasion to do so, but humbly and cordially, as becomes a Daughter of Charity. Observe confidentiality with everyone other than her or me concerning what you have to say about your Sister, your duties, or your trials. Rest assured

---

Letter 2767. - Archives of the Motherhouse of the Daughters of Charity, register entitled: *Recueil de pièces relatives aux Filles de la Charité*, Ms, p. 30.

[1]Anne Hardemont (cf. no. 2768).

[2]Saint Louise.

that, instead of finding elsewhere the remedy or the consolation you seek, you will only make matters worse because you will be acting contrary to the order established by God, who wills that in difficulties which may arise you have recourse to your Superiors. It is also to be hoped, Sister, that you will live on good terms with Sister Anne, act only on her advice, and do nothing against her wishes.

I ask Our Lord to give you a share of His own humility and love.

2768. - TO SISTER ANNE HARDEMONT, SUPERIOR, IN USSEL

January 4, 1659

Dear Sister,

The grace of O[ur] L[ord] be with you forever!

I received two letters from you which have distressed me deeply and with good reason, seeing how you are behaving there. Who, indeed, would not be distressed at seeing a Daughter of Charity—one of the oldest in the Company—brought to Limousin by Divine Providence to do the works of mercy, no sooner arrive on the spot than she wants to return out of sheer caprice and constantly complains of being left there, although she has no difficulties to endure other than the ones she makes for herself?

True, if these complaints did not go outside the Company, there would be no great harm in that; but everyone knows of them; people have written to the Duchess [1] about them, and you yourself tell me of another person who is aware of them. With all that, there is no reason to doubt that the entire province knows of them.

Letter 2768. - Reg. 1, fol. 22v.

[1]The Duchesse de Ventadour.

Now, I ask you to consider the scandal you are giving and the insult which O[ur] L[ord], who has called you to His service, receives from it. Look at the harm you are doing to the Duchess, who brought you to her estates for the relief of the poor and the edification of her subjects. Must she not find your behavior strange and so contrary to her intentions? Must she not be surprised to see your anxiety, to hear your murmurings, and to know that you are not acting in conformity with your vocation? You are doing more harm to the Company in this than any good you have ever done for it. In addition, you are doing great harm to yourself by giving in to nature. Once it has the upper hand you will have a harder time overcoming it in order to live according to the spirit and to do God's Will—which is, however, what we must do to save ourselves. Otherwise, "if you live by the flesh," as Saint Paul says, "you will die."[2]

"But, Monsieur," you will say to me, "I told you from the beginning that I could not last in this region; I dislike it too much." My reply to that, Sister, is that no one likes being in a strange place; yet, they go there and they stay. How many young women who have married far away are unhappy with their homes and their husbands as well! But they do not return to their parents' house because of that. They have to mortify their preference. Do you think that the nuns and the many other girls and women who have gone to Canada[3] really enjoy being in that place? On the contrary, they have a strong aversion to it—and rightly so—still, they remain because God has called them there.

You will tell me also that you do not have enough to do. My

---

[2]Cf. Rom 8:13. (NAB)

[3]When Saint Vincent was writing this letter, Mademoiselle Mance and Sister Marguerite Bourgeois had returned to France from Canada and were trying to find volunteers to go to that distant country to work for the education of children or in health care. (Cf. Étienne-Michel Faillon, *Histoire de la colonie française en Canada* [3 vols., Villemarie: Bibl. parois., 1865-66], vol. II, pp. 306-13.)

reply is that, if you are humble in a few things, God will set you over many.[4] Do well the little you have to do, and rest assured that work will not be lacking to you. Besides, since you are not strong, too much work might overwhelm you, and you would have greater reason to complain about that than you would about having too little to do, which gives you time to think about yourself. Furthermore, you should not always stay in your room, but take turns with your Sister—or go with her—visiting and serving the poor. That is one way of not getting bored.

If you reply that you do not get along well with your Sister, I will tell you that this is a great evil which must be remedied, not by avoiding her—since that would be pleasing the devil who does everything he can to separate you—but by being united by mutual affection. Love one another as sisters; esteem and respect one another as daughters of O[ur] L[ord] made in the image of God; bear with one another's little weaknesses as you would wish to be borne with; lastly, comply graciously with one another's wishes and never argue. Sister Avoie[5] should, above all, take your advice, since you are in charge; but you, for your part, should be humble, gentle, and wise in your leadership.

In the name of God, Sister, be patient; try to enter into the sentiments of this letter, and make up your mind never to do your own will; otherwise, you will fall into the misfortune of souls who are being lost because they do not submit themselves to the persons God has established to direct them in the ways of their salvation. And with regard to this, you must never lose the confidence you should have in Mademoiselle. She is your mother, who has the right to give you the instructions she thinks advisable, and she has received graces from God to do so. Yet, you are so displeased by this that you say you no longer wish to write to her. Beware, Sister. That is the resolution of a rebellious, proud spirit, capable of

---

[4]Cf. Mt 25:23. (NAB)
[5]Avoie Vigneron.

depriving you of the graces of God, who gives them only to the humble and peace-loving. I ask His Divine Goodness to include you in that number.

I am, in His love, Sister, your very affectionate brother and servant.

VINCENT DEPAUL,
i.s.C.M.

2769. - TO LOUIS RIVET, SUPERIOR, IN SAINTES

January 5, 1659

You speak of returning on mission, but I ask you not to be in such a rush; wait until you have fully recovered, and then moderate your efforts for the love of Our Lord. It is better to have some strength left over than not to have any at all, and God will bless your work—even if it seems little to you—if you avoid overwork in order to serve Him better. True, it is a great happiness to die in the actual practice of charity, as you hope to do, and this will undoubtedly happen to you, since you want to live only to work at this.

It is also true that something extra is given at table four times a year at Saint-Lazare—an egg on Easter, a cake for the Epiphany, a little pâté on the feast of the patron saint, and a few fritters on Quinquagesima Sunday. You may have the same given at your house.

We must never accept any remuneration for our missions, either from persons absent or present, rich or poor. I am not saying that you may not accept money as an alms if anyone sends you some, but you may not accept it for having given a certain mission or on condition of giving one.

Letter 2769. - Reg. 2, p. 115.

2770. - TO PIERRE DE BEAUMONT, SUPERIOR, IN RICHELIEU

January 5, 1659

You tell me that you decided during your retreat not to ask again to be relieved of the office of Superior but to be content with representing your inadequacy to God. That is what should be done, Monsieur. Value this practice and continue to govern as you have done in the past. All has gone well with God's blessing, and all will go even better with the trust you will have in His grace and the experience you have acquired. It is not that we do not need you elsewhere, but we are waiting for a greater need before taking you from Richelieu, where a wise, vigilant, gentle, regular man like you is needed.

I do not know how M. [Liège] [1] has the nerve to dare to show his face in Richelieu, where he has given reason for gossip against his reputation, and I know even less on what grounds he claims to base the dispensation from his vows. As for me, I cannot release him from them without a legitimate reason, and his so-called infirmities—even if they were genuine—must not be taken into account, no more than his mental upsets, which proceed only from his allowing nature to get the upper hand. When God gives him a firm determination to return to the Company, He will also give him indifference with regard to houses and the desire to stay away from places which now give him pleasure.

Letter 2770. - Reg. 2, p. 187.

[1] As mentioned in no. 2692 (October 20, 1658), M. Liège had recently left the Company. Saint Vincent had given Pierre de Beaumont specific instructions on how to deal with him.

2771. - TO FATHER PHILIPPE-EMMANUEL DE GONDI

[January 9, 1659] [1]

My Lord,

My declining state of health and a slight fever I had cause me to take this precaution in your regard, My Lord, in the uncertainty of what is to come. I would like to prostrate myself in spirit at your feet to ask your pardon for the displeasure I have given you by my boorishness and to thank you most humbly, as I now do, for your charitable forbearance in my regard and the innumerable favors our little Congregation and I in particular have received from your kindness. Rest assured, My Lord, that, if God is pleased to continue to grant me the power to pray to Him, I will use it in this world and in the next for you and your family, desiring to be, in time and eternity, your. . . .

2772. - TO CARDINAL DE RETZ

[January 9, 1659] [1]

Monseigneur,

I have reason to think that this is the last time I will have the honor of writing to Your Eminence because of my age and an ailment I have, which perhaps are going to lead me to the judgment seat of God. In this uncertainty, Monseigneur, I most humbly entreat Your Eminence to forgive me if I have displeased you in any way. I have been wretched enough to do so unwittingly, but I never did so intentionally.

Letter 2771. - Reg. 2, p. 92.
[1]Date given by Collet, *op. cit.,* vol. II, p. 61.

Letter 2772. - Reg. 2, p. 92.
[1]Date given by Collet, *op. cit.,* vol. II, p. 61.

I also venture, Monseigneur, to recommend to Your Eminence your Little Company of the Mission, which you have founded, maintained, and favored. Since it is the work of your hands, it is also most submissive and very grateful to you, as to its father and Prelate. In addition, while it will be praying on earth for Your Eminence and the house of Retz, I will recommend the one and the other to God in heaven, if His Divine Goodness grants me the grace of welcoming me there, as I hope from His mercy and your blessing, Monseigneur, which I ask of Your Eminence. Prostrate in spirit at Your feet, I am, in life and in death, in the love of Our Lord. . . .

2773. - TO SAINT LOUISE

Tuesday evening

I thank Mademoiselle Le Gras most humbly for her care of me and for the little remedies she in her charity suggests. Recently M. Dalencé [1] told me that frequent purging is not good for my condition. Brother Alexandre[2] wanted me to take a little something from him tomorrow. Nevertheless, I offer a thousand wishes that Mademoiselle Le Gras and her dear Daughters will be more and more sanctified, and I recommend myself to her prayers.

Letter 2773. - Archives of the Motherhouse of the Daughters of Charity, original autograph letter.

[1]A renowned surgeon, whose name is linked to the story of the miracles attributed to the Holy Thorn (la Sainte Épine) of Port-Royal.

[2]Alexandre Véronne, infirmarian of Saint-Lazare.

2774. - TO JEAN MARTIN, SUPERIOR, IN TURIN

Paris, January 17, 1659

Monsieur,

The grace of O[ur] L[ord] be with you forever!

I thank God a thousand times for the extraordinary benefits that have come from your latest mission and for the fact that all of you have returned in good health and just in time to welcome the Visitor and the visitation. I hope the house will receive both good results and consolation from them.

The outcome of the affair being pursued in Rome [1] depends more on what God wants than on the recommendation of men. That is why we must trust in God alone and ask Him to settle it according to His good pleasure. That is what we will do. We must await patiently your entire establishment. God's works are not done all at once, but little by little.

We have no news here. I have been sick but am better now, thank God. I offer you frequently to Him, in whom I am, Monsieur, your most humble servant.

VINCENT DEPAUL,
i.s.C.M.

Addressed: Monsieur Martin, Superior of the Priests of the Mission, in Turin

---

Letter 2774. - Archives of the Mission, Turin, original signed letter.

[1] The Sant'Antonio affair (cf. no. 2670).

2775. - TO FIRMIN GET, SUPERIOR, IN MARSEILLES

Paris, January 17, 1659

Monsieur,

The grace of O[ur] L[ord] be with you forever!

While awaiting your letter from the last regular mail, I am sending you a bill of exchange from Messieurs Simonnet on Messieurs Napollon for 1966 livres. They come from the Attorney General,[1] who is giving them as alms to the hospital for the convicts. I received them in payment of the bill of exchange the Administrators sent me on M. Bruand, agent for the Attorney General. This note was for 2000 livres; however, I am sending you only 1966. The reason is that, on the one hand, Messieurs Simonnet took 20 livres for the exchange at the rate of one per cent, contrary to their usual way of acting, saying that money was scarce in Marseilles, and, on the other, 14 livres were missing from a bag of 1000 francs.

When Madame Fouquet's man, who brought it here, saw the miscount, he wanted to take it back to M. Bruand to have this rectified, which I was unwilling to allow him to do. I felt we should not haggle over such a trifle with persons of their caliber and for something that is a gift. Despite our request that he say nothing about it, the man still mentioned it to Madame. Then he went off and complained to M. Bruand and to his agent, who told him that, if he brought his bag back, he would give him a full one and that he knew well from whom he had received it. So he returned here yesterday on behalf of Madame to ask for the bag in order to have it exchanged, but we had already sent it to Messieurs Simonnet. These are the reasons for the lesser amount.

Letter 2775. - Archives of the Mission, Paris, original signed letter.

[1]Nicolas Fouquet.

We received 4 livres 10 sous for a convict named Lesueur on the *Ducale;* I am notifying M. Huguier of this so he will give them to him.

I just received your letter of the seventh. You say you have heard nothing from Barbary, and M. Le Vacher[2] tells me that Brother Barreau is a prisoner. If that is the case, God be praised! Things are not as bad as I feared. I am glad M. Le Vacher is ministering to the sick in the hospital. May God in His mercy bless you and your work!

I am, in His love, Monsieur, your most humble servant.

VINCENT DEPAUL,
i.s.C.M.

Addressed: Monsieur Get

2776. - *SAINT LOUISE TO SAINT VINCENT*

[January 1659] [1]

A young man came and told us quite simply of his obligation to see that a baby, twenty-one months old, who had been taken from its mother, be well brought up. The man wants to join a religious Order and has set forth the terms he is willing to meet to be relieved of his responsibility. He will pay seven livres a month to the hospital and make an outright gift of one thousand livres to the child, to be invested for the time when he is old enough to learn a trade.

Some sensitive persons in the Company have a repugnance for the term Confraternity *and want only* Society *or* Community. *I took the liberty of saying that that word [Confraternity] was essential for us and could be very helpful in remaining firm against innovation. I also said that it signified* secularity *for us; and since Providence had added to it the words*

---

[2]Philippe Le Vacher.

Letter 2776. - Archives of the Motherhouse of the Daughters of Charity, original autograph letter.

[1]Date added on the back by Brother Ducournau.

Society *and* Company, *we understood by this that we must live regular lives by observing the Rules we received at the time of the establishment of our Confraternity, as has been explained to us. I think, Most Honored Father, that M. Portail should discuss this with Your Charity. I ask that, if you think it advisable, this be done without it being obvious that I said anything to you about it.*

Sister Louise Ganset's[2] *money is cleared to be handed over. However, since it changed hands on the death of Monsieur Bézé, the person who has it wants to hear from M. du Fresne.*[3] *If you judge it appropriate, I most humbly entreat you, Most Honored Father, kindly to let him know. Sister is growing weaker by the day, and we are afraid she will not last much longer. What she wants to give to the Company might then be lost.*

I think I am obliged to take this little precaution and to ask your pardon most humbly for all the trouble I have caused you recently. This is my usual way of acting; with your assistance, I want to correct it along with all my other faults. I am, Most Honored Father, your most humble daughter and very grateful servant.

L. DE MARILLAC

Addressed: *Monsieur Vincent*

2777. - TO FIRMIN GET, SUPERIOR, IN MARSEILLES

Paris, January 24, 1659

Monsieur,

The grace of Our Lord be with you forever!

We have received ten livres for Charles Ballagny, a convict on

---

[2]A native of the environs of Villepreux, she was sent to Richelieu in 1638 and remained there until 1644, when she returned to Paris to work with the galley slaves. In 1657 she was sent to Maule.

[3]Charles du Fresne, Sieur de Villeneuve, former secretary of Queen Marguerite de Valois, was one of Saint Vincent's closest friends. After the Queen's death in 1615, he became secretary, then intendant, of Philippe-Emmanuel de Gondi.

Letter 2777. - Archives of the Mission, Paris, copy made from the original in the Hains Family Collection, Marseilles.

the galley *Princesse de Morgue.* I ask M. Huguier to pass them on to him.

Enclosed is a bill of exchange for three thousand livres from Messieurs Simonnet on Messieurs Napollon, payable in your name. This money is to be used for the Missionaries of Tunis and Algiers, where you will send it at the first opportunity in two installments. I greatly fear that no safe way will present itself for a long time, but we finally have the wherewithal to maintain our poor confreres. It is up to you to figure out how to get this money to them. If M. Le Vacher of Tunis supplied the money for Algiers, it is only right that you send him that amount.

A week ago I sent you another bill of exchange for 1966 livres, which the Attorney General [1] gave us for the hospital for the convicts. If you have not received the first one, the second bill of exchange is enclosed from the same Messieurs Simonnet on Messieurs Napollon.

After writing the above, I received your letter of the fourteenth. I have not yet seen the letters from Algiers, but according to yours we have reason to praise God for the present state of our Brother.[2] It consoled me greatly, and I thank the Divine Goodness for having thus disposed things so well.

Before saying anything more to you on that, I will wait for the translations you lead me to expect, and I think that, before making any decision on M. Le Vacher's[3] return, it will be better to see what reply the King will give the Pasha and the Customs House of Algiers. Meanwhile, if you have the possibility of so doing, you can send Brother Barreau some clothing and whatever he requests, up to two hundred livres. You can take this money from the fifteen hundred earmarked for him in this bill of exchange. I do not know what else to do to prevent him from spending and lending the funds

[1]Nicolas Fouquet.

[2]Jean Barreau.

[3]Philippe Le Vacher.

deposited with him by the slaves; for, even after my writing to him several times not to do so, he still contravenes this order because he lacks firmness.

I cannot reply to M. Le Vacher[4] today.

I am. . . .

2778. - TO CANON CRUCHETTE, IN TARBES

January 29, 1659

I saw, from one of your letters, your remembrance of and your charity for us, especially for me, who do not deserve it, and I thank you most humbly. I am deeply edified, Monsieur, to hear that you are still doing good, enlightening town and country by word and work, and spreading good graces and gentleness everywhere.

It is true that our Little Company was considered for Bétharram;[1] the late M. Charpentier[2] was the first to propose it to me

---

[4]Philippe Le Vacher.

Letter 2778. - Reg. 2, p. 64.

[1]Bétharram is situated in the commune of Lestelle (Pyrénées-Atlantiques), not far from Lourdes. In 1614, Jean de Salettes, Bishop of Lescar, had a chapel built there which, under the direction of the Missionaries of Garaison (1615-21), had rapidly become the center of a very popular pilgrimage. Léonard de Trapes, Archbishop of Auch (1600-29), once led there a pilgrimage of ten thousand persons. He erected three crosses on the top of the hill and left in the sanctuary a statue of the Blessed Virgin, which he himself had carried there. Hubert Charpentier, whom the Bishop of Lescar had put in charge of the chaplains there, was a man of great virtue and integrity. In 1621 he founded in Bétharram the Congregation of the Priests of Notre-Dame-du-Calvaire, which was still serving at the shrine in 1659. The increasing renown of Notre-Dame-de-Bétharram won the favor of Popes and the aristocracy. Louis XIII, Anne of Austria, the Brienne and Montmorency families, and the leading families of Béarn and Gascony became its benefactors. The history of the shrine was written by Canon Dubarat, to whom we owe many valuable works on the Pyrénées-Atlantiques. (Cf. Victor-Pierre Dubarat, *Bétharram et le Mont-Valérien* [Pau, 1897].)

[2]Hubert Charpentier, a graduate in theology of the Sorbonne, was born in Coulommiers on November 3, 1565. After contributing to the foundation of Notre-Dame de Garaison, he founded two shrines honoring the Cross of the Savior: one at Bétharram, the other at Mont-Valérien, near Paris. He died in Paris on December 10, 1650.

almost twenty years ago, and it has been discussed with us from time to time. Up until now, however, God has not found us worthy to serve Him in that holy place; furthermore, it is true that we are only poor folk, as you know. Still, people persist in wanting us there, especially some gentlemen from the Parlement of Navarre; and M. de Laneplan, a gentleman delegated to the Court by the Estates of Béarn, explained to us recently that he was responsible for finding out what we think. I was told that the Bishop of Lescar,[3] who has just been consecrated, wants to do me the honor of coming to talk it over with me. Now, to tell you my thoughts on the question:

(1) I fear that our insignificance, which is great as to the number, quality, and virtue of the workers, will prevent us once again from accepting the honor being offered to us.

(2) The custom of those priests in Bétharram is to wait for penitents to come there, and ours is to go and seek them out where they are. It would be difficult for our priests, who have given themselves to God to go from village to village to evangelize the poor, to renounce giving missions in order to attach themselves to a single church, and to work only for the devotion of people who come and go and cannot receive properly the necessary instructions to be converted to God. All of them, however, could go to the house on major feast days when there is a large crowd, but a means would have to be found in between times so that, while some of them would take care of obligations in the house, the others could work at exterior ministries.

(3) Only three priests in the chapel are willing to yield their places to us, and there are four who do not want to admit us; yet, they must all give their consent for us to be established there; otherwise we could not agree to this. If those who have a hard time with this want to continue to live and perform their spiritual

---

[3]Jean du Haut de Salies (1658-81).

exercises in that house and still consent to our being brought in, we could in that case come to an agreement with them about what is needed for their upkeep, and they could live with us, as did the religious who received us at Saint-Lazare.

(4) Lastly, Monsieur, I have great difficulty with the vigils that are often held at night in that church. I am well aware that the intention in having them is good, and I want to believe that no distressing trouble has occurred with them; but I am also aware that this could happen and that it is not without good reason that the Church, which allowed these vigils in the beginning, has stopped them since then. I entreat you to let me know how often they have them in Bétharram and on what days they take place.

Since you wish to be informed about the state of this affair, I am very glad to tell you, Monsieur, the difficulties involved. In addition, I can assure you that, if they can be eliminated, the plan could also be carried out. In which case, it will be a great blessing for us to be able to contribute something to the honor rendered to Our Lord and His glorious Mother in this holy place and to know that we will receive there your protection, your help, and your advice, as you offer us in advance.

2779. - TO DOMINIQUE LHUILLIER, IN CRÉCY

Saint-Lazare, January 31, 1659

I received your letter and learned of your illness, which has grieved me deeply. I have prayed and have had others pray for you that it may please God to restore you to health and, in the meantime, to grant you the grace to make good use of your present state for yourself and for others. Since it seems that Our Lord loved God and redeemed humanity more through suffering than in any other

---

Letter 2779. - Archives of the Mission, Paris, Marseilles manuscript.

way,[1] He has shown His servants that they can serve humanity more effectively by this same means. You must, however, do all in your power to get well, and I ask you to do whatever depends on you for this purpose.

And because you are not in a place where you can be properly cared for, we thought of bringing you here, and I am sending the bearer of this letter for the express purpose of finding out how to do this. See, Monsieur, if you are well enough to go to Meaux to get a seat in the coach, or if you could stand the fatigue of traveling on horseback, or if we should send a stretcher for you, which I will do as soon as I am told which way. Please consider it a duty to do so without waiting for any further decision from us. On Monday morning we will send a priest to take your place; he will arrive in the evening.

I repeat to you that I am deeply grieved by your illness; *mais quoi!* we must conform ourselves to God's good pleasure, and hope from His goodness that it will be nothing serious. It will be a great joy for me and for the whole house to see you.

2780. - TO JEAN BARREAU, CONSUL, IN ALGIERS

Paris, January 31, 1659

Dear Brother,

The grace of O[ur] L[ord] be with you forever!

I received your letter sent on three dates, the last being the second of this month. For a long time we were between hope and fear in your regard, but hope always prevailed because it was founded in God who protects His own.[1] He has indeed delivered

---

[1]Cf. Heb 2:10. (NAB)

Letter 2780. - Archives of the Mission, Turin, original signed letter.
[1]Cf. Ps 31:24-25. (NAB)

you—not only from death and the acts of violence we feared, but even from the prison where they put you because of the Bastion. Even though you are not yet free from the claim of the Turks in this matter, they will perhaps leave you in peace in their hope that the men M. Picquet[2] kidnapped will be returned to them. We are working on that.

I will say nothing in particular to you regarding the things you tell me except that we will extricate you, God willing, from your former commitments and from those you mention in your new list. But you must practice a little patience until there is a safe way of sending you the money. Right now, we do not feel there is one, whatever the Turks may pretend, and there is certainly wisdom in waiting until the present obscure matters are cleared up. You have reason to fear not only Picquet's creditors but Rappiot's as well, who are undoubtedly on the watch to see if anything will be sent to you so they can pounce on it. We are being advised not to send anything by way of Tunis either, until M. Le Vacher[3] assures us that there is nothing to fear. He has not written for a long time, which is a bad sign.

A week ago I sent M. Get three thousand livres for the living expenses of the Missionaries in Algiers and Tunis. If M. Le Vacher has advanced any money for you, it is only right for you to reimburse him from your share; if not, M. Get will forward your half to you by the first safe occasion.

Dear Brother, please manage well what the good God is sending you and be exact in keeping the deposits so you can return them on demand. It is the money of the slaves that is entrusted to you; their freedom—and perhaps their salvation—depends on it. If you are going to use this money for other purposes or lend it out to ransom other slaves, to the prejudice of those to whom it belongs, you put yourself in the grave danger of being unable to give it back when

---

[2]Thomas Picquet, Governor of the Bastion of France.

[3]Jean Le Vacher.

they need it. Consequently, you will make yourself blameworthy before God and before others. All you need is a little firmness to rid yourself of those obtrusive persons who borrow from you. Tell them you have nothing of your own nor the means of paying your own debts, that you are forbidden to commit yourself for others, and similar reasons against which you cannot act in conscience.

I had your letters delivered to your brother. Everything is going very well here. We have prayed hard for you and will continue to do so, God willing. If the Bastion is reestablished, we will have the interests of the Consul recommended.

I embrace you with all the tenderness of my heart, filled with gratitude to God in His goodness for the patience and protection He gives you. I am, in His love, Monsieur, your most humble servant.

VINCENT DEPAUL,
i.s.C.M.

2781. - *SAINT LOUISE TO SAINT VINCENT*

February 1, 1659

Most Honored Father,

If God did not make me insensitive to my suffering at seeing myself so forsaken, I would be enduring great pain. The one that does affect me is that of not having sufficient light to make good use of this according to God's plan and to make this deprivation—which I have perhaps merited—useful to me. This opportunity is a consolation to me, since I can ask for your blessing for myself and for all our Sisters, as I now do, especially for Sister Marie of the Hôtel-Dieu, Sister Anne of Angers,[1] *who has been in*

Letter 2781. - The original autograph letter was formerly the property of the Daughters of Charity, 28 rue Louis Ulbach, Troyes. Its present location is unknown.

[1]Anne Vallin, of whom little is known; she was in Paris in 1659.

the Company for eighteen years, and Sister Geneviève from ncar Maule.[2] *After their recent retreat, they expressed to Monsieur Portail their desire to be allowed to renew their vows tomorrow. The Sister who came from Brienne*[3] *with Sister Catherine*[4] *very humbly asks for the simple attire of the Daughters of Charity.*

Several persons recommend to your prayers a matter of very great importance for the glory of God and the salvation of souls redeemed by the blood of His Son. You are aware of my need for them as well. That is sufficient for me, since I am, Most Honored Father, your most humble daughter and very obedient servant.

L. DE MARILLAC

2782. - TO DENIS LAUDIN, SUPERIOR, IN LE MANS

February 5, 1659

We are sending you a Brother who is new in the Company but not in virtue. We could not give you one more clearly called by God, more firmly grounded in his vocation, or more suited to your need. He is upright and prudent, and I hope, Monsieur, that since he will edify your family, you will take care to see that he is not disedified by it, for nothing repels and unsettles beginners more than to see that their seniors do not give them good example.

---

[2]Geneviève Caillou, a native of Saint-Germain-en-Laye, entered the Daughters of Charity in 1638. In March 1640 she left the Motherhouse for Angers, where she remained until the end of 1644, when she returned to Paris. During 1645-46 she was Sister Servant at Saint-Gervais parish; in May 1646 she went to Le Mans but returned to Paris because of the difficulties experienced in trying to establish the Daughters of Charity there. She subsequently served in the parishes of Saint-Médard, Saint-Roch, and Saint-Benoît, and on August 8, 1655, was among those who signed the Act of Establishment of the Company. In May 1680 her health failed, and she left active duty to reside in the house in Pantin.

[3]Brienne-le-Château (Aube).

[4]Catherine Baucher, born in Épone (Yvelines), was stationed in Nantes (1649-53) and in Brienne (1654-59). In September 1660 she was sent to Poland, where she remained until she died unexpectedly some time after 1682.

Letter 2782. - Reg. 2, p. 170.

2783. - TO PIERRE DE BEAUMONT, SUPERIOR, IN RICHELIEU

February 6, 1659

We have recommended to the Daughters of Charity here never to allow men into their rooms—not only laymen but diocesan priests and the members of our Congregation as well. Even if I myself were to present myself to enter their rooms, I have asked them to shut the door in my face. I forgot to tell you that, and I am doing so today so you will recommend the same thing to the Richelieu Sisters and inform all the members of your house of it, who might otherwise sometimes go into their rooms, and that is inadvisable. I make an exception for when the Sisters are ill; for, in case of necessity, your infirmarian may go there on your orders, accompanied by a priest, and a priest may go with a Brother, but never otherwise.

I have been informed that your Sisters know everything that goes on in your house. This may stem from the fact that some of our confreres have too many contacts with them. It takes only one who tells one Sister everything for others to know it, too. This must be avoided; when they happen to meet them or otherwise, they should speak to them only of necessary matters.

Since writing to tell you not to send any confessor to the monastery you know,[1] I have spoken to a priest of the Order, who is aware of the disorder in that house. He told me we should not refuse to go to the aid of those souls when they call on us and that it would be a great pity if, when the ordinary means for saving themselves are lacking, the extraordinary ones were denied them. In line with that, Monsieur, I approve of your going or sending someone to them, whenever you are asked to do so, to hear only one of them each time—or two at the most—and, if possible, to do so secretly so the others will not know it.

Letter 2783. - Reg. 2, p. 188.

[1]Possibly the Monastery of the Sisters of Notre-Dame in Richelieu.

2784. - *JACQUES PESNELLE, SUPERIOR IN GENOA, TO SAINT VINCENT*

February 6, 1659

We have just given two small missions, which God has blessed abundantly, especially the last one.

It was a parish of only 240 communicants in a very isolated spot; yet, for the general Communion more than seven hundred persons came from neighboring places that were very far away. Among the reconciliations is the case of an extraordinary peace made by a father, whose eldest son had recently been murdered in his sleep for no reason. Several prominent persons had used their influence to get him to forgive the man who had committed the murder, but to no avail. The very day before, he had refused me when I tried to make the same request of him, and he asked me never to mention it to him again. But God accomplished by His grace what men had been unable to do by their remonstrances and pleading; for, the following day I took the risk of asking him once again, with prayers and tears, to extend this pardon and peace for the love of Our Lord. Suddenly he was a changed man and granted me what I was asking, doing so with truly Christian sentiments that brought tears to the eyes of all those who were present.

2785. - TO FIRMIN GET, SUPERIOR, IN MARSEILLES

Paris, February 7, 1659

Monsieur,

The grace of O[ur] L[ord] be with you forever!

I just received your letter of January 28. I will send someone to ask the Duchesse d'Aiguillon and Madame Fouquet to entreat the Attorney General to get the state to provide money for the salaries at the hospital and have some of it sent to the Administrators soon.

Letter 2784. - Abelly, *op. cit.*, bk. II, chap. I, sect. IV, p. 72.

Letter 2785. - Archives of the Soeurs Augustines de l'Assomption, 18 rue de Lourmel, Paris, original signed letter.

If another boat is leaving for Tunis, you will have reason to console M. Le Vacher by sending him the fifteen hundred livres you have for him. If he has supplied Brother Barreau with anything, you can forward to him what is due him on the other fifteen hundred livres. I praise God for the good news he sends us.

Do not expect anything from the Mercedarian Fathers for the avania endured by the Consul in Algiers on their account. They have let us know that, if the collections taken up for him here are not sufficient to get him released, they will pay the eight hundred écus they owe, but not otherwise.

I thank God for the peace and joy He has given the city of Marseilles by keeping the new Consuls.[1]

You think it advisable to send Brother Barreau some help at the first opportunity—at least the amount of what he received to ransom some slaves but used for his own affairs—so he can free those poor people and save his own reputation.[2] That seems right in one sense but, because it is to be feared that he may use that money for other things that are more urgent—as he did with other sums I had very particularly entrusted to him—I think we must be patient until we see a little more clearly how to settle this affair safely. If M. Le Vacher of Tunis has not advanced him any money,

---

[1]Despite a decree of the Council, postponing the elections of the Consuls, the people of Marseilles had appointed Bausset, Vacon, and Lagrange to that post on October 28, 1658. This displeased the King, who forbade the new magistrates to carry out the duties of their office and ordered both the Consuls and the rebel leaders to give an explanation to the Court in Lyons. He received them coldly but had the good sense not to take any harsh measures against them. An amnesty was granted the culprits, and it was decided that the Duc de Mercoeur, Governor of Provence, would go to Marseilles to have new elections carried out in his presence. Anxious above all else to avoid further trouble, the Duke had the wisdom to give the majority of votes to the Consuls who had been named the previous October 28. (Cf. Augustin Fabre, *op. cit.*, vol. II, pp. 280-85.)

[2]The rest of this paragraph is in the Saint's handwriting.

you can send him his share of the three thousand livres, or part of it.

Your most humble servant.

VINCENT DEPAUL,
i.s.C.M.

It has been some time since I asked the Pastor in Le Havre if you should have the one hundred livres intended for Nicolas Renouard from Le Havre, who has returned to France, given to his son, who is still a slave. I have not received any answer to that. I will have someone write to him again.

Addressed: Monsieur Get

2786. - TO SISTER ANNE HARDEMONT, SISTER SERVANT, IN USSEL

Paris, February 9, 1659

Dear Sister,

The grace of O[ur] L[ord] be with you forever!

We have seen that good gentleman who brought us your letter. He made his retreat here and plans to enter the Bons-Enfants Seminary afterward.

You ask my advice on the request a lady made you to go to nurse her in her home in her illness. Let me tell you, Sister, that I am pleased with your reluctance to do anything extraordinary without our orders. The Daughters of Charity are only for the sick poor who have no one to help them, and not for ladies who have the means of getting someone to nurse them. When some ladies in Paris of the upper and middle classes were sick, they asked us for some of

---

Letter 2786. - Archives of the Motherhouse of the Daughters of Charity, original signed letter.

your Sisters. We excused ourselves from that for many reasons, and whenever the same request is made to you, I ask you, Sister, to excuse yourself as well, unless you have express permission from Mademoiselle Le Gras or from me. Have no fear that the Duchess [1] will complain about this, for she certainly wants you to keep your Rules. If she wishes you to disregard them on some occasion, she will ask us to write to you about it.

I praise God, Sister, that you are striving to overcome yourself in your difficulty, and I think His Divine Goodness is very pleased with the way you are resisting nature in its inclination for change. After such a long trial, God can only give you peace and quiet. I really hope it will be in the way you wish, but you see clearly how hard it would be to send a Sister such a long distance to take your place. Nevertheless, if the opportunity to do so presents itself, and if you continue to find life wearisome, we will willingly do so to give you this satisfaction. But, in the name of God, be patient in the meantime and do not rebel against Mademoiselle Le Gras any longer by refusing to write to her. She loves and esteems you, and you must give her an account of yourself and your exercises. So, please do so, and pray to Our Lord for me. I am, in His love, Sister, your most affectionate servant.

VINCENT DEPAUL,
i.s.C.M.

Addressed: Sister Anne Hardemont, Daughter of Charity, in Ussel

---

[1] The Duchesse de Ventadour.

2787. - TO SISTER FRANÇOISE MÉNAGE,[1] IN NANTES

Paris, February 12, 1659

Dear Sister,

The grace of O[ur] L[ord] be with you forever!

I praise God for the good dispositions He gives you to make yourself more and more pleasing in His eyes. You will attain this happiness if you practice faithfully humility, gentleness, and charity toward the poor and toward your Sisters. I ask Our Lord, who has given us the example of these virtues,[2] to grant you this grace.

It suffices to renew your vows for one year, after which you may renew them for another year, if you have this devotion.[3] I give you permission for that. You ask me if you may make this renewal monthly; however, if you do it for a year, you do it for twelve months at a time, so it is not necessary to do it every month. Still, you can make it during this year as often as you like—not to assume a new obligation to live them, since the first one is commitment enough to do so, but to witness to God that you are happy to have given yourself entirely to Him and to spur yourself on to renew your desire to be faithful to Him.

There is no need for anyone to tell me about your conduct, for I know it is good and that you want to make it even better. You do well to consider yourself weak and, if you really believe this, Our Lord will be your strength. Continue to mistrust yourself and to trust in Him.

Letter 2787. - Archives of the Motherhouse of the Daughters of Charity, original signed letter.

[1]Françoise Ménage was from an excellent family of Serqueux; she and three of her sisters—Madeleine, Marguerite, and Catherine—became Daughters of Charity. Françoise nursed the sick for several years at the Nantes hospital, where she had been sent in 1650. When the Sisters withdrew in 1664, she went immediately to the Montpellier hospital where she remained until 1692.

[2]Cf. Mt 11:29. (NAB)

[3]The Daughters of Charity still renew their vows annually on the day the Church celebrates the feast of the Annunciation.

The two Sisters you have in the Company[4] are striving to be virtuous, thank God, and are very much attached to their vocation, as you are to yours. May it please God to preserve and bless you in it!

I thank God for the trust you have in your Director and that he is helping you with so much concern and charity.

I am not sending the medal you requested because I do not have any. When they send me some from Rome, I will send you some of them. Meanwhile, I recommend myself to your prayers. I am, in the love of O[ur] L[ord], Sister, your most affectionate brother and servant.

VINCENT DEPAUL,
i.s.C.M.

Addressed: Sister Françoise Ménage, Daughter of Charity, in Nantes

2788. - TO SISTER NICOLE HARAN, SUPERIOR, IN NANTES

Paris, February 12, 1659

Dear Sister,

The grace of O[ur] L[ord] be with you forever!

I received your letter of the first of this month. The next time I am speaking to Mademoiselle Le Gras we will see if it is time to relieve you of your office of Sister Servant, or whether it is advisable to leave you there awhile longer. I will also suggest to her to do now what was done in the beginning, namely, to appoint an Assistant. Furthermore, I will point out to her your need for some

---

[4]Since Marguerite Ménage had died in Calais in 1658, Saint Vincent is referring here to Madeleine and Catherine.

Letter 2788. - Archives of the Mission, Paris, original signed letter.

help, since there are only six Sisters for two hundred twenty patients. That is a lot of work for such a small number of nurses. May God be pleased to strengthen you and to establish great union among you; for you will be even stronger if you are all closely united!

Do not worry if your duties prevent you from being exact to prayer and the Rules because, since charity is the queen of virtues, we must leave everything for it; but, when it allows you to observe the Rules without being detrimental to the care of the sick, you must do so in order to make yourselves more pleasing to God and, consequently, more apt to procure the salvation and relief of the poor.

I am most grateful for the consolation and kindness you receive from the Assistant at Sainte-Croix. May God render to him the charity he renders to you, and may He grant you the grace to merit its continuation and to profit from his good advice!

M. Alméras is no longer in a state of being able to go to see you, as we were hoping a while ago. He is too weak to travel. However, we will send you someone else in his place.

Mademoiselle Le Gras is very well, thank God, and so am I, although I have been a little ill and am confined to my room because of my bad legs.

It is true that we have promised to send two or three priests—and no more—on the next ship leaving for Madagascar; as for Sisters, however, I have heard no talk of them. If some are going on this voyage, as you have been told, they are not from your Company, which God in His mercy continues to bless. I ask Him to fill you with His patience, wisdom, and goodness.

I am, in His love, Sister, your most affectionate servant.

VINCENT DEPAUL,
i.s.C.M.

Addressed: Sister Nicole Haran

2789. - TO GUILLAUME DESDAMES, SUPERIOR, IN WARSAW

Paris, February 21, 1659

Monsieur,

The grace of O[ur] L[ord] be with you forever!

I already expressed to you my dread that the plague, which carried off your sacristan, might have other disastrous effects on your family. This has caused us to redouble our prayers for your preservation and that of M. Duperroy.[1] Your letter of February 9 consoled us greatly because you say there is no more danger and also because of the strength and grace God is giving both of you to preach and act for the service of God and of souls. This is all the more highly to be esteemed because several times you almost lost your health and your life, and only God alone could have preserved them for you. Likewise, only He alone knows the good results He can claim from them.

The zeal He gives you for giving missions causes me to hope that He will use you, as two solid rocks, for the foundation of this good work in Poland. By it His Providence will provide for the instruction and betterment of the people and will inspire other workers from that country to join you and, in a word, to do all the works of the Company in various places.

We must, however, be peaceful and resigned in awaiting that time. The one who is faithful in a few things will be placed over many.[2] Continue to make good use of the present opportunities and leave future ones to God. Do not worry about the foundation in Warsaw; that is more O[ur] L[ord]'s affair than ours because, by His grace, we want only what He wills. If He allows the benefice of Saint-Roch, which was promised to you, to be given to a secular

---

Letter 2789. - Archives of the Mission, Krakow, original signed letter.

[1]Nicolas Duperroy.

[2]Cf. Mt 25:23. (NAB)

priest, *in nomine Domini,* perhaps He is reserving something better for you. I am glad you did not make a journey there to prevent this but were satisfied with writing to have the business postponed until spring. My advice, then, is that you leave matters at that so as to be faithful to the maxim of the Company, which acts passively rather than actively in such circumstances.

I praise God that you have taken possession of Holy Cross again. That has given you the opportunity to tell me your fear that the Bishop[3] might one day confer this benefice *ad vitam*[4] on some priest from outside, to the prejudice of the Company. If that cannot be prevented, we must abandon ourselves to the guidance of God, who perhaps will never allow such a thing to happen; however, if you see some remedy for it, we should know what it is and whether it is time to try it.

You are urging us a little to send you some men, especially Brothers, and my zeal urges me even more to help you out. Rest assured, Monsieur, that we will do so, God willing; but I find it very hard to send anyone there until peace and good health are firmly established. May God be pleased to send both of these there! We will see about it this spring. Meanwhile, prostrate in spirit at your feet, I embrace you and good M. Duperroy.

I am, in the love of O[ur] L[ord], Monsieur, your most humble servant.

VINCENT DEPAUL,
i.s.C.M.

Addressed: Monsieur Desdames, Superior of the Priests of the Mission of Holy Cross, in Warsaw

---

[3]Albert Tholibowski.
[4]*For life.*

2790. - *SAINT LOUISE TO SAINT VINCENT*

February 27, 1659

I thought I would be consoling Sister Jeanne Lepeintre [1] *by telling her that I did not think her ailment seemed too serious, but I did not make myself clearly understood.*

I cannot find out the location of that hospital for the mentally ill, but I entreat Your Charity to recall that you do not think it advisable to send one of our Sisters by herself. Furthermore, you know we do not have any to give, and I think they might ask for Sisters for Saint-Eustache[2] *because the servants of their poor have left them. There is, however, a little opposition to this.*

Most Honored Father, please give me your holy blessing, as to your most obedient daughter and very humble servant.

L. DE M.

Addressed: *Monsieur Vincent*

Letter 2790. - Archives of the Motherhouse of the Daughters of Charity, original autograph letter.

[1]Jeanne Lepeintre had been sent to the Daughters of Charity by her mistress, Madame Goussault. Saint Vincent says elsewhere that she was "a very fine, wise, and gentle girl." Both he and Saint Louise had great confidence in her because of her intelligence and organizational skills. She was first sent to the school of the Charity in Saint-Germain-en-Laye (1642). In the spring of 1646, after installing the Sisters in the Le Mans hospital, she returned to Paris, where she was put in charge of the Motherhouse while Saint Louise was establishing the house in Nantes. Jeanne then became Sister Servant in Nantes (1646), where great difficulties were being encountered. In 1654 she made the foundation in Châteaudun and, in 1657, at the Salpêtrière (cf. *Spiritual Writings*, L. 64, p. 77, n. 1). In *Recueil de pièces relatives aux Filles de la Charité*, Ms, p. 24, preserved in the Archives of the Motherhouse of the Daughters of Charity, we read: "During the lifetime of Mademoiselle Le Gras, she seemed to be a hypochondriac. Moreover, she could not be made to do anything she did not like, nor would she accept opinions other than her own." She was reprimanded for this fault more than once by Saint Vincent. Her last years were sad ones spent at the Nom-de-Jésus hospice, where she had to be committed because of mental illness.

[2]A parish in Paris.

2791. - TO SAINT LOUISE

[March 1659] [1]

I am ashamed for having taken so long to thank Mademoiselle Le Gras for her many kindnesses to us. I do so now with all the gratitude of my heart, and I ask Our Lord to be her reward.

She is right to reject the proposal of those kinds of Sisters who are separated and are dressed differently from the others, and she will do well to let her officers know from time [to time] [2] how she feels about it. I will do likewise whenever the opportunities present themselves, God willing.

Is she going to send for Sister Georgette to find out the particulars of this affair[3] and see whether to send her back to Richelieu or to somewhere else? If she has no objection, it would seem desirable that this be done as soon as possible, before the wife of the Maréchal d'Estrées, who is the Lady of Nanteuil,[4] goes to see her, which must be soon.

I am feeling better, thanks to God's grace and your assistance. I had a bout of fever caused by the cold, which gave me the usual chills and fever. This is a type of fever to which I am very susceptible. One of my legs, which has been bad for about a year, is now healed, so I no longer bandage it; the other one is better, thank God. I have it dressed in the way Mademoiselle has instructed. As for my ulcers, which have been draining a lot for some

---

Letter 2791. - Archives of the Mission, Paris, original autograph letter.

[1]This letter is from the same date, or nearly the same date, as the one from Saint Louise to Sister Nicole Georgette, dated March 28, 1659 (cf. Appendix 4 of the present volume; also, *Spiritual Writings*, L. 614, pp. 634-35).

[2]Words omitted by the Saint.

[3]Nicole Georgette (Georget), a member of the Company of the Daughters of Charity from its beginnings, was not getting along with the Pastor in Nanteuil. She had served in Richelieu before being sent to Nanteuil.

[4]Anne Habert de Montmaur, widow of Charles de Thémines. In April 1634 she married François Annibal, Duc d'Estrées, Comte de Nanteuil-le-Haudouin, Peer and Maréchal de France, former Ambassador to Rome.

time now, I attribute their improvement to her. I prefer to believe that it is the result of her prayers and the novena she in her charity made for me. Never has her kindness seemed so worthy of esteem and so amiable. God be praised for manifesting Himself so well through the kindness of Mademoiselle, whom I thank once again with all the gratitude of my heart!

What I said about my ulcerated leg does not mean that I should expect it to be completely healed.

Addressed: Mademoiselle Le Gras

2792. - TO MONSIEUR DUPONT-FOURNIER, LAWYER, IN LAVAL

March 5, 1659

Monsieur,

The grace of O[ur] L[ord] be with you forever!

Your son,[1] who is in Cahors, sent me a letter to be delivered to you; at the same time, he asked me to support your plan to retire to a seminary. I would gladly do so, Monsieur, were it not for the difficulties I see in this:

(1) Room and board must be paid everywhere, and this is expensive. I do not know anyone to whom I could turn who might be willing and able to contribute to paying yours, as I myself have already had the honor of writing you.

Letter 2792. - Reg. 1, fol. 42, copy made from the original signed and annotated letter.

[1]François Fournier, born in Laval (Mayenne) on February 2, 1625, entered the Congregation of the Mission on August 12, 1644, took his vows on September 24, 1646, and was ordained a priest on September 25, 1650. He was professor of theology at the Agen Seminary (1649-58) and in Cahors (1658-63), Secretary General of the Congregation (1663-77), and Assistant General from 1667 to April 4, 1677, the day he died. The life of Saint Vincent, commonly and correctly attributed to Abelly, was erroneously thought to have been written by Fournier. It is possible and even probable that, as Secretary General, he helped prepare the material, but that is the extent of his role. Brother Ducournau may well have contributed much more than he. (Cf. *Notices,* vol. I, pp. 247-67.)

(2) Your advanced age does not allow you to discipline yourself to life under a Rule and to subject yourself to the exercises of a seminary.

(3) For the same reason, I would consider it a matter of conscience to do anything to have you take Holy Orders, especially priesthood, because it is a misfortune for those who enter it by the window of their own choice and not by the door of a legitimate vocation. Yet, the number of the former is high because they consider the ecclesiastical state a soft way of life, in which they seek rest rather than work. This has been the source of the scandalous havoc we see in the Church, for the ignorance, sin, and heresies that devastate it are attributed to priests. That is why Saint John Chrysostom [2] has said that few priests will be saved. Why? Because God gives the graces needed to fulfill the obligations of this sacred state only to those whom His Goodness has called to it, and He never calls anyone in whom He does not see the requisite qualities or to whom He does not intend to give them. For everyone else, He lets them act and, as a punishment for their temerity, permits them to do more evil than good, and ultimately they are lost.

So, one must be called by God to this holy profession. This can be seen in O[ur] L[ord] Himself, who was the Eternal Priest [3] and who, nevertheless, did not will to assume the exercise of this state until after this testimony of the Eternal Father who said, "This is my beloved Son, listen to Him." [4] This example, together with my experience of the disorders produced by priests who have not made the effort to live according to the holiness of their specific character, causes me to advise those who ask my opinion about receiving it, not to do so unless they have a genuine call from God and a pure intention of honoring O[ur] L[ord] by the practice of His virtues

---

[2]Saint John Chrysostom (347-407), Father and Doctor of the Church and Patriarch of Constantinople.

[3]Cf. Heb 7:26;8:6. (NAB)

[4]Cf. Mt 17:5. (NAB)

and the other sure signs that His Divine Goodness is calling them to it. I feel so strongly about this that, if I was not already a priest, I never would become one. I often say this to such applicants, and I have said it more than a hundred times when preaching to the country folk.

Accordingly, Monsieur, I venture to tell you, in the name of O[ur] L[ord], that I think it will be a good idea for you to remain in the state in which God has placed you and to be reconciled to the difficulties you have in it. This is your cross, and perhaps your salvation is attached to it. You have reason to believe this is the case because you have always lived in that state as an honorable and upright man. God is reserving the fruits of this for you in the next life, since He allows you to find nothing but bitterness in your old age. Happy are those who suffer in this world, for they will be consoled in the next.[5] This is a saying of the Son of God, after which I have nothing more to tell you, except that I ask His Infinite Majesty to be your strength so that you may walk to the end on the path He has marked out for you to reach your last end, which is God. I am, in Him, Monsieur, your. . . .

2793. - TO GUILLAUME DESDAMES, SUPERIOR, IN WARSAW

Paris, March 8, 1659

Monsieur,

The grace of O[ur] L[ord] be with you forever!

Your letter of January 16 consoled me in a most extraordinary way, informing me of the return of the King and Queen to Warsaw and the good prospect of peace. May it please God to grant it to us

---

[5]Cf. Mt 5:10. (NAB)

Letter 2793. - Archives of the Mission, Krakow, original signed letter. The postscript is in the Saint's handwriting.

for the benefit of Their Majesties and the great consolation of the people! We pray constantly to God for that because it is for His glory.

You told me you were leaving for Krakow to secure the little benefice of the hospital, from which the possessor was evicted. We will be waiting to hear the outcome of your journey so as to prepare some help for you, in the event that it has to be sent promptly. Otherwise, my opinion will continue to be that you should wait until peace is made and decontamination confirmed, for I do not think you are completely rid of the plague—I mean the entire country—as is all of Warsaw, since, by the grace of God, Their Majesties are now there.

God be praised that the little family is in good health and still filled with zeal for the service of our Divine Master!

We now have the ordinands here in this house and a band of workers out in the country. All our houses, thank God, are working zealously everywhere, with blessings both on the missions and in the seminaries. The latter are fuller than ever. Pray to God for the Company and its needs.

I am, in His love, Monsieur, your most humble servant.

VINCENT DEPAUL,
i.s.C.M.

We are getting everything ready to send you some men. What do you think of M. Guillot? I am a little worried about sending people during the war. Please let me have a word of advice quickly.

Addressed: Monsieur Desdames, Superior of the Priests of the Mission of Holy Cross in Warsaw

2794. - TO A COADJUTOR BROTHER [1] OF THE ROME HOUSE

I cannot tell you the consolation my heart received when word reached me from time to time that God was continuing to bless you, and you were continuing to be faithful to Him. All I can do now is to thank His Divine Goodness for this, as I have always done, because your progress—as well as your soul—is very dear to me. Therefore, if you absolutely want to return, you may do so; we will welcome you with open arms. I, however, do not see that this is God's Will because:

(1) His Providence has brought you to Rome;

(2) He has granted you the grace of succeeding well in your duties there;

(3) it would be contrary to the advice of your Superiors, by whom God makes known what He wills and does not will;

(4) it is difficult for you to be able to render greater service to Our Lord elsewhere than you do there.

Perhaps you will tell me, dear Brother, that you plan to come only in order to become more skilled in your art so as to do even better what you have already done. I laud your intention and even more the humility that makes you acknowledge that you know very little. Still, the truth is that those who have seen you at work say that you know a great deal both in theory and in practice. Then, too, is not Our Lord the sufficiency of those who trust in Him? When He consoled us by your entrance into the Company, you had no plans to become more skilled as a surgeon, but rather to be prompter and more submissive to His good pleasure.

Perhaps you will go on to tell me that your present experience makes you fear that you may be guilty if some accident happens to

---

Letter 2794. - Reg. 2, p. 346.

[1]Probably Philippe Patte. Born in 1620 in Vigny, Rouen diocese, he entered the Paris Seminary of the Congregation of the Mission as a coadjutor Brother on April 5, 1656, and took his vows there on April 16, 1658, in the presence of M. Delespiney. In 1659 he went to Madagascar, where he proved himself an excellent surgeon. Along with M. Nicolas Étienne, he was massacred on March 4, 1664. (Cf. *Notices,* vol. III, pp. 369-71.)

the patients through your fault. My reply to that is that, when you do what you honestly think you should do to relieve them, you are in no way responsible for the rest. A doctor who prescribes remedies according to his skill and his conscience is free in the sight of God, even though his remedies may have results contrary to what he intends.

You know all that well enough; so remain at peace and please reflect a little on what Our Lord replied when two young disciples of His asked His permission to return home, one to bury his deceased father, the other to sell his property and give it to the poor.[2] They were fine prospects; yet, this Divine Master preferred that they stay where He put them. He has no use for our knowledge or our good works if He does not have our heart, and He does not want that heart if we give it to Him away from the place where He asks for it.

In the name of God, dear Brother, let us truly belong to Him; we can be no better off. Let us humble ourselves more and more; and the more we see our own inadequacy, let us think that we have even more than we deserve. I ask His Infinite Mercy to pour itself abundantly on you and your work so as to draw from them in the end the sanctification of your soul and the accomplishment of His eternal plans. Do me the charity of imploring this for me, who am a great sinner and am always, in His love, your. . . .

2795. - JEAN MARTIN, SUPERIOR, IN TURIN, TO SAINT VINCENT

March 12, 1659

Ever since the Missionaries evangelized the places near Mondovi, homicides, which occurred quite often, have ceased. In one of those very

---

[2]Cf. Lk 9:59-62. (NAB)

Letter 2795. - Abelly, *op. cit.*, bk. II, chap. I, sect. VI, p. 89.

sparsely populated areas there were forty bandits. All of them have done penance; before approaching the Holy Table, they expressed regret for their crimes by their tears and other external signs of repentance in the presence of the Blessed Sacrament.

2796. - TO EDME JOLLY, SUPERIOR, IN ROME

March 14, 1659

The Nuncio [1] did me the honor of coming to see me to tell me that, since the Fathers of Christian Doctrine [2] have obtained the favor of making simple vows as we do, they also want to give missions as we do. He also said he was coming to ask me if we had any objection to that. I replied that, far from being troubled by it, we would be very glad if they and many other religious worked earnestly for the instruction and salvation of the people. Whereupon he asked me for a written declaration on that and added that those good Fathers would be very glad if our Company would share with them by communication[3] the privileges it has.

This gave me reason to tell Monseigneur that, if those good

Letter 2796. - Reg. 2, p. 244.

[1]Celio Piccolomini (1656-63).

[2]The Institute of the Priests of Christian Doctrine, founded in 1592 by Jean-Baptiste Romillion and Venerable César de Bus for the instruction of the poor, the ignorant, and the people of rural areas, was approved by Pope Clement VIII in 1597.

Jean-Baptiste Romillion, born in Isle (Vaucluse) in 1553 of Huguenot parents, was converted in 1579, became a priest in 1588, and died on July 14, 1622. (Cf. Abbé Claude Bourguignon, *La vie de P. Romillion, prestre de l'Oratoire de Jésus et fondateur de la Congrégation des Ursulines de France* [Marseille: B. Garcin, 1649].)

César de Bus was born in Cavaillon (Vaucluse) on February 3, 1544. After having lost and regained his faith, he entered the priesthood. He became blind at the age of forty-nine, died on April 15, 1607, and was declared Venerable on December 8, 1821, by Pope Pius VII. (Cf. P. Giloteaux, *Le Vénérable César de Bus: Fondateur de la Congrégation des Prêtres de la Doctrine Chrétienne (1544-1607)* [Paris, 1961].)

[3]Communication of privileges implies an act of competent ecclesiastical authority extending to certain persons privileges which have already been granted to others.

Fathers give us in writing what they would like from us, we will see what we will have to do. I thought I should inform you of this so as to get your opinion on it.

2796a. - TO FIRMIN GET, SUPERIOR IN MARSEILLES

Paris, March 14, 1659

Monsieur,

The grace of O[ur] L[ord] be with you forever!

I think your mission in Sisteron [1] will deprive me of your letters in this regular mail, but I willingly accept this deprivation for such a good cause, and I ask Our Lord once again to bless your work and to give you strength.

I hope the Administrators will borrow money to maintain the hospital rather than abandon the patients, since they are assured of getting the alms of the foundation for this year, as I told you, and as the Coadjutor of Narbonne[2] also did me the honor of telling me in writing three days ago.

Letter 2796a. - Archives of the Mission, Paris, copy made from the original in the Haines Family Collection, Marseilles. In his unpublished notes, Coste states that this letter is from 1659, and not from 1658. For this reason it has been repositioned here from no. 2552, placing it in its correct chronological order.

[1]Principal town of a canton in Alpes-de-Haute-Provence (Provence).

[2]François Fouquet was the son of another François Fouquet, Comte de Vaux, and Marie de Maupeou, a Lady of Charity most admirable for her zeal and her devotion to Saint Vincent. Fouquet's brothers were Nicolas, Superintendent of Finances, and Louis, Bishop of Agde; his sister, Louise-Agnès, was a nun in the First Monastery of the Visitation. François, named Bishop of Bayonne in 1636, was not consecrated until March 15, 1639. He was transferred to the Agde diocese in 1643, appointed Coadjutor of Narbonne on December 18, 1656, and Archbishop of that diocese in 1659. Relegated to Alençon in 1661, he died in exile on October 19, 1673. He brought the Priests of the Mission to Agde and Narbonne and established the Daughters of Charity in the latter town. A very zealous Prelate—too zealous perhaps—he found Saint Vincent's slowness hard to understand, but he greatly admired his virtue. The Saint's death affected him deeply; as soon as he received news of it, he wrote to the priests of Saint-Lazare: "However prepared I may have been for M. Vincent's death, since he was advanced in age, I

We received one écu for Renaud Le Page[3] and another for Lesueur, a convict on the *Ducale;* I ask M. Huguier to give them to them.

I am, in Our Lord, Monsieur, your most humble servant.

VINCENT DEPAUL,
i.s.C.M.

I just received thirty livres and a letter for Martin de Lancre; please give them to him. Enclosed is another twenty-one livres that have been brought to us for Vincent Traverse; I am writing to ask M. Huguier to give them to him.

2797. - *LOUIS SERRE, SUPERIOR IN SAINT-MÉEN, TO SAINT VINCENT*

1659

By the grace of God, our mission in Plessala [1] is now over. God was pleased to shower it so abundantly with His blessings that all those who ministered during it agree that they have never yet seen any in which so much good was apparent.

It was noted that crowds of people came from seventeen neighboring parishes. In presenting themselves for confession, several men told me they had been waiting in the church for ten days, and I think the same thing happened to more than five hundred persons.

Much good was done by way of reconciliations, especially among the

---

assure you that I did not hear the news of his passing without surprise and without being moved by great sorrow, humanly speaking, at seeing the Church deprived of a most worthy subject, the Congregation of its very dear Father, and myself of a very charitable friend to whom I am so deeply indebted. I think that, of all those whom his charity caused him to embrace as his children, there is no one to whom he showed greater affection and gave more signs of friendship than to me."

[3]A galley slave in Toulon.

Letter 2797. - Abelly, *op. cit.*, bk. II, chap. I, sect. II, §6, p. 43.

[1]Commune in the district of Loudéac (Côtes-du-Nord).

nobility. Baron du Rechau was a big help to us in this. He has a house in this parish, to which he had come from Saint-Briant, his usual place of residence. Having heard our first sermon, he and his wife came to see us at the house where we were staying, and he told us he would not be going home until the mission ended. I asked him at the same time to help us to settle the disputes that are so common here and to bring about reconciliations, especially among the noblemen. In this he had the most extraordinary success.

The days of the carnival were spent in exercises of piety. A solemn procession took place on Monday, in which the Bishop of Saint-Brieuc [2] *carried the Blessed Sacrament. All the people, walking four abreast, took part in it with such great devotion and respect and were so orderly that, even though it rained almost constantly for the nearly two hours that it lasted, no one fell out of line. On the following Tuesday, the church was filled with persons going to Communion. Because there was no room in it, the same Prelate administered Confirmation in the cemetery, in the midst of the wind and the rain.*

2798. - TO FIRMIN GET, SUPERIOR, IN MARSEILLES

Paris, March 21, 1659

Monsieur,

The grace of O[ur] L[ord] be with you forever!

I received your letters of March 4 and ll, and I am glad you have celebrated some Masses for your late benefactress.[1] Please continue to do so until I can send you a copy of the extract from her will, where you will see the Masses of obligation.

---

[2]Denis de la Barde (1642-June 22, 1675).

Letter 2798. - Archives of the Mission, Paris, original signed letter.

[1]Dame Laurence Veyrac de Paulian, Baronne de Castelnau, widow of Melchior Dagouz de Montauban, Marquis de Vins, Maréchal of the King's troops. She died in Paris on February 20, 1659. By her will, drawn up on May 29, 1655, she left eighteen thousand livres to the Marseilles house for the maintenance of two Missionaries. There is an excerpt of this act in the Archives Nationales (S 6707).

I praise God for the disposition of Abbé Félix regarding the garden he wants to buy. He must be allowed to do so, just as you thought, even if there were no other advantage in it for you than to have him as a neighbor.

I agree with you about the Bastion project and that the less we get involved in it, the better. I still sent the Duchesse d'Aiguillon the letter from M. Le Vacher.[2] It contains some fine proposals but does not give much hope of success.

I informed you that the twelve thousand livres for the hospital were to be paid by the state, not for this year, as I thought, but for the year 1660, since the King has used for other things the entire amount of the salt taxes up to that time. The state has even handed the money over to M. Amat, the Chief Tax Collector, who personally assures that payment is certain and there is nothing more to fear. Since the state has placed the matter in his hands, he is free to see that it is carried out and that the allotted amount will no longer be taken and used for other purposes.

Accordingly, it is to be hoped that the Administrators will maintain the hospital and will advance or borrow money on the amount to be received so as to be able to operate modestly until then. I am taking the honor of writing to them. The four thousand livres for the chaplains' stipends are also being levied on the state and will be paid as agreed—on condition that[3] they will live as a community. It will, however, be difficult for them to do so, if the galleys from Toulon do not return to Marseilles. We will have to wait and see.[4]

With regard to Toulon, the new Bishop[5] is getting ready to go

[2]Philippe Le Vacher.

[3]First redaction: "and will surely be paid. It will have to be stated that this is on condition. . . ." The correction is in the Saint's handwriting.

[4]This last sentence is in the Saint's handwriting.

[5]Pierre Pingré (1659-62).

there. He is very zealous and is going off filled with holy intentions. He has worked very hard to put the affairs of the galleys and the hospital in good order here. When he arrives, it will be appropriate for you to go to see him to offer him the modest services of the Company and to thank him for his great charity toward the poor convicts. He is a fine Prelate and is very cordial.

You sent me an account for 320 livres, and along with this amount you would like us to send you something for your living expenses. We will try to do so as soon as possible.

We received one écu for Antoine Auroy; I ask M. Huguier to give it to him.

I am, in O[ur] L[ord], Monsieur, your most humble servant.

VINCENT DEPAUL,
i.s.C.M.

Addressed: Monsieur Get, Superior of the Priests of the Mission, in Marseilles

2799. - *SAINT LOUISE TO SAINT VINCENT*

March 25 [1659] [1]

I had promised myself the honor and blessing of receiving Holy Communion at your Mass, Most Honored Father, but I do not deserve it. It is already a great deal that Providence reminded Your Charity to kindly grant me a quarter hour's time afterward, otherwise I would have been in great difficulty.

All our Sisters, both near and far, who have had the happiness of taking their vows, and I, though unworthy, entreat you, Most Honored Father, to offer us to God in this sovereign mystery so that we may renew our vows

---

Letter 2799. - Archives of the Motherhouse of the Daughters of Charity, original autograph letter.

[1]Year added on the back of the original by Brother Ducournau.

well, particularly the twelve Sisters who will have the grace of assisting at the Mass you will offer. We hope to have a share in it for the needs Your Charity knows we have, and we ask in all humility for your paternal blessing.

Allow me also to recommend my children[2] *to you and to call myself, Most Honored Father, your most humble servant and very obedient daughter.*

L. DE M.

Addressed: *Monsieur Vincent*

2800. - TO GUILLAUME DESDAMES, SUPERIOR, IN WARSAW

Paris, March 28, 1659

Monsieur,

The grace of O[ur] L[ord] be with you forever!

I will be writing to you only very briefly this time. I praise God that you made the Krakow trip in good health and for the Bishop's[1] reply to you. Since we must not undertake anything unless we are resigned to God's good pleasure, we must also receive refusals and a lack of success willingly, especially the latter, in which God's special Providence is obvious. The reason is that, if the establishment had been made, you would have found it hard to supply the men and the maintenance required for the two houses. That

---

[2]Her son Michel Le Gras, her daughter-in-law, and her granddaughter. Michel was born on October 19, 1613. The instability of his character and his vacillation about a vocation to the priesthood were a cause of great anxiety to his mother. Ultimately he left the seminary at the age of twenty-seven (1640). After ten years of further wavering, he married Demoiselle Gabrielle Le Clerc on January 18, 1650, in Saint-Sauveur Church in Paris. Saint Vincent witnessed the marriage contract. Their daughter Renée-Louise was born in 1651. Michel Le Gras died in February 1696.

Letter 2800. - Archives of the Mission, Krakow, original signed letter.

[1]Andrzej Trzebicki.

makes me even more convinced of the maxim we have always had, namely, not to take too much initiative to establish ourselves in places and employments before being called to them by those who have the authority to do so, but rather to wait until God's Will is made known to us through them. That will come to you with time, when people will know the Company by its fruit more than by a recital of its works.

God grant that you may soon be able to give some missions! We will try to send you the men you request for this purpose, God willing. Meanwhile, let us ask O[ur] L[ord] to send good workers into His vineyard [2] and to perfect those who are already in the Company. I ask Him above all to preserve you and to fill you with His Spirit.

I am, in His love, Monsieur, your most humble servant.

VINCENT DEPAUL,
i.s.C.M.

2801. - TO JACQUES PESNELLE, SUPERIOR, IN GENOA

March 28, 1659

Here in this house we are given a little something extra at table three or four times a year, namely, an egg at Easter; some hors d'oeuvres on the feast of the patron saint; a little cake on the Epiphany; and two or three fritters on Quinquagesima Sunday. You may do the same at your house and eliminate the other days on which you are accustomed to give something extra.

I do not know if I told you that it is the custom in the Company for local Superiors to sign all the official documents they issue—

---

[2]Cf. Mt 9:37-8. (NAB)

Letter 2801. - Reg. 2, p. 210.

not as procurators designated by the community, but as Superiors appointed by the General. They sign those documents—receipts, farm land leases, etc.—without calling anyone else in, except for important affairs such as buying or selling real estate, setting up annuities, or signing contracts for large amounts of money. In those cases, the Superior asks the advice, not of the whole community, but of some of the leading members of the family, who co-sign with him.

The Superior is responsible for all the duties of a house; but, since he cannot do them all, he is given assistants to act as his council, a procurator to handle business affairs under him and on his orders, and instructors to teach and direct under his guidance. It is not, as you thought, up to the community to elect the procurator—or the other officers either—but they must be appointed by the General or the Visitor. I felt I should give you this clarification because I think you understand it differently.

2802. - *SAINT LOUISE TO SAINT VINCENT*

March 30 [1659] [1]

Most Honored Father,

The Baronne de Mirepoix told me she would be very happy to participate in the general meeting.[2] *Would you like me to inform her of the time and place, when I know them? I refused once again her offering of ten écus for the retreat. However, she forced one of our Sisters to take it, but the latter slipped it into the dress of her lady-in-waiting, who then left it on the ground by the front door. I was not there. Most Honored Father, does Your Charity think it appropriate for me to return the money when I send her our Rules for her consideration and inform her about the meeting?*

Letter 2802. - Archives of the Motherhouse of the Daughters of Charity, original autograph letter.

[1]Year added on the back of the original by Brother Ducournau.

[2]Of the Ladies of Charity.

We have not yet given an answer to Abbé de Vaux, [3] *whose letter I sent to Your Charity; nor have we answered the confessor of our Sisters in Nantes with regard to Sister Nicole Haran's suggestion that we increase the number of Sisters and send an Assistant. I await your orders on these matters and humbly ask for your holy blessing, since I am, Most Honored Father, your most humble daughter and very obedient servant.*

L. DE MARILLAC

Addressed: *Monsieur Vincent*

2803. - TO A NOBLEMAN

(Now Vol. VI, no. 2237.)

---

[3]Guy Lasnier, Abbé de Vaux, was one of the most remarkable priests of Anjou during the seventeenth century. For a long time his sole ambition was to satisfy his vanity and his passion for hunting and other worldly amusements. In February 1627, he was appointed to the Saint-Étienne de Vaux Abbey in Saintonge; in 1628 he was named Vicar-General of Angers, then Canon of Notre-Dame de Paris. In spite of the obligations imposed on him by these dignities, he continued to lead a very worldly life. In 1632, like many others, he was curious as to what was going on in the convent of the Ursulines of Loudun. [It was rumored that some of the nuns were possessed; Richelieu ordered their exorcism and the execution of the Pastor, Urbain Grandier, for the practice of witchcraft.] Abbé de Vaux had cause to rue the day. It is alleged that, to his great confusion, one of the nuns, penetrating his interior life, revealed faults that he had never mentioned to anyone. From then on, he was a new man. In 1635 he made a retreat at Saint-Lazare, where he met Saint Vincent, with whom he remained in contact. He also had dealings with Saint Jane Frances de Chantal, Jean-Jacques Olier, and Baron de Renty. In his city, Angers, he established a Visitation convent, richly endowed the seminary, and founded the ecclesiastical conferences in his diocese. He was a prudent counselor and devoted protector of the Daughters of Charity of the Angers hospital and gave hospitality to Saint Vincent, Saint Louise, and Jean-Jacques Olier. De Vaux died on April 29, 1681, at the age of seventy-nine.

We have only one of the letters Saint Vincent wrote to him (cf. vol. I, no. 416), but there are about one hundred addressed to him by Saint Louise. (Cf. François Chamard, *Les vies des saints personnages d'Anjou* [3 vols., Paris: Lecoffre, 1863], pp. 279-303.)

2804. - TO DENIS LAUDIN, SUPERIOR, IN LE MANS

Paris, April 2 [1659] [1]

Monsieur,

The grace of O[ur] L[ord] be with you forever!

On Friday I will write to Rome to have M. d'Eu change the orders he gave you. Meanwhile, please suspend all proceedings for his affairs.

In my opinion, you should not receive the good young man from Lignières [2] to become a Brother—I mean for the present—but rather as a servant for a time, if he is willing, so you can judge better his vocation. Ordinarily, Brothers who have begun to study are not successful; they are tempted to resume their studies and to change their state of life.

I praise God that your workers have returned in good health and for the glory God has drawn from their work. In spirit I embrace them and the [whole] family most affectionately.

Please tell M. Herbron that I received his [letter and] will reply to him one [of these days]; I will do the same for M. Turpin,[3] [since I cannot do so] today.

Has M. Molony resumed his duty as procurator? Let me know if you have spoken to him about this and what he said to you so that, if a Brother has to be sent to look after business matters, we will try to send you one. We have none in whom there is not something to be desired.

Letter 2804. - Archives of the Mission, Paris, original signed letter. The document is in very poor condition; reconstructed text is enclosed in brackets.

[1]Year indicated by the contents, especially the parts referring to Louis d'Eu, Thady Molony, Jean Descroizilles, and the Irish priests.

[2]François Fichet, born in Lignières-la-Doucelle (Mayenne) in 1636, entered the Congregation of the Mission on September 8, 1659, in Le Mans, where he took his vows in October 1663, in the presence of M. Laudin.

[3]Pierre Turpin, born in Roye (Somme) on April 9, 1629, entered the Congregation of the Mission on September 16, 1655, and took his vows in Le Mans on October 6, 1658. He had left the seminary for health reasons but was readmitted.

We have discussed here at other times reducing your general lease to individual ones, which we found difficult at the time. Let me know what advantage you hope from this.

Since the theology classes at Saint-Lazare are already in progress, Brother Descroizilles would not be able to study with the others. He has to wait until they start again.

Since Brother Taillié [4] does not have a dimissorial for tonsure from his Bishop, I do not see how he can take part in this ordination, as he proposes.

We are trying [to obtain from] Rome a permission [on behalf] of the Irishmen, so that they may [be admitted] to Orders.

I am, in O[ur] L[ord], Monsieur, your most humble servant.

VINCENT DEPAUL,
i.s.C.M.

At the bottom of the first page: Monsieur Laudin

2805. - TO JACQUES PESNELLE, SUPERIOR, IN GENOA

Paris, April 4, 1659

Monsieur,

The grace of O[ur] L[ord] be with you forever!

I received your letter of March 16. I praise God that you have agreed on mediators for the dispute over the inheritance.[1] I ask His

---

[4]Patrick Taylor (Patrice Taillié), born in Dublin around September 29, 1631, entered the Congregation of the Mission on July 9, 1657. As happens often enough, there are variations in the spelling of his name: *Notices*, vol. I, p. 487, has *Tallier*; vol. V (Supplement), p. 584, lists him as *Tailler*.

Letter 2805. - Archives of the Mission, Paris, original signed letter. The document is in very poor condition toward the end of the letter, which necessitated some reconstruction of the text as indicated by the brackets.

[1]The inheritance from Jacques Pesnelle's father.

Divine Goodness to let them see what is just and to render justice to the one to whom it is due.

You should hold as an infallible prophecy, uttered first by Jesus Christ and then by His saintly Cardinal of Genoa,[2] that, if you continue to seek God's glory and to establish His reign in souls through the functions of our vocation, and do so in the same spirit that has been evident in the Company until now, you will lack nothing.[3] May God be pleased to fill all of us with this faith so we will abandon ourselves to His Providence and His service!

I will be sorry, on the one hand, if His Eminence leaves, but, on the other hand, I will adore the guidance of God if He calls him to Rome, where he will be useful not only to one diocese, but to the whole Church, especially since His Holiness probably wants to have him near him.

After Easter, a ship is supposed to leave Brittany for Madagascar. We are hoping to send three of our priests on it to go to the rescue of good M. Bourdaise, if God has chosen to preserve him.

I already wrote you that quartan fever really upsets people and that you should not pay too much attention to the odd behavior of the priest from Savoy, provided he shows good will in trying to correct himself and to work at virtue when he is cured. However, because you fear that, besides these traits, he may have others that are inappropriate for our way of life, it is up to you to take the bull by the horns and admit or dismiss him as you judge advisable.

You ask me if you should accept into the Internal Seminary those who present themselves, when you think they have the requisite qualities, as I have allowed M. Le Juge to do. Let me say that, since this permission was given him at a time when he was responsible for the family, it ceased to be his and was passed on to you when you took over the office. He must no longer have

[2]Stefano Durazzo.
[3]Cf. Mt 6:23. (NAB)

anything to do with it,[4] but you can use it, setting down as a basis, in this and in all other circumstances, that duties and prerogatives of subjects are all in reference to the Superior, just as those of the local Superiors are in reference to the General.

You suggest to me once again having some of your seminarians pursue their studies before they have completed their two years in the seminary. I persist in telling you, Monsieur, that this could be an impediment to taking their vows validly, that they must be given their full two years of seminary to work only at virtue, [and they] will study better afterward. I hope that [God] in [His goodness] will provide for your lack of workers. [I] ask [Him this] with all my heart. I a[m, in the love] of O[ur] L[ord], Monsieur, your most humble [servant].

VINCENT DEPAUL,
i.s.C.M.

Addressed: Monsieur Pesnelle, Superior of the Priests of the Mission, in Genoa

2806. - TO EDME JOLLY, SUPERIOR, IN ROME

Paris, April 4, 1659

Monsieur,

The grace of O[ur] L[ord] be with you forever!

I received your letter of March 4. We are going to send our Rules to the Apostolic Commissary through an address we have for the approval of agreements.

---

[4]First redaction: "prevail."

Letter 2806. - Archives of the Mission, Paris, original signed letter.

I had the *perquiratur* [1] you sent for the Bishop of Sarlat [2] given to him and have had forwarded to M. Serre the marriage dispensation for which he was waiting. We paid your small bill of exchange for 53 livres 10 sous.

Thank you for the Brief of indulgences you sent us for the ordinands.[3] The ones we now have here will begin to enjoy this favor, in accord with the permission we obtained for this from the Ordinary of Paris.

May God be merciful to those deceased persons you mentioned to me, especially that wretched man who took his own life, if he had a few moments to repent.[4]

God be praised that the Pope has been pleased to grant the Bishop of Pamiers [5] the first of his requests, without denying him the others! I hope you will manage to get all of them.

I never thought the Saint-Sépulcre affair would succeed, and what you write me about it should cause us to consider the Prior's resignation null and void.[6]

---

[1]A *perquiratur* is an order or commission given by the Cardinal Datary for a single examination of dates in the registries of the Datary. The Apostolic Datary took care of certain business relating to non-consistorial benefices.

[2]Nicolas Sevin.

[3]This decree, dated March 1, 1659, was given *ad septennium*, that is, *for seven years.*

Jacques-Bénigne Bossuet was giving this particular retreat for those preparing for ordination.

[4]From what Saint Vincent says about Pierre Escart in no. 2813, the Saint is probably referring to him here. The words "if he had a few moments. . ." are in the Saint's handwriting.

Pierre Escart, born in the canton of Valais (Switzerland) in 1612, entered the Congregation of the Mission on March 6, 1637, and was ordained a priest the following year. He was stationed in Annecy and later sent to Richelieu. At the beginning of his stay in Annecy, he made a good impression on Saint Jane Frances de Chantal, who said of him, "M. Escart is a saint." He was indeed virtuous, zealous, and very austere, and would have continued to please Saint Jane Frances if he had known how to moderate his zeal, to be more tolerant with the defects of others, and to judge his confreres, especially Superiors, with greater fair-mindedness. His temperament carried him to extremes, and in a fit of passion he killed one of his friends. He went to Rome to seek absolution for this murder but died tragically there some time before 1659.

[5]François-Étienne Caulet.

[6]Efforts had been made to unite the Saint-Sépulcre Priory in Annecy to the Community's seminary in that town.

I am sending you the copy of the Bishop of Alet's[7] letter, or rather a report he made of what happened [8] regarding the censure of the *Apologie des Casuistes,*[9] in which he justifies his way of acting. I thought that the death of the Archbishop of Narbonne,[10] which occurred a short time ago, would moderate the complaints being made against this censure; but, from what I hear, there are other Prelates who are very agitated about it and want to put an end to this affair [11] contrary to the appeal of the Bishop of Alet.

In my preceding letter I mentioned a book M. Abelly wrote,[12] and I sent you three volumes of it [13] by the Lyons mail coach so

---

[7]Nicolas Pavillon was born on November 17, 1597. As a very young priest he placed himself under the direction of Saint Vincent, who had him teach catechism and work in the missions and the Charities, where his presence was deemed useful. More than once he entrusted him with the conferences and retreats for priests. Appointed to the diocese of Alet in 1637, Pavillon accepted it only upon the Saint's urging. This new office did not deter him from his apostolic works: he gave a mission in Rueil at Richelieu's invitation, then in Saint-Germain-en-Laye at the King's request. He was consecrated at Saint-Lazare on August 22, 1639, and went to his diocese accompanied by Étienne Blatiron. A zealous, intelligent Bishop, dedicated to reform, he justified the expectations placed on him. His episcopate would have been more fruitful had he been more on his guard against Jansenistic ideas. Saint Vincent begged him in vain to sign the formulary against Jansenism. Pavillon died on December 8, 1677. There are several biographies of him, notably that of Étienne Dejean, *Un prélat indépendant au XVIIe siècle, Nicolas Pavillon, évêque d'Alet* (1637-1677) [Paris: Plon-Nourrit, 1909].

[8]First redaction: "I am sending you a letter from the Bishop of Alet, or rather a report of what happened."

[9]*Apologie pour les casuistes contre les calomnies des jansénistes* (Paris, 1657) by a theologian and professor of canon law [Georges Pirot, S.J.]. Rarely has a book caused such an uproar; indignant protests arose from all sides. It was censured by the Vicars-General of Paris, by the Archbishops of Sens, Rouen, and Bourges, by Alain de Solminihac, and by many other Bishops. The Bishops of Pamiers, Bazas, Comminges, and Couserans met with Nicolas Pavillon in Alet to discuss the terms of a condemnation. They signed the condemnation on October 24, 1658, and published it in Toulouse under the title: *Censure d'un livre anonyme intitulé: Apologie pour les Casuistes.* The censures most telling for the author of the *Apologie* were those of the faculty of theology of Paris (July 16, 1658) and of Pope Alexander VII (August 21, 1659). In *Bibliothèque de la Compagnie de Jésus,* reedited by Father Carlos Sommervogel (9 vols., Brussels: Oscar Schepens, 1895) under the entry *Pirot* (vol. VI, col. 856ff.), is the long list of writings motivated by the publication of *Apologie.*

[10]Claude de Rebé had died on March 17, 1659.

[11]The rest of the sentence is in the Saint's handwriting.

[12]*Défense de la hiérarchie de l'Église et de l'authorité légitime de N.S.P. le Pape et de nos seigneurs les évesques contre la doctrine pernicieuse d'un libelle anonyme* (Paris: Josse, 1659).

[13]Three copies.

you could present one of them to the Pope. I am now sending you a letter from the author to give you the means of responding to any objection that might be made to you.

M. Pesnelle tells me that the Cardinal of Genoa is leaving them to go and live in Rome. The Pope probably wants to have him near His Holiness. His Eminence even told M. Pesnelle that, if our house in Genoa is losing something by his going away, the one in Rome will gain from it because he will see that some Cardinals among his friends will take care of the foundation. All that, however, will be as God pleases.

I am, in His love, Monsieur, your most humble servant.

VINCENT DEPAUL,
i.s.C.M.

Addressed: Monsieur Jolly

2807. - TO THE LORD OF GUESPREYRE

Paris, April 6, 1659

Monsieur,

The grace of O[ur] L[ord] be with you forever!

The memory of the late M. de Vincy [1] is too precious for us not to welcome with joy the opportunities of serving all the members of his family, especially you, Monsieur, who are one of its most distinguished members and who show us such kindness by the letter you did me the honor of writing to me. I thank you most humbly for it.

In reply, I will tell you, Monsieur, that we receive here only two

---

Letter 2807. - Archives of the Mission, Paris, original signed letter.

[1]Antoine Hennequin, Sieur de Vincy, priest-brother of Mademoiselle du Fay and nephew of Marie de Marillac, an aunt of Saint Louise. A great friend of Saint Vincent, he died in 1645, four hours after being received into the Congregation of the Mission.

sorts of persons: (1) those who wish to make a general confession and to prepare themselves to serve God well, each according to his state of life. We try to help them in this for just seven or eight days, after which they leave; and (2) those who want to give themselves to God for their whole life in our Company, which is not a religious Order but a Community of secular priests dedicated to the service of the poor country people.

Sometimes other priests come to ask if they might spend some time with us to be formed in the duties of their state. We direct them to the Bons-Enfants Seminary, where they are received as paying boarders and instructed in all the appropriate matters for as long as they wish. If the young man you do me the honor of mentioning to me is of this sort and is willing to go there on the same conditions as the others, I will recommend him to the Superior so that the latter will take special care of him. If he wants to become a Missionary, we would have to know whether it is to be a coadjutor Brother—especially since we cannot accept him for that state because we have more than we need—or whether it is to enter Holy Orders, in which case he must have a title and have studied at least as far as philosophy; otherwise, we could not admit him among us.

I venture to tell you the state of affairs, Monsieur, so that you will kindly excuse us if we are unable to act contrary to our usual custom. You know that the good order of Communities depends on the observance of their Rules. If any other occasion arises on which I can obey you, I will do so with respect and affection, since I am, in the love of O[ur] L[ord], Monsieur, your most humble and very obedient servant.

VINCENT DEPAUL,
i.s.C.M.

Addressed: Monsieur de Guespreyre, Lord of the said place, in Guespreyre

2808. - TO NICOLAS PORCHER, OFFICIALIS OF PARIS

[April 1659] [1]

Vincent de Paul, priest and Superior General of the Congregation of the Mission, humbly petitions, stating that he negotiated by an agreement of January 7, 1632, with Brother Adrien Le Bon, Prior of the Saint-Lazare house,[2] and the monks of that house and domain dependent on it, to unite it to the said Congregation of the Mission and to have them remain with the priests of the said Congregation established in that house, in accord with the responsibilities and conditions stated in the said agreement. King Louis XIII, of happy memory, granted his letters patent, under date of the said month of January, confirming the said agreement. By an act of March 24 of the said year, the Provost of Tradesmen and the Magistrates of this city of Paris gave their consent to it. However, because the monks, Abbot, and convent of Saint-Victor, and the Pastors of this city and faubourgs of Paris opposed the said union, the court of the Parlement, disregarding the said opposition, ordained by its decree of August 21, 1632, that it would examine the said agreement and letters patent. By another decree of the following September 7, it ordained that the said agreement and letters patent would be registered in the registers of the said court to allow the said priests of the Congregation of the Mission to enjoy its effects and contents, and that they should go to the Archbishop of Paris [3] to obtain letters of union and establishment in perpetuity of

---

Letter 2808. - Arch. Nat., M 212, no. 7, copy, courtesy of the ecclesiastical court of Paris.

[1]This petition was presented to the Officialis on April 8, 1659, as he himself states in *Procès verbal de l'estat des bastimens, cloistres, jardins et clos de Saint-Lazare*, June 27, 1659 (cf. Arch. Nat., M 212, no. 7).

[2]Adrien Le Bon, Canon Regular of Saint Augustine, was born in Neufchâtel (Seine-Maritime) and died at Saint-Lazare on April 9, 1651, in his seventy-fourth year. As Prior of Saint-Lazare, he supervised the transfer of the priory to Saint Vincent and the Congregation of the Mission. He also donated a number of farms for the support of the Congregation.

[3]Jean-François de Gondi.

their Congregation in the said Saint-Lazare house, under the conditions of the said agreement, with the responsibility to take in lepers and to fulfill the obligations of foundations. These letters of union were conferred by the said Archbishop under date of December 31 of the said year and were confirmed and approved by other letters patent by the late King in the month of January 1633. They were registered in the registers of the said Parlement the following March 21, and in the Chamber of Accounts and the Court of Aids, together with the first letters patent, on October 11, 1633, and January 9, 1634.

Desiring that the said agreement be legally ratified in the court of Rome and that confirmation be obtained there of the said letters of union of the said Archbishop of Paris and the approval of the introduction and establishment of the said priests of the Congregation of the Mission in the said Saint-Lazare house, the petitioner had the necessary applications made in the said court of Rome. When the affair had been examined by the congregation of Cardinals in charge of the affairs of Regulars, Pope Urban VIII, on their advice, signed the petition, dated at Saint Peter's in Rome, on the ides of March, in the twelfth year of his pontificate, which according to our reckoning is March 15, 1635. As the Bulls were not expedited in his time nor during the time of his successor, Innocent X, the petitioner obtained them from Our Holy Father the Pope, presently reigning,[4] in the form called *Rationi congruit,* dated at Saint Peter's in Rome, in the year of the Incarnation of Our Lord one thousand six hundred fifty-five, the fourteenth of the Kalends of May, in the first year of his pontificate, which according to our reckoning is April 18, 1655. By these Bulls His Holiness declares that the favor granted by his predecessor, Urban VIII, is effective

---

[4]For this Bull of Pope Alexander VII, reapproving the union of Saint-Lazare to the Congregation of the Mission see vol. XIII, no. 112. Many of the other documents mentioned in this letter are in the same volume.

from the day of its date, March 15, 1635, just as if the Bulls had been expedited on it by his predecessor.

You have been mandated by the said Bulls to approve and confirm in perpetuity the said union and agreement, to assign once again to the said Priests of the Mission the said priory or hospice of Saint-Lazare, of which the petitioner and the priests of the said Congregation of the Mission have been in possession and peaceful enjoyment since the year 1632, at which time they were admitted and established there by the Archbishop of Paris, in the sight and with the consent of the interested parties and with all the aforesaid solemnities.

In consideration of this, Monsieur, and since the truth of the statement in the petition presented to the late Pope Urban VIII is evident to you from the attached documents, may it please you by apostolic authority to officially announce and ratify the said Bulls and, by so doing, to approve and confirm once again and in perpetuity the said union and agreement formerly made of the said priory and house of Saint-Lazare, its appurtenances, and its dependencies, to the said Congregation of the Priests of the Mission; and you will do well.[5]

VINCENT DEPAUL,
i.s.C.M.

Addressed: The Officialis of Paris, Commissary delegated by our Holy Father the Pope

---

[5]Nicolas Porcher acceded to Saint Vincent's request. On April 30 he had the prescribed notices posted at the ecclesiastical court building and at Saint-Lazare to apprise the lawful claimants. Since no one came forward to object, he went to Saint-Lazare on June 27, drew up "a report on the state of the buildings, cloisters, gardens, and enclosure," and heard the testimony of those called to voice their opinions: André Guignard, Principal of the Collège de Navarre; Charles de Baignolz, Doctor of Theology and priest of the Community of Saint-Nicolas; Louis de Chandenier, Abbé de Tournus; Claude de Chandenier, Abbé de Moutiers-Saint-Jean; and Claude de Blampignon, Abbé de l'Aumône. Nicolas Porcher confirmed the Bulls of union on July 21; on August 7, Saint Vincent took possession, before witnesses, of the Saint-Lazare house. In March 1660 the King gave his consent by letters patent, which the Parlement registered on May 15, 1662. (Cf. Arch. Nat., M 212.)

2809. - TO EDMUND BARRY, SUPERIOR, IN NOTRE-DAME DE LORM

Paris, April 9, 1659

Monsieur,

The grace of O[ur] L[ord] be with you forever!

I just received your letter of March 29. I praise God for having preserved you from the fire with which someone tried to torment you. You are right to trust in the protection of God and the Blessed Virgin. I also hope they will deliver you from the evil designs someone may have on your house.

I agree that you should get back the assets of . . . [1] sold by M. Bajoue, by returning to the purchaser the fifty-five livres he paid; but get some advice on a sure way to do that.

You say that M. Agan[2] has two thousand livres on hand to be used for the seminary the Bishop[3] wants to transfer to Montauban, but that, since this is borrowed money, the Bishop wants you to make a commitment to pay, along with him and the syndic of the clergy, the interest and the principal. I will tell you my thoughts on this a week from now, God willing.[4]

Meanwhile, I recommend myself to your prayers and to those of your little family, whom God is showering with His blessings. I am in a hurry and am, in the love of O[ur] L[ord], Monsieur, your most humble servant.

VINCENT DEPAUL,
i.s.C.M.

Letter 2809. - Archives of the Mission, Paris, original signed letter.

[1]Because of the poor condition of the original letter this word is illegible.

[2]Vicar-General of the Montauban diocese.

[3]Pierre de Bertier.

[4]The promised reply is not extant.

2810. - TO GUILLAUME DESDAMES, SUPERIOR, IN WARSAW

Paris, Good Friday [1] 1659

Monsieur,

May the Holy Passion of the Savior cause us to do and suffer all things for love of Him!

I received your letter of March 6. You gave me pleasure by speaking frankly about the reinforcements you had requested of us. We were seriously preparing a few men to go and join you, but, on your advice, we will wait until you have the wherewithal to maintain them and can keep them busy. I admit that idleness is often a stumbling block and that Missionaries, more than anyone else in the world, should avoid it, since they are cut out for work; however, their happiness does not consist in always being busy but in doing unceasingly the Will of God, as Our Lord did. Now, He did so in various ways, actively and passively, by doing and by not doing.[2] I am sure, Monsieur, that you are suffering from having been deprived for so long of doing the principal works of the Company; but, aside from the fact that you do them in part, in so far as you are serving souls for eternity and are showing priests how they should act, by the virtues you practice, you also have the means of honoring the inactivity of Our Lord by not forging ahead—I mean with all your zeal—in the enormous tasks of apostolic workers.

Be patient, Monsieur; some day you will be placed over many things because you are faithful in a few.[3] I say the same to

---

Letter 2810. - Archives of the Mission, Krakow, original signed letter.

[1]April 11.

[2]Cf. Jn 6:38. (NAB)

[3]Cf. Mt 25:23. (NAB)

M. Duperroy,[4] whom I embrace most affectionately at the foot of the cross of O[ur] L[ord]—I mean both you and him. I am, in His crucified love, Monsieur, your most humble servant.

VINCENT DEPAUL,
i.s.C.M.

Addressed: Monsieur Desdames, Superior of the Priests of the Mission of Holy Cross, in Warsaw

2811. - TO EDME JOLLY, SUPERIOR, IN ROME

Paris, Good Friday [1] 1659

Monsieur,

May the Holy Passion of the Savior cause us to do and suffer all things for love of Him!

I received your letter of March 11 and have forwarded the ones you wrote to the Bishops of Le Puy [2] and Pamiers.[3] I also gave M. Gicquel the letter of provision you obtained at his request and ours. I see clearly that we are overworking you by asking you to take care of business other than our own; but it is also the least we can do. There are persons and occasions concerning which we cannot refuse to write you.

I will send to Troyes the extract [from your letter] [4] which

[4]Nicolas Duperroy.

Letter 2811. - Archives of the Mission, Paris, original signed letter.

[1]April 11.

[2]Henri de Maupas du Tour.

[3]François-Étienne Caulet.

[4]These words have faded from the original.

mentions the dispensation requested by the Bishop.[5] M. Dupuich[6] told me recently that they are anxious to have it to avoid certain difficulties.

I hope, God willing, that the official proclamation of all our Bulls[7] will be done before what you fear may happen.[8] We are working toward that.

I praise God for the return of your workers in good health, for the good results they had, and for the new mission you are going to give. May it please His Divine Goodness to be glorified by all that!

I gather from your letter that M. Le Gouz is now a priest, and I hope from the goodness of God that he will be a good one. You should not be surprised at not seeing in him as much external devotion as is to be desired, for that does not prevent him from being a good soul. He always seemed to us here to be a very wise young man, although not so recollected; and I think it would be a good idea for you to encourage him by signs of esteem and cordiality.

I praise God for all the things you tell me [about the] abbey [9] requested for the Turin mission. This affair is in God's hands; He will settle it according to His good pleasure and, consequently, according to our will, since we want no other will than His.

I say the same thing with regard to your housing. As you say, the time for that has probably not yet come.

I fully agree that you should accept the offer made you of a little church and modest lodgings in the town of Palestrina so you can go there during the summer. It is imperative that you leave Rome during the very hot weather, and I ask you to do so especially because your health is the most important affair we have or could

---

[5]François Malier du Houssay.
[6]François Dupuich.
[7]Especially the Bull for the union of Saint-Lazare.
[8]First redaction: "before a change of pontificate."
[9]Sant'Antonio Abbey.

have. So, forget about what might happen during your absence. As for me, I hope your leadership will be no less blessed in the place where you will be than your presence would be blessed in Rome, since it is Our Lord who is governing in and through you. It is also in and through Him that I am, Monsieur, your most humble servant.

VINCENT DEPAUL,
i.s.C.M.

Enclosed is a letter and report from Abbé Ribier, who is just finishing his retreat in our Richelieu house. Since he is so good to us, I could not refuse to ask you to do this for him. As for what he requests, however, do whatever you judge advisable.

Please thank M. Legendre [10] for us for the three hundred livres his brother brought us today.

At the bottom of the first page: Monsieur Jolly

2812. - TO ANTOINE CAIGNET [1]

Paris, April 13, 1659

Monsieur,

The grace of O[ur] L[ord] be with you forever!

I am quite embarrassed to be so late in replying to the letter you

---

[10]Renault Legendre, born in Tours on September 30, 1622, entered the Congregation of the Mission on August 16, 1643, and was ordained a priest in March 1647. He took his vows in Rome in November 1647 and was still in that city in 1659.

Letter 2812. - Unsigned autograph rough draft, Besançon Library, Ms. 1442.

[1]The name of the recipient is not indicated on the rough draft, but everything points to Antoine Caignet, Vicar-General of Meaux, author of a collection of sermons published in August 1659 (*L'année pastorale contenant des prédications familières ou prosnes sur les épistres et sur les évangiles de la Messe, pour servir aux curez et aux prédicateurs apostoliques d'entretiens aux peuples les cinquante-deux dimanches de l'année* [Paris: Jean de la Caille, 1659]).

did me the honor of writing me on February 4. You in your goodness will please forgive me, although I give you no reason other than my usual wretchedness, which does not excuse me from meeting my obligations on time, due to my typical laziness, and to my old age that is slowing me down both in body and mind.

I begin this letter, Monsieur, by thanking you for your interest in my illness and for the prayers you have said for a miserable sinner at the very moment of the elevation of the Holy Sacrifice, and I ask Our Lord to be Himself your reward.

I am ashamed, Monsieur, of what you tell me with regard to your preaching. You know well enough to what extent my ignorance makes me unworthy of contributing something to that work of your hands. *Mon Dieu!* Monsieur, how greatly the diocese is indebted to you, and what blessings will you not have for this work, as a result of all the good you do in the diocese both by your leadership and the exemplary life you lead in it!

What shall I say to you about the report enclosed in your letter except that Our Lord lays the groundwork of your interior life on the meaning of the words of the Psalmist: *quoniam ego sum pauper et mendicus;* [2] and this spirit is the spirit of humility, which is an antidote to pride.[3]

---

[2]*Because I am poor and needy.* Cf. Ps 40:18. (NAB)

[3]First redaction: "I read the report enclosed in your letter and am deeply moved by it. It would appear, Monsieur, that the opinion you voice comes from the God of enlightenment and is based on the words of the Psalmist: "because I am needy and poor." The circumstances of your retreat and of the time and place, the sentiments you had then, the fact that they have lasted until now, and the good results show that God. . . . " We eliminated from the second redaction five useless words, which the Saint obviously decided to change, even though he did not delete them: "or for better" before "the words of the Psalmist" and "the one" before "which is an antidote."

2813. - TO PIERRE DE BEAUMONT, SUPERIOR, IN RICHELIEU

Paris, April 16, 1659

Monsieur,

The grace of O[ur] L[ord] be with you forever!

I am replying to two of your letters. Thank you for the report from Loudun. I delivered it to the person who was waiting for it.

Since the student who is asking to enter the Company is hunchbacked and deformed, he would not be able to come and go on foot to give missions, as Missionaries must do. So you can thank him for his good will, Monsieur, and apologize for me to the Grand Archdeacon of P[oitiers, who] sent him to you.

We must be submissive to God and humble ourselves, in view of our unworthiness, for the cooling off of the Bishop of Poitiers [toward us].[1] If he allows you to work only half of the time in his diocese, you must be satisfied with that. If he does not allow you to work there at all, be patient and go to other dioceses where the door will be open to you.

That good Prelate is a gentle, charitable man; how is it then that he changed so soon, after seeming to you to be so pleased about your works? This change does not come from him but rather from his officials, who are hostile toward the Company. I do not know why, unless it is due to the notice we had served in the past on the Officialis because he was trying to find out what happened to the late M. Escart,[2] about which you have heard. I think that has always rankled him since then, and he has passed his resentment on to others.

Letter 2813. - Archives of the Mission, Paris, original signed letter.

[1]Gilbert de Clerambault de Palluau (1659-80).

[2]He was stationed in Richelieu when the problems arose that necessitated his trip to Rome, where he took his own life some time before 1659.

But what can be done? If by chance you find an opportunity to speak to them, you can tell them that it was senseless to listen to a deranged man. We had him confined as a madman, and he had indeed lost his mind. He made this only too clear after his escape; for, on returning to his native region, he killed another priest—a friend of his—in cold blood; and he died in Rome, after going there to receive absolution for this crime.

I sent M. Jolly the letter and report from Abbé Ribier.

We will send you a Visitor as soon as we can. It cannot be right after Easter, as you wish, because M. Berthe, whom we are planning to send, is still in Annecy—unless he has left there within the past three or four days—and has to make the visitation of some other houses on the way back. Consequently, I do not see how he can go to visit you before two or three months from now. Meanwhile, write me what is making it so urgent for you to have this visitation. I suspect it is M. F.[3]

I am, in the love of O[ur] L[ord], Monsieur, your most humble servant.

VINCENT DEPAUL,
i.s.C.M.

Addressed: Monsieur de Beaumont

---

[3]The "M. F." here is probably M[onsieur] F[érot]. In September 1659 Saint Vincent wrote to Jean Dehorgny that he was awaiting Férot's return from Richelieu (cf. vol. VIII, no. 2992).

Claude Férot, born in Saint-Quentin on July 6, 1630, entered the Congregation of the Mission on October 3, 1647, took his vows on October 15, 1649, and was ordained a priest in Agen in March 1656. He was Superior in Montmirail (1662-66).

2814. - *PIERRE LOISEL,[1] PASTOR OF SAINT-JEAN-EN-GRÈVE, TO SAINT VINCENT*

Monsieur,

Since my absence does not excuse me from attending to the concerns of Saint-Jean parish, and since, from time to time, I must provide workers who can minister effectively there, I readily cast my eyes on an upright diocesan priest from Reims named M. Daisne.[2] From the outset I was all the more pleased with him on hearing that he had spent some time in two of your houses and had been prepared there to carry out the duties of his priesthood well.

That is why, Monsieur, I am taking the honor of writing to you from the place where I have been relegated,[3] and I ask you to do me the favor of letting me know what I might expect from him, how he conducted himself with your men, and why he left a Congregation that obliged him only to teach and to practice the Gospel. Your opinion, Monsieur, will carry all the weight it merits because of your zeal and example in this opportunity for our church. Furthermore, it is indebted to you and will greatly appreciate the kindness you will have in contributing to my consolation in my exile, for the good of the souls God has entrusted to me and from whom I find myself still separated.

I am pleased, Monsieur, to be able to assume the title of your most humble and very obedient servant.

LOISEL,
Pastor of Saint-Jean

Compiègne, April 17, 1659

Letter 2814. - Archives of the Mission, Turin, original signed letter.

[1]Pierre Loisel, born in Compiègne on June 6, 1606, qualified as a Doctor of the Sorbonne on June 26, 1636. He was Pastor of Saint-Jean-en-Grève parish from June 26, 1637, to May 20, 1679, the day of his death; Chancellor of the University of Paris and Rector seven times.

[2]This name is barely legible under the scratching out that covers it.

[3]Pierre Loisel had been consigned to Compiègne in 1654 for rejoicing too openly at Cardinal de Retz's escape from his imprisonment in the Château of Nantes.

2815. - TO EDME MENESTRIER, SUPERIOR, IN AGEN

Paris, April 18, 1659

Monsieur,

The grace of O[ur] L[ord] be with you forever!

I deeply regret having missed the opportunity of seeing the Pastor of Saint-Caprais.[1] I was told that he came here twice, and I assure you that while he was here I knew nothing about it. I would have dropped everything to have the blessing of speaking with such a good servant of God, so filled with zeal and virtue, and to have the honor of expressing to him my entire gratitude for his charity toward us and especially toward your house. Please assure him of my sentiments in this regard, Monsieur, togeth[er with the respect] and obedience I will have for him all my life.

Since you want to sell only some extra copies of books, and to do so in order to buy others that you do not have, well and good, I give my consent for M. Chrétien to purchase them.

One of our maxims is that we do not accept any new Brothers—and servants even less—as long as we have enough other Brothers. Accordingly, Monsieur, since you have enough with two Brothers and a servant, and the houses in Cahors and La Rose have a sufficient number, I do not agree to your holding on to that good young man M. Cuissot sent back to you, unless you prefer to keep him as a servant in place of the one you already have. In that case you may do so, and send the other one back. This will give you the means of testing even more whether he will have the grace and vocation to be a Brother, and with time we will be able to accept him.

I cannot consent, however, to your getting rid of Brother Robin[2]

Letter 2815. - Archives of the Mission, Paris, original signed letter.

[1]Saint-Caprais-de-Lerm, commune in the district of Agen (Lot-et-Garonne).

[2]Jacques Robin, born in Mortiers (Charente-Maritime), entered the Congregation of the Mission as a coadjutor Brother on March 8, 1644, and took his vows on September 7, 1648.

to make room for a servant, or of an older Brother to get a young one. I can believe you when you say that good Brother Robin is not very suitable for your house; but will he be any more so for the Cahors house, which does not need him? Must he be rejected on that account? No, but he must be borne with as he is, and you must try gently and patiently to get from him whatever services you can.

Oh! but M. Cuissot has a real knack for getting what he wants and for getting rid of the rest. That may well be, although I have not yet noticed it. But, since you acknowledge that what he does is not right, why do you want to imitate him? Why not give him this example of charity and forbearance toward the weak? I ask you, Monsieur, to give it to the entire Company; for it is true that everyone naturally wants what is best for himself, whereas O[ur] L[ord] wants us to prefer the worst.[3]

M. Admirault[4] is writing to you; he does not explain clearly to you the diet that he and Messieurs Alméras, Bourdet,[5] Bécu, and Gorlidot are following. He says that all they take is milk; yet, they eat a fair amount of bread whenever they like. They do not, however, eat anything else, and they drink nothing but milk. They are all doing well with this, and M. Gorlidot, who was the first to begin, has recovered from a condition in which we expected him only to die, and right now he is very well. If M. Admirault has discontinued it, it is because he has a natural aversion for milk.

The late Marquise de Vins, who was from Provence, died in Paris last March. She left eighteen thousand livres to our Marseilles house for the maintenance of two priests who would give missions. She also wanted all the members of the Company to celebrate one Mass for her intention after her death. I ask you, Monsieur—you

---

[3]Cf. Lk 14:10-11. (NAB)

[4]Charles Admirault.

[5]Étienne Bourdet, born in Saint-Babel (Puy-de-Dôme) on April 27, 1615, entered the Congregation of the Mission on October 9, 1638, and was ordained a priest on June 2, 1640. He was Superior in Toul (1641-42) and took his vows on June 10, 1648.

and M. Admirault,[6] whom I embrace with all the tenderness of my heart—to carry this out in a spirit of gratitude because it is her just due.

I am, in the love of O[ur] L[ord], Monsieur, your most humble servant.

VINCENT DEPAUL,
i.s.C.M.

At the bottom of the first page: Monsieur Edme

2816. - TO EDME JOLLY, SUPERIOR, IN ROME

Paris, April 18, 1659

Monsieur,

The grace of O[ur] L[ord] be with you forever!

I received your letter of March 18. I praise God for the good will He is giving the young man you have received into your seminary, and I pray that He will give him the necessary spirit and perseverance. I gave his letter to M. Éveillard [1] to be sent to his father.

---

[6]Claude Admirault. He and Charles were brothers.

Letter 2816. - Archives of the Mission, Paris, original signed letter.

[1]Jacques Éveillard, born in Nogent-le-Bernard (Sarthe), entered the Congregation of the Mission on October 12, 1647, at sixteen years of age, took his vows on October 13, 1650, and was then sent to Poland. Recalled to France the following year because of political unrest in Poland, he was given the chair of philosophy at Saint-Lazare by Saint Vincent. René Alméras appointed him Superior of Saint-Charles Seminary in 1662 but sent him during the year to Noyon in the same capacity. In 1668 he put him in charge of the Collège des Bons-Enfants. Éveillard left there in 1674 to become Superior of the Warsaw house. He found such favor with the King, Queen, and Ministers that Edme Jolly, who was dissatisfied with his administration, had to use great circumspection to recall him. Because Éveillard continued to scheme in order to remain in his position, the Superior General expelled him from the Congregation, notifying the Visitors of this in a circular letter dated June 29, 1680.

The person who complained to you about the reconciliation brought about by M. d'Eu most likely has the kind of mind you indicate to me. In the future, then, you will have to be careful to do nothing outside confession [without our] [2] advice.

As for the other complaint you mention, it is an obvious calumny, instigated by some evil-minded person to make the Bishop of Geneva[3] even more hostile toward us. It is sufficient for us that God sees our hearts and knows our desire to see that the servant of God, Bishop de Sales,[4] is soon canonized. Nevertheless, when you have occasion to speak about this, it is advisable for you to show by your words that you are eager for it, in order to remove the contrary impression that false rumor may have created. In addition, you should refrain from seeing the Promoter of the Faith about the matter of which the Bishop of Le Puy [5] has written you. I, for my part, will try to dissuade him from writing to you again about it, if by chance he wants to do so.

You tell me that people there think the Bishop of Clermont[6] was authorized to make the official proclamation of our Bull in place of the Officialis. I would really like to know the persons to whom you mentioned this and who are of this opinion.

I am sending you unsealed the reply I am giving M. Le Mercier so you will know what is going on and can act accordingly. I mean that you should please receive him, if he so desires, on the conditions I am laying down for him.

I am, in the love of O[ur] L[ord], Monsieur, your most humble servant.

VINCENT DEPAUL,
i.s.C.M.

Addressed: Monsieur Jolly

---

[2]This place on the original has been damaged by insects.

[3]Charles-Auguste de Sales.

[4]Saint Francis de Sales.

[5]Henri de Maupas du Tour.

[6]Louis d'Estaing.

2817. - TO MONSIEUR LE MERCIER, IN ROME

Paris, April 18, 1659

Monsieur,

The grace of O[ur] L[ord] be with you forever!

I received the letter you wrote me, which was sent to me by your mother. I am deeply touched by the sentiments God is giving you, and I thank His Divine Goodness for your disposition to enter into the freedom of the children of God,[1] that is, to have no will of your own, as is necessary in our vocation. Please let me know if you are firmly determined to renounce your own sentiments in order to submit yourself always and in all things to your Superiors, and whether you are ready to go back to the seminary, for that is necessary to bind you firmly to the Company because you left it. If so, you can assure M. Jolly of this, and he will welcome you into his house, or you can go to Richelieu, as I wrote you in the first letter I sent you, which is still in Lyons with M. Delaforcade. I leave the choice of these houses up to you so that you will find less difficulty following the call of God. This presupposes, however, that you are fully determined to allow yourself to be guided with regard to your studies [2] and about recommencing the seminary exercises.

By these means, Monsieur, you will enjoy great peace and will receive a thousand blessings from God for the service of His Church, since He has already given you in advance many graces to prepare you for that. I ask Our Lord to accomplish His holy Will in you.

Letter 2817. - Archives of the Mission, Paris, original signed letter.

[1]Cf. Rom 8:21. (NAB)

[2]The Saint himself added, in his own handwriting: "with regard to your studies."

I am, with all my affection, in His love, Monsieur, your most humble servant.

VINCENT DEPAUL,
i.s.C.M.

Addressed: Monsieur Le Mercier, Priest, in Rome

2818. - TO FIRMIN GET, SUPERIOR, IN MARSEILLES

Paris, April 18, 1659

Monsieur,

The grace of O[ur] L[ord] be with you forever!

I hope this letter will find you back from your mission—or rather, from your missions; for, from what I hear, you have given two of them. Would it not have been better to work in the Marseilles diocese? Are there no parishes there where the mission has not yet been given? I say this to you for the future so that you will always give preference to the diocese in which you are established and where you have the greatest obligation.

We failed to send you today the one hundred écus for M. Le Vacher of Tunis, which we received for him from the Comtesse de Tonnerre [1] but will do so without delay, God willing. I will send them to you at the first opportunity, together with the 320 livres you paid out for us, according to your little account. We will add another 320 or 330 livres to this. That is what remains to us from the money sent by the Pastor of Saint-Malo[2] for Étienne Le Huby, who is no longer in Algiers but is home now. M. Le Vacher[3] will

---

Letter 2818. - Archives of the Motherhouse of the Daughters of Charity, original signed letter.

[1]Marie Vignier, wife of François, Comte de Clermont and de Tonnerre.
[2]Guillaume Le Gouverneur (1640-67).
[3]Philippe Le Vacher.

use them according to the latest instructions of the said Pastor. We were not able to send them today because of a lost key. Meanwhile, Monsieur, if by chance a boat leaves for Tunis before you receive this money, please send the one hundred écus to M. Le Vacher.

Have you received any reply from him about the twelve hundred livres you sent him last September for the ransom of Amable Coquery, who was recommended to us by the Superior of the Oratory in Dijon? [4] He has not yet made any mention of this to me in his letters.

This past February 14 I asked you to send M. Le Vacher fifty livres to be given to M. de Romilly[5] from his mother. I do not think you did so, since M. Le Vacher tells me that, in order to give this amount to M. de Romilly, he had to take sixteen piastres from the five hundred we sent him for his living expenses. Please send them to him together with those three hundred livres; for you are charging them to us in your accounts.

I am waiting for a bill of exchange for two thousand livres that is supposed to be sent to me. The Attorney General[6] is giving them as an alms to the hospital for convicts to keep the Administrators from abandoning the patients. You will see the letter I am taking the honor of writing them on this subject.

Get a good rest after so much hard work, Monsieur, and take care of your health.

I am, in the love of O[ur] L[ord], Monsieur, your most humble servant.

VINCENT DEPAUL,
i.s.C.M.

Enclosed is the bill of exchange payable to you.

Addressed: Monsieur Get

---

[4]Father Chaduc.

[5]Chevalier de Romilly, a slave in Tunis.

[6]Nicolas Fouquet.

2819. - TO JEAN LE VACHER, CONSUL, IN TUNIS

Paris, April 18, 1659

Monsieur,

The grace of O[ur] L[ord] be with you forever!

Today I received your dear letter of March 20, and in replying to it, I will reply also to the ones I recently received, dated January 14 and February 3 and 9.

Tomorrow I will send M. de Lafargue the receipt for the money he sent you for the ransom of Martissans de Celhay. Then he will see that he has been ransomed and that you wasted no time sending him back to his own country.

Mon Dieu! Monsieur, when are you going to send us a similar receipt for Dominique de Lajus? And when are you going to send him home to his poor wife and five or six children? Is there no way to persuade his master to release him for less than six hundred piastres? That is really an exorbitant ransom for someone who has nothing and to whom the money you have received for him was given as pure alms. Please ransom him as soon as you can and send him back to France at the first opportunity. Advance whatever is required—borrow it, if need be; I will reimburse you as soon as you let me know what you spent. M. Delaforcade has given us his word on this, even if the 180 piastres you mention are necessary, along with the 460 you say you have left over. Remember to get a receipt for everything.

Have you not received the twelve hundred livres M. Get says he sent you last September for the ransom of Amable Coquery, who was recommended to us by Father Chaduc, Superior of the Oratory in Dijon? You make no mention of them to me. There should be

---

Letter 2819. - Archives of the Mission, Paris, copy written in part by the secretary, who added on the back: "Copies of the letters written by M. Vincent to M. Le Vacher on April 17 and 18, 1659."

no further talk about Alexandre de Guerre; his slanders have gone up in smoke; people knew what he was like and no one mentions him anymore. I did not fail to send the Duchesse d'Aiguillon your letter and attestation.

We will heed the advice you give me about not sending anyone to Barbary until past disorders have been remedied. Your brother would still like to return to Algiers, but I fear, as you do, that they will take whatever he has and mistreat him.

I praise God that you received the one thousand écus we sent you and have given half to Brother Barreau. M. Get is supposed to repay you the sixteen piastres you took from your half for the Chevalier de Romilly because he has received—or will soon receive—fifty livres for that purpose.

You say that Brother Barreau drew a bill of exchange on you for 450 piastres, which the Governor of Tabarka [1] owes him, in the hope the Governor had [given him of reimbursing him] that amount. He has not done so, and I strongly fear he will not do so.

I do not know why that poor young man allows himself to be tricked like that into lending not only his own money but that of others. If you have not paid that bill of exchange, I advise you not to pay it until you get the money.

You tell me that, like him, you too are beginning to commit yourself and that you owe twelve hundred écus. This really disturbs me. You attribute the cause to the little profit you received from the consulate last year. I see clearly that this has contributed to it, but you should have reduced your expenses proportionately. Nevertheless, you increased them to more than two thousand écus, although only 720 came in.

Your food alone for just two persons comes to almost twelve hundred écus. This scares me. I am well aware that you have servants, but why several? Can you not do with one? I also know that you have unexpected guests to whom you cannot refuse a meal;

---

[1] Jean-Marie Canalle.

but to keep open house for everyone, and to feed and lodge in your house people who pay you no room and board, is something you should not do, be they French or foreigners, poor or rich, recommended or not recommended, especially when you cannot cover this expense on your own. For you cannot in conscience borrow money to appear splendid and generous, not even to do acts of charity, since I have asked you not to do so. You tell me that in your position it is difficult to refrain from doing so. I reply that it will be even more difficult for us to send you the money to pay and that, if you knew how poor we are, you would have no trouble making your own poverty known to those who make demands on you, since your receipts and expenditures have to be regulated and balanced.

In the name of God, Monsieur, take these measures in the future. God does not ask you to go beyond the means He gives you. I thank Him that in His infinite goodness He has preserved you from the avania with which you were threatened.

The Comtesse de Tonnerre has repaid us the one hundred écus you gave her son the Chevalier. I am forwarding them to M. Get to be sent to you. I sent your letter to that Lady; if she gets the reply to me before nightfall, you will find it in this packet. She told us recently that M. Guerraut, a banker in Malta, had instructions to give the Chevalier the four thousand piastres he needs for his ransom; but, according to what you say, it would be safest to send him the money from here.

I can only be deeply grieved by the intense sufferings of the poor slaves and by my inability to procure some relief for them; may it please God to have pity on them!

I doubt very much that a safe conduct can be obtained for Isaac and Jacob Alcalay for the time you wish, since M. de Brienne refused it to Madame d'Aiguillon for more than one year.

I had someone deliver the letters the Chevalier de Ravelon [2] sent

---

[2]Jean Coquebert de Ravelon, a Knight of Malta.

me. I think M. Poussay has replied to him, and all the others will do so. A member of our Company saw President Coquebert in Reims; he told him he would be coming to Paris soon and would see me about the Chevalier. It remains to be seen if he will do so.

Our Lord is treating you as He treated the saints, having led them to sanctity and glory through various tribulations. He is not satisfied with the extraordinary labors you endure in His service but, from what I see, He tests you also by interior trials, which are more troublesome than bodily ones. May His Divine Goodness be pleased to increase His grace in proportion as He multiplies your crosses, so that you may carry them courageously! I will not fail to offer you often to God for this intention, Monsieur.

Yesterday I wrote you a short letter [3] at the request of M. Langlois to ask you once again to do what you can to help M. de Beaulieu, his agent in Tunis, and also to stand surety for him up to six thousand livres. He told me he would send his promise today to vouch for all you could guarantee for his man—which he has not done. Perhaps he will send it to me before this letter goes out; in which case, I will let you know. Otherwise, I do not agree to your committing yourself for anything for M. de Beaulieu; for, if he does not keep his word, I am not obliged to keep mine.

2820. - TO LUKE PLUNKET, IN SAINT-MÉEN

Paris, April 19, 1659

Monsieur,

The grace of O[ur] L[ord] be with you forever!

I heard you have had a little trouble teaching chant and the

---

[3]This letter is not extant.

Letter 2820. - Archives of the Mission, Paris, seventeenth-century copy.

ceremonies; this does not surprise me, since everyone finds some difficulty in doing good actions, even the best. What distresses me, however, is that you are allowing yourself to give in to nature and to yield to its suggestions. Do you not know, Monsieur, that Christian virtue lies in mastering them and that, if you refuse to render this small service to God, you make yourself unworthy of rendering Him greater ones, according to this saying of the Savior: "If you are not faithful in small things, you will not be so in greater ones." [1] Yet, you say that you did not come to the Mission for that. Why not? Did you not come to obey? Did you not promise God to do so? Did you not come to do what the other Missionaries do? Have you not promised the Company to do so? Now, you are well aware that they are not here simply to give missions, but also to teach priests the things they should know and practice in their state of life. Consequently, if you do not fulfill the duty you have in the seminary, someone else has to do it because it is obligatory.

Now that you are a priest, Monsieur, and more obliged than ever to be useful to the Church, is it possible for you to refuse to carry out the functions that contribute to the formation of good priests? What will you say to that? That if you work in the places and in the manner that best fall in with your spirit, you will be more successful than you now are? But you cannot promise yourself this; on the contrary, you should fear that, if you shake off the yoke of holy obedience, God may take His Spirit from you and abandon you to your own judgment. And where will you go then? What will you do? If you remain in France, you will be in danger of being out on the street like so many other priests from Ireland. If you return to your own country, what will you do there? Other workers are having a very hard time there—not only to survive but to work—because of the persecution of the heretics. So, no matter where you turn, you will be in danger of leading a sad life and of having painful remorse of conscience at the time of your death.

---

[1]Cf. Lk 16:10. (NAB)

Reflect seriously on this, Monsieur, and do now what you would like to have done then. You lack nothing for your maintenance in your present state; in addition, you find in it every adequate means to assure your salvation and to procure that of your neighbor. Do not render yourself unworthy of these advantages, but give yourself to God to observe the Rules and to practice virtues such as humility, submission, and indifference to duties, of which we should make a more particular profession. If you do so, Monsieur, as I am hoping, you will draw down fresh graces on yourself. I ask you, then, to let yourself be guided, and I ask Our Lord to give you His Spirit.

I am, in His love, Monsieur, your most humble servant.

VINCENT DEPAUL,
i.s.C.M.

2821. - TO FRANÇOIS HERBRON, IN LE MANS

Paris, April 19, 1659

Monsieur,

The grace of O[ur] L[ord] be with you forever!

I have put off answering your letter because I was waiting to hear from someone to whom I had written about the Madagascar voyage. I have finally heard that it will not take place this spring. The Maréchal de la Meilleraye, who has no ships, had sent to Holland to get one, but he was refused. This has obliged him to postpone the departure until the fall. I do not know if there will be any further delay even then. Men propose; God disposes,[1] and

---

Letter 2821. - Archives of the Mission, Paris, unsigned rough draft in the secretary's handwriting.

[1]Cf. Prv 16:1. (NAB)

Providence has already upset their plans and obstructed this scheme so many times that we must not set our hopes on anything.

As far as we are concerned, however, we must continue to aspire to carry out this endeavor, since it concerns the glory of the Master whom we serve and who often grants to perseverance the success He has refused to give to the first attempts.[2] In addition, He is pleased to try His workers a great deal before giving difficult works over to them; He does so in order to have them merit, by the practice of their faith, hope, and love, the grace of going to diffuse these virtues in souls who do not have them. I thank God, Monsieur, that these three lamps are not only always burning within you, but that they are more and more ablaze with the desire to go and enlighten those far-off peoples who live and die in the darkness of infidelity. I ask His Divine Goodness to accomplish His good pleasure in you for this purpose.

I still do not know His disposition regarding the choice of you, but I hope you will be always ready to answer His voice, in the event that He calls you to foreign lands. Even if He should not call you there, you would still have the reward of an Apostle and, along with it, the glory of dying for the salvation of your own homeland. I would like to say the same to M. Turpin; but, because I am unable to write two letters, I ask that this one be for you and for him. I am, for both of you in O[ur] L[ord], Monsieur, your most humble and affectionate servant.

At the bottom of the first page: Monsieur Herbron

---

[2]Cf. Mt 15:22-28. (NAB)

2822. - TO PIERRE LOISEL, PASTOR OF SAINT-JEAN-EN-GRÈVE

April 21, 1659

Monsieur,

I received with special respect and keen consolation the letter you did me the honor of writing me. I did so because it is your letter and because of the great kindness you show me, although I am the poorest and most useless of your servants.

I do not know well enough the priest you mention to me, Monsieur, to be able to give you any testimonial on him, although he entered and left our Company twice.

I think the time has come, Monsieur, when God wants to reinstate you in your own place. This is in keeping with the desires and prayers of countless persons, especially of the most insignifi-

---

Letter 2822. - Archives of the Mission, Turin, copy. This copy was made by the secretary, subsequent to the letter of Pierre Loisel, published as no. 2814. The secretary added the following comment to his copy: "One day while M. Vincent was dictating this letter to a Brother, in the presence of Messieurs Portail, Dehorgny, and Alméras, whom he had called together to discuss the most important affairs of the Company as was his custom, M. Dehorgny interrupted to say that the Pastor of Saint-Jean, to whom the Saint was writing, might be very surprised if he told him he did not know well enough a priest who was under his direction. To which M. Vincent replied, 'I am well aware of that, Monsieur; but even though Our Lord knew perfectly well all kinds of persons, He still said to some, "I do not know you;" and He will say this on Judgment Day because *He does not know with the knowledge of approval.*' [For the interpretation of this, see Thomas Aquinas, *Summa Theologica,* Bk. 1, Q. I, Art. 14, 8c.] In making that statement, M. Vincent was actually saying enough to make himself understood by that Pastor, without revealing the faults of the priest. In addition to the countless acts of charity and prudence I saw this great man practice, I wanted to stress this one, which is charitable because it preserves the reputation of a priest who had not been an edifying subject in the Company, and which is prudent because he simply made known his instability, without putting it into words. He gives this Pastor reason to think that the man was not suitable for his flock or, should he want to use him, he would have no reason to complain about his answer if, in fact, he became dissatisfied with the man. It is also worthy of note that these acts of charity and prudence testify not only to the wisdom of M. Vincent but still more to his practice of drawing on the living source of the words and actions of Our Lord for everything he says and does and to regulate himself in all things according to the spirit of the Gospel, to which, however, few persons pay attention." (The priest in question here was Chrétien Daisne.)

cant among them, who is, however, the one most disposed to obey you. And he is, Monsieur, your most humble and very obedient servant.

VINCENT DEPAUL,
i.s.C.M.

2823. - TO EDME JOLLY, SUPERIOR, IN ROME

Paris, April 25, 1659

Monsieur,

The grace of O[ur] L[ord] be with you forever!

I received your letter of March 25. I sent to Troyes the extract of your preceding letter, which refers to the attestation of poverty or the money necessary for the marriage dispensation.

You will do a great act of charity for that poor priest, the Pastor in the Sens diocese, by having him reinstated.

The letter I sent you for M. Le Mercier [1] replies to what you write me about him.

Thank you for allowing me to share in the fruits of all your missions. I ask O[ur] L[ord] to continue to bless your leadership and your workers.

In His mercy He is blessing the works of the Company everywhere, and it is going along as usual. We are being asked for in many places, but we do not have enough men. We have many young ones who are students—some in theology, some in philosophy—and even more of them in the seminary. I have recommended your seminary to the prayers of this community.

M. Desdames, who until now has been urging us to send priests

---

Letter 2823. - Archives of the Mission, Paris, original signed letter.

[1]Cf. no. 2817.

to Poland, asked me in his last letter not to do so. This is because they would not have the wherewithal to feed them as long as the war is going on, and also because the Bishop of Krakow objects to establishing us in his city and in a hospital some persons were offering us.

The departure for Madagascar that was supposed to take place this spring has been postponed until the fall.

We have a few invalids [2] who are on a brand-new kind of diet. Some are doing well on it, especially one man, who is almost cured. The others are not doing badly by it. It consists in this: they eat only bread and drink only milk. It is a remedy that has been used in Paris for some time now; it has had very good results and never bad ones. A lot of cow's milk is drunk to make up for the nourishment that comes from bread, of which very little is eaten. Nothing else is eaten and only milk is drunk.[3]

The Nuncio[4] did us the favor of coming to see us, but nothing worth writing to you occurred during the visit.

I am, in O[ur] L[ord], Monsieur, your most humble servant.

VINCENT DEPAUL,
i.s.C.M.

Addressed: Monsieur Jolly

---

[2]Cf. no. 2815.

[3]The words "nothing else is eaten, etc." are in the Saint's handwriting.

[4]Celio Piccolomini.

2824. - TO GUILLAUME DESDAMES, SUPERIOR, IN WARSAW

Paris, April 25, 1659

Monsieur,

The grace of O[ur] L[ord] be with you forever!

I have received no letters from you for three or four weeks now. The last letter is the one in which you informed me of what took place during your visit to Krakow, and I have not written to you since my reply to that one. In it you saw that we have decided to postpone sending you any men until Providence provides the occasion to put them to work and support them there. That may happen when we are least thinking of it.

God's works are not governed according to our views and wishes. We must be satisfied with making the best use of the few talents He has given us without troubling ourselves about having greater or more extensive ones. If we are faithful in little things, He will place us over great ones; [1] but that is up to Him and is not a result of our efforts. Let us allow Him to act and let us go back into our own shells. The Company began without any intention on our part; it has grown solely by God's guidance; it was called to Poland by higher orders, and all we contributed to it was obedience. Let us continue, Monsieur, to act in the same way; God will be very pleased with this abandonment, and we will be at peace.

The spirit of the world is restless and tries to do everything. Let us leave it as it is. We do not want to choose our own ways but to walk in those it will please God to set down for us. Let us consider ourselves unworthy of being used by Him and of having others think of us, and then we will be well off. Let us offer ourselves to Him to do and suffer all things for His glory and the building up of His Church. He wants nothing more. If He desires results, they are

---

Letter 2824. - Archives of the Mission, Krakow, original signed letter.

[1]Cf. Mt 25:21. (NAB)

His and not ours. Let us open wide our hearts and wills in His presence, not deciding to do this or that until God has spoken. Let us ask Him to grant us the grace of working in the meantime at the practice of the virtues O[ur] L[ord] practiced during His hidden life. I ask Him to animate you and good M. Duperroy [2] with His Spirit so that you may possess all of them to the highest degree.

I am for both of you, in the sole good pleasure of God, Monsieur, your most humble servant.

VINCENT DEPAUL,
i.s.C.M.

Addressed: Monsieur Desdames, Superior of the Priests of the Mission of Holy Cross, in Warsaw

2825. - TO DENIS LAUDIN, SUPERIOR, IN LE MANS

Paris, April 26, 1659

Monsieur,

The grace of O[ur] L[ord] be with you forever!

I received three letters from you. I really wanted to answer your first two sooner but was unable to do so.

I praise God, Monsieur, that the compromise between the Administrators and us seems likely. Oh! how heartily will we abide by the decision of three Parisian lawyers, one to be named by them, another by us, and the two of them making the choice of the third. I thank M. de la Bataillère [1] a thousand times for opening the way to this and for the zeal he is bringing to it. I ask Our Lord to bless

---

[2]Nicolas Duperroy.

Letter 2825. - Archives of the Mission, Paris, original signed letter.

[1]Administrator of the Le Mans Hospital.

him with the blessedness He has promised to peacemakers.[2] You may, then, act in accord with this settlement.

Since you are being given good references for M. Faussard, I consent to your hiring him as a salaried servant to look after your temporal affairs, on condition that you stipulate that he is not to keep any documents for himself but, when he has obtained the ones he needs from you or from the attorney, or gets them from the notary or from your lawyer, procurator, or bailiff, he will hand them over to you as soon as he has finished with them. You will have to be very careful of this. It is not advisable to accept him just now to become a Brother; we will see about that with time.[3] If you were to admit him as a Brother first, you should not put him to work too soon at business affairs.

As for the young man you have already taken as a servant, since he seems hard-working and well-intentioned you may accept him to try him out as a Brother. It might not be a bad idea to delay him for a while longer, the better to test him; I leave that to your discretion.

I have nothing to say about accepting the notary M. Le Vayer presented to you, since that has already been done.

I, like some other persons, do not think you should convert your general lease into individual ones. You have enough financial difficulties without adding to them, and the profit might not be worth the trouble. See if you can find an upright, solvent farmer who will give you as much as the late M. Aubert.[4] If the vines are damaged by frost, as they are here, that will work against you.

I am consoled that you sent someone else to give a mission and you stayed at home, where your presence is still needed. Furthermore, your health does not allow you to do the work of preaching.

---

[2]Cf. Mt 5:9. (NAB)

[3]The records available to us give no indication that he was ever received into the Congregation of the Mission.

[4]Pierre Aubert, a merchant in Le Mans.

I am also very glad that you sent M. Le Blanc[5] to give that mission, since he conducted himself in the seminary in the way you told me. I am pleased, too, that you have put M. Molony in charge of your boarders. Tell him that I know he is in this duty, I consent to his remaining in it, and I request that he do so. If, by chance, he asks to leave it to do something else, simply let me know about his desire for a change when he indicates this, and I will write him a letter to tell him what I think about it.[6]

When you see someone who does not carry out the duties of his office or keep the Rules, you should reprove him, even though you may think he will not receive your admonition well—and even if you are sure of this from experience—provided it be done properly and always in a spirit of gentleness; otherwise, he might think he was doing the right thing or assume that you approve of his infractions.

So, you should not allow anyone to do by halves the things he has to do, and even less should you do what he neglects, in order to make up for his negligence, for that would overwhelm you. Your principal duty is the overall guidance of the family and business matters; you must supervise everyone and see that all is done as it should be done. If, after that, you still have some time to study, fine! It will be a good idea for you to apply yourself to that. "But," you will tell me, "I have no free time for that." If such is the case, Monsieur, rest assured that, when Our Lord sees you busy with other things for love of Him, He Himself will be your competency and will help you to speak effectively when you preach. Indeed, it is not the most learned persons who have the best results but rather those who have greater grace from God. Now, who has more of it than those who detach themselves from everything to be united to

---

[5]Charles Le Blanc.

[6]First redaction: "If, by chance, he asks to leave it to do something else, help him to realize that obedience is essential in the Company and that we prefer to see outside, rather than inside, a man who is willing to do only what pleases him."

His Divine Goodness, as you do, by bearing lovingly the burden He has imposed on you?

Since that good Pastor who asks to work on your missions has remained at your house, and you think he will do a good job of it, you can give him that consolation and your workers this relief. But, as for the proposal from the Archdeaconry of Tréguier for the union, do not even think about it because the dignities of a cathedral are not to be united to other bodies. Thank him, however, for his good will. When you have seen the Pastor of Mamers,[7] let me know his plan.

I say nothing to you about Brother Descroizilles; we will see if the mission will change him.

I am, in O[ur] L[ord], Monsieur, your most humble servant.

VINCENT DEPAUL,
i.s.C.M.

At the bottom of the first page: Monsieur Laudin

2826. - TO JEAN PARRE, IN LAON

Paris, April 26, 1659

Dear Brother,

The grace of Our Lord be with you forever!

I received your letter from Reims, and I am writing to you in Laon to tell you that no further orders were given at our last meeting. Furthermore, I do not think there will be any for another two or three weeks because a mission will be given at the Hôtel-

---

[7]Pierre de Grougnault.

Letter 2826. - Archives of the Mission, Paris, original signed letter.

Dieu, in which the Ladies are to participate. After that we will see if they can send you something. Meanwhile, I ask God to give you an ever greater share in His Spirit.

We have no news here.

I am, in O[ur] L[ord], dear Brother, your most affectionate servant.

VINCENT DEPAUL,
i.s.C.M.

Addressed: Brother Jean Parre, of the Mission, at the home of the Cantor, in Laon

2826a. - TO CHARLES-AUGUSTE DE SALES, BISHOP OF GENEVA

Paris, April 29, 1659

Excellency,

I learned from M. Berthe that Your Excellency is willing to hear the facts of our dispute with M. Donyer [1] and to do us the favor of being the judge of the case. I thank you most humbly for this, Excellency, and assure you that we will proceed in it unquestioningly in the way Your Excellency ordains.

He also informs me, Excellency, that M. Coglée is in danger of losing his sight if he remains any longer in Annecy, where the

---

Letter 2826a. - Property of Count de Roussy de Sales, Thorens-Glières, France, original signed letter. The editors are indebted to Sister Marie Patricia Burns, VSM, archivist of the Visitation monastery of Annecy, for providing us with a copy.

The original did not indicate the addressee, but the contents leave little doubt that it was Charles-Auguste de Sales, Bishop of Geneva, who was always favorable to the Missionaries stationed in Annecy.

[1] It is uncertain whether this M. Donyer is the unnamed lawyer mentioned in no. 2532 or the person of evil intent mentioned in no. 2816. Saint Vincent seems to be alluding here to the problems the confreres in Annecy, especially M. Le Vazeux, were experiencing with the union of Saint-Sépulcre Priory to the Congregation of the Mission.

climate is very harmful to his eyes; he himself has written me the same thing. This obliges us, Excellency, to recall him here and to ask M. Charles [2] to replace him in the interim.

I most humbly entreat Your Excellency to accept the renewal I make him of my perpetual obedience, since I have the honor to be, Excellency, by the goodness of God and your own, in His love, your most humble and very obedient servant.

VINCENT DEPAUL,
i.s.C.M.

2827. - TO PIERRE CABEL, IN SEDAN

Paris, April 30, 1659

Monsieur,

The grace of O[ur] L[ord] be with you forever!

I am writing in answer to your letter of April 17. I would like to think that you are now back from the journey to Reims. God grant that you have returned in good health!

It will be a good idea for you to write to the Suffragan Bishop of Trèves [1] to find out whether you should welcome or should send away the penitents from his diocese, so as to do nothing in this matter that is not proper and in accord with the Will of God.

The Marquise de Vins, who was from Provence, died in Paris

---

[2]François Charles, born in Plessala (Côtes-du-Nord) on December 10, 1611, entered the Congregation of the Mission on March 12, 1640, and was ordained a priest during Lent of 1641. He was Director of Retreatants and of the coadjutor Brothers at Saint-Lazare and died on January 26, 1673. In the circular letter addressed to the entire Company to announce his death, Edme Jolly, Superior General, greatly praised his virtue. (Cf. *Notices*, vol. II, pp. 245-46.)

Letter 2827. - Archives of the Mission, Paris, original signed letter. This is probably the letter mentioned by Collet (*op. cit.*, vol. II, p. 539, note); he read *Caset* instead of *Cabel*.

[1]Trier, in what is now part of Germany.

last month. She left the Marseilles house eighteen thousand livres for the maintenance of a few priests who are to give missions and she wanted all the priests of the Company to celebrate one Mass for her intention after her death. I ask you and your men, Monsieur, to please render her this duty in a spirit of gratitude.

I am, in the love of O[ur] L[ord], Monsieur, your most humble servant.

VINCENT DEPAUL,
i.s.C.M.

Addressed: Monsieur Cabel, Priest of the Mission, in Sedan

2828. - TO FIRMIN GET, SUPERIOR, IN MARSEILLES

Paris, May 2, 1659

Monsieur,

The grace of O[ur] L[ord] be with you forever!

Your short letter of April 22 contains nothing to which I have not already replied, and I think you have now received the assistance you requested for the hospital. It is very doubtful that the Administrators will get anything else (the Attorney General [1] has explained this) until they receive payment [2] from the King's alms, which is on the books of the State for next year. Therefore, they will do well to use those two thousand livres carefully and, if that amount is insufficient, to borrow whatever more they need; for, alas! could they allow the patients to die for want of making this little effort to help them?

Letter 2828. - Archives of the Mission, Paris, original signed letter.

[1]Nicolas Fouquet.

[2]First redaction: "the Administrators must not expect any more until they receive payment. . . ." The correction is in the Saint's handwriting.

I sent you two bills of exchange a week ago, one for a thousand and the other for five hundred fifty livres. I will say nothing to you now about how they are to be used because my last letter explained this to you in detail.

When we have received something from your little revenue—which will be soon, God willing—we will send it to you. As you know, it is from the coaches and it continues to decrease.

I am sending you single copies of the foundations of the Duchesse d'Aiguillon and the late Marquise de Vins. You will see in them to what they obligate your house.

We received here two écus for Pierre Le Gros, called Lapointe, a convict on the *Capitaine.* I am writing to tell M. Huguier to give them to him. We also received fifty livres from Madame de Romilly for her son the Chevalier, which I will send you at the first opportunity. Meanwhile, if some ship is leaving for Tunis, please advance this amount and send it to M. Le Vacher in Tunis to be given to that slave. I also ask M. Huguier to give three livres to Antoine Auroy, a convict on the *Grimaldi.*

Your most humble servant.

VINCENT DEPAUL,
i.s.C.M.

Addressed: Monsieur Get

2829. - TO JACQUES PESNELLE, SUPERIOR, IN GENOA

Paris, May 2, 1659

Monsieur,

The grace of O[ur] L[ord] be with you forever!

I received your letter of April 7, which consoled me immensely.

Letter 2829. - Archives of the Mission, Paris, seventeenth-century copy.

You have given me great pleasure by your firmness in not hearing the confessions of French persons in your chapel, and I ask you to continue because the permission I gave was only in case of necessity. In addition, I also presumed that there was no church within a quarter or half of a league outside the city because, if there were, my opinion was that we should go there to hear the confessions of those poor people, who could not go elsewhere. The proposal had been made to me in a somewhat roundabout way, which was very different from the aspect you give it.

I do not think that the unassuming manner and limited learning of the Italian priest who is presenting himself for admission should keep you from accepting him, if he also has a certain ability, common sense, and the best of wills, as you lead me to understand.

I praise God that your little nursery continues to grow in numbers and in virtue. It is better for M. Antoine Bruno, and all those who will take their vows at the end of their seminary, to take them in your presence, while you are celebrating Holy Mass—when you can do so—and not in the presence of someone else who is not the Superior.

I am not sorry that you recognize your need for God's grace because that keeps you in a state of awe and humility, from which we should never depart. I ask Our Lord to ground us firmly in them and then to fill us with confidence in His paternal goodness so we will ask and obtain from Him all the help necessary to fulfill our plan of procuring simply His glory in ourselves and in others. I ask Him especially to give you the fullness of His Spirit so you may diffuse it on the country Pastors who are at your house—or who are to come there—for their retreats, according to the Cardinal's order.

I have no news at all of your brothers, and I do not know if the one who had gone to Rome has returned from there; there is no way of settling your business without him. Let me know if he is still in Italy; in case he is in Rouen, write to both of them about your plans, and we will act accordingly. Send me your letters unsealed.

The late Marquise de Vins, who was from Provence, died in

Paris a month or two ago. She left the Marseilles house eighteen thousand livres for the maintenance of a few priests who are to give missions. She also wanted all the priests of the Company to celebrate one Mass for her intention after her death. I ask you, Monsieur, to see that the men in your family render her this duty in a spirit of gratitude.

I am, in the love of O[ur] L[ord], Monsieur, your most humble servant.

VINCENT DEPAUL,
i.s.C.M.

2830. - TO EDME JOLLY, SUPERIOR, IN ROME

Paris, May 2, 1659

Monsieur,

The grace of O[ur] L[ord] be with you forever!

I received at the same time two letters from you, dated April 1 and 7. We are waiting for the letter of provision for Chavagnac and the dimissorial for Brother Butler, for which you lead me to hope.

I think I told you that the Madagascar voyage is postponed until the month of September.

Your reply to me about the Fathers of Christian Doctrine is right, namely, that we cannot share by communication our privileges with them. The death of Father Hercules, their former General, means that perhaps they will not think about this any longer. The Nuncio, who came here recently, did not mention it to me again—or perhaps they can take care of their business without us.

Letter 2830. - Archives of the Mission, Paris, original signed letter.

We will try to pay your bill of exchange and to give you a little[1] help later on with paying the expenses of your little seminary, in which you tell me you are soon to admit a young Italian priest.[2] I praise God for this.

While we are on the subject, I will tell you, Monsieur, that it is greatly to be feared that the Frenchmen you have admitted will not persevere because this is contrary to the usual custom of other Communities—even the Jesuits, I think—who ordinarily send postulants back to their own provinces. They find it disadvantageous to admit them otherwise because of the difficulty Frenchmen have in getting along with Italians. Another reason is that those who go to Rome may enter with you because they do not know what to do with themselves, have no means of meeting their own needs, and want to take cover in the meantime. Or else they are gadabouts and somewhat flighty, trying now one state of life, now another.

I have been told that the last man you admitted is like that, and I think I detected a little of this in his letters. That is why I ask you, Monsieur, to send us from now on the Frenchmen who express a desire to enter the Company—unless the person is someone whose virtue is above suspicion and whose vocation is known to you.

I sent the last letter—and the one before it—from that young man from La Ferté-Bernard[3] to his relatives, and I will ask M. Éveillard to find out about his father's accident so he can write him the truth about it.

I already told you that you could make an effort to obtain authorization for the General of the Company to have, when he

---

[1]In the preceding text, the Saint made a few additions. He himself inserted: "until the month of September," "former," "or perhaps they can take care of their business without us," and "a little."

[2]Tommaso Robiolis, born in Nice (Alpes-Maritime) on August 23, 1634, entered the seminary of the Congregation of the Mission in Rome on July 30, 1659, and took his vows there on July 30, 1661, in the presence of M. Simon. Robiolis served a time as Assistant General and died on August 5, 1701.

[3]A town in Sarthe.

deems it appropriate, some members of the Company, who will not and cannot have any patrimonial title, admitted to Sacred Orders under that of *mensae communis,*[4] since Father Hilarion[5] was of this opinion.

I praise God that the preacher has softened his stance about trying to prevent Messieurs d'Eu and Baliano[6] from working in the place where he was preaching, and for the moderation those two used in this unfortunate incident, thanks to your good advice. Above all, I thank God that, since the needs there are very great, the results of their spiritual exercises are also great. I am consoled that you sent Messieurs Legendre and Morando[7] to another place, and if it were possible for you to send yet others elsewhere, as Cardinal Ginetti[8] would like, I am sure you would do so, both on account of his authority and because of the need those poor people have of this help.

I praise God that M. Le Gouz [9] is now a priest and is feeling better.

I feel much relieved of my anxiety concerning Cardinal Bagni's illness (since you told me he was recovering from his ailment). People here led us to think it was more serious than you tell me it is. May it please God to continue to preserve him for His Church!

I am sending you the attestation from the Bishop of Troyes [10] of

---

[4]*Common table;* title under which the support of a member of the Congregation of the Mission is guaranteed; such a guarantee is required to receive the sacrament of Holy Orders.

[5]Hilarion Rancati.

[6]Pietro Paolo Baliano, born in Genoa on February 3, 1628, entered the Congregation of the Mission there on November 1, 1649, was ordained during Lent of 1652, and took his vows on September 8, 1652.

[7]Antonio Morando, born in Croce, Tortona diocese (Italy), on January 13, 1613, was ordained a priest on September 20, 1636. He entered the Internal Seminary of the Congregation of the Mission in Genoa on March 25, 1650, took his vows in September 1652, and died on July 15, 1694. His obituary (cf. *Notices,* vol. II, pp. 439-47) is a great tribute to his virtue.

[8]Martio Ginetti was appointed Cardinal on January 19, 1626, then Legate in Ferrara, Legate *a latere* in Germany; Bishop of Albano, Sabina, and Porto. He was also Cardinal-Vicar and sub-Dean of the Sacred College when he died at eighty-six years of age on March 1, 1671.

[9]Jacques Legouz.

[10]François Malier du Houssay.

the poverty of the parties for whom he is requesting a marriage dispensation. Included with it is an informative report, in reply to the questions you posed.

M. Dupuich wanted to write to you for another dispensation, but I told him you had too much to do and to go to the bankers.[11] M. Serre is writing to you for a document similar to the one you sent him. I will write him the same thing so that he will not take on such affairs anymore. Enough of that for this time!

I am always, in the love of O[ur] L[ord], Monsieur, your most humble servant.

VINCENT DEPAUL,
i.s.C.M.

Addressed: Monsieur Jolly

2831. - TO JEAN PARRE, IN RETHEL

Paris, May 3, 1659

Dear Brother,

The grace of O[ur] L[ord] be with you forever!

I received your letter from Laon. I see in it that you were retracing your steps to Rethel to achieve here what you were unable to begin there. Everything will be done with time, if God wills it. I have not yet sent your letters to Madame Talon [1] and Mademoi-

[11]In this context "bankers" means "forwarding agents" at the Court of Rome. These officials were responsible for sending out all the Bulls, dispensations, and other documents issued in the Roman Court.

Letter 2831. - Archives of the Mission, Paris, original signed letter.

[1]Françoise Doujat, widow of Omer Talon, Solicitor-General at the Parlement. She died on April 17, 1667.

selle Viole because it was only today that I opened your packet.

Since our Ladies are taking part in the mission being given at the Hôtel-Dieu, we had no meeting last week, so I have nothing to tell you. We will see if they meet on Wednesday.

The grain is damaged by frost in many places, along with the vines, which are damaged everywhere. May it please God to have pity on the poor people! If Providence afflicts us in that way, God's goodness consoles us in another because people are saying that peace has already been concluded; that will be an immense blessing for the poor border areas.[2]

I am, in the love of O[ur] L[ord], dear Brother, your most affectionate servant.

VINCENT DEPAUL,
i.s.C.M.

A week or so ago, one of your relatives passed by here on his way to Liesse[3] with some other persons from your region. I think he said he was your brother-in-law. Ducournau told him he could find you in Laon because we had heard at the time that you were supposed to be going there. Most likely, however, those poor people did not find you, since you were there such a short time.

Addressed: Brother Jean Parre, of the Congregation of the Mission, in Rethel

---

[2]The Treaty of the Pyrenees (between France and Spain) was being drawn up and, after prolonged discussion, would be signed on November 7, 1659. The areas in which Jean Parre was working would now know peace after the long periods of devastation.

By this treaty Louis XIV married the Spanish Infanta, Maria Teresa, eldest daughter of the Spanish King, Felipe IV. This treaty marked the end of the Spanish ascendancy in Europe, which now passed to France.

[3]Notre-Dame-de-Liesse (Aisne).

2832. - *ALAIN DE SOLMINIHAC TO SAINT VINCENT*

Mercuès, May 3, 1659

Monsieur,

I am making a great effort in writing to you in my own hand, due to my present weakness. I feel obliged to do so, however, to tell you that it is necessary for you to take up once again the arms you so long had in hand to combat Jansenism—not to combat Jansenism again, but rather the most pernicious doctrine that could ever appear in the Church. People are trying to introduce it under the pretext of combating Jansenism, but that is a ruse. I am speaking of that abominable monster, the Apologie des casuistes.[1]

I think you know that, when the General of the authors of this book heard that the Sorbonne and a large number of Prelates had condemned it, he ordered them to disclaim it. They have done so verbally but, in fact, they are defending it so strongly that they will stop at nothing to have it received as containing true doctrine. I am not saying this because I heard it but because of what transpired between me and my people.

About six weeks ago the Provincial of this province came to see me. He and his companion were well prepared to debate that doctrine with me, and he began to propound it. When I told him my sentiments about it in a few words, he tried at the same time to engage in a dispute, but I stopped him short, telling him that Bishops are the teachers and they are the disciples, with whom they do not discuss matters. His companion said that the most learned Prelates in the kingdom were writing in defense of this book. I replied that this was not true and that no upright man approves it. And turning to the Provincial, I told him that, if he or his men tried to uphold it, I would never see them. With that, he turned on his heels and left.

A few days later, he came back to see me, bringing me a letter from his General telling the Provincials of this kingdom to have nothing to do with that book and expressly forbidding all the members of the Company to write to uphold it. Nevertheless, they continue to use all [sorts] of means to justify it. Since that time, they have had one of their men, named Father

---

Letter 2832. - Archives of the Diocese of Cahors, Alain de Solminihac Collection, notebook, copy made from the original.

[1]For information about this book see no. 2806, n. 9.

Ferrier,[2] *write a treatise on the probability of opinions* [3] *to show that a person may follow the opinion of a Doctor or scholar in certain cases—which no one denies. He attempts to prove this by citing a number of authorities and, in passing, establishes probability in a certain important question, using their authors as proof of this proposition, the goal for which they are aiming. He has also had this work approved by two Doctors of the Sorbonne residing in Toulouse. They proclaim that, if probability as they establish it is accepted, the whole* Apologie *will also be, since it is based entirely on it. That is what he told one of my men.*

Twice I sent the Prior of the Convent of Canons Regular of Cahors to the Rector of the collège in that town to ask him which casuists were teaching the doctrine he is putting in that book to support that of the Apologie; *but he could not tell him any of them, so it has to be the members of that Company who invented and are teaching it. I ask you to note where we would be if it were accepted that people might follow—even when it is a question of our salvation—an opinion that would be supported by some weighty argument.*

They persuaded the Archbishop of Toulouse[4] *and the Bishops of Vabres*[5] *and Montpellier*[6] *to write in favor of probability—as if those who*

---

[2]Jean Ferrier, born in Valadi (Aveyron) on January 20, 1614, entered the Society of Jesus on April 22, 1632, was appointed confessor to the King in 1670, and died in Paris on October 29, 1674. He was the author of several works against the Jansenists.

[3]Jean Ferrier, *Les sentimens des plus considérables casuistes sur la probabilité des opinions dans la morale* (Toulouse, 1659). The work is dedicated to Pierre de Marca, Archbishop of Toulouse at the time (1654-62).

Probabilism is a theory that any solidly probable course may be followed in disputed moral questions, even though an opposed course of action is or appears more probable.

[4]Pierre de Marca born in Gans (Basses-Pyrénées) on January 24, 1594 became a magistrate and, on April 16, 1631, a widower with the care of four children. He was a Councillor and then Minister of State. Although he had decided to enter the priesthood, he was sent to Catalonia as Visitor and Intendant-General (1644-51). He was confirmed as Bishop of Couserans at the consistory of January 13, 1648. In Barcelona he received Minor Orders on March 25, 1648, subdiaconate on March 28, diaconate on March 29, and priesthood on April 2. De Marca was consecrated a Bishop in Narbonne on October 25, 1648, and continued his service in Catalonia until he took possession of the Couserans diocese on August 3, 1651. On March 23, 1654, he was promoted to the office of Archbishop of Toulouse. Although named Archbishop of Paris on June 5, 1662, he died on June 29 of the same year and was buried in the Archbishops' crypt of Notre-Dame Cathedral.

[5]Isaac Habert (1645-68).

[6]François de Bosquet, Administrator for Justice in Languedoc, who later became Bishop of Lodève (1648-57), then of Montpellier (1657-76). He died on June 24, 1676. (Cf. Abbé Paul-Émile-Marie-Joseph Henry, *François Bosquet* [Paris: Ernest Thorin, 1889].)

censured the Apologie *were denying it, which is not the case, but simply the way it is explained and drawn up. They are doing their utmost to prevent the Prelates from censuring this harmful book. They are writing to Rome that, since these censures have been made, Jansenism is getting bolder in opposing the authority of the Pope in order to oblige His Holiness, by this means, to reserve to himself examination of it.*

In a word, they are acting with as much precaution and passion to defend this pernicious book as if there were question of the loss of the Company. In the judgment of the most clear-sighted and those who are interceding (?) and—even more—of our dear Holy Father, they are trying to create a division among us.

That is why I ask you to call together at your house the Pastor of Saint-Nicolas du Chardonnet [7] *and the Marquis de Magnac*[8] *(it would be most desirable to have some Bishop there, too) to see what means should be taken to thwart the plans of those persons. I will be part of this meeting, please, which must be kept very secret, and I ask you to allow me to tell you my opinion in advance, namely, that you should go to see the Nuncio and make it quite clear to him that this* Apologie *is a very dangerous book, which all upright persons abhor, and that it is not true that the Bishops are writing to defend this book, nor that the Jansenists are becoming bolder in opposing the authority of our Holy Father. I also feel that it must be censured by as many Bishops as we can get and by the monks in general as soon as possible. I think, too, that this would be best because it is obvious that it merits a severe censure.*

It seems to me that it would be advisable to write to the Bishop of Alet,[9] *asking him to explain the censure by a declaration. He can do this on what he publishes, as if he had censured the authors who wrote that one might follow a probable opinion. In a word, we must not drag our feet in preventing the evils that this harmful book will cause if we do not put a stop to it. Discredit it constantly as a very dangerous work, which aims at destroying the spirit of Christianity.*

---

[7]Hippolyte Féret.

[8]Antoine de Salignac, Marquis de Magnac, Lieutenant-General in the government of Upper and Lower Marche. He was also Fénelon's uncle.

[9]Nicolas Pavillon.

My weakness constrains me to finish by assuring you that I am, Monsieur. . . .

ALAIN,
Bi[shop] of Cahors

Extract of two letters from a religious to the secretary of the Bishop of Cahors: "I am sending you a short treatise on the probability of opinions, composed by a very knowledgeable, highly respected Prelate who does not sign his name to it. He promises other important volumes on these matters, as you will see by the lines at the end of this study in different writing. Someone wrote us that the Archbishop of Toulouse is still working on this same material and will soon produce his work. We have also been informed that an appeal for censures against the Apologie *has been made to Rome, where resides the common Father of the faithful and the sovereign judge of decisions regarding faith and morals and Church policy. The disputes, however, are encouraging the Jansenists. The Pope saw the letter from that priest from Languedoc and strongly approved of it. He ardently awaits the works of the Prelates who are studying these questions."*

"I share with you the news that was sent me about the matters that constitute today most of the quarrels of the curious, scholars, and zealots:

(1) From Rome they write that the Pope has seen, read, and highly praised the letter of the Bishop of Mirepoix,[10] *translated into Latin—as you have read it—as well as in French. There are three renowned, learned Prelates who are working hard on this material, and whose works the Pope will welcome with as much approval and pleasure as the Bishop of Mirepoix's letter.*

(2) The Pope considers this affair of Poland against the Jansenists and its repercussions as a matter of great consequence for what concerns the Church and the Holy See. He has indicated this through his advisor in Rome to persons of great learning and eminent virtue. One of the reasons provoking such thoughts and concerns for the Pope is that the Jansenists are becoming so insolent with it that they are beginning to speak with disrespect about the authority of the Pope and his sovereignty over the whole universal Church.

(3) The Pope has named eight Cardinals and as many Doctors of Theology to examine this Apologie des casuistes *against the Jansenists.*

---

[10]Louis de Lévy de Ventadour (1655-79).

(4) The Vicar-General of the Bishop of Bourges[11] *is the instigator of the censure that comes from that area. He is a very upright man but, by some misfortune which I really regret, he took about forty propositions from the writings of some professor at the University of Bourges and, after having misstated them, inserted them into his own work. That is going to give him a great deal of trouble because it will doubtless be taken to Rome, where resides the sovereign oracle of the faithful. I pity him, for he is an excellent man. I have in my hands a beautiful treatise on the probability of opinions composed by one of our theology professors in Toulouse; if you want to see it, I will send it to you."*

Monsieur, show the Bishop of Sarlat,[12] *the Coadjutor of Cahors, my letter and the copies of those that the Rector of the Jesuit collège in Cahors wrote to my secretary, which I am sending you. I think it is very important for you to write and ask M. Jolly to find out if it is being said publicly in Rome that there are some Bishops in France who are writing in defense of the* Apologie des casuistes *and that, since the Prelates have censured it, the Jansenists are becoming bolder in opposing the authority of the Pope. If that is the case, tell him to be sure that the one saying it is not someone who has access to our Holy Father, so that the latter may be informed of the truth. Have him let you know what he finds out. I did not deem it advisable to ask the Bishop of Sarlat to come to the meeting about which I am writing you because I did not know whether he might be reluctant to do so.*

As a reply to my letter, simply have your secretary write on a sheet of paper what you decide, without signing it. I will understand you clearly, even though you may be speaking in veiled terms. I do not mean this for what concerns me but rather for you; for I would say publicly, if needs be, what I am writing you.

Please write notes to the Bishop of Sarlat, our Coadjutor, and M. de Magnac, asking them to come to your house so you can share with them my letter and the two copies of the ones from the Rector of the collège of Cahors, which aim at dissuading me from publishing the censure I have made of that harmful book. The appeal it mentions is a ridiculous fantasy.

---

[11]The Bourges diocese was headed by Anne de Lévy de Ventadour (1651-62).
[12]Nicolas Sevin.

2833. - TO JEAN MONVOISIN, IN MONTMIRAIL

Paris, May 5, 1659

Monsieur,

The grace of O[ur] L[ord] be with you forever!

I received your letter of April 20. You must, then, be patient regarding Madame de Melun's [1] modest revenue. Still, you should continue to write to her about it from time to time.

As for what the King's Procurator in Neuilly-Saint-Front [2] received—or is to receive—from the farmer on the land of the late M. François Vincent, there is no harm in seeking an explanation and representing to him that it was given by the deceased to the Company. Depending on his reply, we will see what has to be done.

I do not agree to your giving a power of attorney to anyone to act for you in the matter of that land. You should even forbid the farmer to pay anyone but you. I would be very glad to know when his lease expires.

When you can go back to that place, inquire tactfully—either of others or of the man himself—who was the previous farmer on that property; see how many acres it should really cover and, if there are twenty-six, find out what happened to the five that people are complaining about, and who took them. If it was the fault of the farmer who was enjoying their use, he should be made to pay on twenty-six acres, since he is bound to do so; but it is not fair for him to pay for more than twenty-one, if that is all he has. Find out also whether the land is good and what it is worth in ordinary years; for example, what is the yield per acre. I am sure you will find that it is not more than three livres eight sous in the case of the farm

---

Letter 2833. - Archives of the Mission, Paris, original signed letter. The postscript is in the Saint's handwriting.

[1]Ernestine de Ligne-Aremberg.

[2]Principal town of a canton in Aisne.

held under the first lease. That little farm used to be worth fifty écus a year.[3]

Send Brother Pinson[4] back to us, since you do not need him.

Let me know if your vines are damaged by frost, as they are everywhere else; and if you have any wine, keep it.

The late Marquise de Vins, who was from Provence and died in Paris last March, left our house in Marseilles eighteen thousand livres for the maintenance of two priests who are to give missions. She wanted all the priests of the Company to celebrate one Mass for her intention after her death. I ask you and your men, Monsieur, to render her this duty in a spirit of gratitude.

I embrace all of you with all the tenderness of my heart. I am, in the love of O[ur] L[ord], Monsieur, your most humble servant.

VINCENT DEPAUL,
i.s.C.M.

Find out when the farmer's lease is up.

Addressed: Monsieur Monvoisin, Priest of the Mission, in Montmirail

---

[3]This sentence is in the Saint's handwriting.

[4]Denis Pinson, born in Villers-sous-Saint-Leu (Oise) in 1630, entered the Congregation of the Mission as a coadjutor Brother on July 17, 1654, at twenty-four years of age.

2834. - TO GUILLAUME DESDAMES, SUPERIOR, IN WARSAW

Paris, May 9, 1659

Monsieur,

The grace of O[ur] L[ord] be with you forever!

I am beginning to be anxious about not receiving any letters from you. I have not had one for five or six weeks, I think, and I cannot believe that you have not written me any. Oh well, I must be patient! Perhaps I will receive three or four at a time. I am worried only about your health and that of M. Duperroy,[1] who will learn about his brother's health in the enclosed letter.

We have nothing special to tell you that is worth writing, except that God is pleased to continue to shower His blessings on the poor Little Company.

The late Marquise de Vins, who was from Provence and died in Paris last March, left our house in Marseilles eighteen thousand livres for the maintenance of two priests who are to give missions. She wanted all the priests of the Company to celebrate one Mass for her intention after her death. I ask you and your men, Monsieur, to render her this duty in a spirit of gratitude.

I am, in the love of O[ur] L[ord], Monsieur, your most humble servant.

VINCENT DEPAUL,
i.s.C.M.

Since writing the above, I received your letter of April 9. What consolation it gave me! It is too late to reply to it at this hour.

Addressed: Monsieur Desdames, Superior of the Priests of the Mission of Holy Cross, in Warsaw

---

Letter 2834. - Archives of the Mission, Krakow, original signed letter. The postscript is in the Saint's handwriting.

[1]Nicolas Duperroy.

2835. - TO FIRMIN GET, SUPERIOR, IN MARSEILLES

Paris, May 9, 1659

Monsieur,

The grace of Our Lord be with you forever!

From the enclosed letter from M. Durand you will see the proposal made to him by the Bishop of Montpellier [1] and M. Durand's thought concerning you. We here have studied it and have felt that you, Monsieur, and M. Parisy are among the most suitable men we could find in the Company to lay the foundations of such an important work. Because of the person who is asking for the Company, it seems clear that its call to that place comes from God. This, together with the importance of the formation of the clergy in that region, where heresy has been entrenched for so many years, seems to oblige us to give ourselves to God for this purpose. The only thing that holds me back and concerns me is Marseilles and the need of that house for your presence. M. Le Vacher,[2] who has filled in for you in your absence, will please continue to do so until we can send someone else in your place.

I most humbly entreat you, Monsieur, to make this sacrifice of yourself to our good God. I ask you also to put the business affairs in the best possible state and to inform M. Le Vacher about them, then leave for Agde as soon as possible so you can discuss everything with M. Durand. I have no specific advice to give you on that point; I will wait to see the plan and state of everything before telling you my humble thoughts.

It is not advisable for you to take your final leave of the Bishop of Marseilles or of any other persons to whom you owe this; it will suffice to say that you have been instructed to go to Montpellier.

Letter 2835. - Archives of the Mission, Paris, original autograph letter; formerly the property of the Carmelite monks of Rennes.

[1]François de Bosquet (1655-76).

[2]Philippe Le Vacher.

Then, too, you will perhaps find that things have changed. See that one key to the strongbox is given to M. Le Vacher, and you keep the other; you will not be so far away as to be unable to be there, if need be, to open the strongbox when the time comes.

Go then, Monsieur, *in nomine Domini.* I ask His Divine Goodness to fill you with His Spirit so that you may communicate it to souls. May Divine Providence watch over your leadership!

I am, in His love, Monsieur, your most humble servant.

VINCENT DEPAUL,
i.s.C.M.

For several reasons, it w[ould be] des[irable] for you to have a Brother—if this can be done—and to have him go to Montpellier, whenever you think it advisable.

I am once again. . . .[3]

I am not sure if you wrote me about M. Bidre's[4] behavior. Let me know; I will write to him accordingly.

I have been overwhelmed with transacting business affairs and have not had time to write to M. Le Vacher. Share with him this letter, in which I ask him to replace you in your absence and to follow all your ways of acting. Give him a brief account of the sums of money you have received in the past year and those you have sent to Tunis and Algiers; what you owe—if anything—what is due you, and what you are leaving with him. Please send me a copy of all that.

Brother Get [5] is the best of the eighteen students we have for philosophy, and we think he will be able to teach it at the end of the present term.

Addressed: Monsieur Get

---

[3]After the letter had been signed, this first part of the postscript was inserted in the blank section on the original between "I am, in His love" and "your most humble servant."

[4]First redaction: "M. Beaure's." Jacques Beaure is listed in the personnel catalogue, but there is no Bidre.

[5]Nicolas Get, Firmin Get's brother.

2836. - TO FIRMIN GET, SUPERIOR, IN MARSEILLES

Paris, May 9, 1659

Monsieur,

The grace of O[ur] L[ord] be with you forever!

I received a letter dated April 29. I forwarded to the Duchesse d'Aiguillon the one from M. Le Vacher [1] and to the Attorney General[2] the one from the Administrators.

Last week the Brother forgot to put into the packet the extracts from the foundations of the Duchesse d'Aiguillon and Madame de Vins so you could see your obligations; so, we are sending them to you now.

I have nothing to say about what you tell me concerning the missions, except that it is to be hoped that, in the future, as far as possible, preference will be given to the Marseilles diocese over any other.

I greatly fear, as you do, that M. Constans[3] will play his last hand against the Consul, when he sees him taking his place; and God grant that this agent will do no harm to the work of God, since it is difficult to serve two masters! [4]

You will see that the foundation of Madame de Vins must be considered as capital and is not payable for three years; I doubt, therefore, that you can take from that money the three hundred écus you need to have the water the city has given you brought into your garden. If, however, you could wait a year, you could take that money from the one thousand livres the heirs or executors of that Lady's will will give you at that time as income for the first year

---

Letter 2836. - Archives of the Mission, Paris, copy made from the original in the Hains Family Collection, Marseilles.

[1]Philippe Le Vacher.

[2]Nicolas Fouquet.

[3]François Constans, Chancellor of Brother Jean Barreau, the Consul in Algiers.

[4]Cf. Mt 6:24. (NAB)

of this foundation. We will think about that, or, if we find any money to borrow, we will do so.

We received one écu for Nicolas Bonner and eight for M. Gardon, a convict on the *Saint-Philippe.* I ask M. Huguier to give each one his share, and I ask you to credit him for those twenty-seven livres, as we will do for you.

I ask M. Le Vacher to excuse me for not writing to him this time; it is eight o'clock in the evening. If there is any news of poor Bernusset,[5] Abbé de Chandon will be glad if we could share it with him, and I will be glad if you let me know if the money sent him will be enough for his ransom.

I am, in O[ur] L[ord], Monsieur, your most humble servant.

VINCENT DEPAUL,
i.s.C.M.

2837. - TO JACQUES PESNELLE, SUPERIOR, IN GENOA

Paris, May 9, 1659

Monsieur,

The grace of Our Lord be with you forever!

Since your letter of April 22 was filled with reasons for consolation, I do not know where to begin to thank God for them. I have already done so in general and in particular for the special graces God gave you during the missions and, through you, to sinners—and to the most hardened among them—for the outstanding large

---

[5]Vital Bernusset, a slave held in Nauplia (Návplion), a town and port in the Peloponnesus (Greece).

Letter 2837. - Archives of the Mission, Paris, seventeenth-century copy.

donation given you by Signor Brignole,[1] and for the plan of the members of the Senate to send Missionaries to Corsica and to allocate a sum of money annually for this purpose. Since I am unable on my own to thank God for this in the way I would like to do, I have asked the members of the Company to help me with this just obligation and have given them all those blessings from heaven as dessert.

I have no words—and I do not expect to find any, Monsieur—to express my gratitude to that virtuous, charitable gentleman for the exceptional charity he has done you. I ask O[ur] L[ord] to make it known to him. I will take the honor of attesting to it in some way by letter, as soon as God gives me the leisure to write to him; I cannot do so today. I will try to write another one to the Cardinal at the same time. We are indebted, after God, to His Eminence for this benefit and for all the others.

We cannot offer ourselves to Signor Brignole to go and give a mission in his marquisate unless it is the good pleasure of the Cardinal, nor should you make any commitment to go to minister in Corsica without his consent. We are not obliged simply to follow his orders but also to comply with his wishes. Furthermore, God's goodness to the Company is very great in thinking of it for His service in so many places and in so many ways, and, because of the modest services we render the poor, to inspire the rich and the powerful to help—and even to urge—us to continue it and to extend ourselves.

If Our Lord allows the plan that has been formulated for the instruction and salvation of those island people to materialize, fine; we will have to answer the call. We must, however, hold to the maxim God has given us the grace to keep until now of never

[1]Coste originally identified this man as Maria Emmanuele Brignole, Marchese di Grappoli, in Tuscany, son of Antonio Giulio Brignole, who had entered the Jesuits on March 11, 1652. In a later unpublished note on this, Coste states that it was "the son of Rodolfo Maria who made the donation. M. Pesnelle was unaware that he had doubtlessly acted without his parents knowledge."

making the first move to have any works given us, either directly or indirectly. We should lament before God at seeing so many needs in the Church, and ask the Divine Goodness to be pleased to remedy them and to send good workers into His vineyard.[2] We must, however, be very careful not to offer our services to anyone for any place before being called there. What we have to do, Monsieur, is to humble ourselves profoundly and abandon ourselves entirely to God.

You give me reason to go back to M. Emmanuel Brignole, regarding the deep affection you say he has for our insignificant Congregation, and to tell you that one of the things that amazes me is that a nobleman of his rank and piety should set his heart on such a lowly site to raise our unworthiness to the honor of his benevolence and the effects of his goodness. We will ask God to be his reward for this. Our house in Rome will be highly blessed if he chooses to make use of it for his holy intentions.

I praise God for the new seminarians you have admitted. I think that, far from doing wrong, you have done the contrary in using your influence with the Cardinal to have accepted into his seminary—provided they pay their room and board—the two young clerics who asked you if they might enter the Company but are not sufficiently educated to do so. This will be a means for them to attain that to which they aspire and for you to get to know them better in order to judge whether God wills it.

Regarding the young men who want to be coadjutor Brothers, since you have received one to test him,[3] that suffices for now because you do not need any more. So, instead of refusing the others, you can have them wait.

Have no doubt, Monsieur, that I offer you often and tenderly to God, together with your leadership, your family, and your spiritual

---

[2]Cf. Mt 20:1. (NAB)

[3]Giovanni Lavanino (or Langino), born in the village of San Marco, Genoa diocese on December 27, 1641, entered the Congregation of the Mission in Genoa as a coadjutor Brother on October 9, 1659, and took his vows there on October 20, 1667, in the presence of M. Pesnelle.

exercises. Nor am I satisfied with that, but I recommend to the Company to do likewise so that God may be your spirit, your strength, your success, and your glory. As for me, I am, in His love, Monsieur, your most humble servant.

VINCENT DEPAUL,
i.s.C.M.

2838. - TO EDME JOLLY, SUPERIOR, IN ROME

Paris, May 9, 1659

Monsieur,

The grace of O[ur] L[ord] be with you forever!

I received your letter of April 14. You must not be surprised if there is no longer any talk of giving you a house; that is God's affair; He will take care of it in unexpected ways and with extraordinary means, and perhaps when we are not thinking about it at all. What we have to do is to abandon ourselves to His guidance and consider ourselves fortunate to be able to honor in some way the poverty of O[ur] L[ord], who had nowhere to lay His head.[1] If it had never been heard or seen that anyone who served God and trusted in His goodness lacked the things suitable to his state, we would have some reason to be anxious about our needs; but we have only to commend them to His Providence, be faithful to our obligations, and be convinced that sooner or later God will provide what He knows we need for His plan for us. What more do we have to do?

I ask you, Monsieur, to help us thank God for the charity that a nobleman from Genoa[2] has done for our family in that same place

---

Letter 2838. - Archives of the Mission, Paris, original signed letter.

[1]Cf. Lk 9:58. (NAB)

[2]Rodolfo Maria Brignole (cf. no. 2837, n. 1).

by promising it two thousand livres a year for living expenses while he is alive. Who but God could have inspired him to do that? The Cardinal had some part in it, but the grace of this decision can come only from heaven.

You have delighted me by assuring me that Cardinal Bagni[3] is now cured. Please assure him that I could not receive a more tangible consolation and that we are asking God to preserve him for His Church for the purpose that all upright men here desire.

I praise God for the missions your workers are giving and for the graces God bestows on them and, through them, on the poor. Both you and they can count on the prayers of the Community here, which offers them frequently to O[ur] L[ord] for your good health and for blessings on your work.

I am sending you a report on behalf of the Bishop of Chartres.[4] It suffices to tell you that it is from him in order to persuade you to do what he wishes. Nevertheless, I personally ask you to do so.

We have only good news here, thank God, except that frost has ruined the vines almost everywhere in this kingdom, and most of the rye as well. God has willed to temper by these losses the joy we had of a general peace, which we feel is certain.

I am, even more assuredly in the love of O[ur] L[ord], Monsieur, your most humble servant.

VINCENT DEPAUL,
i.s.C.M.

Addressed: Monsieur Jolly

---

[3]Nicolò di Bagno.

[4]Ferdinand de Neufville de Villeroy had been Coadjutor to his uncle, Achille de Harlay de Sancy since 1644. When the latter died (November 20, 1646), Neufville succeeded him, remaining Bishop of Saint-Malo until 1657, when he was named Bishop of Chartres.

2839. - TO JEAN PARRE, IN RETHEL

Paris, May 10, 1659

Dear Brother,

The grace of O[ur] L[ord] be with you forever!

Only a few Ladies were at our last meeting, which allocated nothing for you, for lack of funds. They simply ask you—and I along with them—to get some rest and take the remedies the doctor will deem advisable to cure you, and to get a horse to take you from one town to another whenever you need one.

I am, with the heart God knows, in His love. . . .[1]

We welcomed your nephew here and had him rest for two or three days. I had him given two écus for his journey. I did not want to use the interest he is requesting from your property, since it is his father who keeps it.

I saw M. Carlier; he had dinner here one day.

I am, in O[ur] L[ord], dear Brother, your most humble servant.

VINCENT DEPAUL,
i.s.C.M.

Addressed: Brother Jean Parre, of the Congregation of the Mission, in Rethel

---

Letter 2839. - Archives of the Mission, Paris, original signed letter.

[1]Originally, these words were followed by the ones at the end of the letter, "dear Brother, etc." before the signature, which was separated from them by a large blank space. After the letter was finished, the secretary inserted in that space the news about Parre's nephew and M. Carlier. That is why the phrase "I am, with the heart God knows, etc." seems incomplete.

2840. - TO A DAUGHTER OF CHARITY

May 14, 1659

My very dear Sister,

The grace of Our Lord be with you forever!

I ask your pardon for having taken so long to reply to your letter of February 15. My minor ailments and sometimes my urgent occupations have been partly the cause of this. I must tell you frankly, however, that I did it somewhat on purpose because of the things you wrote to me, which did not require an immediate reply.

You told me of your trials and tribulations of spirit so that I might give you some quick remedy to alleviate them. I have learned, however—even from long experience—that it is not advisable to bandage fresh wounds right away because that would do them more harm than good. On the contrary, when we give a little leeway to nature to act on its own, the condition clears up sooner, especially when the wound has bled profusely and discharged all its pus. That is what you did when you wrote me what was rankling you and causing you to suffer. That is also what I did when I left you without an answer until the present, and what I am now doing through the little advice I am giving you to help to allay your troubles—if you still have any.

I am convinced that the same God who delivered you in the past from similar trials, when you thought there was no remedy for the difficulty, will likewise safeguard you from this other interior trial, since you, for your part, have done what you should and could have done to cooperate with His grace. You did this when you were in Liancourt, and things turned out very well.

And what did you do then? You were prompt in sharing your interior life by letter with your Director; you had recourse to God,

---

Letter 2840. - Archives of the Motherhouse of the Daughters of Charity, *Conférences spirituelles tenues pour les Filles de la Charité*, SV 17, p. 648.

to the Blessed Virgin, and to the saints, while waiting to hear from me; you tried to humble yourself, to trust in God, and to put into practice the resolutions you had taken during your retreat and the advice I had given you there. And after that, when you received my letter, you were already healed of your ill even before reading it.

How did that happen? As I just said, God never fails to come to our rescue in our time of need, when we, for our part, have done what we could—as you did. And even if your difficulties should continue up to the present, I would not want to take the trouble to try to free you from them, since they spring from such a good root—mistrust of yourself—and produce such good fruit—the lowly opinion you have of yourself. All that is a great means of helping you to grow in holy humility and, consequently, in the perfection your vocation requires of you. So, you have reason to rejoice over your suffering rather than to be distressed by it.

If you had sought through curiosity to go to the place where you now are, or had schemed through ambition to have the duty you now have, or had failed through sheer laziness or malice to fulfill your office, you might fear that God would make you render an account of all that some day. I know, however, that you are quite far from that, and, on the contrary, that you affirm only your incompetence and the too great esteem your Superiors have of you. Furthermore, it is God who placed you there, since you are in that office through obedience, and consequently are certain of doing the Divine Will in that. For all these reasons, I say, you should be at peace, adoring His Providence and being resigned—in this as in everything else—to His Holy Will. If, despite all that, your troubles continue, do not worry, and be content to do simply whatever you can. And if the thought comes to you that you are good for nothing and all you do is spoil everything, say: "Oh, well! so much the better! Since God habitually makes use of the poorest instruments to do great things, there is reason to hope that things will go better than if I were very intelligent and virtuous because, by this means, I will have greater reason to humble myself and to attribute to God alone the glory of all the good resulting from it, and I will not be so tempted to boastful vanity and presumption."

So, Sister, my very dear daughter in Jesus Christ, this is what I would want to say to myself if I were suffering in a similar manner. I have gone on longer than I had intended to do and have said more than was necessary, since I am convinced that a word of encouragement might have sufficed to console you and put your mind at rest. Still, I have written you this letter because, if you do not need it right now, it can be a help to you at a future time, when similar and worse difficulties assail you. We have to expect these if we lay claim to paradise.

Do not think, however, that the advice that is on this paper can diminish your sufferings; God must give His Spirit to it, and we must await everything from His infinite goodness. Pray often for that, as I do now, asking God to be Himself your strength, your courage, and your guidance everywhere and in all things. I wish the same for your dear companion, to whom I send respectful greetings. I recommend myself to her prayers and yours, being for both of you, in the love of Our Lord and His Holy Mother, etc.

2841. - TO LOUIS DUPONT, SUPERIOR, IN TRÉGUIER

May 14, 1659

Monsieur,

The grace of O[ur] L[ord] be with you forever!

I have not received any of your dear letters since the one dated March 30. To my distress, it has also been a long time since I have written to you, although I would like to console myself more often with you for the graces God gives you, and through you, to your

---

Letter 2841. - Archives of the Mission, Paris, original signed letter.

diocese.[1] Whenever I think of it, I cannot help but rejoice before God and thank Him for it. I thank Him especially for the happiness you have of working under such a good Prelate,[2] who contributes in so many ways by his example and concern to the sanctification of his clergy and the salvation of his people. May it please God to preserve him and to fill you with His Spirit so that you will be able to correspond with his holy intentions!

I am glad that Brother Butler is helping you and satisfies you. I really expected that. We are trying to find the means of having him receive Holy Orders.

I praise God likewise that those other priests, ministering with you in God's work, are comporting themselves in it with the devotion and zeal God demands and with the requisite edification both at home and abroad. That, Monsieur, is the means of drawing down new blessings on you and your work. Please take good care of their health and your own.

God is pleased to continue to grant His protection and graces to the Little Company and to gather everywhere some fruit from its modest services. He offers us many opportunities to render him new ones, even in places where we have not yet ministered, but we do not have the personnel. In this, God is making known to us our need, obliging us to ask Him to send good workers into His vineyard.[3] The men you have sent us are doing very well, thank God.

The late Marquise de Vins, who was from Provence, died in Paris last March. She left eighteen thousand livres to our Marseilles house for the maintenance of two priests, who are to give missions. She also wanted all the priests of the Company to celebrate one

---

[1]First redaction: "to the whole diocese." The correction is in the Saint's handwriting.
[2]Balthazar Grangier de Liverdi.
[3]Cf. Mt 9:38. (NAB)

Mass for her intention after her death. I ask you and your men, Monsieur, to render her this duty in a spirit of gratitude.

I am, in the love of O[ur] L[ord], Monsieur, your most humble servant.

VINCENT DEPAUL,
i.s.C.M.

I just received your letter of April 26, which gives me new reasons to praise God for the material and spiritual growth of your seminary.

Addressed: Monsieur Dupont, Superior of the Priests of the Mission of Tréguier, in Tréguier

2842. - TO JACQUES PESNELLE, SUPERIOR, IN GENOA

Paris, May 16, 1659

Monsieur,

The grace of O[ur] L[ord] be with you forever!

I received your letter of April 29. I am sure that the crosses of your office seem to you such as you tell me; but, in my opinion, they are great only because you consider them as such. They are not extraordinary, to say the least, for all those in leadership positions have similar ones. They have persons difficult to govern and men of different temperaments who are inclined to do various and often unconventional things. These must be tolerated, but they must still try to guide them gently, patiently, and adroitly to the love of the Rule and of obedience.

Letter 2842. - Archives of the Mission, Paris, original signed letter.

Continue to act in this way, as you have done until now. With all that, Monsieur, abase yourself before God, acknowledging that you are nothing but a useless instrument,[1] capable of spoiling everything. However, abandon yourself, just as you are, to His divine guidance, full of confidence that He will be the guide of your own leadership, your strength of mind and body, and the soul of your family. So, please be courageous and hope that all will go well, even when it seems the contrary to you.

I am greatly consoled by the honor the Republic does us by considering the Little Company to minister in its kingdom of Corsica. We likewise have the desire and obligation to obey it, and may it please God to make us worthy of this! There are, however, two difficulties with the proposed establishment, besides the ones you pointed out:

The first is that just now we do not have men ready to send there. You know they have to speak Italian. Where will we get them? You need your own men, and the Rome house needs the ones it has, as does Turin.

The second reason is that we cannot minister effectively in dioceses if we are not put to work by the Bishops and supported by them. Now, a contrary result might occur on that island, if the living expenses of the workers are taken from the persons on whom they should depend, because that would cause the latter to look on them in a bad light.

For these reasons, it is to be hoped that this project will be deferred and they will be satisfied with a mission like the one the late M. Blatiron gave there. You could give it at the most convenient time, provided the Cardinal agrees to it; and perhaps the Rome house could help you out.

---

[1]Cf. Lk 17:10. (NAB)

I praise God for the v[ows] M. Antoine Bruno has taken,[2] and I ask His Divine Majesty to grant him the grace of living in conformity with those promises.

I am, in His love, Monsieur, your most humble servant.

VINCENT DEPAUL,
i.s.C.M.

I am taking the honor of writing to the Cardinal.

The official from Genoa[3] did us the honor of coming here to this house. Since I am in no condition to go to his residence, I sent M. Alméras to him today. He returned filled with admiration for his gracious manner, his great courtesy, his intelligence, and his kind nature.

Addressed: Monsieur Pesnelle

2843. - TO EDME JOLLY, SUPERIOR, IN ROME

Paris, May 16, 1659

Monsieur,

The grace of O[ur] L[ord] be with you forever!

I can only praise God for all the things you tell me in your letter of April 21. I thank you especially for accepting to work on the Loreto business for the Duchesse d'Aiguillon, for having fixed the date the Bishop of Sarlat [1] wanted, for the letter of provision for Chavagnac, for the absolution from irregularity we received for that Pastor from the Sens diocese, and for working on a quick

---

[2]Antonio Bruno had taken his vows on April 28.

[3]Marchese Durazzo, who had arrived in Paris on April 6.

Letter 2843. - Archives of the Mission, Paris, original signed letter.

[1]Nicolas Sevin.

settlement for the affair of the Bishop of Pamiers,[2] which you lead us to hope for.

As for what Cardinal de Sainte-Croix[3] told you, we can only humble ourselves profoundly before God, always adoring the ways of His guidance over us, without troubling ourselves about what concerns us but simply fulfilling well our duty toward O[ur] L[ord] and the souls He has redeemed.

Earlier we sent you the description of Brother Étienne's[4] left hand, which is so deformed that it does not resemble a hand. It is like a mass of rounded flesh on which only the tip of the thumb and of another finger can be seen, but he can still use it for certain things.

When we admitted him into the Company, it was on condition that we would not make a priest of him, and he himself still does not expect to become one, although he shows an inclination for that because of the zeal God is giving him to go to evangelize unbelievers. Because, however, he has for a long time felt this impulse to leave his own country and to engage his property and his life for the propagation of the faith; because he has always worked hard to acquire virtue and has even studied theology; because he has the

---

[2]François-Étienne Caulet.

[3]Marcello di Santa Croce.

[4]The personnel catalogue states: "Nicolas Étienne, born on September 17, 1634, was admitted on August 8, 1653, provided he remain a seminarian all his life because of the serious deformity of one of his hands. He took his vows on August 8, 1655, and with a dispensation was ordained a priest on August 31, 1659, on condition that he go to Madagascar." (Cf. *Notices*, vol. I, p. 480.) Étienne had already applied to go as a catechist; it was Saint Vincent who sought the dispensation for his ordination. He set off the first time in 1660 but could not land and had to return to France. In May 1663 he left again, arriving in Madagascar in September. His apostolate was short-lived: Dian Mananghe, a Malagasy chief who had promised to receive Baptism, invited him to dinner, then imprisoned and murdered him, along with Brother Philippe Patte and some indigenous Christians.

Coste and *Notices*, vol. V (Supplement), p. 218, give February 27, 1664, as the date of the massacre. *Notices*, vol. III, pp. 350-68, gives a fuller biography of Étienne: on p. 350 it states that he died on March 4, while on p. 367 it says "in the first week of Lent 1664." A short account of Brother Patte is given on pp. 369-71 of the latter, which states that he died with Étienne on March 4. In both instances, *Mémoires de la Congrégation de la Mission. Madagascar*, vol. IX, is cited; Coste specifies pp. 374-494.

signs of a true vocation for distant lands; and because we have decided to send him to Madagascar on the first ship that sails; we thought he might serve God more effectively there if he were a priest, and that perhaps, in consideration of this, he might be dispensed from his irregularity.

Please make an effort to obtain this dispensation for him, which I am sure will be sent to the Vicars-General of Paris. In which case, it will be up to them to judge whether there is any risk in having him receive Holy Orders, and by this means the Will of God will be made known to us. Perhaps we will send you a pencil sketch of this deformed hand very soon.

If this dispensation is refused, Monsieur, please try to obtain for him at least permission: (1) to baptize in the Church with the ceremonies, in the absence of any priests; (2) to touch sacred vessels and objects; (3) to read books on the Index; (4) to exorcize possessed persons; (5) to receive the four Minor Orders; (6) to preach in church; (7) to carry the Sacred Host on his person, as it used to be carried in the early Church, so he can receive Holy Communion in the absence of any priests. He asks you also to request for him the blessing of our Holy Father the Pope and a plenary indulgence for the hour of his death, and please send him an Arabic grammar, dictionary, and catechism.

If you are granted the first favor—which covers almost all the others—namely, that he be raised to the holy priesthood, I ask you to send us at the same time an *extra tempora* to allow him to receive all the Orders between now and the month of September, when the ship is supposed to leave.

I am sending you separately a short memorandum for a few other *extra tempora* we need and for a dispensation because of age for Brother de Marthe,[5] whom we can send on this foreign mission; he

---

[5]Ignace-Joseph de Marthe, born in Arras on March 19, 1637, entered the seminary of the Congregation of the Mission in Paris on July 7, 1654, and took his vows on October 14, 1656, in the presence of M. Berthe. He was Superior in Noyon (1668-74) and Toul (1678-83).

also feels attracted to it. He will be a very good subject. I make no mention of faculties for anyone, since we have not yet definitely decided whom we will send there. I will give you their names some time before their departure.

I have been told that two ships will make this voyage: one sent by the Maréchal de la Meilleraye, and the other by the Company of the Indies, which began trading long ago with this island but discontinued sending ships there a few years ago because of some misunderstanding—perhaps also because the Maréchal encroached on their rights. We think they now want to send a ship to bring back the men they left there or to try to maintain their people and their authority there. The Bishop of Heliopolis[6] has arranged with them to take him and his men to India, where they are going to minister. We are most anxious to find out on which of these ships we are supposed to send our men. I think they will certainly be on this latter one, but if those gentlemen do not sail again, and the Maréchal is no longer willing to accept us on his ship because we disagreed with him on that occasion, we would no longer be able to send anyone to that country. We shall see.

I was hoping to send you today a letter for the Pope but cannot do so until next week. I want to join my most humble request to those made to him on all sides for the canonization of the great servant of God Francis de Sales. Those who are promoting it wanted my support; I think it is because of what you did for the Bishop of Le Puy.[7] While you await my letter and once you have

---

[6]François Pallu, born in Tours in 1626, was a Canon of Saint-Martin and one of the founders of the Foreign Missions Society [Société des Missions-Étrangères]. In 1655 he went on a pilgrimage to Rome with some friends, but a letter from the Duchesse d'Aiguillon influenced him to approach Pope Alexander VII and Cardinal di Bagno for the erection of Vicariates Apostolic in the Far East. The Pope received the suggestion favorably and appointed a commission of four Cardinals to study it. On May 13, 1658, Propaganda Fide approved the report presented to it and, on August 14 François Pallu was appointed Titular Bishop of Heliopolis and Vicar Apostolic of Tonkin, Laos, and southwest China. He died in Moyang, China, on October 29, 1684. (Cf. manuscript life of François Pallu, Archives of the Missions-Étrangères, vol. 106.)

[7]Henri de Maupas du Tour.

received it, it is advisable for you to act accordingly—I mean zealously—to do whatever you can so that the Holy See will declare the sanctity of that worthy Prelate, who lived like a saint. If you cannot do anything else, show at least by your words the desire that you, I, and the entire little Congregation have for this great benefit, which will greatly console the whole Church.

I am, in O[ur] L[ord], Monsieur, your most humble servant.

VINCENT DEPAUL,
i.s.C.M.

Addressed: Monsieur Jolly, Superior of the Priests of the Mission of Rome, in Rome

2844. - TO JEAN PARRE, IN REIMS

Paris, May 17, 1659

Dear Brother,

The grace of O[ur] L[ord] be with you forever!

I do not know why you did not receive my letter written last Saturday. I wrote you then, as I do again today, that the Ladies have not met for a long time—except for two or three of them—because of the mission at the Hôtel-Dieu in which they are taking part. Consequently, nothing has been allocated for the poor of the border areas, for want of funds.

In your letter of the eleventh, I saw what you did in Rethel to initiate the [Confraternity of] Charity of the Ladies and to get them started on visiting and comforting the sick. God be praised for this, and may it please Him to bless this good work!

Letter 2844. - Archives of the Mission, Paris, original signed letter.

You write me that M. Marteau, the Pastor in Sorbon,[1] told you that someone promised him one hundred livres to rebuild his church. You should find out who made this promise because I for one do not remember, and you know we have always informed you of what people have managed to do for the churches.

I am writing to you in Reims, and I continue to offer you to God and to recommend myself to your prayers.

Brother Alexandre [2] received the basket you sent him, and M. Carlier is responsible for bringing you the holy cards depicting the presence of God.

I am, in the love of O[ur] L[ord] and His glorious Mother, dear Brother, your most humble servant.

VINCENT DEPAUL,
i.s.C.M.

Addressed: Brother Jean Parre, of the Mission, at the home of Monsieur de Séraucourt, Lieutenant for Criminal Affairs, in Reims

2845. - TO LOUIS RIVET, SUPERIOR, IN SAINTES

Paris, May 18, 1659

Monsieur,

The grace of Our Lord be with you forever!

I am a little late answering your most recent letters of April 13 and 20. I am really worried about the restlessness of the persons you mention. As I write to you now, I see no other remedy on your

[1]Near Rethel (Ardennes).
[2]Alexandre Véronne.

Letter 2845. - Archives of the Mission, Paris, seventeenth-century copy.

part than prayer and patience, which will be more acceptable to God for their welfare and the preservation of the Company than the means they are proposing or any we could think of.

I ask O[ur] L[ord] to draw His glory from the mission you are now giving, as He is doing for the one in Arces.[1] I ask Him also to preserve you and to strengthen your health for the salvation of the people. *Mon Dieu!* Monsieur, what good reason you have to thank His Divine Goodness for the grace and opportunities He gives you of contributing, together with Jesus Christ, to the redemption of souls, applying to them the infinite merits of His sorrowful death and His Precious Blood, of which most people do not know how to avail themselves. May God, in His mercy, be pleased to fill all of us with faith, charity, and zeal for rendering some small service to His Church! Happy are those who, on these foundations, hope in God and consume themselves for charity!

The late Marquise de Vins, who was from Provence, died in Paris last month. She left our house in Marseilles eighteen thousand livres for the maintenance of two priests who are to give missions, and she wanted all the priests in the Company to celebrate one Mass for her intention after her death. I ask you and your men, Monsieur, to please render her this duty in a spirit of gratitude.

It is true that Brother Robineau has received some money for you. I asked him to make a list of what he spent on your expenses and to send it to you with the rest of the money, if there is any left. He will do so as soon as he can.

Meanwhile, I am, in the love of Our Lord, Monsieur, your most humble servant.

VINCENT DEPAUL,
i.s.C.M.

I am not writing to those two persons; I am turning to Our Lord,

---

[1]A small locality near Saintes (Charente-Maritime).

asking Him to restore to them the spirit by which He called them to the Company. Please give them my recommendations. Pray and have others pray for them.

2846. - TO PROPAGANDA FIDE

[May 1659] [1]

Most Eminent and Most Reverend Lords,

Vincent de Paul, Superior General of the Congregation of the Mission, humbly represents to Y[our] E[minences] that the last ship that sailed for the island of Madagascar [2] was captured at sea, and four priests of the Congregation of the Mission, named Apostolic Missionaries for that island, were on that ship. Because one of these priests is now not in a state to be able to make this voyage, the said petitioner humbly proposes to Y[our] E[minences] the preacher, Pierre Turpin, a priest of the same Congregation, asking that they name him an Apostolic Missionary to that island to work there for the glory of God and the salvation of souls. And the said petitioner will receive it as a special favor from Y[our] E[minences].

Whom God, etc.

Addressed: The Sacred Congregation of Propaganda Fide, for Vincent de Paul, Superior General of the Congregation of the Mission

---

Letter 2846. - Archives of Propaganda Fide, *Africa 9-10, Madagascar-Morocco,* no. 252, original in Italian.

[1]The request made in this petition was granted on May 27, 1659.

[2]Cf. nos. 2616-17 and 2619-20.

2847. - TO LUKE PLUNKET, IN SAINT-MÉEN

Paris, May 21, 1659

Monsieur,

The grace of O[ur] L[ord] be with you forever!

I have received no reply from you to the letter I wrote you,[1] nor any report that you have done as I asked you, namely, to let yourself be guided. On the contrary, I hear that you are unwilling either to teach chant or go to the Divine Office, regardless of how much you are needed or how strongly you are urged to do so, and all this because you want to go off and give missions.

But what shall we do to remedy this disorder, Monsieur? As for me, I fear that God may remedy it Himself by punishing you in some way. I would be very sorry about that because my heart truly esteems and loves you. That is why I ask His Divine Goodness to open your eyes to see the wrong you are doing and the danger in which it puts you. Thus, you may rise above it and, by this means, merit that God will preserve you in your vocation and continue to grant you the graces necessary for the service of His Church.

Do you not know, Monsieur, that we are as much obliged to form good priests as to instruct country people and that a Priest of the Mission who wants to do one but not the other is only half a Missionary, since he has been sent to do both? I say further that, when he refuses to obey in one thing in order to push his way into a work in which it has been felt inadvisable to place him, he is not one at all. It is very strange that you have no sooner become a priest by the kindness of the Company than you are beginning to resist it and, when you have a greater obligation of practicing humility, obedience, and gratitude, it is then that you commit greater faults

---

Letter 2847. - Archives of the Mission, Paris, seventeenth-century copy.

[1]Cf. no. 2820.

against these virtues, to the great scandal of the house and to my own regret.

Mon Dieu! Monsieur, what are you trying to do? You are not ready to give missions just yet, since you are not fluent enough in our language to speak in public. We had a hard time understanding you here; how, then, could the poor people understand you? And do you think that, when you are not obedient in one office, we would dare to assign you to another that requires no less obedience? Do you not think that it is the duty of Superiors to restrain an individual who leaves the ranks and, when he rejects the duties entrusted to him, to refuse him the important ones he is seeking?

In the name of O[ur] L[ord], Monsieur, humble yourself, ask His pardon for the bad example you give the seminary and your confreres, and rest assured that the Company will be indulgent enough to forget the past and to give you the satisfaction you desire, when it sees that you are indifferent to duties and very exact to the things recommended to you.

The point now is that you should sing in choir when necessary and teach chant and the ceremonies to the priests who are in Saint-Méen to learn them. With all the tenderness of my heart I ask you to do so, Monsieur. We have already taken you from Tréguier, thinking that you would do better in the place where you now are. If you do not, what hope will you give us of being better if we send you to another house! Change of place does not change the person. And if you are determined to stay as you are, attached to your own opinions and unwilling to submit to the orders of those whom God wills to guide you, what good will you be? And what will a Community that is maintained only by correction and dependence do with someone who will not accept them?

Please reflect on all this, Monsieur, and let me know your dispositions. Mine are to be all my life, in the love of O[ur] L[ord], Monsieur, your most humble servant.

VINCENT DEPAUL,
i.s.C.M.

2848. - TO GUILLAUME DESDAMES, SUPERIOR, IN WARSAW

Paris, May 23, 1659

Monsieur,

The grace of O[ur] L[ord] be with you forever!

I received your letter of April 9 two weeks ago, after writing to you the same day. I was very much consoled by it, and I thank God now as I did then for the good state of affairs in general and of your own in particular. May it please God to give peace to the entire kingdom and a thousand blessings to Their Majesties! Peace between France and Spain is deemed certain here.[1]

You tell me your reasons for wanting one or two priests plus a Brother. I agree that it will be a good idea to send them to you, and we are going to think about the choice of persons and what they will need for their journey.

Regarding what you tell me about M. Duperroy's [2] belief that he could get better in France, please let me know the state of his wound. I imagine that it is still running and, in that case, will do more good than harm to his health. Doubtless God has sent him this condition for his own good; and since the fluid has run its course through the wound, it would flow into other areas if it were stopped, and other difficulties would arise. That is why so many noblemen and other persons in France who were wounded in those areas during the war and were unable to be treated immediately prefer to keep the wound open. They suffer no great inconvenience from it and prefer this to closing it with a risk to their life or some other

---

Letter 2848. - Archives of the Mission, Krakow, original signed letter. There is also an unsigned letter, perhaps a rough draft, in the Archives of the Mission, Paris.

[1]The Saint was well informed because the preliminaries of the peace treaty were signed on June 4. The negotiations, begun in 1658, lasted another several months; the Treaty of the Pyrenees was signed on November 7, 1659.

[2]Nicolas Duperroy.

unfortunate accident.[3] I ask Our Lord to be Himself the surgeon who will heal him and the preserver who will keep both of you safe.

We have no news here. Everything is going along very well, thank God.

I embrace M. Duperroy and you, too, Monsieur, with all the affection of my heart. I am, in the love of O[ur] L[ord], Monsieur, your most humble servant.

VINCENT DEPAUL,
i.s.C.M.

At the bottom of the first page: Monsieur Desdames

2849. - TO JACQUES PESNELLE, SUPERIOR, IN GENOA

Paris, May 23, 1659

Monsieur,

The grace of O[ur] L[ord] be with you forever!

I see from your letter of the sixth that the Corsica project is urgent. If, however, it has not yet been settled and can be deferred, please postpone it for two reasons. This first is that you do not have the men needed for this establishment. I doubt that the Rome house can furnish you with any, and it is questionable whether M. Le Juge

---

[3]Following this, the secretary had first written: "Then, too, has anyone ever seen a Polish person come to France expressly to have his wounds dressed? That seems to be a temptation." He then crossed it out and added: "Nevertheless, if we could be sure that such a long journey would not make this good Missionary unwell and he could be completely cured once he was here, we would be delighted to see him and to give him this satisfaction. It would be for the good of the Company and the glory of God. But, given the doubt and appearances to the contrary, I think he should abandon himself to the holy guidance of God and remain in peace. I embrace him with all the affection of my heart, and you as well, Monsieur, for whom I am, in the love of O[ur] L[ord], your most humble servant." This ending did not satisfy Saint Vincent, who had the letter rewritten and concluded it in another way.

Letter 2849. - Archives of the Mission, Turin, original signed letter.

would be suitable for it, even though he manifests a desire to go there.

You have heard of the great blessing God bestowed on the mission given on that island a few years ago. I thought it was one of the most remarkable, richest ones I ever saw. But please note the quality of the workers—Messieurs Blatiron, Martin, and others—some of the best. I ask you to notice the contrast between the ones you suggest sending there and those men and to see if you can hope that they will have the same success. Yet, Monsieur, that is what should be desired in these early stages—or at least that there might be one or two rather strong men, whom you do not have and whom we cannot send you.

The second reason is that it is one of our maxims (perhaps you do not know this) never to request or seek out any new establishment. We wait until we are called or are sent, and we let those whose business it is take action, except when things are in progress and we are asked to carry them out. Then we see if that is within our power and if the conditions are reasonable, and we do what we can to further the project, in so far as we see that God wills it. Never, however, do we make the first move or hasten such proposals, thank God.

Your arbitration is important enough for you to interrupt your missions so that you might inform your judges clearly, and I think the Cardinal will accept your having remained in Genoa to apply to them until the verdict.

I am consoled by the devotion you have in honor of Saint Joseph to obtain good Missionaries from God. If the priest from Chiavari does not adapt to the exercises in your seminary after you have been patient for some time and reproved him, you can ask him to let someone else have his place.

I ask O[ur] L[ord] to be your strength and your spirit to do and suffer whatever is His good pleasure. I am, in His love, Monsieur, your most humble servant.

VINCENT DEPAUL,
i.s.C.M.

Addressed: Monsieur Pesnelle, Superior of the Priests of the Mission of Genoa, in Genoa

2850. - TO JEAN MARTIN, SUPERIOR, IN TURIN

Paris, May 23, 1659

Monsieur,

The grace of O[ur] L[ord] be with you forever!

I was greatly consoled to receive your letter of the first of this month, since I had not received any for a long time. I was also consoled to see in it that God continues to bless you and to give you good health. I thank Him for this with all my heart, and I thank you, Monsieur, for having recommended me to the prayers of the Marchese, your founder. I have great confidence in his charity and great need of such help. I am very well just now, except for my legs which can hardly support me any longer. God still grants me the grace of saying Holy Mass, but I no longer go into the city.

Since the preservation of that good nobleman is so necessary, I often ask it of God and, at the same time, the greatest sanctification of his soul. Our entire Little Company is obligated before God to concern itself with this because of his great kindness to us and especially to you and your family. Even if negotiations for the abbey [1] are not successful, we will still be eternally indebted to him

---

Letter 2850. - Archives of the Mission, Turin, original signed letter.

[1]Sant'Antonio Abbey.

because he is sparing nothing in that matter. But God be praised that things are in such a good state! M. Jolly told me the same thing as you concerning that.

The conversion of heretics and sinners alike is a result of the absolute mercy and omnipotence of God alone, and it comes about when we are not thinking about it rather than when we are seeking it. Still, we must not stop working at it when the opportunities present themselves because God wills this, and one of two things may happen: either those souls who have gone astray will profit by the good seed being sown in their hearts, or God will use it on judgment day to justify the death sentence He will pronounce against them, when He says to them, "What could I have done that I did not do to bring you back to the right path? "

We will continue to ask God to draw glory from your work and to bless in a special way the mission you are giving in Cherasco[2] on the Madame R[oyale]'s lands.

The late Marquise de Vins, who was from Provence, died in Paris last March 18. She left our Marseilles house eighteen thousand livres for the maintenance of two priests, who are to give missions. She also wanted all the priests of the Company to celebrate one Mass for her intention after her death. I ask you and your men, Monsieur, to render her this just duty in a spirit of gratitude.

We have no news here; everything is going along very well, thank God. We have no one sick or infirm, other than the usual ones, namely Messieurs Alméras,[3] Bécu, Bourdet,[4] Admirault,[5] and Gorlidot. They are following a brand-new diet and are doing quite well on it. The last-named, who was the first to adopt it and

---

[2]A town in Piedmont. With regard to this mission see Abelly, *op. cit.*, bk. II, chap. I, sect. VI, p. 90.

[3]René Alméras the younger.

[4]Étienne Bourdet.

[5]Charles Admirault.

whom we expected to die rather than to have his health restored, is completely cured, and he preached to us yesterday in fine style. They eat only bread and drink only milk and take no other remedy.

You tell me that a young priest, a member of the Congregation of Saint Philip Neri,[6] is presenting himself for the Company and that, even though you have urged him to stay where he is and have explained our objection to admitting persons from other Communities, he persists in asking to join us. You say he wants to distance himself from his relatives to give himself totally to God and that he asked permission to leave for this reason but did not get it. These reasons do, in truth, seem plausible; but, even if there were more cogent ones, there must be no thought of admitting him; experience has shown us that a person who leaves one Community to enter another is successful in neither. This is so well known that our priests of the Tuesday Conferences are unwilling to accept among them those who have been members of some other group.

I am, in the love of O[ur] L[ord], Monsieur, your most humble servant.

VINCENT DEPAUL,
i.s.C.M.

Addressed: Monsieur Martin, Superior of the Priests of the Mission, in Turin

[6]The Oratory of Saint Philip Neri.

2850a. - TO EDME JOLLY, SUPERIOR, IN ROME

Paris, May 23, 1659

Monsieur,

The grace of Our Lord be with you forever!

I received your letter of April 28. In reply, I can only thank God for the things you tell me and thank you for all your concern, as I now do with all my heart, particularly for the blessing God is bestowing on the ministry of your workers and on the little family through the grace He has given you. May it please His Divine Goodness to accept the little services that all of you are striving to render Him.

I gladly consent to your welcoming into your house M. Emmanuel Brignole whenever he chooses to go there. This opportunity to be of service to him will be a blessing to the Company, considering our great obligation to do so, not only because of his personal merit but also because of the gratitude we owe him as an outstanding benefactor of the Genoa house. Furthermore, we do so to obey Cardinal Durazzo who desires this. You should pray fervently, and we will do so on our part, that God will grant you the grace to be a real help to that young man in preparing him to receive the priestly spirit together with Holy Orders. That is all I have to tell you at this time. May God preserve you.

I am, in His love, Monsieur. . . .[1]

This letter will scarcely arrive in Rome when it will be time for you to leave for the country to go to the house offered you in Palestrina, Frascati, or elsewhere. Please do so, Monsieur, and be sure to inform fully the person who is to replace you; give him your

---

Letter 2850a. - Ducournau Archives, Eastern Province of the Congregation of the Mission, Saint Vincent's Seminary, Philadelphia, Pennsylvania (USA), original signed letter; gift of St. John's University, New York. Its authenticity was verified by the antiquarian Giovanni Puccinelli (1922) and, more recently by Father Angelo Coppo, C.M.

[1]The rest of the letter is in the Saint's handwriting.

instructions concerning all the letters I shall write you, and whether there is anyone going to or coming from Rome to the place where I think you will be.

VINCENT DEPAUL,
i.s.C.M.

At the bottom of the first page: Monsieur Jolly

2851. - TO THE MARQUIS DE FABERT, IN SEDAN

May 24, 1659

Enclosed is a letter, My Lord, that M. [Coglée] [1] wrote to you from Lyons. He followed closely after it because he arrived here yesterday. He wrote me one at the same time to tell me he is planning to leave us, and he hopes that, if I do not provide him with a situation to earn his living outside our Company, you will kindly give him one.

Now, My Lord, he has no reason to leave us. You know that he himself wanted to return here from Sedan on account of his eye trouble. Everything possible was done to cure him. After that, we sent him to Savoy as Superior of one of our houses,[2] where he told the Visitor[3] he wanted to leave, that he was mistrusted, that most of the persons there had been instructed by me to spy on him, and that the same thing happened at Saint-Lazare when he was here. He even went so far as to say that I had written him some letters in which there was some cryptic writing, by which I was letting him know that he would one day be a Bishop.

Letter 2851. - Reg. 2, p. 53.

[1]The copyist of Register 2 omitted the name of Mark Cogley, to whom this letter obviously refers.

[2]The Annecy house.

[3]Thomas Berthe.

In these and in a few other things he has manifested some slight mental aberration, causing the Visitor to fear that people outside the Company might notice this. For that reason he wrote to me in haste asking me to recall him to Paris, which I did.

I thought it my duty to tell you this, My Lord, so you will not be surprised by his decision. If, however, you do him the honor of writing to him, you might encourage him to stay; otherwise, since his mind is disturbed, we will have a hard time holding him back. He already left once before, ten or twelve years ago,[4] although no weakness was apparent in him at that time. I think he would like to return to Sedan, but this is in no way advisable, for fear that his condition may worsen and scandal may result from it. We will try to satisfy him in everything else. He will not abuse the freedom we will give him; for, in the midst of his delusions, he is very reserved and has a great fear of God.

Forgive me, My Lord, for taking too much liberty in informing you of this. I do so, knowing that, if anyone in the world is capable of removing those pressures from that good priest, it is you, My Lord. This is so because of his esteem and respect for you and the kindness you have shown him and all the members of our poor, insignificant Company, which is extremely indebted to you, and I am especially so.

2852. - TO JEAN PARRE

Paris, May 24, 1659

Dear Brother,

God be praised that you are feeling better! The Ladies—and I

---

[4]This departure is mentioned in a letter of October 1646 to Gilbert Cuissot (cf. vol. III, no. 879).

Letter 2852. - Archives of the Mission, Paris, original signed letter.

more than anyone else—are consoled by this. I ask God to keep you well.

When you are coming and going, look at the churches that are most devastated and draw up a short report on them as well as on the most needy poor. You must, however, do this discreetly so that no one will be aware of it. That is all they wanted me to tell you this time.

I am, in O[ur] L[ord], dear Brother, your affectionate servant.

VINCENT DEPAUL,
i.s.C.M.

2853. - TO A PRIEST OF THE MISSION

[1659] [1]

. . . . His Superior [2] tells me he[3] led a most exemplary, innocent, gentle, and harmonious life, was loved by all, did a great deal of work unobtrusively, and conducted well all the business outside the house. He adds that the Bishop himself had him work on his private affairs, entrusting to him matters that he was unwilling to entrust to others, and was very well satisfied with him. For twelve or fourteen years, he always went into town—often several times a day because their house is in the suburbs—and was so sober and regular that persons outside the Company could never prevail on him to take a drop of wine, although there were frequent opportunities to do so. Please do not fail to offer your prayers and Holy Sacrifices for the repose of his soul, as is the custom.

Letter 2853. - Lyons manuscript.

[1]Apparently, the person in question here was mentioned prior to this segment of the Lyons manuscript, as indicated in n. 3. If this is correct, and because of the panegyric nature of the contents, 1659 can be presumed for the date of this letter.

[2]If Brother Nicolas Perrin is the person eulogized here, then his Superior in Troyes would be François Dupuich.

[3]Nicolas Perrin, born in Troussey (Meuse), entered the Congregation of the Mission in Paris on January 11, 1642, at twenty-five years of age. He took his vows on November 20, 1646, in the presence of M. Berthe, and renewed them in 1656. Perrin died in Troyes in 1659.

2854. - TO A BROTHER OF THE MISSION

Paris, May 28, 1659

Dear Brother,

The grace of O[ur] L[ord] be with you forever!

I received your letter telling me of the difficulty you were experiencing. I really think God is making you feel the distressing consequences of a change that was requested. For, it is His custom to make known to those who have undertaken to serve Him that their peace is in obedience and never in doing their own will. Remember that you will never find your peace of mind in following Our Lord unless you renounce yourself because He Himself has said that this renunciation is necessary to come after Him and to carry His cross daily.[1]

You have heard that a hundred times; yet, you do not apply that lesson to yourself. At least you have shown the contrary by your frequent urgent requests to leave . . . , regardless of the entreaties made to you to be patient. You encountered a few difficulties there, and I told you that there were some everywhere. In the end we had to satisfy you; but that satisfaction was short-lived, as you yourself told me. Our Lord calls the observance of His maxims a yoke to tell us that it is a state of submission and a state difficult to bear for those who try to shake it off, but a gentle, light one for those who love Him and submit to it.[2]

Dear Brother, if you want to have peace of heart and a thousand blessings from God, do not listen any longer either to your own judgment or your will. You have already made a sacrifice of them to God; be very careful not to take back the use of them. Allow yourself to be guided, and rest assured that God will be the one who

---

Letter 2854. - Archives of the Mission, Paris, seventeenth-century copy.

[1]Cf. Lk 9:23. (NAB)

[2]Cf. Mt 11:30. (NAB)

guides you; but where? To the freedom of His children,[3] to a superabundance of consolations, to great progress in virtue, and to your eternal happiness.

I say all this to you because you suggest once again that I change you; otherwise, I would have imitated God in His goodness, who never reproaches us the faults He has forgiven us. I would not have given another thought to yours if I did not see you in danger of committing a similar one again. That is why I point out to you the trouble this will cause you, if the experience of the one you are now suffering does not make you more submissive. You can be certain that, if we send you back to . . . because you request it, you would no sooner arrive there than you would say what you are saying where you are now: that you are there by your own choice rather than by the Will of God, since you obliged your Superiors to send you there against their better judgment, and this thought would disturb you constantly.

So, if you want to get rid of this worm of conscience in the place where you now are, stay there because holy obedience orders you to do so, and do not feel any longer that you are there by your own will but rather by that of God. Ask His forgiveness for the past, and do not think about it again. If you do not want to be led astray, resolve not to listen to your own mind anymore, for its nature is such that it will upset you everywhere; take my word for it.

I ask Our Lord to animate you with His own Spirit. He was so submissive that He compared Himself to a beast of burden,[4] which is so indifferent that people do to it whatever they want—anywhere, any time. If we were in this disposition, God would soon lead us to our perfection.

I am, in His love, dear Brother, your most affectionate servant and brother.

VINCENT DEPAUL,
i.s.C.M.

---

[3]Cf. Rom 8:21. (NAB)
[4]Cf. Mt 21:5. (NAB)

2855. - TO DENIS LAUDIN, SUPERIOR, IN LE MANS

Paris, May 28, 1659

Monsieur,

The grace of O[ur] L[ord] be with you forever!

I am answering your letter of the twenty-first. You acted wisely regarding the hut, allowing the Administrators to act, without saying anything to them, since they are ready to come to an agreement. As to this settlement, however, if by chance they make no further mention of it, it will be a good idea for you to mention it to them yourself, or have someone speak to them about it from time to time.

May God in His mercy bless the ministry of your workers!

We are trying to send you someone to act as procurator. Since M. Molony is no longer willing to be involved with this, you can give him the care and instruction of the seminary.

You pleased me by taking from Brother Pintart the outfit he wanted to make for himself. Most of our Brothers here wear black linen during the summer. It is really bold of him to choose the fabric and to want to be different from the others. He has always seemed a little vain to me, and this is a proof of it; that is why it will be a good idea to humble him.

I hope to send you in a month or two the Visitor you are requesting, but it will not be to look into your conduct regarding your discontented seminarians. I quite believe what you tell me about them. I ask Our Lord to send you others who are more apt to profit by your good advice.

The late Marquise de Vins, who was from Provence, died in Paris last March. She left our Marseilles house eighteen thousand livres for the maintenance of two priests, who are to give missions. She also wanted all the priests of the Company to celebrate one

---

Letter 2855. - Archives of the Mission, Paris, original signed letter.

Mass for her intention after her death. I ask you and your men, Monsieur, to render her this just duty in a spirit of gratitude.

We have no news here. I am writing you in haste. Please deliver the enclosed to M. Herbron.

I am, in the love of O[ur] L[ord], Monsieur, your most humble servant.

VINCENT DEPAUL,
i.s.C.M.

At the bottom of the first page: Monsieur Laudin

2856. - TO JACQUES PESNELLE, SUPERIOR, IN GENOA

Paris, May 30, 1659

Monsieur,

The grace of O[ur] L[ord] be with you forever!

In reply to your letter of the thirteenth, let me tell you that the Cardinal must be obeyed in the matter of the retreats he wants you to give for the two houses of Sisters, even though one of our maxims and customs is to distance the Company from any kind of ministry with Sisters because of the little good we can do and the bonds that are contracted with them—at least in France. You ask me what you should tell His Eminence, if he orders you to do the same thing in other monasteries. My reply is that, when you find a favorable opportunity, you should try to anticipate this by informing him of our Rule and practice. If, after that, he wants you to disregard them, you will have to do so.[1]

Letter 2856. - Archives of the Mission, Paris, original signed letter.

[1]Next came the words, "... because we would rather follow his order than our determination," which were crossed out.

Since you find it more of a disadvantage for your seminarians from the outside to go into town to take care of their business on recreation days rather than on other days, I agree to your following the old custom established by the late M. Blatiron.

It is true that the men who come into this house from the country go to the refectory for supper the evening they arrive. The abuse of eating in the infirmary, which has sprung up—and has really grown— has obliged us to remedy it by doing away with that custom. You say, however, that it is difficult for you to do likewise because all of you go on foot and, since you have mountains to climb, you arrive very tired. That being the case, you may continue awhile to do as you have done in the past, until further orders.

As for the Corsica foundation, I have already told you my little thoughts on that. If God in His Providence has already obligated you to this affair, Monsieur, see how you can meet the commitment. We thought that, whether or not it is made,[2] it is advisable for M. Lej[uge] to be separated from you, since his type of mind and present indisposition cause us to see many problems in keeping you together on good terms, and we feel that the best thing to do is to send him to Rome for a time. Please discuss this with the Cardinal to see if he will agree to this change. I say *change* because I am informing M. Jolly that he should send up another priest in his place—a French one, if possible.

So, if His Eminence gives his approval, after you have told him the reasons for this, please have M. Lej[uge] leave promptly so he will arrive in Rome before the very hot weather, and give him the letter I am writing him to that effect.

If the Corsica affair is settled,[3] that makes this change difficult; but, assuming that His Eminence thinks it expedient for the Supe-

---

[2]The first establishment of the Priests of the Mission on the island of Corsica was in Bastia in 1678.

[3]The rest of this letter is in the Saint's handwriting.

rior to be French, it seems advisable for M. Jolly to send a Frenchman from Rome, whose place M. Lej[uge] will be able to fill. There still remains the problem of the three Italians—or at least of two of them—because you tell me you will give someone from your seminary. I do not know if M. Jolly and M. Martin can furnish you with them; I am writing to M. Jolly about it. Is M. Pinon well enough prepared to be the second man in your house? But who will help you with your missions? It is important for you to act in this, as in everything else, with as much humility and gentleness as possible, and with the advice of your consultors (God usually has a part in the resolutions taken with them) or at least with the advice of your admonitor.

Your most humble servant.

VINCENT DEPAUL,
i.s.C.M.

Addressed: Monsieur Pesnelle, Superior of the Mission, in Genoa

2857. - TO EDME JOLLY, SUPERIOR, IN ROME

Paris, May 30, 1659

Monsieur,

The grace of O[ur] L[ord] be with you forever!

I have had your letter delivered to Abbé Ribier, along with his document. He has not sent us the eleven livres it costs. It will be well for you to charge persons outside the Company for the postage on their Briefs, Bulls, and packets, since we have to pay it.

Thank you for the *extra tempora* for Brother Butler, which I also received with your letter of the fifth.

Letter 2857. - Archives of the Mission, Paris, original signed letter.

All the letters I receive from you give me new reasons to praise God for your attention and your leadership and for the grace that accompanies them. I cannot express to you the joy this gives me, nor my gratitude to His Divine Goodness, to whom I often recommend you, asking that He be pleased to bless you more and more and to keep you in good health.

Speaking of which, the hot weather that you find so difficult to bear is now upon you. I have asked you—and I ask you again—not to stay in Rome during it but to spend this time in Palestrina or Frascati, leaving the care of the family and business matters to whomever you judge most suitable and who will not do anything without your orders.

Since Cardinal Brancaccio was in Rome when you wrote me, I want to think that the matters for which you have so long awaited him will be settled or advanced by the time you receive this letter. May it please God to arrange them for the best!

I am not sure if the Duchesse d'Aiguillon wants her Loreto vow changed. I have not yet informed her of what you wrote me concerning it; before doing so, I will wait until I know the Pope's reply to the proposal the Cardinal Datary [1] was supposed to discuss with him. Whatever His Holiness ordains in that matter, please do nothing until you know the Lady's intention for her foundation regarding both the past and the future.

I am sending you a letter written to me by Abbé de Vaux, Vicar-General of Angers, who is very good to us. If you know the priest he mentions, you can find out what he thinks about the subject of that letter, and please let me know.

It is absolutely necessary to separate M. Lejuge and M. Pesnelle. That is why I am asking the latter to send the other to you as soon as possible. I am also asking two things of you, Monsieur. The first is to welcome him as warmly as possible into your house. He

---

[1]Giacomo Corradi.

is capable of many things, especially of working on the missions; and, if well guided, he will be of service to God and to the Company. Furthermore, since he respects you, I hope you will get him to do whatever you want. The second thing I ask of you is to send M. d'Eu or some other French priest to Genoa[2] for a while.

Our Lords of the Genoa Senate want to open a house of four Missionaries in Corsica. I stated the objections I have to that just now, both with regard to a Superior—whom the Cardinal thinks should be French—and with regard to the other Missionaries, who should be Italian. Please reflect on that before God and give me your advice on it. I am afraid M. Pesnelle moved too quickly in this affair.

They are complaining that he is a little too rigid and stingy regarding the food of the mission. If you think it advisable to say something to him about this, as coming from yourself, please do so; above all, take care of your health. I ask Our Lord to keep you well.

Your most humble servant.

VINCENT DEPAUL,
i.s.C.M.

Addressed: Monsieur Jolly

2858. - TO JEAN PARRE

Paris, May 31, 1659

Dear Brother,

The grace of O[ur] L[ord] be with you forever!

This is the second time I have written to you in Laon without

---

[2]The letter written by the secretary stopped here; the rest is in the Saint's handwriting.

Letter 2858. - Archives of the Mission, Paris, original signed letter.

knowing whether you have arrived there, since I received no letters from you this week. You told me you were supposed to go there a day or two after you last wrote me from Reims. God grant that nothing disastrous has befallen you! I have been worried about your health since you wrote me that you were cured of your cold; I ask you once again to take care of yourself. I am not asking for news of you, since I know that you will not have failed to send me some; but the postal agents sometimes delay a long time in bringing us your letters.

The Ladies, very few of whom were at the last meeting, have allotted you two hundred livres for Laon; you can draw them on Mademoiselle Viole.

May God bless you! I am, in His love, dear Brother, your most affectionate servant.

VINCENT DEPAUL,
i.s.C.M.

At the bottom of the first page: Brother Jean Parre

2859. - ***SAINT LOUISE TO SAINT VINCENT***

June 2, 1659

Madame de Glou [1] most humbly entreats you, Most Honored Father, to give her a little time to speak with you tomorrow morning, at an hour that is convenient for you.

Allow me to ask you if every year, during this Pentecost season, we should hold the election of Officers, either to elect new ones or to extend the terms of those already in office. If so, although we might perhaps have to elect some Sisters who are not in Paris, will Your Charity please let us

---

Letter 2859. - Archives of the Motherhouse of the Daughters of Charity, original autograph letter.

[1]A Lady of Charity in Paris.

know the day? Remember also that my pride or foolishness still prevents me from presenting my needs to you, even though they are important for my salvation and the accomplishment of God's Will. Therefore, kindly help me to surmount my difficulties and make better use of my remaining days so that I may not be filled with shame on the last day.

I hope for this from the goodness of God, entreating Him with all my heart to grant it as I entreat Your Charity to give me some time for this purpose, since, for many years, it has been through you that I have been assured of fulfilling God's Will in doing what I have been directed to do. I desire this grace until the end, although I am unworthy of it, and to call myself, in His most holy love, Most Honored Father, your most humble, most obedient, and very grateful daughter.

L. DE M.

Addressed: *Monsieur Vincent*

2860. - TO EDME JOLLY, SUPERIOR, IN ROME

Paris, June 6, 1659

Monsieur,

The grace of O[ur] L[ord] be with you forever!

I received your letter of May 12. Brother Le Mercier passed through Lyons, and I think he is now in Richelieu.

It is not necessary for you to seek further opportunities to speak in favor of the canonization of Bishop de Sales, unless you are asked to do so.

I am very glad that you went to Palestrina to see the little house being offered you. I strongly hope that this letter finds you in that place and that you will remain there for the duration of the hot weather.

Letter 2860. - Archives of the Mission, Paris, original signed letter.

We received the Bull for the Bishop of Pamiers [1] and the Brief for Abbé Ribier; I have had them delivered to each of them.

I accepted your two small bills of exchange, and we will try to pay them, God willing.

We are busy with the ordination [retreat], which God is blessing. His Divine Goodness is also pleased to bless the work of the Company elsewhere, both the missions and the seminaries.

I think I told you[2] we would send you a pencil sketch of Brother Étienne's hand, but we will not do so, for a special reason. Do not fail to do whatever you can with the description you have of it.

I am, in the love of O[ur] L[ord], Monsieur, your most humble servant.

VINCENT DEPAUL,
i.s.C.M.

Addressed: Monsieur Jolly, Superior of the Priests of the Mission, in Rome

2861. - TO EDME JOLLY, SUPERIOR, IN ROME

Saint-Lazare, June 6, 1659

Monsieur,

The grace of O[ur] L[ord] be with you forever!

The Mothers of the Visitation wanted me to write a letter to our Holy Father the Pope for the canonization of Blessed Francis de Sales, joining my most humble and unworthy prayers to those of so many very important persons. I have done so both to obey them

---

[1]François-Étienne Caulet.
[2]In no. 2843.

Letter 2861. - Archives of the Mission, Paris, seventeenth-century copy.

and to express the esteem and special veneration I have for such a great saint, whose great virtues I myself witnessed on several occasions.

If they send you the packet to be given to him, please do so, Monsieur, and use your influence for this good work in every other way they will stipulate. In this you will be doing something that is extremely pleasing to me. I ask Our Lord to bless the attention you will give to it. I am, in His love, Monsieur, your most humble servant.

At the bottom of the first page: Monsieur Jolly, Superior, in Rome

2862. - TO POPE ALEXANDER VII

[June 6, 1659] [1]

Most Holy Father,

I know that all of France and many nations are urgently petitioning Your Holiness to deign to inscribe in the number of the saints the Most Illustrious and Most Reverend Francis de Sales, Bishop of Geneva. I know also that you, Your Holiness, filled with admiration for the outstanding virtues that shone in him and the books of such lofty devotion that he published, hold his memory in the highest veneration and, consequently, seem disposed to carry out this intention, with no need of petitions coming from others and especially from a man as wretched and unknown as I am.

Nevertheless, Most Holy Father, since I had a very close relationship with this excellent servant of God, who deigned to con-

---

Letter 2862. - Archives of the Mission, Paris, unsigned rough draft, original in Latin.

[1]This date has been assigned because Saint Vincent mentions this letter to Pope Alexander VII in two other letters that he wrote on June 6 (cf. nos. 2861 and 2863).

verse frequently with me, either concerning the Institute of the Visitation Nuns of Sainte-Marie, which he established and founded, or other pious matters, I admired in him so many great virtues that it is very difficult for me to keep silence on this occasion and to be the only person to say nothing.

Faith, hope, charity, and other Christian virtues, both cardinal and moral, seemed almost innate in him. Taken together, they formed in him—at least to my way of thinking—such goodness that, during an illness that came upon me shortly after speaking with him, I often reflected on his gentleness and exquisite meekness, repeating [very frequently to myself these] words: "Oh! how good God is, since [the Bishop of Geneva i]s so good! "

If I were the only one in the world to think this of him, Most Holy Father, I might believe that I was deceiving myself. Since, however, everyone shares these sentiments with me, what more could be desired to complete such a holy work, Most Holy Father, than that the will of Your Holiness agree to place Francis de Sales in the catalogue of the saints and to propose him to the veneration of the entire world? This is what all the priests of our Congregation and I myself, prostrate at the feet of Your Holiness, ask of you by our most humble petitions. May God, who is the best and the greatest, deign to preserve you for many years for the welfare of His Church!

I am, Most Holy Father, of Your Holiness. . . .

2863. - TO MOTHER LOUISE-EUGÉNIE DE FONTAINE [1]

Saint-Lazare, June 6, 1659

Dear Mother,

The grace of O[ur] L[ord] be with you forever!

Since you wanted me to write to Our Holy Father for the canonization of the blessed Bishop of Geneva, I am doing so, although with shame, being so unworthy of obtaining such a favor. Nonetheless, I do so with great joy because I hold in such honor the memory of that blessed man, whom I consider one of the greatest saints in heaven, and also because I am glad to support your good intentions and to try to be of service to you on this occasion. I am sending you the letter, therefore, to have it forwarded by whatever way you please. I am also enclosing one addressed to M. Jolly—if you want him to be the one who presents it—so that in all events he will do whatever he can to contribute to this good work.

I am also returning to you the copies of the letters written by other persons more important than I, who am but a wretched sinner. I am, however, filled with the desire to serve you in every circum-

---

Letter 2863. - Archives of the Mission, Paris, rough draft in the secretary's handwriting.

[1]Louise-Eugénie de Fontaine (Fonteines) was born in Paris of Huguenot parents on March 13, 1608, and entered the Visitation Monastery (rue Saint-Antoine) in 1630, seven years after her abjuration of heresy. She soon became Mistress of Novices; after her election as Superior in 1641, she was reelected so often that the convent had her at its head for thirty-three years. In 1644 she went to La Perrine Abbey near Le Mans to establish the renewal. On her return, the Archbishop of Paris asked her to work on the Rule of Port-Royal Abbey. Saint Vincent, who observed her behavior in certain difficult situations, stated that "an angel could not have comported herself with more virtue." (Cf. *Sainte Jeanne-Françoise Frémyot de Chantal. Sa vie et ses oeuvres* [8 vols., Paris: Plon, 1874-80], vol. VIII, p. 446, *note*.) She died September 29, 1694, at the age of eighty-six, leaving the reputation of a holy religious. "God always blessed her leadership and her undertakings," states the *Book of Professions* (Arch. Nat. LL 1718). Her biography has been written by Jacqueline-Marie du Plessis Bonneau, *Vie de la vénérable Mère Louise-Eugénie de Fontaine, religieuse et quatrième supérieure du premier monastère de la Visitation Sainte-Marie de Paris* (Paris: F. Muguet, 1696).

stance and to prove to you that I am, in the love of Our Lord, dear Mother, your most humble. . . .

At the bottom of the first page: The Mother Superior of Sainte-Marie of Paris

2864. - TO JACQUES PESNELLE, SUPERIOR, IN GENOA

Paris, June 6, 1659

Monsieur,

The grace of O[ur] L[ord] be with you forever!

I received your letter of May 20. You must not be surprised if, among those whom you admit to the Internal Seminary, you are obliged to send some away; for it is advisable to do so, since all are not suitable for the Company. Neither should you find it strange to see some inconstancy in the most determined and the wisest among them, since the human spirit is never in the same state. And, although Brother Caron [1] told you he did not enter your house with the intention of staying there, you should still admit him to vows at the end of his seminary, provided he is disposed at that time to take them in the right way.[2]

As for the money you will give those who leave of their own accord, we usually return to them what they brought with them. If they do not have the wherewithal to get back home, in the event that they live somewhat far away, you can also give them a demi-écu or an écu.

Letter 2864. - Archives of the Mission, Paris, original signed letter.

[1]In the personnel lists that are available to us, there is no listing for a *Caron.* We know from no. 2870 (June 13, 1659) that he was to be ordained, but we learn from a number of letters in vol. VIII that he left the Company.

[2]The last four words are in the Saint's handwriting.

Missionaries have no other Pastor than their Superior, so you may give Holy Communion as Viaticum to the sick in your house, without asking the Pastor of the parish, unless the Cardinal expressly wishes you to do so.

Your letter requires no other reply, nor can I tell you anything else right now because I am in a hurry.

I am, in O[ur] L[ord], Monsieur, your most humble servant.

VINCENT DEPAUL,
i.s.C.M.

Addressed: Monsieur Pesnelle, Superior of the Priests of the Mission, in Genoa

2865. - TO EDME MENESTRIER, SUPERIOR, IN AGEN

Paris, June 8, 1659

Monsieur,

The grace of O[ur] L[ord] be with you forever!

I have nothing to tell you except that I received your letter of May 16 and will try to have someone visit the Bishop of Agen [1] before he leaves for his diocese. I myself am in no state to go to see him, since I have not gone out for five or six months.

I ask O[ur] L[ord] to bless and keep you and the entire little family, whom I greet. I am, in His love, Monsieur, your most humble servant.

VINCENT DEPAUL,
i.s.C.M.

Letter 2865. - Archives of the Mission, Paris, original signed letter.

[1]Barthélemy d'Elbène.

I just received your letter of May 30. I am going to send to your uncle the one you addressed to him. Read the one I am enclosing for Brother Didolet.

2866. - TO PIERRE CABEL, IN SEDAN

Paris, June 11, 1659

Monsieur,

The grace of O[ur] L[ord] be with you forever!

I received two letters from you together with the ones from the Maréchal.[1] I took the honor of informing him that M. Coglée has returned and that we welcomed him with great joy.

Be very careful not to urge the person you mentioned[2] to be more attentive to the affairs of the parish; he is wiser than we are.

God be praised for the help the Maréchal is procuring for the Venetians[3] and for the services he renders to the Church in so many ways! May it please His Divine Goodness to preserve him and to bless more and more his plans and his guidance!

The grumbling of certain individuals must not deter you from dealing cordially with them and, still less, from being firm in maintaining good order and discouraging them from making useless visits.

Letter 2866. - Archives of the Mission, Paris, original signed letter.

[1]Maréchal de Fabert.

[2]Maréchal de Fabert.

[3]Saint Vincent seems to think that a plan which was still only a proposal had been realized. The Marquis de Fabert had told Mazarin he would go, as leader of the officers and soldiers made available by the general peace, to help the Venetians, who were at war with the Turks. On May 11, he wrote to his friend d'Andilly: "Before dying, I am determined to make a foray against the Turks. The peace now in place between France and Spain should convince me that men of my profession are now useless to the King. If his Majesty decides to send an army to Venice, I am fully resolved to ask to go there." Mazarin was satisfied with the good will of the Governor of Sedan. The expedition took place in June 1660, but with only a small contingent of soldiers and without the Marquis de Fabert (cf. Bourelly, *op. cit.*, vol. II, pp. 226-33).

The goal of the family is to glorify God, to perfect itself, and to edify the neighbor. Now, you must always aim at achieving that, but by gentle means. It is the duty of those who govern to put up with the bad humor of those they guide and to correct them when they stray. They must not weary of admonishing them gently and respectfully, provided the time and place are right, and the matter merits it. M. Berthe is going off to make a visitation of your house, and he will straighten things out.

I am, in the love of O[ur] L[ord], Monsieur, your most humble servant.

VINCENT DEPAUL,
i.s.C.M.

Addressed: Monsieur Cabel, [Priest] of the Mission, in Sedan

2867. - TO EDME JOLLY, SUPERIOR, IN ROME

Paris, June 12, 1659

Monsieur,

The grace of Our Lord be with you forever!

Since I am one of those who have had the greatest esteem for the blessed Bishop of Geneva and the greatest zeal for his canonization, I feel confident in expressing both of these to Our Holy Father the Pope in the letter I am taking the honor of writing him, as so many Prelates and other persons remarkable for piety and

---

Letter 2867. - Jules Gossin, *Saint Vincent de Paul peint par ses écrits* (Paris: J.J. Blaise, 1834), p. 467, copied from the original made available by Alexandre Martin. This letter is very similar to no. 2861 of June 6, written to Edme Jolly, which the Saint included in the one to Mother Louise-Eugénie de Fontaine (cf. no. 2863) to be enclosed with her packet of petitions to be sent to Rome. The Saint seems to have written this second letter (no. 2867) to be sent directly to M. Jolly; perhaps no. 2861 was never mailed.

merit have done. And, although I am only a poor, very unworthy priest, I nevertheless owe this testimony to the truth and to the desire of our Mothers at Sainte-Marie, especially since I had the happiness of seeing and admiring the lofty virtue of their holy patriarch. I witnessed this not only in his admirable works but in his holy person, having seen him act and heard him speak on many occasions, both in public and in private.

If those good Mothers send you my packet, Monsieur, please present it yourself and use your influence for this holy work in whatever ways they wish. In this you will be doing something most pleasing to our Little Company and most gratifying to me, since I am filled with reverence for the memory of that great Prelate and most eager to be of service to his holy Order of the Visitation.

I am also, in Our Lord, Monsieur, your most humble servant.

VINCENT DEPAUL,
i.s.C.M.

2868. - TO FIRMIN GET, SUPERIOR, IN MARSEILLES

Paris, June 13, 1659

Monsieur,

The grace of O[ur] L[ord] be with you forever!

I received your letter of the third. I thank God for what occurred on your arrival and for the way you acted in the matter. I see clearly that I was too hasty, but the pressure put on me to send someone there obliged me to ask you to see to this, thinking that everything had been arranged there.

It is contrary to good order and to our custom for us to take on a commitment in any place temporarily and not permanently. If,

---

Letter 2868. - Archives of the Mission, Paris, original signed letter.

however, God wants us in Montpellier, He will certainly find the means of establishing us there, and if He does not will it we must not desire it. Whatever the case, the servant who is faithful in few things will be placed over many.[1] You are fortunate to be working under a Prelate of such eminent merit [2] and so full of good intentions, in a diocese where heresy, having established its throne, gives you a broad scope for doing your part in laying solid foundations of piety there.

In the education of priests, your principal aim must be to form them to the interior life, prayer, recollection, and union with God, especially since the people of that area[3] are inclined by nature to be undisciplined. You will find it difficult, but God's grace and your own example will be a great help. This is not the work of a day but of several years, nor is it an undertaking that succeeds with all sorts of persons. However, they will all be able to profit by it to a greater or lesser degree, and some will become spiritual men and masters in virtue, capable of teaching its practice afterward in the places where they will be.

You will also have to suffer in temporal matters, but be patient; the beginnings of important works are always difficult. You are now in a situation of honoring the uncertainty of means of subsistence in which Our Lord Himself was, and He willed that the Apostles experience it as well, at the time the Church was established.

We have not yet assigned anyone to Marseilles; but, since you are staying in Montpellier, we are going to give serious thought to sending a few men there, including a Brother, who can leave them in Avignon and go on to be with you in Montpellier. May it please God to give you strength of mind and body for the guidance and

---

[1]Cf. Mt 25:21. (NAB)

[2]François de Bosquet.

[3]The words "that area" are scratched out in the original. Apparently, this was not done either by the Saint or by his secretary.

success of His work! You will have special need of forbearance and great gentleness with those whom the Providence of God will entrust to your care so that they will have confidence in you and you can win them over to God. If those now in the seminary should leave, perhaps that will be for the best; do not worry about it; others will come to you.

I am sending [M. Le Va]cher,[4] by [an opportunity that has presented itself,] five hundred livres for living expenses [for the house in Marseil]les, along with the fifty livres you [requested for M. . .]milly and eighty livres for the money you have adva[nced] up to the present.

I am, in the [love of Our Lord], Monsieur, your [most humble] servant.

VINCENT DEPAUL,
i.s.C.M.

The Bishop of Montpellier did me the honor of writing to me; but, since it was in reply to the letter I had the honor of writing him, I will not bother him with a second letter so soon.[5]

Addressed: [Monsieur Get, Superior of the Priests of the Mission] of [Marseilles] at present at the Montpellier [Seminary]

---

[4]Philippe Le Vacher.

[5]The postscript is in the Saint's handwriting.

2869. - TO ANTOINE DURAND, SUPERIOR, IN AGDE

[1659] [1]

I share your anxiety over the person who is the cause of your writing to me.[2] I want to believe he acted in good faith but I think that, when he reflects on all the circumstances involved in this event, he will see clearly that he must not return there often and that you, Monsieur, will recognize this as a little trial Our Lord has sent you to form you to become a good leader of the persons who will be entrusted to you.

That will make you realize Our Lord's great goodness in bearing with His Apostles and disciples when He was on earth, and how much He had to put up with from both the good ones and the bad. It should even make you see that the office of Superior, like all other positions, has its thorns and that Superiors who try to do their duty well by word and example have much to suffer from their subjects—not only the troublesome ones but also the best among them.

Accordingly, Monsieur, let us give ourselves to God to serve Him in that capacity, seeking no satisfaction from others. Our Lord will give us enough, if we work as we should at being very exact in the observance of the Rules and the acquisition of the virtues proper to true Missionaries, especially humility and mortification.

I also think it will be well for you, Monsieur, when that good priest makes his communication, or on some other occasion, to ask him to remind you of your failings, since perhaps you commit many faults in your present duty, not only as Superior but also as a Missionary and a Christian. Tell him not to be deterred, even

---

Letter 2869. - Reg. 2, p. 139. Abelly states (*op. cit.*, bk. III, chap. XXIV, sect. 1, p. 346) that the original was in the Saint's handwriting.

[1]Nos. 2908 and 2957 (vol. VIII) give us reason to think this letter was probably written in 1659. It is certainly posterior to Antoine Durand's assignment to Agde (1656).

[2]Perhaps François Brisjonc or Brother Jean Thierry (cf. vol. VIII, no. 2908).

Thierry, born in Cahors, entered the Marseilles Seminary of the Congregation of the Mission as a coadjutor Brother in 1648, at twenty years of age.

though at first you may seem naturally to blanch or blush or allow some word of impatience to slip out. The greatest saints usually have this first reaction because our animal nature, always alive in us, blocks our reason in this way. With the help of grace, however, reason draws inexpressible advantages from the reproofs given us in charity.

I think you will also do well, Monsieur, to declare to your family from time to time that not only will you accept being reminded of your faults by your admonitor but would be sorry if he did not reprove you and if he failed to write to me, as the Rule ordains and is the custom in all well-regulated Companies. Assure them also that you will not read the letters they will write to me nor those I will write to them. O Monsieur, how great is human misery and how necessary is patience for Superiors!

I conclude by recommending myself to your prayers, which I ask you to offer so that God will pardon me the incomparable faults I commit every day in the position I hold—I who am the most unworthy of all men and worse than Judas was toward Our Lord.

2870. - TO JACQUES PESNELLE, SUPERIOR, IN GENOA

[Paris, June 13, 1659] [1]

Monsieur,

The grace of O[ur] L[ord be with you forever!]

At the end of [last] week, I received your letter of May 27, which hardly [needs] a reply. I [praise God] for the good results He has drawn from your mis[sion to the] Penitents, and I ask Him to draw [His glory] from the ordination [retreat], if it is taking place during

---

Letter 2870. - Archives of the Mission, Paris, original signed letter. The document is in very poor condition.

[1]Date written on the back of the letter by the secretary.

these Ember Days. I ask Him also to preserve the Cardinal, whether he goes to Rome or remains in Genoa. That is what we are asking God and, along with that grace, all those he may wish. We do so because of the gratitude we owe him as one of the greatest benefactors of the Company.

Since you have deemed it appropriate to have Brother Caron ordained a priest, well and good. As for Brother de Lagrange,[2] it will be a good idea to give him time to study, although he is a fine young man and I think you can count on having him take Holy Orders when he reaches the required age. We can [also request for him an *extra tem]pora*. [I am consoled by your] readiness to abandon yourself [entirely to the] guidance of God; [I ask Him] to establish you firmly in this [state], in the certainty that nothing [happens] except by His Will, [with the exception of] sin, and that He draws His glory and our good [from everything], when we are [totally] resigned to Him. He even changes the [greatest] evil into good.

On your part, do purely and simply whatever depends on you to make things go well. As for what others do or say, however, or for unfortunate occurrences, do not worry about them; confide all to God and trust in Him. This is the basis of all good leadership and the peace and enrichment of your soul. I ask O[ur] L[ord] to establish all of us in it.

I am, in His love, Monsieur, your most humble servant.

VINCENT DEPAUL,
i.s.C.M.

Addressed: Monsieur Pesnelle, Superior of the Priests of the Mission of Genoa, in Genoa

---

[2]Robert de Lagrange, born in Lille (Nord) on November 1, 1636, entered the Congregation of the Mission at the Paris Seminary on October 19, 1655, and took his vows on October 19, 1657, in the presence of M. Delespiney.

2871. - TO JEAN MONVOISIN, IN MONTMIRAIL

[June 1659] [1]

M[onsieur,]

The grace [of Our Lord be with you for]ever!

You [tell me in your letter] of the fifth that [M.] Berthe has led you to hope for [a visitation from him.] Since, however, he has gone [to the town] of Toul, and is [planning to go to] Sedan afterward, you will have given that mission before he comes back. So, if you are ready to undertake it, you have time.

I praise God that M. Cornuel[2] is recovering from his ailment and that Brother Pinson is out of the distressing state he was in. May it please God to keep all of you in perfect health!

I really would prefer to have the son of M. de Noirmoutiers[3] in Fontaine-Essart. . . .[4]

We have no news here. Everyone is very well, thank God. I ask Him to continue to grant and increase His blessings to you. I am greatly consoled by the services you render Him and the good results the poor are receiving from your work. God be praised for this!

I am, in His love, Monsieur, your most humble servant.

VINCENT DEPAUL,
i.s.C.M.

At the bottom of the first page: Monsieur Monvoisin

Letter 2871. - Archives of the Mission, Paris, original signed letter.

[1]Date of M. Berthe's visitation of the house in Toul.

[2]Superior of the Montmirail house.

[3]The Duc de Noirmoutiers and his wife Renée-Julie Aubery had three children: one daughter, named Yolande-Julie, and two sons.

[4]The six or seven lines that follow in the original are too incomplete for us to reconstruct the text. There is some question in them about a lease.

2872. - TO JEAN PARRE, IN SAINT-QUENTIN

[June 14, 1659] [1]

Dear Brother,

The grace of O[ur] L[ord] be with you [forever!

I have] received your letter wr[itten from Saint-Quentin.] [2] I praise God that you arrived safely and that [you have] put the Charity of La Fère on its feet again.

Our Ladies have allotted you . . . livres; [please] get them, and draw them as usual on Mademoiselle [Viole]. They ask you, however, to use them well because they have no more money. They also want to tell you that more bolting cloth than ever is being brought to Paris, and the workers should know that it has to be very dark if it is going to sell.

As for the devotion and crowds of people coming for the statue that was found,[3] the Bishop or the Vicars-General should be advised of this so they will be aware of any alleged miracles and put a stop to the abuse, if there is any.

I am, in the love of O[ur] L[ord], dear Brother, your most affectionate servant.

VINCENT DEPAUL,
i.s.C.M.

Addressed: Brother Jean Parre, of the Congregation of the Mission, in Saint-Quentin

---

Letter 2872. - Archives of the Mission, Paris, original signed letter. The upper right-hand corner is badly damaged by mildew.

[1]Date given by Collet (*op. cit.*, vol. II, p. 145). The year is given on the back of the letter.

[2]A town in Aisne.

[3]On April 20, 1659, a two-hundred-year-old lime tree was felled in Fieulaine, near Saint-Quentin. Workers who were cutting it down uncovered a small statue of the Blessed Virgin, to which rumor attributed some miracles. This was the origin of the pilgrimage to Notre-Dame-de-Paix. A chapel was soon built near the site, and people flocked to it. (Cf. [Charles Bourdin], *Histoire de ce qui s'est passé de plus remarquable à l'occasion d'une image de la sainte Vierge, dite Notre-Dame-de-Paix, nouvellement trouvée au village de Fieulaine* [Saint-Quentin: C. Lequeux, 1662].)

2873. - TO PIERRE DAVEROULT, IN LISBON

Paris, June 16, 1659

Monsieur,

[The grace] of O[ur] L[ord] be with you forever!

It was only yesterday that [we re]ceived your letter of [last] December 29, but it gave me very great consolation [because] I see you are healthy in both mind and body. I thank God for this, Monsieur, [and] especially for the fact that you continue to want to give yourself to His Divine Goodness in the best possible way for the salvation of the poor souls of the Indians, for whom Our Lord died.[1]

Today or tomorrow I should receive the money you are sending me, namely, four pistoles and thirty-five and a half patagons,[2] which I will forward as soon as possible to your good sister, together with the letter you are writing to M. Cochet. I have given three receipts for them, which will serve as only one, to M. Emmanuel Seissez, Intendant of the house of the Ambassador of Portugal to this Court.

Blessed be God, Monsieur, that the Comte d'Obidos welcomed you into his home and is treating you so well! He himself did me the honor of informing me of this by letter in the month of April, and I am venturing to thank him most humbly for it by a note I am sending him in reply. Please [present to him the offer] of the respects and services that our Little Company, and [I in particular, make to him.]

I can conclude only where I [began], namely, with the thanks

Letter 2873. - Archives of the Mission, Paris, original signed letter. The poor condition of the original obliged us to reconstruct several sentences.

[1]The words, from "for the salvation. . . ." are in the Saint's handwriting.

[2]A Spanish coin; at that time, the patagon was worth about three livres tournois.

[we owe] to God for all the favors He does [for you] and for the determination with which He [is inspiring] you to make the voyage to Madagascar, [if such] is His good pleasure. A ship is being readied in France to go there this September, and it is hoped that sailings will be more frequent than they have been.

So, come whenever you like, Monsieur; come to Paris. We will be greatly consoled to see and embrace you, and then we will see whether it is advisable for you to make this voyage with some other priests of the Company or whether you will serve God here; for we have plenty of suitable work for you everywhere. Messieurs Le Blanc, Arnoul, and de Fontaines have returned [to France]. They were taken by a [man-of-]war, which captured their ship [a few] days after they [had] left you in Lisbon.

Try to ke[ep well], Monsieur, and write to us [as] often as possible, while you are waiting to return. I ask Our Lord to bring you safely home to Saint-Lazare and to honor you everywhere with His blessings.

I am, in His love, Monsieur, your most humble and affectionate servant.

VINCENT DEPAUL,
i.s.C.M.

I would like you to return as soon as possible. If you do not have money for the journey, I hope M. d'Obidos in his incomparable [kindness] [3] will lend you what you need, and I will repay it here to the Agent of Portugal to be forwarded to him.

If you arrive by land in Bayonne, the Bishop[4] will have someone give you what you need, as he had his Vicar-General do for Messieurs de Fontaines and Arnoul. If you arrive by sea at La

[3]A word left out of the original.

[4]Jean Dolce.

Rochelle, the Bishop[5] will do the same; if at Nantes, it will be M. Couplier; and if at Le Havre de Grâce, it will be the Governor, upon presentation of this letter to the above-mentioned noblemen and those two gentlemen.[6] So come, Monsieur, and make it as soon as you can; I will be impatient until I embrace you in fact, as I do now in spirit.[7]

At the bottom of the first page: Monsieur Daveroult

2874. - TO THE COMTE D'OBIDOS

[Sain]t-Lazare, the fifteenth day before the Kalends of July,[1] 1659

[Most Illustrious Lor]d,

I received with all possible respect and submission [your let]ter, which was filled with the exceptional sentiments of deference and benevolence y[ou profess] in my regard. I was deeply embarrassed by it, seeing how [far I] am from the eminent qualities you, in the [good]ness of your heart, attribute to me, without my ever having done anything to deserve it. What indeed is there to praise, I ask you, in a man lacking everything, and whose father was a poor farmer?

---

[5]Jacques-Raoul de la Guibourgère, born in 1589, was the widower of Yvonne de Charette and father of several children when he was ordained. In 1631 he succeeded his uncle as Bishop of Saintes, then went on to Maillezais, and finally to La Rochelle when the episcopal See was transferred there. Very few other bishops were so closely associated with Saint Vincent. He died in 1661.

[6]In a note that filled the last page of the Saint's letter, which was blank, Pierre Daveroult himself informs us that a Frenchman named Lasserre lent him in Lisbon the money he needed for his journey (143 livres 15 sols) and asked that this amount be reimbursed to the Superior of the Franciscans of Toulouse, who was supposed to use it in "the service of Our Lady" in their convent chapel.

[7]The postscript is in the Saint's handwriting.

Letter 2874. - Archives of the Mission, Paris, seventeenth-century copy, written in Latin.

[1]June 17.

Nonetheless, that will not prevent me, Most Illustrious Lord, from offering most humbly to Your Most Illustrious Lordship the homage of our Little Company and the services of my humble person. We are all the more inclined to do so (believe me) because we would not wish to seem ungrateful and appear to have forgotten the great benefits you have lavished upon us, especially your kindness in giving hospitality to our confrere and doing countless acts of charity for him.

And since I feel incapable, Most Illustrious Lord, of acknowledging so many devout services other than by the avowal of my absolute powerlessness to show my gratitude for them, I beg Almighty God to reward Your Most Illustrious Lordship according to your merit and to enrich your soul daily with the most splendid treasures of His divine grace. I urgently entreat Him also to grant your desires in the order of His Providence, to increase your virtues, and to shower His choicest gifts on your most noble and most illustrious family.

These are our daily wishes and the earnest prayers offered to Our Lord by the one who, in his insignificance, is the most humble and most respectful servant in Jesus Christ of Your Most Illustrious Lordship.

2875. - TO MONSIEUR DEMURARD[1]

Paris, June 17, 1659

[Monsieur,]

This is the second letter I have [had] the honor of writing you. The first [was about] one of your younger children [who was

---

Letter 2875. - Archives of the Mission, Paris, unsigned rough draft in the secretary's handwriting. The document is in poor condition.

[1]Seigneur de Saint-Julien and Treasurer for France in Lyons.

st]udying at our Saint-Charles Seminary; this one concerns your second son, who is now in your disfavor. My knowledge of his conduct gives me confidence to speak to you about this. I entreat you, Monsieur, to allow me to do so.

About two months ago he came here to tell me about his situation. He explained to me that he was the holder of a benefice and yet did not feel disposed to live as a priest, since he has a greater inclination for marriage than for celibacy. He asked my advice to find out the best thing to do. I did not wish to give an opinion on this question and was content with telling him that it was a matter to be decided between God and himself. I said that, if he were to make a spiritual retreat to consult God about it, there was reason to hope that His Divine Goodness would make known to him His good pleasure.

Some time afterward, your eldest son, whom I did not know, also came to speak to me to see if we could admit to this house a young man who was rebelling against his father's wishes. I said that, provided it was ordered by the magistrate, we would admit him. And in fact, when he was brought here, with permission to confine him, we did admit him. This young man [allowed himself to be confined] and had me subsequently informed that he was the one [who had come] recently to get my advice, and had been [thus ill]-treated because he had [resigned his] benefice.

When I [had] him brought to me, I recognized him; and [he related] how he had made his retreat at Saint-Sulpice, where he had decided, [on] the advice of his director, to marry rather than to burn, according to the counsel of Saint Paul.[2] He added that, since he did not think he could hand over his benefice to one of his brothers, in accord with your wishes, Monsieur, because he did not judge him competent, he had resigned it in favor of a person who was competent, in order to safeguard his conscience, and that was why you had him arrested.

---

[2]Cf. 1 Cor 7:9. (NAB)

Immediately following that, I sent someone to ask your eldest son to come and see me. I told him that, if he took my word, he would set his brother at liberty once again because I was sure that when the Parlement heard his reasons, it would have him removed, and it was better that you and he, rather than the law, be responsible for his leaving. He agreed to this, after consulting others. I had them embrace one another in my presence, and they went off together for the city.

[I] now feel bound to entreat you, [Monsieur, to] forgive this second son if he has been at [fault in any] way, to consent to the resignation he has made [and the marria]ge he wishes to contract, to restore to him [the rights] nature has given him, and to honor him with [your fatherly af]fection, for the following reasons:

(1) You will be imitating God's clemency toward us, who are His children—ungrateful and sinful children—on whom He has mercy whenever we turn to Him.

(2) Your title of father urges you to acknowledge as your child this young man who has done nothing to render himself unworthy of this favor.

(3) The circumstances of his way of acting make him more worthy of praise than of blame. He saw himself perishing like a drowning man, and he sought the means of saving himself; for, if he disobeyed you by handing over the benefice to someone other than the one to whom you ordered him to do so, he believed it was his duty rather to follow the intention of God and the Church, which obliged him to choose the most capable person. If he marries against your will, he does so on a good principle, which is to avoid offending God; he does so also because he is of an age to marry, and some wise, devout persons have counseled him to do so.

(4) In a word, Monsieur, you will one day regret having brought a man into the world and abandoning him—especially if you see that he is in need—by favoring, in a way prejudicial to him, other children who are no more yours than he is.

Perhaps, Monsieur, you will tell me that [it would really be] just to give him nothing [as far as] your estate is concerned. M[onsieur,

I ask] Our Lord to take [this thought] from you, if [it comes] to your mind through some natural resentment, because, since the [allocation] of a temporal and patrimonial good has been demanded . . . to compensate for a benefice which is . . . it would make you guilty, Monsieur, of a manifest [injustice], were you to wish to take advantage of it, God forbid!

In the name of Our Lord, Monsieur, seek the advice of some wise, disinterested persons so as not to do anything in this matter but what you would wish at the hour of your death to have done. This is the most humble request I make of you, Monsieur, begging you most humbly to forgive me for taking the liberty of writing to you on this matter which affects you so closely. My commitment to your service and the peace of your family obliges me to do so because Our Lord has made me, in His love. . . .

2876. - TO DENIS LAUDIN, SUPERIOR, IN LE MANS

[Paris, June 18, 1659] [1]

Monsieur,

The grace [of O[ur] L[ord] be with you forever!]

About [. . . ago, the Lieutenant] for Criminal Affairs in Le M[ans did me the honor of] coming to see me to discuss a dispute [between the two of you over] repurchasing rights, [and he] showed [me] a very old title. [Please] let me know what [this is all about], if it is a matter that cannot be settled by arbitration here.

When M. Le Blanc [2] returns from giving the mission, it will be a good idea for you to ask him to resume charge of the seminary and to assist at the Divine Office. It will also be well for you to

---

Letter 2876. - Archives of the Mission, Paris, original signed letter.

[1]This date is also written on the back of the original.

[2]Charles Le Blanc.

inform the Visitor, who will be with you in one or two months, of any of his failings in these matters and of his excessive fastidiousness about his body, so he can admonish him for that. . . . [3]

Do [what] you can to get [him] to attend to the business of the procurator's office. Let me know whether, if we give him a Brother to work under him to help him, he will be willing to take charge of it.

May God in His infinite goodness continue to give you strength of body and the working of His Spirit to carry out His plans!

I am, in His love, Monsieur, your most humble servant.

VINCENT DEPAUL,
i.s.C.M.

I almost forgot to ask you to go or to send someone, when convenient, to visit the Charity in Domfront,[4] which I hear is not getting on very well.

Addressed: Monsieur Laudin, Superior of the Priests of the Mission, in Le Mans

2877. - TO GUILLAUME CORNUEL, IN MONTMIRAIL

Paris, June 19, 1659

Monsieur,

The grace of O[ur] L[ord] be with you forever!

I am writing to inquire about the state of your health and to find

---

[3]The five lines that follow in the original cannot be deciphered.

[4]Domfront-en-Champagne (Sarthe), near Le Mans.

Letter 2877. - Archives of the Mission, Paris, unsigned rough draft. The text is mutilated; the few words that are missing are found in Reg. 2, p. 122.

out how God will inspire you with regard to the proposal I am about to make. There is question of a foundation of the Company in a place of great devotion—if it is not the second, it is at least the third most frequented one in the kingdom. It is Notre-Dame-de-Bétharram, where miracles frequently take place. We are being called there by the Bishop of Lescar [1] and the Parlement of Navarre. There is a gentleman in this city, a deputy of Béarn,[2] who has been instructed to make this proposal to us. Eight priests have consented to give their places to us.

It was the late M. Charpentier who established them there and promoted that devotion. That good servant of God wanted to establish us there more than twenty years ago, and he spoke about it to me from time to time, but God never brought the plan to the stage at which it now is. Nonetheless, those proposals of long ago have greatly served to persuade us that the resolution now taken comes from God and that we should offer ourselves to His Divine Majesty to serve Him in that place.

So, it is a question of carrying this out. We are planning to send four priests and a Brother there and have cast our eyes on you to be in charge, especially since some priests from that area, who knew you at the Bons-Enfants Seminary, would like to have you there. The place is situated at the foot of the Pyrenees and is a very beautiful site; this, in itself, inclines people to devotion. The air is a little thin, and I would be afraid of it for you if I did not know that it is at least as thin in Montmirail.

It now remains for you, Monsieur, to raise your heart to God and to listen to what He will say to you on this matter. I have been told that there is an income of four thousand livres. Of those who are serving the chapel, four will remain and the others will leave.

Our duties will be to hear confessions and preach in the house, direct a seminary, and give missions in the diocese. Please let me

---

[1]Jean du Haut de Salies (1658-81).

[2]M. de Laneplan.

know as soon as possible, Monsieur, your disposition of mind and body concerning this holy undertaking. There is reason to hope that the sanctity of the place, the merits of the glorious Virgin, and the great good you can do there will draw down special graces on you and your governance. I ask Our Lord to give all of us the grace to correspond always and everywhere with His adorable Will. As for myself, I am with all my heart, in His love. . . .

2878. - TO JACQUES PESNELLE, SUPERIOR, IN GENOA

[Paris, June 20, 1659] [1]

Monsieur,

The grace of [O[ur] L[ord] be with you] forever!

I [received your letter of. . . .] I am glad [you had the retreat for] the ordinands.

Yes, Monsieur, there is every reason [to think] that, since God has put you in [charge of] the family, He will give you the requisite qualities for fulfilling that office well. Let Him do so, and do not be upset when things go other than you desire. Pay special attention to not being troublesome to anyone, but a consolation to all.

Since the Cardinal thinks that the four hundred écus for Corsica can be raised and given to the Company without making us odious to the Bishops, well and good; you cannot fail to follow the advice of His Eminence. The major difficulty now is to find suitable men. I wrote to M. Jolly asking him to try to give you one, and I am writing again to him about it today.

Letter 2878. - Archives of the Mission, Paris, original signed letter.

[1]Date written on the back by the secretary.

If M. Jolly does not need that good lad from Marseilles you offered him. . . .[2]

[I a]m, in His [love], Monsieur, your most humble servant.

VINCENT DEPAUL,
i.s.C.M.

Addressed: Monsieur Pesnelle, Superior of the Mission, in Genoa

2879. - TO GUILLAUME DESDAMES, SUPERIOR, IN WARSAW

Paris, June 20, 1659

Monsieur,

The grace of O[ur] L[ord] be with you forever!

I [received your letter of] April 30. It greatly consoled me by assuring me of your good health and that of M. Duperroy.[1] I thank God for this and for the donations the King and Queen have made to your church. I admire their piety and the attention Their Majesties give to your needs. God alone can make known to them my sentiments of esteem and reverence for them and my gratitude for their benefits. All I can do is to assure the Queen through you, Monsieur, that we ask God very frequently to be pleased to preserve their sacred persons, bless their plans, and give peace to their States.

The Bishop of Poznan[2] has good reason to want to see the Company exercising its ministry in his diocese, after its having been established there for such a long time; however, you would not have delayed so long before doing so, had it not been for the events that occurred, depriving you of the men and the means you

---

[2]Only three words of the four lines that followed on the original remain.

Letter 2879. - Archives of the Mission, Krakow, original signed letter.

[1]Nicolas Duperroy.

[2]Albert Tholibowski.

had for that purpose. God so ordained matters for reasons we must adore in Him without knowing what they are. There is cause to hope that it will be the same with you as with fruit trees, for the more a long, hard winter constricts them and prevents them from growing, the deeper they take root and the more fruit they bear.

You tell me that this good Prelate has a church in mind for you in his episcopal town, where he wants to establish you with time. God be praised for that! I am sure that some day the same thing will happen there as happened with us here, namely, that there will be more foundations to be made than we can accept, for lack of workers. Few persons with the proper dispositions are coming forward to give themselves to God in the right way, and among those who start out, there are even fewer who persevere.

O Monsieur, how very precious is a good Missionary! God must raise him up and fashion him; that is the work of His omnipotence and His great goodness. That is why Our Lord has specifically recommended that we ask God to send good workers into His vineyard; [3] for in fact there will be no good ones if God does not send them, and very few of these are needed to accomplish a great deal: twelve sufficed to establish the universal Church, despite human wisdom, the power of the world, and the rage of demons. Let us ask Our Lord, Monsieur, to give the apostolic spirit to the Company, since He has sent it to carry out that ministry.

I am deeply distressed by what is happening with the Daughters of Charity. When the opportunity presents itself, it will be a good idea for you to send Sister Françoise[4] back to France, but get the Queen's approval beforehand.

Everything is going very well here, and God in His mercy continues to bless the Company and all the houses. Pray to His Divine Goodness for all our needs and for mine in particular.

---

[3]Cf. Mt 9:37-38. (NAB)
[4]Françoise Douelle.

I embrace you and good M. Duperroy with all the tenderness of my heart, and I am, in O[ur] L[ord], Monsieur, your most humble servant.

VINCENT DEPAUL,
i.s.C.M.

Addressed: Monsieur Desdames, Superior of the Priests of the Mission, in Warsaw

2880. - *ALAIN DE SOLMINIHAC TO SAINT VINCENT*

June 1659

Monsieur,

I was glad to learn that those gentlemen with whom you shared my letter are determined to use their influence in the affair I mentioned to you.[1] *In so doing, you and they will render an immense service to God and to the Church, for I think those persons or their Company are prepared to ruin it.*

I am very glad you are on good terms with the nobleman to whom I felt you should speak. It is important that you yourself be the one who speaks, and I think that, if you send him one of your men to explain to him that you have some matters of importance to the Church to tell him, he will go to see you. I see no risk in that; for, it does not affect you or your men, and you yourself will do that much better than by acting through someone else. I know those persons are striving to get that infamous work[2] *approved by Rome and will spare nothing for that purpose. That is why it is of the utmost importance to inform Our Holy Father clearly and, above all, to see that His Holiness designates no one to examine it except persons of whom he is very sure, and has it examined afterward in his presence. It is, then,*

Letter 2880. - Archives of the Diocese of Cahors, Alain de Solminihac Collection, notebook, copy made from the original.

[1]Cf. no. 2832.

[2]The *Apologie des casuistes.*

absolutely essential that the said gentleman be fully informed of everything so he can write to him and give him the necessary information on it.

The most perceptive people fear the consequences of this affair—and with good reason—because of the extremes to which those persons are going, making every effort to uphold a doctrine that is so harmful and so contrary to that of Jesus Christ. That should compel all true children of the Church to spare nothing to oppose it and to hinder their plan.

That obliges me to tell you that I think it is important for the Marquis [3] *to inform the Queen fully of the importance of this affair and entreat her to be willing to be of service to the Church on this occasion. She can do so by recommending this affair to the Nuncio, asking him to make His Holiness understand clearly the harm this bad book is doing and the disorder and scandal it would cause in both Church and State if it were approved, etc. Those persons have caused quite a stir in Toulouse, but that work is so offensive that the reaction they have received from it is public hatred. Several of them are writing because of this prohibition. Forbidding them to write any more of those articles might be very important, and I think it will have to be done.*

I am always, Monsieur. . . .

ALAIN,
B[ishop] of Cahors

2881. - TO EDME JOLLY, SUPERIOR, IN ROME

[Between June 13 and 30, 1659] [1]

Monsieur,

The grace [of Our Lord be with you for]ever!

[Thank] you [for the information] you give me [concerning the Saint-]Pourçain [affair]. We will [apply] to. . . .

---

[3]Antoine de Salignac, Marquis de Magnac.

Letter 2881. - Archives of the Mission, Paris, original signed letter.

[1]The passage referring to Cardinal Durazzo of Genoa shows that this letter was written after no. 2870 and before no. 2885.

It will be well for you to settle [the business] with the chap[ter] of Saint Peter's and [to see the] chaplain about Loreto.

It is up to those who govern in France and in Savoy to remove the obstacle hindering the Pope in the Sant'Antonio affair, and we should want what God wants, and nothing more.

I spoke to our senior members who are familiar with the house offered by Cardinal Maldachini,[2] but they have two objections to taking it: the first is that it is intended to house the plague-stricken; the other is that it is too far from the city to receive the ordinands there. In addition, for those members of the Company who would have to come and go during the summer, we need a place that is accessible. It is, then, hardly likely that we will negotiate for that far-off house because we would be obliged to have another one in the city—unless that one is given to us outright, and given by Providence, with no move on our part. . . .

[If the Cardinal] of Genoa arrives [in Rome before] you leave,[3] t[ell him that] I asked you to go [for a rest] during the very hot weather, on the advice of the doctors, who felt you were risking your life by staying in Rome. If you have already gone, have someone tell him the same thing; otherwise, he might find it strange not to see you there.

I am, in O[ur] L[ord], your most humble servant.

VINCENT DEPAUL,
i.s.C.M.

Addressed: Monsieur Jolly

---

[2]Francesco Maldachini, born in Viterbo on April 12, 1621, was created Cardinal on October 7, 1647, and died in Nettuno in 1700.

[3]Cardinal Durazzo had been in Rome since June 14.

2882. - TO DOMINIQUE LHUILLIER, IN CRÉCY

Paris, June 26, 1659

Monsieur,

The grace of O[ur] L[ord] be with you forever!

This is the person I asked you to welcome into your house and who is leaving to go to stay there. I recommend him to you. He will tell you why he is making that retreat, including the following reason: that he is prone to go to taverns in Paris. Now, so that this does not happen in Crécy, please watch him carefully. He really wants to be prevented from going.

He is talking about giving you five hundred livres. Take whatever he gives you and see, meanwhile, if you can get along with him, and he with you. He is recommended to us by a very devout Abbé to whom we are greatly indebted.

I am, in the love of O[ur] L[ord], Monsieur, your most humble servant.

VINCENT DEPAUL,
i.s.C.M.

Addressed: Monsieur Lhuillier, Priest of the Mission, in Crécy

2883. - TO FIRMIN GET, IN MONTPELLIER

Paris, June 27, 1659

Monsieur,

The grace of O[ur] L[ord] be with you forever!

Letter 2882. - Archives of the Mission, Paris, original signed letter.

Letter 2883. - Archives of the Mission, Paris, original signed letter.

I admit once again that we moved too quickly, but we were led to understand things other than they are; and it seemed that all would have been lost if we had delayed ever so little. Oh well! there is no use talking about it any longer; the mistake has been made. It will teach us another time to look more closely and to take more time with what we have to do. God, who knows how to draw good from evil, will see that all that turns to His glory. One mistake should not be corrected by another, nor should you leave the place where you now are, after having undertaken to render service there to God and to the diocese. So you should continue, and I ask you to do so. If the work that has begun does not succeed, it should not, however, depend on us but on God [1] to bring it to completion, since it is His Providence that has committed us to it.

I am really worried about the Bishop's [2] condition, and I ask Our Lord to bless the baths he has gone to take.

I thank Father Baurème most humbly for the honor he did me through your letter. Please recommend me to his prayers and assure him of my obedience.

You can have the long cloaks you left in Marseilles brought to Montpellier, or get them yourself when you go there. Have no doubt that all the living expenses for your men will have to be taken from the four hundred écus offered you, as well as money for linen, clothing, and food. If this sum does not suffice, you will have to explain to the Bishop that you do not have the means of getting anything more from somewhere else. As for the vestments and books you need, you must be patient and think about what Our Lord and the Apostles, who had none, did. This should help you enter into their spirit and, as far as possible, into the practice of their simplicity and poverty, trusting in the mystical vision of God, who will not fail to inspire you with the things you have to say and

[1]First redaction: "it will not depend on us, God willing, but on God."
[2]François de Bosquet.

teach—I mean He Himself will do it, when He will not be teaching you them by books. Still, do not fail to ask the Bishop for any necessities, as I am asking God for an abundance of His graces for you and M. Parisy, whom I embrace cordially.

I am, in the love of O[ur] L[ord], Monsieur, your most humble servant.

VINCENT DEPAUL,
i.s.C.M.

Addressed: Monsieur Get, Superior of the Priests of the Mission of Marseilles, at present at the Montpellier Seminary, in Montpellier

2884. - TO JEAN BARREAU, CONSUL, IN ALGIERS

Paris, June 27, 1659

Dear Brother,

[The grace of Our Lord] be with you forever!

[I received your lett]er of May 3, which [consoled] me [greatly, seei]ng that the Turks have been appeased and things [have turned out well]. God be praised for that! [I fear, however,] that they are not as they appear to be. [Mon]ey will ever be a source of anxiety, and since they will always be [remembering] something from the past, I am afraid that some day they will settle accounts [with the Fren]ch for what is due them, whenever they c[an do so] to their advantage. I am writing to tell M. Le [Vach]er [1] to get information on any ships coming from Algiers, and whether we can be sure of

Letter 2884. - Archives of the Mission, Paris, original signed letter. Because the letter is torn, part of the text is missing.

[1]Philippe Le Vacher.

them, and that I will seek advice in the meantime from some farsighted men in public life to see if we will be able to send M. Le Vacher back to you soon with the money—or part of it. Believe me, dear Brother, I want that as much as you do.

I am very distressed—more than I can tell you—to know that you are alone and in such financial straits. Until now, however, God has shown that the delays of the past were in the order of His Providence, and we still cannot see clearly His good pleasure concerning the help you are expecting—I mean, with regard to the time and manner of giving it to you. All I know is that, since we are seeking only His will alone, He will grant us the grace of finding in it your deliverance and our peace of mind. Meanwhile, I ask Him to give you the patience to wait [a little longer].

I thank His Divine Goodness that, [by His grace], you have maintained [all your influen]ce with the slaves, for whom you h[ave so much charity]. It is of the utmost importance for [you to be careful] always to do the same. [Avoid] diverting sums of money for anything other than the int[ention for which] they have been sent to you. [Do not take] from one to give to the other, [but keep for] each one what belongs to him so that you [will be in a position to] give it to him whenever he wishes. The ob[ligations of] justice have priority over those of c[harity.

As for] your saying that there are some slaves whose freedom is being de[manded] by the merchants, to whom you cannot refuse the thirty piastres they need to return home, I will tell [you] that, if you have any money left over—I mean, of your own—you may make these advances; but you must never borrow any or take it from what belongs to someone else, or stand surety or take on a commitment for anyone whomsoever; otherwise, we would have to begin all over again. What is worse, it would be impossible for us to extricate you a second time.

Having a collection taken up in Paris for your needs must never be mentioned again. It is up to you to support yourself or to leave. Supporting yourself will be easy, if you take my advice: do not get involved in anything outside your own duty; do no trading or business with anyone, except what your office obliges you to do; and undertake nothing beyond your own strength.

[As for the comm]ission business Messieurs de Gastines and Campou [want to gi]ve you, it can be done in two [ways: either by] using persuasion with the Turks and urging them [to do what those] gentlemen wish, or simply. . . . I do not [agree to your] taking responsibility for their affairs. [It is better to sug]gest the first way, [namely, using] persuasion. It will be a good idea for them to send [someone else] to Algiers for that purpose. I do, however, think it [very wise] for you to act on their behalf in the form [of a propo]sal, being satisfied with pointing out to the [authorities] the reasons and intentions of your principals [and] urging them to follow them. Thus they will not be able to reproach you with having committed them to do something against their will or profit. The angels take care of us in this latter way: they inspire us gently and almost imperceptibly to do good, and then leave us full liberty to do it or not.

I have good reason to ask you not to get involved any longer in anything but consular business; for, in addition to your previous trading in diamonds and other things, I noticed that you recently took it upon yourself to have some pearls sent in from France and wrote to your brother about it. All that, dear Brother, is inappropriate and contrary to the Will of God, who has called you to that place only for the office and not for trading.

I ask His Divine Goodness to protect and bless you. I am, in His love, dear Brother, your most humble servant.

VINCENT DEPAUL,
i.s.C.M.

Addressed: Monsieur Barreau, French Consul, in Algiers

2885. - TO EDME JOLLY, SUPERIOR, IN ROME

[End of June 1659] [1]

[Monsieur,]

[The grace of Our Lord be with you forever!]

[God be praised for all] the [steps you have taken regarding the Saint-]Méen [affair, and for your] diligence concerning the young man's [call to] Orders. I thank you [for this] with all my h[eart].

We will return to M . . . the ten pistoles he left you.

I am waiting until you have finished the Loreto business to inform the Duchesse d'Aiguillon about it.

I heard that the Cardinal of Genoa left for Rome on the ninth of this month. I think he will arrive soon enough to be of help to you with the business regarding the approval of the conditions of our vow of poverty; I hope he will use his influence willingly and effectively in this. And God grant that it be in such a way that the incident of the Minims [2] may not . . .[3] persons of every class and from every country.

Letter 2885. - Archives of the Mission, Paris, original signed letter.

[1]The sentence that reads: "I heard that the Cardinal of Genoa left for Rome on the ninth of this month," shows clearly that the letter is from the month of June; since it took at least two weeks for the mail from Genoa to arrive, it can only have been written at the end of the month.

[2]The French Friars Minor had a convent in Rome, at Trinità del Monte, which was under the protection of the French Kings. Having heard that Jean Guillard, the new Vicar-General of the Order, intended to make a visitation of their house—although the preceding one had taken place less than six years before—some of the Friars protested loudly and declared that they would not submit to it. The visitation took place, and the Visitor thought it advisable to take strong measures against the malcontents. It was no sooner finished when Étienne Gueffier entered the monastery in his capacity of Agent of the King and ordered two of the Friars to go to the Court of the King of France to give an account of their actions. This occurred on May 24, 1659. Such was the origin of the sad affair which, for two years, caused strife between the pontifical authorities and the royal power. (Cf. Archives des Affaires étrangères, Rome 137, *pièces diverses,* especially the documents in fols. 546 and 576.)

[3]Of the six lines that follow in the original, only isolated words remain, and it is difficult to make any connection between them.

I was overjoyed to learn of the blessings God is giving your family and your leadership, and I ask His Divine Goodness to continue them and to strengthen you.

I am, in His love, Monsieur, your most humble servant.

VINCENT DEPAUL,
i.s.C.M.

Addressed: Monsieur Jolly

2886. - TO A SEMINARIAN OF THE MISSION

Paris, June 28, 1659

Monsieur,

[The grace of] O[ur] L[ord] be with you forever!

[It was a] joy for me to receive your letter, and I was [grate]ful to God in His goodness when I [saw] your readiness to go to preach the Gospel and administer the sacraments to people in distant lands. This holy seed that O[ur] L[ord] has sown in your heart will be able to bear fruit in due time, and fruits of eternal life. Cultivate it carefully but without departing from the holy indifference you must have for places and works. And since you are now engaged in studying, make it your principal concern, after that of pleasing God and making yourself ever more pleasing in His sight by the practice of the virtues. Strive to become very competent in all the functions of the Company; then we will think about you.

I am, in O[ur] L[ord], Monsieur, your most humble servant.

VINCENT DEPAUL,
i.s.C.M.

Letter 2886. - Archives of the Mission, Paris, seventeenth-century copy.

2887. - TO DENIS LAUDIN, SUPERIOR, IN LE MANS

Paris, June 28, 1659

[Monsieur,]

[The grace] of O[ur] L[ord] be with you [forever!]

Here is Brother [Jean Proust whom] we are sending to you. [I] told [him] that it was to do [whatever] you find advisable [for him] to do, and that, if you put him to work at business matters, he is to render you each evening an account of what he did that day and get your instructions for what he will have to do the next day. It is indeed advisable, Monsieur, to do things in this way, at least in the beginning. Please act in conformity with this so that he may become accustomed to it and do nothing on his own initiative, as I recommended to him, but discuss everything with you and follow your orders. When he [has nothing to do] outside, [he] can work [in the house like] the other Broth[ers. He understands] business affairs, since he was Procurator at the Bishop's residence in Fon[tenay. I think] he will be a hel[p to you and you will be] pleased with him.

I ask Ou[r Lord] to animate you more and more with His humility, gentleness, patience, vigilance, zeal, and goodness. I ask Him also to pardon me for the faults I commit against these virtues. I am, in His love, Monsieur, your most humble servant.

VINCENT DEPAUL,
i.s.C.M.

A minor ailment I now have[1] prevents me from replying to your last letter—and even from reading it. I have not yet opened it.

Letter 2887. - Archives of the Mission, Paris, original signed letter. The original has deteriorated. The bracketed words are taken from Register 2, p. 17.

[1]An inflammation of the eyes.

APPENDIX

1. - RENÉ ALMÉRAS TO NICOLAS DUPERROY, IN WARSAW

Paris, January 18, 1658

Monsieur,

The grace of O[ur] L[ord] be with you forever!

Since M. Vincent is not feeling very well today, he instructed me to reply to the letter you wrote him and the one you wrote me concerning your brother.[1] He wanted me to tell you that he was greatly consoled by his entrance into the Company and for the time he spent in it, since he was so edifying, and was very sorry about his ailment and subsequent departure. He also says that he is deeply consoled to hear how he is conducting himself in the world and by his continued love for the Mission. He sincerely hopes he will fully recover his health and, if he perseveres and asks to return, he will receive him then with great joy. He does not deem it advisable, however, to encourage him to do so, nor to take any steps for that purpose.

After telling you this on behalf of M. Vincent, it is only just that I, on my part, thank you for the trouble you took to write to me and for your continued affection for me. I do so now, Monsieur, with all my heart, asking Our Lord, who has preserved you in the midst of so many disasters of war and of the plague and has given you

---

Appendix 1. - Archives of the Mission, Krakow, original autograph letter. Since this letter and the two that follow were written in the name and by order of Saint Vincent, they have been included in the Appendix.

[1]Victor Duperroy.

the patience and constancy to suffer all that so generously, to strengthen you more and more for His glory and the good of those with whom you are working there.

These are the wishes of him who is, in the love of Our Lord, Monsieur, your most humble servant.

ALMÉRAS,
i.s.C.M.

2. - BERTRAND DUCOURNAU TO SAINT LOUISE

[After March 1657] [1]

I wish Mademoiselle Le Gras as her New Year's gift the fullness of the Spirit and, for her Company, that of the preservation of such a good mother, that she might give them an ever greater share of the gifts of this Spirit.

M. Vincent does not think she should send anyone to Mademoiselle,[2] as Madame de Brienne [3] suggests, unless she has to inform her of something special. It is true, he says, that there are Communities who visit important people, but he adds that there is not much advantage in that for them.

If Mademoiselle has a third Sister to give her,[4] she will do well in that case to send two Sisters to inform her of this and to find out

---

Appendix 2. - Archives of the Motherhouse of the Daughters of Charity, *Recueil de pièces relatives aux Filles de la Charité*, p. 682.

[1]This date has been assigned because of the reference to the Saint-Fargeau Hospital, to which the Sisters were called by the Duchesse de Montpensier in March 1657.

[2]Anne-Marie-Louise d'Orléans, Duchesse de Montpensier.

[3]Louise de Béon, a Lady of Charity devoted to Saint Vincent and his work, was the daughter of Louise de Luxembourg-Brienne and Bernard de Béon, Intendant of Saintonge, Angoulême, and the territory of Aunis. She was also the wife of Henri-Auguste de Loménie, Comte de Brienne, Secretary of State. The Daughters of Providence owed much to her charity. Louise de Béon died on September 2, 1665.

[4]For the hospital.

more specifically what she wants. If, however, she does not have a third Sister at present, it will suffice for her to ask Madame de Brienne to make her excuses to her.

3. - BERTRAND DUCOURNAU TO SAINT LOUISE

[January 9 or 10, 1659] [1]

M. Vincent approves of Mademoiselle Le Gras' receiving for a retreat the person mentioned by the Pastor of Saint-Nicolas;[2] she may also give written permission to the Sisters of the Hôtel-Dieu to go and bury the Lady after her death, as she desires.

4. - SAINT LOUISE TO SISTER NICOLE GEORGETTE, IN NANTEUIL

March 28, 1659

Dear Sister,

I have truly felt your suffering in all the matters you mentioned to me, although we should not find strange all the ill-natured things people will try to say about us by telling lies, since we are Christians

---

Appendix 3. - Archives of the Motherhouse of the Daughters of Charity, original unsigned letter.

[1]The note given below, which Saint Louise received from Hippolyte Féret, allows us to assign this date.

[2]Hippolyte Féret. He had written the following to Saint Louise: "Paris, January 9, 1659. Mademoiselle Le Gras is very humbly requested to admit the bearer of this note into her house for an eight-day spiritual retreat. She plans to become an associate of the Sisters of the Charity of the parishes, if her vocation is recognized as such. Your most humble servant, H. FÉRET." Both notes are written on the same sheet of paper.

Appendix 4. - Archives of the Motherhouse of the Daughters of Charity, original autograph letter.

and Daughters of Charity as well. This obliges us to endure everything, as we have been taught by that great lover of the sufferings of Jesus Christ.

What saddens me somewhat is that it seems you have had a misunderstanding with the Pastor, who leads such a holy life and is so learned, and to whom we are greatly indebted for the charity and good will he in his charity has always had for our Sisters. I shared your letter with M. Vincent, who knows how virtuous he is. He instructed me to ask you to show him always the respect we owe him. As for the other matters, you know that His Charity does not always reply immediately. I can simply assure you that, our Sisters, far from removing anything—books or otherwise—have always been faithful to their obligations, by the grace of God.

I am sorry you defended yourself by making fun of another person. *Mais quoi!* our weakness should not allow us to be discouraged. I do not think you should teach our Sister [1] or permit someone else to teach her; she is incapable of that, and I would not want to put anyone at risk from her attempts.

I am sending you the cross you want, from which you will learn to accept willingly the ones Our Lord is pleased to send you.

I recommend myself to your prayers and to those of Sister Marie. I am, in His most holy love, my very dear Sister, your most humble sister and very affectionate servant.

L. DE MARILLAC

Addressed: Sister Nicole Georgette, Daughter of Charity, Servant of the Sick Poor, in Nanteuil

[1] To do bloodletting.

INDEX

This index proposes to facilitate reference to the biographical data used in this volume and to the explanation of places and terms which recur frequently in the text and which have been explained in the footnotes when first used. Names of persons are in bold print (alternate spellings are given in brackets); those of terms or places appear in *italics*. The accompanying numbers indicate the letters to which the reader should refer for the desired information.

A

B

R

S

T

V

W